Adobe® Acrobat® 7
PDF Bible

Adobe® Acrobat® 7 PDF Bible

Ted Padova

WILEY

Wiley Publishing, Inc.

Adobe® Acrobat® 7 PDF Bible

Published by
Wiley Publishing, Inc.
10475 Crosspoint Boulevard
Indianapolis, IN 46256
www.wiley.com

ISBN: 0-7645-8378-6

Manufactured in the United States of America

10 9 8 7 6 5 4 3 2

1B/RX/QS/QV/IN

Published by Wiley Publishing, Inc., Indianapolis, Indiana
Published simultaneously in Canada

For general information on our other products and services or to obtain technical support, please contact our Customer Care Department within the U.S. at 800-762-2974, outside the U.S. at 317-572-3993 or fax 317-572-4002.

Wiley also publishes its books in a variety of electronic formats.

Library of Congress Cataloging-in-Publication Data: Available from Publisher

About the Author

Ted Padova is the former Chief Executive Officer and Managing Partner of The Image Source Digital Imaging and Photo Finishing Centers of Ventura and Thousand Oaks, California. He has been involved in digital imaging since founding a service bureau in 1990.

Ted has taught university and higher education classes over sixteen years in graphic design applications and digital prepress at the University of California, Santa Barbara, and the University of California at Los Angeles. He has been and continues as a conference speaker nationally and internationally at PDF conferences.

Ted has written over a dozen computer books on Adobe Acrobat, Adobe Photoshop, and Adobe Illustrator. Recent books published by John Wiley and Sons include *Adobe Acrobat PDF Bible (versions 4,5, and 6), Creating Adobe Acrobat PDF Forms, Teach Yourself Visually Acrobat 5,* and *Adobe Acrobat 6.0 Complete Course*. He also co-authored *Adobe Illustrator Master Class — Illustrator Illuminated* for Peachpit Press. He is also host of the Total Training video series on Acrobat 6.0.

Credits

Acquisitions Editor
Michael Roney

Project Editor
Kenyon Brown

Technical Editor
Lori DeFurio

Copy Editor
Paula Lowell

Editorial Manager
Robyn Siesky

Vice President and Executive Group Publisher
Richard Swadley

Vice President and Publisher
Barry Pruett

Project Coordinators
April Farling
Erin Smith

Graphics and Production Specialists
April Farling
Lauren Goddard
Denny Hager
Joyce Haughey
Jennifer Heleine
Heather Ryan
Amanda Spagnuolo
Ron Terry
Erin Zeltner

Quality Control Technician
Laura Albert
John Greenough
Leeann Harney
Jessica Kramer
Joe Niesen
Brain Walls

Proofreading and Indexing
TECHBOOKS Production Services

Preface

*A*dobe Acrobat 7 PDF Bible* is written for a cross-platform audience. Users of Microsoft Windows 2000 with Service Pack 2, Windows XP Professional or Home Edition, Tablet PC Edition, and Apple Macintosh Computers running OS X v10.2.8, 10.3 and above will find references to these operating systems.

About This Book

Most of the chapters in this book illustrate screenshots from Acrobat running under Windows. The user interface is closely matched between Windows and the Macintosh; therefore, Macintosh users will find the same options in dialog boxes and menu commands as found in the screenshots taken on a Windows machine. Where significant differences do occur, you'll find additional screenshots taken on a Macintosh to distinguish the differences.

How to read this book

I have to admit this publication is not a page turner that leaves you grasping for more time to finish up a chapter before retiring at night. After all, it's a computer book and inasmuch as my editors at Wiley always strive to get me to add a little *drama* to the text, few people will pick up this *Bible* and read it cover to cover. This book should be thought of more as a reference where you can jump to an area and read over the contents to help simplify your work sessions in Acrobat Standard or Professional version 7.0.

Because Acrobat is such a behemoth program and can do so many things for almost any kind of work activity, most people won't use every feature the program provides. You may be interested in converting files to PDF and setting up reviews, or you may devote more attention to the area of prepress and printing, or perhaps it's accessibility or PDF forms that's part of your work. Therefore, you may ignore some chapters and just want to jump to the area that interests you most.

Regardless of where you are in Acrobat experience, you should be able to gain much insight and skill at using the new version of Acrobat by studying in detail those areas that interest you most. However, don't completely ignore chapters that cover features you think you won't use. You can find many related concepts falling under headings that are not exclusively related to the general topic for each chapter. For example, you may not be interested in creating accessible PDFs for screen readers. However, what is covered in the Accessibility chapter also includes document structures and tagging, which will be important if you need get the content of a PDF back out to an authoring application.

Because many chapters may include features that relate to the work you want to perform, studying over the most important features of interest to you and skimming over those chapters that appear to be less beneficial for you works best.

To begin, I recommend you look closely at the section in this Introduction covering new features in Acrobat 7.0. No matter where you are in Acrobat skill, be certain to understand PDF navigation, as things have changed for moving around PDF files and creating cross-document links. Look closely at the help documents and the Help features in Acrobat 7.0. Pay particular attention to Chapter 3, which explains the new features that have been added to Adobe Reader. In some cases you need to add functionality in Acrobat and save the PDF before Reader users can take advantage of some new exciting tools and commands. Carefully look over the details covering PDF file creation and support for converting more authoring application documents to PDF; become familiar with using Acrobat Find and Search and editing PDF documents. Then jump into your particular area of interest and read over the chapters that can help you get up to speed using this new release. As a final step, browse the remaining chapters to see what other features can help you in your workflow.

Throughout the book are sections called *Steps*. If you find the contents of a given series of steps interesting, follow the steps to see whether you can replicate what is covered in that section.

Icons

What would a Wiley and Sons Bible book be without icons? The use of icons throughout the book offers you an at-a-glance hint of what content is being addressed. You can jump to the text adjacent to these symbols to get extra information, be warned of a potential problem, or amplify the concept being addressed in the text. In this book you'll find icons for the following.

A caution icon alerts you to a potential problem in using Acrobat, any tools or menus, or any supporting application that may be the origination of a document to be converted to PDF. Pay close attention to these caution messages to avoid potential problems.

A note icon signifies a message that may add more clarity to a text passage or help you deal with a feature more effectively.

Where workflow solutions are particularly applicable you'll see an icon indicating that the text describes tasks or features that apply to workgroups and workflows. This icon will be an important signal for people in large businesses, government, and education where large workgroups with common tasks exist.

Much support is offered in version 7.0 for the prepress and printing market. If you're a design professional, service bureau, or print shop, take note of these messages for information related to prepress and printing.

Tips are handy shortcuts. They help to more quickly produce results or work through a series of steps to complete a task. Some tips provide you with information that may not be documented in the Help files accompanying Acrobat Professional.

The Cross-Reference icon indicates a cross reference to another area in the book where more information can be found on a topic. Walking you through Acrobat in a linear fashion is almost impossible because it has so many interrelated features. Covering all aspects of a single feature in a contiguous section of the book just doesn't work. Therefore some common features for a command, a tool, an action, or task may be spread out and discussed in different chapters. When the information is divided between different sections of the book, you'll find a Cross-Reference icon that cross-references the current passage to another part of the book covering related information.

The book contents

Almost all of what you can do with Acrobat is contained within the chapters that follow. I've made an effort to address many different uses for all types of users. This book covers Acrobat features and how to work with Adobe Acrobat Professional, Adobe Acrobat Standard, Adobe Reader, and companion products. Individual industries such as office occupations, digital pre-press, engineering, enterprise workflows, and multimedia and Web publishing are covered. Regardless of what you do, you should be able to find some solutions for your particular kind of work. Whether you are an accounting clerk, a real estate salesperson, a digital prepress technician, an engineer, a Web designer, or a hobbyist who likes to archive information from Web sites, there's a reference to your needs and Acrobat will provide a solution.

To simplify your journey through the new release, the book is broken up into six separate sections. A total of 29 chapters address Acrobat features and some individual purposes for using the software. The six sections include the following:

Part I: Welcome to Adobe Acrobat. To start off, I offer some discussion on the PDF format and its new revision. Acrobat 7.0 has new help features that enable you to find help fast within the program. I cover tools, menus, and palettes to help you get an understanding for many Acrobat 7.0 features. This section covers the distinctions between different viewer types, navigating through PDFs, and using the new Find tool and the Search pane to search PDF files.

Part II: Converting Documents to PDF. There are many different ways to create a PDF document and all these methods are thoroughly covered in Part II. I begin by discussing the ease of creating simple PDF files that might be used by office workers and travel through to much more sophisticated PDF file creation for more demanding environments. In addition, I discuss how many application software manufacturers are supporting PDFs through direct exports from their programs. The Adobe Creative Suite is discussed and how you can integrate PDF with the CS applications. The advantages and disadvantages of using all these methods are also discussed.

Part III: Editing PDFs. This section covers editing, modifying, and enhancing PDF files for many different purposes. Also covered are how to modify content and how to flow content between Acrobat and authoring programs. I also discuss scanning in Acrobat and converting scans to text with Optical Character Recognition (OCR). Document repurposing is covered in this section for users who want to modify files for different output mediums.

Part IV: PDF Interactivity. Part IV covers interactivity with PDF documents for workgroups through the use of Review and Comment tools, adding interactive elements such as multimedia, and links and buttons. I address the layer features in Acrobat Professional and include a chapter devoted to making PDF documents accessible.

Part V: PDF Publishing. This section covers distribution of PDF files in some of the more common means available today. I begin with security and authentication as your first step in document distribution and then move on to PDF workflows. I discuss creating PDFs for different kinds of distribution, such as presentations, and offer complete coverage of all the new printing and prepress features. I also offer information about eBooks in Part V. Hosting your PDFs on the Web, sending them via e-mail, and writing collections of PDFs to CD-ROMs and DVDs are also covered in this section.

Part VI: Acrobat PDF Forms. This section covers PDF forms and data. For Windows users I cover using the new Adobe Designer for forms authoring. Forms creation and editing in Acrobat is also covered as well as how to fill out and manage Acrobat PDF forms. An introduction to JavaScript and writing simple JavaScript routines are also included in this section.

Staying Connected

It seems like new products and new upgrades are distributed about every five minutes. If you purchase a software product, you can often find an updated revision soon after. Manufacturers rely more and more on Internet distribution and less on postal delivery. You should plan on making routine visits to Adobe's Web site and the Web sites of third-party product manufacturers. Any software vendor who has a Web site will offer a product revision for downloading or offer you details on acquiring the update.

Internet connection

At times I feel a *required* Internet connection is either a blessing or a curse. I have about six computers I use for different things. My laptop is a computer I just haul around to conferences, and I don't want an Internet connection on the computer I use to demonstrate software. Yet, at other times, I welcome an Internet connection on my computers, which allows me to easily update a software product.

With newer releases of computer software, having an Internet connection is now essential. Programs, including Acrobat, prompt you routinely to check for updates over the Internet. To optimize your performance with Acrobat, you should run the software on a computer that has an Internet connection.

Registration

Regardless of whether you purchase Acrobat Professional, Acrobat Standard, or Acrobat Elements, or download the free Adobe Reader software, Adobe Systems has made it possible to register the product. You can register on the World Wide Web or mail a registration form to Adobe. If you develop PDF documents for distribution, Adobe likes to keep track of this information. You will find great advantage in being a registered user. First, update information will be sent to you, so you'll know when a product revision occurs. Second, information can be distributed to help you achieve the most out of using Acrobat. Who knows, some day you may be requested to provide samples of your work that might get you a hit from Adobe's Web site. By all means, complete the registration. It will be to your benefit.

Web sites to contact

Obviously, the first Web site to frequent is Adobe's Web site. When Acrobat and the Acrobat plug-ins are revised, downloads for updates will become available. You can also find tips, information, and problem solutions. Visit Adobe's Web site at www.adobe.com. Also make use of the Help ➪ Adobe Expert Support menu command in all Acrobat viewers. 'This command opens a Web page where you can order technical support for a nominal fee.

Acrobat tips are available on many Web sites — all you need to do is search the World Wide Web for Acrobat information. The best source for information as well as a comprehensive collection of third-party plug-ins is Planet PDF. You can visit them at www.planetpdf.com.

If learning more about Acrobat is your interest, you can find regional conferences sponsored by DigiPub Solutions Corporation. If you want to meet and discuss PDF issues with some of the world's experts, look for a conference in your area. You can find information at www.pdfconference.com.

The American Graphics Institute offers another PDF conference program . You can find out more information by logging on to www.AGItraining.com.

The Open Publish conference in Sydney, Australia, is an annual conference for design and creative professionals. This organization hosts many PDF-related seminars and workshops annually. Find out more at www.openpublish.com.au/.

Another conference with the same name is the Open Publish conference held in the U.S. This conference covers printing and publishing. You can find its site at http://www.open-publish.com.

If video training helps complement your learning, you can purchase training CDs developed by Total Training Systems. Each video set covers specific areas of Acrobat 7.0 and comes along with tutorial files to help you get up to speed fast in the new release. You can find a sample of the Total Training Acrobat 7.0 video series on this book's CD-ROM. For more information visit the Total Training Systems Web site at www.totaltraining.com/home.html.

Whatever you may desire is usually found on some Web site. New sites are developed continually so be certain to make frequent searches. And now with Acrobat 7.0 you can narrow your searches to look for just PDF files on the Internet.

Contacting Me

If, after reviewing this publication, you feel some important information was overlooked or you have any questions concerning Acrobat, you can contact me and let me know your views, opinions, hoorahs, complaints, or provide information that might get included in the next revision. (If it's good enough, you might even get a credit line in the acknowledgments!) By all means, send me a note. Send your e-mail inquiries to ted@west.net.

If you happen to have some problems with Acrobat, keep in mind that I didn't engineer the program. Inquiries for technical support should be directed to the software manufacturer(s) of any products you use. This is one more good reason to complete your registration form.

There you have it — a short description of what follows. Don't wait. Turn the page and learn how Acrobat can help you gain more productivity with its amazing new features.

For Brandon

Our love and memories of you shall continue
throughout our lives . . . and for those you left behind:
my dear niece, Bonnie; father, Mark, and sisters, Brittany and Courtany.

Acknowledgments

I would like to acknowledge some of the people who have contributed in one way or another to make this edition possible. Mike Roney, my Acquisitions Editor at Wiley and Sons; my Project Editor, Kenyon Brown; Copy Editor, Paula Lowell; and Editorial Manager, Robyn Siesky; as well as all the Wiley and Sons crew who participated in the project.

A very special thank you to my technical editor Adobe PDF Evangelist, Lori DeFurio. Because of Lori's comments, suggestions, and assistance, I believe this version of the *Adobe Acrobat 7 PDF Bible* is the best to date.

Much appreciation and thanks also go to Leonard Rosenthal of PDF Sages. Leonard graciously jumped in to help Lori with some of the technical editing, and his comments were invaluable.

I feel very fortunate in having so much support from many people at Adobe Systems who were continually available for comments, suggestions, and favors over a five-month period of time while Acrobat 7.0 was in development. The energy and enthusiasm of the engineering and marketing teams throughout the development period was evident from a group of people with passion and excitement for their work.

I'd also like to thank my friends at Planet PDF — Karl DeAbrew, Kurt Foss, and Daniel Shea; and Johanna Rivard of pdfZone .

Contents at a Glance

Contents

Part I: Welcome to Adobe Acrobat — 1

Chapter 14: Repurposing PDF Documents 421

Part IV: PDF Interactivity   439

Chapter 15: Review and Markup 441

Introduction

This book is the fourth edition of the *Acrobat PDF Bible 2005 Edition*. As a result of many users' feedback, this edition is an effort to add a little more coverage in some topics missed in the last version or in areas where users asked for more amplification. As you will see by browsing the contents of the book or launching the new version of all the Acrobat viewers, including Adobe Reader, Adobe Acrobat Standard, and Adobe Acrobat Professional, there are many changes in the programs. As such, I've made an effort to cover as much of the new version as is possible in this single, comprehensive book.

What Is Adobe Acrobat?

We've come a long way in Acrobat evolution, and those users of Adobe Acrobat are familiar with the distinctions between the Adobe Reader software and Adobe Acrobat (either Standard or Professional). However, among the many users of Adobe Reader, there still exists some confusion about what Reader can and cannot do. When acquiring Adobe Reader, many folks think the viewing of PDF documents with Adobe Reader is the extent of Acrobat. Now in version 7, Adobe Reader can do much more in terms of editing PDF documents. The additions to the new Adobe Reader may add a bit more confusion to the general user population, and it's important for all Acrobat users to know the differences between features of all Acrobat viewer products.

For those who don't know the difference, I explain in Chapter 2 that Adobe Reader is only one small component of Acrobat. Other programs included in the suite of Acrobat software provide you with tools for creating, editing, viewing, navigating, and searching Portable Document Format (PDF) information. Regardless of your familiarity with previous versions of Acrobat, you should carefully review Chapter 2. In Chapter 3, you'll find some detail on all the new features added to Adobe Reader and how you can add to PDF documents some new Reader Extensions that enable the Adobe Reader user much more functionality than was available in all versions prior to version 7.

Acrobat has evolved with many different changes both to the features it offers you and often to the names associated with the various components. In earlier versions of Acrobat, names like Acrobat Professional, Acrobat Exchange, and then simply Acrobat were used to refer to the authoring application. Version 7.0 of Adobe Acrobat, fortunately, continues with the same product names as found in Acrobat 6. The high-end performance application is referred to as Adobe Acrobat Professional. In release 7 as was the case in version 6, there is also a lighter Acrobat version with many of the same features found in Acrobat 5.x. The lighter version, also the same as was available in Acrobat 6, is called Adobe Acrobat Standard. This program has all the features you find available in Acrobat Professional with the exception of forms authoring, high-end printing and prepress, and some differences in tools and menu commands. As you follow the pages in this book, you can apply most of what is contained herein to either Acrobat Standard or Acrobat Professional. With the exception of Chapters 26-29 where I cover Acrobat PDF forms, and parts of Chapter 25, in which I discuss commercial printing, you'll find that most of the remaining chapter contents cover topics that pertain to either viewer.

One more product you can purchase from Adobe Systems in the Acrobat family is Adobe Acrobat Elements. Elements is a low-cost PDF creation tool designed for enterprises, and it requires purchasing a site license of a minimum of 1,000 copies. The Adobe Acrobat Reader software remains a free download from Adobe Systems and offers you many more features than found with previous versions of the Acrobat Reader software.

Nomenclature

The official name for the new release of Acrobat is Adobe(r) Acrobat(r) Professional. You'll notice the registered marks appearing in the name. For the sake of ease and clarity as you read through the book and see a reference to Acrobat, Adobe Acrobat, and Acrobat Professional (also called Acrobat Pro), please realize that the reference is to Adobe Acrobat Professional. For the other authoring application, the official name is Adobe (r) Acrobat (r) Standard. When referring to this product I may use terms like Acrobat Standard or simply Standard. Where it makes sense I'll say it like it is supposed to be used; otherwise, I'll use an abbreviated name.

The official name for the lighter version is Adobe Acrobat Elements, and the free downloadable software is Adobe Reader. Again, for the purposes of communication and ease, I may refer to the applications as Elements or Reader. Please realize, however, that the official name should prevail when you communicate in writing about these products.

Why is this important? Adobe Systems, Inc. has spent much time, labor, and money on developing branding for their products. With the different changes to product names and the different components of the software, some people using the products don't completely understand the differences or where the product came from. An Adobe Reader installer can appear on CD-ROMs distributed legitimately by users and some end users may not know that it is a product available for upgrading at the Adobe Systems, Inc Web site. Therefore, using the formal name can help users understand a little bit more about the software.

And, there's a very good reason for helping Adobe Systems with the recognition and marketing of these products. If the product doesn't do well in the marketplace, you might one day see it disappear. You won't want that to happen because when you start working with the new release, you'll easily see many great new features and much more polish added to the programs. Adobe Systems has done well in bringing the entire Acrobat family of products to maturity and I'm certain you'll find many more new uses for Acrobat.

Adobe Systems and the Acrobat mission

Adobe Systems, Inc. began as a company serving the graphic design and imaging markets. With the release of PostScript, its first product, much development in the early years of its history was devoted to imaging programs, font libraries, and tools to help service graphic design professionals. When you speak to graphic designers and advertising people, they connect Adobe Systems with products like Adobe Photoshop, Adobe Illustrator, Adobe InDesign, Adobe Premiere, and so on. With some of these flagship programs experiencing long histories and large installed user bases, some people may think that a product like Adobe Acrobat takes a back seat to the high-end graphics and multimedia programs.

Where does Acrobat fit into Adobe's mission and view of its product line? According to some interviews posted on the www.planetpdf.com Web site in late 2002, Adobe Chairman and CEO Bruce Chizen was quoted as saying that he expects the Acrobat family of products to weather economic storms in the software market. Acrobat is Adobe's fastest growing product, experiencing between 40 to 60 percent growth in year-over-year sales. Chizen was also quoted as saying that more than 60 percent of Adobe's worldwide sales and marketing personnel were diverted to Acrobat-related products during the Acrobat 5 lifecycle.

Adobe sees Acrobat as an integral part of its future and is investing much energy on Acrobat's growth. With more than 500,000,000 installed users of the Adobe Reader software, Acrobat and the PDF file format are among the most popular software products available today.

Acrobat has become a standard in many different industries. In the publishing market many large newspaper chains, publishing houses, and book and magazine publishers have standardized on the PDF format for printing and prepress. The prepress industry has long adopted PDF as a standard for commercial and quick print houses. Almost every software manufacturer includes last-minute notes, user manuals, and supporting information in PDF format on CD-ROM installer disks. The U.S. federal, state, and city governments and U.S. government contractor organizations have standardized on PDF for everything from forms, applications, notices, and official documents to intra-office document exchanges.

With the introduction of the Acrobat 6 product line, Adobe Systems expanded existing markets and targeted new markets. The features in Acrobat 6 and 7 Professional appealed to all kinds of engineering professionals. With the support for layers and direct exports from programs like Microsoft Visio and Autodesk AutoCAD, engineers, planners, and architects welcomed the new additions to Acrobat. Enterprises, in which document flows include different workgroups for almost any industry, welcomed additions to the comment and review tools in Acrobat Professional. The already standardized prepress market applauded new features for printing to high-end imaging devices without the use of third-party plug-ins. New features were added to support the eBook market where Adobe expects to expand PDF as a standard for this industry. All the great new features in Acrobat 6 have now been amplified in version 7, and you find additional support for users in almost every industry. With the addition of more functionality for Adobe Reader users, Acrobat is reaching out to more than one-half billion people using the Adobe Reader software in new ways.

PDF workflows

The definition of a workflow can mean different things to different people. One of the nice features of working with Acrobat is the development of a workflow environment. Quite simply, workflow solutions are intended to get out of a computer what the computer was designed for: Productivity in a more automated and efficient fashion. Editing page by page and running manual tasks to change or modify documents could hardly be called workflow solutions. Workflows enable office or production workers a means of automating common tasks for maximum efficiency. Batch processing documents, running them through automated steps, and routing files through computer-assisted delivery systems are among workflow solutions.

The exchange and delivery of documents are part of any office workflow. With Adobe Reader's new review and markup capabilities, office workers find many new additions to help workgroups exchange, comment in, review, revise, and publish documents. New editing tools help people in workgroups modify, refine, and polish legacy files as well as newly created documents, and in version 7 you are introduced to the new PDF/A format used for archiving documents.

In addition to building on what was introduced in version 6 of Acrobat, the new version supports integration with Adobe Creative Suite programs. For workflow environments, Adobe Version Cue has been added to Acrobat 7, enabling users to save different versions of the same document. You'll find a complete description for using Version Cue in Chapter 9.

New Features in Adobe Acrobat Professional

The changes to Acrobat in version 7.0 represent much more polish to an already impressive product. Just about everything you could do in the last version is still available in version 7.0, but there have been many additions to existing features and some new options for editing PDF files. The user interface remains consistent with Acrobat 6, but you'll find some new tools added to the toolbars and some new menu commands. Before you tackle the chapters ahead, take a close look at the brief description of the many new features listed here. As you poke around the new release, don't get frustrated if you can't find a particular feature you're used to in Acrobat. Come back to this section and skim over the new features list to help you find what you think you may have lost.

All the features highlighted here and more are covered in the chapters ahead. This brief coverage gives you an idea for some of the new features found in Acrobat Professional; many are also included in Acrobat Standard. If you're an experienced Acrobat user, the reasons for upgrading to the newest version will be obvious. If you're a new user, you'll find the current version of Acrobat to be a program that offers you tools to help you with almost anything related to viewing, archiving, and sharing documents among your workgroup, clients, colleagues, and friends.

Accessibility

More enhancements have been made for creating and viewing accessible documents. Reflowing text is now available for untagged files, enabling you to transport documents to handheld devices without creating tagged files. A new Setup Assistant is available for controlling accessibility options; a new Touchup Reading Order dialog box combined with the Order Navigation tab offers a much cleaner method for changing page reading order than found in the Tags palette.

Application support

Deployment and maintenance for Acrobat installations for Windows users has been greatly improved in Acrobat 7. A much improved UI (user interface) enables you to add PDF Maker to programs installed after Acrobat has been installed. Optional installer caching helps IT managers easily patch or repair the application. On the Macintosh an Uninstaller has been added so you can easily delete all those associated files nested in various Library folders.

Attaching files

The ability to attach files to PDF documents has been greatly improved. A new Attachments pane has been added to the panel where the Comments pane appears. File attachments can be easily viewed, managed, and searched in the Attachments pane. File attachments can be separately secured and extracted in Adobe Reader, which is another great support item for Reader users participating in reviews. (See "Review and comment" later in this section for more about commenting in Adobe Reader.)

Audio reading

Audio reading has been improved in Acrobat and now features the ability to read aloud form fields.

Authoring application support and PDF creation

PDF creation gets another boost with new support for JDF Job Definition Files, XML PDF, more AutoCAD support for AutoCAD Inventor and reduced file sizes for AutoCAD files (Windows), Microsoft Publisher support (Windows), Microsoft Visio support (Windows), Microsoft Access support (Windows), and support for archiving MS Outlook files and messages. The overall performance of the PDF Maker has been improved for all applications that use it. Improved support has been added for PDF creation from MS Internet Explorer on Windows with single-click conversion of multiple URLs. Macintosh users can now make use of the Create PDF from Clipboard command that was previously only available to Windows users in Acrobat 6. A new Create PDF From Document Template feature has been added to the Create PDF Task Button menu commands. Adobe provides some template files that you can open via the Create PDF From Document Template command, and you can add your own design templates to the DocTemplates folder contained within the Acrobat folder. As new templates are added to the folder, the names derived from the Title metadata field are listed in the submenu.

Autosaving files

Acrobat 7 offers you a new preference option for automatically saving and updating your document within an editing session.

Browser-based reviews

Browser-based reviews are now supported on the Macintosh.

Document repurposing

The PDF Optimizer has been improved and now provides transparency flattening, optimization of scanned images, and selective image compression based on color content. Discarding objects and cleanup have been separated into two panes.

eBook maintenance enhancements

My Bookshelf has been replaced by My Digital Editions and is now accessed from the Advanced menu. eBooks are now viewed in the My Digital Editions window as well as the new Organizer window (see "Organizing files" later in this section).

eEnvelopes (Secure ePaper Mail)

You can attach any document to an eEnvelope template, memo, or placeholder template from a simple menu command; set up a password and select permissions options; and apply a compatibility setting all from within a single document. You can send your file along with the attachment to users of the Adobe Reader software, who can then extract the file attachments. (See "Authoring application support and PDF creation" earlier in this section).

Fast launch

The first thing you notice about Acrobat 7 is a great speed improvement in launching the program. Both Adobe Reader and the commercial Acrobat viewers open super fast on both the Macintosh and Windows.

Faster searches

Much improved speed performance has been added to searching non-indexed PDFs.

Foreign language support

This release continues support for foreign languages, and now offers an Accents/Diacritics option when searching PDF files. There is now support for additional character sets, including Hebrew, Thai, and Vietnamese, in both Acrobat and Reader as well as support for "Hanko" stamps for Japanese customers.

Forms

Adobe Designer (a separate form design program) ships with Acrobat Professional on Windows; the Acrobat installer installs both Acrobat Professional and Adobe Designer. Designer can be launched as a separate executable application from within Acrobat via several different menu commands found in the new Form Task Button (Windows only). With Designer you can create XML-based forms designed for completion in Acrobat or as HTML documents. The graphical UI facilitates form design by using drag and drop assets for creation of all the form fields common to Acrobat. In addition, Designer offers many data-capture and data-handling solutions where forms authors can easily tie data to back-end databases without the need for complex programming routines. Data can be read, captured, routed, and validated from easy-to-use menu commands and tools in Designer. Additionally, Designer can integrate PDF documents in existing workflows by binding forms to XML schemas, databases, and Web services.

Headers and footers

A new option in the Headers and Footers window is available for preventing page resizing and positioning when printing. You can now more easily replace or remove headers and. The improved UI makes adding custom text to headers and footers, adding number pages, and adding special codes in the entry window easier than before.

Help

The How To window is still present, offering help information found in Acrobat 6. New menu commands offer you direct links to Adobe's Expert Support Center and a forum where you can find accessibility information. The How To Task Button, now relabeled more intuitively as *Help,* organizes help information in a neater package by offering direct help links for engineering features, comment and markup, and forms features.

JavaScript

New JavaScript support features include a complete dialog box running with a number of controls to help debugging, an XML parser with full DOM and XPath support, XSLT for XML transformations, and a much improved SOAP implementation.

Layers

Multimedia now placed on a separate layer is now editable only when that layer remains in view. Acrobat treats media placed on a layer specific to that layer as opposed to making the video accessible when viewing other layers.

Linking documents

The process of creating cross-document links has been simplified. You accomplish linking to cross-document pages and different views via the Go to page view action. The Go to page in another document and Go to Snapshot view actions have been eliminated in the Actions tab for links and buttons.

Multimedia enhancements

Problems associated with viewing video clips as a floating window when in Full Screen mode on the Macintosh has been fixed; this feature now behaves the same as viewing video in Full Screen mode in Windows.

Organizing files

A new Organizer window has been introduced in Acrobat 7 that behaves similar to the File Browser found in Adobe Photoshop. You can view thumbnails of all pages in a PDF document in the Organizer without opening the document in Acrobat, change thumbnail view sizes, sort documents according to metadata, view a history of files last opened over time incremented periods, print files, send files for e-mail review, or simply e-mail documents — all from within the Organizer window.

PDF standards

Support for creating PDF/A files for archiving purposes has been added to Acrobat Distiller. PDF/X standards have been extended to PDF/X 1a 2003 and PDF/X3 2003.

Prepress and printing

A host of new tools has been added for creative professionals, including gamut warning previews, rich black warnings, previews for minimum and maximum dot sizes, total ink coverage warnings, and the ability to convert color spaces within Acrobat. Also included are tools for flattening transparency without printing, trapping as well as creating trap presets, remapping spot colors, fixing hairline widths, and managing JDF (Job Definition Format) information. New reporting methods have been introduced for communicating problems between vendors and clients. The pre-flight window has had a complete overhaul, and now features a new sizable window with a new interface for selecting, editing, and creating new profiles.

Review and comment

A few new tools have been added to the impressive review and comment tools that were introduced in Acrobat 6. A new Callout tool and Dimensioning tool have been added. Online comments are now supported on the Macintosh. But perhaps the most impressive new feature is the ability to create PDF files that can be commented on in Adobe Reader. Be certain to look over Chapters 3 and 15 to learn how to create PDF documents with Reader Extensions for commenting and adding text within Adobe Reader.

Searching PDFs

A new Find tool has been added to Acrobat 7. You can use the tool to search PDF documents without opening the Search pane. Searching non-indexed files now features a much welcomed speed improvement. Searching XMP data has been improved and new features for searching object-level metadata have been added.

Security and digital signature enhancements

The capability to apply and verify digital signatures has been improved, and new standards are supported in Acrobat 7. XML signatures are supported. One of the most impressive features for securing files is a new feature for time stamping documents where users can no longer access a PDF after an expiration date.

Version Cue support

Support for Version Cue introduced with the first version of the Adobe Creative Suite has been added to Acrobat. You can save different versions of a PDF and promote the desired version to the top level.

Watermarks and backgrounds

The Watermark & Backgrounds dialog box now supports adding custom text that can be viewed and printed or hidden from view and printing. Importing files for watermarks and backgrounds remains the same as was available in Acrobat 6.

Web browser support

Acrobat 7 offers more Web browser support for Macintosh users and supports inline viewing with Apple's Safari.

Welcome to Adobe Acrobat

✦   ✦   ✦   ✦

✦   ✦   ✦   ✦

Getting to Know Adobe Acrobat

I f, after perusing your local bookstore, you decided to lay down your money at the counter, carry away this ten-pound volume, and take it to bed with you tonight, you probably already know something about Adobe Acrobat. Why else would you buy this book? If you're at the bookstore shelf and you haven't bought it yet, then you're probably wondering how in the world anyone could write so many pages for such a simple application.

What Is Adobe Acrobat?

Assuming you know little about Adobe Acrobat, I start with a brief description of what Acrobat is and what it is not. As I explain to people who ask about the product, I usually define it as the most misunderstood application available today. Most of us are familiar with the Adobe Reader software, which is a product from Adobe Systems Incorporated that you can download free from the Adobe Web site (www.adobe.com/acrobat). You can also acquire the Adobe Reader from all the installation CD-ROMs for other Adobe software. You can even acquire Adobe Reader from other users, as long as the Adobe licensing requirements are distributed with the installer program. The Adobe Reader, however, is *not* Adobe Acrobat. Adobe Reader is a component of a much larger product that has evolved through several iterations over more than a decade.

You're probably a little more sophisticated and realize there is a major difference between the applications noted previously and you may wonder why I even spend any time discussing the difference between Acrobat and Adobe Reader. Interestingly enough, I attended a PDF conference not too long ago. The conference coincided with a worldwide technology conference and one of the speakers at the PDF conference took a video camera and microphone to the other conference and interviewed random attendees, asking questions like, "What is Adobe Acrobat?" and "What is PDF?" Surprisingly, most of the computer-savvy interviewees could not provide a correct answer. Inasmuch as Acrobat has come a long way, many people still confuse what you purchase from Adobe Systems and what you can download free.

To add a little more confusion, this iteration of Acrobat includes the three different kinds of viewer applications found in the last release and many new features added to the Adobe Reader software. Adobe Reader software remains a free download from Adobe's Web site.

The other two Acrobat viewers are software products you need to purchase from Adobe Systems or from software vendors. They include Adobe Acrobat Standard and Adobe Acrobat Professional. As I talk about Adobe Acrobat in this chapter, I'm referring to both Acrobat Standard and Acrobat Professional.

Note   There are distinctions between the Acrobat Standard product and the Acrobat Professional product in terms of tools and commands. Most editing tasks can be handled in either viewer; however, Acrobat Professional does provide more editing features than Acrobat Standard. Throughout this book I delineate the differences and point out when an Acrobat Professional feature cannot be accomplished in Acrobat Standard.

Adobe Acrobat (either Standard or Professional) in version 7 is the upgrade from Adobe Acrobat 6 (Standard or Professional) and both viewers are the subject of the remaining chapters of this book. Acrobat is the authoring application that provides you tools and commands for a host of features outlined in the following chapters. If you haven't yet purchased a copy of Acrobat, either the Standard version or the Professional version, you might want to look over Chapter 2 and observe some of the comparisons between the viewers. If fewer tools and features suit your purpose, you might find the Standard version satisfactory. Although some of the features differ between the viewers, they both provide many features for editing, enhancing, printing, and working with PDF documents.

Acrobat is an authoring application but it has one little feature that distinguishes it from almost any other authoring program. Rather than starting from scratch and creating a new document in Acrobat, your workflow usually involves converting a document, created in just about any program, to a Portable Document Format (PDF) file. Once converted to PDF you use Acrobat to edit and refine the document, add bells and whistles and interactivity, or prepare it for professional printing. In addition to the Acrobat program, Acrobat Professional ships with companion programs such as Adobe Acrobat Distiller and Adobe Acrobat Catalog, and Adobe Designer (Windows only). Acrobat Standard ships only with Acrobat Distiller. These companion products are used to convert PostScript files to PDF, create search indexes, and author XML-based forms.

Cross-Reference   For information related to Acrobat Distiller see Chapter 8. For more information on Acrobat Catalog, see Chapter 5. For more information related to Designer, see Chapter 26.

Acrobat solutions are greatly extended with other supporting programs from Adobe Systems and many different third-party vendors. If Acrobat can't do the job, chances are you can find a plug-in or companion program to handle all you want to do with a PDF file.

Cross-Reference   For information related to Acrobat plug-ins and companion products see Chapter 2.

What Is PDF?

PDF, short for *Portable Document Format,* was developed by Adobe Systems as a unique format to be viewed through Acrobat viewers. As the name implies, it is portable, which means the file you create on one computer can be viewed with an Acrobat viewer on other computers, handheld devices and on other platforms. For example, you can create a page layout on a Macintosh computer and convert it to a PDF file. After the conversion, this PDF document can be viewed on a UNIX or Windows machine.

Multiplatform compliance (to enable the exchange of files across different computers, for example) is one of the great values of PDF documents.

So what's special about PDF and its multiplatform compliance? It's not so much an issue of viewing a page on one computer created from another computer that is impressive about PDF. After all, such popular programs as Microsoft Excel, Microsoft Word, Adobe Photoshop, Adobe InDesign, Adobe FrameMaker, and Adobe Illustrator all have counterparts for multi-platform usage. You can create a layout on one computer system and view the file on another system with the same software installed. For example, if you have Adobe InDesign installed on a Macintosh computer and you create an InDesign document, that same file can be viewed on a PC with InDesign running under Windows.

In a perfect world, you may think the capability to view documents across platforms is not so special. Document viewing, however, is secondary to document integrity. The preservation of the contents of a page is what makes the PDF so extraordinary. To illustrate, suppose you have an InDesign document created in Windows using fonts generic to Windows applications. After it's converted to PDF, the document, complete with graphics and fonts intact, can be displayed and printed on other computer platforms. And the other computer platforms don't need the fonts or graphics to print the file with complete integrity.

This level of document integrity can come in handy in business environments, where software purchases often reach quantum costs. PDF documents eliminate the need to install all applications used within a particular company on all the computers in that company. For example, art department employees can use a layout application to create display ads and then convert them to PDF so that other departments can use the free Adobe Reader software to view and print those ads for approval.

The benefits of PDF viewing were initially recognized by workgroups in local office environments for electronic paper exchanges. Today users have much more opportunity for global exchange of documents in many different ways. As you look at Acrobat and discover some of the features available for document comment and markup, comparing documents, support for layered files (which adds much more functionality to Adobe Reader), and preparing PDFs for screen readers, you'll see how Acrobat and the PDF have evolved with new technologies.

Cross-Reference

The term *screen reader* is used extensively throughout this book. When you see a reference to "screen reader," I'm referring to either a hardware device or special software (JAWS, Kurzweil, and so on) used to convert visual information to audio format. For more information on screen readers and making documents accessible to the readers, see Chapter 20.

Document repurposing

The evolution of the computer world has left extraordinary volumes of data that were originally designed to be printed on paper on computer systems. Going all the way back to UNIVAC, the number crunching was handled by the computer and the expression was the printed piece. Today, forms of expression have evolved to many different media. No longer do people want to confine themselves to printed material. Now, in addition to publishing information on paper, we use CD-ROMs, the Internet, and file exchanges between computers. Sometimes we use motion video, television, and satellite broadcasts. As high-speed access evolves, we'll see much larger bandwidths, so real-time communication will eventually become commonplace. And the world of tomorrow will introduce more communication media. Think of outputting to plasma, crystal, and holograms, and then think about having a font display or link problem with one of those systems!

Technology will advance, bringing many improvements to bandwidth, performance, and speed. To enable the public to access the mountains of digital data held on computer systems in a true information superhighway world, files will need to be converted to a common format. A common file format would also enable new documents to be more easily *repurposed,* to exploit the many forms of communication that we use today and expect to use tomorrow.

Acrobat Professional has added more tools for helping users repurpose documents. Tools for repairing problem files, downsizing file sizes, porting files to a range of different devices, and eliminating unnecessary data are part of the many features found in Acrobat Professional. In addition, the new PDF/A format available in Acrobat 7 is designed specifically for archiving documents. A standards committee has developed this format so documents viewed on computer systems 100 years from now will be compatible with future operating systems.

PDF and Adobe PostScript

The de facto standard of almost all printing in the graphics industry is Adobe PostScript. Ninety-nine percent of North America and about seventy-five percent of the rest of the world uses PostScript for all high-end output. Adobe developed this page description language to accurately display the design created on your computer screen to the printed page. If graphics and fonts are included in your files and you want to print the pages to high-end professional devices, then PostScript is the only show in town. The Adobe PostScript language was responsible for the rise of so many software and hardware manufacturers. If you stop and think about it, PostScript ranks up there with MS-DOS and Windows in terms of its installed user base.

Okay, so how does PostScript relate to PDF? In the initial release of Acrobat, all PDF conversion began with a file that was created as a PostScript file. Users selected the Print command in an authoring program and printed the file to disk — thus creating a PostScript file. This file was then opened in the Acrobat Distiller program and Distiller converted the PostScript to a PDF.

Distiller is still a part of Acrobat. In some cases, creating a PDF from a PostScript file rather than through any of the many other means available may be preferable. It could be that you have a problem with exporting to PDF from a program, such as fonts not appearing embedded, or you may need to create a PDF for a special purpose like printing and prepress. In such circumstances using Acrobat Distiller may be your best solution for generating a PDF document to properly suit the purpose.

Cross-Reference   For information related to printing PostScript files and using Acrobat Distiller see Chapter 8.

Printing to PostScript and opening PostScript files in Distiller is used much less today because now so many programs support PDF creation through one-button clicks or using the Save As command. However, many of these one-button clicks still use the Distiller application in the background to create the PDF file. You may not see Distiller launched when PDFs are created in the background, but the program is working away to convert your authoring application document to a PDF file.

PostScript can be a problem solver for you, and you may have an occasional need to use it even if your workflow does not require its use all the time. The more you know about PostScript and Acrobat Distiller, the more often you might be able to rescue problem files that don't seem to properly convert to PDF.

PDF versions

Acrobat is now in version 7. The version number indicates the number of releases of the product. PDF is a file format and with it you'll also find a version number. The PDF version relates to the specifications of the file format; for the end user it's usually not so important to understand all the specifications as much as it is to know what it does for you or what you can expect from it. If you create PDF documents for users of older Acrobat viewers and use the newer PDF format, your users may not be able to view your PDF files. Conversely, creating PDF files with the older version might prohibit you from using some newer features in the recent release.

With PDF file conversion you have choices for creating and saving PDF documents with your choice of version number. Depending on which version you select you'll have different specifications assigned to the file. To give you an idea for how PDF format has changed, look over Table 1-1.

Table 1-1: PDF Version Compatibility Differences

Acrobat 3.0	Acrobat 4.0	Acrobat 5.0	Acrobat Professional 6.0	Acrobat Professional 7.0
Supports PDF version 1.2.	Supports PDF version 1.3.	Supports PDF version 1.4.	Supports PDF version 1.5.	Supports PDF version 1.6.
PDF files can be opened by Acrobat viewers 3.0 and later.	PDF files can be opened by Acrobat viewers 3.0 and later.	PDF files can be opened by Acrobat viewers 3.0 and later.	PDF files can be opened by Acrobat viewers 3.0 and later.	PDF files can be opened by Acrobat viewers 3.0 and later.
	Minor viewing problems with earlier viewers may be experienced.	Some viewing problems with earlier viewers may be experienced.	Some viewing problems with earlier viewers may be experienced.	Some viewing problems with earlier viewers may be experienced.
Page size is limited to 45 inches × 45 inches.	Page size is available up to 200 inches × 200 inches.	Page size is available up to 200 inches × 200 inches.	Page size is available up to 200 inches × 200 inches.	Page size is available up to 200 inches × 200 inches.
Document conversion is limited to 32,768 pages.	Document length is limited only by RAM and hard drive space.	Document length is limited only by RAM and hard drive space.	Document length is limited only by RAM and hard drive space.	Document length is limited only by RAM and hard drive space.
Color conversion supports CalRGB.	Color conversion supports sRGB.	Color conversion supports sRGB.	Color conversion supports sRGB.	Color conversion supports sRGB, supports color conversion of RGB to CMYK.
ICC Profile embedding supported.	ICC Profile embedding supported.	ICC Profile embedding supported.	ICC Profile embedding supported.	ICC Profile embedding supported.

Continued

Table 1-1 *(continued)*

Acrobat 3.0	Acrobat 4.0	Acrobat 5.0	Acrobat Professional 6.0	Acrobat Professional 7.0
DeviceN color space is converted to an alternate color space.	DeviceN color space is supported.	DeviceN color space is supported.	DeviceN color space with 32 colorants is supported.	DeviceN color space with 32 colorants is supported.
Smooth shading is converted to images.	Smooth shading is supported.	Smooth shading is supported.	Smooth shading is supported.	Smooth shading is supported.
Patterns display at 50 percent but print correctly.	Patterns display accurately and print correctly.	Patterns display accurately and print correctly.	Patterns display accurately and print correctly.	Patterns display accurately and print correctly.
Places halftone information in the PDF.	Will place halftone information only when the Preserve Halftone information is selected in the Color Job Options.	Will place halftone information only when the Preserve Halftone information is selected in the Color Job Options.	Will place halftone information only when the Preserve Halftone information is selected in the Color Job Options.	Will place halftone information only when the Preserve Halftone information is selected in the Color Job Options.
Preserve, remove, and apply Transfer functions are supported.	Preserve and remove Transfer functions are supported but NOT apply Transfer functions.	Preserve, remove, and apply Transfer functions are supported.	Preserve, remove, and apply Transfer functions are supported.	Preserve, remove, and apply Transfer functions are supported.
Masks do not display or print properly.	Masks are supported in viewing and printing.	Masks are supported in viewing and printing.	Masks are supported in viewing and printing.	Masks are supported in viewing and printing.
Photoshop 6.0 layers and transparency are not supported.	Photoshop 6.0 layers and transparency are not supported.	Photoshop 6.0 layers and transparency are supported in Save as PDF from Photoshop only.	Photoshop 6.0 layers and transparency are supported in Save as PDF from Photoshop only.	Photoshop 6.0 and above layers and transparency supported in Saves as PDF from Photoshop only.
Illustrator 9.0 transparency is supported.	Illustrator 9.0 transparency is supported.	Illustrator 9.0 transparency is supported in Save as PDF from Illustrator only.	Illustrator 9.0 transparency is supported in Save as PDF from Illustrator only.	Illustrator 9.0 and above transparency supported in Save as PDF from Illustrator only.
Cannot embed double-byte fonts.	Can embed double-byte fonts.	Can embed double-byte fonts.	Can embed double-byte fonts.	Can embed double-byte fonts.
TrueType fonts cannot be searched.	TrueType fonts can be searched.	TrueType fonts can be searched.	TrueType fonts can be searched.	TrueType fonts can be searched.

Acrobat 3.0	Acrobat 4.0	Acrobat 5.0	Acrobat Professional 6.0	Acrobat Professional 7.0
Supports 40-bit encryption.	Supports 40-bit encryption.	Supports 40-bit encryption and 128-bit encryption.	Supports 40-bit encryption and 128-bit encryption.	Supports 40-bit, 128-bit, and 256-bit encryption.
No PDF/X support. No PDF/A support.	No PDF/X support. No PDF/A support.	No PDF/X support. No PDF/A support.	PDF X/1-A and PDF X/3 are supported. No PDF/A support.	PDF X/1-A, PDF/X1-A 2003, PDF X/3, PDF/X3 2003, PDF/A are supported.
No Adobe PDF Layer support.	No Adobe PDF Layer support.	No Adobe PDF Layer support.	Support for Layers from certain authoring applications.	Support for Layers from certain authoring applications. Supports object level metadata.

Table 1-1 lists a comparison of attributes of the different PDF versions and should not be confused with certain features you can employ in one release that may make the PDF unusable to users with earlier versions of Acrobat. For example, embedding movie clips in a PDF document or using a JavaScript that won't work in earlier versions is not a function of the PDF version. Rather, they are features added to the program and employed after the PDF has been created.

One of the nice new features of Acrobat Professional with the current PDF version is support for PDF/A files. If you want to be certain your files are saved in an archive format that can be opened several years in the future, you'll want to know more about the new PDF/A archiving format.

Cross-Reference   For information related to PDF/A, see Chapter 8.

Acrobat Environment

Experienced Acrobat users will immediately notice the user interface (UI) in Acrobat 7 appears very similar to the UI introduced in version 6. If you're updating from Acrobat 4 or 5 then the UI is probably overwhelming to you. There's a lot to absorb when looking at the Acrobat window and you'll need some initial help to understand all the changes. Fortunately you bought this book and, together with Adobe Systems and the new help features in all Acrobat viewers, I'll walk you through the many different items located in the Acrobat workplace.

Acrobat provides you with features such as menu commands, toolbars, and palettes to accomplish work for whatever goal you hope to achieve with PDF documents. When you launch the program you see many of these features in the Acrobat window. Just so you know what is being referred to when I discuss accessing a feature in Acrobat, take a look at Figure 1-1 to understand the names used to describe the various areas of the new Acrobat workplace.

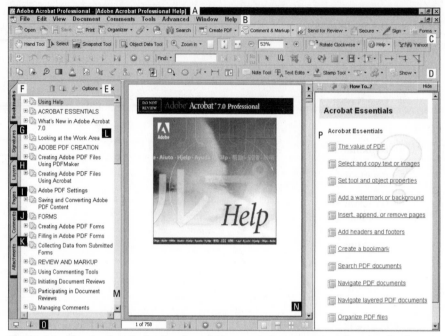

Figure 1-1: The Acrobat Professional workplace contains menus, toolbars, and palettes.

A   Title bar: By default, the name of the file you open appears within parentheses in the Title bar. The title appearing in the Title bar can change according to an option for displaying the Document Title in the Open Options dialog box.

For information related to Open options and displaying Document Titles, see Chapter 5.

B   Menu bar: The menu bar contains all the top-level menu commands. These menu choices are also available from various actions associated with links and form fields when you choose the Execute a menu item command in the Actions Properties dialog box for links, form fields, and other features that permit associating an action with a command.

For information related to link actions and the Execute a menu item command action type, see Chapter 17. For more information on actions with form fields, see Part VI.

C   Toolbar: A number of individual toolbars are nested below the menu bar. Individual toolbars are marked with a vertical separator bar at the left side of the toolbar. This bar can be selected and dragged to move it out of the Toolbar Well.

For information related to working with toolbars, see the "Tools and toolbars" section later in this chapter.

D Toolbar Well: The Toolbar Well houses the toolbars. You can drag toolbars away from the Toolbar Well or add other toolbars and expand the Toolbar Well to house your new additions. When you drag a toolbar away from the Toolbar Well, the toolbar is "undocked" and becomes a floating toolbar. When you drag a floating toolbar and drop it in the Toolbar Well, the toolbar becomes "docked."

E Palette pull-down menu: Individual tabs can be tucked away in the Navigation pane (see Navigation pane later in this list) or appear anywhere in the Acrobat window. Each palette contains its own menus accessible by clicking the down-pointing arrow. These menus are referred to as palette pull-down menus in all subsequent chapters.

F Bookmarks tab: The first of the default tabs appearing in the Navigation pane is the Bookmarks tab. If bookmarks are contained in the PDF document they appear in the palette when the palette is open, as is shown in Figure 1-1.

Cross-Reference

For information related to creating bookmarks from authoring programs, see Chapter 7. For information related to creating and managing bookmarks in Acrobat, see Chapter 17.

G Signatures tab: If digital signatures are included in your PDF document, they can be viewed in the Signatures tab.

Cross-Reference

For information related to digital signatures, see Chapter 21.

H Layers tab: Acrobat supports layers that have been created from some authoring applications and exported as a PDF file with layers intact in versions 6 and 7. The Layers tab enables you to view or hide layers when they are present in the PDF.

Cross-Reference

For information related to working with layers, see Chapter 19.

I Pages tab: Users of versions of Acrobat prior to version 6 will notice there is no tab for Thumbnails. The Thumbnails tab was renamed in version 6 to the Pages tab. When you open the Pages tab, you'll see thumbnail images of each page in your document and you'll find many page-editing features available to you from the Pages tab palette pull-down menu.

Cross-Reference

For information related to using the many options available in the Pages tab, see Chapter 12.

J Comments tab: A major overhaul to the Comments tab was made in version 6, and Acrobat version 7 continues with the same palette design. When you open the Comments tab, the display of comments and reviews is shown horizontally at the bottom of the Acrobat window.

Cross-Reference

To learn how to use the Comments tab options, see Chapter 15.

K Attachments: A new pane has been added in Acrobat version 7 to display all file attachments in a document. When usage rights are permitted for Adobe Reader users, the attachments are accessible in Adobe Reader.

Cross-Reference

To learn how to use file attachments, see Chapter 15. To learn how to deploy usage rights for Adobe Reader users, see Chapter 3.

L **Bookmarks:** Figure 1-1 shows the Bookmarks tab opened with bookmarks listed in the palette. Bookmarks enable you to jump to the page view associated with the bookmark. In addition, you can assign attributes other than views to bookmarks, such as opening/closing files, running a menu command, invoking a JavaScript, and many other actions.

Cross-Reference

For information related to link actions associated with bookmarks, see Chapter 17.

M **Navigation pane:** The Navigation pane can be expanded or collapsed. The view in Figure 1-1 is an expanded view where the Bookmarks tab is the active pane. To open the Navigation pane you can click a tab to display the respective information associated with that tab in the expanded palette window. Clicking again on the tab collapses the view. You can also use the keyboard shortcut F4 to expand and collapse the Navigation pane.

N **Document pane:** The Document pane is the container for PDF files you see in Acrobat. When no file is open, the Document pane is empty. When you open a PDF document, the document appears in the Document pane.

O **Status bar:** The status bar contains viewing tools for zooming, page navigation, page modes, and page layout, and displays information about your PDF document. You can see the current zoom level and the number of pages in the open PDF at a glance in the status bar, as shown in Figure 1-1 where page 1 of 758 is displayed. You can navigate pages in the status bar by clicking on a navigation tool (represented by the arrows), entering a number in the status bar, and pressing Enter/Return on your keyboard. You can change page layout views by selecting one of the four tools on the far right side of the status bar.

Cross-Reference

For information related to navigation with the status bar, see Chapter 4.

P **How To pane:** The How To pane enables you to obtain instant help with menu commands, tools, palette options, and many selected tasks you perform routinely. When you invoke a search in Acrobat the How To pane is replaced with the Search pane. By default, the How To pane opens when you first launch Acrobat. You can toggle the pane off by deselecting the check box for Show How To Window at Startup on the home page in the How To pane.

Cross-Reference

For information on using the How To pane, see the "Accessing Help" section later in this chapter.

For more detail on specific menu commands, tools, and palettes, see the related chapters to discover the different options available to you. All of the items discussed here are explained in more depth in subsequent chapters.

Menus

Like any program operating on a computer system that supports a windows type of environment, you'll notice menu commands at the top level of the Acrobat window. Users of previous versions will notice different menu commands have been relocated under different menu headings. If at first glance you don't see an option you used in Acrobat 6, poke around the menus. None of the Acrobat 6 features have been eliminated; they may just be in a different place or referred to by a different name.

File menu

File The File menu is where you open and close documents, create PDF files, import and export certain data, access print commands, and find some other nifty new additions in Acrobat. The Mac and Windows operating systems display recent files in different menus. On the Mac in OS X you'll find recently viewed documents by choosing File ➪ Open Recent File. This command opens a submenu where you can access recent documents. On Windows, a list of the recently viewed documents is located at the bottom of the File menu, as shown in Figure 1-2.

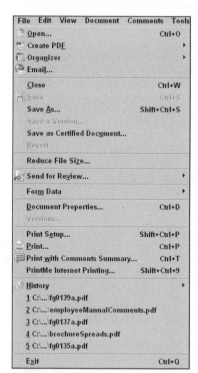

Figure 1-2: Recently opened files in Windows appear at the bottom of the File menu. Macintosh users can display a list of recently viewed files by choosing File ➪ Open Recent File.

Note The Form Data menu command, shown in Figure 1-2 is only available in Acrobat Professional. Save a Version and Versions appear only in Acrobat Professional when Version Cue is enabled.

You'll note that the My Bookshelf command has been eliminated and a new file management tool called *Organizer* now appears in the File menu.

Cross-Reference For information related to using the Organizer, see Chapter 4. For information about saving versions, see Chapter 9.

Edit menu

Edit As shown in Figure 1-3, the traditional Cut, Copy, and Paste commands are located in the Edit menu along with other familiar commands from Acrobat 6. No changes appear in the Edit menu in Acrobat 7 than were present with Acrobat 6.

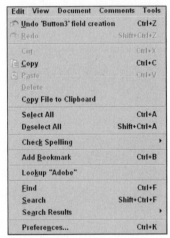

Figure 1-3: The Edit menu contains the same commands found in Acrobat 6.

View menu

View The View menu (see Figure 1-4) contains all the commands you'll use for viewing PDF documents. Additions to the View menu include items such as Wireframe and Tracker. Wireframe mode displays all lines at one point for easier viewing when you zoom out on drawings. You can launch the Review Tracker from either this menu command or the Tracker command in the Comment & Markup Task Button.

Note Wireframe, Grids, Guides, and Rulers are available only in Acrobat Professional.

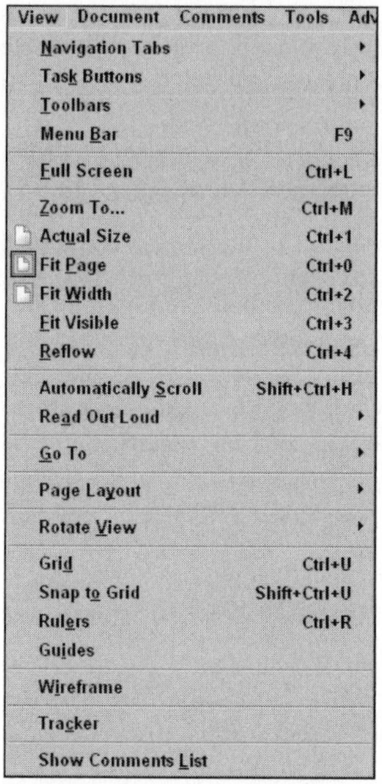

View	Document	Comments	Tools	Adv

Navigation Tabs ▶
Task Buttons ▶
Toolbars ▶
Menu Bar   F9

Full Screen   Ctrl+L

Zoom To...   Ctrl+M
Actual Size   Ctrl+1
Fit Page   Ctrl+0
Fit Width   Ctrl+2
Fit Visible   Ctrl+3
Reflow   Ctrl+4

Automatically Scroll   Shift+Ctrl+H
Read Out Loud ▶

Go To ▶

Page Layout ▶

Rotate View ▶

Grid   Ctrl+U
Snap to Grid   Shift+Ctrl+U
Rulers   Ctrl+R
Guides

Wireframe

Tracker

Show Comments List

Figure 1-4: The View menu contains commands for viewing PDF documents and navigating through pages and different PDF files. This menu contains the commands for many of the new features appearing in Acrobat Professional.

 Cross-Reference   For information related to Wireframe viewing see Chapter 4. For information on tracking reviews, see Chapter 16.

Document menu

Document   The Document menu (see Figure 1-5) contains a collection of commands specific to document handling. Options in the Document menu have changed substantially in Acrobat 7 compared to the options in Acrobat 6. Notice a new command — Attach a File — at the top of this menu handles attaching files to PDF documents. This command does not create a file attachment as a comment as you might use with the Attach a File as a Comment tool. Recognize Text Using OCR is a new label for Paper Capture (used in Acrobat 6) and now more intuitively describes the function. Set Page Transitions is a new command in this menu and simply duplicates the same command contained in the Pages pane. Below Set Page Transitions you'll find various commands for handling pages. These commands were previously displayed in the Pages submenu in Acrobat 6.

For information related to attaching files, see Chapter 15. For information related to deploying documents for Reader users to extract attachments, see Chapter 3. For information related to Print Production, see Chapter 25. For information on recognizing text as OCR (optical character recognition), see Chapter 13. For information on setting page transitions, see Chapter 23.

Menu commands that have been eliminated from the Document menu in Acrobat 7 compared to Acrobat 6 are the Pages submenu, Import Comments, Export Comments to Word, Add a Comment (which now appears in the Comment & Markup Task Button described as Add a Note), and Summarize Comments. The Preflight command has also been eliminated from the Document menu and relocated to the Tools ⇨ Print Production submenu.

Most of the aforementioned Comments-related commands have now been moved to the new Comments menu. For example, this is where you go to print comments with a summary. The Summarize Comments command is also available in the Comments pane Options menu as in Acrobat 6. In Acrobat 6 you opened a dialog box to manage comments. In Acrobat 7 you manage comments in the new Comments menu.

For information related to adding comments, summarizing comments, and using the Comments menu, see Chapter 16. For information related to Print Production and pre-flighting, see Chapter 25.

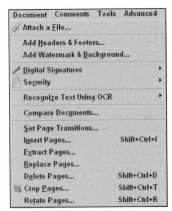

Figure 1-5: The Document menu reflects several changes in Acrobat 7.

Comments menu

Comments New in Acrobat 7 is a separate menu for handling comments. In addition to the Comments pane that also provides tools and menu commands, the Comments menu (see Figure 1-6) provides access to commenting tools as well as commands for importing and exporting comments, adding a note, opening the Comments pane, enabling commenting for Adobe Reader users, printing documents with comments, opening the commenting preferences, and access to help information related to commenting.

For details on all the menu commands in the Comments menu, see Chapter 15.

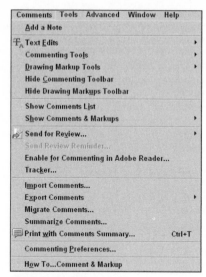

Figure 1-6: The new Comments menu offers commands specific to review and markups.

Tools menu

Tools The Tools menu (see Figure 1-7) in Acrobat logically places access to many editing tools in a single convenient menu. You can access certain tools from the Acrobat toolbars (explained in the section "Tools and toolbars" later in this chapter) or you can use a context menu to access toolbars from the Acrobat Toolbar Well. The difference between the menu command in the Tools menu compared to both the View menu and a context menu is the Tools submenus give you direct access to individual tools as opposed to toolbars. When you load a toolbar, several individual tools appear in the bar.

Figure 1-7: The Tools menu contains a collection of tools accessed from submenus. Select a tool group from the menu options to open a submenu.

Note   Measuring, Drawing Markups, and Print Production tools are available only in Acrobat Professional.

Advanced menu

Advanced The Advanced menu (see Figure 1-8) contains a collection of menu commands considered to be advanced Acrobat features. A few of these tools are not available to users of Acrobat Standard such as Batch Processing and access to Acrobat Catalog. Some menu names have been changed and some commands found in Acrobat 6 such as the PDF Optimizer have been relocated to other menus.

Figure 1-8: The Advanced menu offers menu commands related to advanced editing features.

Cross-Reference

For information related to Batch Processing, see Chapters 14 and 29. For information on using Acrobat Catalog, see Chapter 5.

Window menu

Window The Window menu (see Figure 1-9) provides menu commands to assist you in viewing documents. A new Spreadsheet Split view has been added to Acrobat 7 where you can split a document into several panels for viewing similar to spreadsheet views.

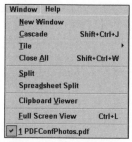

Figure 1-9: The Window menu handles all the window views such as tiling, cascading, and the new feature for displaying a split window.

For information related to window views and the split window views, see Chapter 4.

Help menu

Help The traditional help files added to your Acrobat folder at installation are found in the Help menu (see Figure 1-10). The previously named How To pane is now labeled Help and offers the same access to the complete Acrobat Help document installed with your application. Topics have been reorganized in the Help pane and now give you quick access to many different Acrobat features, including new help topics such as Forms, Print Production, and Engineering tasks. As is the case in Acrobat 6, you can use the Complete Acrobat 7.0 command to open a complete help document that you can search so you can find help information fast.

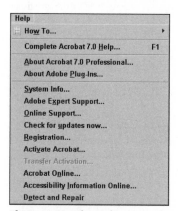

Figure 1-10: The Help menu gives you access to Help information on selected topics as well as access to the complete Acrobat Help document.

Cross-Reference For information related to Help documents and Help menus, see the "Accessing Help" section later in this chapter.

Submenus

An extensive number of submenus appear in menus contained in the top-level menu bar and from many different tools contained in toolbars. Note that on individual toolbars you see a down-pointing arrow. Clicking the arrow opens a menu; some menus contain submenus. A submenu is denoted in Acrobat by a right-pointing arrow on the right side of a given menu command. Select a command with one of these arrows adjacent to the command name and a submenu opens. In a few cases, you can find nested submenus where another right-pointing arrow may be visible in a submenu, as shown in Figure 1-11. If you want to access the second submenu, move the cursor to the menu option containing a right-pointing arrow. To make a selection from a submenu command, move the cursor to the desired menu command. When the menu command highlights, click the mouse button to execute the command.

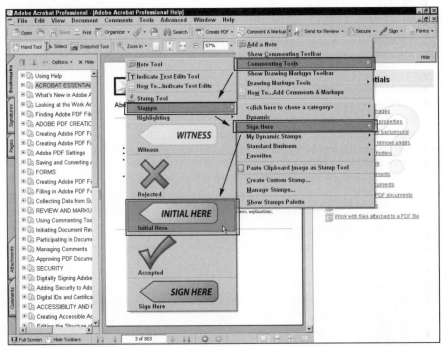

Figure 1-11: To access a submenu, move the cursor to the command containing a right-pointing arrow and slide the cursor over to the submenu options. Click the desired command in the submenu to execute the command.

Context menus

Wherever you are in the Acrobat window — the toolbars, palettes, Document pane, or the Help menus — you can gain quick access to menu items related to your task by opening a context menu. Context menus pop up in an area where you either click the right button on the mouse or use an appropriate key modifier. In Windows, right-click the mouse button to open a context menu. On a Macintosh, when not using a two-button mouse, press the Control key and click the mouse button. Context menu options relate to the particular tool you have selected from a toolbar. By default the Hand tool is selected when you launch Acrobat and open a PDF document. When you right-click the mouse button (Windows) or Control+click (Macintosh), a context menu pops up where you click the mouse as shown in Figure 1-12.

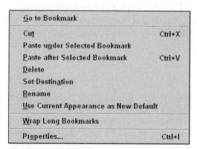

Add Note	
Add Bookmark	Ctrl+B
Allow Hand Tool to Select Text	
Zoom Tools	▶
Next Page	Right Arrow
Previous Page	Left Arrow
Select All	Ctrl+A
Deselect All	Shift+Ctrl+A
Print...	Ctrl+P
Search	Shift+Ctrl+F

Figure 1-12: With the Hand tool selected, right-clicking (Windows) or Control+clicking (Macintosh) the mouse button opens a context menu. From the menu, scroll the list and select the desired menu command.

If you change tools in a toolbar and open a context menu, the menu options change to reflect choices with that particular tool. Likewise, a context menu opened on a palette offers menu options respective to the palette, as shown in Figure 1-13.

Go to Bookmark	
Cut	Ctrl+X
Paste under Selected Bookmark	
Paste after Selected Bookmark	Ctrl+V
Delete	
Set Destination	
Rename	
Use Current Appearance as New Default	
Wrap Long Bookmarks	
Properties...	Ctrl+I

Figure 1-13: When a palette is open in the Navigation pane and you open a context menu, the menu options reflect tasks you can perform respective to the palette.

Note   In order to open a context menu on a palette, the palette must be open in the Navigation pane. Clicking the tab for the palette name doesn't open a context menu.

Context menus are a great benefit during your Acrobat sessions and using them helps you work much faster. Throughout this book I often make references to the different choices you have in selecting a tool or command. In most incidences, you find mention of context menus. Be certain you know how to open a context menu in Acrobat on your computer. For the remainder of this book I'll mention opening context menus without walking through the steps for how to open the menu.

Keyboard shortcuts

Pressing one or more keys on your keyboard can also open menus and invoke different commands. When you become familiar with keyboard shortcuts that perform the same function as when using a menu or context menu, you'll find yourself favoring this method for making different menu selections or grabbing a tool from a toolbar. Fortunately, you can learn as you work when it comes to memorizing keyboard shortcuts. As I'm certain you know, several shortcut combinations are noted in menu commands. You can learn these shortcuts when you frequently use a particular command. However, the keyboard shortcuts you see in the menu commands are just a fraction of what is available in Acrobat for quick access to commands and tools. For a complete list of all keyboard shortcuts, look over Appendix A. You can use the appendix to refresh your memory on shortcut keys as you work through the program.

Note

Pressing a single key to access a tool requires you to have your Preferences set to accept single keystroke shortcuts. See the steps for "Setting up the Acrobat environment" later in this chapter for the proper Preferences settings.

Tools and toolbars

Tools are grouped together in separate toolbars in the Toolbar Well below the menu bar. The default view when you launch Acrobat contains several toolbars visible in the Toolbar Well. You can remove various toolbars from the Well, move them around the Acrobat window, close them, and add different toolbars to the Toolbar Well. The Toolbar Well, where the toolbars are contained, is collapsed and expanded according to the number of toolbars you add to it. When a toolbar is contained within the Toolbar Well, it is said to be *docked*. When a toolbar is dragged away from the Toolbar Well and rests atop the Acrobat window, it is said to be *undocked*.

Toolbars often contain nested tools accessible from pull-down menus. When you see a down-pointing arrow adjacent to a tool, you can click the arrow to open the menu. Many menus contain an Expand This Button menu command. Selecting this command (see the example shown in Figure 1-14), expands the toolbar enough to accommodate additional tools. In Figure 1-15 you can see the File toolbar expanded after the command was selected.

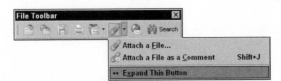

Figure 1-14: Several tools contain pull-down menus with an Expand This Button menu command, which you use to expand the toolbar to accommodate more tools.

Default toolbars

When you launch Acrobat for the first time or you set the toolbars to the default view, six different toolbars are docked in the Toolbar Well. The default toolbars include

✦ **File toolbar:** These tools are used for general document handling. The File tools activate commands for Open, Open Web Page, Save, Print, Open Organizer, Attach a File, Attach a File as a Comment, Email, and Search. In Figure 1-15 the File Toolbar is expanded.

Figure 1-15: The File Toolbar contains tools for document handling, such as opening PDF documents, saving documents, and printing files.

✦ **Tasks Toolbar:** Task tools are used for editing tasks and document handling. The tools handle Acrobat tasks such as Create PDF, Comment and Markup, Send for Review, Security, Digital Signatures, and Forms. All of these tools have toolbar pull-down menus. Notice in Figure 1-16 the down-pointing arrow appearing to the right of all the tools in this group, indicating they all have pull-down menus.

Figure 1-16: The Tasks Toolbar contains tools used for specific Acrobat tasks such as creating PDFs, reviewing documents, adding digital signatures, and so on.

✦ **Basic Toolbar:** Among the Basic tools, shown in Figure 1-17, are the Hand tool, Select tool, and the Snapshot tool. In Acrobat 7 the Select tool combines tasks for selecting either text or graphics. The order of selection in terms of what is selected first (either text or graphics) is controlled with a Preferences setting.

Figure 1-17: The Basic Toolbar contains tools for selecting text and graphics. The default Hand tool is selected when you open Acrobat at the start of each session.

Cross-Reference

For more information on changing Preferences, see "Understanding Preferences" later in this chapter.

✦ **Zoom Toolbar:** The tools in this group (see Figure 1-18) are used to zoom in and out of pages in the Document pane.

Figure 1-18: The Zoom tools handle zooming in and out of the current active document.

✦ **Rotate View Toolbar:** The Rotate View tools, shown in the expanded toolbar in Figure 1-19, are used to rotate pages in the Document pane. When these tools are used to rotate pages, the rotated views cannot be saved.

 Figure 1-19: Use the Rotate View tools to temporarily rotate pages while viewing a document.

✦ **Help Toolbar:** Help topics are readily available to you in Acrobat via the Help pane. A list of Help items is contained in the pull-down menu shown in Figure 1-20 as well as access to the complete Acrobat Help document.

Figure 1-20: The Help Toolbar enables you to obtain help for many common editing tasks in Acrobat.

Managing default toolbars

As mentioned previously, toolbars can be moved, docked, and undocked from the Toolbar Well. Here's a list of some of the things you can do with the default toolbars and any other toolbars you decide to view:

✦ **Undocking toolbars:** Toolbars can be relocated from within the Toolbar Well to another area within the Acrobat window. For example, you might find it more convenient to move a toolbar you frequently access during an editing session so it is positioned at the bottom of the Document pane. If so, just place the cursor on top of the vertical separator bar adjacent to the first tool in a toolbar and drag it away from the Toolbar Well, as shown in Figure 1-21. This vertical line is the *hot spot* used to select the toolbar instead of a tool in the group. Clicking anywhere else in the toolbar selects a tool.

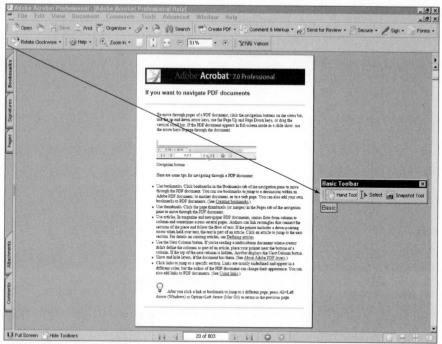

Figure 1-21: Move toolbars around the Acrobat window by selecting the vertical separator adjacent to the first tool in a toolbar and dragging it away from the Toolbar Well.

✦ **Docking toolbars:** To dock a toolbar back in the Toolbar Well once removed, drag the toolbar, again by the vertical separator bar adjacent to the first tool, on top of the Toolbar Well. The toolbar snaps to an available position in the well. If you drop the toolbar between two other toolbars, the toolbar you relocate back to the Toolbar Well snaps in position between the two docked toolbars.

Toolbars can also be docked vertically on the left and right sides of the Document pane and at the bottom of the Acrobat window below the status bar. For example, if you drag a toolbar to the left of the Navigation pane and release the mouse button, the toolbar snaps to a docking station and the tools display vertically. In Figure 1-22 you can see toolbars docked on the left, right, and bottom of the Acrobat window with one floating toolbar in the Document pane.

✦ **Resetting toolbars:** You can position toolbars around the Acrobat window and return them to the default positions with one menu command. This is particularly helpful if multiple users work on a single computer or you frequently change editing tasks that require using different tools during different editing sessions. In many cases it's easier to reset toolbars to the original default view, than open tools needed for a specific editing task. To set toolbars to their defaults, open a context menu from any toolbar or in the Toolbar Well by right-clicking (Control+clicking on Macintosh), and select the menu item Reset Toolbars as shown in Figure 1-23.

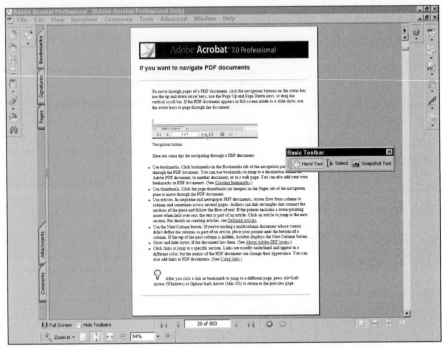

Figure 1-22: Toolbars can be docked on all four sides of the Acrobat window.

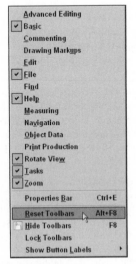

Figure 1-23: To return toolbars back to the default view, open a context menu from any toolbar or in the Toolbar Well and select Reset Toolbars.

Note

When you dock a toolbar on the left, right, and/or bottom of the Acrobat window, the empty area surrounding the toolbar becomes a Toolbar Well. Context menus can be opened from any Toolbar Well and menu commands appear the same as shown in Figure 1-24.

✦ **Hiding all toolbars:** Toolbars can be hidden from view to offer you more room when editing a PDF document or browsing the contents of PDFs. If you master some of the keyboard shortcuts shown in Appendix A, you can move about PDF files in the Document pane or perform many different editing tasks without the toolbars in view. To hide the toolbars from view, open a context menu from the Toolbar Well and choose Hide Toolbars. When toolbars are hidden you won't have access to a context menu to get the toolbars back in view. Instead, choose View ⇨ Toolbars ⇨ Show Toolbars or press the F8 key on your keyboard to make all toolbars reappear. (Note that using this menu command also hides toolbars.) Alternately, you can click the Hide/Show toolbars in the lower left corner of the Status Bar.

✦ **Hiding a single toolbar:** You can hide a toolbar after it has been undocked from the Toolbar Well. Click the X in the top-right corner of the toolbar (Windows) or the small circle on the top-left side of the toolbar (Macintosh) to close it, and it disappears from view. From a context menu opened on any toolbar or the Toolbar Well you can open the toolbar and display it in the Acrobat window again.

✦ **Locking toolbars:** The vertical separator bar used to move toolbars disappears when you select Lock Toolbars from a context menu. The toolbars cannot be inadvertently moved after you lock them. To unlock the toolbars, open a context menu and select Lock Toolbars again. The check mark alongside the menu command becomes unchecked and the toolbars are unlocked in the Toolbar Well. If the toolbars are locked and you drag an undocked toolbar on top of the Toolbar Well, it won't dock. You need to first unlock the toolbars before you can redock them.

Note

You can also lock toolbars that are undocked outside of the Toolbar Well. The separator bar on the toolbar disappears on floating toolbars the same as it does for toolbars docked in the Toolbar Well. However, locking undocked toolbars does not prevent you from moving them around the Acrobat window. You can click and drag the title bar for any undocked toolbar and move it to another location.

✦ **Setting new toolbar defaults:** If you decide to reposition your toolbars and want to keep them fixed as new defaults, Acrobat can do so for you automatically. Move the toolbars to the desired locations and go about your work. When you quit Acrobat and reopen the program, the toolbar positions remain as you last arranged them. Unfortunately, Acrobat does not have a Save Workspace command like you find in several Adobe Creative Suite applications.

Tip

If you are unfamiliar with many Acrobat tools, you can change the tool labels to show you a more descriptive label for each tool that offers you a hint of what the tool does. To show more descriptive labels, open a context menu on the Acrobat Toolbar Well and choose Show Button Labels ⇨ All Labels. The toolbars expand and show a text description for each tool's name. Keep this option active until you are familiar with the tool names.

Understanding advanced toolbars

The default toolbars represent less than half of the tools available to you in Acrobat. Many of the other toolbars remain hidden from view. The reason for this is obvious when you load all the toolbars in the Toolbar Well. You lose a lot of viewing real estate when all toolbars are docked in the Toolbar Well. Unless you have a large display monitor or a second monitor, working on a file in the Document pane when all toolbars are in view gives little room to see document pages. Fortunately, by managing the toolbars you can elect to show only the tools you want to work with and you can move them around the Acrobat window, allowing for the best view.

Cross-Reference   Turn back to Figure 1-1 in this chapter to see all the toolbars docked in the Toolbar Well.

You open toolbars from menu commands in the Tools menu or by opening a context menu. If you're a seasoned Acrobat user, your first encounter with Acrobat viewers 6 and above might be a bit frustrating if you don't know how to access the tools you want to use. "Where is that Form tool?" you may ask. Don't worry; it's there. You just have to poke around and search for it, or better yet, look over the following descriptions to understand more about how these other tools are grouped into separate toolbars.

Acquiring advanced toolbars

For the purpose of discussion, I'll refer to the non-default toolbars as advanced toolbars. Acrobat does not refer to all these tools as advanced tools. Some of the tools labeled in the menu commands are not referred to as advanced tools. For clarity in this chapter, though, consider all the following toolbars as advanced toolbars.

You can use three methods for displaying toolbars not visible when you open Acrobat. You can open the View ⇨ Toolbars menu where you find a list of tools in submenus. Select a submenu item to open a toolbar as a floating toolbar in the Acrobat window. Another method is to open a Task Button pull-down menu and select a menu command to show a toolbar. Not all the toolbars are accessible from Task Buttons so you need to use other methods if a toolbar you want to open is not contained in a Task Button pull-down menu. The third method, and perhaps the easiest way to access tools, is to open a context menu on the Toolbar Well. As a matter of routine, you should use this option, as it's the fastest method for opening and closing tools. All tools except the Form tools (Acrobat Professional only) are accessible from the context menu.

Advanced Editing tools

When you open either the View ⇨ Toolbars submenu menus or a context menu on the Toolbar Well, the first menu option is Advanced Editing. Select the menu option and the Advanced Editing tools open in their own toolbar.

Down arrows in the toolbar denote where you can open pull-down menus. Click a pull-down menu, and various other tools appear as additional choices. When you click the down arrow to open a pull-down menu adjacent to the Button tool (Acrobat Professional only) as shown in Figure 1-24, the menu options show the different Form tools and a menu command for showing the Forms toolbar. The Forms toolbar needs to be opened from this menu command as it's not accessible in either the View ⇨ Tools submenu or from a context menu opened on the Toolbar Well.

The Advanced Editing tools offer you a set of tools to edit documents with articles, crop pages, add form fields, add movies and sound (Acrobat Professional only), and edit text.

Cross-Reference   Advanced Editing tools are described throughout Parts III and IV.

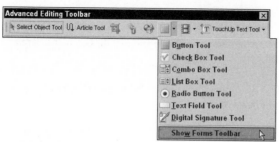

Figure 1-24: Selecting the down-pointing arrow adjacent to the Button tool opens a menu where you select form tools.

Commenting tools

The Commenting tools, shown in Figure 1-25, are used in review sessions to mark up and comment on documents, much like you might use pens, highlighters, and diagrams in an analog review session.

Cross-
Reference

To learn how to use each of the Commenting tools, see Chapter 15.

Figure 1-25: Use the Comment tools to mark up documents during a review.

Drawing Markups tools

Acrobat divides the comment tools into two categories. The tools in the Commenting Toolbar are used typically with office documents, reports, manuals, letters, and so on commonly found in regular business environments. The Drawing Markups tools shown in Figure 1-26 can be used in these environments as well, but the intent for the use of these tools is focused on engineers and technical professionals.

Cross-
Reference

To learn how to use the Drawing Markups tools, see Chapter 15.

Figure 1-26: Drawing Markups tools are used to mark up technical documents during a review.

Edit tools

The Edit tools, shown in Figure 1-27, are limited to spell checking (comment notes and form fields only), and Undo, Redo, and Copy a selection. These simple edit commands are found in most programs running on Windows and the Macintosh.

Figure 1-27: The Edit Toolbar contains tools for spell checking, and Undo, Redo, and Copy a selection.

Find tool

Early versions of Acrobat had a Find tool used to find text in open documents. In Acrobat 6, the Search pane was used to find text in open documents as well as to run searches across documents and through search index files. In Acrobat 7, the Find tool returns, as shown in Figure 1-28. Use of this tool is limited to searching text in an open document.

Figure 1-28: Use the Find tool to search text in the active open document.

To learn how to use the Find tool and understand more about using Search in Acrobat viewers, see Chapter 5.

Measuring tools

The Measuring tools include the Distance tool used for measuring linear distances, the Perimeter tool for measuring linear distances of angles and objects, and an Area tool for measuring the surface area of objects. The Measuring Toolbar, shown in Figure 1-29, might be used for examining measurements in engineering and scientific drawings.

For more information about using the Measuring tools, see Chapter 15.

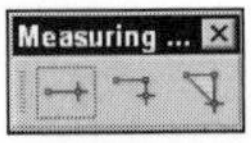

Figure 1-29: The Measuring Toolbar offers three tools to measure distances and areas on a PDF page.

Navigation tools

Because so many different ways exist for paging through PDF files, having the Navigation tools visible as a default isn't really necessary. The status bar contains all the navigation tools you need. Nonetheless, the Navigation Toolbar is available to you and might be used in instances where the document window controls have been hidden. In this case, you might open the toolbar, shown in Figure 1-30, to navigate pages.

Figure 1-30: The Navigation Toolbar is not visible when Acrobat opens with default toolbars in view. To access the Navigation tools choose View ➪ Toolbars ➪ Navigation or use a context menu.

Cross-Reference For more information regarding navigating PDFs, see Chapter 3. For information on hiding window controls, see Chapter 4.

Object Data tool

The Object Data tool (see Figure 1-31) is used to select objects on a document page. When you select an object that has object data associated with it, the Object Data dialog box opens. This dialog box contains object metadata that was added by PDF authors using programs such as Microsoft Visior Project, Autodesk AutoCAD, and other programs that support support object data. Object Data might include asset information on objects that are shown on diagrams such as costs, object attributes, inventory, catalog information, and so on.

 Cross-Reference For a greater understanding about object and document metadata, see Chapter 4. For information on using the Object Data tool, see Chapter 7.

 Figure 1-31: Use the Object Data tool to select objects and view file attributes associated with the selected object.

Print Production tools

The Print Production tools (see Figure 1-32) enable you to make adjustments on the PDF or alter the content. This toolbar contains tools for assigning traps, pre-flighting, converting colors, assigning color profiles, adding crop marks, cropping pages, fixing hairlines, transparency flattening, and assigning Job Definitions.

Figure 1-32: Use the Print Production tools to open dialog boxes where you can preview and change PDF documents to accommodate prepress and commercial printing.

 Cross-Reference For more information on using Print Production tools and preparing files for commercial printing, see Chapter 25.

Properties Bar

You use the Properties Bar (see Figure 1-33) in conjunction with several different tools. After you create comments, links, buttons, and similar content in a PDF document, the selected comment, link, button, and so on displays current properties such as colors, fonts, and line weights in the Properties Bar. You can make changes in the Properties Bar without visiting the Properties dialog box. You can quickly open the Properties Bar with a keyboard shortcut (Ctrl/⌘) or via context menu.

Figure 1-33: The Properties Bar offers a quick solution for editing item properties without the need for opening dialog boxes.

Customizing the Acrobat workplace

Whether you're an Acrobat pro or a new Acrobat user, seeing all those toolbars scattered across the Toolbar Well the first time can be very intimidating. As you poke around and possibly feel a little frustration when trying to identify the right tool icon to select the right tool for the task at hand, please realize that Acrobat is a multifaceted program serving a huge array of needs for different users. Not all the tools and features are designed for use in a single Acrobat session. You may be a PDF forms author and need only Basic tools, Navigation tools, and Form tools. In another session you may be a reviewer and only have need for the Comment and Markup tools. You might be an eBook author and need to work with many features for creating and viewing eBooks, or you might want to edit PDF pages and post modified PDFs on your Web site.

When learning all the tools and commands contained in Acrobat Professional, be certain to look over all the chapters where tools are discussed. Learn how to access toolbars and organize them in the Toolbar Well. When you begin a new Acrobat session, set up your environment so you can easily select a tool from toolbars you dock in the Toolbar Well. Frequently return to Appendix A and look over the keyboard shortcuts to learn how to quickly access the tools you use most frequently.

As a starting point, you can configure Acrobat to provide you with immediate feedback related to tools selection and keyboard shortcuts. As you first start using Acrobat Professional, follow the steps in the next section to help you customize your environment for more efficient editing and less frustration. In this example, an environment for engaging in a commenting session is used. You can change the toolbars to meet needs in PDF editing or PDF creation, or add tools for some other kind of work you do.

STEPS: Setting up the Acrobat environment

1. **Return to toolbar defaults.** Open Acrobat. Position the cursor on any toolbar or an empty area in the Toolbar Well and right-click to open a context menu (Ctrl+click for Macintosh) and select Reset Toolbars.

2. **Show a toolbar.** Open the Tools menu and select the first toolbar you need to add to the Toolbar Well for easy access to the tools you intend to use. In this example, I select Tools ➪ Commenting to open the Advanced Editing toolbar.

3. **Dock the toolbar in the Toolbar Well.** Click the separator bar on the floating toolbar in the Acrobat window and drag it toward the Toolbar Well. Release the mouse button when the toolbar is on top of the Toolbar Well.

4. **Add additional toolbars for tools you intend to use.** If you need more tools, follow the previous steps and add just the toolbars containing the tools you expect to use in your editing session. In this example I open a context menu on the Toolbar Well and select Drawing Markups and then return to the context menu and load the Measuring toolbar. Open a context menu on the Acrobat Toolbar Well and select Properties Bar.

5. **Dock the floating toolbars.** To use another method for docking toolbars, open a context menu on the Toolbar Well and select Dock All Toolbars.

6. **Show all button labels.** Open a context menu on the Toolbar Well and select Show Button Labels ➪ All Labels. Showing all the labels provides you a clear description for the tools contained in the Toolbar Well.

7. **Open the Preferences dialog box.** Many tools can be accessed using keyboard short-cuts. In order to use keyboard shortcuts, you need to adjust a preference setting in the Preferences dialog box. On Windows, choose Edit ⇨ Preferences. On the Mac, choose Acrobat ⇨ Preferences. You can also use the keyboard shortcut Control/⌘+K.

8. **Enable single-key accelerators.** Click General in the left pane of the Preferences dialog box. In the Miscellaneous section in the right pane, check the box for Use single-key accelerators to access tools. When this check box is selected, you can press a single key on your keyboard to access respective tools. For example, press the H key to select the Hand tool. Press the Z key to select the Zoom In tool. Pressing Shift+Z toggles all the zoom tools each time you press the keys.

9. **Exit the Preferences dialog box.** After making your preference choices, click OK in the dialog box. New preference choices take effect without your having to restart the program. In Figure 1-34 you can see the Acrobat Workplace configured for working with comment and markup. Note that many tools are accessible only when you have a PDF document open in the Document pane.

Figure 1-34: Toolbars are loaded and docked in the Toolbar Well.

Tool Tips

When you select All Labels from a context menu or preference setting, you see tool descriptions on many tools. However, not all tools describe the tool with a label. For example, look at the Zoom In tool (the magnifying glass with a plus symbol). It should be apparent to you what the tool does by viewing the icon in the toolbar. Other tools' functions, however, may not be so apparent from viewing the tool icons. Fortunately, you have some extra help in the form of Tool Tips. To view a Tool Tip, place the cursor over a tool in the Toolbar Well or on a floating toolbar, and pause a moment before selecting the tool. A Tool Tip appears inside a yellow box directly below the cursor with a label describing the tool. In Figure 1-36 you can see the Tool Tip that appears when the cursor is placed over the Snapshot tool. As you move the cursor over different tools, the Tool Tips change to reflect the description of the targeted tool as well as the keyboard shortcut used to make the tool active. Note the (G) in Figure 1-35, indicating that pressing the G key on your keyboard selects the Snapshot tool.

 Figure 1-35: Place the cursor over a tool and pause a moment before selecting the tool. A Tool Tip describing the tool opens below the mouse cursor.

As you become familiar with the tools, you can return to the context menu opened from the Toolbar Well and choose Show Button Labels ⇨ No Labels. When No Labels is active, your toolbars shrink in size and offer you more room in the Toolbar Well.

Palettes

Other tools available to you in all Acrobat viewers are *palettes*. Palettes are similar to toolbars in that they can be docked to a docking station called the Navigation pane; they can be undocked and floated around the Acrobat window; they can contain pull-down menus for selecting more options; a series of default palettes appears docked in the Navigation pane; and you can open additional palettes from menu commands.

A couple distinctions between toolbars and palettes are that palettes can be placeholders for information, and tools can appear inside a palette. Whereas tools are used in the Document pane, many palette operations can take place directly in the palette. Toolbars remain relatively fixed in size, but palettes can be sized and stretched along the Acrobat window to provide you with more room to work within the palette or view the information contained within the palette. In addition, some palettes contain their own tools where edits can be made in the palette and dynamically reflected on the document page. Palettes help you organize content, view specific content across many pages, and provide some tools for global editing of PDF files.

Default palettes

Like toolbars, Acrobat displays a series of palettes docked in a well when you first launch the program. Palettes are contained in the Navigation pane along the left side of the Acrobat window. By default, the Navigation pane is collapsed; however, you can save PDF documents in such a manner where a palette expands when a file is opened in any Acrobat viewer. These settings are document-specific and can be toggled on or off for individual PDF documents.

For more information about setting opening views for palette displays, see Chapter 3.

Bookmarks

The topmost default palette tab in the Navigation pane is the Bookmark tab. You can save PDF documents in a manner where the bookmarks are visible when the file opens in Acrobat. A good example of such a file is the Acrobat Help file. When you open the Acrobat or Adobe Reader Help file, bookmarks are visible in an open Navigation pane, as shown in Figure 1-36. You can open and close the Navigation pane by pressing F4. You can also grab the vertical separator bar at the right edge of the Navigation pane and move it left and right to size the pane.

Bookmarks are navigation buttons that can launch a page, a view, or one of many different Action types similar to link and button actions. Anyone familiar with Acrobat already knows much about bookmarks and how to navigate pages by clicking individual bookmarks in the palette.

To learn how to create and manage bookmarks and add actions, see Chapter 17.

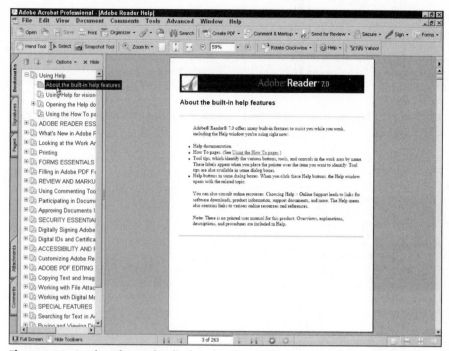

Figure 1-36: Bookmarks can be displayed in the Navigation pane when a file opens.

Signatures

The Signatures tab in the Navigation pane has been repositioned to occupy the second tab spot from the top of the pane. Users of earlier versions of Acrobat will remember that Comments followed Thumbnails in Acrobat 5 viewers and appeared third in the list in Acrobat 6.

Digital signatures help you manage signed documents; the Signatures tab enables you to perform tasks such as displaying signatures in the Signature pane, verifying signatures, clearing them, deleting them, and so on. All these editing tasks with signatures are still available in Acrobat Professional as is signature validation, which is also available in other Acrobat viewers.

Cross-Reference

For a complete description of creating and managing digital signatures, see Chapter 21.

Layers

Adobe PDF layers are supported in Acrobat 6 and 7. Earlier Acrobat viewers cannot display layer views. If you create a PDF document with layers and open the file in viewers earlier than version 6, the layers are merged into a single layer view also known as *flattening layers*. The Layers palette offers you menu options for managing layers as well as turning on and off individual layers.

Cross-Reference

For a complete description of working with layers, see Chapter 19.

Pages

Acrobat users have been familiar with the thumbnail view of each page since the early days of Acrobat. A mini view of each page in the active PDF document is displayed in the Pages pane, as shown in Figure 1-37. The Pages pane offers you menu options for arranging, deleting, inserting, and editing pages in a number of ways. You can zoom in to the thumbnail views as large or even larger than a page viewed in the Document pane.

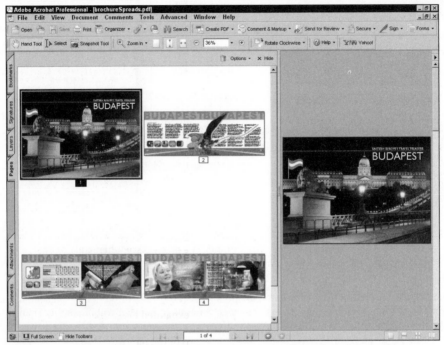

Figure 1-37: Thumbnails are found in the Pages pane in all Acrobat viewers. The thumbnail view of document pages can be sized larger and smaller using context menu commands.

Cross-Reference

For a complete description of working with pages (thumbnails), see Chapter 12.

Attachments

The new Attachments pane (see Figure 1-38) in all Acrobat viewers is used to display, manage, and extract file attachments. Now you can attach files in Acrobat Standard and Professional and extract file attachments using Adobe Reader.

Cross-Reference

For a complete description of adding file attachments to PDF documents, see Chapter 15. For more on extracting attachments from within Adobe Reader, see Chapter 3.

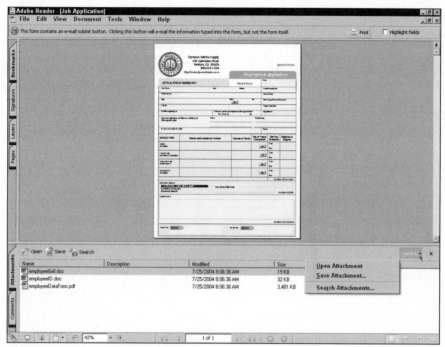

Figure 1-38: The Attachments pane provides options for managing file attachments. Attachments can be extracted from within Adobe Reader.

Comments

The Comments palette shows you comments in an expanded horizontal view, just like the Attachments pane. When you click the Comments tab, you'll notice a number of pull-down menus (signified by down-pointing arrows at the top of the pane), a list of comments that can be expanded and collapsed, and a host of tools within the palette, as shown in Figure 1-39.

Figure 1-39: The Comments palette

Cross-Reference   For a complete description of creating and managing comments, see Chapters 15 and 16.

Hidden tabs

As with toolbars, you can choose to view additional tabs through menu commands. You can choose to display a number of other tabs in the Acrobat window and dock them in the Navigation pane. To open a hidden tab, choose View ▷ Navigation Tabs. From the submenu, you'll find all the tabs available. In Figure 1-40, the list shows Navigation tabs available in Acrobat Professional. The list includes the default tabs. If you select a default tab, the Navigation pane opens and the tab is selected. When you select a hidden tab, in other words, a tab other than those docked in the Navigation pane when you first launch Acrobat, the tab opens in the Acrobat window as a floating palette with one or more tabs contained in the window.

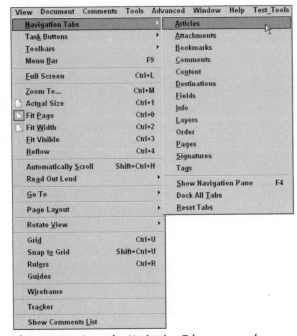

Figure 1-40: Open the Navigation Tabs menu and a submenu displays all Navigation tabs.

To dock a tab from a floating palette to the Navigation pane, select the tab to be docked and drag it away from the floating palette. Move the tab on top of an expanded Navigation pane or on top of one of the tabs in a collapsed Navigation pane. When you release the mouse button the tab is docked in the Navigation pane. If you dock a tab in the Navigation pane and quit Acrobat, the tab will be in the same position when you launch Acrobat in your next session.

Articles

The first of the hidden palettes listed in the Navigation Tabs submenu is Articles. Choose View ▷ Navigation Tabs ▷ Articles to open a floating palette. When you open the Articles palette, both the Articles tab and the Destinations tab appear in the window as shown in Figure 1-41. Most of the palettes include pull-down menus where you select options.

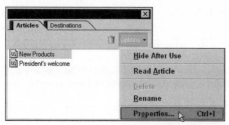

Figure 1-41: When you select Articles in the Navigation Tabs submenu, the Articles tab opens in a palette with the Destinations tab.

Articles enable you to create article threads to help users follow passages of text in a logical reading order. You won't find any new features added to the Article tool since Acrobat 5.

For information on creating article threads and managing them, see Chapter 12.

Destinations

The Destinations tab is contained in the same palette as the Articles tab. Destinations work similarly to bookmarks, in that specific views are captured and listed in the tab. Clicking a destination opens the associated page in the Document pane, whereas clicking a bookmark opens the associated view (page and zoom).

For information on creating destinations and managing them, see Chapter 17.

Content

A palette designed for managing the structural content of PDF documents is found in the Content tab. When you choose View ➪ Navigation Tabs ➪ Content, the Content palette opens in a floating palette with the Fields, Tags, and Order tabs, as shown in Figure 1-42. Content features help you reflow tagged PDF files and manipulate the structure of tagged documents.

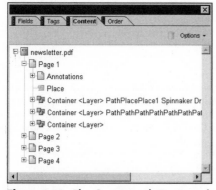

Figure 1-42: The Content palette opens in a floating palette alongside the Fields, Tags, and Order tabs.

For information on working with the Content palette and tagged PDF documents, see Chapter 20.

Fields

The Fields tab enables you to manage form fields on Acrobat PDF forms. You can list all form fields in the tab and execute menu commands from the pull-down menu and context menu opened from within the palette.

For information about Acrobat forms, see Part VI.

Tags

Tagged PDF files provide more editing capability with PDF documents, and the files can be made accessible to adaptive devices such as screen readers. For adding, editing, and annotating tags in PDF documents use the Tags tab. Together with the Content tab options, you have much control over document accessibility.

To understand accessibility and the advantages of creating tagged PDF documents, see Chapter 20.

Info

The Info tab displays the x,y position of the mouse cursor as you move it around the Document pane. From this tab you can choose to display from among three different units of measure—inches, points, and millimeters. No changes have been made to the Info palette in Acrobat viewers.

For information on working with the Info tab, see Chapter 3.

Order

You use the Order tab to manage reading order of documents. This tab also relates to document accessibility, like the options available in the Tags tab. The Order tab enables you to add tags to a document, clear tags, and reorder a page's contents to change a reading order that might be read aloud by a screen reader.

For information on working with the Order tab, understanding screen readers, and document accessibility, see Chapter 20.

Palette menus

Each of the tabs contains its own pull-down menu. When a tab is open in the Navigation pane or in a floating window, select the Options down-pointing arrow to open a pull-down menu, as shown in Figure 1-41. Menu commands found in tabs may or may not be available from the top-level menu bar. Additionally, some tabs, like the Attachments and Comments tabs, offer you several pull-down menus.

Context menus

Context menus can display different options for palette choices depending on where you open a context menu. If you move the cursor to an empty area when all text and objects in a palette are deselected and open a context menu, the menu options may be different than when you select text or an object in a palette. However, this is not always the case because a few palettes provide you with the same options regardless of whether something is selected or not. In Figure 1-43 a context menu is opened within the Pages tab. No page is selected in the palette, and you can see the context menu offers you few options.

Figure 1-43: When all page thumbnails are deselected and a context menu is opened from within the Pages palette, only a few menu choices appear in the open menu.

Compare Figure 1-43 with Figure 1-44. In Figure 1-44, a page is selected in the Pages palette. When the context menu opens, you can see that many more options are available from the menu list than when all pages are deselected.

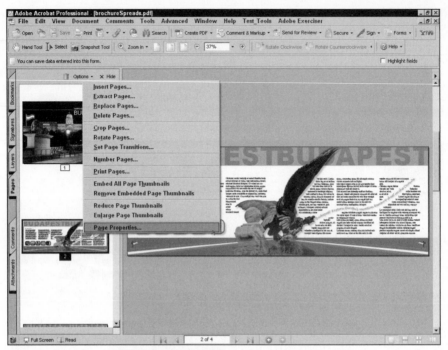

Figure 1-44: When a page is selected in the Pages palette and a context menu is opened, more menu choices are available than when no page is selected.

Accessing Help

You can see the number of different commands and tools available in Acrobat are extraordinary—and you haven't yet looked at all the submenu options or different preference options accessed from the top-level menu bar. With all these features available to you, your initial Acrobat sessions can sometimes be overwhelming. Fortunately, the great engineers and program designers at Adobe Systems thought about you and they decided to provide some help.

Help with learning more about Acrobat comes in several forms and you can choose from several help methods to find the one that works well in your workflow. This section covers different options for getting help in an Acrobat session.

How To menus

When you launch any Acrobat viewer for the first time, you see a window on the right side of the Acrobat window. It occupies more than a quarter of the horizontal view, and on smaller monitors, there won't be much room to work in the Document pane.

The window is intended for you to toggle the view on and off as you need help in using Acrobat on specific limited topics. To hide the menu, click the Hide button at the top of the How To pane as shown in Figure 1-45. To open the pane when it's not in view, click the Help Task button in the Acrobat Toolbar Well or press Shift+F4. If you want the pane to remain hidden from view when you launch Acrobat, deselect the check box at the bottom of the pane.

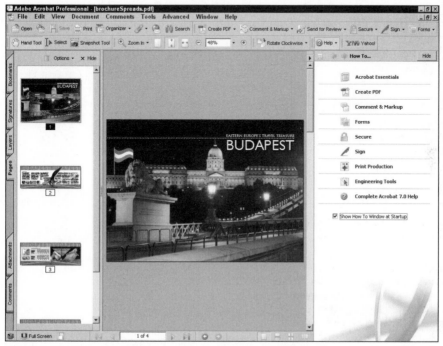

Figure 1-45: When the How To pane is visible it occupies more than a quarter of the horizontal width of the Acrobat window. If you do not want the How To pane to open when launching Acrobat, deselect the box for Show How To Window at Startup.

When the How To pane is open, several topics are listed as hot links that take you to definitions of the respective items. These items are a condensed version of a more comprehensive help document explained a little later in this chapter. Keep in mind that not all the Acrobat features are contained in the How To pane.

Click any blue text or the icons adjacent to the blue text to open a view inside the How To pane that provides you with a topical listing to assist in refining your search. If you click an item like Comment & Markup, you can see a contents list for specific items related to help on working with comments, as shown in Figure 1-46.

Figure 1-46: Click a category in the How To pane, and the window information changes to reflect information about the topic.

Note   When you see a page icon in the How To window adjacent to a topic, clicking on the icon or text takes you to help information in the How To window. When you see an icon appearing as a question mark, clicking on the icon or adjacent text opens the Complete Acrobat Help document.

When you arrive at the contents list page, as shown in Figure 1-46, click again on any text displayed in blue to go to information about the subtopic. Using the example of Comment and Markup as a category, you could choose to click the Add a note comment link. The window displays the page containing a description of how to add notes in a PDF file, as shown in Figure 1-47.

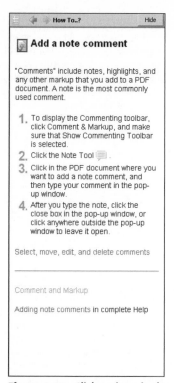

Figure 1-47: Click an item in the contents page and you are linked to a page where a description appears that explains how to perform a task.

In some cases you'll see a text description informing you how to go about archiving a result for the item you searched. In other cases you can find dynamic links to the complete Acrobat Help file. Click a link to open the topic in the Complete Acrobat Help file for a more detailed description for performing the task.

Docking the window

The How To window is docked on the right side of the Acrobat window by default. You can move the window to the left side by opening a context menu on the title bar to the left of the Hide button. When you open a context menu from the title bar, select the Docked Left option. The How To window moves to the left side of the Acrobat window. When the How To pane is docked on the left, the Navigation pane and Document pane slide to the right.

The size of the How To window is fixed and you can't change the horizontal width. Be certain to deselect the check box for Show How To Window at Startup after you become familiar with accessing help.

Navigating the How To window

You can return to the opening view of the How To window, called the *Homepage,* by clicking the icon in the top-left corner of the window. The left and right arrows move to the previous and next window views, respectively. If you navigate through a series of pages and click the Homepage button, it resets the viewing history and you aren't able to use the arrow buttons to retrace your last views. A vertical scrollbar is displayed on the right side of the How To window when the description is longer than can be viewed on your monitor. If the description is short, you won't see a scrollbar.

At the bottom of some descriptions you can find more information related to the topic you searched. Again with hot links, click the text or an icon to open another page offering you related information. If you want to return to the contents, click another button, also visible at the bottom of a description page, indicating you will return to the topics.

If you want to open another topic without being on the Homepage, you can open the pull-down menu from the Help Task Button. The down-pointing arrow opens a menu with the specific help topics listed. Selecting a topic reopens the How To pane and a help page associated with the topic selected from the menu.

Acrobat help

The How To window contains a select group of common Acrobat features about which you can find help within the listed topics on the Homepage. You can also access more topics by selecting various topics from the Help Task Button. However, Acrobat is a monster program with many features and listing all the methods for working in the program is not the intent for the How To help pane. To browse through a comprehensive help guide you need to access a different document. The comprehensive help guide contains more than 800 pages covering just about everything you want to know about Acrobat. There are, in essence, two flavors of the Acrobat Help guide. You can access the Complete Acrobat 7.0 Help document from the Homepage in the How To pane or you can open the Acrohelp.pdf file in Acrobat. These two documents are different in that the Complete Acrobat Help document is a PDF file using a custom interface. The Acrohelp.pdf file is a standard PDF document contained in the Acrobat folder. Depending on which one you open, you have some different methods for viewing and navigation.

Complete Acrobat 7.0 Help

You open the Complete Acrobat 7.0 Help from the Help Task Button. Open the pull-down menu by clicking the down-pointing arrow and select Complete Acrobat 7.0 Help. When you open this document without a PDF file open in the Document pane, you'll immediately notice you have no access to tools and menu commands. That's because the document is a PDF file designed with a special user interface. It appears similar to files you open in Acrobat with a Navigation pane on the left side of the window and the page contents to the right. It can be sized and scrolled, but the file is not confined to the Document pane like other PDF files. It behaves more like a floating window on top of the Acrobat window. When you select the menu command to open the document, three tabs appear in the top-left side of the window as shown in Figure 1-48. Click the Contents tab to show bookmarks, Search to search for keywords, and Index to see an alphabetical list of indexed topics.

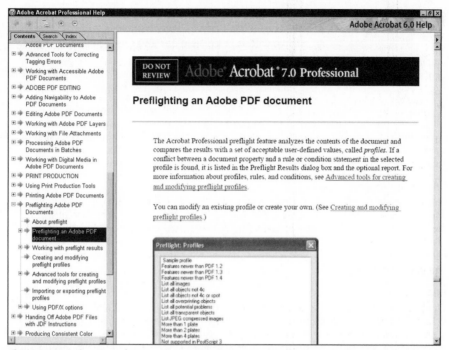

Figure 1-48: The Complete Acrobat 7.0 Help opens as a floating window with three tabs—Contents, for listing bookmarks; Search, for keyword searches; and Index, for an alphabetical topic list.

Contents tab

By default the Complete Acrobat 7.0 Help document opens with the Contents tab exposed as shown in Figure 1-48. In the Navigation pane you'll find a table of contents for the document shown in a very similar manner to the way bookmarks are listed in a PDF document. To expand the parent item, click the plus symbol (Windows) or right-pointing triangle (Macintosh). Subtopics appear when you expand a parent topic. To collapse a parent item, click the minus sign or down-pointing triangle adjacent to the parent item you expanded. Click one of the parent or child topics listed in the Contents tab to see the respective book-marked page in the Topic pane.

Search tab

You can use the Search tab to find any word(s) in the help document, as shown in Figure 1-49. Click the Search tab and the Navigation pane changes to display a field box where you type your search criteria. Type one or more words in the field box and click Search. The results then appear in the Search tab. All text appearing in blue is linked to the page that opens in the Topic pane.

Figure 1-49: The Search tab enables you to search for words contained anywhere in the help document. Type the search criteria in the field box and click Search.

Index tab

The Index tab is similar to any index you find in a manual or book. When you click the tab, a list of alphabetical characters (A to Z) appears in the Navigation pane. The alpha characters are parent markers that you can expand like the Contents items. Click the plus sign or triangle to expand the category. Click a child item in the expanded list to open the page link in the Topic pane.

Navigating topics

The arrows at the top of the Navigation pane enable you to move forward and back to the pages you view during your search. The review history remains in memory until you close the document. If you close the help file, the review history is flushed from memory and you need to begin again to find information on the same topics. On the right side of the Topic pane is a scroll bar. Use the arrow keys and elevator bar to view documents as you do in any application document.

Printing topics

The Print tool located at the top of the Navigation pane opens the Print dialog box. In the Print dialog box you can choose to print a single page, a page range, or the complete help document. Print controls enable you to fit the page to standard paper sizes, tile pages, and scale them. These options are handy, as many pages in the help document don't conform to standard US Letter size pages.

Cross-Reference   For information on printing PDF documents and using the Print dialog box, see Chapter 25.

Acrohelp.pdf

When you open the Complete Acrobat 7.0 Help from the How To window you access a file called ACROHELP.pdf. The file is a PDF document, but when opened using the How To menu command, the file opens with a custom user interface. This file can also be opened in Acrobat and viewed with the normal Acrobat user interface. If you want to use navigation tools or perform a sophisticated search with Boolean operators, the Complete Acrobat 7.0 Help file needs to be opened in Acrobat using the Open command. To open the file, click the Open tool or select File ⇨ Open and navigate to the Acrobat 7.0 folder open the Help folder and then open ENU. Double-click on the file labeled ACROHELP.

Tip   You can make comment notes on the Complete Acrobat 7.0 Help document. Select the comment tool you want to use, and then click the Help Tasks Button and open the Complete Acrobat 7.0 Help document. The last tool you selected in the Acrobat Toolbar Well is active when you view the help file.

Cross-Reference   For information on searching PDF files and using Boolean expressions, see Chapter 5.

When you open the Acrohelp.pdf file the file opens like any other PDF. The PDF document opens with bookmarks visible in the Bookmarks pane in the Navigation pane and these bookmarks contain descriptions identical to the contents in the Complete Acrobat 7.0 Help file. You also have an index to help you search for topics from an alphabetical list.

In addition, using the tools and viewing the file like any other PDF document, you can search for information within the PDF file by entering your search criteria in the How To window. Type the word(s) to be searched for and click the Search button. The search results are reported in the How To window. Additionally, you can use the new Find tool in Acrobat to search the active open document. Type your search criteria in the Find tool field box and press the Enter/Return key on your keyboard to jump to the first occurrence of the searched word.

Cross-Reference   Many distinctions exist between using the Find toolbar and the Search tool in Acrobat viewers. For a complete description of the use of both tools, see Chapter 5.

Advanced search is available to you using Acrobat Search. An index for the file has been created for you and is also installed with your Acrobat installation. You need to load the index before using more advanced search tools and then you can refine your search with many more search features.

More help

In addition to the help file that covers working in Acrobat, some other help PDF files are located in the Help folder inside your Acrobat folder. These help documents are specific to certain tasks, such as pdfmark and Distiller parameters. To view the help documents, open your Acrobat folder and open the Help\ENU folder. The files are PDF documents and can be opened in any viewer.

Online help is available to you as well from Adobe Systems. If you choose Help ➪ Online Support, your default Web browser launches and the Adobe Acrobat support page opens from Adobe's Web site. This Web page and links to the page are continually updated so be certain to make frequent visits to the Acrobat Online help Web pages.

Note   When accessing Adobe's Online Support, your Web browser opens in the foreground while Acrobat Professional remains open in the background. When you finish viewing Web pages and quit your Web browser, the Acrobat window returns to view.

Additional help links to Web pages at Adobe's Web site are also contained in the Help menu. Find support by selecting menu items such as Adobe Expert Support and Online Support. You can also get help information on document accessibility by selecting the Accessibility Information Online command.

Understanding Preferences

Preferences enable you to customize your work sessions in Acrobat. You can access a Preferences dialog box from within any Acrobat viewer and from within a Web browser when viewing PDFs as inline views. A huge number of preferences exist that all relate to specific tool groups or task categories, and it would not make as much sense to cover them here in the opening chapter as it would within chapters related to using tools and methods influenced by preference choices.

Some general things you should know about preferences is that they are contained in a dialog box as shown in Figure 1-50. You make a topic selection in the list on the left side of the dialog box and the related preferences are shown to the right side of the list. You make choices for preferences by selecting check boxes or making menu selections from pull-down menus. When you complete making your preference choices, click OK at the bottom of the dialog box.

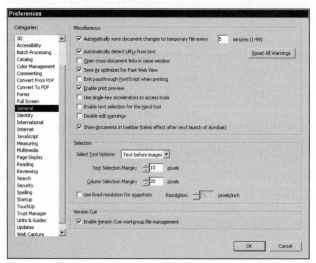

Figure 1-50: Press Control/⌘+K to open the Preferences dialog box. Click a category on the left and the choices are reflected to the left of the categories list.

Almost all the preferences you change in the Preferences dialog box are dynamic, which means you don't need to quit Acrobat and relaunch the program for a preference choice to take effect. Preferences remain in effect until you change them again. If you quit Acrobat and relaunch the program, the preferences you last made are honored by Acrobat. However, if for some reason the program crashes and you don't shut it down properly, any new preference changes will not be recognized when the program is launched again.

If you find some operation in Acrobat not working as you think it should, first take a look at the Preferences dialog box. In many cases you'll find a check box or menu command not enabled to permit you to perform a task. As you become familiar with specific tool groups and menu commands, make a habit of routinely visiting the Preferences dialog box so you understand all the toggles and switches that affect tool and viewing behavior.

Summary

This chapter offers you a general introduction for working in both Acrobat Standard and Acrobat Professional and helps you understand the environment, the user interface, and some of the many new features added to the commercial Acrobat products. At the very least, you should know how to go about finding help when you first start working in the program. Some of the more important points discussed in this chapter include the following:

✦ Adobe Acrobat is a multifaceted program designed to provide solutions for many different business professionals. Several types of Acrobat viewers exist, ranging in features to suit different user needs. The most sophisticated of the three viewers is Acrobat Professional, now in version 7. Acrobat Standard offers fewer tools and menu commands than Acrobat Professional.

✦ PDF, short for Portable Document Format, was developed by Adobe Systems and was designed to exchange documents between computers and across computer platforms while maintaining file integrity.

✦ The PDF language format has changed version numbers along with the Acrobat viewers. The current PDF version is 1.6.

✦ Tasks are performed through the use of menus, tools, and palettes that can be accessed through mouse selections and keyboard shortcuts.

✦ The extensive list of tools appears in an abbreviated form when you open Acrobat and view the default toolbars. You can open additional toolbars from menu commands. You can dock toolbars in the Toolbar Well or float them around the Acrobat window.

✦ Palettes are similar to toolbars in that they can be docked and undocked from a well called the Navigation pane. Palettes contain pull-down menus, and some palettes contain tools.

✦ You can customize the Acrobat workplace to suit your work style through the use of different preference choices. When preferences, palettes, and toolbars are changed from their default views, the new views are saved when you quit your Acrobat session. They remain unchanged until you change them again or reset them to defaults.

✦ Acrobat Professional provides you extensive assistance through the use of help documents. You can gain immediate help on selected topics through choices in the How To pane or by expanding your list of categories to seek help in the Complete Acrobat 7.0 Help window.

✦ Preferences are settings that apply globally to Acrobat and influence the behavior of tools and menu commands.

✦   ✦   ✦

Using Acrobat Viewers

In Chapter 1 you got a feel for some of the tools and menu commands provided in Acrobat Standard and Acrobat Professional. If you're a PDF author and you use Acrobat Standard or Professional, knowing the capabilities of one viewer versus another is important for both job efficiency and productivity, as well as usefulness to the end user. You may be a forms designer and want your forms to reach a large audience. Therefore, you need to know what authoring tool is needed to create PDF forms. You may be sending out a document for review and want to solicit comments. Therefore you need to know what viewer a user needs to send comments back to you.

At times you may find that neither Acrobat Standard nor Professional can help you do some editing tasks needed in your workflow. Fortunately, you have options for acquiring Acrobat plug-ins developed by third-party manufacturers that add much more functionality to the Acrobat tools and menu commands.

Many of the chapters ahead give you an idea of the distinctions between Acrobat Standard and Acrobat Professional and the tools accessible from one viewer versus the other. This chapter introduces you to the Acrobat viewers, points out some differences between them, and shows you how to use Acrobat plug-ins when you need more features than the viewers provide.

Viewer Distinctions

Adobe Reader, the two Acrobat products and Elements are designed to serve different users with different purposes. It should be obvious to you that Adobe Reader, as a free download from Adobe's Web site, is much more limited in features and performance than the products you purchase. It should also be obvious that because of the low cost of Acrobat Elements, it is much more limited in features than Acrobat Standard and Acrobat Professional.

For a general overview, take a look at the following descriptions of the Acrobat products.

Acrobat Elements

Acrobat Elements is only available for site license purchasing of 1,000 or more copies. The unit costs are very aggressive and are lowered with higher volume purchases. This product is intended to offer large companies and enterprises a means for employees to create PDF files. The primary features of Acrobat Elements include

✦ **Viewing and printing:** For viewing PDFs, the Adobe Reader software is used as the viewer. Elements in and of itself is not an Acrobat viewer.

✦ **PDF creation:** The PDF creation capability available from Elements is limited to creating PDF documents from Microsoft Office products or printing files to the Adobe PDF printer.

Adobe Reader

Adobe Reader is available for download from Adobe's Web site free of charge. The Adobe Reader software is distributed for the purpose of viewing and printing PDF files created by users of Acrobat Elements, Acrobat Standard, or Acrobat Professional. The major features of Adobe Reader include

✦ **Viewing and printing:** These features are common across all Acrobat viewers. You can view, navigate, and print PDF documents with Adobe Reader.

✦ **Forms completion and submission:** Adobe Reader enables you to complete forms but not save the form field data. Forms are submitted through the use of a Web browser or buttons created on forms for e-mailing or submitting data to Web servers.

✦ **Reader Extensions Server:** If an organization uses the Adobe Live Cycle Reader Extensions Server product available from Adobe Systems to enhance PDF files, Adobe Reader users can digitally sign documents, and save form data.

✦ **Reader-enabled usage rights:** A new addition in Acrobat 7 offers you the ability to add usage rights for more functionality in Adobe Reader. In Adobe Reader 7 you can comment on documents, extract file attachments, and save documents to update files. These features are document-specific and need to be enabled in Acrobat Professional on a document-by-document basis.

In addition to the preceding, Adobe Reader provides support for eBook services and searching PDF documents, as well as extended support for working with accessible documents.

 Cross-Reference   For more information on using tools in Adobe Reader, see Chapter 3.

Acrobat Standard Versus Acrobat Professional

Acrobat Standard is the lightweight of the authoring programs. However, Acrobat Standard still offers you many tools for PDF creation and authoring. Without going into every tool that differs between Acrobat Standard and Acrobat Professional, the major differences include the following limitations:

✦ **Form field authoring:** No form tools or form field authoring is available with Acrobat Standard. JavaScripts on form fields cannot be created in Acrobat Standard. However, if a JavaScript is contained in an area accessible to Acrobat Standard (such as Bookmark Properties or Link Properties), the JavaScript can be edited. You can write JavaScripts on Page Actions in Acrobat Standard.

Cross-Reference

For information on writing JavaScripts, see Chapter 29.

✦ **Professional printing:** Acrobat Standard does not provide options for soft proofing color, pre-flighting jobs, or commercial printing using such features as color separations, frequency control, transparency flattening, and so on. All these print controls are contained only in Acrobat Professional.

Cross-Reference

For information on pre-flighting, soft proofing color, and commercial printing, see Chapter 25.

✦ **Adding Adobe Reader usage rights:** You can add usage rights enabling Adobe Reader users to add comments and extract file attachments to PDF documents in Acrobat Professional. Acrobat Standard does not support adding usage rights to PDF files for Reader users.

Cross-Reference

For information on adding usage rights for Adobe Reader users, see Chapter 3.

✦ **Batch processing:** Acrobat Standard does not support batch processing and running batch commands.

Cross-Reference

For information on creating batch sequences, see Chapter 14.

✦ **Creating index files:** Acrobat Catalog is not part of Acrobat Standard. You can create index files only with Acrobat Professional through a menu command that launches Acrobat Catalog.

Cross-Reference

For information on creating index files, see Chapter 5.

✦ **Creating PDFs:** Acrobat Standard offers an impressive range of file types that can be converted to PDF. The limitations include producing PDFs from AutoCAD, Microsoft Visio, and Microsoft Project. Acrobat Standard does use Acrobat Distiller, but the Acrobat Standard Distiller does not support PDF/X and PDF/A compliance.

Cross-Reference

For information on using Acrobat Distiller, see Chapter 8.

✦ **Engineering tools:** Acrobat Standard does not support tools used by engineers and technical illustrators, such as the measuring tools, certain drawing tools, and advanced features related to managing layers.

Cross-Reference

For information on using the measuring tools and working with layers, see Chapter 19.

The preceding items are some of the major differences between the two commercial viewers. You will discover subtle differences as you work with the programs. For example, Acrobat Standard has fewer zoom tools, doesn't have support for drawing or measuring tools, doesn't support comparing documents, does not contain the PDF Optimizer for repurposing files, and so on.

If your mission is to recommend the product for purchase or make the decision for your own use, be aware of the four primary distinctions between the products: Acrobat Standard does not support forms authoring, professional printing, engineering tools, or adding Adobe Reader usage rights for review and comment. If your work is in one of these areas, you need to purchase Acrobat Professional.

Using Plug-ins

All Acrobat viewers support a plug-in architecture. Plug-ins are installed during your Acrobat installation and loaded when you launch Acrobat. Many of the features you find when exercising commands and using tools are made possible by the use of plug-ins. To view the current plug-ins loaded with the viewer you use, choose Help ➪ About Adobe Plug-ins. The About Adobe Plug-Ins dialog box opens as shown in Figure 2-1.

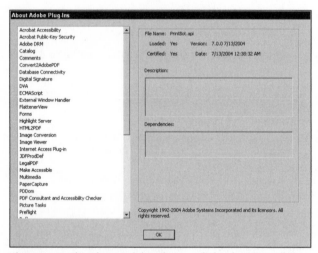

Figure 2-1: The About Adobe Plug-Ins dialog box lists all the plug-ins accessible to your viewer.

The list in the left side of the dialog box lists the names of the installed plug-ins. Click a name to see a description for the plug-in, including whether the plug-in is certified, the version number, creation date, text description, and dependencies. To examine different plug-ins, select them in the left pane and view the description on the right side of the dialog box.

Adobe plug-ins are developed by Adobe Systems and third-party manufacturers. All plug-ins developed by Adobe Systems are *certified* plug-ins. No third-party plug-ins are certified. Some features in Acrobat require that only certified plug-ins be loaded before the feature is enabled. Working with eBooks is one example where only certified plug-ins can be used.

Note   Any time a document has Adobe DRM (Digital Rights Management) protection such as eBooks and/or documents protected with the Adobe Policy Server, the viewer is launched in *certified plug-in mode*.

In order to instruct your Acrobat viewer to open with only certified plug-ins, open the preferences dialog box by choosing Edit ➪ Preferences. Select Startup in the left pane and select the Use only certified plug-ins check box, as shown in Figure 2-2. When you quit your Acrobat viewer and relaunch the program, only certified plug-ins will load.

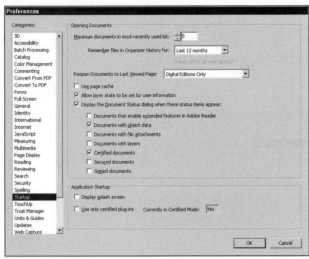

Figure 2-2: Select Use only certified plug-ins to open Acrobat to allow only certified plug-ins to load.

Plug-ins developed by third-party developers can also be loaded. The list of available resources for adding to Acrobat functionality in the form of add-ons and plug-ins is almost limitless. As you review all the chapters in this book and find that something you want to accomplish in your workflow is not covered, look for a plug-in developed by a third-party manufacturer. Chances are that you can find a product well suited to do the job.

Plug-ins for Acrobat are far too numerous to mention in this book. For a single source where you can view a list of plug-ins, download demonstration copies, and make purchases, visit the Planet PDF store at www.pdfstore.com. On the Planet PDF Web site you'll find product descriptions and workflow solutions for almost any third-party product designed to work with Acrobat. When you visit the Web site and review the products, be certain the product you purchase is upgraded to work with Acrobat 7 and the viewer you use. All products are listed with links to the manufacturer's Web sites, so you can find information on product descriptions, version numbers, and compatibility issues.

Installing plug-ins

Most plug-ins you acquire from third-party manufacturers are accompanied by an installer program. Installing plug-ins is easy. Open the folder for a plug-in you download from a Web site and double-click on the installer icon. The installer routine finds the plug-ins folder inside your Acrobat folder and the plug-in is loaded when you launch Acrobat.

If a plug-in is not accompanied by an installer program, you need to manually add the plug-in to your Acrobat plug-ins folder. On Windows, open the Program Files\Adobe\Acrobat 7\Acrobat\plug_ins folder. Copy the plug-in you want to install to this folder.

On the Macintosh, open your Applications folder. Open the Acrobat 7 Professional (or Standard) folder from within the Applications folder. Press and hold the Control key and click the program icon (Adobe Acrobat 7 Professional or Adobe Acrobat 7 Standard) to open a context menu, as shown in Figure 2-3. From the menu items, select Show Package Contents.

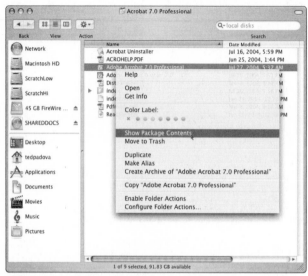

Figure 2-3: Open the Package Contents on the Macintosh to gain access to the Plug-ins folder.

When you open the Package Contents, the Contents folder appears in a single window. Double-click the folder to open it. Several folders appear within the Contents folder, one of which is named Plug-ins. Open this folder and copy your plug-in to it.

Uninstalling plug-ins

If your plug-in is not accompanied by an uninstaller program, you need to either disable the plug-in or physically remove it from the Acrobat plug-ins folder. A temporary solution is to disable third-party plug-ins by opening the Preferences dialog box, clicking on Startup, and selecting the check box for Use only certified plug-ins, as shown earlier in Figure 2-2.

To permanently remove a plug-in, open the plug-ins folder as described in the previous section, "Installing plug-ins," and drag the plug-in out of the Acrobat plug-ins folder.

Caution   Some plug-ins are installed in their own folder. To remove a plug-in, drag the folder where the plug-in is installed out of the Acrobat plug-ins folder. Be certain not to remove the Acrobat plug-ins folder from within the Acrobat folder. Doing so disables all tools and menu commands using plug-ins.

Resolving plug-in conflicts

At times you may find a plug-in conflict among several third-party products or a plug-in that may have a bug. If your Acrobat functionality is impaired and you can't launch the program, hold down the Shift key while double-clicking the program icon to launch your viewer. All plug-ins are disabled when you use the modifier key. Open the Preferences dialog box again and select the Use only certified plug-ins check box. Quit and relaunch the program, and the offending plug-in is eliminated during startup.

If a plug-in is creating a problem, you may need to use a process of elimination to figure out which one it is by opening your plug-ins folder and removing all plug-ins. Then add several plug-ins at a time back to the plug-ins folder and launch your viewer. Keep adding plug-ins back to the plug-ins folder until you discover which plug-in produces the error.

Working with a plug-in

As an example for how plug-ins can help you work with PDF files, take a look at a real-world example of a problem and how a plug-in can provide a solution. Suppose you have a large PDF document that needs to be divided into separate smaller files. You could manually extract pages from the file and save the extracted pages together as a separate file and repeat the process for each group of pages you want to save as individual files. This process could take quite a bit of time.

Cross-Reference For more information about extracting pages from PDF files, see Chapter 12.

As an alternative to using manual methods for extracting pages in Acrobat, you can find a plug-in to do the job. ARTS PDF is a third-party provider that distributes a tool called ARTS PDF Split & Merge. ARTS PDF Split & Merge is an Acrobat plug-in designed to break apart PDF documents and save the divided pages into separate PDF files. With ARTS PDF Split & Merge you can save each page as a separate PDF document or you can use divisions in your file such as bookmarks to break up the file according to bookmark headings.

Like many Acrobat plug-ins, you can download ARTS PDF Split & Merge and use it for a trial period to evaluate the tool before you make a purchase. To see how a plug-in like ARTS PDF Split & Merge works with Acrobat Professional or Standard, perform the following steps.

STEPS: Using an Acrobat plug-in

1. **Download a plug-in for trial use.** Open your Web browser and log on to the Planet PDF Store site at www.pdfstore.com. Scroll the Web page to find the Go to Product pop-up menu. From the menu select ARTS PDF Split & Merge Lite to go to the download page for this product. Select your platform (Win or Mac) from the Platform menu. Click "Get Demo." Fill out the requested information on the next page and click Submit to commence the download. Wait for the download to complete before moving to the next step.

2. **Install the plug-in.** Be certain you quit Acrobat before attempting the installation of any plug-in. ARTS PDF Split & Merge Lite uses an application installer program to install the plug-in in your Acrobat plug-ins folder. Double-click the executable file and fill in the requested information.

Note   When you launch the installer a dialog box offers you an option for installing either ARTS PDF Split & Merge Lite or ARTS PDF Split & Merge Plus (a more advanced version of the tool that offers enhanced features). Select the radio button for ARTS PDF Split & Merge Lite to follow these steps.

3. **Launch Acrobat.** Open Acrobat by double-clicking the program icon or alias of the program. When you open Acrobat, notice a new menu appears in the top-level menu bar titled Plug-Ins.

4. **Open a PDF document.** Open a document containing bookmarks if you have one available. If not, just be certain to open a file with multiple pages.

5. **Open the plug-in tool.** From the Plug-Ins menu, choose ARTS PDF Split & Merge Lite ➪ Split File, as shown in Figure 2-4.

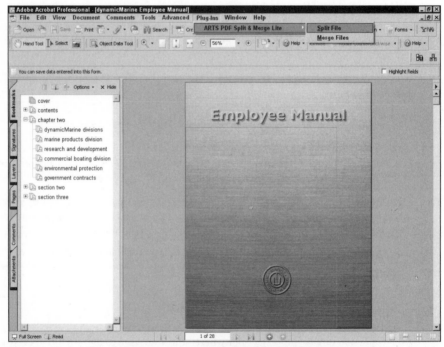

Figure 2-4: Acrobat plug-ins are conveniently listed in the Plug-Ins menu that appears in the top-level menu bar when at least one third-party plug-in is installed.

6. **Select attributes for splitting a file.** In the ARTS Split & Merge – Split PDF File dialog box that appears, select the attributes for your file conversion. In the dialog box shown in Figure 2-5, you can choose to split a file by page, page range, or according to bookmarked pages. In this example, I use a bookmarked document and select the radio button for By bookmarks starting at Level. Notice that you can divide documents according to different bookmark levels. Leaving the default at Level 1 divides the document into separate files following the order of the top-level bookmarks.

Cross-Reference For information related to bookmark levels and nesting orders, see Chapter 17.

7. **Select a folder where the files are to be saved.** At the bottom of the ARTS Split & Merge – Split PDF File dialog box, click the Browse button to open a dialog box where you can target a location for your saved files. If you want to create a new folder, click the Make New Folder button. Click OK and the folder path is reported back to you in the dialog box, as shown in Figure 2-5.

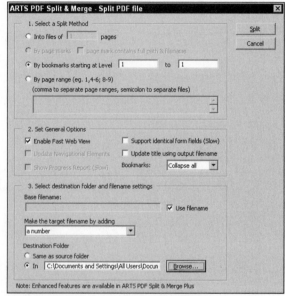

Figure 2-5: Make choices for how a file is split and the folder location for the saved files.

8. **Split the document.** Click the Split button at the top right side of the ARTS PDF Split & Merge – Split File dialog box. A progress bar appears in the lower-left corner of the Acrobat window as files are saved to the target location.

9. **Open a saved file.** Click the Open button in the Acrobat Toolbar Well or choose File ⇨ Open and navigate to the folder where you saved files after splitting the document. Select one of the files and click Open in the Open dialog box.

10. **Expand bookmarks.** Click the Bookmarks tab in the Navigation pane to open the Bookmarks pane. Notice that if you split a file containing bookmarks, all the bookmarks are listed in the Bookmarks pane, as shown in Figure 2-6. Also notice in Figure 2-6 that the document is only one page, as denoted in the status bar at the bottom of the page. Inasmuch as the document is one page, the bookmarks are active to open other documents containing the remaining pages.

Note When you use a trial demo plug-in, often the results in your edited file show a stamp across each page indicating that you used a demo software product. When you purchase the commercial version, the stamp is not imposed on pages in your document.

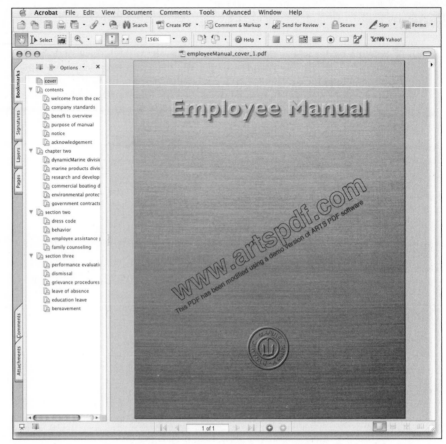

Figure 2-6: Files split with ARTS PDF Split & Merge retain links for bookmarks, links, and buttons.

11. **Click a bookmark.** Original bookmarks, links, and buttons from the original file link to the same views in the new split files. ARTS PDF Split & Merge preserves all link destinations.

As you can see, a task like splitting documents and saving pages as new files can be greatly simplified by using an Acrobat plug-in offering you much more editing power than you find using default methods in Acrobat. ARTS PDF Split & Merge Plus offers you a bonus by preserving all file links that were contained in the original document and performs the task of splitting PDF files in a fraction of the time you might spend using manual methods.

Whenever you find tasks in Acrobat to be cumbersome or unattainable, visit the PDF Store and browse the third-party plug-in descriptions on the Planet PDF Web site. The many hours of editing you save on large jobs in Acrobat can justify some of the low-cost solutions available from third-party developers.

Summary

✦ Adobe Systems introduced four Acrobat products with the release of Acrobat 7.0. The viewers include Adobe Reader, Acrobat Standard, and Acrobat Professional. The Adobe PDF creators include Acrobat Elements, Acrobat Standard, and Acrobat Professional.

✦ Adobe Reader is a free download from Adobe's Web site. All other products require purchase. Acrobat Elements is available only in site license quantities of 1,000 or more.

✦ Acrobat Standard offers fewer features than Acrobat Professional. Among the primary limitations with Acrobat Standard are no support for Forms creation, commercial printing tools, engineering tools, or creating PDFs with Adobe Reader usage rights. These features are only available in Acrobat Professional.

✦ Acrobat plug-ins are additions to Acrobat that offer features and tools for adding more functionality to Acrobat viewers. Plug-ins are installed with Acrobat from sources developed by Adobe Systems.

✦ Plug-ins are available from third-party software manufacturers. A complete list of plug-ins and demonstration products is available at the Planet PDF Store.

✦   ✦   ✦

Getting Familiar with the New and Improved Adobe Reader

As a PDF author you need to be aware of the capabilities and the limitations of the Adobe Reader software. In some situations you can distribute PDF documents to users of the free Adobe Reader software for active participation in your workflow without all your clients and colleagues needing to purchase the full version of Acrobat Standard or Acrobat Professional. In other situations where the Adobe Reader software does not contain tools or commands to properly edit a file for a given workflow, you may need to recommend to others which commercial viewer they need to purchase. Regardless of where you are with PDF creation and editing, at one time or another you'll be called upon to explain some of the differences between the viewers.

Adobe Reader has matured as a product, and the newest release offers users much more functionality than any previous version. Features that have long been requested by users such as being able to add a comment note and save a document to update changes have now been added to Adobe Reader 7. However, the features are document-specific and require at least one person in a workflow attempting to use these new tools to author a file in Acrobat Professional. The relationship between the viewers and how to grant usage rights as well as all the capabilities within Adobe Reader is the subject of this chapter.

Adobe Reader Tools

In addition to knowing the distinctions between Adobe Reader and other viewers, you should also become familiar with the tools available to Reader users. Knowing what the user can do with these tools and what features are available in Reader is helpful if you intend to distribute documents to Reader users.

All tools available in Adobe Reader have counterparts in Acrobat Standard and Acrobat Professional. The Reader tools are the same in the other viewers; however, some of the Adobe Reader tools offer more limited features than the same tool used in the other viewers. The Adobe Reader tools include the following:

✦ **File Toolbar:** The File tools include Open, Save a Copy, Print, E-mail, and Search. The Save a Copy tool saves a duplicate copy of the PDF document. You might use the tool for saving a PDF from an inline view in a Web browser. Saving a copy of files from Adobe Reader does not permit the Reader user to save form data.

For information related to using the e-mail tool, see Chapter 16. For information related to using the Print tool, see Chapter 25. For information related to using the Search tool, see Chapter 5.

✦ **Basic Toolbar:** The Basic tools include the Hand tool, the Select tool, and the Snapshot tool. In previous versions of Acrobat this toolbar contained the Select Text and Select Image tools. Now in version 7, all Acrobat viewers host a single tool used for selecting both text and graphics. The order of what is selected first (text or graphic) is determined in a Preferences setting.

For information related to using the Select tool, see Chapters 10 and 11.

✦ **Object Data Toolbar:** The Object Data Toolbar, explained in Chapter 1, is used to select objects containing object metadata on a document page. When you select an object with this tool, the Object Data dialog box opens and displays information about an object that was originally supplied in an authoring program. The Object Data tool only works with objects where certain metadata was originally supplied in another program such as AutoCAD or Microsoft Visio.

For information related to using the Object Data tool, see Chapter 5.

✦ **Zoom Toolbar:** The Zoom tools include Zoom In, Zoom Out, and Dynamic Zoom. Page zooms appear as Actual Size, Fit Page, and Fit Width, selectable from the page icons in the toolbar. The field box is editable and shows a readout for the current zoom. The field box also contains a pull-down menu where preset fixed zoom levels are selected. On either side of the field box are symbols (minus and plus) used for zooming out and in on the document shown in the Document pane. The advanced zoom tools found in Acrobat Professional, such as the Loupe tool and the Pan and Zoom tool, are not available in Adobe Reader or Acrobat Standard.

For information related to using the Zoom tools, see Chapter 4.

✦ **Tasks Toolbar:** The Tasks tools include Digital Editions, which you use for acquiring and managing eBooks; the Forms task button, which you use to acquire help information related to forms completion; and the Picture Tasks button, which appears in the Tasks Toolbar only when files of certain file types are opened in an Acrobat viewer. By default, the Picture Tasks button does not appear in the toolbar.

For information related to using the Digital Editions tool, see Chapter 24. For information related to using the Picture Tasks button, see "Using Picture Tasks" later in this chapter.

✦ **Rotate View Toolbar:** Rotate Clockwise and Rotate Counterclockwise tools, provide temporary viewing rotations only. Rotated views cannot be saved.

✦ **Find Toolbar:** The Find tool enables you to perform a text search in the open PDF document.

For information related to using the Find Toolbar, see Chapter 5.

✦ **Navigation Toolbar:** This toolbar contains the First Page, Previous Page, Next Page, Last Page, Previous View, and Next View tools, To view this toolbar, choose View ➪ Toolbars ➪ Navigation. This toolbar is not loaded by default.

 For information related to navigating PDF documents, see Chapter 4.

✦ **Properties Bar:** Even though Adobe Reader does have a Properties Bar, none of the default tools have options available in the tool. The Properties Bar is used in PDF documents carrying usage rights when you're using the Adobe Live Cycle Reader Extensions Server or with PDFs enabled for usage rights for commenting with Acrobat Professional. This toolbar has been opened on a PDF document enabled for commenting in Adobe Reader. When a comment tool is selected, attributes for comment notes are edited in the Properties Bar.

For more information on plug-ins, see Chapter 2. For more information on using the Properties Toolbar, see Chapter 15.

In addition to the aforementioned tools, Adobe Reader contains tabs docked in the Navigation pane. Users of earlier versions of Adobe Reader will immediately notice the addition of the Attachments tab and the Comments tab. The Navigation tabs not shown by default in the Navigation pane include the Layers tab, the Bookmarks tab, and the Articles tab. If no Bookmarks are contained in a document, the Bookmarks tab does not open. Likewise, if a file contains no layers, the Layers tab does not open and the same holds true for the Articles tab and Signatures tab when no articles or signatures are present. Adobe Reader is intelligent and shows tabs in the Navigation pane when content in the PDF uses data managed by a respective tab. To manually open a tab when it is not shown by default, choose View ➪ Navigation Tabs and select from the submenu the tab you want to open.

For more information on using the Articles tab, see Chapter 17.

Using Picture Tasks

 Picture Tasks is a feature available in all Acrobat viewers. It uses the Image Viewer plug-in, which is installed by default with Acrobat viewers for the purpose of extracting images. If you look for the Picture Tasks tool in the Toolbar Well, you won't find it. Nor will you find the Picture Tasks tool listed among the toolbars in the View ➪ Toolbars or Task Buttons submenus. The Picture Tasks tool opens only in an Acrobat viewer Toolbar Well when certain file types are opened in the viewer. Files created from Adobe Photoshop Album and files saved as PDF Presentations from Photoshop CS are file types that support Picture Tasks.

Cross-Reference For information on converting Adobe Photoshop Album files to PDF, see Chapter 18. For information on using Photoshop CS to convert files to PDF Presentations, see Chapter 7.

When you open a file where Picture Tasks are accessible, you'll be immediately informed with a dialog box providing information related to Picture Tasks, as shown in Figure 3-1. If you want to open files without the dialog box appearing each time a Picture Tasks–enabled document opens, select the Don't show again check box.

Figure 3-1: Files that support Picture Tasks open with a dialog box indicating the Picture Tasks tools are accessible.

When a Picture Tasks–enabled document opens, the Picture Tasks task button is loaded in the Toolbar Well. From the task button a pull-down menu offers you choices for handling the images contained in the open PDF document, as shown in Figure 3-2.

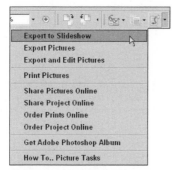

Figure 3-2: A pull-down menu on the Picture Tasks task button offers several Picture Tasks–related commands.

Getting help

To help you understand more about using the Picture Tasks commands, some help information is available in the How To pane. To open the How To pane with Picture Tasks help, open the pull-down menu on the task button and select How To...Picture Tasks. The How To pane opens with a list of the commands available for Picture Tasks and a brief description for each command, as shown in Figure 3-3.

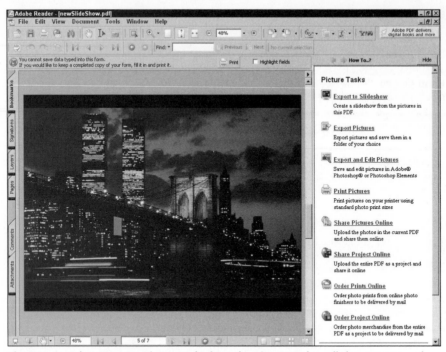

Figure 3-3: Select How To...Picture Tasks from the Picture Tasks pull-down menu and the How To pane opens with a brief description for using the commands.

Export to Slideshow

The first command in the How To pane and the Picture Tasks pull-down menu is Export to Slideshow. When you select the command from either location, the Export to Slideshow window shown in Figure 3-4 opens. Choices in the window offer options for creating a slideshow from a selected range of pages in the open document.

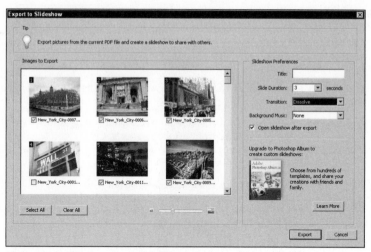

Figure 3-4: The Export to Slideshow window offers options for creating a new slideshow from all or a selected range of pages.

The options in the Export to Slideshow window include

✦ **Images to Export:** Thumbnail images are displayed in the window. Beside the image name a check box appears. Select the check box to include the selected thumbnail in the exported slideshow.

✦ **Select All:** Click the Select All button to check and target all thumbnail images for export. You can click Select All and then deselect those images you want to exclude by removing the check mark on the associated thumbnails.

✦ **Clear All:** If you want to deselect all selected thumbnails, click the Clear All button.

✦ **Zoom slider:** Move the slider below the thumbnail list to zoom in and out of the thumbnail views.

✦ **Title:** A field box enables you to enter a title for the slideshow. The text typed in the field box is displayed on the opening slide. The title text has nothing to do with the filename.

✦ **Slide Duration:** Preset values are selectable from a pull-down menu for the number of seconds each slide remains onscreen before the next slide appears. You can choose from the presets or enter a value between 1 and 32767.

✦ **Transition:** Transition effects include None, Fade, Dissolve, Wipe Up, Wipe Down, Wipe Left, and Wipe Right. Exporting Picture Tasks offers many fewer transition effects than you can assign in Acrobat.

Cross-Reference

To learn more about applying transitions to PDF documents, see Chapter 23.

✦ **Background Music:** From this pull-down menu click Select to open the Choose Audio File dialog box, in which you can navigate your hard drive to select a sound file to import. Files saved as .wav and .mp3 are supported. When the slideshow is exported, the sound begins to play at the first slide and continues play through the duration of the slideshow.

✦ **Open slideshow after export:** Check the box if you want to see the slideshow immediately after exporting.

✦ **Learn More:** Click the Learn More button to see more information on Adobe Photoshop Album and how to acquire the software from Adobe Systems. Clicking on the button opens your default Web browser and takes you to Adobe's Web site where more information is offered about acquiring Adobe Photoshop Album.

✦ **Export:** After you set all the options for the slideshow you want to create, click the Export button. A Save As dialog box opens where you can target a folder location and save your file. The name you provide for the exported file appears in the title bar of the slideshow when viewing the pages in a normal view.

✦ **Cancel:** Click Cancel to exit the Export to Slideshow window without creating a slideshow.

When you export a slideshow using Picture Tasks, Adobe Reader or Acrobat does more than simply save a new file. All the transition effects, music, and controls applied with JavaScripts are added to the slideshow by your Acrobat viewer. The slideshow defaults to a Full Screen mode with the controls appearing on the opening slide, as shown in Figure 3-5.

Figure 3-5: Exporting to a slideshow from any Acrobat viewer displays the slideshow in Full Screen mode as well as a set of control buttons created through the export sequence.

Exporting pictures

Adobe Reader, as well as the other viewers, can export images from a file compatible with Picture Tasks. If you want to export a single image, a group of images, or all images to save as separate JPEG images, select Export Pictures from the Picture Tasks pull-down menu or from the Export Pictures link in the How To pane. Selecting either item opens the Export Pictures dialog box shown in Figure 3-6.

Figure 3-6: Select Export Pictures from either the Picture Tasks pull-down menu or the How To pane and a dialog box opens where you select the pictures to export.

Click the Select All button to select all images. If you want to export a single image, select the check box or the thumbnail image. Make noncontiguous selections by holding down the Ctrl/⌘ key and clicking the thumbnails in the Export Pictures dialog box. Alternatively, you can click the check boxes to select slides to export. For contiguous selections, click a thumbnail and Shift+click another thumbnail, and all images between the first and second click are selected.

Click the Change button at the top of the dialog box to locate a folder where you want to save the exported images. In the Browse For Folder dialog box you navigate your hard drive to find a destination folder.

If you want the filenames to use a base name derived from your original filename, select Original Names. If you want to change the base name, select Common Base Name and enter the name you want to use in the field box. The Acrobat viewer uses a base name plus 1, 2, 3, and so on plus a .jpg extension. All files are exported as JPEG images.

Note that the Select All button, Clear All button, and zoom slider are the same options you have available when exporting a slideshow. See the section "Export to Slideshow" earlier in this chapter.

After making the selections and determining the destination and filenames, click the Export button. All images are exported as single JPEG files.

Exporting and editing pictures

When you select the third menu command, Export and Edit Pictures, from the Picture Tasks pull-down menu, you need to have a program installed that can open JPEG files. Ideally you would use an image editor to edit an image, but the export options extend beyond image editors. You can use programs such as Adobe Illustrator, CorelDraw, or Macromedia Freehand to open the files. Additionally, you can use programs such as Windows Photo Editor, or Apple's iPhoto as your default editor. Programs that import JPEG files (as opposed to *opening* them) are not supported. For example, you don't have an option for exporting from Picture Tasks to Adobe InDesign because it imports files as opposed to opening them.

The first dialog box you encounter when making the menu selection is the Export and Edit Pictures dialog box. Make selections in the dialog box like you do when exporting pictures. A button appears for Change in the Editing Application area of the dialog box. Click on Change and the Choose Image Editor dialog box opens. Navigate your hard drive and locate the image editor you want to use. Click the Edit button in the Export and Edit Pictures dialog box and the selected image(s) opens in your image editor.

Note   If you have Adobe Photoshop CS installed on your computer, Photoshop CS is selected as your default image editor.

After making edits to images, you save the files from the image editor as new files. If you use a program such as Adobe Photoshop CS or Photoshop Elements or similar image editor, you can choose any file format supported by the program. When you save files, the original PDF document opened in the Acrobat viewer remains unchanged. That is to say, no dynamic updating in the PDF document occurs when you use the Picture Tasks commands. This feature is much different than using image editors with PDF images when you select Edit Image from a context menu opened with the TouchUp Object tool.

Cross-Reference   For information on editing images using the Edit Image command in Acrobat, see Chapter 11.

Printing pictures

A marvelous way of printing images supporting Picture Tasks is via the Print command from the Picture Tasks task button pull-down menu or from the How To pane. The options with Picture Tasks offer you more layout flexibility for photo albums and traditional photo prints obtained from photo-finishing centers than using the Print command in Acrobat viewers.

Cross-Reference   For information on printing PDF files, see Chapter 25.

Select Print Pictures from the Picture Tasks task button or the How To pane to open the Print dialog box. Select the pictures you want to print and click the Next button at the bottom of the dialog box. The Print dialog box shown in Figure 3-7 opens. In this dialog box you make selections for the layout options you want for your prints. Among the choices are:

Note   The Print dialog box opened from the Picture Tasks command is substantially different than the Print dialog box that appears when you choose File ➪ Print. For a comparison between the two Print dialog boxes, compare Figure 3-7 to the Print dialog box shown in Chapter 25.

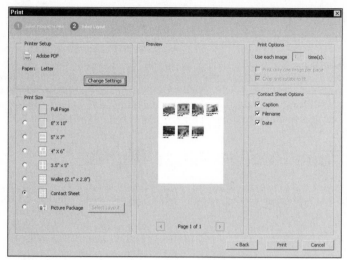

Figure 3-7: Select Print Pictures from either the Picture Tasks pull-down menu or the How To pane to open a dialog box where you select the pictures to print and the layout options for the printed pages.

✦ **Printer Setup:** Click the Change Settings button and the Printer Setup dialog box opens where you can select a printer attached to your computer or network and change properties for the target printer such as page setup, page size, orientation, and so on.

✦ **Print Size:** Select the size of the prints in this section. Notice the sizes match traditional photo-finishing sizes. The Full Page item sizes the photo to the maximum size available for the selected page size assigned in the Print properties.

✦ **Preview (arrows):** Click the left and right arrows below the thumbnail of the pages to see a preview of each page.

✦ **Use each photo [ ] time(s).** For dupes, enter the number of duplicate images you want to print. If a single image is what you want, be certain to leave the default at 1. The field box is editable for multiple copies of each page for all print sizes except Contact Sheet and Picture Package.

✦ **Crop and rotate to fit:** The photo is sized to match the selected Print Size. This choice fills the Print Size as much as possible and eliminates any white borders that might otherwise print. Note, however, that the files need to be proportional to the Print Size to print borderless prints. If one side or the other does not fit the Print Size, you'll see a white border on that side.

✦ **Contact Sheet Options:** To add a caption, filename, and/or date, select the respective check boxes. All three options may be selected together.

✦ **Print:** After making choices for the kind of prints you want, click the Print button to commence printing and exit the dialog box.

Using online services (Windows only)

The remaining menu commands for Picture Tasks relate to services you can order online on Windows only. Select the menu option for Share Pictures Online or Share Project Online. Sharing pictures offers you options for selecting which pictures in the open file you want to share. Sharing a project online uploads the entire file. The Order Prints Online and Order Project Online options enable you to order photo prints from an online service provider and order photo merchandise online. Choose a menu command to open a dialog box that instructs you as to how to place your order for any one of the online choices.

Enabling Adobe Reader Usage Rights

One of the best new additions to the Adobe Reader software is the ability to edit and save PDF documents that have been deployed with certain usage rights. To create a Reader-enabled document for certain usage rights, you need Acrobat Professional or Adobe Live Cycle Reader Extensions Server. In Acrobat Professional you can add usage rights that enable an Adobe Reader user to comment on a PDF file, save the comments, and invite Reader users to participate in an e-mail–based review or an e-mail for approval session.

Cross-Reference For a complete description of using comment tools, starting an e-mail review, or creating an e-mail for approval session, see Chapter 16.

All the comment usage rights are enabled in Acrobat Professional. When you want to distribute a document for Reader users to mark up and comment, choose Comments ➪ Enable for Commenting in Adobe Reader, as shown in Figure 3-8. A Save As dialog box opens where you can select a folder for the new saved file. Saving the document in the Save As dialog box opened from this menu command enables the file with usage rights for Reader users.

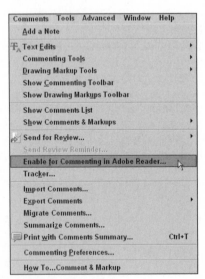

Figure 3-8: Choose Comments ➪ Enable for Commenting in Adobe Reader. After you save the file, Adobe Reader users can comment and save the PDF with updated edits.

Commenting in Adobe Reader

Be certain you are aware of the fact that you need to grant a PDF document usage rights in Acrobat Professional by choosing Comments ➪ Enable for Commenting in Adobe Reader before a Reader user can make comments. When the file is enabled with usage rights, comment tools, as shown in Figure 3-9, are loaded in the Reader application. If an Adobe Reader user opens a PDF document without usage rights enabled, the comment tools are not accessible.

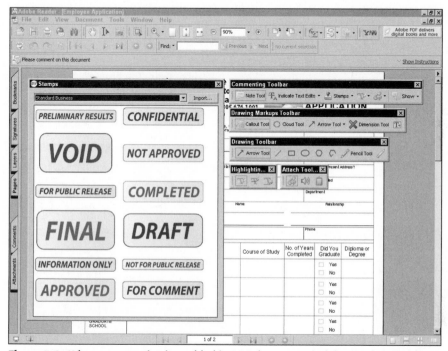

Figure 3-9: When commenting is enabled in PDF documents, Adobe Reader users have access to the comment and markup tools.

Notice in Figure 3-9 that Adobe Reader users have access to all comment and markup tools, as well as the ability to create and use custom stamps. When an Adobe Reader user marks up a document with the commenting tools, the file can be saved and the comments preserved. Documents enabled with usage rights also include a File ➪ Save command. By default, Adobe Reader only permits saving an unedited copy of a PDF document if usage rights are not enabled.

Cross-Reference

For information on using the comment and markup tools and creating custom stamps, see Chapter 15.

Using file attachments

A file attachment is an external file that can be a PDF document or any other document saved from any program. The PDF acts as a wrapper container for the file attachment. File attachments can be extracted and saved to disk outside the PDF or opened in the native application in which the original document was created. In order to view a document in a native application, the original authoring program must be installed on your computer.

Cross-Reference   For information on attaching and extracting files, see Chapter 15.

Another nice new addition to Adobe Reader is the ability to extract file attachments. Files can be attached to a PDF by a Reader user when a PDF document is enabled with commenting usage rights for Adobe Reader users. When an Acrobat user attaches a file to a PDF, Adobe Reader users can extract the file attachments. A separate tab in the Navigation pane enables the Reader user to open, save, and search file attachments. Click the Attachments tab, shown in Figure 3-10, to open a pane where you can access tools to manage the attachments.

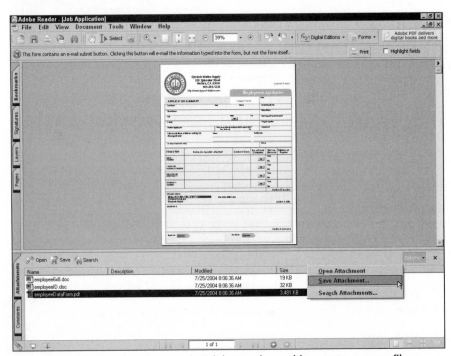

Figure 3-10: The Attachments pane in Adobe Reader enables you to manage file attachments.

One great feature now in all Acrobat viewers is the ability to attach any file type to a PDF document and secure the PDF with password protection. After a PDF has been encrypted with password security, the end user needs the access password in order to either open the PDF document or extract the attachment. With the process now accessible to Adobe Reader users, business professionals in all industries will find much greater use for Adobe Reader 7.

For information on adding permissions rights with Acrobat security, see Chapter 21.

Adding More Functionality to Adobe Reader

You may look over the new Adobe Reader 7 and wish for more features or wonder why Adobe Systems didn't add more to the newest release. If the thought occurs to you, keep in mind that Adobe Systems offers the Reader software free of charge. As a free program, Adobe Reader is certainly one of the most feature-rich applications than can be acquired without purchase. A large company can purchase Adobe Acrobat Professional that is needed for all PDF authors and install the free Adobe Reader software for hundreds of other employees who can then participate in comment and review sessions. That kind of power is a generous contribution from a software developer.

If you want more from Adobe Reader you do have other purchase options available to you from Adobe Systems. From PDF creation to saving form data, Adobe does make these features available to you in the form of online services and server-side solutions.

Creating PDFs online

If your clients or colleagues don't have Acrobat Standard or Acrobat Professional and they need to create an occasional PDF file, they can download the free Adobe Reader software and choose File ➪ Create Adobe PDF Online. Create Adobe PDF Online is a Web service from Adobe Systems that permits users to upload documents of several different file types. The user uploads the file(s) to Adobe's Web site, where it is then converted to PDF and sent back to the user. A free trial period enables you to create your first five PDFs free of charge. After the fifth PDF creation, the cost is $9.99 (US) per month or an annual subscription of $99.99 (US) per year.

Create PDF Online supports many different file formats. The native document formats include

- ✦ **Microsoft Office:** All Microsoft Office files for Mac and Windows.

- ✦ **Other Microsoft formats:** Microsoft Publisher is supported.

- ✦ **Adobe formats:** Those programs not supporting direct export to PDF, such as earlier versions of PageMaker without the PDF plug-in, are supported. All Creative Suite programs now support export to PDF and using a service to create PDF files is not necessary.

- ✦ **AutoDesk AutoCAD:** AutoCAD is supported.

- ✦ **Corel WordPerfect Office formats:** Corel WordPerfect files can be converted to PDF.

- ✦ **Adobe PostScript formats:** Any program you use that's capable of printing can be printed to disk as a PostScript file. You can submit the PostScript file for conversion to PDF.

- ✦ **Text formats:** All ASCII (American Code for Information Interchange) and Rich Text Format (RTF) files can be converted to PDF.

- ✦ **Image formats:** Most of the common image formats such as Windows bitmap (.bmp), GIF (.gif), JPEG (.jpg/.jpeg), PCX (.pcx), PICT (Macintosh) (.pct/.pict), PNG (.png), RLE (.rle), and TIFF (.tif) can be converted to PDF.

Cross-Reference   For information on converting native application documents to PDF, see Chapters 7 and 8. For information on printing PostScript files and converting PostScript files to PDF, see Chapter 8.

Understanding Adobe Reader Extensions

The advanced tools in Adobe Reader for comment and markup are features that are available through the Adobe Reader Live Cycle Extensions Server (ARES). For users of earlier versions of Acrobat, Reader Extensions enable users of Adobe Reader versions below 7.0 to comment and mark up. ARES is an enterprise solution intended for large companies that have the technology and resources to offer cost effective solutions for many users. As an example, for 250 users, individual costs break down to about $60 USD per user.

In addition to comment and markup, Reader Extensions also provide solutions for enabling documents for saving form data and adding digital signatures. As is the case with Adobe Reader–enabled usage rights, the Reader Extensions are added to PDFs on a document-by-document basis.

For information about Adobe Reader Extensions Server, log on to Adobe's Web site at www.adobe.com/products/readerextensions/main.html. You'll find more information about the server-side software and how to acquire it for your company.

Summary

- ✦ Picture Tasks are used with files that originated in Adobe Photoshop Album, Adobe Photoshop Elements, or PDF slide presentations created in Photoshop CS.

- ✦ The Picture Tasks task button only appears in an Acrobat viewer Toolbar Well when you open one of the file types listed in the preceding bullet.

- ✦ Picture Tasks enable you to print, extract, and edit JPEG images. The online services menu options provide a means of sending your photos and PDF creations to online service providers for printing and other packaging.

- ✦ Adobe Reader usage rights are enabled in Acrobat Professional. When a PDF has been enabled with commenting usage rights, Reader users can comment and mark up a document, participate in an e-mail–based review, and save comment updates.

- ✦ File attachments can be extracted from within Adobe Reader. When usage rights have been enabled in a PDF document, Adobe Reader users can attach files to PDFs.

- ✦ Adobe Systems provides an online service for converting files saved in a number of different formats to PDF. You can easily access the online service from within Adobe Reader by choosing File ➪ Create Adobe PDF Online.

- ✦ Adobe Live Cycle Reader Extensions Server is a server-side solution intended for large companies or Web hosting documents for public use. With the Reader Extensions Server you can enable PDF documents for saving form data and digitally signing PDFs from within Adobe Reader.

✦   ✦   ✦

Viewing and Navigation in Adobe Acrobat Professional

Acrobat viewers provide you with many different kinds of tools to view pages and move around PDF documents. As a visitor to PDFs created by other PDF authors you can use many tools within the program to browse pages and find information quickly. As a PDF author you can create viewing options and links to views you know will help the end user explore your files. In this chapter I cover all viewing tools, pages, documents, and the different kinds of viewing options you have available in Acrobat viewers. I leave the authoring items and how-to methods to other chapters. For now, just realize this chapter is an abbreviated form of looking at a huge list of possibilities for viewing and navigation. The amplified explanations follow in several other chapters.

Some new features have been implemented in Acrobat and some changes have been made from earlier versions of the program. If you're an experienced user, don't pass this chapter by. The latest release of Acrobat contains new viewing tools and provides new methods for viewing documents. Also, some of the dialog boxes and menu options for viewing have changed.

Setting Up the Work Environment

At the beginning of all subsequent chapters, I begin the chapter by offering suggestions for setting up your work environment. As you can see in Chapter 1, all the Acrobat viewers contain many tools and palettes, and most of these tools and palettes are hidden when you first launch the program. Because Acrobat can do so many things for so many different working professionals, Adobe Systems didn't intend for you to use all the tools and palettes in each editing session. Therefore, you have the opportunity to open and hide different tools and palettes depending on the kind of edits you want to make. As you begin each chapter, look over the section related to setting up the work environment for suggestions on what tools and palettes should be loaded to follow along as you read a chapter.

When viewing PDF documents you'll want to use tools that help you easily navigate pages and files. By default, navigation tools are not loaded in the Acrobat Toolbar Well. Choose View ➪ Toolbars ➪ Navigation. When the Navigation toolbar opens in the Document pane, open a context menu from the Toolbar Well and select Dock All Toolbars.

As is explained in this chapter, several tools and menu commands provide a means for navigating pages and documents. When you're familiar with alternative methods, you can leave the Navigation toolbar hidden, especially if you're using other toolbars that occupy a lot of room in the Toolbar Well. If you're new to Acrobat, keep the Navigation toolbar open as you work through this chapter.

Note   Consider opening and docking the Navigation toolbar an exercise in learning how to access toolbars and dock them in the Toolbar Well. In reality, the Navigation toolbar is not necessary as you have identical tools available in the status bar below the Document pane. The Navigation toolbar is addressed here just so you know it's available. However, as you work in Acrobat, you'll find using it to be unnecessary.

Navigating PDF Documents

You navigate pages in an Acrobat viewer via several means. You can scroll pages with tools, menus, and keystrokes; click hypertext links; and use dialog boxes to move through multiple documents and individual pages. Depending on how a PDF file is created and edited, you can also follow Web links and articles through different sections of a document or through multiple documents. All Acrobat viewers have many navigation controls and several ways to go about viewing and navigating PDF pages.

Navigation toolbar

Navigation tools are found in a toolbar and in the viewer status bar. By default, the Navigation toolbar is hidden. If you want to open the toolbar and keep it around the Acrobat window in either the Toolbar Well or a comfortable place beside the Document pane, choose View ➪ Toolbars ➪ Navigation. The toolbar opens in the Acrobat window as shown in Figure 4-1.

As in many other applications, the icons for these navigation tools resemble the buttons on VCRs, CD players, and tape recorders, which when clicked move you through the media. For the most part, the icons will be familiar if you've ever dealt with video frames in applications on your computer or worked a VCR. If you change your preferences settings to show all labels for toolbar properties as I explain in Chapter 1, you won't need to rely on remembering what the icons represent. A text description explains what each tool does within the toolbar, as shown in Figure 4-1.

Figure 4-1: The Navigation Toolbar shows the icon and name for each tool when the Show Button Labels ➪ All Labels menu selection is made in the Preferences dialog box or from a context menu command opened from the Toolbar Well.

The tools for navigation in Acrobat Professional and other Acrobat viewers include the following:

✦ **First Page:** In the current active document, the First Page tool returns you to the first page in the document.

✦ **Previous Page:** The Previous Page tool moves you back one page at a time.

✦ **Next Page:** The Next Page tool scrolls forward through pages one page at a time.

✦ **Last Page:** The Last Page tool moves you to the last page in the document.

✦ **Go to Previous View:** The Go to Previous View tool returns you to the last view displayed on your screen. Whereas the four preceding tools are limited to navigation through a single open document, the Go to Previous View tool returns you to the previous view even if the last view was another file.

✦ **Go to Next View:** The Go to Next View tool behaves the same as the Go to Previous View tool except it moves in a forward direction. Use of the Go to Previous View and Go to Next View tools can be especially helpful when navigating links that open and close documents. The Next Page and Last Page tools confine you to the active document; whereas the Go to Previous View and Go to Next View tools retrace your navigation steps regardless of how many files you have viewed.

The Navigation toolbar can be docked horizontally in the Toolbar Well, vertically along either side of the Document pane, or horizontally below the status bar. If you dock the toolbar vertically by dragging it to the right side of the Document pane, the toolbar docks to the left side of the How To window. If you drag and dock to the left side when the Navigation pane is open, the toolbar docks vertically to the left side of the Navigation pane. If the How To window is closed, the Navigation pane docked on the right side appears on the far right side of the Document pane.

Cross-Reference For docking toolbars below the status bar, see the discussion on the status bar later in this chapter.

Clicking one of the tools in the toolbar invokes the action associated with the tool. If you want to move through pages left or right, click the left or right arrows. If you want to go to the first or last page in the file, click the respective tools described earlier.

Tip The Navigation toolbar is handy if your operating system status bar (Dock on Macintosh) is positioned at the bottom of your monitor and set to auto-hide. As you move the cursor toward the Acrobat status bar, the operating system status bar interferes with your clicking on navigation tools. If this is a problem for you when viewing PDFs, open the Navigation toolbar and use the tools in the toolbar.

Context menus

Acrobat viewers make limited use of context menu commands for page navigation. This is a big change over versions of Acrobat prior to version 6 when you had many choices for page navigation and page viewing. In Acrobat 6 and 7 page navigation from a context menu is limited to moving between opening the next page and the previous page. To use a context menu for these navigation commands, select the Hand tool and click the right mouse button (Windows and two-button Macs) or Control+click (Macintosh) to open the context menu as shown in Figure 4-2.

Figure 4-2: Context menus opened on a document page using the Hand tool offer navigation commands limited to moving forward and backward one page at a time.

Navigation menu commands

The View menu contains all the page navigation commands formerly listed under the Document menu in Acrobat 6 and earlier viewers. You can use these commands to achieve the same results as using the Navigation tools when viewing pages in a PDF file. Notice that the View menu clearly describes viewing operations, and new users should be easily able to find menu commands associated with views.

When you open the View menu you can select menu commands that perform the same operations as those performed with the Navigation toolbar. However, many users would certainly opt for using the toolbar or keyboard shortcuts to navigate pages because other methods for page navigation are much easier than returning to menu commands. The real value in the View menu is all the other viewing commands you have accessible. The View menu contains many commands for viewing not only pages, but also toolbars and task buttons. When you choose View ➪ Go To, the page navigation commands appear in a submenu, as shown in Figure 4-3.

Those viewing commands apart from the same options you have for navigation with the Navigation toolbar include commands for viewing tools, for various page views, and alternatives to viewing such as reading and scrolling pages automatically. Following is a list of what you can find in the View menu.

Task Buttons

Task Buttons don't have anything to do with PDF viewing; rather, they are used for PDF editing. However, you toggle the visibility of these tools on and off in the View menu. Unlike the other toolbars that contain several different tools in a single palette, the Task Buttons are individual tools contained in the Tasks Toolbar that can be toggled on and off. If you deselect a Task Button, the tool disappears but the Tasks Toolbar remains in view in the Toolbar Well or as a floating toolbar. Choose View ➪ Task Buttons as shown in Figure 4-4 and select the tools you want to view or hide.

Note   You cannot pull a single Task Button out of the Tasks Toolbar and dock it or float it on the Acrobat window by itself. The tools are fixed to the Tasks Toolbar, but you can make them visible or hide them from the Tasks Toolbar by selecting the respective menu commands.

Figure 4-3: The View menu contains many different commands for viewing pages, toolbars, and task buttons.

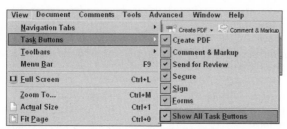

Figure 4-4: Choose View ➪ Task Buttons to open a submenu where you can toggle the Task Buttons view on or off.

Users of Acrobat 6 will notice the absence of the eBooks Task Button and the Advanced Editing Task Button. eBooks are now referred to as Digital Editions in Acrobat 7 and you access them by choosing Advanced ➪ Digital Editions. You handle all management for eBooks in the My Digital Editions window that was previously referred to as My Bookshelf in Acrobat 6. The Advanced Editing tools are still available in Acrobat 7, but now are removed from the Tasks Toolbar and appear within the Advanced Editing toolbar.

The different Task Buttons include

✦ **Create PDF:** Displays the Create PDF Task Button. Use the pull-down menu on this tool to select different file formats for PDF conversion within Acrobat Standard and Acrobat Professional. On the Mac, Create PDF From Clipboard Image has been added to the Task Button.

Cross-Reference

For information about using the Create PDF tool and PDF conversion from different file formats, see Chapter 6.

✦ **Comment & Markup:** The pull-down menu on the Comment & Markup Task Button contains several commands for accessing comment tools, tracking reviews, and managing comments.

Cross-Reference

For information related to using the Comment & Markup tools and menu commands, see Chapter 16.

✦ **Send for Review:** You use the Send for Review Task Button for sending documents for Email-based reviews, and Browser-based reviews.

Cross-Reference

For more on reviews and approval, see Chapter 16.

✦ **Secure:** Menu options from the Secure Task Button enable you to encrypt your document with security policies. You can manage security policies, remove security from a document, display security settings, and obtain help information related to document security.

Cross-Reference

For more information on file encryption and security policies, see Chapter 21.

✦ **Sign:** This Task Button enables you to digitally sign a document, validate digital signatures, and create signature fields.

Cross-Reference

For information related to signing documents with digital signatures, see Chapter 21.

✦ **Forms:** The Forms Task Button has been added in Acrobat 7. Use the pull-down menu on this button to initiate data collection workflows, create spreadsheet data files, and gain help information related to Acrobat PDF forms. On Windows, you can choose commands that launch Adobe Form Designer which are used for designing PDF forms.

Note

Adobe Form Designer ships with Acrobat Professional on Windows only.

Reflow

Document reflow enables users to view PDF documents on adaptive devices for the visually impaired, and it is used when porting PDF files to handheld devices and tablets. When you reflow text onscreen or when using other devices, the text in the PDF wraps according to the zoom level of the page or the device viewing area. Therefore, when you zoom in on a paragraph of text and the text moves off the viewing area of your screen, you can use the Reflow command to make the text automatically scroll to your window size.

Reflow only works with tagged PDF documents in Acrobat viewers earlier than version 7. Acrobat 7 viewers can now reflow any PDF document whether it is a tagged file or not. When you copy PDF documents to handheld devices such as Palm Pilots, Adobe Reader for Palm software wraps text to fit the width of the screen for untagged as well as tagged documents.

Cross-Reference   For information about tagging PDF documents, see Chapters 7 and 20.

Automatically Scroll

Automatic scrolling scrolls pages in the open file at a user-defined speed in all Acrobat viewers. When you select the command, Acrobat automatically switches the Page Layout view to Continuous view, and the pages in the document scroll up, permitting you to read the text without using any keys or the mouse. Attribute changes for automatic scrolling include

✦ **Changing scrolling speed:** To change the scrolling speed, press a number key from 0 (being the slowest) to 9 (being the fastest) on your keyboard or press the up or down arrow keys to speed up or down in increments.

✦ **Reverse scrolling direction:** Press the hyphen or minus key.

✦ **To jump to the next or previous page and continue scrolling:** Press the right or left arrow, respectively.

✦ **Stopping:** To stop the scrolling, press the Esc key.

Note   The Page Layout view automatically switches to Continuous when you choose View ➪ Automatically Scroll. When you stop the scrolling, the Page Layout view remains in Continuous view. If you want to go to Single Page view, use the Single Page tool or select View ➪ Page Layout ➪ Single Page.

Cross-Reference   For information related to page layout views, see the "Page Layout" section later in this chapter.

Read Out Loud

This command is a marvelous accessibility tool in all Acrobat viewers. You can have Acrobat PDF documents read aloud to you without having to purchase additional equipment such as hardware or software screen readers. If you want to turn your back on the computer while doing some other activity, you can have Acrobat read aloud any open document. For entertainment purposes, you can gather the family around the computer and have an eBook read to you.

Cross-Reference For information on screen readers, see the sidebar "About Screen Readers" later in this chapter.

When you choose View ➪ Read Out Loud a submenu opens with four menu commands. The menu commands all have keyboard shortcuts associated with them, so you can use these shortcuts or the actual menu commands. For pausing and stopping the reading, you may want to remember these keyboard shortcuts. The commands include

✦ **Read This Page Only** (Shift+Ctrl+V or Shift+⌘+V): The current active page in the Document pane is read aloud. Reading stops at the end of the target page.

✦ **Read To End of Document** (Shift+Ctrl+B or Shift+⌘+B): The reading starts on the active page and continues to the end of the document. If you want to start at the beginning of your file, click the First Page tool before selecting this menu command.

✦ **Pause/Resume** (Shift+Control+C or Shift+⌘+C): After the reading begins, you see the Pause command active in the submenu. Select Pause or press the keyboard shortcut keys and Resume appears in the menu. Use the same menu command or shortcut to toggle Pause and Resume.

✦ **Stop** (Shift+Control+E or Shift+⌘+E): To stop the reading aloud, select the command or use the keyboard shortcut.

You change attribute settings for reading aloud in the Preferences dialog box, which you open by choosing Edit ➪ Preferences in Windows, Acrobat ➪ Preferences in Mac OS X, or use the keyboard shortcut (Control+K or ⌘+K). In the left pane shown in Figure 4-5, Reading is selected. The Reading preferences are displayed in the right pane. Preferences settings include

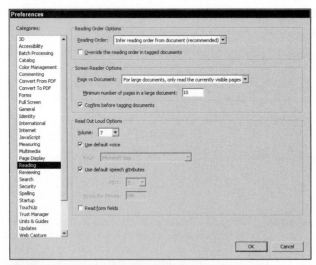

Figure 4-5: To open Reading preferences, choose the Preferences command or press Ctrl+K or ⌘+K. Click the Reading item in the list at the left side of the Preferences dialog box.

✦ **Reading Order:** Three choices are available from the Reading Order pull-down menu. When in doubt, use the default setting to Infer reading order from document (recommended).

- **Infer reading order from document (recommended):** With this choice Acrobat makes some guesses about the order for what items are read on the page. If you have multiple columns and the layout is not clearly set up as a page with no lay-out attributes, the reading order may need some finessing. Acrobat will do its best to deliver the reading in an order compliant to the page layout.

- **Left-to-right, top-to-bottom reading order:** Reading order delivers the reading, ignoring any columns or heads that may be divided across a page. This choice might be best used for a book designed as text only in a single column.

- **Use reading order in raw print stream:** Delivers words in the document in the order recorded in the print stream.

✦ **Override the reading order in tagged documents:** Tagged PDF documents contain structural information and they are designed to be accessible with reading devices so the proper reading order conforms to the way one would visually read a file. Tagged PDF documents have a designated reading order based on the tree structure. If the PDF document is a tagged PDF with a reading structure defined and you want to ignore the order, deselect the check box. You might make this choice if the tagged PDF does not accurately support the proper reading order and the delivery is more problematic than delivering an untagged file.

✦ **Page vs. Document:** Choices include Only read the current visible pages, Read the entire document, or For large documents, only read the currently visible pages. The dif-ference between the first and last command is when the last item is selected (For large documents, only read the currently visible pages), the field box below the pull-down menu becomes active where you can specify the number of pages to be read.

✦ **Confirm before tagging documents:** If a document is tagged before reading aloud, a confirmation dialog box opens confirming the file is a tagged document.

✦ **Volume:** You adjust volume settings in the Volume pull-down menu. Choose from 1 to 10 to lower or raise the volume.

✦ **Use default voice:** By default the Use default voice check box is enabled. If you want to change the voice, deselect the check box and open the pull-down menu adjacent to Voice. The voice availability depends on voices installed with your operating system. Your text-to-speech default voice installed with your operating system is used. By default you may only have a single voice available. If you want additional voices, con-sult your operating system manual. If no additional voices are installed, you won't be able to change the voice. If you have multiple voices installed, select a voice from the pull-down menu.

✦ **Use default speech attributes:** The speech attributes are settings for the pitch and the speed the voice reads your file. If you want to change the pitch and/or reading rate, deselect the check box. Pitch can be changed to a value between 1 and 10. To com-pletely understand what's going on with the pitch settings, experiment a little and lis-ten to the various pitch changes with the voice you select from the Voice pull-down menu. Words Per Minute enables you to slow down or speed up the reading. The default is 190 wpm. If you want to make a change, type a new value in the field box.

✦ **Read form fields:** This setting is designed for use with Acrobat PDF forms. Check the box to have form field default values read aloud.

For more information about setting form field default values, see Chapters 27 and 28.

For more information on screen readers, tagged PDF files, and accessibility, see Chapter 20.

Go To

The commands that are equal to the actions you perform with the Navigation tools are contained in the Go To submenu. You can choose any of the Navigation commands in this menu and the results are the same as using tools, the status bar, and keyboard shortcuts. You'll probably avoid using the Navigation commands because using any one of the other methods to scroll through pages is so much easier. The exception is the Page command in this submenu. When you select Page or press Shift+Ctrl+N or Shift+⌘+N, the Go To Page dialog box opens as shown in Figure 4-6.

Figure 4-6: The Go To Page dialog box enables navigation to a page you type in the field box.

Enter a value for a page number and click OK. The Page view opens a page respective to the number you typed in the dialog box.

See "Status Bar" later in this chapter for information on jumping to a page from a number typed in the status bar field box.

Page Layout

The Page Layout view can be any one of four different layout types. Choices for page layout are contained in the View ➪ Page Layout submenu. Depending on the way a PDF file has been saved and depending on what preference choices are made for the Initial view, a PDF layout may appear different on different computers depending on each individual user's preference settings. Regardless of how you set your preferences, you can change the Page Layout view at any time.

For more information on setting Initial view preferences, see "Initial View" later in this chapter.

About Screen Readers

The term *screen reader* as used in this book refers to specialized software and/or hardware devices connected to computers that enable the reading aloud of computer files. Software such as JAWS and Kurzwiel, and a host of other specialized software programs are sold to people with vision and motion challenges for the purpose of voice synthesizing and audio output. Many of these devices deliver audio output from proprietary formatted files or a select group of software applications. Some screen readers read raster image files saved in formats such as TIFF by performing an optical character recognition (OCR) on-the-fly and reading aloud text as it is interpreted from the image files. This method makes scanning pages of books and papers and having the scanned images interpreted by the readers easy.

Because Acrobat has implemented many tools and features for working with accessible files for the vision and motion challenged, screen reader developers have been supporting PDF format for some time. When a PDF is delivered to a reader and you select Read the entire document, the entire PDF file is sent to the reader before the first page is read. If you have long documents, you can choose to send a certain number of pages to the screen reader to break up the file into smaller chunks. When you select For long documents, only read the currently visible pages and the default of 10 pages is selected, 10 pages are sent to the screen reader and the reading commences. After the pages are read, another 10 pages are sent to the screen reader and read aloud, and so on.

The four page layout views are shown in Figure 4-7. They are

- ✦ **Single Page:** Single Page views place an entire page in view when the zoom level is set to Fit Page. When you press the Page Down key or the down-arrow key to scroll pages, the next page snaps into view.

- ✦ **Continuous:** Continuous page layout views show pages in a linear fashion, where you might see the bottom of one page and the top of another page in the Document pane as you scroll down. The difference between this view and Single Page views is that the pages don't snap to a full page when viewed as Continuous.

- ✦ **Facing:** This view shows two pages side by side — like looking at an open book. When the zoom level is set to Fit Page or lower, only two pages are in view in the Document pane.

- ✦ **Continuous – Facing:** This page layout view displays a combination of the preceding two options. When the zoom level is zoomed out, the view displays as many pages in the Document pane as can be accommodated by the zoom level.

Figure 4-7: From left to right the four page layout views available in the View ⇨ Page Layout submenu include Single Page, Continuous, Facing, and Continuous – Facing.

Rotate View

If your PDF opens in Acrobat with a rotated view, you can rotate pages clockwise or counter-clockwise from two submenu commands. The same rotations are also available in the View menu. Rotate View tools rotate all pages in your PDF document and come in handy if the PDF pages are rotated on the Initial view or if you want to view PDFs on eBook readers, tablets, or laptop computers. However, changes made with the Rotate View tools or the View menu commands are temporary and any saves you make do not record the rotated views. Another set of rotation commands are available in the Document menu. When you select Document ➪ Rotate Pages and rotate the views, the rotations can be saved with the file.

Grid (Acrobat Professional only)

If you need to examine drawings, a grid may help in your analysis. In Acrobat Professional, you can choose to view your file displaying a grid. Grids can be useful when you're authoring PDF files, particularly PDF forms. For viewing purposes they can be useful where relationships to objects require some careful examination. To show a grid, choose View ➪ Grid. By default the grid is shown in the Document pane as blue lines at fixed major and minor gridlines, as shown in Figure 4-8.

If you want to change the distances for the major gridlines and the number of divisions for the minor gridlines, open the Preferences dialog box and select Units and Guides in the left pane. The preference settings enable you to change the units of measure and attributes for the grid layout as shown in Figure 4-9.

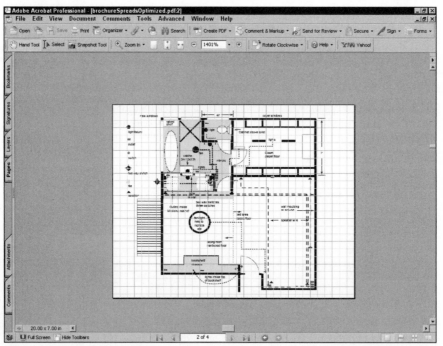

Figure 4-8: Choose View ➪ Grid or press the Ctrl+U or ⌘+U to access the grid. You can change the grid lines for major and minor divisions in the Preferences dialog box.

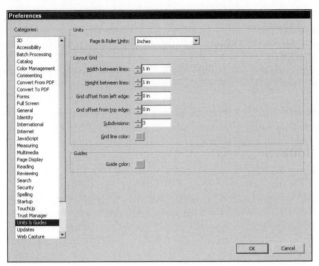

Figure 4-9: Preference choices for Units and Guides offer you options for changing the units of measure and the grid layout.

The Units and Guides preference settings are also used for changing attributes for the grid layout and rulers. The attribute choices include

✦ **Page & Ruler Units:** Five choices are available from the pull-down menu. You can choose Points, Picas, Millimeters, Centimeters, or Inches. Whatever you choose here is reflected in the rulers when you display the rulers. Choices here also affect the units of measure found in the Info palette discussed in Chapter 1.

✦ **Width between lines:** The horizontal distance between the major gridlines is determined in the field box for this setting. You can click on the arrows, enter a number between 0.03 and 139.89 in the field (when inches are selected for the unit of measurement), or press the up- or down-arrow keys to change the values.

Note

The limit of 139.89 relates to inches. If you change the units of measure, the limits are roughly the same as the 139.89-inch limit. In points, the range measures between 2 and 10,000.

✦ **Height between lines:** You can change the major gridlines appearing vertically with this field. Use the same methods of changing the values here as for the lines for the Width option.

✦ **Grid offset from left edge:** Each grid has x and y coordinates indicating where the grid begins on a page. You set the x-axis in this field.

✦ **Grid offset from top edge:** Use this field to set the starting point of the y-axis.

✦ **Subdivisions:** The number of gridlines appearing between the major gridlines is determined in this field. The acceptable values range between 0 and 10,000 (when units are set to points).

✦ **Grid line color:** By default, the color for the gridlines is blue. You can change the grid color by clicking the color swatch. When you click the blue swatch for Grid Line color, a pop-up color palette opens as shown in Figure 4-10. Select a color from the preset color choices in the palette or click Other Color. If you click Other Color, the system color palette opens, in which you can make custom color choices. The Windows and Macintosh system color palettes vary slightly, as shown in Figures 4-11 and 4-12.

Figure 4-10: Click the color swatch for the Grid line color to choose from a selection of preset colors, or select Other Color to open the system color palette.

✦ **Guide color:** Guides are created from ruler wells, and you can manually position them in the Document pane. If you have ruler guides and a grid, you'll want to change one color to easily distinguish the guides from the grid. Both default to the same blue. To change the guide color, click the Guide Color swatch and follow the same steps as described for Grid line color.

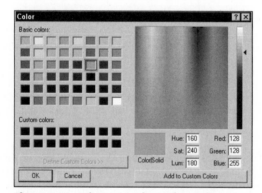

Figure 4-11: When you select Other Color on Windows, the Windows system color palette opens.

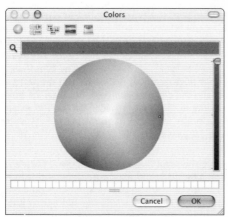

Figure 4-12: When you select Other Color on the Macintosh, the Macintosh system color palette opens. Inasmuch as the palettes differ in appearance, you can make the same custom color choices on both platforms.

Snap to Grid (Acrobat Professional only)

When you choose View ➪ Snap to Grid, objects you draw snap to the major and minor grid-lines. This feature can be particularly helpful with form designs and engineering drawings.

Cross-Reference

For more information on Snap to Grid, see Chapter 26.

Rulers (Acrobat Professional only)

Acrobat Professional supports viewing rulers, and you can turn them on via the View menu or using the keyboard shortcut Control/⌘+R. When you choose View ➪ Ruler or use the key-board shortcut, rulers appear on the top and left side of the Document pane. Inside the top and left ruler is an inexhaustible supply of guidelines. To add a guideline on the document page, place the cursor within the top or left ruler, press the mouse button, and drag away from the ruler to the Document pane. Continue adding as many guidelines as you want by returning to the ruler wells and dragging out more guidelines.

Tip

You can also add guidelines by double-clicking a ruler. If you want guides positioned at 1-inch increments, as an example, move the mouse cursor to a ruler and double-click the mouse button on each 1-inch increment. Guidelines appear on the page in the Document pane with each double-click of the mouse button. If you attempt to create a guideline out-side the page area, Acrobat sounds a warning beep. Guides are not permitted outside the page area.

If you want to move a guideline after it has been placed in the Document pane, select the Hand tool and place the cursor directly over the guideline to be moved. The cursor changes from a hand to a selection arrow. Press the mouse button and drag the line to the desired position.

Tip   If you have multiple guidelines to draw on a page at equal distances, use the Units and Guides preferences and set the major guides to the distance you want between the guides. Set the subdivision guidelines to zero. For example, if you want guidelines two inches apart, set the major Height and Width guides to 2 inches and enter **0** (zero) in the subdivisions. Click OK and you save some time dragging guidelines from ruler wells.

To delete a guideline, click the line when you see the selection arrow described earlier and press the Delete key on your keyboard. You can also click and drag a guideline off the document page and back to the ruler well to delete it. If you want to delete all guides on a page, open a context menu (see Figure 4-13) on a ruler and select Clear Guides on Page. If you select Clear All Guides, all guides drawn throughout your document are deleted.

The context menu for rulers also enables you to hide the rulers; you can also use the shortcut keys Ctrl/⌘+R or revisit the View menu. Hidden rulers don't affect the view of the guides that remain visible. Notice that the context menu also contains choices for units of measure, which makes changing units here much handier than returning to the preference settings mentioned earlier. The context menu also offers the option to show and hide guides.

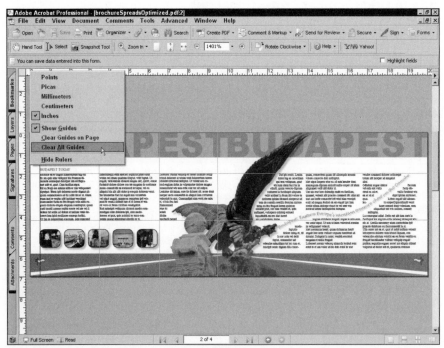

Figure 4-13: To clear guides on a page or throughout all pages, open a context menu on a ruler and make a choice for the desired task from the menu commands.

Scrolling

Anyone familiar with window environments is no stranger to scrolling. Fortunately, scroll bars behave in a standard fashion among computer platforms and various computer programs. Page scrolling works the same in an Acrobat viewer as it does in Microsoft Word (or any other Microsoft product for that matter), or any illustration, layout, or host of other applications that you may be familiar with. Drag the scroll bar up and down or left to right to move the document within the active window. Click between the scroll bar at the top or bottom of the scrolling column to jump a page segment or full page. The arrow icons at the top, bottom, left, and right sides allow you to move in smaller segments in the respective directions.

Note   When you drag the scroll bar up or down in a multiple-page PDF file, a small pop-up Tool Tip displays a page number associated with the scroll bar position as well as the total number of pages in the document. The readout is in the form of "*n* of *n* pages." The first number dynamically changes as you move the scroll bar between pages. This behavior only works when you view a document in Single or Facing layout mode.

Cross-Reference   For information on auto scrolling see the "Automatically Scroll" section earlier in this chapter.

Status bar

The status bar at the bottom of the Acrobat window provides you with navigation and viewing tools in all Acrobat viewers. The tools for First Page, Previous Page, Next Page, and Last Page (reading left to right in the status bar) are identical to the tools you find in the Navigation toolbar. Additionally, the Previous View and Next View tools appear on the right side of the other navigation tools.

The Go To menu command enables you to jump to a specific page number. However, the status bar provides an easier method for navigating to a specific page. Click the cursor in the page numbers readout in the status bar and highlight the numbers. Type a new page number you want to go to and press the Enter/Return key. Acrobat opens the page you supplied in the status bar.

Note   When you click and drag across numbers in the field box to highlight them, and then type a new value, the highlighted items are replaced with the new values you type on your keyboard.

The Page Layout tools are located at the far right of the status bar. You can click one of these tools to view your pages as Single Page, Continuous, Continuous – Facing, and Facing. Changing page layout views using the status bar is much easier than opening the View menu and Page Layout menu to access a different page layout view.

When the How To window is open, the Document pane shrinks in size and the status bar travels with it. Notice that when the How To window is open, the Page Layout tools slide to the left to make room for more viewing area in the How To window.

Document status bar

In Figure 4-13 notice the space between the Document pane and the Toolbar Well. On the left side of the window you see the text *You can save data entered into this form*. This area of the Acrobat window is called the Document status bar. If you're working with forms, a check box on the right enables you to turn on and off form field highlights. However, you may see the bar open as it appears in Figure 4-13 when your document is not a form. At times you'll want to eliminate the bar from view for more convenient viewing and navigation. To close the bar, drag the separator bar appearing below the text and check box up. You can also double-click the separator bar to close the Document status bar.

Cross-Reference   For more information about the Document status bar, see Chapter 21.

Read Mode

In the status bar at the bottom of the Acrobat window is a tool that is used to hide toolbars. This handy new tool introduced in Acrobat 7 enables you to easily toggle views between Edit mode and Read mode. Read mode eliminates all toolbars from view, enabling you to see more of your document in the Document pane. The Navigation tabs are accessible and the top-level menus are in view when you click the Hide Toolbars tool in the status bar. To return to edit mode where all the toolbars are brought back in view, click the Show Toolbars tool. Note that when you click Hide Toolbars, the tool name changes to Show Toolbars.

When you change the view to Read mode, the Hand tool appears in the status bar adjacent to the Show Toolbars tool. From a pop-up menu adjacent to the Hand tool you access zoom tools and the Select tool. Clicking the Show Toolbars tool hides the Hand tool and pop-up menu in the status bar.

Cross-Reference   For more information about using Read mode, see Chapter 24.

Full Screen Mode tool

To the left of the Hide Toolbars tool is the Full Screen Mode tool. Click this tool to hide all toolbars, navigation tabs, and menus from view. This view gives you the maximum viewing area for a document. To return to Edit mode and bring back the toolbars, menus, and navigation tabs, press the Escape (Esc) key on your keyboard.

Cross-Reference   There's much more to viewing documents in Full Screen mode than described here. For a complete discussion about using Full Screen mode, see Chapter 23.

Zooming

Zooming in and out of document pages is a fact of life with many different programs. Even when you type text in a word processor, you often need to zoom in on text that is set in a style suited for printing, but looks horrible at a 100% view on your computer monitor. The same holds true for spreadsheets, all the imaging and layout programs, and any kind of program where page sizes grow beyond a standard letter-size page.

Because Acrobat accommodates a page size of up to 200 × 200 inches, PDF documents sporting large page sizes need some industrial-strength zoom tools. Acrobat Professional contains a few more tools than the other Acrobat viewers; however, all viewers enable you to zoom in and out of document pages using some tools consistent across all the viewers. The Zoom In and Zoom Out tools used in all viewers permits views from 8.33 percent to 6,400 percent of a document page.

Several tools are available for zooming. By default the Zoom In tool appears in a toolbar docked in the Toolbar Well. If you select the Zoom In tool pull-down menu, you can select from one of five different Zoom tools in Acrobat Professional. Three of the five tools are available in Acrobat Standard and Adobe Reader.

In all viewers, you can also zoom by clicking the Zoom In or Zoom Out icons in the viewer toolbar (represented by a + and – symbol) or editing the zoom percentage field in the toolbar — just type a new value in the field box and press the Enter/Return key to zoom. When you click the down-pointing arrow, the preset pull-down menu opens.

The View menu also has a Zoom To command. Select it and the Zoom To dialog box opens where you can select fixed zoom levels from a pull-down menu or type in a value from 8.88 to 6,400 percent. However, this menu command is redundant because you can also use the Zoom toolbar in the same manner.

 Tip   At first glance you may think that the menu command is useless and unnecessary. However, when viewing PDF documents where the menu bar is hidden or viewing files in Full Screen mode, you can use the keyboard shortcut Ctrl/⌘+M to open the Zoom To dialog box. You can then change zoom levels without making the menu bar visible or exiting Full Screen mode.

Zoom In tool

The Zoom In tool functions, as you might expect, like similar tools in other authoring applications. Select the tool in the Zoom toolbar and click a page in the Document pane. For temporary access to the Zoom In tool when another tool is selected, you can use the shortcut keys Ctrl/⌘ + Spacebar. When you release the shortcut keys, you return to the selected tool. You can also temporarily access the Zoom Out tool when the Zoom In tool is selected by holding the ctrl/⌘ keys down and then adding the Alt/Option key and clicking the mouse button. The cursor inside the magnifying glass changes to a minus sign indicating the Zoom Out tool is selected.

When you click to zoom in or out, the page zoom follows the same zoom presets found in the pull-down menu from the Zoom toolbar. If you need zoom levels between the presets, type a number in the field box in the Zoom toolbar and press the Enter/Return key.

If you want to target a specific area to zoom in on, you can drag open a rectangle while the Zoom In tool is selected. The area you marquee zooms to view in the Document pane when you release the mouse button. Zoom levels are also accessible from a context menu while a Zoom tool is selected. Open a context menu and you see the same preset zoom levels and page views found in the Zoom toolbar.

Zoom Out tool

Zoom Out ▾   The Zoom Out tool works in exactly the same way as the Zoom In tool only it zooms out rather than in. It also has the same options associated with it as are associated with the Zoom In tool. You can access the tool with the same modifier keys as the Zoom In tool (Control/⌘+spacebar), but with the addition of the Alt/Option key. Be certain to first press the Control/⌘ key, and then add the Alt/Option key. The same presets, context menu, and ability to marquee an area are available with the Zoom Out tool.

Dynamic Zoom tool

Dynamic Zoom ▾   When you first use the Dynamic Zoom tool you may feel like you're watching a George Lucas sci-fi movie. It's downright mesmerizing. This tool is available in all Acrobat viewers and is much handier than drawing marquees with the Zoom In or Zoom Out tools.

To use dynamic zooming, select the tool from the Zoom toolbar pull-down menu adjacent to the Zoom In tool. Click and drag in any direction toward the page edge in the Document pane to zoom in or toward the middle of the page to zoom out. As you move the cursor you see the page zoom dynamically. Stop at the desired zoom level by releasing the mouse button. Acrobat displays a proxy view while zooming in and out and only refreshes the screen when you release the mouse button. Using this tool, therefore, is much faster because each zoom increment does not require a new screen refresh.

Loupe tool (Acrobat Professional only)

Loupe ▾   If you use other Adobe programs, such as Adobe Photoshop, Adobe Illustrator, or Adobe InDesign, you know about the Navigator palette. In Acrobat Professional, the Loupe tool works similarly to the Navigator palette found in other Adobe programs but with a little twist. Instead of viewing a complete page in the Loupe Tool window, you see just the zoom level of your selection while the page zoom remains static. This tool can be a great benefit by saving you time to refresh your monitor when you change screen views.

To use the Loupe tool, select the tool from the Zoom toolbar pull-down menu, or press the Z key on your keyboard and then press Shift+Z until the Loupe tool comes in view in the toolbar. Move the cursor to an area on a page you want to zoom to and click the mouse button. The Loupe tool window opens and displays the zoomed area you selected, as shown in Figure 4-14.

Cross-Reference   When using keyboard shortcuts for accessing tools you need to enable the *Use single-key accelerators to access tools* preference setting. For more information on setting preferences for using keyboard shortcuts, see Chapter 1.

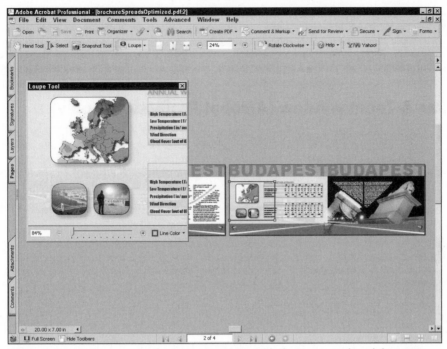

Figure 4-14: Click an area in the Document pane with the Loupe tool, and the target area is viewed at a zoom level in the Loupe window.

You can increase or decrease the magnification of the zoom area by adjusting the slider bar in the Loupe window or clicking the minus or plus symbols in the window. Clicking these symbols offers you smaller incremental changes than when using the same symbols in the Zoom toolbar. If you want the Loupe tool to show a larger portion, you can resize the Loupe Tool dialog box by grabbing a corner of the box and dragging.

When you click in the Document pane with the Loupe tool, a rectangle appears around the area zoomed into the Loupe window. You can place the cursor inside this rectangle and move it around the Document pane to view different areas at the same zoom level. As you zoom in, the rectangle reduces in size. At some point it would be impractical to select the rectangle on the page. If you can't find it, zoom out a little in the Loupe tool window until you see the rectangle on the page. Click and drag it to a new position and you can adjust your zoom.

A new feature added to Acrobat 7 now permits you to size the rectangle on the page. In Figure 4-14 notice the four handles (squares) on the corners of the rectangle marking the Loupe tool zoom area. You can drag the handles in or out to zoom in or out, respectively.

If you have oversized documents that take a long time to refresh, using the Loupe tool helps speed up your PDF viewing. You can keep the document page in the Document pane at a reduced view while using the Loupe tool to examine areas in detail, which won't necessitate screen refreshes.

Tip   The Loupe window displays the zoom level on an open document and remains fixed to that document until you target a new area. When you have multiple documents open, you can zoom in on one document and switch views in the Document pane to another document; the zoom display in the Loupe tool window remains fixed to the original document view. What you wind up with is like a picture-in-picture view such as you might see on a television set.

Pan & Zoom window (Acrobat Professional only)

Whereas the Loupe tool displays the zoom view in its own window and the page in the Document pane remains static, the Pan & Zoom window works in the opposite manner. The zoom level changes on the page in the Document pane while the original page view remains static in the Pan & Zoom window. The zoom area is highlighted with a red rectangle in the Pan & Zoom window. In Acrobat 7 you can change the default red color of the zoom rectangle by opening the Line Color pull-down menu in the window and choosing from preset colors or choosing a custom color.

To use the Pan & Zoom window, select the tool from the Zoom toolbar pull-down menu. The window displays a full page and the red rectangle showing the zoom area. If you open the Pan & Zoom window when your PDF page is in Fit Page view, the page and the red rectangle are the same size.

Note   You can select all the zoom tools with keyboard shortcuts (by pressing Z and then Shift+Z to toggle the tools) except the Pan & Zoom window. You must access the tool via the Zoom toolbar pull-down menu.

To zoom a view in the Pan & Zoom window, select one of the four handles on a corner of the rectangle and resize the rectangle by dragging in or out to zoom in or out, respectively. The page thumbnail view in the Pan & Zoom window remains the same size while the rectangle is sized, as shown in Figure 4-15.

Also contained in the Pan & Zoom window are navigation buttons. You can establish a zoom view and then scroll pages in your document with the page tools in the window. As you do so, the page views in the Document pane hold the same zoom level you set in the Pan & Zoom window.

Zoom tool behaviors

A few specific differences exist between the Loupe tool and the Pan & Zoom tool that you should know. The Loupe tool targets an area on an open document and the zoom is fixed to that document while it remains open or until you target a new area. Regardless of the number of files you open, the Loupe tool window displaying your target view stays intact even if another document is brought to the front of the Document pane. If you close a file where the Loupe tool was set to view a zoom, the Loupe tool window clears and displays no view.

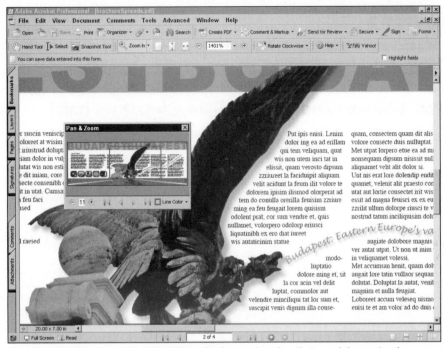

Figure 4-15: The Pan & Zoom window displays a thumbnail view of the entire document page. The rectangle in the window shows the zoom level corresponding to the page zoom view.

The Pan & Zoom tool always shows a target view of the active document brought forward in the Document pane. If you have multiple documents open, open the Pan & Zoom tool, then close a file, the page in view in the next file appears in the Pan & Zoom window. If you close all files, the Pan & Zoom window clears.

If you close a file during an Acrobat session, both the Loupe tool and the Pan & Zoom tool return you to the same views. The Pan & Zoom tool displays the opening page at the same zoom level as was last established in the window. The Loupe tool displays the same view last created with the tool. For example, if you zoom to 200 percent on page 25 of a file, close the file, and then reopen it, the Loupe tool window displays page 25 at 200 percent while the Document pane displays the opening page.

You can use both tools together to display different views in different documents. If the page in view in the Loupe window is not the current active document brought forward in the Document pane, you can still manage zooming on the hidden page. Use the slider of the minus/plus symbols to change zoom levels.

Page Views

The page views for Actual Size, Fit Page, and Fit Width are static views that you want to access frequently when navigating through a PDF document. Acrobat viewers provide several ways to change a page view. Three tools appear in the Zoom toolbar for toggling different page views, as shown in Figure 4-16. The different views include

✦ ☐ **Actual Size:** Displays the PDF page at actual size (a 100 percent view).

✦ ☐ **Fit Page:** Displays the page at the maximum size that fits within the viewer Document pane. If the Acrobat viewer window is sized up or down, the Fit Page view conforms to the size of the Document pane.

✦ ☐ **Fit Width:** The data on a PDF page is displayed horizontally without clipping. If the page is large and data only appears in the center of the page, the page zooms to fit the data. The white space at the page edges is ignored.

Figure 4-16: Page view icons for Actual Size, Fit Page, and Fit Width.

One of the keyboard shortcuts you'll want to remember is Ctrl/⌘+0 (zero). This enables you to view a page in a Fit Page view. As you browse pages in a PDF document, the page views are specific to the individual pages and not the document. Therefore, scrolling PDF files with different page sizes may require you to frequently change views if you want to see the full page in the Document pane. By using the keyboard shortcuts, you can reset page views much faster.

Page views can be established for the opening page and user specified. Setting these attributes was referred to as Open Options in earlier versions of Acrobat. In Acrobat 6 and 7 they are referred to as Initial View. These and other kinds of page views available in Acrobat are covered in the following section, "Initial View."

Initial View

Initial View is the page view you see when you first open a PDF document. You can set several different attributes for an opening view and you can save your settings with the document. These views are document specific so they only relate to a document where you save the settings. When no settings have been saved with a file, the file is saved with a default view.

Cross-Reference To understand more about default views, see "Understanding Initial View preferences" later in this chapter.

Coincidentally, even though previous versions of Acrobat provided you with options to save an initial view, most PDF authors rarely use them. You can find thousands of PDF files on the Internet and most of them have no settings enabled for an opening view other than the program defaults. Hopefully by the time you finish this section, you can see some advantages for saving a particular initial view for the PDF documents you create and edit.

To set the attributes for the opening view, choose File ➪ Document Properties or use the keyboard shortcut Ctrl/⌘+D. The Document Properties dialog box opens, displaying a row of tabs at the top. Click the Initial View tab as shown in Figure 4-17.

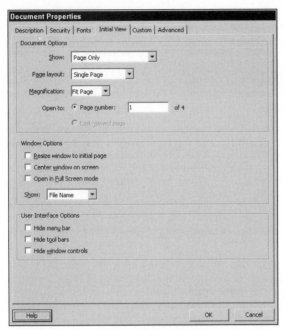

Figure 4-17: To set the attributes for the opening view, choose File ➪ Document Properties and click the Initial View tab when the Document Properties dialog box opens.

Note   Initial View settings are not available nor can they be changed in Adobe Reader even when usage rights have been added to the PDF. When Initial Views are saved from Acrobat Standard or Professional, PDFs open with the saved views in all Acrobat viewers.

Acrobat provides you with many different choices for controlling the initial view of a PDF opened in any Acrobat viewer. Settings you make on the Initial View tab can be saved with your document. When you establish settings other than defaults, the settings saved with the file override the user's default settings. The options on this tab include the following:

✦ **Document Options:** The default opening page is the first page of a PDF document. You can change the opening page to another page and you can control the page layout views and magnification by selecting choices from the Document Options section. The choices include

• **Show:** Five choices are available from the Show pull-down menu. Select Page Only to open the page with the Navigation pane collapsed. Use the Bookmarks Panel and Page option to open the Bookmarks tab when the file opens. Use the Pages Panel and Page option to open the Pages tab where the thumbnails of pages are viewed. Use Attachments Panel and Page to open the Attachments tab when the file opens, and Use Layers Panel and Page to open the Layers tab when the file opens.

- **Page Layout:** The default for Page Layout is noted in the pull-down menu as Default. When you save a PDF file with the Default selection, the PDF opens according to the default value a user has set for page viewing on the user's computer. To override the user's default, you can set a page layout in the opening view from one of four choices. Choose Single Page to open the PDF in a single page layout. Choose Continuous to open in a continuous page view. Use Facing to open with facing pages or use Continuous – Facing to open in continuous facing pages view.

- **Magnification:** Choose from preset magnification views in the pull-down menu. If you want the PDF document to open in a fit-in-window view, select Fit Page. Choose from other magnification options or edit the field box for a custom zoom level. If Default is selected, the document opens according to user preference magnification settings.

- **Open to Page number:** You can change the opening page to another page by entering a number in the Page number field. This setting might be used if you want a user to see a contents page on page 2 in a document instead of a title page that appears on page 1.

- **Open to Last-viewed page:** You can also choose for the opening page to be the Last-viewed page. When this option is enabled, the last page viewed when the file was closed opens in a subsequent Acrobat session. This setting is intended for eBooks, where you might begin reading a novel and want to mark the page like a bookmark and then later return to the page where you left off.

Cross-Reference For more information on eBooks and marking the last-viewed page, see Chapter 24.

✦ **Window Options:** The default window for Acrobat is a full screen where the viewing area is maximized to occupy your monitor surface area. You can change the window view to size down the window to the initial page size, center a smaller window onscreen, and open a file in Full Screen mode. If you enable all three check boxes, the Full Screen mode prevails.

- **Show:** From the pull-down menu choose either File Name or Document Title. If you select File Name, the title bar at the top of the Acrobat window shows the filename. If Document Title is used, the information you supply in the Document Properties dialog box for Document Title is shown in the title bar.

Cross-Reference Document titles are very important when you're archiving volumes of PDFs and creating search indexes. For information on creating document titles and how they are used, see Chapter 5.

✦ **User Interface Options:** The Interface Options in the Initial View Document Properties dialog box have to do with user interface items in Acrobat viewers, such as menu bars, toolbars, and scroll bars. You can elect to hide these items when the PDF document opens in any Acrobat viewer. You can hide any one or a combination of the three items listed under the User Interface Options. When all three are enabled, the PDF appears as shown in Figure 4-18. If you elect to save files without any of the user interface items in view, then creating navigational buttons so users can move around your document is a good idea.

Figure 4-18: When toolbars, the menu bar, and window controls are hidden, navigating pages requires keyboard shortcuts or navigational buttons on the pages.

The window controls you see in Figure 4-19 include the scroll bars, the status bar, and the Navigation pane. If you hide the toolbars and menu bar but elect to leave the window controls visible, users can access tools for page navigation.

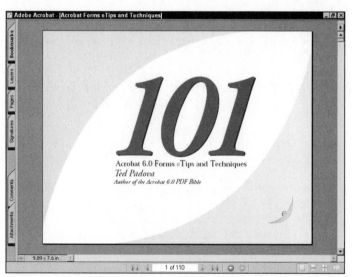

Figure 4-19: If window controls are visible, users can access tools for page navigation.

Caution   If you elect to eliminate the toolbars and menu bar from view and later want to go back and edit your file, you need to use shortcut keys to get the menu bars and toolbars back. Be certain to remember the F8 and F9 keys — F8 shows and hides the toolbars and F9 shows and hides the menu bar.

Understanding Initial View preferences

If you don't assign Initial View attributes in the Document Properties dialog box and save the file to update it, initial views are determined from individual user preferences. Because each user can set preferences differently, the same PDF may appear with a different page layout mode and a different zoom level on different computers. Depending on the design of your documents and how you want them viewed by end users, potential inconsistency in document views might make viewing difficult for those who view your files.

Users set initial view preferences in the Preferences dialog box. Open the Preferences dialog box by pressing Ctrl/⌘+K, and then click Page Display in the left pane. At the top of the right pane, a pull-down menu appears for Default page layout; at the bottom of the right pane another menu appears for Default zoom. You can select different page layout and default zoom views from the menus. In Figure 4-20 the Default page layout view is set to Single Page and the Default zoom is set to Fit Page. When you click OK to accept these changes, all PDF documents that have initial views set to Default will open on your computer with the views derived from your preference choices. Other users may choose different options from the pull-down menus, thereby displaying PDF documents with default views according to the choices they made in the Page Display preferences.

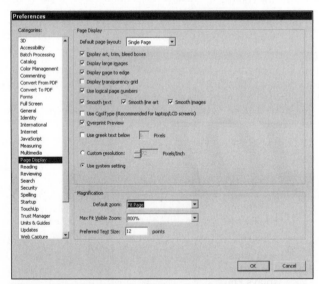

Figure 4-20: Changing the Default page layout to Single Page and the Default zoom to Fit Page opens all PDFs saved with default initial views with your new preference settings.

Be aware that the initial views you set in a PDF file from the Document Properties override the user preferences in the Page Display preferences pane. Therefore you can control the initial views for all the PDFs you create. Doing so means your documents will be viewed consistently across all computers regardless of the differences between individual user preference choices.

Saving the Initial View

When you decide what view attributes you want assigned to your document, you can choose one of two save options. The first option updates the file. Click the Save tool in the Acrobat File toolbar or choose File ➪ Save. Any edits you make in the Initial View properties activates the Save command. The Save command is inactive and grayed out by default until you make any changes to your file or reset any kind of preferences that can be saved with the document. The option is to use Save As. When you select File ➪ Save As you completely rewrite the file when you click the Save button in the Save As dialog box.

Cross-Reference You have different choices for saving files using either Save, Save As, or saving a version. For a more complete understanding of saving, updating, and saving versions of PDFs, see Chapter 9.

Viewing Files with the Window Menu

If you open a PDF file and then open a second PDF, the second file hides the first document. If several PDFs are opened, the last opened document hides all the others. Fortunately, the Acrobat viewers have made it easy for you to choose a given document from a nest of open files.

When you load an Acrobat viewer with several open files, you can use tools to help you manage them. If you need to visually compare documents, several different viewing options are available.

The Window menu contains options for helping you manage document views, and in particular, multiple documents. The options you find in the Window menu won't be found with tools or in the status bar, so you'll find yourself visiting this menu frequently if you work with multiple open files in Acrobat or if you need to create more than one view in the same document.

New Window

New Window is a new feature in Acrobat 7 Professional. When you open a document and select New Window, a duplicate view of your existing document is opened in the Document pane. You can change views and pages in one window while viewing different page views in another window. This feature is handy for viewing a table of contents in one window while viewing content on other pages in the same file.

When you select New Window, Acrobat adds an extension to the filename in the title bar. If you have a document open in Acrobat with a filename like Employee Application, and then select New Window, the title bar displays Employee Application:1 on one view and Employee Application:2 on the second view. In Figure 4-23 later in this chapter you can see the filenames on the title bar in two windows.

Cascade

If you have several files open and choose Window ➪ Cascade, the open files appear in a cascading view with the title bars visible, as shown in Figure 4-21. You can see the name of each file and easily select from any one shown in the Document pane. Click a title bar to bring the document forward.

Figure 4-21: Cascaded views provide you with immediate access to any one of several files open in the Document pane.

After bringing a file forward, if you want to see the title bars in a cascading view again, choose Window ➪ Cascade again. The document currently selected in the foreground will appear first when you use this command.

The Window menu also lists the open files by filename at the bottom of the window. When you have multiple files open, the files are numbered according to the order in which they were opened, with the filename appearing in the list, as shown in Figure 4-22. Select any filename from the list in the Window menu to bring the file forward in the Document pane.

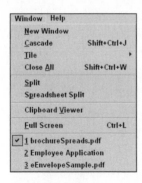

Figure 4-22: Acrobat lists all open files in the Window menu. To bring a document forward in the Document pane, choose the name of the file you want to view from the Window menu.

Tile

You can also choose to have your documents tiled horizontally or vertically via the Tile sub-menu in the Window menu. When you choose Window ⇨ Tile ⇨ Horizontally or Vertically, the PDF files appear in individual windows arranged to fit within the Acrobat window in either a horizontal or vertical view. If you have more than three documents open at one time, the display for Tile Horizontally and Tile Vertically appear identical. With any number of documents displayed in tiled views, the Navigation pane is accessible for each document. Also, when you choose Window ⇨ New Window and open a second view of the same document, and then tile the views, each window appears in the tiled documents. In Figure 4-23 two views (top and bottom) on the left side of the Acrobat window are the same file with different page views.

Tiling documents can be helpful when you need to edit documents and exchange pages between two or more PDF files or when you need to compare changes among documents.

Cross-Reference

For information related to editing files, see Chapter 12. For more information on comparing documents, see Chapter 15.

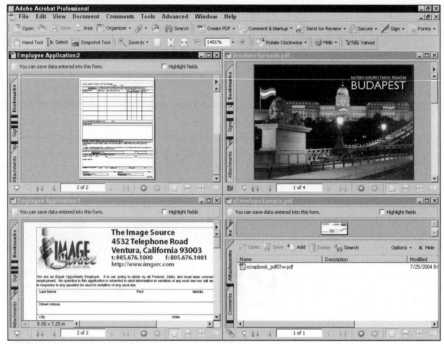

Figure 4-23: Tiling views neatly displays all open documents adjacent to each other within the Acrobat window.

Split

Choose Window ➪ Split and the Document pane splits into two horizontal views of the active document, similar to the way you might see a split view in a word processing or spreadsheet program. The two views are independent of each other and offer you much flexibility. You can view the same page in two different zoom views or you can view two different pages at the same zoom level or different zoom views. You can view one pane in a Single page layout and the other pane in Continuous, Facing, or Continuous – Facing page layout. You can also combine the Split and Tile option to view two or more documents, each with split views tiled horizontally or vertically. You can adjust the window division by moving the horizontal bar up or down, thereby showing a larger view in one pane and a smaller view in the other pane.

Spreadsheet Split

Spreadsheet Split is the same concept as using a Split view except you now have four panes, as shown in Figure 4-24. Just choose Window ➪ Spreadsheet Split. Click inside the pane whose view you want to change and then zoom in and out and navigate pages as needed. Move the divider bars horizontally and vertically to size the panes to accommodate your viewing needs. Position the cursor at the intersection of the separator bars and you can move the bars vertically and horizontally together.

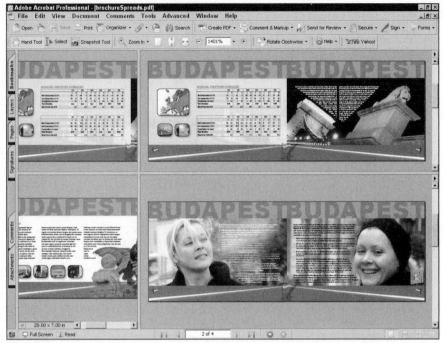

Figure 4-24: Spreadsheet Split enables you to see four different views of the same document. Pages can be viewed in four separate panes with different zoom levels.

Remove Split

Choose Window ➪ Remove Split to eliminate either the Split or the Spreadsheet Split view. You can also remove either view by clicking on a separator bar.

Full Screen

Another viewing option found in the Window menu is the Full Screen View. Full Screen View displays your PDF document like a slide show and temporarily hides the menus, toolbars, and window controls. You can set up the Full Screen View for automatic page scrolling and then walk away from the computer — you'll have a self-running kiosk. You can give a presentation and automatically scroll pages or set preferences for pausing between slides.

Cross-Reference

There's a lot to Full Screen viewing. To learn more about working with Full Screen views, see Chapter 23.

Links

For the purpose of discussion, links in Acrobat are *hot spots* where you click somewhere in the Acrobat window and some action takes place. With regard to viewing PDF documents, clicking the mouse button on a link takes you to another view, opens a document or Web page, or executes some sort of action. Links can be any one of a number of items, including elements on a PDF page such as buttons, articles, fields, and so on, or they can be part of the user interface such as thumbnails and links you create from options in palettes. In this chapter I stick to link behavior in Acrobat as it relates to page viewing and where you can find links.

Cross-Reference

For information on creating links and buttons that execute a variety of different actions, see Chapter 17.

Navigation pane

The Navigation pane contains the default tabs discussed in Chapter 1, and most of these palettes have associated with them certain capabilities for linking to views and other kinds of actions that can be invoked with the click of a mouse button. In some cases a single click takes you to another view and in other cases a double-click takes you to another view. The palettes that contain some form of linking to views include

Cross-Reference

To learn more about the Navigation tabs, see Chapter 1 and Chapter 3.

✦ **Bookmarks:** Any Bookmarks created in the PDF file are displayed in a list beside the Bookmarks tab. With a single click of the mouse button, a Bookmark may take you to another page or view, or invoke an action.

Cross-Reference

For information on creating Bookmarks and setting link actions to them, see Chapter 12.

✦ **Layers:** The Layers tab shows all Adobe PDF Layers contained in a document by layer names. If the pane is empty, no layers are contained in the file. You use the Layers pane to show and hide layers, set layer properties, and manage layers.

Cross-Reference

For more information on using Adobe PDF Layers, see Chapter 19.

✦ **Pages:** To view thumbnails of each page, click the Pages tab in the Navigation pane. The page thumbnails are links to the respective pages. A single mouse click on a page thumbnail displays the respective page in the Document pane.

Cross-Reference

For information on working with the Pages tab, see Chapter 12.

✦ **Signatures:** The Signatures tab contains a list of all digital signatures in a PDF document. You can open the Signatures pane and navigate to pages where signatures have been added to the file.

Cross-Reference

For information on creating digital signatures, see Chapter 21.

✦ **Comments:** The Comments tab contains any annotations added to the open file. You can navigate to any page where a comment has been added by clicking on a comment in the Comments tab.

Cross-Reference

For information on working with comments, see Chapter 15.

✦ **Attachments:** The Attachments tab contains a list of all file attachments. Double-clicking an attachment does not navigate to the page where the attachment is placed, however. Use the Attachments pane to search for the page where the attachment appears because double-clicking an attachment opens the attached file.

Cross-Reference

For information on working with file attachments, see Chapter 15.

Navigation tabs

The additional tabs you can access from the View ➪ Navigation Tabs submenu described in Chapter 1 contain links to the content you create from various tab options. The tabs not yet discussed that appear in the Navigation Tabs submenu include

✦ **Articles:** Article threads are like link buttons. You can create article threads in a PDF file and the threads are listed in the Articles tab. Use the tab to open an article thread and click the mouse button inside the article to follow the thread.

Cross-Reference

For information on creating articles, see Chapter 17.

✦ **Content:** Document content can be displayed in the Content tab. When you open the tab and select individual items, you can highlight the respective content item on the document page. In essence the Content tab is linked to the content appearing on the PDF pages according to the natural reading order of the PDF file.

Cross-Reference

For information on using the Content tab, see Chapter 20.

✦ **Destinations:** Destinations are similar to Bookmarks and are linked to a specific location in an open PDF document or to secondary PDF documents. When you click a destination, the view associated with the destination opens in the Document pane.

Cross-Reference

For information on destinations, see Chapter 17.

✦ **Fields:** The Fields tab lists all form fields created in the open document. Click a field name in the tab and the field becomes highlighted in the Document pane.

Cross-Reference

For information on creating form fields, see Chapters 27 and 28.

✦ **Info:** The Info tab offers pull-down menu choices for changing the units of measure in a document. Choose from Points, Inches, or Millimeters. The information displayed in the status bar reports the page size in the units selected from the Info tab. As you move the cursor around the Document pane, a read-out in the Info palette shows the cursor's x,y position on the page. For example, X: 3 and Y: 2 informs you the cursor is positioned 3 inches from the left side of the page and 2 inches up from the bottom of the page when the unit of measure is in inches.

Cross-Reference

For information on using rulers, guides, and measuring tools according to units of measure, see Chapter 19.

✦ **Order:** The Order tab is new in Acrobat 7. When you click the tab and open the Order pane, the reading order of your pages is displayed in the pane and on the document pages. You can easily change the reading order by moving the references in the Order pane around much like you would reorganize Bookmarks.

Cross-Reference

For information on using use the Order tab, see Chapter 20.

✦ **Tags:** Tags list all the structural content in a PDF document. You can highlight an element from within the Tags pane to locate a tagged element. Whereas the Contents tab identifies all the page content in any PDF file, the Tags tab only shows the structure and elements of tagged PDF files. Together with the Order tab, Tags are used with accessible documents.

Cross-Reference

For information on using the Tags tab and making documents accessible, see Chapter 20.

Hypertext links

In an Acrobat viewer, hypertext references enable you to move around the PDF or many PDFs, much like surfing the Net. You've probably become so accustomed to clicking buttons on your desktop computer that link navigation is commonplace and needs little instruction. Invoking the action is nothing more than a click with the mouse. What the actions do in Acrobat is simply remarkable. To help you gain an understanding of how Acrobat has employed hyperlinks, the following sections describe all the link actions as they can be created in Acrobat and executed in any viewer.

Buttons

Hypertext references, or *buttons,* are easily identified in a PDF document. As you move the mouse cursor around the document window, a Hand icon with the forefinger pointing appears when you position the cursor over a button or a link. You click, and presto!—the link action is executed!

Link actions can be assigned to any one of several items in Acrobat. You can set a link action to links, fields, Bookmarks, and Page Actions. The link action types have changed a little in Acrobat 7 compared to Acrobat 6. The action types available in Acrobat Standard and Acrobat Professional include

Note   All the Link Action types are available with both Acrobat Standard and Acrobat Professional. Form fields can only be created with Acrobat Professional. Link Actions can be assigned to links, Bookmarks, and Page Actions in both Acrobat Standard and Acrobat Professional.

✦ **Execute a menu command:** This action links to commands found in the Acrobat menus. For example, you can create a button field or link to execute the Save As command. The Save As dialog box would open from the link action just like it would from using the menu command.

✦ **Go to a 3D view:** For PDF documents supporting 3D views, you can set an action to a specific 3D view.

✦ **Go to a page view:** The Go to a page view action opens another view on the existing page, a view to another page in the same document, a view to a named destination, or a view in another document.

✦ **Import form data:** This action imports data exported from other forms into the active document where form field names match those from where the data were exported.

✦ **Open a file:** The Open a File link opens any kind of document. PDFs open in Acrobat. Other file types require having the authoring program installed on your computer. For example, if the link is to a Microsoft Word document, you need Word installed on your computer to open the link.

✦ **Open a web link:** Opens a URL in your default Web browser.

✦ **Play a sound:** Plays a sound imported into the active PDF.

✦ **Play Media (Acrobat 5 Compatible):** Plays a movie file saved in formats compatible with Acrobat 5 and lower viewers. Note: Acrobat 5–compatible media cannot be embedded in a PDF document.

✦ **Play Media (Acrobat 6 and Later Compatible):** Plays movie files saved in newer formats compatible with Acrobat 6 and 7 and movie clips embedded in Acrobat.

✦ **Read an article:** This action navigates to the specified article in the open PDF document or another PDF document.

✦ **Reset a form:** All the fields or user-specified fields on a form are cleared of data.

✦ **Run a JavaScript:** Executes JavaScripts written in Acrobat.

Cross-Reference   You can create JavaScripts with links, Bookmarks, and Page Actions in Acrobat Standard. The JavaScript Editor, however, is not accessible from a menu command in Acrobat Standard. For information on using the JavaScript Editor in Acrobat Professional, see Chapter 29.

✦ **Set layer visibility:** This action can be set to either hide or show a layer.

✦ **Show/hide a field:** With form fields, fields are hidden or made visible on a page.

✦ **Submit a form:** This action is used for submitting data in user-prescribed formats to a specified URL (Uniform Resource Locator).

The preceding list is a simplified brief description of action types that can be associated with tools that support link actions. Two action types have been eliminated in Acrobat 7 that were previously available in Acrobat 6. No longer do you have an action for Go to snapshot view or

Open a page in another document. However, you can open pages in secondary documents using the Go to a page action type in Acrobat 7 as I describe in Chapter 17.

Cross-Reference   For more detail on how to create link actions and a host of attributes you can assign to them, see Part IV and Part VI.

Accessing PDF documents

 Like most computer programs you already use on either Windows or the Macintosh, you know that files are generally opened via the File ⇨ Open command. In many programs the keyboard shortcut used to open files is Ctrl/⌘+O. Acrobat uses the same menu and keyboard shortcuts to access the Open dialog box where you browse your hard drive, open folders, and ultimately select a file to open. When you double-click a filename or click the Open button when a file is selected, the file opens in Acrobat.

All Acrobat viewers also offer you a tool to open files. Click the Open tool in the File toolbar and the Open dialog box appears just as if you had used the Open menu command or keyboard shortcut. Any one of these methods opens a PDF document or a document of one many different file types that can be converted to PDF on-the-fly while you work in Acrobat.

Cross-Reference   For information related to opening files that are converted to PDF with the Open command, see Chapter 6.

Opening recently viewed files

When you launch Acrobat and view and/or edit PDF documents, Acrobat keeps track of the most recently opened files. By default, Acrobat keeps track of the last five files you opened. In the Startup preferences you can change the value to as many as ten recently viewed files. The files are accessible at the bottom of the File menu (Windows) or the File ⇨ Open Recent File submenu on the Macintosh. In Figure 4-25 you can see five filenames at the bottom of the File menu from Acrobat running under Windows.

You have another option for viewing files that were previously opened in an Acrobat session. As shown in Figure 4-26, the History menu command appearing over the recent file list offers you submenus for viewing files from a history as long as the previous 12 months. Until you clear the History by selecting the Clear History menu command, all the files you viewed over the last 12 months are displayed in a scrollable list. You can break down the history according to the files viewed Today, Yesterday, the Last 7 Days, the Last 14 Days, and the Last 30 Days as well as the Last 12 Months.

Macintosh users can find the History submenu command appearing at the top of the list of files when you choose File ⇨ Open Recent File.

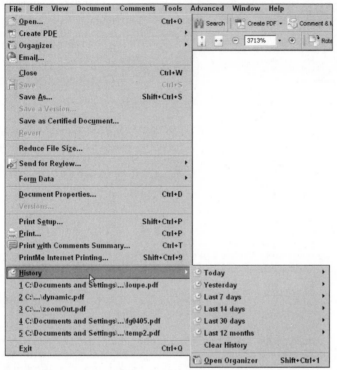

Figure 4-25: The most recently viewed files appear in the File menu (Windows) or File ➪ Open Recent File submenu (Macintosh).

Using the Organizer

The Organizer is a tool similar to the File Browser in Photoshop CS. Although not all features within Photoshop's File Browser are available in Acrobat's Organizer, it has many impressive tools and commands that help you manage and access documents from within Acrobat. To open the Organizer, choose File ➪ Organizer ➪ Open Organizer or click the Organizer tool in the File toolbar. (On Windows you can also choose File ➪ History ➪ Open Organizer.) When you select any of the options, the Organizer, shown in Figure 4-26, opens.

Figure 4-26: Click the Organizer tool or select Open Organizer from a menu command to open the Organizer window in Acrobat.

The Organizer window contains three panes, a number of tools, and menu commands that you select from context menus. When you first open the Organizer, you find three panes in the Organizer window divided by two separator bars. On the left side of the window is the Categories pane. In the center you find the Files pane and the right side holds the Pages pane. You can adjust the size of the panes by clicking a separator bar and dragging it to the left or right. As one pane is sized down, the adjacent pane is sized up. You can adjust the size of the Organizer window by dragging the lower-right corner of the window.

Using the Categories pane

The Categories pane in the Organizer contains three types of categories. At the top of the pane is History followed by My Computer and at the bottom you find Collections. The History category offers you the same choices for viewing history as you find in the File menu in Windows as described in the earlier section "Opening recently viewed files." As you click one of the History options, the files listed in the Files pane reflect the history period you choose.

The My Computer category shows you a view of your hard drive and all servers and drives connected to your computer, similar to a Windows Explorer view or a Macintosh Finder view. You can select a folder, and all PDFs within that folder are listed in the Files pane regardless of whether they appear in the view history. Below your accessible hard drives and servers you find Favorite Places. If you keep documents within folders you frequently access, right-click (Windows) or Control+click (Macintosh) to open a context menu over Favorite Places or click the *Add Favorite Place* button at the bottom of the Categories pane. The Browse For Folder dialog box, shown in Figure 4-27, opens (Windows) or the Select a folder to add to your favorite places dialog box opens on the Macintosh. Adding Favorites in this fashion is similar to adding Favorites in your Web browser.

Figure 4-27: Open a context menu on Favorite Places in the Open Files category and a dialog box opens where you target a folder to add as a favorite place.

After you select a folder and click OK, the folder you selected appears at the bottom of the Favorite Places list.

The Collections category works similarly to Favorite Places, except that instead of adding folders to a list, you can select individual files and add them to a collection. You can add files to collections from different folders on your hard drive. By default, Acrobat offers you three collections Collection 1, Collection 2, and Collection 3.

You manage collections through the use of a context menu. Open a context menu from any collection name in the Collections category and the menu options appear as shown in Figure 4-28.

Figure 4-28: To manage collections, open a context menu on any collection name.

The menu selections should be self-explanatory. Select Create a New Collection to add another collection to the list. Select Rename Collection to rename a collection. Select Delete Collection to remove the collection. Click Add Files to add documents to your collection. After you add documents to a collection and click the collection name, all files added to the collection appear in the Files pane.

Tip   After installing Acrobat you may want to rename the default collection names to more descriptive names used in your workflow. Open a context menu on each collection name and select Rename Collection. The collection name is highlighted and ready for you to type a new name.

Using the Files pane

The Files pane contains a list of all files derived from the choice you made in the Categories pane. For example, click a History category, and all files viewed within the selected history timeframe appear in a list sorted by metadata that you select from the Sort by pull-down menu. In addition to the file list you have tools at the top of the pane and context menu commands when opening a context menu on a file in the list.

Beginning with the tools at the top of the pane, you find

✦ **Open:** By default, the first file in the pane is selected. Click the Open tool to open the selected file. If no file is selected in the pane, the Open tool, as well as all other tools, are grayed out. A condition where you might not have a file selected is when you click a collection that contains no file in the collection folder or when viewing a folder that contains no PDF documents. Otherwise, the first file, by default, is always selected when files are shown in the list.

✦ **Print:** Click a file in the list and click the Print tool to print the file. When you click Print, the PDF document opens and the Print dialog box opens in the foreground. Make your print attribute choices in the Print dialog box and click Print to print the file.

✦ **Email:** Select a file in the list and click the Email tool, and your default e-mail application opens with the selected file attached to a new e-mail message.

✦ **Create PDF From Multiple Files:** Click this tool to open the Create PDF From Multiple Documents dialog box. In the dialog box you can select PDF documents to combine into a single file or select a variety of different file formats that can be converted to a PDF. The tool works the same as selecting the From Multiple Files command from the Create PDF Task Button pull-down menu.

Cross-Reference To learn how to convert files to PDF with the Create PDF From Multiple Files command, see Chapter 6.

✦ **Send for Review:** Select a file in the list and choose from the pull-down menu options to Send By Email for Review or Upload for Browser-Based Review.

Cross-Reference To learn how to send files for reviews and approval, see Chapter 16.

Below the tools is a pull-down menu used for sorting files. Files can be sorted on metadata contained within the file. From the pull-down menu, shown in Figure 4-29, you have several choices for sorting files.

Figure 4-29: Open the Sort by pull-down menu to sort files according to file metadata.

Sorting by Filename is the default and lists files in an alphabetical ascending order. The Title, Subject, Author, and Keywords items are part of the Document Properties Description that you supply at the time of PDF creation from some authoring programs or that you later add in Acrobat. Creator and Producer are part of the Document Description supplied by Acrobat and relate to the original authoring program and the application producing the PDF file. Number of Pages, File Size, and Modified Date are data that Acrobat adds to the Document Properties derived from the structure of the file. The Last Opened Date sorts the files according to the last time you viewed them in Acrobat with the most recent file listed first and in descending order.

Cross-Reference   To learn more about Document Descriptions and Document Properties, see Chapter 5.

You can also manage files from a context menu opened on a file in the list. This menu has commands to perform the same tasks handled by the tools at the top of the pane. In Figure 4-30 you can see the top portion of the menu, duplicating the tools' functions, such as Open, Print, Email, Create PDF From Multiple Files, and Send for Review.

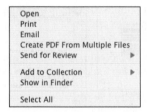

Figure 4-30: Open a context menu on a file listed in the Files pane and the menu options offer additional commands for managing files.

The Add to Collection menu item contains a submenu that lists all the collections in the Categories pane. As you add new collections to the Categories, they dynamically appear in the Add to Collection submenu. After you add a file to a collection, the context menu changes and displays a few more menu commands. In Figure 4-31 note the addition of Move to Collection and Remove from 'Collection 1.' The item within the single quotes denotes the collection name where a file has been added.

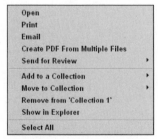

Figure 4-31: After you add a file to a collection, opening a context menu on a filename displays additional options for moving a file to another collection and deleting a file from a collection.

Select Move to Collection and the submenu displays all your collection names. Select a collection and the file is moved to the collection you choose in the submenu. Select Remove from '*n*' (where *n* represents the name of a collection) and a dialog box opens prompting you to confirm the deletion. When you delete a file from a collection, the file is deleted from the collection list but is not deleted from your hard drive.

The last menu item, Show in Explorer (Windows) or Show in Finder (Macintosh) takes you to Windows Explorer (Windows) or switches to Finder view (Macintosh) and opens the folder where the file is located.

Using the Pages pane

By default, the Pages pane displays the first page in a PDF document of a file selected in the Files pane. One of the great features of the Organizer is that it shows multiple pages in the Pages pane for all files containing more than one page (see Figure 4-27). When you select a multipage document, all pages are displayed in thumbnail view in the Pages pane before you open the file. At the bottom of the pane is a zoom slider. Drag the slider left to display smaller thumbnails and to the right to make the thumbnail views larger. The minus and plus buttons display thumbnails smaller and larger, respectively, in zoom increments.

As you view multipage documents in the Pages pane, you can double-click any page thumbnail to open the respective page in Acrobat. Select a page thumbnail and open a context menu, and a single menu command appears enabling you to open that page.

Another nice feature in the Pages pane is the display of a Document Status icon that appears when you save files that have a special status or special feature. Such features might include a document saved with layers, a file in a commenting review, or a certified document. In addition to the Document Status icon, some files may display a security key representing files that have been password secured. When you see an icon to the right of a filename in the Pages pane, click to select the file to see what special features are contained within the file before you open it. In Figure 4-32, a context menu is opened displaying a message window for a file containing layers.

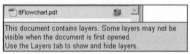

Figure 4-32: Select an icon to the right of a filename in the Pages pane to open a window reporting special features contained within the document.

Bookmarking Web-hosted PDFs

As I explain in Chapter 22, Acrobat is well integrated with many different Web services and support. The new Organizer is no exception when it comes to supporting Web-related services. You can add anything you can view in Acrobat as a PDF document to your Organizer. When you add a document to a collection from a Web-hosted PDF, the link is made to where the file is hosted. In this particular case, it's a link to a URL which you can create as easily as adding files from your hard drive to your collections.

The first step is to view a PDF document as an inline view in a Web browser. Both Apple Safari and Microsoft Internet Explorer are supported. When you view a PDF in a Web browser, many Acrobat tools appear below your browser's tools. In Figure 4-33 you can see the Organizer tool in the top-left corner of the Acrobat window inside Microsoft Internet Explorer. When you click the Organizer tool, the Add to Favorites dialog box opens. Click a collection and click OK to add the link to your collection.

Cross-Reference   For more information on inline viewing in Web browsers, see Chapter 22.

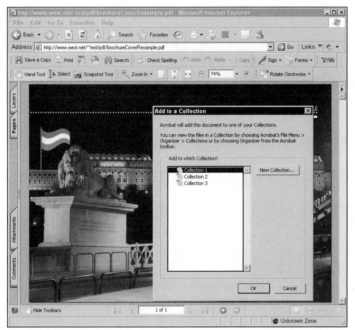

Figure 4-33: Click the Organizer tool inside a Web browser to add the URL link to a collection.

When you return to Acrobat, you can view the URL link in the respective collection. Open the Organizer and click the collection name where you added the link. In the Files pane you see all documents added to the collection. Those files added from Web URLs appear with a different icon than standard PDF documents, as you can see in Figure 4-34. You can add files from PDFs on your hard drive and view them from within a Web browser (something you might do when working with browser-based reviews), or from URL addresses on the Web. In the Files pane adjacent to the document icon, you see the URL address from where the document was retrieved.

Cross-Reference   For more information related to browser-based reviews, see Chapter 16.

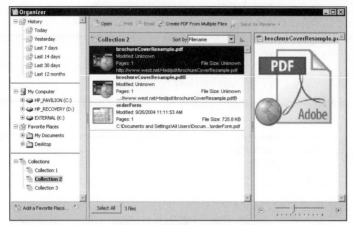

Figure 4-34: PDFs linked to URLs appear with a different document icon.

Double-click any Web-linked file and your default Web browser opens, takes you to the URL, and loads the PDF in the browser window.

Summary

This chapter offers you a brief overview of how to go about moving around PDF documents, using viewing tools, palettes, and pages, as well as opening and managing files. As you can see, the list is long and there's quite a bit to understand in regard to viewing, navigation, opening, and managing files. Some of the more important points include the following:

✦ Page navigation tools are available in a toolbar not visible by default. You can place the toolbar in view and dock it to the left, right, top, or below the Document pane for easy access to navigation tools.

✦ Task Buttons can be hidden and viewed from menu commands in the View menu. Task Buttons are contained in the Tasks toolbar. These tools offer you quick access to commonly used tasks.

✦ PDFs can be read aloud and pages can be autoscrolled without the need for any special equipment.

✦ PDF pages can be viewed in several different layout modes, with grids, guides, and rulers.

✦ The status bar contains tools for easy page navigation and changing page layout views.

✦ Acrobat Professional contains five tools used for zooming views. In addition to the Zoom In, Zoom Out, and Dynamic Zoom tools found in all Acrobat viewers, the Loupe tool and the Pan & Zoom are unique to Acrobat Professional.

✦ Initial Views of PDF documents can be displayed with pages and palettes, at different zoom levels, with or without menus, tools, and window controls. These settings are document specific and can be saved with different options for different documents. The settings are established in the Initial View document properties dialog box.

✦ Links are built into many different Acrobat tools and they can be assigned to items created in Acrobat. Different action types can be assigned to many tools and object elements.

✦ Links can be made to Web pages and URLs.

✦ PDF files are opened through menu commands or by using the Open tool. The most recently opened files are listed in the File menu (Windows) or the File ➪ Open Recent File submenu (Macintosh).

✦ The Organizer introduced in Acrobat 7 helps you manage files and access a file history of documents opened in Acrobat up to the previous 12 months. The Organizer enables you to view page thumbnails of PDF document pages before you open files and can be sorted on metadata, added to collections, and added to a Favorite Places list.

✦ You can add PDFs hosted on Web sites to collections in the Organizer.

✦   ✦   ✦

Searching PDF Files

Acrobat 7 builds on the wonderful search tools added in Acrobat 6 where you can search PDF documents with or without an index file. In addition to all the search features, Acrobat 7 reintroduces the Find tool that was once present in earlier versions of Acrobat, but eliminated in Acrobat 6.

You are able to find information contained in PDF documents either with the Find tool or the Search pane for open documents. The search extends to PDFs scattered around your hard drive and all over the Internet and without the assistance of a search index. However, Acrobat Catalog and searching index files is still available to you for more sophisticated searches. In this chapter I cover all the tools and features available in Acrobat viewers for searching through PDF files and creating and searching index files.

Setting Up the Work Environment

The File toolbar and the Find toolbar contain the specific tools used for searching PDF documents using Yahoo. In addition, the new Search the Internet tool in Acrobat 7 is used to search HTML and PDF files using the Yahoo search engine. If the tool is not loaded, open a context menu on the Toolbar Well and select Search the Internet. For searching text in PDF documents you don't need any other tools. The best way to start this chapter is to first reset your toolbars to their default positions by opening a context menu on the Toolbar Well and selecting Reset Toolbars. By default, the File and Search the Internet using Yahoo toolbars are visible when you reset the toolbars.

To open the Find toolbar, choose Edit ➪ Find or press Ctrl/⌘+F. The Find toolbar opens as a floating toolbar. After opening the toolbars, open a context menu on the Toolbar Well and select Dock All Toolbars. The Find toolbar then docks in the Toolbar Well as shown in Figure 5-1.

Figure 5-1: Dock the Find and Search the Internet toolbars in the Toolbar Well.

Using the Find Toolbar

In order to use the Find toolbar, you must have a document open in the Document pane. If you have more than one document open, you can search only the active document appearing in the foreground. Type a word in the field box in the Find toolbar and press the Enter/Return key. Acrobat searches the current active document and highlights the first occurrence of the found word. When a word is found, the Previous and Next buttons in the toolbar become active. Click the Next button in the toolbar, and Acrobat searches for the next occurrence and stops on the page where the word is highlighted again. Clicking Previous takes you to the last found word in the open document (if you click the button after the first search). When you click Next, and then click the Previous button, the search takes you to the previous found word. For example, if you search for a word in a 100-page document and the word appears on page 5, 6, and 99. The first time you execute the Find, you stop at page 5. Clicking the Previous button takes you to page 99. However, if you click Next while on page 5, the next found word appears on page 6. Clicking Previous on page 6 takes you back to page 5.

The Find toolbar also includes a pull-down menu, as shown in Figure 5-2, containing several menu commands to assist you in narrowing your search. Click the down-pointing arrow to see the following menu commands:

Figure 5-2: Enter the word(s) to be searched in the Find toolbar and press Enter/Return. Acrobat stops at the first occurrence of the word and highlights it.

✦ **Whole words only:** Returns words that match whole words only. For example, if you search for a word like *cat*, this command avoids returning words like catalog, catastrophe, category, and so on.

✦ **Case-Sensitive:** Finds words that match the letter case of the word typed in the Find toolbar.

✦ **Include Bookmarks:** Finds words in Bookmark descriptions.

✦ **Include Comments:** Finds words in comment notes.

✦ **Open Full Acrobat Search:** Opens the Search pane. This command performs the same function as clicking the Search tool.

You can choose one or a any combination of the first four options to perform your search. For example, you can select Whole words only, Case-Sensitive, Include Bookmarks, and Include Comments, and Acrobat returns the first occurrence of only whole words matching the letter case in the search criteria whether it be in a Bookmark, comment note, or on a document page.

Using the Find toolbar also makes active two other menu commands. After invoking a find, the Next Result and Previous Result commands appear active in the Edit ➪ Search Results submenu. These commands are the same as using the buttons in the Find toolbar. They also are accompanied by keyboard shortcuts (Ctrl/⌘+G for Next Result and Ctrl/⌘+Shift+G for Previous Result. Note that the other two options in the submenu (Next Document and Previous Document) are grayed out when you use the Find toolbar. These commands are only active when you use the Search tool.

Using the Search Pane

 You perform searches by accessing a menu command, by choosing the Search tool in the File toolbar, or by using shortcut keys. To search from the menu, choose Edit ➪ Search, or open a context menu with the Hand tool, and select Search. To use the toolbar, click the Search tool. To use the keyboard shortcut, press Ctrl/⌘+Shift+F. These all allow you to search for a word in an open document, in a collection of PDF files stored on your hard drive, or any type of external media. When you invoke a search, the Search pane opens on the right of your screen in the How To window. The Search pane actually uses the How To window space and replaces the How To menu items with search-related options, as shown in Figure 5-3.

Cross-Reference

For information on using the How To pane, see Chapter 1.

Note

In Acrobat 6 you accessed the Search command by pressing Ctrl/⌘+F. Because Acrobat 6 had no Find toolbar, using the Shift key in the keyboard shortcut was not necessary. Now that Acrobat 7 has the Find toolbar, therefore you must add the Shift key to the shortcut to distinguish the difference between your wanting to access a Find versus a Search.

Figure 5-3: When you use the Search menu command or the Ctrl/⌘+Shift+F keyboard shortcut, the Search pane opens in the How To window. All the options in the pane change to search-related options.

At the top of the Search pane are left and right arrows used for navigating through various search results. When a search is invoked, results appear in the Results window. If you want to return to the default view where you supply search criteria, click the left arrow. Clicking the right arrow moves you back to the search results list.

Basic search options

When the Search pane is in view, you type a word or words to be searched for in the field box that appears at the top of the pane. You are limited to the actual word(s) you want to find when you perform a simple search. You cannot use Boolean (AND, OR, and NOT) operators or any kind of search expressions if performing a simple search.

Cross-Reference   For more sophisticated searches where you can use Boolean operators, see "Doing advanced searches" later in this chapter.

Note   The area where you type words and phrases to be searched is in the field box following the text *"What word or phrase would you like to search for?"* in the Search pane. Rather than describe this field box by name, the term *first field box* or *search field box* is used throughout this chapter. When you see such a reference, realize it refers to the area where you type words and phrases to be searched.

If you type more than one word in the search field box, the results are reported for all words typed in the field box regardless of whether all the words appear together in a document. For example, if you search for *Adobe Acrobat Professional*, all the occurrences of Adobe, Acrobat, Professional, Adobe Acrobat, and Acrobat Professional are reported in the results list.

In the Search PDF pane, you choose where you want to search and the options to narrow the search from the list following the first field box. The following sections describe several choices that are available.

Where to search

The question presented to you is *Where would you like to search?* Two radio buttons appear where you choose whether to search the current open file or search locally on your hard drive, a network server, or a media storage device attached to your computer such as removable media or CD-ROMs. If you select the second radio button for *All PDF Documents in*, you can narrow the search to a directory, drive, or media device by opening the pull-down menu and choosing from the hierarchy of drives and folders appearing in the menu options.

Acrobat also permits you to search through Bookmarks and Comments like the Find toolbar does. Check boxes appear below the pull-down menu for these items. If Bookmarks and Comments are to be part of your search, check the respective item(s). After you choose the options you want, click the Search button.

The results appear in the Search pane as shown in Figure 5-4. The total number of found instances for your search are noted at the top of the pane and hot links appear in the scrollable list for the words found in the documents according to the search options you selected. Click any text in blue and the respective document page opens in the Document pane with the first occurrence of the searched word highlighted.

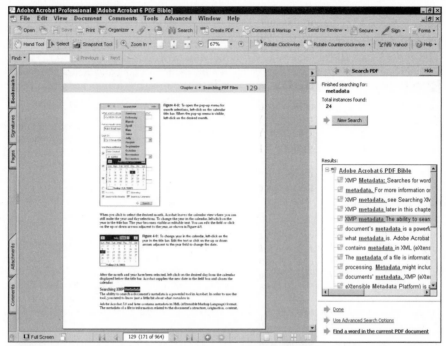

Figure 5-4: Search results are reported in a scrollable list for all occurrences in a single PDF or all occurrences in all documents searched. Click any blue text in the Results list window to open a page where Search found words matching your criteria.

Navigating search results

Menu commands are also available for navigating through search results. Choose Edit ➪ Search Results to open a submenu where you find four menu commands used with searches. The Next Result and Previous Result items are discussed in the "Using the Find Toolbar" earlier in this chapter. These other two items are

✦ **Next Document** (Ctrl/⌘+]): Click Next Document to bypass all found instances in the currently viewed file and open the next file listed in the Search results list.

✦ **Previous Document** (Ctrl/⌘+[): This command offers the opposite response as Next Document — it moves backward through previously viewed documents.

Note   Next Result and Next Document are not available until you first invoke a search. Next Document becomes active only when a search result exists in two or more documents. Previous Result and Previous Document become active only after you have visited a result in a document more than once so as to retrace your steps backward to see previously viewed results.

Stopping a search

When you start a new search, a button appears in the Search pane so you can Stop the search. Click Stop and the results found prior to stopping are listed in the scrollable list. After you click Stop a button for Done appears at the bottom of the Search pane. DO NOT CLICK DONE! If you click Done, Acrobat thinks you are finished searching and clears your search history and returns you to the original Search pane. All your search results are flushed and you need to search again if you want to continue searching more files.

Tip   In Acrobat 6, clicking the Hide button in the Search pane erased your history and you needed to perform another search to regain the search results. In Acrobat 7 you can hide the Search pane and click the Search tool or use a menu command to open the Search pane to keep your Results list intact.

Displaying results

The results list is neatly organized for you in the Search pane. If you search the open document, the search results report found words beginning at the front of the document and lists occurrences as they are found on following pages. If you search multiple documents, the occurrences are listed in groups according to the individual documents where the words are found. The hierarchy is similar to that of Bookmarks. A plus symbol in Windows or a right-pointing arrow in Macintosh is shown for each document where results have been found. Click the icon, and the list expands the same way bookmarks and comments expand. The icon changes to a minus symbol in Windows or a down-pointing arrow in Macintosh when a list is expanded. Click the icon again to collapse the list.

Note   You can use Search or the Find toolbar to find words in the open document. Using Search offers more search criteria options and shows a list of results. As a general rule, using Search is much more efficient than using the Find toolbar.

Cross-Reference   For information on displaying Bookmarks, see Chapter 12. For information on displaying comments, see Chapter 15.

Searching files and folders

If you search through a large collection of PDF files, Search works away loading up the results window. Clicking a link to open a page where results have been found won't interrupt your search. You can browse files while results continue to be reported. To search a hard disk, a media storage device, a network drive, or a folder in any of these locations, open the pull-down menu below *All PDF Documents in* and select a folder location. The moment you select a folder, the *All PDF Documents in* radio button is activated.

The pull-down menu lists the drives and servers active on your system. If you want to search a particular folder, select the item denoted as Browse for Location (Windows or Macintosh) at the bottom of the pull-down menu. The Browse For Folder (Windows) or Choose a folder to search (Macintosh) dialog box opens as shown in Figure 5-5. Navigate your hard drive like you would when searching for files to open. When you find the folder to be searched, click the folder name and click OK.

Figure 5-5: Select the folder to be searched in the Browse For Folder (Windows)/Browse for Location (Macintosh) dialog box. Select the folder name and click OK (Windows)/Choose (Macintosh) to return to the Search pane.

After you click OK in the Browse for Folder/Choose a folder dialog box, the Search pane returns. The search does not begin until you click on the Search button. Before clicking Search, you can examine the name listed as the target folder. The selected folder is displayed in the Search pane by folder name. If all looks as you expect, click Search.

Searching PDFs on the Internet

Below the search results scrollable list is a link to your default Web browser. The criteria you establish in the Search pane is used to conduct a search on the Internet. You can choose to search PDFs on the Internet using the Yahoo search engine. When you click the link to search for PDFs on the Internet, Acrobat is no longer in control. It is merely a means for launching your Web browser and searching PDF files on the Internet for the words you typed in the Search pane. If you are not in Acrobat, you can manually search for PDF content by adding **filetype:PDF** to your search criteria in a search engine in your Web browser. For example, you could type **Acrobat 7 filetype:PDF** in either the Yahoo or Google search engine and the same results occur as when you click the link in the Search pane and search for the same words.

By default, a tool appears in the Toolbar well that enables you to search the internet using the Yahoo search engine. Click the Search the Internet using Yahoo tool. (Figure 5-6) and your default Web browser opens the Yahoo Search page. Clicking this tool invokes the same actions as when selecting Search the Internet using Yahoo in the Search pane.

Figure 5-6: Click the Search the Internet using Yahoo tool to search for PDF on the Internet.

After clicking the button or tool for searching the Internet, you can change your criteria or continue with the search. Furthermore, you can check the box to search only in PDF files. Doing so returns results where selected words are contained only in PDF documents. The actual launching of the Web browser does not occur until you click the Search the Internet button that comes into view after you click the link at the bottom of the Search pane. When you click Search the Internet, the search results are reported in the Yahoo search engine. Click any link listed in the Yahoo search results window to open the linked PDF document in your Web browser.

If you check the box for Search only in PDF files, the list you see in the Yahoo search engine is made up of links to PDF documents containing the information you are searching for. The searched words can appear on any page in the PDF file listed from the search results. The PDF opens as an inline view inside your Web browser. Within the Web browser window you have access to many different Acrobat tools, including the Search tool. When you click the Search tool, you can search the PDF contained in the browser window using the same or different search criteria.

Cross-Reference

For a better understanding of inline views in Web browsers, see Chapter 16.

Note

Macintosh users can now see inline views in Web browsers. This feature was not available in Acrobat 6. Acrobat 7 supports Macintosh Web browsers including Apple's Safari v1.2.3 and above.

Acrobat remains open in the background as you navigate a Web browser. When you quit your Web browser, the Acrobat window moves forward and you're ready to continue more searches or work on any other Acrobat-related tasks.

When you return to the Search pane, the current search mode is set to search PDFs on the Internet. If you want to search an open PDF document or a folder of PDFs, click the link at the bottom of the Search pane where you see Search Across Local PDF Documents. You are then returned to the view where the radio buttons appear for selecting searches in open files or the pull-down menu for searching documents on hard drives and in folders.

Performing advanced searches

In all Acrobat viewers, you can search PDF documents with selected criteria without the assistance of a search index. To take advantage of searching with advanced options, click the Use Advanced Search Options link at the bottom of the Search pane. When you click the link, a series of advanced options appear in the Search pane, as shown in Figure 5-7.

Figure 5-7: Click Use Advanced Search Options to take advantage of more search options. When you select an open PDF file for the search, the options in this figure are available. If you search a collection of PDFs, the Advanced Search Options change.

Note When you click the link to show the advanced search options, the link at the bottom of the Search pane changes to Use Basic Search Options. Click this link or click the Back arrow at the top of the pane to return to searching with the basic options.

Depending on whether you search an open PDF document or a collection of PDFs stored on drives and external devices, the Advanced Search Options change, offering you different options.

Cross-Reference Advanced search offers you options for searching index files as well as PDF files. For information on searching index files, see the section "Searching an index" later in this chapter.

Searching the open PDF file with Advanced Search Options

When you select the Current PDF Document from the Look In pull-down menu, the search options shown in Figure 5-8 are available to you. These options include

- ✦ **Whole words only:** When checked, the search results return whole words. If you search for *forgiven,* the search ignores words like *for* and *give* that make up part of the whole word. If the check box is disabled, various stems and parts of a whole word are included with the search results.

- ✦ **Case-Sensitive:** Letter case is ignored if the check box is disabled. If enabled, then the search results return only words matching the precise letter case of the searched word.

- ✦ **Proximity:** Proximity is a powerful tool when performing searches. If you want to search for two independent words that may appear together in a given context — for example, *Acrobat* and *PostScript* — the Proximity option finds the two words when they appear within 900 words of each other in a PDF. You can change the proximity range in the Search preferences.

- ✦ **Stemming:** If you want to search for all words stemming from a given word, enable this option. Words such as *header* and *heading* stem from the word *head* in the English language. If you type *head* in the first field box and select the Stemming option, all PDFs containing the search criteria from the word *stem* are listed.

- ✦ **Include Bookmarks:** When bookmarks are checked the search results report the found instances in the bookmarks and the document pages.

- ✦ **Include Comments:** Text in comment notes and text on document pages are returned when this option is checked.

- ✦ **Include Attachments:** All PDF document file attachments are searchable. Select the Include Attachments check box and found results are reported in the Results list for all occurrences of the searched word. Clicking a search result opens the attached file in the Document pane.

When all the search criteria have been established, click the Search button. The results are reported in the Search pane like the searches performed with the Basic Search Options.

Searching multiple PDFs with Advanced Search Options

When you change the search parameters to search through a collection of PDF documents, the Advanced Search Options change, offering you more options to help narrow down your search, as shown in Figure 5-8. These options include

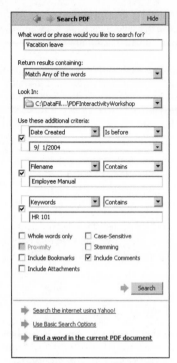

Figure 5-8: Advanced Search Options offer you additional criteria when searching through multiple PDF documents.

✦ **Return results containing:** Four options are available from this pull-down menu. These include

• **Match Exact word or phrase:** If you search for something like *Human Resource Forms*, only these three words together in a PDF document are returned as results. The results report the precise order of the words.

• **Match Any of the words:** Using the same example, words like Human, Resource, Forms, Human Resource, Resource Forms, Human Forms, and Human Resource Forms would be reported in the results. Any one of the words or any combination of words in a phrase is reported.

• **Match All of the words:** In this case, all the words need to be contained in the document, but not necessarily in the order described previously. You might see returns like Forms Human Resource returned from the search.

• **Boolean query:** You can search PDF collections using Boolean expressions (AND, OR, NOT) without the assistance of a search index created with Acrobat Catalog. Note that Boolean queries are not available when you search an open document. You need to use the Advanced Search Options to search through a drive, external media, or a folder.

For more detail on using Boolean queries, see the "Boolean queries" section later in this chapter. For more information on Acrobat Catalog, see "Creating Search Indexes (Acrobat Professional Only)" later in this chapter.

✦ **Use these additional criteria:** Three check boxes offer you one or a combination of several different options to help you refine your search. From the first pull-down menu you select the primary category. The second pull-down menu to the right of each primary category helps refine that particular category. The options for each of the three check box pull-down menus are the same. You might, for example, choose Date Created from the first check box option and define the date from the options contained in the adjacent pull-down menu. You then might add another criterion and ask for the Keywords option. Adjacent to Keywords, you might specify that the file does not contain certain words. In the field box you type any descriptions for the menu choices you make.

All the preceding items require that you supply at least one character in *What word or phase would you like to search for?* The options that follow enable you to search for specific content related to the option of choice and you do not need to supply a word in the first field box in order to execute a search. When you move around adjusting criteria, the Search button will appear active or grayed out. If it is grayed out, know you can't perform a search on the options you chose. In some cases, the missing option is a word or phrase that needs to be added to the first field box.

From the criteria selection pull-down menu, the choices available to you include

- **Date Created:** If you look for PDF documents that you know were created before or after a certain date, use the Date Created menu option. You have four choices for options associated with this category available in the second pull-down menu adjacent to the first menu choice. These options include Is exactly, Is before, Is after, and Is not. These four options are self-explanatory. When you make the choices from the two pull-down menus, your next step is to type the date criteria in the field box appearing below the pull-down menus. If, for example, you select Date Created and Is not, you then add the date you want to exclude from the search. As an additional aid to you, Acrobat offers a calendar when you select the pull-down menu from the field box, as shown in Figure 5-9. Make a date selection from the calendar and move to the option you want to change or click the Search button.

- **Date Modified:** The modified date searches for the date the PDF file was last modified. If you create a file on January 1, 2004 and then save some edits on July 1, 2004, the modified date is July 1, 2004. The manner in which you specify a date is the same as searching for the creation date.

- **Author:** The information is derived from the Document Properties in the Description pane. Any data typed in the Author field is searched. This choice and the remaining options offer two menu options in the second pull-down menu. You can select from Contains or Does not contain. In essence your search includes or excludes the data you supply in the field box immediately following the pull-down menu choices.

Figure 5-9: After making date selections from the pull-down menus, open the pull-down menu from the field box to open a calendar to help you find the date parameters to be searched.

Cross-Reference

For information related to document descriptions, see the "Document Descriptions" section later in this chapter.

- **Title:** Same as the Author search except the Title field is used in the document description.

- **Subject:** Same as the Author search except the Subject field is used in the document description.

- **Filename:** The name you provide for the PDF document is searched.

- **Keywords:** Same as the Author search except the Keywords field is used in the document description.

- **Bookmarks:** When you select this option, Acrobat searches for the words in both the PDF document and in Bookmarks. The results list includes the found words in both Bookmarks and pages.

- **Comments:** Same as Bookmarks, but the comment notes are searched. The results report the found words appearing in comment notes.

- **JPEG Images:** Narrows the search for files meeting the search text criteria and where JPEG images are contained within the PDF.

- **XMP Metadata:** Searches for words or phrases contained in the document metadata.

- **Object Data:** Certain images contain metadata created from an original authoring application, such as MS Visio, Microsoft Project, and AutoDesk AutoCAD. Select an object with the Object Data tool and click . The metadata information displayed in the Object Data dialog box is searchable as well as the data contained in the Object Data dialog box. If you know certain attributes for images contained in a file, you can narrow your search by searching the image metadata.

Cross-Reference For more information on XMP and object metadata, see "Searching Metadata" later in this chapter.

Below the Use these additional criteria pull-down menus are additional options. These options are the same as those used for the advanced searches on open PDF documents. Jump several pages back in this book to review the descriptions for the items listed at the bottom of the Search pane.

Searching dates

To help you target the precise date with the field box and the calendar, Acrobat offers you several options. To change the year, you can edit the field box and type the year for the date to be searched. In the field box you can change dates by clicking the day, month, and year, and then use the up or down arrow keys to scroll dates. The dates revolve like an odometer. Select a day, and then click the month to highlight the value and press the arrow keys again until you find the correct month. Move to the year and follow the same steps to select the correct year. You can also select any one of the three values and type new values you want to search when the text is selected. The text you type replaces all selected text. Acrobat only accepts a legitimate value, so if you type a value not permitted for a date search, for example, entering 33 in the day field, Acrobat will not accept it.

To change dates with the calendar, click the down arrow in the pull-down menu adjacent to the date in the field box to open the calendar. For a month change, left-click in the title bar of the calendar on the month name. For example, if July appears listed in the title bar, click July. Be careful not to left-click the mouse below the title bar because doing so selects a day and closes the calendar. When you left-click on the month name in the title bar, a pop-up menu displays the months of the year. Move the cursor to the desired month and left-click again.

Note You can also change months by scrolling the calendar backward or forward. Click the left arrow in the title bar to scroll backward or the right arrow to scroll forward. As you reach a year beginning or end, the next month in date order is opened. For example, scrolling backward from January 1996 opens December 1995.

When you click to select the desired month, Acrobat leaves the calendar view open so you can still make the year and day selections. To change the year in the calendar, left-click on the year in the title bar. The year becomes visible as editable text. You can edit the field or click the up or down arrows adjacent to the year, shown in Figure 5-10.

Figure 5-10: To change year in the calendar, left-click on the year in the title bar. Edit the text or click the up or down arrows adjacent to the year field to change the date.

After you select the month and year, left-click on the desired day from the calendar displayed below the title bar. Acrobat supplies the new date in the field box and closes the calendar.

Searching metadata

The ability to search a document's metadata is a powerful tool in Acrobat. In order to use the tool, you need to know just a little bit about what *metadata* is.

Adobe Acrobat 5.0 and later contain metadata in XML (eXtensible Markup Language) format. In Acrobat 7 object metadata is accessible. The metadata of a file or an image is information related to the document structure, origination, content, interchange, and processing. Metadata might include, for example, the document author's name, the creation date, modified date, the PDF producer, copyright information on images, color space on images, and more. When you click Search, the search results report all files where the searched words are contained in the a document's metadata.

XMP (eXtensible Metadata Platform) is an XML framework that provides all Adobe programs a common language for communicating standards related to document creation and processing throughout publishing workflows. XMP is a format, and document metadata viewed in XML source code can be exported to XMP format. Once in XMP, it can be exchanged between documents.

To take a look at the XML source code of the XMP metadata for a document, choose File ➪ Document Properties and click the Description tab. In the Description pane click on Additional Metadata to open the dialog box shown in Figure 5-11. Click Advanced and expand the listed items by clicking the symbol adjacent to each listed item.

At the bottom of the dialog box are buttons used for replacing, appending, saving, and deleting data. Click Save to export the XMP data that can be shared in workflows across many different file types. For the purposes of searching information, any of the text you see in the source code in the Advanced list can be searched.

Searching layers

The search criteria discussed on the preceding pages works for documents containing layers. When you invoke a search in documents containing layers, Search automatically searches through all layers for the criteria you specify in the Search pane. The results list contains items on any hidden layers as well as all visible layers. When you click a result associated with a hidden layer, Acrobat prompts you in a dialog box, as shown in Figure 5-12, asking whether you want to make the layer visible.

Figure 5-11: To see document metadata click the Additional Metadata button in the Description preferences pane.

Figure 5-12: If searched words are found on hidden layers, Acrobat asks whether you want to make the hidden layer visible.

If you click Yes in the dialog box, the layer is made visible and the search stops at the found word. If you select No, the layer remains hidden and you are taken to the next search result.

Boolean queries

The *Return results containing* pull-down menu in the Search PDF pane contains a Boolean query menu option for searching with Boolean expressions. Boolean expressions include AND, OR, and NOT. Acrobat recognizes these Boolean operators when you invoke a search. You can use all the previously listed criteria when you want to use the Boolean expressions option.

✦ **AND operator:** AND lets you search for instances of two words appearing together in a document. For example, a search on *Adobe AND Professional*, reports all found instances of the two words appearing together. However, the AND operator is not really necessary because you can produce the same results by using the Match All of the words menu command.

When using Boolean operators, the text is not case-sensitive. Uppercase letters for the Boolean expressions are used here to denote a Boolean operator as opposed to text. You can use lowercase letters and the results are reported the same as long as the Boolean query pull-down menu item is selected.

✦ **OR operator:** When you use OR, either word or phrase is returned in the search results. A search for *Acrobat OR JavaScript* returns all found instances of both terms.

✦ **NOT operator:** When NOT is used, words in a phrase that contain the NOT word are skipped. A search for *Adobe NOT Acrobat* returns all PDF documents where Adobe is found and those with Adobe Acrobat are not reported in the found list.

✦ **Multiple words:** Words appearing together like *Acrobat PDF* can be included in quotes. You would supply *"Acrobat PDF"* in the field box and all instances where these two words appear together are reported in the search results. If the words are not contained within quotes, the words *Acrobat, PDF,* and *Acrobat PDF* would all be returned in the search results. This behavior is similar to how you perform searches in Web browsers.

✦ **Searching and, or, not:** If you want to search for a term where these three words are part of the term, you can distinguish between words you search for and using operators. To search for something like *Ben and Jerry's* as a term, you would type *"Ben and Jerry's"* within quote marks. If you want to search for two terms and a Boolean operator you might use *"Ben and Jerry's" AND "Ice Cream" NOT yogurt*. The results report back to you the documents where the words *Ben and Jerry's* and *ice cream* are contained in the files and the words *Ben and Jerry's yogurt* are not reported in the search results.

Search preferences

To open preference settings for Search, choose Edit ➪ Preferences (Windows) or Acrobat Preferences (Macintosh). In the left pane select Search. The preference options available to you are shown in Figure 5-13.

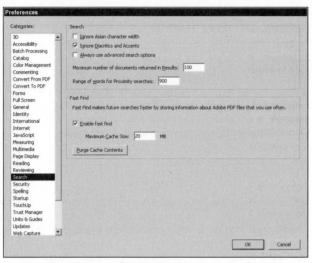

Figure 5-13: Choose Edit ➪ Preferences to open the Preferences dialog box. Click Search in the list at the left to display preference settings for using Search.

The preference choices listed on the right side of the dialog box include

✦ **Ignore Asian character width:** This setting ignores Asian character width and finds both half-width and full-width instances of Asian language characters.

✦ **Ignore Diacritics and Accents:** A diacritic is an accent mark like you might use on a word like *resumé* or the cedilla on a word like *façade* to indicate a special phonetic value. These and other accents are ignored during a search unless you check the box; so for example, if you have it checked Acrobat will find both *resume* and *resumé*. If it is unchecked, Search will only look for resumé

✦ **Always use advanced search options:** Sets the Advanced Search Options as the default. When the check box is enabled you don't need to keep clicking the Use Advanced Search Options button in the Search pane. Enable this setting if you find yourself always using the Advanced Search Options.

✦ **Maximum number of documents returned in Results:** The acceptable range is between 1 and 10,000. Enter a value and the results are limited to this number.

✦ **Range of words for proximity searches:** When using Boolean operators you might want to search for two words within a defined range of words. You can enter a value between 1 and 10,000. Both words need to be within the range when you use a Boolean expression such as AND.

✦ **Enable fast find:** Searches are logged by Acrobat in a memory cache. If you perform a search and later in another session perform a search on the same information, Acrobat returns to the cache for the information, thus speeding up the search. You can edit the cache size by editing the field box for the number of megabytes on your hard drive you want to allocate to the cache. Be certain you have ample hard drive space when enabling the cache and raising the cache size.

✦ **Purge Cache Contents:** The cache occupies as much memory as is available on your hard drive. If you want to clear the cache, click the button to erase all the contents.

After changing any settings in the Preferences dialog box, click OK. The changes you make are dynamically reflected in Acrobat and take effect the next time you perform a search.

Document Descriptions

Document descriptions are user-supplied data fields used to help you identify PDF files according to title, subject, author, and keywords. At the time you create a PDF document, you may have options for supplying a document description. In other cases, you may add descriptions in Acrobat either individually or with Acrobat's batch processing features.

Cross-Reference

To learn how to create batch sequences, see Chapter 14.

After you add descriptions and save your files, the data added to these fields are searchable via advanced searches and index file searches. Developing an organized workflow with specific guidelines for users to follow regarding document descriptions significantly helps all your colleagues search PDFs much more efficiently.

To add a document description, choose File ➪ Document Properties. When the Document Properties dialog box opens, click the Description tab as shown in Figure 5-14.

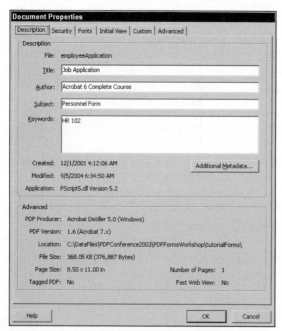

Figure 5-14: You add document descriptions to the Descriptions pane in the Document Properties dialog box.

The four fields for document descriptions include

✦ **Title:** The Title field in this example contains a description of a form. Other forms in a company using a similar schema might use titles such as W-2 Form, Travel Expense, Employee Leave, and so on in its Title field.

✦ **Author:** In the example, the Author field contains the department authoring the form. Notice that an employee name is not used for the Author field. Rather than use employee names, use departments instead. Using departments is a much better choice because a company typically turns over employees more often than it renames departments.

✦ **Subject:** In the example, the Subject field contains Form. The Subject here might be used to distinguish a Form from a Policy, Procedure, Memo, Directive, and so on.

✦ **Keywords:** The first entry in the Keywords field is the form number used by the company to identify the form. Other words in the Keywords field are descriptors related to the form contents. If you want to add an employee author name, add it to the Keywords field.

Note   Users of earlier versions of Acrobat will notice a change in the Document Properties dialog box—tabs are now used instead of a list of categories.

The reason the field information is important for any organization using a PDF workflow is that document description information can be used when a user searches a collection of PDF files. Each field is searchable by the summary title and the words contained in the fields. Therefore, a user can search for all PDF files where the Title field contains the word *Purchase* and the Subject field contains the word *Form*. The search results display all PDF documents where the Title and Subject fields have these words contained in the document description.

As a comparison, imagine searching for the words *Purchase Order.* The search would return all PDFs where these words appear in either the document summary or the text in the PDF files. Purchase Order might be used in memos, policies, procedures, and forms. The user might have to search through many PDFs in order to find the Purchase Order form, thus spending much more time trying to locate the right document.

Searching document descriptions

To search for document descriptions, you need to use either the advanced search or an index file search. Click the Search tool in an Acrobat viewer and click Use Advanced Search Options. Select a folder to search from the Look In pull-down menu.

Cross-Reference   For searching index files, see the section "Searching an index" later in this chapter.

Under Use these additional criteria select one of the description items from the first pull-down menu (Title, Author, Subject, or Keywords). Select either Contains or Does not contain from the pull-down menu adjacent to the first menu. Type the words to be searched in the field box below the pull-down menus. Continue adding additional description fields as desired. In Figure 5-15 two description fields are marked for the search.

Figure 5-15: Two description fields are identified. When you click the Search button, Acrobat searches the document descriptions for matches.

Note that no criteria need to be supplied in the first field box for specific words to be searched in the document. If you click Search in the Search pane with the descriptions shown in Figure 5-15, all PDF files in the designated folder with the words *Purchase Order* in the Title field and *Forms* in the Subject field are returned in the results list for files matching the criteria.

Document descriptions and Boolean queries

You can add Boolean queries when searching document descriptions. You might know some content in PDF files as well as information contained in the document descriptions. In this case you address the additional criteria items in the same manner and add the Boolean query as discussed earlier in this chapter. In Figure 5-16, document descriptions are added to a Boolean query.

Figure 5-16: You can add Boolean queries to searches with additional criteria selections such as document descriptions.

When you click the Search button, the number of results returned in the Search pane is significantly reduced compared to searching for individual words — especially when common words are contained in many PDF documents. What the document descriptions offer you is a method for targeting the exact file you're looking for as fast as possible. If you have 100 PDF documents in the search results list, looking through the list and finding the file you want will take some time. Compare that to two or three files listed. Obviously the document descriptions offer significant time savings as you search PDFs from among very large collections.

Full Text Versus Index Searches

This section represents a pivotal point in this chapter. All of what has been covered so far is information about finding content in PDF documents with a very elaborate *find* feature in Acrobat. The name used in Acrobat to refer to what has been discussed so far is *Search*. Users of earlier versions of Acrobat may take this to mean using Acrobat Search like it was used in Acrobat viewers earlier than version 6.0. What has been covered thus far, however, is a Search of data files that was greatly improved in Acrobat version 6 and is more powerful in returning results in Acrobat version 7. To help understand the difference between the preceding pages and what follows requires a little explanation.

In addition to full-text searches for documents, you can also create a separate index file and search one or more indexes at a time. Index files provide some benefit in that they are still a little faster than full text searches, can be automatically assigned to PDF documents in the Advanced tab in the Document properties, can be automatically loaded from a CD-ROM, and multiple indexes can be searched so files can be scattered somewhat on your hard drive in different folders.

Search Index Procedures

I explain the details for working with search indexes in the remaining pages in this chapter. To provide you with an overall summary for how index file creation and management is dealt with in Acrobat, I give you a short summary of the procedures here.

Using index files to perform searches begins with using a current index file or creating a new one. Users who have been working with index files need to make sure that all your previous indexes are updated for compatibility with Acrobat 7.0 viewers.

Index files are created and updated with Acrobat Catalog with Acrobat Professional only. Catalog is available from a menu selection in the Advanced menu. You open Catalog and make a decision for creating a new index or opening an existing index file for rebuilding or editing in the Catalog window.

After an index file is created or updated, you load the index file into the Search pane. Multiple index files can be loaded and searched. When you search index files, the results are reported in the Search pane like all the searches discussed earlier in this chapter.

Earlier releases of Acrobat offered you options for various menu selections related to managing indexes and loading new index files. Earlier releases of Acrobat also offered you dialog boxes where results were reported and information about an index file could be obtained. In Acrobat 6.0 and 7.0 viewers, you handle all your index file management in the Search pane. Menu commands are limited to viewing search results as described earlier in this chapter.

If you edit PDF documents, delete them, or add new documents to folders that have been indexed, you need to rebuild index files periodically. You can purge old data and re-index files in Acrobat Catalog. Index files can be copied to different hard drive locations, across servers, and to external media. When copying files, you need to copy all files and folders associated with the index file. Failure to copy all the files renders the index inoperable.

Creating Search Indexes (Acrobat Professional Only)

In order to search an index file, you must have one present on your computer, network server, or some media storage device. When you install an Acrobat viewer, a help index file is included during your installation. You can use this file to search for words contained in any of the help documents. If you want to search your own files, you need to create an index. To create an index file you use Acrobat Catalog.

Note   Acrobat Catalog is only available in Acrobat Professional. Search indexes can be used by all Acrobat viewers including Adobe Reader.

To launch Acrobat Catalog from within Acrobat Professional choose Advanced ⇨ Catalog. Catalog is robust and provides many options for creating and modifying indexes. After a search index is created, any user can access the search index in all Acrobat viewers to find words using the Search pane. However, before you begin to work with Acrobat Catalog, you need to take some preliminary steps to be certain all your files are properly prepared and ready to be indexed.

Preparing PDFs for indexing

Preparation involves creating PDFs with all the necessary information to facilitate searches. All searchable document description information needs to be supplied in the PDF documents at the time of PDF creation or by modifying PDFs in Acrobat before you begin working with Catalog. For workgroups and multiple user access to search indexes, this information needs to be clear and consistent. Other factors, such as naming conventions, location of files, and optimizing performance should all be thought out and planned prior to creating an index file.

Note   Adding document descriptions is not a requirement for creating search indexes. You can index files without any information in the document description fields. Adding document descriptions merely adds more relevant information to your PDF documents and aids users in finding search results faster.

Document descriptions

Document description information should be supplied in all PDF files to be searched. As discussed earlier in this chapter, all document description data are searchable. Spending time creating document descriptions and defining the field types for consistent organization will facilitate searches performed by multiple users.

The first of the planning steps is to develop a flow chart or outline of company information and the documents to be categorized. This organization may or may not be implemented where you intend to develop a PDF workflow. If your information flow is already in place, you may need to make some modifications to coordinate nomenclature and document identity with the document summary items in Acrobat.

Document descriptions contained in the Title, Subject, Author, and Keywords fields should be consistent and intuitive. They should also follow a hierarchy consistent with the company's organizational structure and workflow. The document summary items should be mapped out and defined. When preparing files for indexing, consider the following:

✦ **Title:** Title information might be thought of as the root of an outline—the parent statement, if you will. Descriptive titles should be used to help users narrow searches within specific categories. The Title field can also be used to display the title name at the top of the Acrobat window when you select viewing titles in the Initial View properties.

For information on how to set document title attributes in the Initial View dialog box, see Chapter 4.

✦ **Author:** Avoid using proper names for the Author field. Personnel change in companies and roles among employees change. Identify the author of PDF documents according to departments, work groups, facilities, and so on.

✦ **Subject:** If the Title field is the parent item in an outline format, the Subject would be a child item nested directly below the title. Subjects might be considered subsets of titles. When creating document summaries, be consistent. Don't use subject and title or subject and keyword information back and forth with different documents. If an item, such as employee grievances, is listed as a Subject in some PDFs and then listed as a Title in other documents, the end users will become confused with the order and searches will become unnecessarily complicated.

✦ **Keywords:** If you have a forms identification system in place, be certain to use form numbers and identity as part of the Keywords field. You might start the Keywords field with a form number and then add additional keywords to help narrow searches. Be consistent and always start the Keywords field with forms or document numbers. If you need to have PDF author names, add them here in the Keywords fields. If employees change roles or leave the company, the Author fields still provide the information relative to a department.

To illustrate some examples, take a look at Table 5-1.

Table 5-1: Document Summary Examples

Title	Author	Subject	Keywords
Descriptive Titles.	Department Names.	Subsection of Title.	Document numbers and random identifiers.
Titles may be considered specific to workgroup tasks.	Don't use employee names in organizations; employees change, departments usually remain.	Subjects may be thought of as child outline items nested below the parent Title items — a subset of the Titles.	You can supply Forms ID numbers, internal filing numbers, and so on in the Keyword fields. If employee names are a MUST for your company, add employee names in the Keywords field box. List any related words to help find the topic.
Employee Policies	Human Resources	Vacation Leave	D-101, HR32A, H. Jones, policy, employee regulations
FDA Compliance	Quality Assurance	Software Validation	SOP-114, QA-182, J. Wilson, regulations, citations, eye implant device
Curriculum	English Department	American Literature	Plan 2010, Martha Evans, senior English, Emerson High, 11th grade
Receivables	Accounting	Collection Policy	F-8102, M-5433, Finance, collections, payments
eCommerce	Marketing	Products	M-1051, e-117A, golf clubs, sports, leisure

Tip

Legacy PDF files used in an organization may have been created without a document description, or you may reorganize PDFs and want to change document summaries. To quickly (or efficiently) update these documents, you can create a batch sequence to change multiple PDF files and then run the sequence. Place your PDFs in a folder where the document summaries are to be edited. In the Edit Sequence dialog box, select the items to change and edit each document summary item. Run the sequence to update an entire folder of PDFs.

Cross-Reference For more information on creating batch sequences, see Chapter 14.

File structure

The content, filenames, and location of PDFs to be cataloged contribute to file structure items. All the issues related to file structure must be thought out and appropriately designed for the audience that you intend to support. Among the important considerations are

✦ **File naming conventions:** Names provided for the PDF files are critical for distributing documents among users. If filenames get truncated, then either Acrobat Search or the end user will have difficulty finding a document when performing a search. This is of special concern to Macintosh users who want to distribute documents across platforms. As a matter of safeguard, the best precaution to take is always use standard DOS file-naming conventions. The standard eight-character maximum filename with no more than three-character file extensions (`filename.ext`), will always work regardless of platform.

✦ **Folder names:** Folder names should follow the same conventions as filenames. Macintosh users who want to keep filenames longer than standard DOS names must limit folder names to eight characters and no more than a three-character file extension for cross-platform compliance.

✦ **File and folder name identity:** Avoid using ASCII characters from 133 to 159 for any filename or folder name. Acrobat Catalog does support some extended characters in this range, but you may experience problems when using files across platforms. (Figure 5-17 lists the characters to avoid.)

133	à	139	ï	144	É	149	ò	154	Ü
134	å	140	î	145	æ	150	û	156	£
135	ç	141	ì	146	Æ	151	ù	157	¥
136	ê	142	Ä	147	ô	152	_	158	_
137	ë	143	Å	148	ö	153	Ö	159	ƒ
138	è								

Figure 5-17: When providing names for files and folders to be cataloged, avoid using extended characters from ASCII 133 to ASCII 159. Although some of the characters are supported in Acrobat Catalog, you may have problems when copying files across platforms.

✦ **Folder organization:** Folders to be cataloged should have a logical hierarchy. Copy all files to be cataloged to a single folder or a single folder with nested folders in the same path. When nesting folders, be certain to keep the number of nested folders to a minimum. Deeply nested folders slow down searches, and path names longer than 256 characters create problems.

✦ **Folder locations:** Windows users must keep the location of folders on a local hard drive or a network server volume. Although Macintosh users can catalog information across computer workstations, creating separate indexes for files contained on separate drives would be advisable. Any files moved to different locations make searches inoperable.

✦ **PDF structure:** File and folder naming should be handled before creating links and attaching files. If filenames are changed after the PDF structure has been developed, many links become inoperable. Be certain to complete all editing in the PDF documents before cataloging files.

Optimizing performance

Searches can be performed very fast if you take a little time in creating the proper structure and organization. If you don't avoid some pitfalls with the way that you organize files, then searches perform much slower. A few considerations to be made include the following:

✦ **Optimize PDF files:** Optimization should be performed on all PDF files as one of the last steps in your workflow. Use the Save As optimizes for Fast Web View found in the General category in the Preferences dialog box and run the PDF Optimizer located in the Advanced menu (Acrobat Professional only). Optimization is especially important for searches to be performed from CD-ROM files.

For information on PDF Optimizer, see Chapter 14.

✦ **Break up long PDF files:** Books, reports, essays, and other documents that contain many pages should be broken up into multiple PDF files. If you have books to be cataloged, break up the books into separate chapters. Acrobat Search runs much faster when finding information from several small files. It slows down when searching through long documents.

Cross-Reference

For more information on PDF interactivity and creating link buttons to open and close files, see Chapter 17.

Managing Multiple PDF Documents

Books, reports, and manuals can be broken up into separate files and structured in a way that it still appears to the end user as a single document. Assuming a user reads through a file in a linear fashion, you can create links to open and close pages without user intervention. Create navigational buttons to move forward and back through document pages. On the last page of each chapter, use the navigation button to open the next chapter. Also on the last page of each chapter, create a Page action that closes the current document when the page is closed. (See Chapter 17 for creating links and Page actions.) If the end user disables *Open cross-document links in same window* in the General category in the Preferences dialog box, the open file still closes after the last page is closed. All the chapters can be linked from a table of contents where any chapter can be opened. If you give your design some thought, browsing the contents of books will appear to the end user no different than reading a book in the analog world.

Creating search help

You can have multiple indexes for various uses and different workgroups. Personnel may use one index for department matters, another for company-wide information, and perhaps another for a research library. In a search, all relevant keywords will appear from indexes loaded in the Index Selection dialog box. When using multiple indexes, employees may forget the structure of document summaries and what index is needed for a given search.

You can create readme files and index help files to store key information about what search words can be used to find document summaries. You can create a single PDF file, text files, or multiple files that serve as help. Figure 5-18 shows an example of a PDF help file that might be used to find documents related to a company's personnel policies, procedures, and forms.

Widget Company			Title:	HR
Human Resources Index Description			Subject:	Table
			Author:	Table
			Keywords:	Table

Title	Subject	Author	Keywords
Policy	PTO	HR	HR 501
Policy	Maternity	HR	HR 521
Procedure	Maternity	HR	HR 520
Form	Payroll	Accounting	FM 261
Policy	Bonus	Accounting	AC 245
Policy	Manual	Admin	AD 109
Procedure	Grievance	HR	HR 546
Policy	EAP	HR	HR 593
Policy	Hiring	HR	HR 506
Form	ID	HR	FM 505
Chart	HR	Admin	AD 117
Form	Leave	HR	FM 531
Procedure	Pay deduction	Accounting	AC 228
Policy	Benefits	Table	Table
Procedure	Extended Leave	HR	HR 564
Policy	Education Leave	HR	HR 568
Form	Insurance	HR	FM 533
Form	Dental	HR	FM 512
Policy	401K	HR	HR 555

Figure 5-18: A PDF help file can assist users in knowing what keywords they need to use for the Title, Subject, Author, and Keywords fields.

In the top-right corner of Figure 5-18, the document summary for the help file is listed. The Title fields for this company are broken into categories for policies, procedures, forms, and charts. The Subject fields break down the title categories into specific personnel items, and the Author fields contain the department that authored the documents. Form numbers appear for all Keywords fields.

Tip   When creating help files that guide a user for searching document information, use a common identifier in the Subject, Author, and Keywords fields reserved for only finding help files. In Figure 5-18, the identifier is *Table*. Whenever a user searches for the word *table* in the Author field, the only returns in the Search Results dialog box will be help files. When using the Title and Author field together, a user can find a specific help file for a given department. In the previous example, the Title is *HR* and the Author is *Table*. When these words are searched for the document information, the help file for the HR department is returned in the Search Results. If you reserve keywords for the document Summary fields, any employee can easily find information by remembering only a few keywords.

Creating a new index file

After your files are optimized and saved in final form, it's time to create the search index. Choose Advanced ➪ Catalog to open the Catalog dialog box as shown in Figure 5-19. In the dialog box you make choices for creating a new index file or opening an existing index file. Click the New Index button to create a new index file.

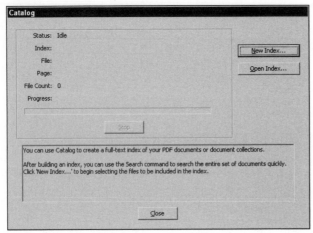

Figure 5-19: Click the New Index button in the Catalog dialog box to create an index file.

The New Index Definition dialog box shown in Figure 5-20 opens, in which you set specific attributes for your index and determine what folder(s) are to be indexed.

Index title

The title that you place in this field is a title for the index, but not necessarily the name of the file you ultimately save. The name you enter here does not need to conform to any naming conventions because in most cases it won't be the saved filename. When you open an index file, you search your hard drive, server, or external media for a filename that ends with a .pdx extension. When you visit the Search pane and select the menu option for Select Index, the Index Selection dialog box opens as shown in Figure 5-21. What appears in the Index Selection dialog box is a list of indexes appearing according to the Index Title names. These names are derived from what you type in the Index Title field in Acrobat Catalog.

Note   When you get ready to build a file, Acrobat prompts you for the index filename. By default the text you type in the Index Title field is listed in the File name field in the Save Index File dialog box. This dialog box opens when you click the Build button in the Catalog dialog box (see the section "Building the index" later in this chapter). In most cases where you supply a name as a description in the Index Title, you'll want to change the filename to a name consistent with standard DOS conventions (that is, eight-character maximum with a three-character maximum extension). Make this change when you are prompted to save the file.

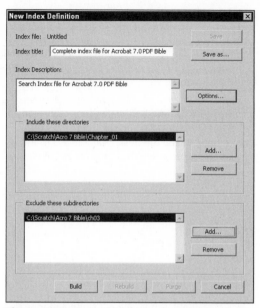

Figure 5-20: You set attributes for your new index file in the New Index Definition dialog box.

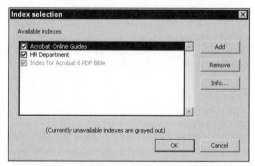

Figure 5-21: Choosing Select Index from the Look In pull-down menu in the Search pane opens the Index Selection dialog box. All loaded indexes are listed according to the index title supplied in Acrobat Catalog at the time the index was created.

Index description

You can supply as many as 256 characters in the Index Description field. Descriptive names and keywords should be provided so that the end user knows what each index contains. Index descriptions should be thought of as adding more information to the items mentioned earlier in this chapter regarding document descriptions. Index descriptions can help users find the index file that addresses their needs.

When an index is loaded, the index title appears in the Select Indexes dialog box. To get more information about an index file, click the Info button shown in Figure 5-21. The Index information dialog box opens as shown in Figure 5-22. The Index information dialog box shows you the title from the Index Title field and the description added in Acrobat Catalog in the Index Description field.

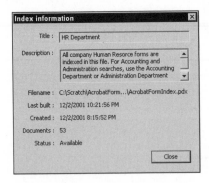

Figure 5-22: The Index Description is contained in the Index information dialog box. Users can click on the Info button in the Index selection dialog box to see the description added in the Index Description field box in Acrobat Catalog.

Include these directories

If you add nothing to the Include these directories field, Catalog won't build an index because it won't know where to look for the PDF files to be included in the index. Adding the directory path(s) is essential before you begin to build the index. Notice the first Add button on the right side of the dialog box in Figure 5-20. After you click Add, a navigation dialog box opens, enabling you to identify the directory where the PDFs to be indexed are located. You can add many directories to the Include these directories list. These directories can be in different locations on your hard drive. When a given directory is selected, all subfolders will also be indexed for all directory locations unless you choose to exclude certain folders. When the directories have been identified, the directory path and folder name will appear in the Include these directories field.

Exclude these subdirectories

If you have files in a subdirectory within the directory you are indexing and want to exclude the subdirectory, you can do so in the Exclude these subdirectories field. The folder names and directory paths of excluded directories appear in the Exclude these subdirectories field as shown in Figure 5-20.

Remove

If you decide to remove a directory from either the Include these directories or Exclude these subdirectories lists, select an item in the list and click the Remove button. You can add or delete directories in either list prior to building an index or when modifying an index.

Saving index definitions

Two buttons appear at the top-right corner of the Catalog dialog box for saving a definition. If you begin to develop an index file and supply the index title and a description and want to come back to Catalog later, you can save what you type in the Index Definition dialog box using the Save As button. The Save button does not appear active until you have saved a file with the Save As option or you're working on a file that has been built. Saving the file only saves the definition for the index. It does not create an index file. The Save As option enables you to prepare files for indexing and interrupt your session if you need to return later. For example, suppose you add an index title and you write an index description. If you need to quit Acrobat at this point, click Save As and save the definition to disk. You can then return later and resume creating the index by adding the directories to be cataloged and building the index.

After you have saved a file you can update the file with the Save button. After a definition is saved, when you return to Acrobat Catalog, you can click the Open button in the Catalog dialog box and resume editing the definition file. When all the options for your search index have been determined, you click the Build button to actually create the index file.

Using Save As or Save is not required to create an index file. If you set all your attributes for the index and click the Build button, Acrobat Catalog prompts you in the Save Index File dialog box to supply a name for the index and save the definition. Essentially, Catalog is invoking the Save As command for you.

If at any time you click the Cancel button in the lower-right corner of the Index Definition dialog box, all edits are lost for the current session. If you add definition items without saving you'll need to start over when you open the Index Definition dialog box again. If you start to work on a saved file and click Cancel without saving new edits, your file reverts to the last saved version.

Setting options

To the right of the Index Description field is a button labeled Options. Click this button and the Options dialog box appears, allowing you to choose from a number of different attributes for your index file, as shown in Figure 5-23. Some of these options are similar to the Preference settings for Acrobat Catalog you made in the Preferences dialog box. Any edits you make here supersede Preference settings.

Cross-Reference For information on setting catalog preferences, see "Setting preferences" later in this chapter.

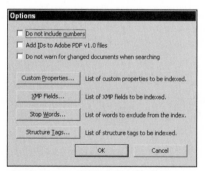

Figure 5-23: Clicking the Options button adjacent to the Index Description field opens the Options dialog box. Here you can assign further attributes to the index file.

Do not include numbers

The first item in the Options dialog box is a check box for excluding numbers. By selecting the Do not include numbers option, you can reduce the file size, especially if data containing many numbers is part of the PDF file(s) to be indexed. Keep in mind, though, that if numbers are excluded, Search won't find numeric values.

Add IDs to Adobe v1.0 files

Because Acrobat is now in version 7.0, finding old PDF 1.0 files that need to be updated with IDs for Acrobat 1.0 files may rarely happen. If you do have legacy files saved as PDF 1.0 format, it would be best to batch process the older PDFs by saving them out of Acrobat 7.0. As software changes, many previous formats may not be supported with recent updates. For better performance, update older documents to newer file formats.

Cross-Reference   For more information on batch processing, see Chapter 14.

If you have legacy files that haven't been updated and you want to include them in your search index, check the box. If you're not certain whether the PDFs were created with Acrobat 1.0 compatibility, check it anyway just to be safe.

Do not warn for changed documents when searching

If you create an index file, then return to the index in Acrobat Catalog and perform some maintenance functions, save the index, and start searching the index, Acrobat notifies you in a dialog box that changes have been made and asks whether you want to proceed. To sidestep the opening of the warning dialog box, check the Do not warn for changed documents when searching option.

Custom Properties

The Custom Properties button opens a dialog box as shown in Figure 5-24. Custom Properties are used when customizing Acrobat with the Acrobat Software Development Kit (SDK). This item is intended for programmers who want to add special features to Acrobat. To add a Custom Property to be indexed, you should have knowledge in programming and the PDF format.

Figure 5-24: You can add custom data fields to Acrobat with the Acrobat Software Development Kit.

You add Custom Properties to the field box and select the type of property to be indexed from the pull-down menu. You type the property values in the field box, identify the type, and click the Add button. The property is then listed in the window below the Custom Property field box.

The types available from the pull-down menu include

✦ **String:** This is any text string. If numbers are included with this option they are treated as text.

✦ **Integer:** The integer field can accept values between 0 and 65,535.

✦ **Date:** This is a date value.

Support for programmers writing extensions, plug-ins, and working with the SDK is provided by Adobe Systems. Developers who want to use the support program need to become a member of the Adobe Solutions Network (ASN) Developer Program. For more information about ASN and SDK, log on to the Adobe Web site at http://partners.adobe.com/asn/developer.

XMP Fields

Click XMP Fields and another dialog box opens where you add to a list of XMP fields. The dialog box is virtually identical to the Stop Words dialog box shown in Figure 5-25. Type a name in the field box and click the Add button. All new XMP fields are added to the list window.

Stop Words

To optimize an index file that produces faster search results, you can add stop words. You may have words, such as *the*, *a*, *an*, *of*, and so on that would typically not be used in a search. You can choose to exclude such words by typing the word in the Word field box and clicking the Add button in the Stop Words dialog box. Click Stop Words in the Options dialog box to open the Stop Words dialog box shown in Figure 5-25. To eliminate a word after it has been added, select the word and click the Remove button. Keep in mind that every time you *add* a word, you are actually adding it to a list of words to be excluded.

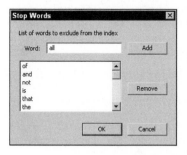

Figure 5-25: You can eliminate words from an index file by adding words in the Stop Words dialog box. Adding a word to the list excludes it from the index file.

Tip

You can create an elaborate list of stop words and may want to apply the list to several index files, but Acrobat (as of this writing) does not include an ability to import or swap a list of words to be excluded from an index file. For a workaround, you can open any existing Index Definition field and change all attributes except the stop words. Add a new index title, a new index description, and select a new directory for indexing. Save the definition to a new file-name and click the Build button. A new index is built using the stop words created in another index. In workgroups you can save an index definition file without adding directories and use it as a template so all index files have consistent settings for the stop words.

Structure tags

If you have a tagged PDF you can search document tags when the tags are included in the search index. Click Structure Tags in the Options dialog box to open the Tags dialog box shown in Figure 5-26. Tagged PDFs with a tagged root and elements can have any item in the tagged logical tree marked for searching. To observe the tags in a PDF file, open the Tags palette and expand the tree. All the tags nest like a Bookmark list. When you want to mark tags for searching, type the tag name in the Tags dialog box and click the Add button. You remove tags from the list window by selecting a tag and clicking the Remove button.

 Cross-Reference   For more information on tagged PDF documents and using the Tags palette, see Chapter 20.

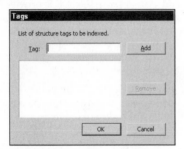

Figure 5-26: You can mark tags for searches in index files by adding tag names in the Tags dialog box.

Building the index

After you've set all the attributes for the index definition, the index file is ready to be created. Clicking the Build button in the New Index Definition dialog box creates indexes. When you click this button, Acrobat Catalog opens the Save Index File dialog box where you supply a filename and target a destination on your hard drive. The default file extension is .pdx. Do not modify the file extension name. Acrobat recognizes these files when loading search indexes.

The location where you instruct Catalog to save your index file can be any location on your hard drive regardless of where the files being indexed reside. You can choose to save the index file inside or outside the folder that Catalog created during the indexing. Therefore you have an index file and a folder containing index resources. The relationship between the index file and resource folder locations is critical to the usability of the index. If you move the index file to a different location without moving the supporting folder, the index is rendered unusable. To avoid problems, try to create a folder either when you are in the Save Index File dialog box or before you open Catalog and save your index file to your new folder. Make the name descriptive and keep the index file together in this folder. When you want to move the index to another directory, another computer, or to an external media cartridge or CD-ROM, copy the folder containing the index and supporting files.

The Structure of Index Files

Users who have created index files in all earlier versions of Acrobat are no doubt familiar with the end product of creating a search index. As you may recall, the index file with a .pdx extension and nine subfolders containing all associated files were produced by Acrobat Catalog for every new index. The relationship between the index file and subfolders in terms of directory paths needed to be preserved in order for the index to work properly. When you copied an index file to another directory or source, you needed to copy all the files together and keep the same relative path between the files.

When you produce an index file in Acrobat Professional, you won't find the same nine folders created during the index build with Acrobat version 5 and earlier. Acrobat 7.0 Catalog creates a single folder where files with an .idx extension resides. The relative directory path is still a factor in relocating files, but in Acrobat 6.0 and 7.0 you need only copy an index file and a single folder to relocate your index and keep it functional.

The .pdx file you load as your search index file is a small file that creates the information in the .idx and .info files. The .idx files contain the actual index entries the end user accesses during a search. When you build an index, rebuild an index, or purge data from an index, the maintenance operation may or may not affect the .pdx file and/or .idx files depending on which option you choose. For specific information related to how these files are affected during index creation and maintenance, see the following pages for building, rebuilding, and purging index files.

Click the Save button in the Save Index File dialog box, and Catalog closes the Index Definition dialog box, returns you to the Catalog dialog box, and begins to process all the files in the target folder(s). Depending on how many files are indexed, the time to complete the build may be considerable. Don't interrupt the processing if you want to complete the index generation. When Catalog finishes the progress bar stops and the last line of text in the Catalog dialog box reads "Index build successful." If for some reason the build is not successful, you can scroll the window in the Catalog dialog box and view errors reported in the list.

Stopping builds

If you want to interrupt a build, you can click the Stop button while a build is in progress. When building an index, Catalog opens a file where all the words and markers to the PDF pages are written. When you click the Stop button, Catalog saves the open file to disk and closes it with the indexed items up to the point you stopped the build. Therefore, the index is usable after stopping a build and you can search for words in the partial index. When you want to resume, you can open the file in Catalog and click the Rebuild button.

Building existing indexes

When files are deleted from indexed folders and new files are added to the indexed folders, you'll want to maintain the index file and update it to reflect any changes. You can open an index file and click Build for a quick update. New files are scanned and added to the index, but the deleted files are marked for deletion without actually deleting the data. To delete data that's no longer valid, you need to use the Purge button. Purging can take a considerable amount of time even on small index files. Therefore, your routine maintenance might be to consistently build a file, and only periodically purge data.

Building legacy index files

When you open an index file created with an Acrobat Catalog earlier than version 6.0, a dialog box opens informing you the index is not compatible with the current version of Acrobat. In the dialog box you have three options: Create copy, Overwrite old index, and Cancel. Click the Create copy button to make a copy of the index file. A new index file is created leaving the original index file undisturbed. You can click the Overwrite old index button and the file rewrites, replacing the old index. If you choose this option your new index file won't be compatible with Acrobat viewers earlier than version 6.0. Clicking Cancel in this dialog box returns you to the Index Selection dialog box, leaving the index file undisturbed.

If you create a search index using Acrobat Catalog version 7, the index file is backward-compatible to Acrobat 6. All Acrobat viewers can use index files suited to the appropriate version.

If you know some users won't be working with the new Acrobat viewers, then be certain to make copies of your index files. Until all users have upgraded to a viewer 6.0 or higher, you may need to organize your indexes according to viewer versions.

Tip

If you work in an organization where many users have different versions of Acrobat viewers, then keeping a complete installation of Acrobat 5.05 installed on a separate computer on your network is to your advantage. If you inadvertently overwrite index files or need to perform some task specifically related to Acrobat versions less than 6.0, you can use the older version to keep compatibility with other users. In addition, you can test many new files you edit in version 6.0 or higher to ensure they work with viewer versions less than 6.0. Ideally, all your colleagues, coworkers, and clients should upgrade to Acrobat 7.0. However, in a real world, we know some users are reluctant to let go of the familiar and convincing all users that upgrading Acrobat is the best solution may take some time.

Building index files from secure documents

In Acrobat versions lower than 6.0 you could not create index files from secure PDFs encrypted with either Acrobat Standard Security or Acrobat Self-Sign Security. Version 6.0 of Acrobat afforded complete access to secure files with Acrobat Catalog if the right permissions were applied. When applying Password Security in either Acrobat 6 or Acrobat 7 you need to enable text access for screen reader devices in order to index a secure file. Creating an index does not compromise your security and doesn't affect all other permissions you set forth when the files are saved.

If you have legacy files that have been secured, you can index them like other files saved in earlier PDF format compatibilities. These files, and any other files you create with Acrobat Professional, can be used only by Acrobat viewers 6.0 and later.

Cross-Reference

For more information on encryption and security, see Chapter 21.

Rebuilding an index

Rebuilding index files completely re-creates a new index. You can open an Acrobat 7.0-compatible index file and click Rebuild. The file rewrites the file you opened much like you would use a Save As menu command to rewrite a PDF document. If a substantial number of PDF documents have been deleted and new files added to the indexed folders, rebuilding the index could take less time than purging data.

Purging data

As indexes are maintained and rebuilt, you will need to perform periodic maintenance and purge old data. A purge does not delete the index file, nor does it completely rewrite the file; it simply recovers the space used in the index for outdated information. Purging is particularly useful when you remove PDF files from a folder and the search items are no longer needed. If you have built a file several times, each build marks words for deletion. A purge eliminates the marked data and reduces the file size. With a significant number of words marked for deletion, a purge will improve the speed when using Search. This operation might be scheduled routinely in environments where many changes occur within the indexed folders.

Tip   When changing options for eliminating words and numbers from indexes or adding tags and custom properties in the Options dialog box, first open the index.pdx file in Catalog and purge the data. Set your new criteria in the Options dialog box and rebuild the index. Any items deleted will now be added to the index, or any items you want to eliminate will subsequently be eliminated from the index.

Setting Catalog preferences

Catalog preference settings are contained in the Preferences dialog box. Choose Edit ⇨ Preferences and click the Catalog item in the left pane as shown in Figure 5-27. Notice that the Index Defaults items use the same settings as found in the Options dialog box from the New Index Selection dialog box. The top three options under Indexing in Catalog preferences are obtained only here in these preference settings.

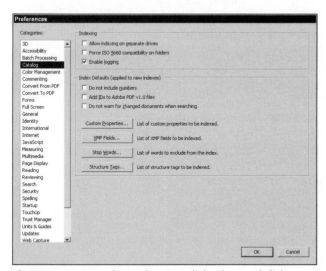

Figure 5-27: Open the Preferences dialog box and click Catalog in the left pane to see the options settings for Acrobat Catalog.

Indexing

The three options found in the Indexing section of the Catalog preferences include

✦ **Allow indexing on separate drives:** When creating index files where you want to include folders on network servers and/or computers on your network, select this item in the Catalog preferences. The indexing option includes indexing files only on local networks. Unfortunately, you can't index files on Web servers and use indexes from within Web browsers.

✦ **Force ISO 9660 compatibility on folders:** This setting is a flag that tells Catalog to look for any folders that are not compliant with standard DOS conventions (eight-character maximum with three-character maximum extensions) for folder/directory names. If Catalog encounters a folder name that is not acceptable, the processing stops and an error is reported in the Catalog dialog box. Folder names and directory paths are listed for all incompatible names. You can review the list and manually rename folders. After changing folder names, try to create the index again.

✦ **Enable logging:** A log file is created during an index build that describes the processing for each file indexed. The file is ASCII text and can be opened in any text editor or word processor. Any errors occurring during the build are noted in the log file. All documents and directory paths are also contained in the log file. If you don't want to have a log file created at the time of indexing, deselect the check box to disable the logging. When you disable logging, you are prevented from analyzing problems when you close the Catalog dialog box.

Index Defaults

The options listed in the Index Defaults area of the Catalog preferences are identical to the options you have available in the New Index Description Options dialog box described earlier in this chapter. These default options settings exist in two locations for different reasons.

When you set the options in the Preferences dialog box, the options are used for all index files you create. When you elect to use the options from the New Index Selection Options dialog box, the settings are specific to the index file you create. When you create a new index file, the options return to defaults.

If you set a preference in the Catalog preferences and disable the option in the New Index Selection Options dialog box, the latter supercedes the former. That is to say, the New Index Selection Options dialog box settings always prevail.

Using Index Files

As I stated earlier, one reason you create index files is for speed. When you search hundreds or thousands of pages, the amount of time to return found instances for searched words in index files is a matter of seconds compared to using the Search tool in the Search pane.

Loading index files

To search using an index file, you need to first load the index in the Search pane. From the Look In pull-down menu, choose the Select Index menu option as shown in Figure 5-28.

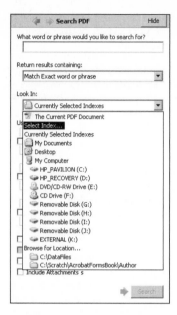

Figure 5-28: Your first step in using indexes is to load the index file(s) by choosing the Select Index menu option from the Look In menu in the Search pane.

The Index Selection dialog box opens after you make the menu selection. Click the Add button and the Open Index File dialog box opens. In this dialog box navigate your hard drive to find the folder where your index file is located. Click the index filename and click the Open button.

After selecting the index to load, you are returned to the Index Selection dialog box. A list of all loaded indexes appears in the dialog box. To the left of each filename is a check box. When a check mark is in view, the index file is active and can be searched. Those check boxes that are disabled have the index file loaded, but the file remains inactive. Search will not return results from the inactive index files. If an index file is grayed out as shown in Figure 5-29, the file path has been disrupted and Acrobat can't find the index file or the support files associated with the index. If you see a filename grayed out, select the file in the list and click the Remove button. Click the Add button and relocate the index. If the support files are not found, an error is reported in a dialog box indicating the index file could not be opened.

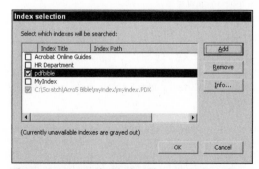

Figure 5-29: Loaded index files are active when a check mark appears adjacent to the index filename. If a file is grayed out, the index is not accessible and may need to be rebuilt.

If you can't open a file, you need to return to the Catalog dialog box and click the Open button. Find the index file that you want to make active and rebuild the index. After rebuilding, you need to return to the Index selection dialog box and reload the index.

Note   If you load an index file from a CD-ROM and the CD is not inserted into your CD-ROM drive, the index filename is grayed out in the Index Selection dialog box. After inserting the CD-ROM containing the index, the index filename becomes active. If you know index files are loaded from CDs, don't delete them from the Index Selection dialog box. Doing so requires you to reload the index file each time you insert a CD.

Attaching an index file to a document

You can associate an index file with a particular document. Open the Document Properties dialog box (Ctrl/⌘+D) and click the Advanced tab. Adjacent to the Search Index item is a Browse button. Click Browse and the Open dialog box appears. Navigate your hard drive to locate the index file created from a folder containing your document, select it, and click Open. When you save your file and reopen it, you can select Currently Selected Indexes in the Look In pull-down menu and your associated index file is automatically loaded for you.

Disabling indexes

If an index is to be eliminated from searches, you can deactivate the index by disabling its check box. In a later Acrobat session, you can go back and enable indexes listed in the Index Selection dialog box. You should always use this method rather than deleting an index if you intend to use it again in a later Acrobat session. However, at times you may want to delete an index file. If the index will no longer be used, or you relocate your index to another drive or server, you may want to completely remove the old index. If this is the case, select the index file to be deleted and click the Remove button. Indexes may be enabled or disabled before you select Remove. In either case, the index file is removed without warning.

If you inadvertently delete an index, you can always reload the index by clicking the Add button. Placing index files in a directory where you can easily access them is a good idea. To avoid confusion, try to keep indexes in a common directory or a directory together with the indexed PDF files. Acrobat doesn't care where the index file is located on your hard drive or server — it just needs to know where the file is located and the file needs to keep the relative path with the support files. If you move the index file to a different directory, be certain to reestablish the connection in the Index Selection dialog box.

Finding index information

When a number of index files are installed on a computer or server, the names for the files may not be descriptive enough to determine which index you want to search. If more detailed information is desired, the information provided by the Index Information dialog box may help identify the index needed for a given search.

PDF Workflow   Index information may be particularly helpful in office environments where several people in different departments create PDFs and indexes are all placed on a common server. What may be intuitive to the author of an index file in terms of index name may not be as intuitive to other users. Index information offers the capability for adding more descriptive information that can be understood by many users.

Fortunately, you can explore more descriptive information about an index file by clicking the Info button in the Index Selection dialog box. When you click the Info button, the Index information dialog box opens, displaying information about the index file as shown in Figure 5-30. Some of the information displayed requires user entry at the time the index is built. Acrobat Catalog automatically creates other information in the dialog box when the index is built. The Index information dialog box provides a description of the following:

✦ **Title:** The user supplies title information at the time the index is created. Titles usually consist of several words describing the index contents. Titles can be searched, as detailed earlier in this chapter, so the title keywords should reflect the index content.

✦ **Description:** Description can be a few words or several sentences containing information about the index. (In Figure 5-30, the description was supplied in Acrobat Catalog when the index was created.)

✦ **Filename:** The directory path for the index file's location on a drive or server is displayed with the last item appearing as the index filename.

✦ **Last built:** If the index file is updated, the date of the last build is supplied here. If no updates have occurred, the date will be the same as the created date.

✦ **Created:** This date reflects the time and date the index file was originally created, and is therefore a fixed date.

✦ **Documents:** Indexes are created from one or more PDF documents. The total number of PDF files from which the index file was created appears here.

✦ **Status:** If the index file has been identified and added to the list in the Index Selection dialog box, it will be Available. Unavailable indexes appear grayed out in the list and are described as Unavailable.

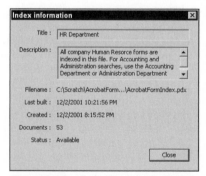

Figure 5-30: The Index information dialog box appears when you select the Info button in the Index selection dialog box.

Searching an index

After your index file(s) is prepared and loaded in the Index selection dialog box, it is ready for use. You search index files in the Advanced Search pane just as you search multiple files explained earlier in this chapter. From the Look In pull-down menu, select Currently Selected Indexes.

All the options discussed earlier for advanced searches are available to you. Select from the Return results containing pull-down menu, enter your search criteria, and select the options you want. Click the Search button and you'll find the search results reported much faster than using other search methods.

Index files can be created from PDF collections contained on external media where the index file can remain on your computer without the need for copying the PDF documents to your hard drive. When you insert a media disk such as a CD-ROM, your search index is ready to use to search the media.

Practice searching your new index file using different options and search criteria. To compare the difference between using a search index file and using the advanced search options, you can choose the Browse for Location menu item and search the CD-ROM for the same criteria. Go back and forth to see the differences between searching folders and searching an index file.

Searching external devices

A computer network server, another computer on your network, a CD-ROM, DVD-ROM, external hard drive, or removable media cartridge are considered external to your local computer hard drive(s). Any of these devices can be indexed and the index file can be located on any of the devices you index. If you want to save an index file on a device different from where the PDF collection is stored, you need to be certain to open the Preferences dialog box for the Catalog preferences and enable the check box for Allow indexing on separate drives. This preference setting enables you to index across media devices.

Note   When you want to write index files to read only media such as CD-ROMs and DVDs, you need to create the index file from PDFs stored on your hard drive. After the index file is created, copy the index file, the supporting files, and the PDFs to your media and burn the disc.

When you want to search an index, you can activate the index in the Index selection dialog box and invoke a search whether your external media is mounted and accessible or not. The search index returns results from the index .pdx file and the .idx files without looking at the PDFs that were indexed. You can examine the results of the search in the Search pane and find the files where the search criteria match the PDF documents in the index collection.

If you want to open the link to the PDF document where a result is reported, you need to have the media mounted and accessible. If a network server or other computer contains the related files, the server/computer must be shared with appropriate permissions and visible on your desktop. If you use external media storage devices, the media must be mounted and visible on your desktop in order to view the PDFs linked to the search results. If you attempt to view a document when the device is not mounted, Acrobat opens an error dialog box.

If you see an error dialog box, click OK in the dialog box and insert your media, connect an external hard drive, or access a computer or network server. You don't need to quit Acrobat to make your device accessible. Wait until the media is mounted and then click a search result. Acrobat opens the linked page and you're ready to continue your search.

A search index file created on one computer can be moved or copied to another computer. To copy an index file to another computer, be certain you copy the index file (.pdx) and all supporting files in the folder created by Catalog. Be certain you maintain the same relative directory path for the index file and the supporting files. If an index file appears in a root folder and the supporting files appear in a nested folder, copy the root folder to other media. If you place the index file in the same folder as the supporting files, copy the single folder containing all files to your media.

You can load the index file and external media on another computer and perform the same searches as were performed where the index file was created. When distributing CD-ROMs and DVDs you can copy these index files to your media and all users can access the index files. If you access an index file on a network server and the PDF collection is stored on an external device such as a CD-ROM, you cannot open files from another computer unless the CD-ROM is mounted. You may see your network server, but the associated devices with the server need to be individually mounted in order to open PDF files remotely.

Summary

✦ Acrobat 7 includes a Find toolbar used for searching the current active document.

✦ Searching PDF files occurs in the Search pane. When a search is requested, the Search pane appears in the How To window.

✦ The Search pane enables basic and advanced searches.

✦ Basic searches are used to search open PDF files but provide more options than the Find command.

✦ Advanced searches enable searching multiple PDFs locally, on external media, and across networks with the use of a search index file.

✦ Acrobat viewers 6.0 and greater support searching content of Bookmarks and comments through advanced searches and index file searches. Acrobat 7.0 supports searching file attachments.

✦ Searches for PDFs on the Internet can be accessed from within Acrobat with a one-click operation that launches a Web browser and searches the Yahoo (www.yahoo.com) Web site for PDF files.

✦ Searches can be made with a variety of options, including Boolean queries, without the use of an index file.

✦ Search index files are created in Acrobat Catalog in Acrobat Professional only. Searching index files returns results for large collections of PDFs much faster than basic and advanced searches.

✦ Document descriptions can be searched with advanced searches and via index file searches.

✦ Index files can be built, rebuilt, and purged with Acrobat Catalog. Old index files created with PDF formats earlier than version 6.0 need to be rebuilt with Acrobat Catalog. Acrobat Catalog 7.0 index files are backward-compatible with Acrobat 6.0.

✦ Tags, XML data, and object data can be searched with advanced searches and from index searches.

✦ Index files can be copied to other computers, network servers, and external media storage units. When copying search indexes, you need to duplicate all supporting files and the relative directory path(s) on the destination units.

✦   ✦   ✦

Converting Documents to PDF

Converting to PDF from Adobe Acrobat Professional

✦   ✦   ✦   ✦

In This Chapter

Setting up the environment

Understanding PDF creation process

Converting files to PDF

Using Document templates

Converting Web pages to PDF

Converting clipboard data

✦   ✦   ✦   ✦

Unlike almost every other computer program, Acrobat does not contain a menu option for creating a new file. Acrobat was never intended for use as an original authoring program. Where Acrobat begins is with file conversion to the PDF format. Users start with a document authored in another program and the resulting document is converted to PDF using tools either from within Acrobat or from tools or commands within programs that support PDF conversion from native documents.

With Acrobat Standard and Acrobat Professional, the number of methods you can employ for converting documents to PDF is enormous. Any program file can be converted to PDF through a number of different methods offered by Acrobat, operating systems, and many different authoring applications. The method you use to convert a document to PDF and the purpose for which the PDF is intended require you to become familiar with a number of different options at your disposal for PDF file conversion. This chapter begins a new part of the book entirely devoted to PDF creation. In this chapter you learn basic PDF conversion methods available in Acrobat Professional and Acrobat Standard. The following chapters in this part cover more advanced PDF creation methods.

Setting Up the PDF Creation Environment

You create PDF documents from within Acrobat with default tools and with menu commands. To regain the default toolbars, open a context menu on the Toolbar Well and select Reset Toolbars from the menu commands or press Alt/Option+F8.

If you intend to edit documents after PDF creation, you need to open toolbars specific to your editing session. Depending on the type of edits you anticipate, open toolbars as needed after you finish converting files to PDF.

Understanding How PDFs Are Created

You can use Acrobat Professional or Acrobat Standard to open various file formats in the viewer; the files are immediately converted to PDF. You can also print a file to the Adobe PDF printer, installed with your viewer, from just about any authoring program, and the native document is converted to PDF. It all sounds like simple stuff, but two very important distinctions exist between these methods of conversion for certain file types that you need to understand before you start converting files to PDF. Quite simply, opening some files in Acrobat Professional or Acrobat Standard does not involve any intervention from companion programs. On the other hand, using some file formats and using the Adobe PDF printer requires some help from the Acrobat Distiller software. To understand the fundamentals of document conversion you need to know a little bit about Acrobat Distiller.

Cross-Reference   Acrobat Distiller is thoroughly covered in Chapter 8, where you'll find information on setting all the options Distiller offers you.

Acrobat Distiller accepts either a PostScript file or an Encapsulated PostScript (EPS) file that it processes to produce a PDF document. Through the processing mechanism, Distiller applies different options during conversion. These options can include image sampling, font handling, color control, PDF format compatibility assignment, document encryption, hypertext linking, and a host of other settings. Each of the settings is designed to produce PDF files for different purposes. Because so many different options can be applied to PDF conversion via the Distiller software, Distiller provides you the capability to save an assortment of specific settings to individual Adobe PDF Settings files. When you save the files to a specific location on your hard drive you can access them from a pull-down menu in Acrobat Distiller or from within authoring programs where Adobe PDF Settings are used.

Note   Adobe PDF Settings was referred to as Job Options prior to Acrobat 6.

In addition to custom settings you can save to Adobe PDF Settings files, Acrobat Distiller, when installed with Acrobat Professional, has nine settings, and Acrobat Standard has four settings. When you create a PDF file that calls upon Distiller to produce the PDF document, the Adobe PDF Settings last used by Distiller control the options for your resulting PDF document. The danger here is that if you intend to have a file created for printing, for example, and the settings are optimized for screen viewing, you wind up with a PDF document that won't be suitable for printing. Therefore, it is imperative that you know what settings are applied to PDFs created with the Acrobat Distiller software.

Prior to the conversion process you'll have an opportunity to make a choice for the Adobe PDF Settings that are applied during distillation. These choices may or may not be available depending on the type of files you convert to PDF. If access to the Adobe PDF settings are not made available when you convert to PDF, the default settings in Acrobat Distiller are used. You need to be certain you open Acrobat Distiller and change the defaults when conversion of a particular file type does not open Acrobat Distiller. Regardless of where you access the settings choices, the same options are always available. Without having saved any custom settings, the defaults appear as shown in Figure 6-1.

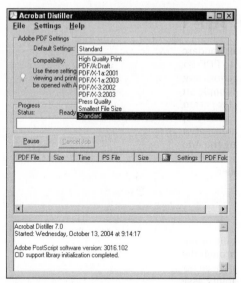

Figure 6-1: The default Adobe PDF Settings are selectable from a pull-down menu in the Acrobat Distiller window in Acrobat Professional. Acrobat Standard does not have PDF/X and PDF/A options.

Cross-Reference For a complete description of the Adobe PDF Settings, see Chapter 8.

In this chapter you look at using the High Quality, Press Quality, Smallest File Size, and Standard settings. Without an elaborate definition of these settings, for the purposes of this chapter, think of High Quality for business office printing, Press Quality as suited for commercial printing. Smallest File Size is suited for Web hosting and screen viewing, and the Standard settings are used for everything else.

Converting Native Documents to PDF

Many authoring programs offer you methods for converting to PDF, such as exporting or saving to PDF directly, or using a utility installed with Acrobat that supports certain authoring programs. However, when these methods are not available you can use the Print command in your authoring program to produce a PDF document. Virtually any document created in an authoring program that allows printing can be converted to PDF through the use of the Adobe PDF printer (Windows and Mac OS X.2 and above).

You access the Adobe PDF printer in the application Print dialog box. Rather than print a file to a printer, you print your file to disk. During this process the file is temporarily saved as a PostScript file and the PostScript is distilled in Acrobat Distiller. The Adobe PDF Settings assigned to Distiller control the attributes of the resulting PDF file. The process is relatively the same on both Windows and Macintosh platforms, but initial printer selection and dialog box selections vary a little.

Adobe PDF printer (Windows)

When you install Acrobat Professional or Acrobat Standard, the Adobe PDF printer is installed in your Printers folder. As a printer driver, the file is accessible from any program capable of printing, including your computer accessories and utilities. Like any other printer you install on Windows 2000, NT, or XP, you can set the Adobe PDF printer as the default printer. Once set as the default printer, you don't need to make a printer selection each time you want to create a PDF document.

Note　　　You may also have the Acrobat Distiller printer installed in your Printer's folder. The features associated with the Adobe PDF printer and the Acrobat Distiller printer are identical.

To convert any application document to PDF, choose File ⇨ Print or access the Print dialog box with the menu command in your authoring program. Some dedicated vertical market programs, such as accounting and other office programs, may have print commands located in menus other than the File menu. When you arrive at the Print dialog box, the various printer drivers installed on your computer are shown. Select the Adobe PDF printer in the Print window as shown in Figure 6-2.

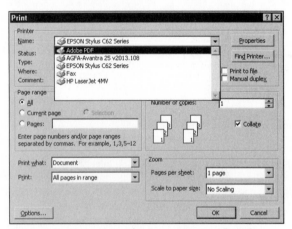

Figure 6-2: From any authoring program, select the Print command, select the Adobe PDF printer, and click OK to convert the open document to a PDF file.

Before printing to the Adobe PDF printer, check your output options by clicking the Preferences button. In Windows 2000 and earlier, you will see Properties appear in the Print dialog box. If you see Properties, click the Properties button. The Adobe PDF Printing Preferences dialog box opens as shown in Figure 6-3. In this dialog box you choose options for the resulting PDF document. Click the Adobe PDF Settings tab to choose the PDF options.

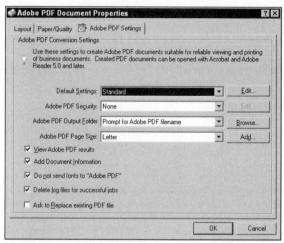

Figure 6-3: Set your PDF options in the Adobe PDF Printing Preferences dialog box in the Adobe PDF Settings pane.

Choices you can make about the PDF file and handling the PDF conversion are contained in the Adobe PDF Settings window. Items you'll want to control include

✦ **Default Settings:** This item relates to the discussion in the previous section concerning the Acrobat Distiller Adobe PDF Settings. The choices you have from the pull-down menu are the same nine preset choices (Acrobat Professional) or four choices (Acrobat Standard) provided with your Acrobat installation and any custom settings, if you've created them. It's important to make the proper choice for the options you want. When you print to the Adobe PDF printer, Acrobat Distiller is used in the background and applies the settings you specify in this dialog box.

Cross-Reference

For a better understanding of Adobe PDF Settings, see Chapter 8.

✦ **Adobe PDF Security:** If you want to password-protect your document, you can apply security settings at the time the PDF is created. Choose the security options from the choices in the pull-down menu. The default choice for None results in PDF documents created without any password protection.

Cross-Reference

To learn how to apply password protection to PDF documents, see Chapter 21.

✦ **Adobe PDF Output Folder:** Choose to save PDF files to a fixed folder and directory path or be prompted for a filename and directory path for the saved file.

✦ **Adobe PDF Page Size:** A pull-down menu offers an extensive list of page sizes derived from the printer driver and not the PPD (PostScript Printer Description file) for your printer. If you don't have a custom size that matches your document page, click the Add Custom Page button adjacent to the pull-down menu. The Add Custom Paper Size dialog box opens where you make choices for the custom page size and to add the new page option in the pull-down menu, as shown in Figure 6-4.

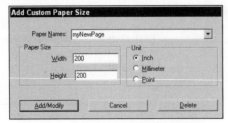

Figure 6-4: The Add Custom Paper Size dialog box enables you to create a page size up to 200 × 200 inches.

Acrobat accepts sizes up to 200 × 200 inches (5,080 × 5,080 millimeters/14,400 × 14,400 points). Enter your new custom page size in the units of measure desired and click the Add/Modify button. Your new page size is added to the Adobe PDF Page Size pull-down menu and selected for you after you click the Add/Modify button. If you want to delete a page after it has been created, click Add Custom Page in the Printing Preferences dialog box and select the page you want to delete from the Add Custom Paper Size dialog box. Click the Delete button and the page is deleted from both pull-down menus. Clicking Cancel (or pressing the Esc key) in the dialog box returns you to the Adobe PDF Document Properties dialog box without affecting any changes.

✦ **View Adobe PDF Results:** When the check box is enabled, the resulting PDF document opens in the Acrobat Document pane. If Acrobat is not open, the program launches after the PDF is created.

✦ **Add Document Information:** If the check box is enabled, a dialog box opens where you are prompted for a Document Description. You add data for the Title, Author, Subject, and Keywords fields in the dialog box. This information is added to the Document Description at the time the PDF is created. If you don't want to add a Document Description, disable the check box and the PDF file is created with the Title field containing the filename of your authoring document and the Author field containing the name derived from your logon name when you sign on to your computer.

For more information on document descriptions, see Chapter 5.

✦ **Do not send fonts to "Adobe PDF":** When this option is enabled, the fonts used in the current document are sent to Distiller for font embedding. If the Adobe PDF Settings are established for font embedding, the fonts are embedded from the fonts sent to the Adobe PDF printer. If the check box is disabled, the fonts are not sent to the printer. Disable this check box as a matter of practice. If fonts are to be embedded, Distiller has its own means of font management, and sending the fonts to Distiller from the Adobe PDF printer is not necessary. If the Adobe PDF Settings are disabled for font management, the fonts are not embedded regardless of whether they are sent or not.

For more information on font management and font embedding, see Chapter 7.

✦ **Delete log files for successful jobs:** During PDF creation the processing information is written to a log file in the form of ASCII text. You can open the log file in any text editor and review the steps used to produce the PDF. Each time a PDF is successfully created, the log file is deleted. In the event you want to review the PDF creation process logged in the text file, disable the check box and open the log file in a text editor.

✦ **Ask to Replace existing PDF file:** If you elect to not have Acrobat prompt you for a filename, the PDF file is created using the authoring document filename. If you make changes in the document and want to create a new PDF document, the second creation overwrites the first file if the check box is disabled. If you're creating different versions of PDF files and want to have them all saved to disk, be certain to enable the check box.

After you review all the options in the Adobe PDF Document Properties dialog box, click OK. You are returned to the Print dialog box and are ready to create the PDF document. Click Print in the dialog box and the PDF is produced with the options you chose in the Adobe PDF Settings dialog box. If the check box was enabled for View Adobe PDF results, the PDF opens in Acrobat.

Because this method of PDF creation uses a printer driver, you can create a PDF document from virtually any application program. The only requirement is that the program is capable of printing. If you use programs such as Microsoft Office, other Adobe programs, certain CAD drawing programs, high-end imaging programs, or a host of other applications, you may have other methods for creating PDF documents depending on the level of PDF support for the program. It is important to understand when to use the Adobe PDF printer and other methods available to you from different applications. Before you integrate using the Adobe PDF printer into your workflow, be certain to review the next two chapters because they discuss other options for creating PDF documents.

Adobe PDF (Macintosh OS X)

Mac OS X and Adobe PDF are married at the operating system level and you can find several ways to convert your authoring files to the PDF format. The Acrobat-supported method uses the same type of printer driver you find on Windows. From any authoring program, select the Print command (most commonly accessed by choosing File ⇨ Print). When the Print dialog box opens, select Adobe PDF from the Printer pull-down menu. From the default selection for Copies and Pages, open the pull-down menu and select PDF Options as shown in Figure 6-5.

The dialog box changes so that you can access Adobe PDF Settings from a pull-down menu, as shown in Figure 6-6. The default selection is Use Default. If you leave this option active, the most recent settings selected in the Distiller application are used to produce the PDF file. The remaining options are the same as those discussed for Windows users. When you add new custom settings, they appear in the Adobe PDF Settings pull-down menus from the Print dialog boxes on Windows and Macintosh operating systems.

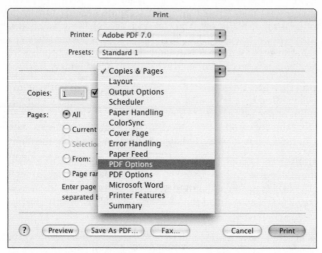

Figure 6-5: PDF Options settings are available after you select the PDF Options pull-down menu command.

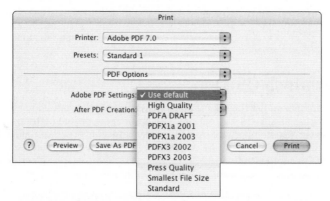

Figure 6-6: Select the Adobe PDF Settings option from the Adobe PDF Settings pull-down menu. All the presets and custom settings are listed in the menu options.

Another setting for viewing the PDF file appears in the pull-down menu: After PDF Creation. You can choose to view your PDF in the default Acrobat viewer or leave the default at Launch Nothing, which allows you to go about your work and view the PDFs later. After you choose the settings, click the Print button to convert the file to PDF using the Adobe PDF Settings you selected from the menu choices.

If you select Output Options instead of PDF Options in the Print dialog box, you see a check box for Save as PDF. Checking this option also creates a PDF file, but the PDF creation is not an Adobe-based PDF creation method. This check box appears in a generic installation of Mac OS X, and creating a PDF this way is supported by the operating system without the use of

Acrobat Distiller. When you use Save As PDF, the PDF is created using the native Mac OS X PDF creation tools, which provide high-quality PDF creation of non-prepress documents. The PDF documents created using this method will work fine for office uses; however, they will be significantly larger than those created by Adobe Acrobat.

 Cross-Reference For more information on PostScript and creating PostScript files, see Chapter 8.

Save As PDF was designed by Apple to provide users with a PDF version of a document to send to people across the Internet for screen viewing and printing. As a matter of practice, using the Adobe PDF printer is your best choice for creating PDFs suited for purposes other than screen displays.

Creating PDFs from Files

Acrobat 5.0 introduced a menu command called Open as Adobe PDF. The menu option enabled you to open files from certain file formats within Acrobat and convert the document to PDF on-the-fly. In Acrobat 6, the Open as Adobe PDF command was replaced with the Create PDF tool appearing in the Tasks toolbar or by choosing File ⇨ Create PDF, and it continues to be the same in Acrobat 7. In addition, you can use another menu command to achieve similar results for file conversion from within Acrobat. Click the Open tool or choose File ⇨ Open to open files saved in a variety of formats. Using any of these tools opens the file in Acrobat and converts it to PDF. The documents open as untitled documents and need to be saved from Acrobat if you want to keep them around as PDFs.

The Create PDF tool Task Button pull-down menu offers several different options for PDF creation as shown in Figure 6-7. You use the first two menu options, From File and From Multiple Files, to convert files saved from authoring documents to the PDF format. Converting to PDF with either of these commands requires you to access files supported by Acrobat's Create PDF option. Although the number of file formats supported by Acrobat through the internal conversion process is greatly expanded in version 7.0, not all files can be converted with the Create PDF tool or menu option.

Figure 6-7: The Create PDF Task Button offers several different options for PDF file creation from within Acrobat.

Supported file formats

To convert files to PDF from within Acrobat you first need to understand all the formats that are supported. You can try to convert any file format to PDF with the Create PDF tool. If the file format is supported, the document is converted to PDF and opens in Acrobat. If the format is not supported, a dialog box opens informing you the format is not supported. It won't hurt to try, but knowing ahead of time what formats are supported is better.

Each file format that is acceptable to Acrobat can also have conversion settings defined by you. Options for the conversion settings are the same as you have available with the Adobe PDF printer, as discussed earlier in this chapter, and they're accessible in the Preferences dialog box. Before you begin converting files to PDF with the Create PDF tool, be certain to choose Edit ⇨ Preferences (Windows) or Acrobat ⇨ Preferences (Macintosh) or use (Ctrl/⌘+K) and click the Convert To PDF item in the left pane. On the right side of the Preferences dialog box you'll see a list of supported file formats, as shown in Figure 6-8.

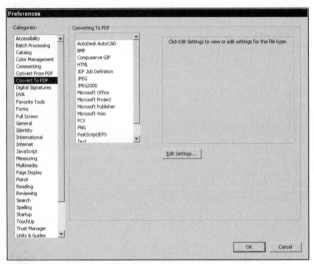

Figure 6-8: When using the Create PDF tool. you assign PDF Settings to different file formats in the Convert To PDF preferences.

The file formats that are supported by Acrobat include

✦ **Autodesk AutoCAD:** Autodesk's AutoCAD files can be opened in Acrobat directly. Layered files are preserved and opened with data on different layers when layer data are created in the AutoCAD file. AutoCAD is also supported with the PDFMaker utility, which installs Acrobat tools and menu options in the authoring application at the time you install Acrobat.

✦ **BMP:** Bitmap is a file format that can be saved from many image editing programs. Bitmap is also commonly referred to as a color mode in Photoshop. As a color mode, the file can be saved in other file formats. For example, a 1-bit bitmap image can be saved as a TIFF formatted file. In regard to Acrobat, the bitmap file format that is capable of rendering images in 1-bit, 4-bit, 8-bit, and 24-bit color depths can be opened as PDF. Furthermore a bitmap color mode saved as any of the compatible formats listed here can also be opened as a PDF.

✦ **Compuserve GIF:** CompuServe's Graphic Interchange Format (GIF) was developed years ago to port image files to and from mainframes and microcomputers. It remains a popular format for Web graphics, and the later version of GIF89a supports interlacing. If using Photoshop, you can either save in the CompuServe GIF87 format or use Photoshop's Save for Web command and choose the GIF89a format. Regardless of what format is used, Acrobat can import either as a PDF.

✦ **HTML:** Hypertext Markup Language files are documents written in HTML for Web pages. You can open any HTML file and the file and file links convert to PDF. Clicking an HTML link in a converted file in Acrobat appends the linked file to the open document.

✦ **JDF Job Definition:** You find JDF files in prepress workflows. The resultant PDF produces a standardized XML-based job ticket with information about the file for commercial printing uses, such as page size, crop and bleed areas, trapping, colorspace, and so on.

✦ **JPEG:** Joint Photographic Experts Group (JPEG) images are also used for Web graphics and file exchanges on the Internet. JPEG compression is a lossy compression scheme that can degrade images rapidly when they are compressed at high levels. These files are already compressed. Adding further compression with the PDF conversion options won't compress files smaller than the original compression. Inasmuch as the Settings button is active in the Open dialog box, you can't actually get more compression out of the file when converting to PDF.

✦ **JPEG2000:** JPEG2000 is a newer compression scheme that offers a lossless option for compressing images. You can use JPEG2000 with lossless compression for the most discriminating quality required in high-end printing.

✦ **Microsoft Access:** The PDFMaker utility or tool is installed in Access and permits you to export databases directly to PDF. Support for Microsoft Access was added with the introduction of Acrobat 7.

✦ **Microsoft Office:** Microsoft Office files are from the office programs of Word, Excel, and PowerPoint. These programs also include installation of PDFMaker, which installs tools and menu options in the authoring applications at the time you install Acrobat, as mentioned in the AutoCAD bullet.

✦ **Microsoft Publisher:** Publisher has been added to the list of supported formats with the introduction of Acrobat 7. The PDFMaker is made available to Publisher.

✦ **Microsoft Visio and Microsoft Project:** These programs also use PDFMaker. Microsoft Visio files with layers can be converted to PDF with the layers intact.

✦ **PCX:** PCX files are native to the PC and were commonly used as an extension for PC Paintbrush. Adobe Photoshop can export in PCX format, but today it is rarely used for any kind of image representation. The advantage you have in opening PCX files in Acrobat is when converting legacy files saved in this format. Rather than your having to do a two-step operation of opening a PCX file in an image editor and saving in a more common format for file conversions, Acrobat can import the files directly.

✦ **PICT (Macintosh only):** The native Apple Macintosh equivalent to PCX (preceding bullet) is PICT (Picture). Photoshop supports PICT file exchanges in both opening and saving. However, Acrobat only supports the format for conversion to PDF via the From File or From Multiple Files commands.

✦ **PNG:** Portable Network Graphics (PNG—pronounced ping) is a format enabling you to save 24-bit color images without compression. The format was designed for Web use and is becoming more popular among Web designers. Older Web browsers need a special plug-in in order to view the images, which has slowed its wide acceptance. Interestingly enough, PNG images are saved from image editors without compression, yet Acrobat can apply image compression when converting to PDF. You can use all the compression options in the Adobe DF Settings dialog box with PNG images to reduce file sizes.

✦ **PostScript/EPS:** PostScript and EPS files were formerly converted only with Acrobat Distiller. In Acrobat 7 you can open the files in Acrobat using the Create PDF tool and Distiller works in the background, handling the conversion to PDF.

✦ **Text:** Text listed in the Convert to PDF preferences relates to plain text files. Unformatted text from word processors, text editors, and any file saved in a text-only format can be opened in Acrobat.

✦ **TIFF:** Tagged Image File Format (TIFF) is by far the most popular format among the print people regardless of platform. TIFF files originate from image editors and scans. When scanning text you can save it as a TIFF, import the file in Acrobat, then convert the image file to rich text with Recognize Text Using (OCR formerly known as Paper Capture).

For more information on the Recognize Text Using OCR feature, see Chapter 13.

Applying settings

Many of the file formats supported by Acrobat can have PDF Options or other settings applied during conversion. These settings are available to all formats except Compuserve GIF, HTML, JDF Job Definition, JPEG2000, Text, and XML PDF. Depending on the file type to be created, you can edit the settings and apply some different options. You edit settings by selecting a file type from those listed in the Preferences dialog box shown in Figure 6-8 and clicking the Edit Settings button. If the settings cannot be adjusted, the Edit Settings button is grayed out.

Settings options for the different file formats include:

✦ **Autodesk AutoCAD/Microsoft Project/PostScript/EPS:** The same settings are available for these file types. Click the Edit Settings button after selecting a file type to open the Adobe PDF Settings dialog box shown in Figure 6-9.

Figure 6-9: The Adobe PDF Settings dialog box offers options for files using PDFMaker and PostScript files.

The Adobe PDF Settings enable you to make selections for the settings applied to Distiller during PDF file creation. These settings are the same as those you can access with the Adobe PDF Printer discussed earlier in this chapter. Adjacent to the pull-down menu for the Adobe PDF Settings is the Edit button. Clicking this button opens the Adobe PDF Settings dialog box where you can edit custom settings and save them as a new setting preference. The options in this dialog box are the same as you find when editing settings in Acrobat Distiller. Users of earlier versions of Acrobat can think of the Edit button as a way to open the Job Options dialog box.

Cross-Reference

For information on adjusting the Adobe PDF Settings, see Chapter 8.

The Adobe PDF Security pull-down menu offers options for adding password protection at the time the PDF file is created. By default, no security is added to PDFs converted from these file types. You have choices for using *None* for adding no security; *Reconfirm Security for each PDF,* which opens a confirmation dialog box after each file is converted to PDF; and a third option for *Use the last known security settings,* which uses the current default Adobe PDF settings for each file converted. Adjacent to the pull-down menu is the Edit button. Clicking this button opens the Acrobat Distiller – Security dialog box where you can further edit security options. Be aware that the first Edit button specifically handles the Adobe PDF Settings and the second Edit button handles the security options.

When you click OK in the Adobe PDF Settings dialog box, any new settings you added become new defaults. Every time you open one of these file formats in Acrobat the same settings are applied until you edit them again.

✦ **BMP/JPEG/PCX/PNG/PICT (Macintosh only)/TIFF:** These file formats all use identical settings. Whereas many other file formats use the Acrobat Distiller application in the background and have Adobe PDF Settings applied during file conversion, these image file formats don't use Distiller and no Adobe PDF Settings are applied during file conversion. Different conversion settings can be applied from the same options lists to each of the file types individually. Therefore, a BMP file, for example, can be converted with one level of image compression and a TIFF file can be converted with another level of compression.

All of these file formats are image formats and the types of settings you apply to them relate to image options, such as file compression and color management. The same set of options available from pull-down menus exists for all the different color modes listed in the Adobe PDF Settings dialog box shown in Figure 6-10.

Figure 6-10: Adobe PDF Settings for image files are available for file compression and color management.

Note

Inasmuch as the Adobe PDF Settings dialog box appears the same for all image formats, some options may be grayed out depending on the type of file to be converted. For example,

TIFF images can have compression applied during PDF conversion, while JPEG images cannot. Therefore, the compression options for JPEG images are grayed out.

The top of the Adobe PDF Settings dialog box offers you options for file compression for monochrome (black-and-white line art), grayscale, and color images. The compression options you can select for each of these color modes include

- **CCITT G4:** CCITT Group 4 compression is only available for monochrome images. This compression scheme, similar to the compression used by fax machines, works best for black-and-white images and results in smaller file sizes without data loss.

- **JBIG2 (Lossless):** JBIG2 is a newer compression scheme for bi-level (black-and-white) images. It offers as much as three to five times the compression as Group 4 compression and is supported in earlier versions of Adobe Reader and all viewers 6.0 and greater. The compression algorithm is lossless and stores images with no perceptible loss of image clarity even when magnified more than 15×.

- **JBIG2 (Lossy):** This compression scheme also offers higher compression than Group 4 and JBIG2 Lossless. As a lossy compression scheme data loss does occur and artifacts are noticeable when you zoom in on PDF files in higher zoom levels.

- **JPEG (Quality: Low/Medium/High/Maximum):** For grayscale and color images you can select from several compression options to specify the acceptable amount of data loss. Medium is sufficient for almost any kind of desktop printing and low-end output. High and Maximum are more suited for high-end printing and digital prepress. Use JPEG for files that need to be exchanged with users of Acrobat versions below 6.0.

- **JPEG2000 (Quality: Minimum/Low/Medium/High/Maximum):** JBIG2000 is a newer compression scheme that offers much better compression and image quality than JPEG. For the amount of compression to be applied, select from the Quality settings for Minimum, Low, Medium, High, and Maximum. High and Maximum settings result in very little data loss that can be visibly seen in printed documents and high magnification levels onscreen. Medium is sufficient for any kind of desktop printing, and the minimum and low compression levels are more suited to screen displays. Use JPEG2000 compression when exchanging files with users of Acrobat 6.0 and later.

- **JPEG2000 (Quality: Lossless):** JBIG2000 lossless offers the most compression without data loss for grayscale and color images.

- **Zip:** Zip compression is a lossless compression scheme. It works best where you have large areas of a common color; for example, a background with one color and a few foreground images with different colors.

The lower section of the Adobe PDF Settings dialog box handles Color Management. You have choices for three color modes: RGB, CMYK, and Grayscale. The Other option at the bottom of the dialog box handles special color considerations such as spot colors you might find in duotones, tritones, and quadtones.

Cross-Reference
For more information on color management and understanding different color modes, see Chapter 25.

The color management polices you can apply to each color mode are identical and they all include options from one of three choices:

- **Preserve embedded profiles:** If you work with images that have been assigned a color profile, choosing this option preserves the profile embedded in the document. Theoretically, no color changes occur when porting the files across platforms and devices.

- **Off:** If a color profile is embedded in an image, the profile is discarded.

- **Ask when opening:** If you select this option, Acrobat prompts you in a dialog box to use the embedded profile or discard it. You can make individual selections as you open files.

✦ **Microsoft Office:** The Microsoft Office options contain the same option choices you have for Adobe PDF Settings and Adobe PDF Security as found with the AutoCAD, PostScript/EPS, Microsoft Project, and Microsoft Visio settings listed earlier. In addition you have options for enabling accessibility, adding Bookmarks from style sheets, and converting an Excel workbook, as shown in Figure 6-11. These options apply to Microsoft Office applications, Microsoft Project, and Microsoft Visio files.

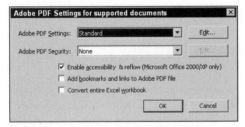

Figure 6-11: Settings for Microsoft Office applications include options for enabling accessibility and converting heads and styles to Bookmarks.

Cross-Reference

Specific uses for enabling accessibility and adding Bookmarks and links to PDFs from Microsoft Office applications are covered in Chapter 7 and Chapter 18.

After making choices for the options you want to use for file conversions, click the OK button in the Preferences dialog box. All the settings are set as new defaults until you change them. These settings are applied to documents you import from a file, from multiple files, and when you use the Open command in Acrobat.

Converting multiple files to PDF

The pull-down menu for the Create PDF Task Button or menu command (File ⇨ Create PDF) contains submenu commands for importing a single file or multiple files in Acrobat. If you want to open one file, use the From File command. You can also open multiple files from the same menu command and have each file converted to PDF in separate documents. When you select Create PDF From Multiple Files, Acrobat concatenates all files into a single PDF document. Either command enables you to import files saved in any of the formats acceptable to the Create PDF command. Therefore you could, for example, import a TIF, BMP, and PDF document (which are the file formats listed on the preceding pages) with either command. When From File is used, the TIF and BMP files are converted to PDF in separate windows and the PDF file opens as it would open with the Open menu command. When you use the From Multiple Files command, the TIF, BMP, and PDF files open in a single PDF document. In essence, the TIF and BMP files are converted to PDF and appended to the PDF document.

Converting to PDF from file

 To convert files to PDF, select the menu option from the Create PDF Task Button pull-down menu and choose From File, or choose File ⇨ Create PDF ⇨ From File. Either of these commands enables you to convert the acceptable file format to PDF. Acrobat opens the Open dialog box where you select the directory and file to be imported. You can make several choices from the Files of type (Windows) or Show (Macintosh) pull-down menu for file type. If you select All Files (*.*) (Windows) or All Files (Macintosh), all files within a directory are displayed in the list in the Open dialog box, shown in Figure 6-12. You can select one or more files to open, but be certain that the file types are supported by Acrobat.

Note You can also convert files using the Open tool, the File ⇨ Open command, and by dragging and dropping files on the Acrobat window, program icon, and an alias of the program icon.

Figure 6-12: From the File of type pull-down menu select the file type to be imported or select All Files (*.*) to view all files within a directory.

Caution You must have the original authoring program installed on your computer when using Acrobat to convert file types that were saved from authoring programs such as Microsoft Office, AutoCAD, and all other similar programs. If you do not have an original authoring program installed, Acrobat won't convert the file.

If you want to open a single file and you know the file type, you have an advantage when you select the file format from the Files of type pull-down menu. If, for example, you want to open a TIFF file, select TIFF (*.tif, .tiff) from the menu options. When you select the file format, the Settings button becomes active. If you want to override the preferences you set for file conversion options, you can access the settings from the Open dialog box. When you select All Files (*.*), the Settings button is grayed out.

For multiple file selection when using the From File command, click a filename in the Open dialog box, hold down the Shift key, and click the next file to be converted. All files between the selected two in a contiguous group are selected. If you want to select files at random in a non-contiguous group, click to select the first file and Ctrl/⌘+click to select subsequent files.

Click the Open button and Acrobat converts the files you selected in the Open dialog box. The files are opened as separate documents in the Document pane. If you want to toggle through the views of the documents, use the Window menu and select the file you want to bring forward.

If a PDF file is open and you close the file without editing, the file is treated like any other PDF document you open with the File ⇨ Open command or by clicking the Open tool in the File toolbar. Acrobat converts all other file types to PDF, but they are not yet saved. When you close a file after converting it to PDF, Acrobat prompts you to save the file. If you elect to not save the file, the file remains in its original format undisturbed. If you save the file, you can save as PDF or as a new file, choosing from many other file formats supported by Acrobat and again leave the original file undisturbed.

Converting to a single PDF from multiple files

Select From Multiple Files from the menu commands in either the Create PDF pull-down menu or the File ⇨ Create PDF submenu to open the Create PDF from Multiple Documents dialog box, as shown in Figure 6-13. You add files to the list in the Files to Combine window. The order displayed in the window is the same order in which the files are concatenated into a single document. The top file in the list is added at the front of the PDF and the following files are added in successive order. To add a file to the list, click the Browse button. You can browse your hard drive or network to add files to the list. Files can be collected from multiple directories, hard drives, external media, networked servers, and workstations.

If you want to remove a file from the list, select the file in the list and click the Remove button. Reorder files by selecting them in the list and clicking the Move Up and Move Down buttons.

At the bottom of the Create PDF from Multiple Files dialog box you'll find a check box and a pull-down menu. The *Include all open PDF documents* item adds any open files in Acrobat to the list in the Files to Combine window. When the check box is enabled, all open files appear in the list. If you want to remove some files, but keep some open files active in the list, select the files to be eliminated and click the Remove button. If no open files are to be added to the new file, deselect the check box.

The pull-down menu enables you to append the most recent files you combined in an Acrobat session. If you want to append files to any recently combined documents, select from the menu the file you want to append.

When you make all the selections, click the OK button to concatenate the files into a new PDF file. If you have an open file in the Document pane that's part of the group, your original file is left undisturbed and a copy of it is included in the new file appearing in the Document pane.

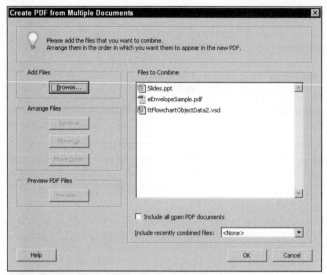

Figure 6-13: The Create PDF from Multiple Documents dialog box offers options for selecting and organizing files to be converted to PDF.

Tip

If you've previously worked with the Insert Pages command to combine PDF documents in Acrobat, you no doubt experienced much frustration over the fact that the PDF pages were imported in a different order than you viewed in your folder containing the files. Rather than use the Insert Pages command, select From Multiple Files from the Create PDF Task Button pull-down menu and organize the PDF documents in the Files to Combine window. Click OK to order the PDFs as you specified in the Create PDF from Multiple Documents dialog box. (To learn more about inserting pages, see Chapter 12.)

Drag and drop

If using the menu commands doesn't suit you, Acrobat enables you to convert all acceptable file types to PDF via drag-and-drop actions. Select one or more files from your desktop and drag them to the open Acrobat Document pane, to the status bar when Acrobat is minimized, or to the program icon when the program is either launched or closed. Files are converted to PDF as when you're using the From File command where each file is opened in a separate window.

Converting Web Pages to PDF

You use the Create PDF From Web Page menu command to convert Web pages to PDF. You can use the command or click the Create PDF From Web page tool in the File toolbar to convert Web pages hosted on Web sites or HTML files stored locally on your computer or networked servers.

Web Capture provides a complex set of preferences and tools with different options for converting Web pages, a Web site, or multiple sites to PDF. A captured Web site converts HTML, text files, and images to PDF, and each Web page is appended to the converted document. Conversion to PDF from Web sites can provide many opportunities for archiving information, analyzing data, creating search indexes, and many more uses where information needs to reside locally on computers.

Web pages containing animation such as Flash animation can be converted to PDF in either Acrobat 6 or Acrobat 7. When animated pages are captured, the animation effects are viewed in the PDF file in any Acrobat viewer.

Web site structure

To understand how to capture a Web site and convert the documents to PDF, you need a fundamental understanding of a Web page and the structure of a site. A Web page is a file created with the Hypertext Markup Language (HTML). There is nothing specific to the length of a Web page. A page may be a screen the size of 640×480 pixels or a length equivalent to several hundred letter-sized pages. Size, in terms of linear length, is usually determined by the page content and amount of space needed to display the page. PDF files, on the other hand, have fixed lengths up to 200×200 inches. You can determine the fixed size of the PDF page prior to converting the Web site from HTML to PDF. After the PDF page size is determined, any Web pages captured adhere to the fixed size. If a Web page is larger than the established PDF page, the overflow automatically creates additional PDF pages. Hence, a single converted Web page may result in several PDF pages.

Web site design typically follows a hierarchical order. The home page rests at the topmost level where direct links from this page occupy a second level. Subsequently, links from the second level refer to pages at a third level, and so forth.

When pages are captured with Acrobat, the user can specify the number of levels to convert. Be forewarned, though; even two levels of a Web site can occupy many Web pages. The number of pages and the speed of your Internet connection determine the amount of time needed to capture a site.

Captured pages structure

One or more levels can be captured from a Web site. You decide the number of levels to convert in the Create PDF from Web Page dialog box. PDF pages are converted and placed in a new PDF file or appended to an existing PDF file. One nice feature with Create PDF From Web Page is it can seek out and append only new pages that have not yet been downloaded.

After pages are converted to PDF they can be viewed in Acrobat. Any URL links on the converted Web page are preserved in the resultant PDF and can be used to append files to the PDF or open the link destinations in your Web browser. The file types that can be converted to PDF include the following:

✦ **Adobe PDF Format:** Although not converted to PDF because they already appear in the format, PDF pages can be downloaded with Create From Web Page.

✦ **FDF:** Form Data Format files can be captured and converted to PDF. An FDF file might be from data exported from a PDF form.

✦ **GIF Image Format (Graphics Interchange Format):** GIF images, as well as the last image in an animated GIF, can be captured when you convert a Web site to PDF. GIFs, like JPEGs within the HTML file, can also appear on separate PDF pages.

✦ **HTML documents:** HTML files can be converted to PDF. The hypertext links from the original HTML file are active in the PDF document as long as the destination documents and URLs have also been converted.

✦ **JPEG (Joint Photographic Experts Group) Image Format:** Images used in the HTML documents are also captured and converted to PDF. JPEGs may be part of the converted HTML page. When captured, they can be part of a captured HTML page and can also appear individually on PDF pages.

✦ **Plain Text:** Any text-only documents contained on a Web site, such as an ASCII text document, can be converted to PDF. When capturing text-only files, you have the opportunity to control many text attributes and page formats.

✦ **PNG Image Format:** Portable Network Graphics (PNG) contained in Web pages can be converted to PDF just like GIF and JPEG images.

✦ **XDP:** Forms can be saved in XDP (XML Data Package) that can be understood by an XFA plug-in. The plug-in is used with high-end forms solutions and an XML Forms plug-in.

✦ **XFDF:** XML-based FDF files typically exported from PDF forms can be converted to PDF.

✦ **Image maps:** Image maps created in HTML are converted to PDF. The links associated with the map are active in the PDF as long as the link destinations are also converted.

✦ **Password-secure areas:** A password-secure area of a Web site can also be converted to PDF. In order to access a secure site, however, you need the password(s).

Accepted file types and links

If a Web page link to another Web page or URL exists, it is preserved in the converted PDF document. Links to pages, sites, and various actions work similarly to the way they do directly on the Web site. However, if a PDF document contains a link to another PDF document, the converted file doesn't preserve the link. When the site is converted, the captured pages reside in a single PDF document. In order to maintain PDF links that open other PDF documents, the destination documents need to be captured as individual pages or extracted and saved from the converted pages.

Links to other levels are also inactive if they have not been converted during the capture. You can append individual linked pages to the converted PDF document by clicking Web links. Selections for converting individual links can be made available in a dialog box opening after clicking a Web link. You can then append one or more links to the converted document. You can find the specifics on how to accomplish this task in "Appending pages" a little later in this chapter.

For executed animation, such as an animation from a GIF file or other programming application, the download contains only the last image in the sequence. A mouseover effect that changes an image is preserved in the converted PDF document as long as you download both the original image and the image associated with the mouseover. Additionally, you can capture sounds contained in documents.

You can also convert form fields to PDF, and field types like radio buttons, check boxes, list boxes, and combo boxes often convert with the data intact. You might want to convert a form that has a list of countries and use the form field in your own PDF forms. The Acrobat implementation of JavaScript varies considerably from JavaScript written for Web pages, so many JavaScripts do not work in converted Web pages.

Cross-Reference For more information on form field types, see Chapter 27.

For Web pages that contain non-English characters, you need to have the appropriate resources loaded in order to download and convert the files. Japanese characters, for example, require installation of the Far East language files and additional system files. Using non-English characters requires you to make additional settings choices for Language Scripts. The options are available in the HTML Conversion Settings dialog box in the Fonts and Encoding tab. For making adjustments in the HTML Conversion Settings dialog box, see the section Conversion Settings later in this chapter.

Bookmarks in converted pages

After you convert a Web site to PDF, you can edit the document in Acrobat as you would any other PDF. Links to pages become editable links — that is, you can modify their properties. When a site has been converted to PDF, all the PDF pages contain Bookmarks linked to the respective pages, as shown in Figure 6-14. The first Bookmark is a regular (unstructured) Bookmark that contains the domain name from which the site was captured. All Bookmarks appearing below the server name are structured Bookmarks linked to the converted pages. With the exception of specific Web applications, you can edit these Bookmarks like any other Bookmarks created in Acrobat. Additionally, you can use structured Bookmarks for page editing by moving and deleting the Bookmarks and associated pages.

Cross-Reference For more information on Bookmarks, see Chapter 17.

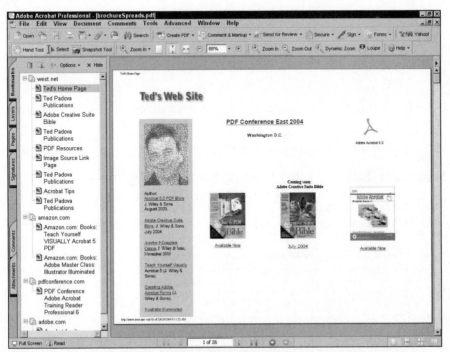

Figure 6-14: A captured Web site converted to PDF displays the domain name server as a normal Bookmark and several structured Bookmarks.

Capturing Web pages

 To begin capturing Web pages, select From Web Page in the Create PDF Task Button pull-down menu, click the Create PDF from Web Page tool, or choose File ➪ Create PDF ➪ From Web Page. The Create PDF from Web Page dialog box opens as shown in Figure 6-15.

Figure 6-15: When you select the From Web Page command, the Create PDF from Web Page dialog box opens.

In the Create PDF from Web Page dialog box, various settings determine many different attributes for how a Web page is converted to PDF and how it appears in the Acrobat Document pane. The first level of controls is handled in the Create PDF from Web Page dialog box. Additional buttons in this dialog box open other dialog boxes where you apply many more settings. If this is your first attempt at capturing a Web page, then leave the default values in the dialog box as shown in Figure 6-17 and supply a URL in the URL field box. Click the Create button and watch the page appear in Acrobat.

Caution　Be certain the Levels field box is set to 1 on your first attempt. Entering any other value may keep you waiting for some time depending on how many pages download from additional levels.

Depending on the site, the number of different links from the site to other URLs, and the structure of the HTML pages, you often need to wade through the maze of dialog boxes that control settings for the PDF conversion from the HTML files. You don't need to memorize all of these settings, but just use the following section as a reference when you capture Web pages.

Settings in the Create PDF from Web Page dialog box

The controls available to you in the Open Web Page dialog box begin with the URL you supplied in the Create PDF from Web Page dialog box when downloading the first Web page. This URL determines the site where the pages, which are converted, are hosted. After you enter the URL, the remaining selections you need to set include

✦ **Get only *x* levels:** Appended pages can contain more than one level. The URL link may go to another site hosted on another server or stay on the same server. Select the levels to be downloaded by clicking the up or down arrows or entering a numeric value in the field box.

Caution　A Web site can have two levels of extraordinary size. If the Home page is on the first level and many links are contained on the Home page, all the associated links are at the second level. If you're downloading with a slow connection, the time needed to capture the site can be quite long.

✦ **Get Entire Site:** When you select this radio button, all levels on the Web site are downloaded.

✦ **Stay on same path:** When this option is enabled, all documents are confined to the directory path under the selected URL.

✦ **Stay on same server:** Links made to other servers are not downloaded when this option is enabled.

✦ **Create:** When you're ready to convert Web pages from the site identified in the URL field box, click the Create button.

✦ **Browse:** Selecting this button enables you to capture a Web site residing on your computer or network server. Click Browse to open a navigation dialog box where you can find the directory where HTML pages are stored and capture the pages.

Although it may not be entirely practical, Web designers who are more comfortable with WYSIWYG (What You See Is What You Get) HTML editors than layout applications may find that creating layout assemblies in their favorite editor is beneficial. You can't get control over image sampling, but you can achieve a layout for screen display. Create the layout in a program such as Adobe GoLive, Microsoft FrontPage, or Macromedia DreamWeaver. When you're finished with the pages, launch Acrobat and select Create PDF from Web Page. Click the Browse button in the Create PDF from Web Page dialog box and navigate to your HTML files. Click the Create button to create your pages to PDF. You can send these pages as an e-mail attachment to a colleague or print them to your desktop printer. It may sound a little crazy, but some people just don't like to leave familiar ground.

Caution   Even though you may browse a folder on your hard drive and convert a local Web site to PDF, any external links launch your Internet connection and capture pages on another site. If you want only local pages converted, be certain to click the Stay on same server button in the Create PDF from Web Page dialog box.

Tip   An alternative to using the Create from Web Page dialog box for a single Web page stored locally on your computer is through drag and drop. Select the HTML document to convert to PDF and drag it to the top of the Acrobat window or program icon. If you have multiple HTML files to convert, you can also use the Create From Multiple Files menu command.

Cross-Reference   You can also create Web pages from tools installed by Acrobat in Microsoft Internet Explorer in Windows only. For information related to converting Web pages to PDF from within Microsoft Internet Explorer, see Chapter 22.

Conversion settings

Clicking the Settings button in the Create PDF from Web Page dialog box opens the Web Page Conversion Settings dialog box. The two tabs in it are where you supply file conversion attributes and page layout settings. The General tab deals with the file attribute settings, as shown in Figure 6-16.

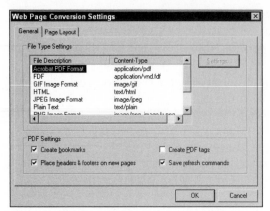

Figure 6-16: The Web Page Conversion Settings dialog box offers controls for file types and how they will be converted to PDF.

Under the File Description heading the file types are listed for those file types discussed in the "Captured pages structure" section earlier in this chapter. Select any file type in the list. Only the file types for HTML and Text offer more options, which you access by clicking the Settings button on the right side of the dialog box. If you select a file type other than HTML or Plain Text, the Settings button is grayed out. At the bottom of the dialog box are four PDF Settings check boxes that include:

✦ **Create bookmarks:** When you enable this option, pages converted to PDF have structured Bookmarks created for each page captured. The page's title is used as the Bookmark name. If the page has no title, Acrobat supplies the URL as the Bookmark name.

✦ **Place headers & footers on new pages:** A header and footer are placed on all converted pages if this option is enabled. A header in the HTML file consists of the page title appearing with the <HEAD> tag. The footer retrieves the page's URL, the page name, and a date stamp for the date and time the page was downloaded.

✦ **Create PDF tags:** The structure of the converted PDF matches that of the original HTML file. Items such as list elements, table cells, and similar HTML tags are preserved. The PDF document contains structured Bookmarks for each of the structured items. A tagged Bookmark then links to a table, list, or other HTML element.

✦ **Save refresh commands:** When this option is enabled, a list of all URLs in the converted PDF document is saved. When the capture is refreshed, these URLs are revisited and new PDF pages are converted for any new pages added to the site. If you want to append new pages to the PDF, you must enable this item for Acrobat to update the file.

If you look again at the top of the dialog box, the two items for which you can edit additional settings include HTML and Plain Text files. When you select HTML in the File Description list and click the Settings button, a dialog box opens for HTML Conversion Settings, as shown in Figure 6-17.

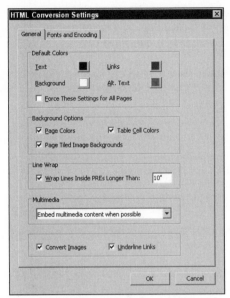

Figure 6-17: When you select HTML in the File Description list and click the Settings button, the HTML Conversion Settings dialog box opens.

The two tabs in the HTML Conversion Settings dialog box are the General tab and the Fonts and Encoding tab. The first group of settings handles the general attributes assigned to the page layout. These include

✦ **Default Colors:** Use this option to assign new default colors for Text, Background color, Links, and Alt Text. You can choose a color from a set of preset colors, or choose the option for custom colors, from a palette that opens after you click the swatch.

✦ **Force These Settings for All Pages:** HTML pages may or may not have assigned color values. When no color is assigned for one of these items this setting defines the unassigned elements with the colors set in the Default Colors section. If this check box is enabled, all colors, including HTML-assigned colors, are changed to the Default Colors.

✦ **Background Options:** These include settings for the background colors used on the Web page, tiled image backgrounds, and table cells. When these check boxes are enabled, the original design is preserved in the PDF document.

Tip If you find table cells, background colors, and tiled background images distracting when you're reading Web pages either in a browser or converted to PDF, disable the Background Options check boxes before converting to PDF. The original design is changed, but the files are easily legible for both screen reading and when printed.

✦ **Line Wrap:** Enables you to choose a maximum distance for word-wrapping the text in an HTML file. When the `<PRE>` tag is used in HTML, the text is preformatted to preserve line breaks and indents. The field box for this option enables you to control the maximum length for text lines in inches.

✦ **Multimedia:** A new feature added in Acrobat 6 and available in Acrobat 7 enables you to set options for handling multimedia clips. From the pull-down menu you can choose from three options:

- **Disable multimedia capture:** Movie and sound clips are ignored. Only the Web pages are converted to PDF and no links to the media are included in the capture.

- **Embed multimedia content when possible:** Acrobat 6 and 7 enable you to embed multimedia clips in the PDF document. Selecting this option captures the Web page and embeds any multimedia files that meet the compatibility requirements of Acrobat. Be aware that embedded multimedia files are available only to Acrobat viewers 6.0 or later.

- **Reference multimedia content by URL:** The captured Web page contains a link to the URL where the multimedia files are hosted.

For more about the new features for handling multimedia in PDF documents, see Chapter 18.

✦ **Convert Images:** If checked, graphics are converted. If unchecked the graphics are not converted.

To produce faster downloads, disable the Convert Images check box. The number of pages to be converted is significantly reduced, thereby reducing the amount of time to capture a Web site.

✦ **Underline Links:** Displays the text used in an `<A HREF...>` tag with an underline. This option can be helpful if the text for a link is not a different color than the body copy.

After you choose the General settings, click the Fonts and Encoding tab to open the Fonts and Encoding portion of the HTML Conversion Settings dialog box. The display appears as shown in Figure 6-18.

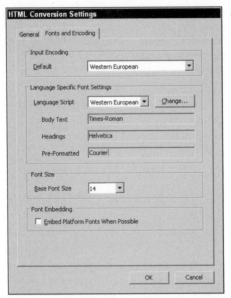

Figure 6-18: When you select the Fonts and Encoding tab in the HTML Conversion Settings dialog box, Acrobat offers options for font handling.

Options for font handling include

✦ **Input Encoding:** Sets the Web page text encoding for body text, heads, and preformatted text. The default is consistent with the language you install. Other supported languages include Chinese, Japanese, Korean, and Unicode characters.

✦ **Body Text, Headings, and Pre-Formatted text:** The items appearing under the Language Specific Font Settings section contain editable fields for changing the text encoding and fonts used for the respective items. You make global changes by clicking the Change button, which opens a dialog box for font selections as shown in Figure 6-19. You choose fonts from all the fonts installed in your system. A pull-down menu is available for body text, headings, and preformatted text. You can assign fonts individually to each item.

✦ **Base Font Size:** You choose font sizes for each of the three text items from pull-down menus or by editing the field boxes.

✦ **Embed Platform Fonts When Possible:** Fonts used to view the pages are embedded when the check box is enabled. File sizes are larger with embedded fonts, but file integrity is preserved and eliminates a need for font substitution. Embedded fonts ensure the display and print of the PDF documents precisely as seen in the Web browser.

Figure 6-19: When you click the Change button a dialog box opens where you can select a system font and point size. The chosen font appears as the new default for text from font sets listed in pull-down menus for body text, headings, and preformatted text.

After choosing all the settings for how to convert HTML files, click the OK button in the HTML Conversion Settings dialog box. The dialog box disappears and returns you to the Web Page Conversion Settings dialog box. The other file format to which you apply settings is Plain Text files. Select Plain Text in the File Description list and click the Settings button (refer to Figure 6-16). The Plain Text Conversion Settings dialog box opens, as shown in Figure 6-20.

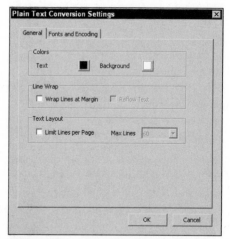

Figure 6-20: In the Web Page Conversion Settings dialog box, select Plain Text in the File Description list and click the Settings button. The Plain Text Conversion Settings dialog box opens where you apply settings for ASCII text file conversion to PDF.

Choices in this dialog box are similar to the choices available in the HTML Conversion dialog box for the Color, Font, and Line Wrap items, which were just discussed. Line Wrap behaves similarly to the Pre-Formatted text discussed earlier in the chapter. One additional item appears in this dialog box:

✦ **Text Layout:** For large bodies of text, the number of lines on the page can be user-defined. Depending on point size, the standard number of lines on an 8.5 × 11 letter-size page is 66. The default in Acrobat is 60 when the Text Layout check box is enabled. You can make a choice for the number of lines by editing the field box only after selecting the Limit Lines per Page check box.

You can also make font choices for plain text files. Click the Fonts and Encoding tab to reveal more options in the Plain Text Conversion dialog box, as shown in Figure 6-21.

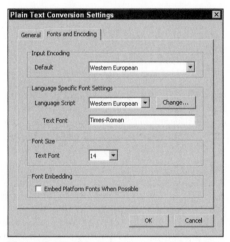

Figure 6-21: Select the Fonts and Encoding tab to apply font options for plain text conversions.

Options available in the Fonts and Encoding tab are similar to the font options you have with HTML page conversions. Make choices in this dialog box for text encoding, text font, and whether the fonts are to be embedded in the resulting PDF. After making changes in the Page Layout dialog box for Plain Text documents, click OK. Once again you return to the Web Page Conversion Settings dialog box.

Page Layout conversion settings

All the settings discussed on the previous few pages were related to the General tab. In the Web Page Conversion Settings dialog box another option is available. Page layout offers you options for describing the physical size and orientation of converted pages. Click the Page Layout tab and the Web Page Conversion Settings dialog box opens, as shown in Figure 6-22.

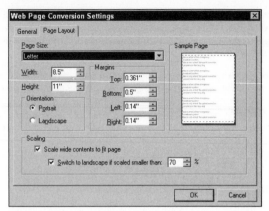

Figure 6-22: The Page Layout options are available from the Web Page Conversion Settings dialog box when you select the Page Layout tab.

Page layout attributes enable you to force long HTML pages into more standard page sizes for viewing or printing. If an HTML page spans several letter-sized pages, you can determine where the page breaks occur and the orientation of the converted pages. Many options are available in the Page Layout tab of the Web Page Conversion Settings dialog box, and they include

✦ **Page Size:** This pull-down menu provides a variety of default page sizes. Acrobat supports page sizes from 1-inch square to 200-inches square. You can supply any value between the minimum and maximum page sizes in the Width and Height field boxes below the pull-down menu to override the fixed sizes available from the pull-down menu. To make changes in the field boxes, edit the text, click the up and down arrows in the dialog box, or click in a field box and press the up and down arrow keys on your keyboard. Press Tab and Shift+Tab to toggle between the field boxes.

✦ **Margins:** In the four Margins field boxes, you can set the amount of space on all four sides of the PDF page before any data appears. You make the changes for the margin sizes via the same methods described in the preceding bullet.

✦ **Sample Page:** The thumbnail at the right side of the dialog box displays a view of the converted page when sizes are established for the Width, Height, and Margin settings.

✦ **Orientation:** You choose portrait or landscape orientation from the radio button options. If a site's Web pages all conform to screen sizes such as 640 × 480, you might want to change the orientation to landscape.

✦ **Scale wide contents to fit page:** Once again, because HTML documents don't follow standard page sizes, images and text can be easily clipped when these documents are converted to a standard size. When this option is enabled, the page contents are reduced in size to fit within the page margins.

✦ **Switch to landscape if scaled smaller than:** The percentage value is user definable. When the page contents appear on a portrait page within the limit specified in the field box, the PDF document is automatically converted to a landscape orientation. The default is 70%. If the default value is used, any vertical page scaled lower than 70% is auto-switched to landscape as long as the orientation is selected for Portrait.

If your workflow is dependent on capturing Web pages routinely, then you'll want to use the same conversion settings for all your Web captures. Educational facilities, government agencies, research institutes, and large corporate offices may have frequent needs for archiving research information found on the Web.

Unfortunately, Acrobat makes no provision for saving and loading Web Capture settings established in the dialog boxes discussed in the preceding pages. To develop a workflow suited to organizations or workgroups, your alternative may be setting up a single computer dedicated to the task of capturing data from the Web. The computer needs to be licensed for Acrobat, but using a single computer ensures all Web captures are performed with the same conversion settings. Users with any Acrobat viewer can retrieve the PDF files that are captured across a network or intranet.

Determining download status

After you choose all settings and options in all the dialog boxes pertaining to converting Web sites to PDF, you can revisit the Create PDF from Web Page command from any one of the three methods discussed earlier. As pages are downloaded and converted to PDF, the Download Status dialog box opens displaying, appropriately, the download status. After the first page downloads, this dialog box, shown in Figure 6-23, moves to the background behind the converted Web pages.

Caution Web Capture places the converted PDF in memory and uses your hard drive space as an extension of RAM. The PDF is not saved to disk until you perform a Save or Save As operation. If your computer crashes or you quit without saving, the file is lost and you'll need to capture the site again.

Figure 6-23: The Download Status dialog box appears momentarily and then disappears as Acrobat continues to download pages and convert them to PDF.

The dialog box actually remains open, but hides behind the PDF pages being converted as the download continues. If you want to bring the Download Status dialog box to the foreground, choose Advanced ➪ Web Capture ➪ Bring Status Dialogs to Foreground. The dialog box opens in the foreground while Acrobat continues to convert pages.

Appending pages

When a PDF file is open in the Document pane, you can append pages from URL links by choosing Advanced ⇨ Web Capture and then selecting the appropriate choice from the submenu commands. You can also append pages via a context-sensitive menu. To open a context-sensitive menu, you must position the cursor over a structured Bookmark and right-click (Control+click on the Macintosh). The context menu in Figure 6-24 includes options for appending Web pages and commands for handling pages. The submenu options from the Advanced ⇨ Web Capture menu shown in Figure 6-25 relate to Web Capture features.

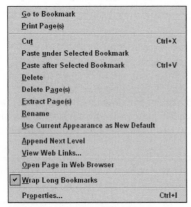

Figure 6-24: A context menu opened on a structured Bookmark offers options for appending pages as well as page-editing commands.

Figure 6-25: When you choose Advanced ⇨ Web Capture, the submenu displays options for treatment of Web captures.

To append pages to the open PDF, make choices from the following selections in the Web Capture submenu:

✦ **Append Web Page:** Selecting this option opens the Add to PDF from Web Page dialog box where you make attribute choices. The dialog box offers the same choices as originally displayed in the Create PDF from Web Page dialog box. When appending pages, you can change the attribute choices for all conversion options such as the URL, number of levels to be downloaded, and so on.

✦ **Append All Links on Page:** When you select this submenu option, no dialog box opens before the download commences. All Web links to other HTML pages are converted and appended to the PDF. Conversion settings are used from the last choices you made in the Create PDF from Web Page dialog box. If you need to change the conversion settings for links to other pages, you can use the View Web Links dialog box.

✦ **View Web Links:** The Select Page Links to Download dialog box opens when you select this menu command. This dialog box lists all Web links according to URL.

The list contains an icon displayed at the far left of the URL list informing you that a link exists to the URL. You can select each of the items in the list. After you select a link, the Properties button on the right side of the dialog box becomes active. Click the Properties button and another dialog box opens. You'll notice in the next dialog box the options for conversion settings appear within three tabs. These options are the same as those you use with the Create PDF From Web Page command.

✦ **Page Info:** This option opens a dialog box displaying information about the current page viewed in the PDF file. As you scroll through pages, the page info changes according to the page viewed. The information supplied in the dialog box includes the original URL, title of the page, creation date, a description of the content, and the preferred zoom level for viewing.

When you open a context menu from a structured Bookmark, the menu options appear as shown in Figure 6-24. The two choices from the menu commands for appending pages to the PDF are Append Next Level and View Web Links.

Tip   You can also append Web pages by clicking a link in the PDF page. If the link destination is not contained in the PDF, the URL is contacted and the page is appended to the PDF. When you position the cursor over a link, the cursor displays a hand icon and index finger pointing upward. If a link has not yet been converted, the icon displays a plus (+) symbol inside the hand and a Tool Tip shows the URL where you can find the link. If the link has been converted to PDF, no plus (+) symbol and no URL are shown. If you want to open a link in your Web browser, press the Control/Option key and click the link.

Refreshing Web pages

You use the Refresh pages command to update a previously captured site. If content has changed, the updated pages are downloaded. Any pages that haven't changed are ignored. To update a PDF file created with Web Capture, choose Advanced ➪ Web Capture ➪ Refresh Pages. The Refresh Pages dialog box opens as shown in Figure 6-26. In order to update pages with the Refresh Pages command, the Conversion Settings in the original Web Page Conversion Settings dialog box must have the Save refresh commands check box enabled, as shown in Figure 6-16 earlier in the chapter.

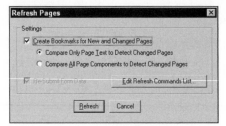

Figure 6-26: The Refresh Pages dialog box
offers options for updating pages in the
open PDF file.

Updates occur according to options you select in the Refresh Pages dialog box. You have two
choices for comparing the page to be downloaded with a page in the PDF document:

✦ **Compare Only Page Text to Detect Changed Pages:** If you are interested in only
changes made to the text on Web pages, then select this radio button. Acrobat ignores
new graphics, colors, backgrounds, and other non-text elements.

✦ **Compare All Page Components to Detect Changed Pages:** When enabled, this option
downloads and converts pages where any changes have occurred.

If you want to selectively update different page links, then click the Edit Refresh Commands List
button in the Refresh Pages dialog box. Another dialog box opens similar to the one opened
with the View Web Links command, which is discussed in the "Appending pages" section of this
chapter. When the Refresh Commands List dialog box opens, all links are selected by default.
Options in this dialog box are similar to those found in the View Web Links dialog box.

If you want all links to be updated, leave the default alone and proceed with the download. If
selected links are to be updated, click the desired link to update. For multiple links hold down
the Shift key as you select the links. For non-contiguous selections in the list, hold down the
Control key (⌘ key on Macintosh) and click the links to be included in the update. Click OK
and exit the Refresh Pages dialog box. The download commences and the Download Status
dialog box disappears. To view the status dialog box, bring it to the front by choosing
Advanced ⇨ Web Capture ⇨ Bring Status Dialogs to Foreground.

Tip   To compare Web pages for obvious changes prior to refreshing the page, visit the Web page
in your browser. In Acrobat, choose Edit ⇨ Preferences ⇨ Web Capture. In the Web Capture
Preferences, select In Web Browser from the Open Web links pop-up menu. Click OK and
click the URL link in the PDF file. The Web page opens in your Web browser. Compare this
page to the PDF page to determine any discrepancies before downloading the pages.

Locate Web addresses

If you have a PDF file that has been converted from a document that contains text formatted
as a URL, Acrobat can convert the text to a Web link. The text must have the complete URL
listing including *http://, or https:.* After the Web link is converted, you can click the link and
append pages by using Web Capture. PDF authors may also create Web links for end users
when distributing files to others.

To create Web links on pages containing URLs, choose Advanced ➪ Links ➪ Create from URLs in Document. A dialog box opens as shown in Figure 6-27.

Figure 6-27: The Create Web Links dialog box enables you to create Web links from text for user-defined page ranges in the open PDF file.

In the Create Web Links dialog box you specify page ranges for where Acrobat should create the links. Acrobat performs this task quickly and creates all links where the proper syntax has been used to describe the URL. If you want to delete links from a PDF document, open the Remove Web Links dialog box by choosing Advanced ➪ Links ➪ Remove All Links from Document. The Remove Web Links dialog box opens where you supply page ranges for eliminating Web links.

Preferences for Web Capture

To access the Web Capture preferences choose Edit ➪ Preferences. In the left pane click Web Capture, and the preference settings shown in Figure 6-28 appear. You can set the additional attributes for Web Link behavior as well as options for converting Web pages to PDF.

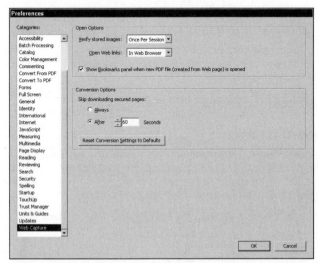

Figure 6-28: The Web Capture Preferences dialog box opens when you choose Edit ➪ Preferences and click Web Capture in the list in the left pane.

The options available in the Web Capture Preferences dialog box include

✦ **Verify stored images:** This pull-down menu contains options for verifying images stored on a captured Web site Once Per Session, Always, or Never. When you select the default setting, Once Per Session, Acrobat checks the Web site to see whether stored images have changed on the site. If changes have occurred, new pages are converted.

✦ **Open Web links:** You can elect to open Web links in either Acrobat or your default Web browser. When you choose the browser option, clicking a Web link in the converted PDF document launches your browser and opens the URL for the associated link. Regardless of whether links are a result of captured pages or authored PDF files, the view appears in the Web browser.

Tip

Regardless of which option you elect to use for opening Web links, you can use the alternate method by pressing the Shift key and clicking the link. For example, if the preference is set to display the link in the Web browser, Shift+click displays the link in Acrobat and vice versa.

✦ **Show Bookmarks panel when new PDF file (created from Web page) is opened:** When this option is enabled, the converted PDF file is viewed with the Navigation pane open and the structured Bookmarks listed in the Bookmarks tab. When this option is disabled, the Navigation pane is closed, but the Bookmarks are still created.

✦ **Skip downloading secured pages:** Secured areas of a Web site can be downloaded, but you must have permission to access the password-protected areas and supply all passwords to gain access to the site. To avoid inadvertently attempting to download a secure area, you can elect to always skip secured pages or skip secured pages at specified intervals ranging between 1 and 9999 seconds.

✦ **Reset Conversion Settings to Defaults:** Clicking this button resets all options in the Conversion Settings dialog boxes to the default settings established when Acrobat was first installed.

Capturing a Web site

The number of options available for converting Web pages and controlling the behavior of Web links may seem overwhelming when you first attempt to capture a site. There is no substitute for practice. The more you use the tools and options discussed earlier in this chapter, the more proficient you'll become at converting Web sites to PDF documents. To help simplify the process, take a look at some steps for converting Web pages.

STEPS: Capturing a Web site

1. **Set the Web Capture preferences.** Before attempting to capture a site, review all the preference settings. To open Web Capture Preferences, choose Edit ⇨ Preferences and click Web Capture in the left pane when the Preferences dialog box opens. Click the Reset Conversion Settings to Defaults button. Click OK after making the changes.

2. **Open the pull-down menu from the Create PDF Task Button.** Select From Web Page from the menu options to open the Create PDF from Web Page dialog box.

3. **Enter the URL for the site to be captured in the Create PDF from Web Page dialog box.** You can use any site on the World Wide Web. If you have a company Web site, use the URL for your site. If not, pick another site. The URL must be complete, so verify the address before proceeding.

4. **Enter the number of levels to capture.** If working with a modem connection, you should first attempt to capture only a single level, especially if you are not familiar with the site structure. If you have a faster connection, try capturing two levels. Enable the check box for Stay on same path, which downloads files under the same path for both levels.

5. **Stay on the same server.** In the Create PDF from Web Page dialog box, enable the check box for Stay on same server. The settings made in the Create from Web Page dialog box should appear as shown in Figure 6-29.

Figure 6-29: The Create PDF from Web Page dialog box displays 2 levels to be captured and the check boxes for Stay on same path and Stay on same server enabled.

6. **Click the Settings button in the Create PDF from Web Page dialog box.** You can elect to use Acrobat's default settings or make some choices for Bookmark attributes and how the HTML and plain text files are converted. When you click the Settings button, the Web Page Conversion Settings dialog box opens.

7. **Create PDF Tags.** In the Web Page Conversion Settings dialog box, three of the four check boxes at the bottom are enabled by default. Add to the enabled check boxes Create PDF tags and place a check mark in the box. With tags you can add new structured Bookmarks that link to the page content. Click OK in the Web Page Conversion Settings dialog box to return to the Create PDF from Web Page dialog box.

8. **Capture the site.** You could navigate to the other options for Conversion Settings, but at this point you'll just look at capturing the Web site with the remaining conversion options at the default values. Click the Create button to begin downloading the site.

9. **View the download progress.** If your connection is slow, and it appears as though the computer is sluggish, files are continuing to download. You can easily determine whether files are downloading by showing a status dialog box. To display a status dialog box, choose Advanced ➪ Web Capture ➪ Bring Status Dialogs to Foreground.

10. **Stop the progress.** If an inordinate amount of time passes and you want to stop the download, click the Stop button in the Download Status dialog box. Acrobat displays all PDFs converted from Web pages before the Stop was invoked.

11. **View the PDF file.** Examine the number of pages and scroll through the document. Open the Navigation pane and view the Bookmarks.

Regardless of whether you downloaded the entire site or stopped the download progress, you'll end up with converted pages appearing in Acrobat. You can edit the PDF document or save it for further use. If you save the file, you can append Web pages in other Acrobat sessions at a later time. If you performed the preceding steps, save the file to use it later for working through some editing steps.

Converting Clipboard Images to PDF

If you're an author, a technical writer, an IT manager, or you create help documents for users of computer software, you'll absolutely love the addition of the Create PDF From Clipboard Image feature. Anyone who needs a screenshot of a dialog box, an image file, a document page, or a desktop can capture the screen data and instantly convert the captured image to PDF format. If you copy a file to the system clipboard, you can convert the clipboard data from any program to a PDF document. You no longer need any kind of third-party utility for screen captures nor do you have to be concerned about compatible file formats when exchanging data.

In Acrobat 7 Macintosh users can enjoy the same options for converting clipboard data to PDFs.

Converting clipboard images

Suppose you have a map contained as part of a layout and you want to clip out the map and send it off to a friend for directions to an event, or perhaps you want to take a screenshot of an ftp client application to show log-on instructions, or maybe you want to clarify the use of a dialog box in Acrobat or another application. All of these examples and many more are excellent candidates for screen captures.

To capture a screenshot of the entire monitor screen in Windows, press Shift+PrtScrn (Print Screen) or PrtSc keys. Macintosh users need to use the Snapshot tool to copy a selection of a PDF page or use the Mac OS X Grab tool to capture a dialog box. (See the next section for "Taking Snapshots.") The keystrokes copy the current view of your monitor to the clipboard. You can launch Acrobat or maximize it and select From Clipboard Image from the Create PDF Task Button pull-down menu. The clipboard data opens as a PDF document in the Acrobat Document pane. If you have a menu or dialog box open, the screen capture includes the foreground items in the capture like the screenshots shown throughout this book. Screens captured on Windows through these methods create 96 ppi (pixels per inch) images; captures on the Mac are 72 ppi.

Cross-Reference   Macintosh users wanting to learn more about the Grab tool can see the Mac Help by selecting the Help menu on your desktop.

If you want to capture a dialog box without the background on Windows, use Alt+PrtScrn (or PrtSc). The dialog box screenshots in this book were all taken by using these key modifiers.

Note   Copying a screenshot to the clipboard works with any program or at the operating system level when capturing desktop or folder views, accessories, or virtually any view you see on your computer monitor. Once data are on the clipboard, you can open Acrobat and convert the clipboard data to a PDF document.

Taking snapshots

In the default Basic toolbar select the Snapshot tool and click on a page. The entire page is copied to the clipboard. You can then create a PDF file From Clipboard Image as described in the previous section. The page you create, however, is a raster image when you convert it to PDF. You lose all text attributes when copying a page in this manner. A better solution for converting an entire page is to use the Extract Pages command.

Cross-Reference   For information on extracting pages, see Chapter 12.

The advantage of using the Snapshot tool is when taking a snapshot of a partial page in Acrobat. You can select the Snapshot tool and drag a marquee in an area you want to copy. When you release the mouse button, the selected area is copied to the clipboard. Choose Create PDF ⇨ From Clipboard Image from the Create PDF Task Button to convert the selection to PDF. Again, you lose all type attributes, but you can use this method if retaining text is not an issue or if you want to crop an image. Using the Crop tool doesn't reduce the page size or file size of a PDF document. Using the Snapshot tool results in smaller file sizes when copying smaller sections of a PDF page.

Snapshots cannot be taken in password-protected files. If a file is encrypted you need to eliminate the file encryption before using the Snapshot tool.

Cross-Reference   For additional information on creating Snapshots and setting resolution for snapshot captures, see Chapter 9. For information on using the Crop tool, see Chapter 12. For linking to snapshots, see Chapter 17. For information on file encryption, see Chapter 21.

Summary

✦ You can create PDF Documents with the Adobe PDF printer. You can use the Adobe PDF printer to apply a variety of Adobe PDF Settings to the PDF conversion. Adobe PDF Settings are used by Acrobat Distiller and the Adobe PDF printer.

✦ You can use Acrobat to convert a variety of different native file formats to PDF using the Create PDF From a File command. Multiple files can be converted to PDF and concatenated into a single document.

✦ You can use Acrobat to download Web pages and convert them to PDF. Web pages residing locally on hard drives can be converted to PDF. All Web page conversions preserve page and URL links.

✦ You can convert data copied to the system clipboard to PDF on both Windows and Macintosh.

✦   ✦   ✦

Exporting to PDF from Authoring Applications

The last chapter covered PDF file creation using built-in features in Acrobat. If you read the chapter, you know that Acrobat offers many more PDF creation methods than earlier versions. Some of the PDF creation options you have from within Acrobat are also available directly from the authoring programs. In other cases, you'll find PDF creation a feature in a program where support is not available from within Acrobat. Adobe Systems has been implementing PDF support for some time in many of its design applications, and other vendors are continually providing support for direct export to PDF.

It stands to reason that the software developer that has implemented the best PDF integration with other programs is Adobe Systems. With the introduction of the Adobe Creative Suite, Adobe Systems has brought to maturity earlier efforts toward a complete integrated document publishing solution, all with PDF at the core.

Other software developers are also adding more support with every program upgrade. Developers such as Corel Corporation, Macromedia, and Quark, Inc., also implement PDF support in their recent program releases. And now Acrobat 7 offers support for more programs, including Microsoft Access and Microsoft Publisher and Auto desk Inventor.

In this chapter I give an overview of some of the more common design and business applications that all export or save to the PDF format.

Setting Up the Environment

This chapter is concerned with creating PDFs; therefore, no toolbars need to be loaded in the Toolbar Well. You can leave your toolbars in Acrobat set to the default view to follow what's covered in this chapter.

Using Acrobat with Microsoft Office Applications

On Windows and Macintosh, Microsoft Word, Excel, and PowerPoint accommodate a tool developed by Adobe Systems called PDFMaker. This same tool is also integrated in other Microsoft applications such as Internet Explorer on Windows, Microsoft Outlook, and Outlook Express, and Autodesk applications. When you install Acrobat, the installer identifies third-party applications on your computer that support PDFMaker and installs the necessary PDFMaker files that enable those applications to convert files to PDF files. If you install such a third-party application after installing Acrobat on Windows, the PDFMaker files are also automatically installed.In all earlier versions of Acrobat you needed to be certain to install Acrobat first and the Office products after installing Acrobat. In version 7, you can install Office applications either before installing Acrobat or after the Acrobat installation.

All the aforementioned programs can also print PostScript files and convert files to PDF with the Acrobat Distiller software. However, you have many more advantages using PDFMaker, and as a matter of practice, you should use this option over using Acrobat Distiller. Among the most important advantages is the ability to produce structured and tagged PDF files, retain layers for programs supporting layers, and retain certain metadata defined in various programs.

Cross-Reference   For more information on using Acrobat Distiller, see Chapter 8. For more information on working with accessible and tagged PDF documents, see Chapter 20.

Microsoft Word

Of all the Office applications, Microsoft Word gives you the best support for PDF file creation. Microsoft Word is the only word-processing application that provides access to the structural data of the document. The structural data of the Word document such as titles, heads, tables, paragraphs, figure captions, and so on can be converted to tagged Bookmarks. Tagged Bookmarks give you much more control over the PDF content. You can navigate to the element structures, and move, copy, extract, and delete pages through menu commands in the Bookmarks tab.

PDFMaker offers several tools to control PDF file creation from within Microsoft Word. After you install Acrobat and later open Word, three Acrobat icons appear on the far left side of the toolbar.

🖼 The first of these three icons is the Convert to Adobe PDF tool. Clicking this icon opens a dialog box where you supply the filename and destination. Enter a name and choose a destination, and then click the Save button to create the PDF.

Note   Three tool icons are installed in Windows. Two tool icons are installed on the Macintosh.

🖼 The second icon is Convert to Adobe PDF and Email. This tool performs the same function as the Convert to Adobe PDF tool and then adds the resulting PDF as an e-mail attachment. The user-defined default e-mail application is automatically launched and the PDF is attached to the message you send. Figure 7-1 shows an e-mail attachment created from the Convert to Adobe PDF and Email tool.

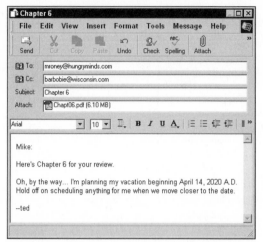

Figure 7-1: After you click the Convert to Adobe PDF and Email tool in Microsoft Word, the PDF is created and automatically placed as an e-mail attachment in your default e-mail application.

 The third tool installed in Microsoft Office Applications is Convert to PDF and Send for Review (Windows only). When you click this tool, the Word document is converted to PDF, and a Send by Email for Review Wizard opens where you proceed through three steps for 1) identifying the PDF to be sent for the review, 2) inviting reviewers where you add the e-mail addresses of recipients, and 3) previewing the review invitation. When you click Finish in the wizard, your file is attached to an e-mail message window in your default e-mail program. In Figure 7-2 you can see the default e-mail message prepared by Acrobat with instructions to recipients for beginning the review.

Cross-Reference   For more information concerning e-mail reviews, see Chapter 16.

In addition to tools, two menus (Windows only) are also installed with PDFMaker. The first is the Adobe PDF menu. The second is the Acrobat Comments menu.

You have the same menu selections in the Adobe PDF menu as you have available for the tools (Convert to Adobe PDF, Convert to Adobe PDF and Email, Convert to Adobe PDF and Send for Review). In addition, a fourth menu command controls the PDF settings where you make attribute assignments for the PDF conversion. Conversion options from the Acrobat PDFMaker dialog box enable you to adjust the attributes for the PDF conversion process. As a matter of practice, you should visit the conversion settings each time you launch Word and prepare to convert documents to PDF to understand what attribute assignments are applied to the resultant PDF documents.

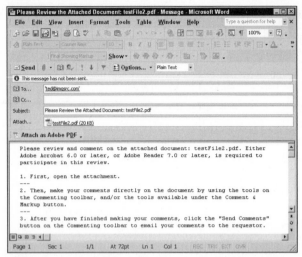

Figure 7-2: After finishing the steps in the Send by Email for Review Wizard, the PDF document appears as a file attachment in a new message window in your default e-mail program.

Changing conversion settings (Macintosh)

Windows users have an elaborate set of conversion settings they can address in menu commands when PDFMaker is installed on Windows. Macintosh users may look for the menus I mention, but they won't find them in OS X. Conversion settings for Macintosh users are much more limited than their Windows cousins and you need to choose your conversion options, as much as can be done, in the Distiller Adobe PDF settings. To learn how to change the Adobe PDF settings, see Chapter 7.

Changing conversion settings (Windows)

PDFMaker prints Word documents to disk and then converts them through Distiller's Adobe PDF Settings. However, the Adobe PDF Settings used in Acrobat Distiller are only some of the attributes assigned to the conversion process. You make the other assignments in Word before the file gets to Distiller. When you choose Acrobat ➪ Change Conversion Settings, the Adobe PDFMaker dialog box opens. In the dialog box, four tabs offer attribute choices for how the PDF is ultimately created. The tabs are Settings, Security, Word, and Bookmarks.

Cross-Reference

Acrobat Distiller is covered in Chapter 7. All subsequent references to Distiller in this chapter are explained in more detail in Chapter 7.

Settings

The Settings tab is the first of the four tabs where you select options. At the top of the Settings tab is a pull-down menu for Conversion Settings. From this menu, you choose the settings Distiller uses to convert the file to a PDF. If you want to edit the settings or create a new Adobe PDF Setting, click the Advanced Settings button shown in Figure 7-3.

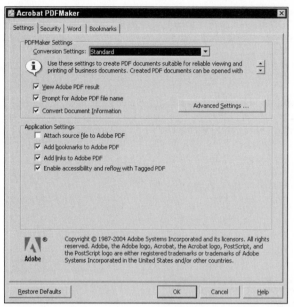

Figure 7-3: The Settings tab offers you choices for selecting the Adobe PDF Settings used by Acrobat Distiller to convert the file.

Options in the Settings tab include

- ✦ **View Adobe PDF result:** When the PDF is created, the document opens in Acrobat if this check box is enabled. If it's disabled, the PDF is created and the Word file remains in view.

- ✦ **Prompt for Adobe PDF file name:** If this check box is enabled, you won't inadvertently overwrite a file with the same name. Leaving this check box enabled is a good idea.

- ✦ **Convert Document Information:** This option ensures document information created in Word is added to the PDF Document Properties.

- ✦ **Attach source file to Adobe PDF:** If you want to attach the Word file from which the PDF was created, enable this check box.

- ✦ **Add links to Adobe PDF:** This option ensures that links created in Word are converted to links in the PDF document.

- ✦ **Add bookmarks to Adobe PDF:** Bookmarks are created from Word style sheets. Select this check box to convert styles and headings to Bookmarks. Make selections for what styles and headings to convert to Bookmarks in the Bookmarks tab.

- ✦ **Enable accessibility and reflow with Tagged PDF:** This option creates document structure tags. Accessibility for the visually challenged and developmentally disabled that are contained in the Word document are preserved in the PDF. Reflowing text enables the Acrobat user to use the Reflow view. As a matter of default, leave this check box enabled. Tagged PDF documents also help you export the PDF text back out to a word processor with more data integrity than when exporting files without tags.

Note   If you enable accessibility and reflow, the file sizes of your PDF documents are larger compared to files exported to PDF without accessibility and tags. If you need to produce the smallest file sizes for specific purposes where you know accessibility and preserving structure are not needed, disable the check box.

Security

Click the Security tab to open options for security settings. Security options for permissions are available only for High-Bit encryption (128-bit). If you choose to add security from the Word options, the PDF document is compatible with Acrobat 5.0 viewers and greater. If you need additional security controls available in Acrobat 6 and Acrobat 7 compatibility options, apply the security in Acrobat.

Cross-Reference   For specific definitions of the security options, see Chapter 19.

Word

Click the Word tab to choose options for Word content as shown in Figure 7-4.

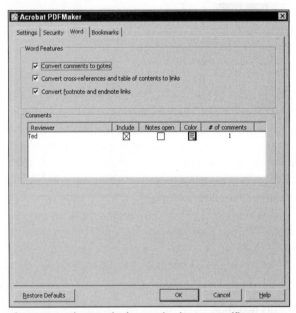

Figure 7-4: The Word tab contains items specific to some of the content in Word that can be converted in the resulting PDF document.

Options on the Word tab include

✦ **Convert comments to notes:** Notes can be converted to annotation comments that will appear in a text note in the PDF file.

✦ **Convert cross-references and table of contents to links:** Any cross-references, such as Table of Contents and indexes, will have links to their respective destinations. These links are preserved in the PDF file.

✦ **Convert footnote and endnote links:** Bookmark links are added for all footnotes and endnotes.

✦ **Comments:** The lower window lists all comments in the file. If you check the box in the Include column, the comments are converted to Acrobat comments. The Notes open column enables you to set the default for note comments with open note pop-up windows.

Bookmarks

In the Bookmarks dialog box shown in Figure 7-5 are two items that can determine what Bookmarks will be created in the PDF file. These are

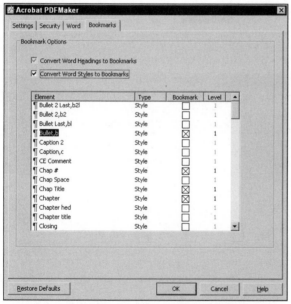

Figure 7-5: The Bookmarks tab offers two choices for determining what Bookmarks are created in the PDF file.

✦ **Convert Word Headings to Bookmarks:** Word headings can be converted to Bookmarks. In the box below the check boxes, a list of all headings and styles contained in the Word document appears. Click the box under the Bookmark column to determine what heads to convert to Bookmarks.

✦ **Convert Word Styles to Bookmarks:** You can select user-defined styles for conversion to Bookmarks. Scroll the list of elements and place a check mark for the styles you want to convert.

After you select the options in the Adobe PDFMaker dialog box, click the Convert to PDF tool or select the menu option to convert the file.

Working with comments (Windows)

The other menu installed with PDFMaker is the Acrobat Comments menu. The commands in the menu address handling comments in Word and exchanging comments with PDF documents. The menu items are

✦ **Import Comments from Acrobat:** The file from which you import comments must have been created with the PDFMaker from Word 2002/XP. When you select the menu item, the Import Comments from Adobe Acrobat help window opens. Read the helpful tips on how to import comments and click the Yes button to proceed. The next dialog box that opens is Import Comments from Adobe Acrobat, as shown in Figure 7-6. In the dialog box, you make choices for what files to select, what comments to import, and whether you want to filter the comments.

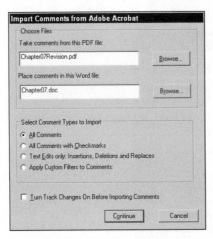

Figure 7-6: The Import Comments from Adobe Acrobat dialog box offers choices for file selection and the comment types to import into the Word document.

✦ **Continue Integration Process:** This continues the integration of PDF comments in the Word document for text edits such as inserts and deletions. If review tracking is on, you can merge tracked changes.

✦ **Accept All Changes in Document:** After the comment integration, select this menu command to accept the comments. Comments such as text marked for deletion are deleted; text marked with insertion adds the inserted comments, and so on.

✦ **Delete All Comments in Document:** All comments imported from the PDF document are deleted from the Word file.

✦ **Reviewing Toolbar:** Comment tools like those you have in Acrobat for comment navigation, review tracking, accepting/rejecting comments, and so on are added to the Word Toolbar Well as shown in Figure 7-7. To hide the tools, uncheck the command by selecting it in the menu.

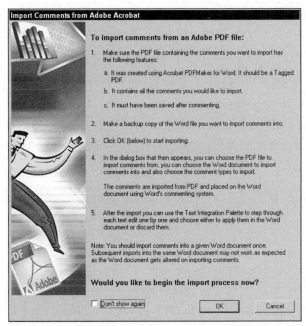

Figure 7-7: When you select the Reviewing Toolbar option in the Acrobat Comments menu, the comment and review tools are made visible in the Microsoft Word Toolbar Well.

✦ **Show Instructions:** The dialog box that opens when you choose the Import Comments from Acrobat command (see the first bullet in this list) also opens when you choose the Show Instructions menu command. See Figure 7-8.

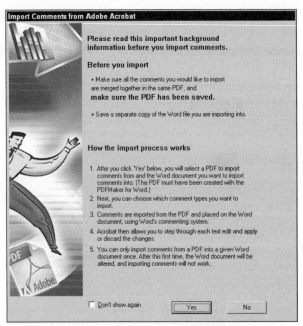

Figure 7-8: You can access the instructions at any time by selecting Show Instructions. In the dialog box, you see steps to follow for importing comments from Acrobat into a Word file.

Cross-Reference   You can also exchange comments from Acrobat to Microsoft Word. To learn more about submitting comments from within Acrobat to Word documents, see Chapter 15.

Working with custom page sizes (Windows)

The many different options available for PDF conversion from Microsoft Word require that you practice a little and become familiar with the settings that work best in your workflow. There's no substitute for spending some quality time studying the settings and observing the results. Many of the options discussed earlier in this chapter are intuitive and should be easily understood. A less intuitive task is creating PDF documents from custom page sizes in Word. To create PDFs from non-standard page sizes requires a little configuration. To understand how to create a PDF document from a Word file with a non-standard page size, follow these steps.

STEPS: Creating PDFs from Word files using non-standard page sizes

1. **Open the Adobe PDF printer.** When you create a Word document with a non-standard page size, you need to add the same page size in the Adobe PDF printer. The first step is to open the Adobe PDF printer from the Start menu by choosing Settings ⇨ Printers and Faxes ⇨ Adobe PDF.

2. **Open the printer properties.** In the Adobe PDF Printer dialog box, choose File ⇨ Properties as shown in Figure 7-9. The Adobe PDF Properties dialog box opens.

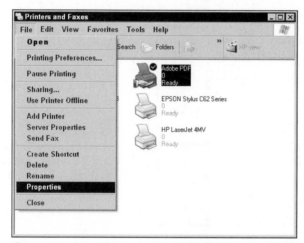

Figure 7-9: Open the Properties dialog box by choosing File ⇨ Properties.

3. **Open the Printing Preferences.** In the Adobe PDF Properties dialog box, shown in Figure 7-10, click the Printing Preferences button.

4. **Add a custom page.** In the Adobe PDF Printing Preferences dialog box, you'll see a button titled Add. Click the button to open the Add Custom Paper Size dialog box, where you define the page sizes.

5. **Set the paper size attributes.** In the Add Custom Paper Size dialog box, supply a name in the Paper Names field. You must add a new name because overwriting fixed paper sizes is not permitted. Add the values for the Width and Height. In Figure 7-11 I created a custom page size for 6 × 9 inches.

6. **Return to MS Word.** Click the Add/Modify button in the Add Custom Paper Size dialog box and click OK through the dialog boxes until you arrive at the original Adobe PDF printer dialog box. Close the window and open Word.

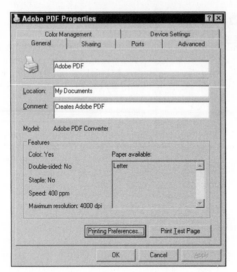

Figure 7-10: In the Adobe PDF Properties dialog box, click the Printing Preferences button to open the Adobe PDF Printing Preferences dialog box.

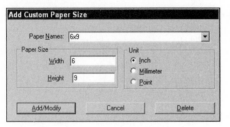

Figure 7-11: Add a name for the new paper size, enter the page size values, and click the Add/Modify button.

7. **Select the new page size.** In Word, choose File ➪ Page Setup. Select the Paper tab. From the pull-down menu for Paper size, select the new paper size you added to the Adobe PDF printer. In Figure 7-12 you can see the 6 × 9 page I added to my Adobe PDF printer. You can begin a new document or open an existing document and reform the pages to the new page size.

8. **Convert to Adobe PDF.** Click the Convert to Adobe PDF tool in the Word Toolbar Well. If you enabled View Adobe PDF result in the Adobe PDFMaker Settings tab, the resulting PDF opens in Acrobat.

Note

Creating custom page sizes is particularly important for programs such as Microsoft Visio, Microsoft Project, and Autodesk AutoCAD where non-standard sizes are commonly used. Acrobat supports a page size of up to 200 inches square. Make certain you have the proper page size defined for the Adobe PDF printer before attempting to Convert to Adobe PDF.

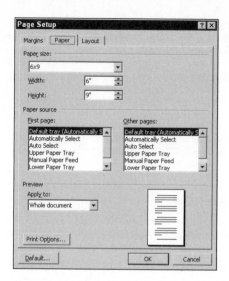

Figure 7-12: In Microsoft Word, choose File ⇨ Page Setup and choose the new paper size in the Paper size pull-down menu.

Microsoft Excel

You can also use PDFMaker with Microsoft Excel. Options for conversion settings are common between the programs with a few exceptions. Excel Bookmarks are created from different sheets in an Excel Workbook or you can select Convert Entire Wordbook from the Adobe PDF menu to convert all worksheets in a workbook and add the bookmarks. Spreadsheets and charts are converted with PDFMaker. The menu options for the Adobe PDF menu are the same in Excel as in Word. Excel doesn't support the Adobe Comments menu, but you can convert Excel files to PDF and send them for an e-mail review.

Cross-Reference Microsoft PowerPoint also uses PDFMaker for conversion to PDF. For information concerning PowerPoint conversions to PDF, see Chapter 23.

Microsoft Publisher

With the introduction of Acrobat 7, Adobe expands PDFMaker support for Microsoft Publisher. The same PDFMaker tools are added to the Publisher window and you can export PDFs directly from within the program or from using the Create PDF From File menu command in Acrobat.

Working with Acrobat and Adobe Creative Suite

The Microsoft programs have long been supported with PDFMaker, and the Adobe/Microsoft alliance for improving integration between Microsoft products and Acrobat PDFs has provided users a seamless workflow between the programs. In addition to working with

Microsoft, Adobe has continually developed PDF integration in its own design applications. In years past, each program was developed individually to take advantage of PDF exports and imports. The culmination of these developments by individual engineering teams has led to the development of an integrated solution where the current products work together with much improved continuity and interoperability. At the core is PDF and the result is the Adobe Creative Suite.

The Adobe Creative Suite (CS) comes in two flavors. The Creative Suite Standard edition includes Adobe Illustrator CS, Adobe InDesign CS, Adobe Photoshop CS, and Adobe Version Cue. The Adobe Creative Suite Premium edition includes these four programs and adds Adobe GoLive and Adobe Acrobat. All the CS applications support PDF documents with direct exports and imports.

Acrobat and Adobe Photoshop

Adobe Photoshop CS supports creating and importing PDFs. When you create a PDF, you use the Save As command and save directly to the PDF format. When you import PDF documents that were not originally created in Photoshop, the files are rasterized. The process of rasterizing files converts all objects, such as type and vector objects, to raster images (pixels).

Saving to PDF from Photoshop

Creating a PDF file from Photoshop is nothing more than choosing the PDF format from the Save dialog box. Photoshop supports many different file formats for opening and saving documents. In versions prior to Photoshop 6.0, you had to flatten all layers before you could save a document as a PDF file. In versions 6.0 and later, you can preserve layers and vector art. When you save a layered file from Photoshop CS as a PDF and open it again in Photoshop, all layers are retained. Type and vector art work the same way. You can create type without rasterizing it and save the file as a PDF. Later, if you want to edit the file, you can reopen it and edit the type. What's more, you can search and edit the type in Acrobat when you save the file as PDF from Photoshop.

To save a multilayered Photoshop image, Photoshop document, or flattened image, you use the Save As command. In Photoshop CS, choose File ⇨ Save As. The Save As dialog box (see Figure 7-13) provides many options for preserving the Photoshop file integrity while saving in PDF format that include

   ✦ **Save As (Mac) File name (Windows):** As when saving any file you supply the filename and destination in the Save (or Save As) dialog box. Note Save As at the top of the dialog box and the File name field (statue.pdf) in Figure 7-13.

   ✦ **Format:** From the pull-down menu you can choose many formats for layered documents and documents containing vector art. However, preserving both can be achieved when saving in the Photoshop PDF format.

   ✦ **As a Copy:** If you use the Save As command, the file you save is a copy of the original document presuming you use a different filename than the original. If you open a PDF file and select Save As, you can select the As a Copy check box to duplicate the file. The filename is automatically extended to include the word *copy* after the filename and before the extension.

   ✦ **Alpha Channels:** The PDF format also retains all Alpha Channel data. Use of Alpha Channels is restricted to Photoshop when you reopen the file in Photoshop. In Acrobat, the use of Alpha Channel data isn't useful.

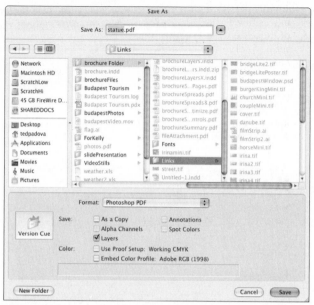

Figure 7-13: To export directly to PDF, use the Save or Save As dialog box in Photoshop. Layers are saved in the PDF document, but they do not appear as layers in the PDF file.

✦ **Layers:** Saving as a Photoshop PDF also preserves all layers. When you reopen the file in Photoshop, you have access to all layer data.

✦ **Annotations:** You can add text notes and audio comments in Photoshop much like when using Comment tools in Acrobat. When you add a comment to the file, it is preserved in the PDF file. If you open the PDF in Acrobat, you can edit or delete text notes and audio comments.

✦ **Spot Colors:** If a Spot Color is included in the Photoshop file, Spot Colors are preserved when you save the file as a PDF.

✦ **Use Proof Setup:** Proof viewing can accommodate different viewing options for color separations. Saving as a PDF displays the document in Acrobat with the Proof Setup enabled.

Cross-Reference

For information on using Proof Setup in Acrobat, see Chapter 25.

✦ **Embed Color Profile:** You can embed the current profile used for the respective color mode in the PDF file.

After you enable all check boxes for the file attributes and click Save, Photoshop opens a second dialog box where you handle settings for the compression, font, and security. Figure 7-14 shows the PDF Options dialog box.

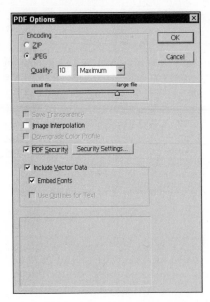

Figure 7-14: After you click the Save button in the Save As dialog box, the PDF Options dialog box opens.

Two choices are available to you for the encoding method:

✦ **ZIP:** ZIP compression is lossless. Files will not be compressed as much as with JPEG, but the data integrity will be optimal. ZIP compression is usually preferred for images with large amounts of a single color.

Note   Acrobat 5.0 eliminated the use of LZW compression in favor of the more efficient ZIP compression. No access to LZW compression exists in either Photoshop 6.0 or Acrobat 5.0 or greater.

✦ **JPEG:** JPEG compression in this dialog box corresponds to the compression amounts you observed in Chapter 6. Depending on your output, the compression amount corresponds to the examples discussed in Chapter 6.

✦ **Save Transparency:** A single-layer image may have transparency on the layer. If you select Save transparency, the PDF viewed in Acrobat appears with the transparent area white — regardless of the background color you used in Photoshop. However, when placed into a layout application or printed, the transparent areas are indeed transparent.

✦ **Downgrade Color Profile:** If you selected an ICC (International Color Consortium) Profile (Windows) or Embed Color Profile (Macintosh) for a version 4 profile, checking this option downgrades the profile to version 2. The option is available only when a profile has been saved with version 4 and, you need to use it only when an application doesn't support version 4 profiles.

✦ **PDF Security:** When you save files from Photoshop to the PDF format, you can secure the files with 40-bit (Acrobat 3 and 4 compatibility), 128-bit (Acrobat 5 compatibility), or 128-bit (Acrobat 6 compatibility) security. The same options available in Acrobat for securing files are also available when you click the Security Settings button adjacent to this check box.

Cross-Reference

For more information on securing PDF files, see Chapter 21.

✦ **Image Interpolation:** Anti-aliasing is applied to lower resolution images for viewing onscreen. If you use higher compression on files, you can somewhat improve appearances by using interpolation.

✦ **Downgrade Color Profile:** Color profiles have been modified through the years and come in versions much like your software versions. A newer version 4 profile assigned to an image may not be usable in some older applications. If you need to downgrade the color profile to version 2, check this box. Only use the option when embedding profiles, and you know you are going to transport the Photoshop PDF to an application not supporting version 4 color profiles.

✦ **Include Vector Data:** Vector data may be in the form of vector objects or type. When either is used, the data are not rasterized. Vector data and type is preserved in the PDF and recognized by Acrobat and Photoshop.

✦ **Embed Fonts:** Font embedding will occur much as it does with Distiller. If you create a Photoshop file and preserve the type layer, embedding the font will eliminate another user from needing the font if he or she opens the file in Acrobat.

✦ **Use Outlines for Text:** Text is converted to outlines (or paths) when this check box is enabled.

Note

Many designers have resigned themselves to always converting type to outlines regardless of the program or fonts used. This habit has developed because of many continuing font problems found when using imaging service centers. Converting type to outlines is not a panacea for resolving all the problems. Fonts converted to outlines put undue burden on RIPs and imaging equipment, not to mention your desktop printers. Avoid converting to outlines whenever possible and reserve the procedure for only those fonts where a known problem exists.

PDF and color modes

Photoshop provides a number of choices for the color mode used to express your image. You can open files from different color modes, convert color modes in Photoshop, and save among different formats available for a given color mode. File formats are dependent on color modes, and some format options are not available if the image data are defined in a mode not acceptable to the format.

Tip

See Table 7-1 later in this section for Photoshop PDF exports supported by the Photoshop color modes and relative uses for each mode.

Color mode choices in Photoshop include the following:

✦ **Bitmap:** The image is expressed in two colors: black and white. In Photoshop terms, images in the bitmap mode are referred to as line art. In Acrobat terms, this color mode is called monochrome bitmap. Bitmap images are usually about one-eighth the size of a grayscale file. The bitmap format can be used with Acrobat Capture for converting the image data to rich text.

✦ **Grayscale:** This is your anchor mode in Photoshop. Grayscale is like a black-and-white photo, a halftone, or a Charlie Chaplin movie. You see grayscale images everywhere, including the pages in this book. I refer to this as an anchor mode because you can convert to any of the other modes from grayscale. RGB files cannot be converted directly to bitmaps or duotones. You first need to convert RGB to grayscale, and then to either a bitmap or duotone. From grayscale, although the color is not regained, you can also convert back to any of the other color modes. Grayscale images significantly reduce file sizes — they're approximately one-third the size of an RGB file, but larger than the bitmaps.

✦ **RGB:** For screen views, multimedia, and Web graphics, RGB is the most commonly used mode. It has a color gamut much larger than CMYK and is best suited for display on computer monitors. A few printing devices can take advantage of RGB — for example, film recorders, large inkjet printers, and some desktop color printers. In most cases, however, this mode is not used for printing files to commercial output devices, especially when color separating and using high-end digital prepress.

✦ **CMYK:** The process colors of Cyan, Magenta, Yellow, and Black are used in offset printing and most commercial output devices. The color gamut is much narrower than RGB; and when you convert an image from RGB to CMYK using Photoshop's mode conversion command, you usually see some noticeable dilution of color appearing on your monitor. When exporting files to PDF directly from Photoshop or when opening files in other applications and then distilling them, you should always make your color conversions first in Photoshop.

✦ **Lab:** Lab color, in theory, encompasses all the color from both the RGB and CMYK color spaces. This color mode is based on a mathematical model to describe all perceptible color within the human universe. In practicality, its color space is limited to approximately 6 million colors, about 10+ million less than RGB color. Lab color is device-independent color, which theoretically means the color is true regardless of the device on which your image is edited and printed. Lab mode is commonly preferred by high-end color editing professionals when printing color separations on PostScript Level 2 and PostScript 3 devices. Earlier versions of PDFs saved from Lab color images had problems printing four-color separations. With Acrobat 6 and above you can print Lab images to process separations.

Cross-Reference   For more information on printing color separations, see Chapter 25.

✦ **Multichannel:** If you convert any of the other color modes to Multichannel mode, all the individual channels used to define the image color are converted to grayscale. The resulting document is a grayscale image with multiple channels. With regard to exporting to PDF, you likely won't use this mode.

✦ **Duotone:** The Duotone mode can actually support one of four individual color modes. Monotone is selectable from the Duotone mode, which holds a single color value in the image, like a tint. Duotone defines the image in two color values, Tritone in three, and Quadtone in four. When you export to PDF from Photoshop, all of these modes are supported.

✦ **Indexed Color:** Whereas the other color modes such as RGB, Lab, and CMYK define an image with a wide color gamut (up to millions of colors), the Indexed Color mode limits the total colors to a maximum of 256. Color reduction in images is ideal for Web graphics where the fewer colors significantly reduce the file sizes. You can export indexed color images directly to PDF format from Photoshop.

Table 7-1: Photoshop Color Modes

Color Mode	Export to PDF	Screen View	Print Composite	Print Separations
Bitmap	Yes	Yes	Yes	No
Grayscale	Yes	Yes	Yes	No
RGB Color	Yes	Yes	Yes*	No
CMYK Color	Yes	No	Yes	Yes
Lab Color	Yes	Yes	Yes	Yes
Multichannel	Yes	No	No	No
Duotone	Yes	Yes	No	Yes
Indexed Color	Yes	Yes	No	No
16-bit	Yes	No	No	No

* When working with high-end commercial devices, CMYK is preferred.

Compression and color modes

When you choose File ⇨ Save or File ⇨ Save As and choose PDF as the format, the PDF Options dialog box opens after you click Save. Choose a level of compression and make other choices as desired in the PDF Options dialog box and click OK. The file is saved as a PDF and can be opened in Acrobat.

Because Photoshop does not have an automatic choice for compression types, you should know that different compression choices are available depending on the color mode of the Photoshop image. Table 7-2 includes the compression types available according to the color mode of the image to be exported.

Table 7-2: Compression Methods According to Color Mode

Color Mode	Export to PDF	Compression Type
Bitmap	Yes	No compression option
Grayscale	Yes	JPEG/ZIP
RGB	Yes	JPEG/ZIP
CMYK	Yes	JPEG/ZIP
Lab	Yes	JPEG/ZIP
Duotone	Yes	JPEG/ZIP
Indexed	Yes	ZIP only
Multichannel	No	N/A

Acquiring PDF files in Photoshop

PDF documents may be composed of many different elements depending on the design of the original file. If you design a page in a layout program for which you create text, import Photoshop images, and also import EPS illustrations, the different elements retain their characteristics when converted to PDF. Text, for example, remains as text, raster images such as Photoshop files remain as raster images, and EPS illustrations remain as EPS vector objects. Although the images, text, and line art may be compressed when distilled in Acrobat Distiller, all the text and line art remain as vector elements. In Photoshop, if you open an illustration or text created in any program other than Photoshop, the document elements are rasterized and lose their vector-based attributes. Photoshop rasterizes PDF documents much as it does with any EPS file.

In Photoshop, you have several methods of handling PDF imports. PDF documents opened in Photoshop are handled with the File ➪ Open command, File ➪ Place command, File ➪ Import command, and through a File ➪ Automate command. Each of the methods offers different options, so let's take the methods individually.

Opening PDF files in Photoshop

When you choose File ➪ Open, the Open dialog box will permit you to choose from formats in a pull-down menu for Files of type. The three file formats listed that specifically reference PDF documents are

- ✦ **Generic PDF:** Any PDF file from any producer application can be opened in Photoshop. Files other than those saved from Photoshop are rasterized by Photoshop's Generic Rasterizer.

- ✦ **Photoshop PDF:** This option opens PDFs originating from Photoshop and those containing layers where vector art and/or type are preserved and appear on different layers. If the PDF was not produced from Photoshop and this file type is selected, Photoshop automatically switches to Generic PDF and prompts you for rasterizing attributes.

- ✦ **Acrobat TouchUp Image:** When working on a PDF in Acrobat, you have an opportunity to edit a raster- or vector-based object in Photoshop or an illustration program. Using the Select Object tool, hold down the Ctrl key (Option Key on Macintosh) and double-click the object or open a context menu and select Edit Image. The respective image opens in one of the supporting applications. The object you open is saved as a TouchUp Image. If you save the file and reopen it in Photoshop, this format is recognized by Photoshop as a file exported from a PDF file.

Cross-Reference   For information on dynamically editing objects and images from PDF documents, see Chapters 8 and 9.

If you inadvertently save a PDF from Photoshop as an Acrobat TouchUp Image, then reopen it and see your image distorted, you can make corrections in Photoshop to resolve the distortion problem. You can often open PDFs in Photoshop at the wrong pixel aspect ratio. If you experience this problem, choose Image ➪ Pixel Aspect Ratio.

From the submenu look for Custom as the current choice. If you see Custom selected, click Square in the submenu. Typically, Photoshop will warn you ahead of time with a warning dialog box as you open a file with pixel ratios distorted, as shown in Figure 7-15.

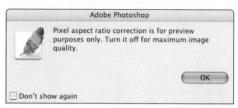

Figure 7-15: If the pixel aspect ratio of a file is not correct, Photoshop alerts you in a dialog box.

I took a screenshot in Photoshop that was saved to PDF. I then opened the file and saved it as an Acrobat TouchUp Image from Photoshop. When it's reopened as shown in Figure 7-16, you can see the obvious distortion. After I choose Image ➪ Pixel Aspect Ratio ➪ Square, the file distortion disappeared, as shown in Figure 7-17.

Figure 7-16: When saving the file as an Acrobat TouchUp Image and reopening it in Photoshop, you need to correct the pixel aspect ratio.

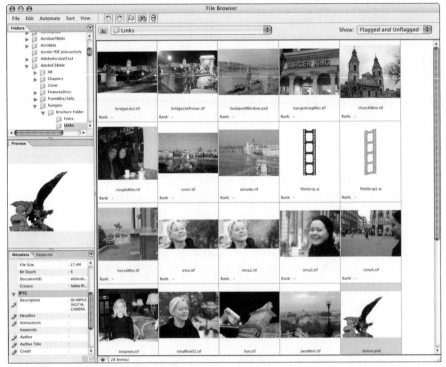

Figure 7-17: After you correct the pixel aspect ratio, the image distortion disappears.

Placing PDF files in Photoshop

Instead of opening a PDF file through the File ➪ Open command, you can use File ➪ Place to add a PDF to an open Photoshop document. Placing PDFs also requires rasterization. The advantage of using Place instead of Open is the placed PDF won't fully rasterize until you finish scaling it. When you choose File ➪ Place, the Place dialog box opens. Locate the file to place in Photoshop and click Place. The file appears within a rectangle containing handles in each corner. Click and drag a handle to resize the placed image. You can size the image up or down in the Photoshop document window. When finished scaling, press the Enter (Windows) or Return (Macintosh) key. Pressing the key lets Photoshop know you have accepted the size. At that point the image is rasterized. The disadvantage of using Place over the Open command is you have no control over resolution and color mode. The PDF is rasterized at the same resolution and mode in the file where the document is placed.

Importing PDFs in Photoshop

When you choose the File ➪ Import ➪ PDF Image command and select a PDF file to open, the PDF Import Image dialog box opens. The file you import, however, won't be a PDF document. Photoshop searches for images contained in the PDF file and permits you to selectively import a single image or all images found in the document. You can navigate thumbnail views before electing to import an image and see a thumbnail in the PDF Image Import dialog box by dragging the scroll bar up and down as shown in Figure 7-18.

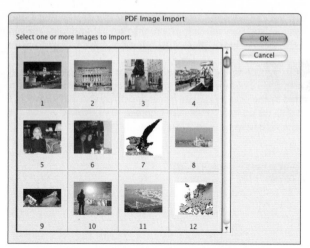

Figure 7-18: The PDF Image Import dialog box displays thumbnails of each image contained in a PDF file. To navigate, scroll with the elevator bar or click the up and down arrows.

When you click the Import All button, all the images contained in the PDF are imported at the original size, resolution, and color mode they were when the PDF was created. Because the images are already raster images, Photoshop's rasterizer isn't used.

Importing multipage PDFs

Figure 7-19 offers several choices for automating the sequence that include

✦ **Choose:** Select the source PDF file by clicking the Choose button at the top left of the dialog box. Photoshop can't use multiple PDF files as a source. You are limited to opening a single PDF document. The document, of course, can have multiple pages.

✦ **Page Range:** You can select all pages in the PDF or a range of pages. The page range choices require you to know ahead of time the number of pages in the PDF file to be converted. If you select pages by clicking the From radio button and choose a range outside the PDF page range, a warning dialog box opens indicating the problem. For example, if you attempt to select pages 21 to 22 in a 20-page PDF file, pages 21 and 22 are out of range. Photoshop opens a warning dialog box to inform you the first page it attempts to convert is out of range. If you attempt to convert pages 18 to 22 in the same example, Photoshop converts pages 18 through 20 and then opens another dialog box, informing you that not all pages within the specified range exist in the PDF document.

✦ **Output Options:** These options are the same as those for single-page conversions. You can choose the resolution, color mode, and whether anti-aliasing is used. One option you do not have available in the dialog box is the capability to choose size and proportions. If you want to size the PSD files, you can set up a Photoshop Action to open the saved files and resize them with values used in creating the Action.

✦ **Base Name:** The base name you specify appears in the filename for the saved PSD files. If you use a name such as *acroFile*, Photoshop saves the PSD files as acroFile0001.psd, acroFile0002.psd, acroFile0003.psd, and so on. Photoshop adds the 000n and .psd extension to the filename you supply as the base name.

✦ **Choose (Destination):** You use the second Choose button for the destination folder or directory. You can highlight a directory name in the hierarchy list and click the Select button, or you can open a directory in the hierarchy list and click the Select button.

The File ➪ Automate ➪ Multi-page PDF to PSD command is similar to a Photoshop Action in that it automatically opens PDF files, rasterizes them in Photoshop, and saves the files to a destination directory specified by the user. When you select this command in Photoshop, the Convert Multi-Page PDF to PSD dialog box opens (see Figure 7-19), enabling you to determine the same rasterizing characteristics as used with the Open command.

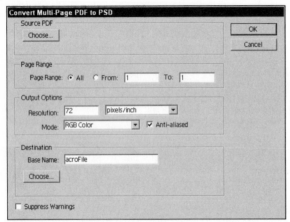

Figure 7-19: The Multi-Page PDF to PSD command enables conversion of several pages within a PDF file to be rasterized in Photoshop.

Rasterizing PDF files

For those conversion methods that require rasterization, such as the Open command discussed in the "Opening PDF files in Photoshop" section, Photoshop opens a dialog box where you supply user-defined rasterization attributes. If you have a multipage document and you use the Open command, the first dialog box that appears is the PDF Page Selector dialog box. Select a page to open and click OK. The second dialog box appearing after you click OK is the Rasterize Generic PDF Format dialog box shown in Figure 7-20.

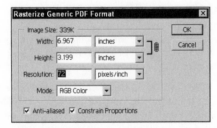

Figure 7-20: The Rasterize Generic PDF Format dialog box enables you to define the rasterization attributes.

If you open a single-page PDF file, the PDF Page Selector dialog box does not appear. Regardless of whether you select a page within a range of pages or a document with only one page, Photoshop wants some information before it rasterizes the PDF page. The rasterization attributes you can control in the Rasterize Generic PDF Format dialog box include

✦ **Width/Height:** You can determine the physical size of the final Photoshop image by changing the width and/or height of the rasterized image. The default size of the original PDF document is shown when the dialog box first opens.

✦ **Resolution:** The default resolution regardless of the size is 72 ppi. You can choose to supply a user-defined resolution in this dialog box. If the original raster images were at a resolution different from the amount supplied in this dialog box, the images are resampled. Text and line art will be rasterized according to the amount you define in the dialog box without interpolation.

Image resampling is a method for tossing away pixels (downsampling) or manufacturing new pixels (upsampling). Either way the process is referred to as *interpolation* where Photoshop makes some guesses as to what pixels to toss or what pixels to create.

✦ **Mode:** Choose a color mode — Grayscale, RGB, CMYK, or Lab color — from the pull-down menu.

✦ **Anti-Aliased:** Use this option to smooth edges of text, line art, and images that are interpolated through resampling. If you disable this option, text appears with jagged edges. Text in PDF files rasterized in Photoshop looks best when anti-aliased and when the display is more consistent with the original font used when the PDF was created.

✦ **Constrain Proportions:** If you change a value in either the Width or the Height field and the Constrain Proportions option is enabled, the value in the other field (Height or Width) is automatically calculated by Photoshop to preserve proportional sizing. When the check box is disabled, both the Width and Height are independent values — that is, they have no effect on each other. If you don't preserve proportions, the rasterized file is likely to be distorted.

One problem you may encounter when rasterizing PDF documents in Photoshop is maintaining font integrity. Photoshop displays a warning dialog box when it encounters a font that is not installed on your system, which presents problems when you attempt to rasterize the font. If such a problem exists, the font can be eliminated from the document or changed after you open the file in Photoshop and edit the type layer.

When files are password-protected, users are prevented from opening a PDF file in Photoshop or any other application. If you attempt to open a secure document, an alert dialog box opens. The dialog box indicates the PDF file can't be parsed. If you encounter such a dialog box, open it in an Acrobat viewer and check the security settings.

For information about Acrobat security, see Chapter 21.

If you want to convert catalogs and lengthy documents to HTML-supported files, the PDF to PSD conversion can be useful. You can set up Actions in Photoshop to downsample images, convert color modes, and save copies of the converted files in HTML-supported formats.

Comments and Photoshop

Photoshop supports the use of Comment tools. You can create a note or sound attachment in Photoshop much like you do in Acrobat. The comment is an object and won't be rasterized with any other Photoshop data. You can delete the annotation at any time by selecting the Note icon or Attach Sound icon and pressing the Backspace (Windows) or Delete (Macintosh) key.

You can also import comments from PDF files into Photoshop. You must use the Comment Note tool because Photoshop does not support the other comment types available in Acrobat. If a Note is contained in a PDF document and you want to import the Note into Photoshop, choose File ⇨ Import ⇨ Annotations. Photoshop can import an annotation only from PDF formatted files.

In addition, Photoshop can import Form Data Format files. Data exported from Acrobat in FDF format can be chosen as another import format from the File ⇨ Import ⇨ Annotations command. Data from FDF files are imported in a comment or a note comment window.

Cross-Reference   For more information about comment notes and sound attachments, see Chapter 15.

Creating PDF presentations

All the features for Photoshop discussed thus far are derived from the top-level menu commands. When you open the Photoshop CS File Browser, you gain access to additional features related to PDF integration. From within Photoshop CS you have support for converting image files to a PDF Presentation. If you have Photoshop, follow these steps to see how to create a PDF presentation complete with transitions:

STEPS: Saving a PDF presentation

1. **Select image files to convert to PDF.** Choose Window ⇨ File Browser to open the File Browser window. In the File Browser, navigate your hard drive to find a folder containing JPEG, TIFF, or other file formats compatible with Photoshop. Select the files you want to use for the presentation. Click an image in the File Browser window and either Shift+click to select a contiguous group of images or press Control/⌘+click to select images in a non-contiguous order.

2. **Set presentation attributes.** Choose Automate ⇨ PDF Presentation in the File Browser window. Click the Presentation button in the Output Options as shown in Figure 7-21. Click Advance Every and type a number for the interval between slides. From the Transition pull-down menu select a transition effect.

3. **View the Presentation.** Check the box for View PDF after Saving in the PDF Presentation dialog box and click the Save button. The Save dialog box opens. Navigate to a folder destination and click Save in the Save dialog box. The file is saved and opens in Acrobat in Full Screen mode.

4. **Exit Full Screen mode.** After viewing the presentation press the Esc key to exit Full Screen mode. Open the Pages pane to see thumbnails of the files included in the presentation, as shown in Figure 7-22. If you want to add sounds to your presentation, you can add a sound to a Page Action by opening the Properties dialog box from a context menu on the first page.

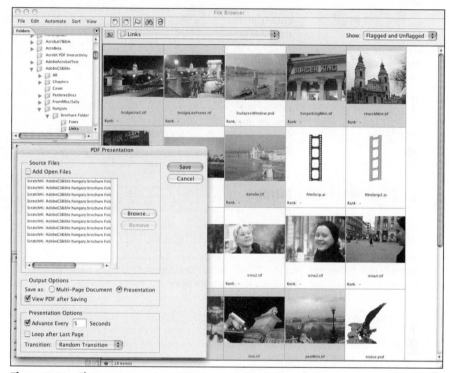

Figure 7-21: Choose Automate ⇨ PDF Presentation in the File Browser menu to open the PDF Presentation dialog box.

Cross-Reference

For information on adding sounds to page actions, see Chapter 23. For more information on using the Pages pane, see Chapter 12.

Figure 7-22: When you exit Full Screen mode and open the Pages pane, you can see thumbnails of the pages added to your presentation.

Adobe Illustrator CS

Adobe Illustrator, like other Adobe programs, is built on core PDF technology. In fact, the native Adobe Illustrator file format is PDF, and as such it is one of the best applications supporting direct export to PDF.

Illustrator has evolved to a sophisticated integration with PDF and supports the following: transparency, editing capability, layers, blending modes, text, and filters. Further integration with the program in non-PDF workflows embraces exports for Web design where its current iteration now supports one-step optimization for formats such as GIF, JPEG, PNG, SWF, and SVG.

Saving PDFs from Adobe Illustrator CS

To export PDF files from Adobe Illustrator, you use the File ⇨ Save command. The format options available to you include the native Illustrator format, Illustrator EPS, SVG (Scalable Vector Graphics), SVG Compressed, and Adobe PDF. In Illustrator, choose File ⇨ Save from a new document window. A Save dialog box opens that enables you to name the file, choose the destination, and select one of the formats just noted. When you select Acrobat PDF and click the Save button, the Adobe PDF Options dialog box opens where various PDF options appear as shown in Figure 7-23.

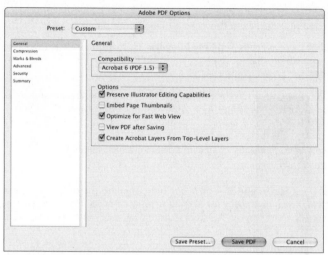

Figure 7-23: When you select the PDF format and click the Save button in the Save dialog box, the Adobe PDF Options dialog box opens, enabling you to select PDF export options.

These options include

✦ **General:** The list on the left side of the dialog box contains six categories. The default options are the General options. The right pane displays the options settings for General.

✦ **Compatibility:** Three choices are available in the File Compatibility section of the options dialog box. Here you can set the file compatibility for Acrobat versions 4, 5 and 6.

✦ **Options:** The Options section of the dialog box includes choices for font handling and color management:

   • **Preserve Illustrator Editing Capabilities:** Those who have attempted to edit PDF files in Illustrator know there have been many problems with nested grouped objects, masking, and handling text. With this option, PDF files are preserved in terms of their editing capabilities once they are saved as PDF and reopened in Illustrator. For all but screen and Web graphics, enabling this check box should be your default.

   • **Embed Page Thumbnails:** Always deselect this option. Page thumbnails are generated automatically in Acrobat viewers 5.0 and greater. If you embed page thumbnails in Illustrator, the page thumbnails add more space to the file size and the thumbnail appearances are severely degraded.

   • **Optimize for Fast Web View:** Always check the box and the file is optimized resulting in smaller file sizes.

- **View PDF after Saving:** If you check the box, Acrobat is launched and the resultant PDF document is shown in the Acrobat Document pane.

  - **Create Acrobat Layers From Top-Level Layers:** This option is only available with Acrobat 6 compatibility. Select Acrobat 6 compatibility and check the box if you want the Illustrator layers converted to Adobe PDF layers.

- **Compression:** Click Compression in the left pane and the options in the right pane show settings for compression settings. The options choice are the same as you find using Acrobat Distiller.

Cross-Reference

For information on setting compression options in Acrobat Distiller, see Chapter 8.

- **Marks and Bleeds:** Click Marks and Bleeds in the left pane and the options in the right pane change to settings you can apply for setting printer's marks. Options are the same as you find when setting marks in the Acrobat Print dialog box.

Cross-Reference

For information on setting printer's marks in the Print dialog box, see Chapter 25.

- **Advanced:** The Advanced options offer settings choices for color profile embedding, font handling, and transparency flattening.

  - **Color:** In order for the check box to be active, you must have an ICC profile identified and available for embedding. If no color management is used in the Illustrator file, the check box remains grayed out. To select color profiles choose Edit ⇨ Color Settings. After determining your color management policies, save the PDF with the selected profiles embedded. Color management must be assigned before you attempt to save the file. If you need to embed a profile and the option is grayed out, cancel out of the dialog box and choose your profile. Return to the Save as Acrobat PDF dialog box and then select the color management options.

  - **Subset fonts when percent of characters used is less than []:** Font subsetting is handled the same way here as it is handled in Acrobat Distiller. The default is set to subset fonts at 100%.

Cross-Reference

For more information on font embedding, subsetting, and font permissions, see Chapter 7.

  - **Overprint and Transparency Flattener Options (PDF 1.3 Only):** The setting is available only when you select Acrobat 4 compatibility (PDF 1.3 compatibility). When PDF 1.3 compatibility is used you can choose to preserve overprints and flatten transparency.

Cross-Reference

For information and options choices available for overprints and transparency flattening, see Chapter 25.

- **Security:** Click Security in the left pane and the options choices for applying security to the saved file are shown. Security settings are the same as you can apply in Acrobat.

Cross-Reference

For more information applying security settings in Acrobat, see Chapter 21.

- **Summary:** The Summary pane lists a summarized version of the settings you apply to the saved PDF documents. You can save the summary and send it to a service provider to accompany the file or save the summary for your own reference.

When you click Save PDF, the document is saved in PDF format. From Illustrator, the file is converted to PDF directly, and Distiller isn't introduced in the background.

Saving layered files to PDF

You can save layered Illustrator CS files to PDF with Adobe PDF Layers. Creating layered PDF documents from Illustrator is supported in Illustrator CS version 1 and above. To create PDF layers you need an authoring program capable of creating layers and capable of saving or exporting to PDF 1.5 format (Acrobat 6 compatibility) and above—Illustrator CS does both.

When saving files with layers to PDF with Adobe PDF Layers, create the default layer view you want to appear in Acrobat. As shown in Figure 7-24, two layers in an Illustrator file are hidden and three layers are visible. The layer visibility you see in Illustrator is the same visibility you'll see in Acrobat when saving as PDF.

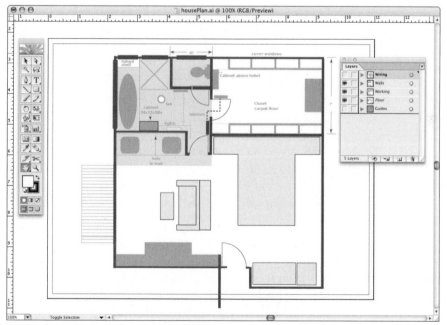

Figure 7-24: When saving to PDF with layers, create the layer view in the authoring program that you want to appear as the default view in Acrobat.

In Illustrator, choose File ➪ Save or Save As and select PDF as the format. In the Adobe PDF Options dialog box select Acrobat 6 or greater compatibility and check the box for Create Acrobat Layers from Top-Level Layers. If the box is not checked, you won't see layers in the resultant PDF document.

When you open the PDF in Acrobat, you see the same layer view as when the file was saved from Illustrator, as shown in Figure 7-25.

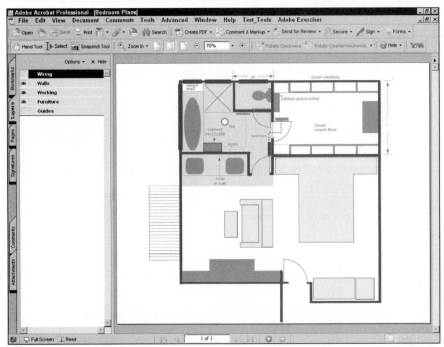

Figure 7-25: The default layer view in Acrobat appears the same as the view from Illustrator when the file was saved.

Cross-Reference For more information on working with layered files in Acrobat, see Chapter 19.

Saving SWF files

Acrobat versions 6 and 7 support many different kinds of media formats including Macromedia Flash SWF files. Using Illustrator CS you can create vector objects as animated sequences to embellish PDFs such as forms, diagrams, electronic brochures, and similar documents where you want to add animation to amplify your messages. To understand a little more about saving SWF files from Illustrator and importing them in Acrobat, follow these steps:

STEPS: Exporting SWF files to Acrobat

1. **Create a sequence in Illustrator.** Either draw vector shapes in Illustrator or drag a symbol from the Symbols palette to the document page. The shape you create is on a layer. Duplicate the shape and paste it to a second layer. Continue adding new layers and shapes to complete a sequence. You can change size, rotations, or shape designs for each shape on a different layer. In my example shown in Figure 7-26, I created a shape on one layer and sized the objects up 25 percent on each new layer.

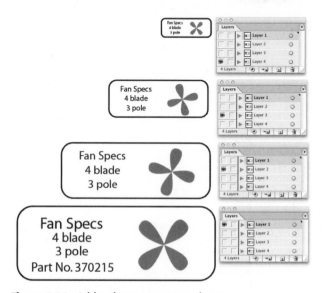

Figure 7-26: Add a shape to separate layers.

> **Tip**
>
> To easily create a sequence for motion objects, drag a symbol from Illustrator's Symbols palette to the document page. Press the Control/Option key and click+drag to duplicate the shape. Press Control/⌘+D several times to repeat the duplication. Select all the objects and open the Layers palette fly-away menu. Select Release to Layers (Sequence) from the palette menu commands. All your objects are distributed to separate layers.

2. **Export to SWF.** Choose File ⇨ Export. In the Export dialog box, select Macromedia Flash (swf) from the Format pull-down menu. Add a filename, select a target folder, and click the Export button. The Macromedia Flash SWF Format Options dialog box opens.

3. **Set the SWF file format options.** In the Macromedia Flash SWF Format Options dialog box shown in Figure 7-27 are choices for the frame rate, exporting HTML compatible files, and various appearance options. Make your choices here and click OK to continue the export to SWF.

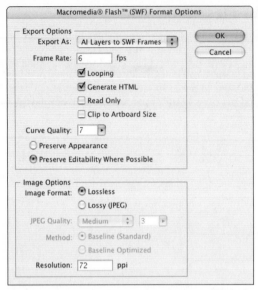

Figure 7-27: Set options in the Macromedia Flash (SWF) Format Options dialog box.

4. **Save the Illustrator file.** When you export to a file format from Illustrator, your file is not yet saved. If you want to return to the document to make additional edits, save the file. Choose File ➪ Save and save the file with Create PDF Compatible File checked.

5. **Import the SWF file in Acrobat (Acrobat Professional only).** Open the Advanced Editing Toolbar and select the Movie tool. Drag a rectangle on the document page where you want to import the SWF file. Click the Browse button in the Add Movie dialog box, locate your SWF file, and import it. When you import the movie, the first frame in the sequence appears within the movie rectangle, as shown in Figure 7-28.

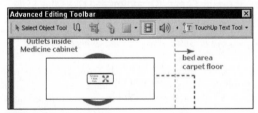

Figure 7-28: Select the Movie tool from the Advanced Editing Toolbar and drag open a rectangle to import a movie clip.

6. **Play the movie clip.** Select the Hand tool and click the movie frame. Figure 7-29 displays the last frame in a sequence. The effect is the message box appears to explode in view as the sequence is played.

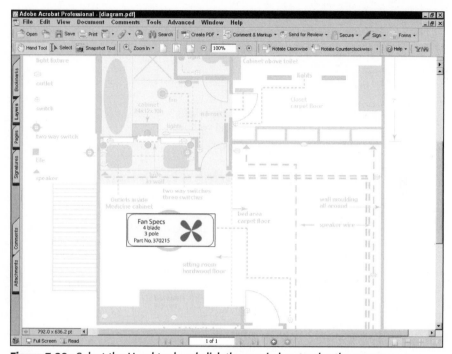

Figure 7-29: Select the Hand tool and click the movie box to play the sequence.

Cross-Reference You can add buttons and links with play Actions to start, stop, and play movie frames, and you can edit the poster image that appears within the movie box. To learn more about working with movie files, see Chapter 18.

Opening Illustrator files in Acrobat

Illustrator native files do not need conversion to PDF to be viewed in Acrobat. Acrobat supports opening native Illustrator .ai documents. When you click the Open tool, choose File ⇨ Open, or select Create PDF From File and select a native Illustrator .ai file, the file opens in Acrobat without conversion to PDF. All this is possible if the original Illustrator document was saved with an option for Create PDF Compatible File. When you save Illustrator files as native documents and click the Save button in the Save or Save As dialog box, the Illustrator Options dialog box opens as shown in Figure 7-30. Under the Options, select the Create PDF Compatible File check box. You can then open the file in Acrobat without converting it to PDF.

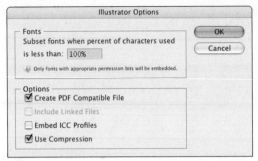

Figure 7-30: Saving with PDF compatibility results in file types that can be opened in Acrobat without conversion to PDF.

Exporting to PDF from Adobe InDesign

Adobe InDesign CS is so far ahead of any professional design program it's in a league of its own. InDesign CS introduced methods of layout and design that require graphic artists and professional designers to rethink the way they handle file formats, colorspaces, layered files, and file attributes. With support for native layered files from Illustrator and Photoshop, native transparency, RGB color conversion, and transparent objects, designers need only to save native files without color conversion and import direct to InDesign to create professional files designed for commercial printing. These methods combined with superior type handling, nested style sheets, table formatting, and exporting to PDF/X make InDesign the premier choice for professional layout artists.

Cross-Reference For more information on PDF/X, see Chapter 8.

To export to PDF from InDesign, choose File ➪ Export. In the Export dialog box, select Adobe PDF from the Format pull-down menu and click Save. The Export PDF dialog box then appears, as shown in Figure 7-31. Options here provide some similar settings as you find with Adobe Illustrator as well as a number of additional attribute choices for handling files designed for print, Web hosting, and screen viewing. You can export Bookmarks that appear in the resultant PDF file, export interactivity with buttons and actions, export HTML and hyperlinks, and create PDF documents designed for commercial printing.

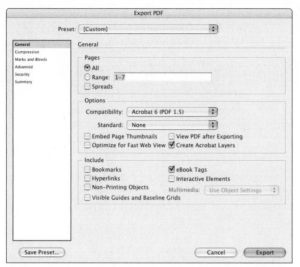

Figure 7-31: InDesign can export documents with options settings to accommodate files designed for print, Web hosting, and interactive screen viewing.

Exporting PDFs for print

The Preset pull-down menu offers you choices for several Adobe PDF Settings that determine how your PDF is created. Among those options are selections for PDF/X files. PDF/X is a format specifically designed for printing and commercial prepress. When you export to PDF/X, you resolve colorspace problems, transparency problems, and other potential problems faced when printing documents on commercial devices.

Cross-Reference   For a detailed explanation of PDF/X and Adobe PDF Settings, see Chapter 8.

When you select one of the PDF/X options for files intended for commercial printing, the PDF compatibility option is selected for you, as shown in Figure 7-32. Note that when selecting PDF/X as a preset you cannot save with Adobe PDF Layers because the PDF/X file compatibility is Acrobat 4 compatibility.

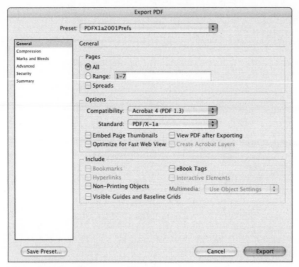

Figure 7-32: When exporting for commercial printing, select a preset for creating a PDF/X file.

Exporting Adobe PDF Layers

Just as when exporting layers from Illustrator, you set the default layer view in InDesign that you want to appear in Acrobat as a default view. You can add interactive buttons in InDesign and export your interactive links that are also recognized by Acrobat. In the Export PDF dialog box shown in Figure 7-31, be certain to check the boxes for Create Acrobat Layers and the Include items such as Bookmarks, Hyperlinks, and Interactive Elements. Click the Export button to export your document to PDF. In Figure 7-33 a layered InDesign CS file with interactive buttons and imported video is prepared for export to PDF.

When you open the file in Acrobat, a modification of the button attributes sets a different layer visibility and plays the imported video as shown in Figure 7-34. These kinds of design opportunities provide artists with tools to create effective presentations and electronic brochures that users who download the free Adobe Reader software can view.

Figure 7-33: A layout is prepared in Adobe InDesign with imported video, interactive buttons, and multiple layers.

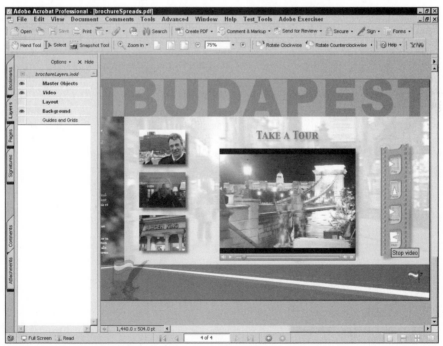

Figure 7-34: A slight modification to the button attributes changes layer visibility and plays the imported video.

Exporting to PDF from Adobe GoLive CS

Adobe GoLive CS is a powerful Web authoring tool. Inasmuch as you can convert Web pages to PDF and use the Create PDF From File command to convert HTML files locally on your hard drive to PDF, you may want to check a PDF view while working in GoLive. To complement the interoperability between the Creative Suite programs, you can export InDesign files to GoLive and export GoLive documents to PDF.

In GoLive, select PDF Preview at the top of the GoLive workspace to convert your file to a PDF view, as shown in Figure 7-35. The view you see is exactly how the GoLive file appears in Acrobat when it's opened as a PDF. If you want to save the document as a PDF after previewing it, choose File ➪ Export ➪ HTML as Adobe PDF. The Save: GoLive dialog box opens in which you can name the file and select a target folder.

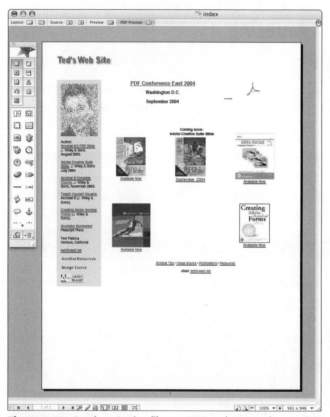

Figure 7-35: Preview GoLive files as PDF and Export the preview to create a PDF file.

Note   You must first preview your GoLive document as PDF before you can export the page to PDF.

Using Acrobat and Design Programs

Other professional programs used for design and layout from both Adobe Systems and other developers provide tools and menu commands designed for exporting documents to PDF. As time moves on in the Acrobat and PDF evolutionary cycle, finding programs that do not support PDF exports or creation becomes difficult. Some of the programs call upon Acrobat Distiller to run in the background as a program exports to PDF while others export to PDF without the assistance of Acrobat Distiller.

Among the more popular programs supporting PDF creation, you find Macromedia FreeHand, CorelDraw, QuarkXPress, Adobe PageMaker, and Adobe FrameMaker. Each program has a unique method for setting attributes and preferences for creating PDF documents. If you use any of these tools look for PDF export capability in the File menus.

Working with Engineering Applications (Windows)

Engineers, technical professionals, and architects are among the many users of programs such as Microsoft Project, Microsoft Visio, and Autodesk AutoCAD. Each of these programs uses Adobe PDFMaker to produce PDF documents. Inasmuch as you can either print PostScript or save as EPS from one or the other and distill the files in Acrobat Distiller, using PDFMaker is a much better choice.

With Microsoft Project you convert files the same way you do other Office files. Only the current view of the Project worksheet can be converted to PDF. From the desktop you can also convert Project files to PDF by right-clicking the document icon and selecting Convert to Adobe PDF.

AutoCAD and Visio offer options for converting the AutoCAD and Visio layers to PDF layers. It is critical to be certain that the Adobe PDF Settings are enabled for converting layers with either program.

From either program, open the Adobe PDF menu and select Change Conversion Settings. The Adobe PDFMaker dialog box opens like it does when you're using Convert to Adobe PDF from Microsoft Office applications. In Figure 7-36, notice the check box disabled for Always flatten layers in Adobe PDF. Be certain to disable the check box if you want layers converted to Adobe PDF layers. If you want the PDF opened in Acrobat with the Layers tab open, select the Open Layers pane when viewed in Acrobat check box.

 Caution Adobe PDF Layers are supported only in Acrobat 6 or greater and when you're creating Acrobat 6 or greater compatible files. Before you attempt to create a PDF file with layers, be certain to click the Advanced button in the Adobe PDFMaker dialog box to open the Adobe PDF Settings dialog box. Select the General tab and verify that either Acrobat 6.0 (PDF 1.5) or Acrobat 7.0 (PDF 1.6) is selected from the pull-down menu for Compatibility. If you use another compatibility setting, the PDF won't contain layers.

Other options are similar to the attributes used with Adobe PDFMaker in Office applications. After setting the options in the Acrobat PDFMaker dialog box, click OK and select the Convert to Adobe PDF tool in the AutoCAD or Visio toolbar. The same tools that are in the Office applications are installed in AutoCAD and Visio.

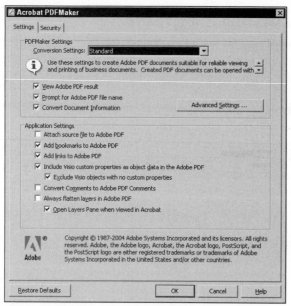

Figure 7-36: When converting AutoCAD and Visio files, disable the check box for flattening layers if you want the layers converted to Adobe PDF layers.

Cross-Reference   For information on working with layers in Acrobat, see Chapter 19.

Working with object data

Engineering and scientific programs often enable you to describe objects in drawings that result in object data that can be added to the metadata in a PDF document. When using PDFMaker you can view certain metadata in the resultant PDF file.

As an example, look at Figure 7-37 where you see a Microsoft Visio document. Objects in Visio are assigned custom properties for associating costs and comments with each milestone in a project. These data elements are added to the individual objects' metadata.

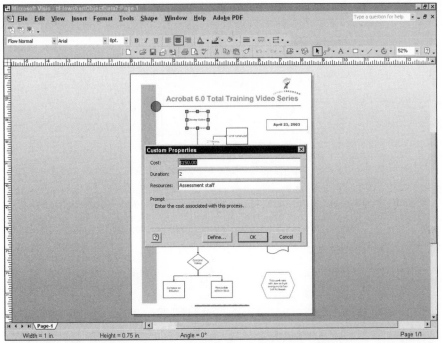

Figure 7-37: Individual objects are assigned object data in a Microsoft Visio document.

Using the Object Data tool

After converting a file to PDF where object data are added in the original authoring program, open the file in Acrobat. The first thing you see in Acrobat is a Document Status dialog box informing you that the file has special features. Included in the message is a remark about object data and another about layers. You can dismiss the dialog box shown in Figure 7-38 in future Acrobat sessions if you select the Do not show this dialog next time this document is opened check box. If you want to be reminded each time the file is opened, leave the check box unchecked.

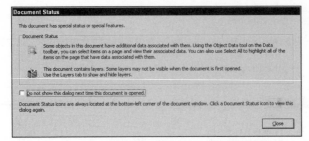

Figure 7-38: Documents containing special features open a dialog box when the file is viewed in Acrobat.

To view object metadata, open the Object Data tool from a context menu on the Acrobat Toolbar Well and select Object Data. The Object Data tool is immediately docked in the Toolbar Well. Select the tool and click an object in the document. If object data has been assigned to an object, the Object Data dialog box opens as shown in Figure 7-39. In the dialog box you can see the custom properties information originally added in Microsoft Visio.

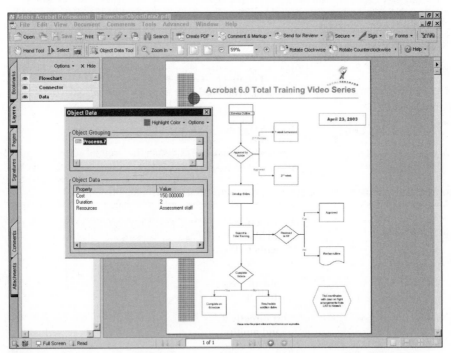

Figure 7-39: Select the Object Data tool and click an object to open the Object Data dialog box.

In order for the Object Data dialog box to open, the object you click with the Object Tool must contain object data. If you click an object without data assigned, nothing happens.

In the Object Data dialog box, the Options menu (shown in Figure 7-40) provides some menu commands for viewing, selecting, and deselecting similar objects, copying data, and searching objects. All the text you see in the Property list is searchable in the PDF document.

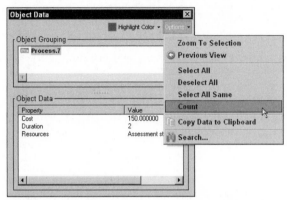

Figure 7-40: Open the Options menu to search and select data.

The additional Count menu command enables you to count objects in your document that have similar data associated with them. When you select the menu command, a dialog box reports the findings.

For other programs, such as those used in engineering and project management, where detailed information is needed to describe objects, you find much support for converting the documents and metadata to PDF when using tools like PDFMaker.

Summary

✦ Microsoft Office applications such as Word, Excel, and PowerPoint export directly to PDF with the assistance of PDFMaker. Office applications retain document structure and convert structured elements to Bookmarks and links in exported PDFs when Adobe PDFMaker is used.

✦ Adobe Creative Suite is a sophisticated solution for file interoperability. All the CS applications export directly to PDF.

✦ Adobe Photoshop can export directly to PDF as separate files and presentations. Photoshop can open single and multiple PDF documents created by any producer and preserve text and vector art when exporting to PDF.

✦ Adobe Illustrator exports Macromedia Flash SWF files that can be imported in PDF documents as movie files.

✦ Adobe Illustrator CS and Adobe InDesign CS export to PDF with layers intact.

✦ Adobe InDesign CS exports links, Bookmarks, and embedded media to PDF.

✦ Other programs such as Adobe PageMaker, Adobe FrameMaker, Macromedia FreeHand, QuarkXPress, and CorelDraw support direct export to PDF.

✦ Programs such as Microsoft Visio and Autodesk AutoCAD export to PDF with native layers converted to Adobe PDF layers. PDFMaker is available to Visio and AutoCAD when Acrobat is installed. If you install the program after Acrobat, the next time you run Acrobat it will '"self-heal"' and add the functionality.

✦ You can examine custom data applied to objects in programs like Microsoft Visio and Autodesk AutoCAD with the Object Data tool in Acrobat.

✦   ✦   ✦

Using Acrobat Distiller

Because PDF file creation has been much simplified in Acrobat 7, you may bypass thoughts of learning what Acrobat Distiller does and how PDF documents are converted with the Distiller application. If you remember the PDF conversion steps discussed in the previous two chapters, the Adobe PDF Settings were mentioned many times. These settings apply to Acrobat Distiller, and also the conversion of documents for many options from within Acrobat and via exports from authoring programs. They all use Distiller's Job Options, now referred to as the Adobe PDF Settings.

In order to successfully produce quality PDF documents, you need to have a basic understanding of how Acrobat Distiller works and what the settings control in regard to converting files to PDF. In some cases Distiller works in the background using Adobe PDF Settings you assign to the distillation process. Therefore, knowing how to change settings and understanding what options are available to you is essential. In this chapter I cover some advantages for using Acrobat Distiller and discuss how to change the Adobe PDF Settings.

Setting Up the Work Environment

You can access Acrobat Distiller in several ways. You can open Distiller from the Advanced menu command in Acrobat Standard and Acrobat Professional, you can launch Distiller from the desktop, or you can drag and drop files to the Distiller program application. None of these methods require loading special tools.

Cross-Reference For a detailed description of the various ways to access Acrobat Distiller, see the section "Accessing Distiller" at the end of this chapter.

When you convert files to PDF you typically create a PostScript file in other applications and convert the PostScript to PDF in Distiller. Therefore, the default view of the toolbars is all you need to follow the instructions throughout this chapter.

Understanding PostScript

Adobe PostScript is a *page description language* — that is, it describes the text and images on your monitor screen in a language. A raster image processor (RIP) interprets this language. Whereas PostScript is the language, the RIP behaves like a compiler. The RIP interprets the file and converts the text and images you see on your monitor to a bitmap image in dots that are plotted on a printing device. In the office environment, you won't see a RIP independent of a PostScript laser printer you use — but it exists. It's built into the printer. With high-end devices such as imagesetters, platesetters, large-format inkjet printers, on-demand printing systems, high-end composite color devices, and film recorders, the RIP is often a separate component that may be either a hardware device or software operating on a dedicated computer.

One of the reasons PostScript has grown to its present popularity is its device independence. When you draw a Bézier curve, rectangle, oval, or other geometric object in a vector art authoring application, the resolution displayed by your monitor is 72 pixels per inch (ppi). This image can be printed to a 300 dots per inch (dpi) laser printer or a 3,600 dpi imagesetter. Through the device independence of PostScript, essentially the computer "says" to the printer, "Give me all you can." The printer responds by imaging the page at the resolution it is capable of handling. When the file is ripped, the laser printer RIP creates a 300-dpi bitmap, whereas the imagesetter RIP creates a 3,600-dpi bitmap.

With all its popularity and dominance in the market, PostScript does have problems. It comes in many different dialects and is known as a *streamed* language. If you have a QuarkXPress file, for example, and import an Adobe Illustrator EPS file and a Macromedia EPS file, you'll wind up with three different flavors of PostScript — each according to the way the individual manufacturer handles its coding. If the same font is used by each of the three components, the font description resides in three separate areas of the PostScript file when printed to disk. PostScript is notorious for redundancy, especially with fonts.

About Imaging Devices

Imagesetters are high-end devices ranging from $10,000 to over $100,000 and are usually found in computer service bureaus and commercial print shops. Imagesetters use laser beams to plot the raster image on either sheet-fed or roll-fed paper or film. The paper is resin coated, and both paper and film require chemical processing through a developer, fix, and wash much like a photographic print. The material is used by a commercial printer to make plates that are wrapped around cylinders on a printing press. These prepress materials are an integral part of offset printing, and much of the printing performed today is handled from a form of digital output to material that is used to create plates for presses.

Direct-to-plate and direct-to-press systems bypass the prepress materials and expose images on plates that are used on print cylinders or directly to the press blankets where the impression receives the ink.

On-demand printing is a term describing machines that bypass the prepress process by taking the digital file from a computer directly to the press. Depending on the engineering of the output device, the consumable materials may consist of toner (as used in copy machines) or ink (as used on printing presses).

As a streamed language, PostScript requires the entire code to be processed by the interpreter before the image bitmap is created. Ever wonder why you need to wait while the RIP is churning for an endless amount of time only to eventually end up with a PostScript error or RIP crash? PostScript can't begin plotting the bitmap image until the entire PostScript stream has been interpreted.

PDF, on the other hand, is like a database file—it has a database structure. PDF eliminates redundancy with file resources. Fonts, for example, only appear once, no matter how many occurrences are used in imported EPS files. In addition, PDF takes all the dialectical differences of PostScript and converts them to a single dialect. Whereas a PostScript file containing many pages requires the entire file to be downloaded to the RIP and ultimately printed, a PDF file is page independent in that each individual page is imaged before proceeding to the next page. In short, PDF is much more efficient than PostScript for printing purposes.

Creating PostScript files

In some ways a PostScript file is very similar to a PDF file. If, for example, you create a layout in Adobe PageMaker, Adobe InDesign, Adobe FrameMaker, or QuarkXPress with images and type fonts, the document page can be printed to disk as a PostScript file. In doing so, you can embed all graphic images and fonts in the file. If you take your file to a service center, the file can be downloaded to a printing device. Assuming you created the PostScript file properly, the file prints with complete integrity.

On desktop printers, printing to a PostScript file is just like printing to a device. On printers in commercial imaging centers, many different requirements need to be considered that are not typically found on a desktop printer. Some of the considerations that need to be understood when printing PostScript files for high-end devices include the following:

 The following items address PDF creation for the purpose of printing files on commercial printing equipment. For more information on commercial printing, see Chapter 25.

✦ **PPD device selection:** In past years it was essential for you to use a device PostScript Printer Description (PPD) file. Today your PPD selection can be either a device PPD, an Acrobat Distiller PPD, or the Adobe PDF Printer that doesn't offer you a separate PPD choice. In some cases you'll find more success in using a Distiller PPD or the Adobe PDF Printer than using a device PPD, especially with PostScript clones and older printing devices.

✦ **Page size:** With desktop printers, you often have only one or two page sizes. With printers that have multiple trays or interchangeable trays, you select the appropriate page size for the tray used. With imaging equipment, you need to be certain the page size is properly selected to include all image data and printer's marks. Assume for a moment a document is created in the standard page size for a letter (8.5×11 inches) page. However, to accommodate printer's marks (registration and color bars), it turns out that the page area needs to be defined larger than a letter page. In the Paper Size area of the dialog box shown in Figure 8-1, the word *Custom* appears, indicating the page is a custom size. The thumbnail on the right in Figure 8-1 shows how the page fits within the defined size. In this example, all data and printer's marks print within the defined page. If your page is too small, some clipping of the data occurs when printed or when a PDF file is generated.

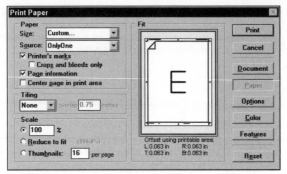

Figure 8-1: The page size was defined as a Custom size to include the printer's marks and page information.

✦ **Font inclusion:** You may need to specifically tell the host application to include fonts in the PostScript file. If the file is printed at a service center, you definitely need to include the fonts in the file you submit for output. If you distill the file in Acrobat Distiller, the fonts need to be loaded on your system in order for you to embed the fonts in the PDF file. When you have options in Print dialog boxes for font inclusion, always choose to embed the fonts.

✦ **Screening:** Halftone frequencies, or *line screens,* can be printed at different settings. With desktop printers the maximum line screen available for the device is often the default. 600-dpi laser printers, for example, most commonly use a maximum line screen of 85 lines per inch (lpi). With imaging equipment, you need to first know the requirements of the commercial printer and take his/her advice depending on the paper, press, and prepress material. Therefore, if your file is ultimately printed at 133 lpi, you must enter this value in the Print dialog box of the application creating the PostScript file.

Setting the halftone frequency is an important issue only if the PostScript file is downloaded to an imaging device where the default screens are not overridden by a technician. For files printed from Acrobat directly to printing devices, the technician who prints the file also sets the frequency in the Acrobat Advanced Printing dialog box.

Screening can also be a particular type relative to the printing device and RIP. Stochastic screening, Crystal Raster, AGFA Balanced Screens, and others are available from a PPD selection for a particular device. For these settings you need to contact your service center for the precise screening options needed and use a device PPD.

✦ **Color:** If separations are to be printed, you must make certain all identified colors are properly named in the host document. There is often an option in a Print dialog box to select separations. As you view a color list of potential separations, it is imperative to verify all colors appearing are those you specified in the document. If a spot color is in the current document, the color doesn't print unless it is an identified color in the Print dialog box. Fortunately, in Acrobat 7 a method is available for previewing separations. Before sending files off to a service center, make a habit of previewing files for printing in Acrobat.

For information regarding separation previews and soft-proofing color, see Chapter 23.

Encoding

Encoding comes in two flavors: Binary and ASCII. Binary encoding results in smaller files and prints faster on PostScript Level 2 and PostScript 3 devices. As a default you'll want to use binary encoding if you see options in the Print dialog box to choose between ASCII and Binary. If no option is available for choosing between ASCII and Binary when you print a PostScript file, the file encoding defaults to Binary.

PostScript levels

PostScript originated sometime in 1976, and later it was updated to a version called Interpress at the Xerox Palo Alto Research Center (PARC). Interpress was designed for output to early laser printers. Xerox abandoned the project, and two of the staff at Xerox PARC decided to take it forth and develop it. In 1981, John Warnock and Chuck Geschke formed Adobe Systems Incorporated, and PostScript was their first product.

On March 21, 1985, the digital print revolution was founded when Apple Computer, Aldus Corporation, Adobe Systems, and Linotype collaborated on an open architecture system for electronic typesetting. Later that year Apple Computer introduced the LaserWriter printer that came with a whopping 13 fonts fried into the printer's ROM chips and a price tag of $6,500. If you were outputting to a PostScript device in 1987, when Adobe Illustrator first appeared, you may still be waiting for that 12K Illustrator file to spit out of your laser printer. PostScript Level 1 was a major technological advance, but by today's standards it was painfully slow. Many in the imaging world remember all too well still waiting at 3:00 a.m. for the final file to print after ripping over eight hours.

In 1990, Adobe Systems introduced PostScript Level 2, which was a more robust version of PostScript and a screamer compared to the first release. In addition to speed, PostScript Level 2 provided these features:

✦ **Color separation:** In earlier days, color was preseparated on Level 1 devices. PostScript Level 2 enabled imaging specialists to separate a composite color file into the four process colors, Cyan, Magenta, Yellow, and Black. Also, there was support for spot color in PostScript Level 2.

✦ **Improved font handling:** In the early days of PostScript imaging, there were more font nightmares than you can imagine. Font encoding for PostScript fonts handled a maximum of only 256 characters. Other font sets such as Japanese have thousands of individual characters. PostScript Level 2 introduced a composite font technology that handled many different foreign character sets.

✦ **Compression:** Getting the large files across a 10-Base-T network was also a burden in the Level 1 days. PostScript Level 2 introduced data compression and supported such compression schemes as JPEG, LZW, and RLE. The files are transmitted compressed, which means they get to the RIP faster, and then decompressed at the RIP. In a large imaging center, the compression greatly improved network traffic and workflows.

In 1996, Adobe introduced PostScript 3 (note *Level* was dropped from the name). Perhaps one of the more remarkable and technologically advanced features of PostScript 3 is the inclusion of Web publishing with direct support for HTML, PDF, and Web content. PostScript 3 also provides the ability to create In-RIP separations. When you send a PDF file to an imaging center using PostScript 3 RIPs you can deliver composite color files that are sent directly to the RIP where they are separated at the imaging device.

Using Acrobat Distiller Preferences

Acrobat Distiller is launched from within Adobe Acrobat Standard or Adobe Acrobat Professional. As a separate executable application, Acrobat Distiller can also be launched from a desktop shortcut or alias or by double-clicking the program icon contained in the Distiller folder inside the Acrobat 7.0 folder.

When you first launch Acrobat Distiller, it looks like a fairly simple application. Examining the menus immediately tells you there's not much to do in the File menu. This menu is limited to opening a file, addressing preferences, and quitting the program. Distiller's real power is contained in the second menu item — the Settings menu. The commands listed in this menu offer all the control for determining how PostScript files are converted to PDF.

Before making choices in the Settings menu, look over the options in the Preferences menu. When you choose File ➪ Preferences on the Distiller Window (Windows) or the top-level Distiller ➪ Preferences (Macintosh) a dialog box opens. The options available are listed among three groups that include Startup Alerts, Output Options, and Log Files as shown in Figure 8-2 for Windows and 8-3 for Macintosh.

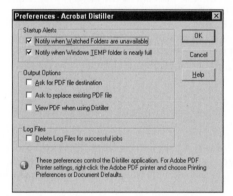

Figure 8-2: Access Acrobat Distiller Preferences by choosing File ➪ Preferences. Preferences enable you to customize startup and output options.

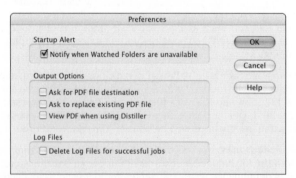

Figure 8-3: On the Macintosh, you select Preferences from the Distiller top-level menu.

Startup Alerts

The two items listed in the Startup Alerts section of the Distiller Preferences dialog box have to do with your initial startup upon launching the Distiller application:

✦ **Notify when Watched Folders are unavailable:** This command enables Distiller to monitor a folder or directory on your computer or network server to automatically distill PostScript files placed in watched folders. In an office environment, you can have different users create PostScript files and send them to a server for automatic distillation.

For more information on working with watched folders, see the "Creating watched folders" section later in this chapter.

✦ **Notify when Windows TEMP folder is nearly full (Windows only):** Distiller needs temporary disk space to convert the PostScript files to PDF documents. If the available hard disk space on your startup volume becomes less than 1 megabyte, Distiller prompts you with a warning dialog box. Leaving this preference setting enabled is always a good idea. The amount of temporary space required by Distiller is approximately twice the size of the PostScript file being distilled.

Output Options

Output Options relate to what you intend to do with the PDF both in terms of where it is saved and what to do after conversion.

✦ **Ask for PDF file destination:** When enabled, this option prompts you for the location of the saved file.

✦ **Ask to replace existing PDF file:** Selecting this option warns you if a PDF of the same name exists in the folder where the new PDF is saved. If you want to use different Adobe PDF Settings and create two PDF files, you may forget that you have a PDF with a filename the same as the new one you are creating. With this option, you are warned if Distiller attempts to overwrite your existing file.

✦ **View PDF when using Distiller:** After the PDF has been created the default Acrobat viewer launches and the PDF opens in the Document pane.

If you are running Adobe Reader and Adobe Acrobat Standard or Professional on the same computer, open the viewer you want to designate as the default viewer. When prompted to set the viewer as the default, click Yes in the dialog box. All subsequent PDF files are opened in the default viewer.

Log Files

A log file describes the sequence of steps used to produce the PDF file. The Log Files section offers an option for what to do with the log file: the Delete Log Files for successful jobs option. A log file is an ASCII text file detailing the distillation process. If an error is produced during distillation, the log file records the error even though the PDF is not created. Viewing the log file can be helpful in debugging problems with files not successfully being converted to PDF. If the PDF is successfully created, there would be no need to keep the log file on your computer. By default, you'll want to enable this check box to eliminate the clutter.

Editing Adobe PDF Settings

In earlier versions of Acrobat, the Adobe PDF Settings were referred to as Distiller Job Options. The various options you have available through several tabs in the Adobe PDF Settings dialog box control how PDFs are produced with Distiller and what attributes are assigned to the files.

When you launch Distiller, a pull-down menu appears for Default Settings, shown in Figure 8-4, for the preset options installed with Acrobat. There are nine separate settings presets in Pro designed to produce PDF files for different purposes. When you distill a PostScript file in Acrobat Distiller, or use Adobe PDF Settings when accessing the Create PDF From File menu commands that addresses different settings, the currently selected setting is used to convert the file. From the pull-down menu you select one of the menu options to produce the PDF suited for your needs. If you want to create a different setting, choose Settings ➪ Edit Adobe PDF Settings in Distiller where you can create and save custom settings.

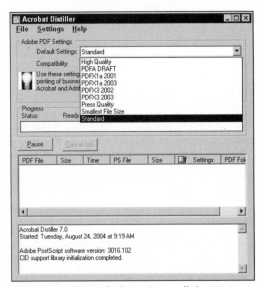

Figure 8-4: The Default Settings pull-down menu lists all currently available settings for converting PostScript files to PDF. By default, nine different preset settings are listed in the menu.

Preset Adobe PDF Settings

The Default choices for Adobe PDF Settings when you install Acrobat include

✦ **High Quality Print:** The preset settings associated with this option are established for the highest-quality images for high-end digital prepress and printing. The lowest levels of compression and downsampling are used to preserve image quality.

✦ **PDF/A:Draft:** PDF/A is a standard for archival purposes. Acrobat Distiller does a minimal check to assure PDF/A compliance hence you have PDF/A Draft as an options choice. Note that *Draft* is included in the preset name because the standard, as of this writing, is not finished.

Cross-Reference

See PDF/A later in this chapter for more detail about the standard.

✦ **PDF/X-1a:2001:** For prepress and printing, PDF/X files are streamlined for print output. PDF/X is an ISO standard developed by a committee outside Adobe Systems. Although Adobe participates in the standards committee, the format is a collaborative effort between members of the ISO standards committee. PDF/X files result in PDF documents that eliminate data not essential for printing. It does not mean the file sizes are necessarily smaller, but they are optimized for printing and produce fewer problems than non-PDF/X files. The PDF/X-1a format supports process (CMYK) and spot color.

Cross-Reference

See PDF/X later in this chapter for more detail about all the variations of the PDF/X format.

✦ **PDF/X1a:2003:** A newer version of the PDF/X-1a subset that supports Acrobat 5 compatible files.

✦ **PDF/X-3:2002:** Like PDF/X-1a, the file format is a subset of the PDF format. PDF/X-3 files support ICC profile embedding. If working in a color-managed workflow, use this flavor of PDF/X.

✦ **PDF/X3:2003:** A newer version of the PDF/X-3 subset that supports Acrobat 5–compatible files.

✦ **Press Quality:** These settings are virtually identical to the settings for High Quality (see first bullet). The difference between the two is that when you use the High Quality settings, any fonts not available for embedding during distillation are noted in the log file but the PDF is produced without the embedded fonts. When you use Press Quality, the job cancels at the first encounter of a font not available for embedding and the PDF is not produced.

✦ **Smallest File Size:** The intent for this option is to produce files for Web hosting, e-mailing, and screen views. The name implies that the file sizes are very small, but in reality, you can create smaller file sizes by editing the downsampling of the images. The sampling resolution only downsamples files above 150 pixels per inch (ppi) to 100 ppi. You can create a new set for smaller file sizes and downsample all images to 72 ppi for Web hosting when the images don't need to be displayed above a 100% view.

✦ **Standard:** The general-purpose setting and quite often the default when accessing settings the first time in Acrobat is the Standard choice. For office desktop color printers, laser printers, photocopiers, and general-purpose printing, the settings create PDF files with no lower than 150 ppi resolutions and embed fonts when necessary.

If one of these preset conditions comes close to producing the type of PDF you want to create, but it doesn't exactly meet your needs, go ahead and select that preset option and then choose Settings ➪ Edit Adobe PDF Settings to open a dialog box where you can make changes. When you finish editing the settings to your satisfaction, you have an opportunity to save your own custom preset file that you can access at a later time. There are six panes where you can choose to change the settings. They are General, Images, Fonts, Color, Advanced, and Standards.

General settings

If you need to make any changes in the Adobe PDF Settings from one of the preset options, or you need to create a new setting, choose Settings ➪ Edit Adobe PDF Settings to open the Adobe PDF Settings dialog box as shown in Figure 8-5. The first of six panes appear, labeled General, which covers some general controls:

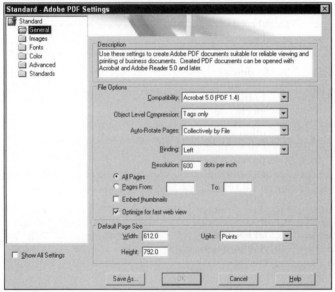

Figure 8-5: The first Adobe PDF Settings that appear when you choose Settings ➪ Edit Adobe PDF Settings are those under the General pane.

✦ **Description:** A field box at the top of the General pane is editable and enables you to add a message description about the new settings you create. Place the cursor in the field box, highlight any existing text, and delete it. Type your new description in the field box. When you save the new setting, the description is saved along with your chosen options.

✦ **Compatibility:** You have choices for Acrobat 3.0, 4.0, 5.0, 6.0, and 7.0 compatibilities. Using earlier compatibility versions may affect the visibility of PDFs with earlier viewers. If you work in an enterprise where a large installed user base is using a particular version of Acrobat, create files for the compatibility version consistent with the site license of the Acrobat version. If you're creating files for mass distribution, think about forgetting Acrobat 3 and 4 compatibilities and focus on versions 5 through 7. Be aware that if you create Acrobat 6 or 7 compatible files and use new features like embedding media clips or working with 2D barcodes, users of earlier versions won't be able to view your files. Excluding older versions is always a trade-off, and you need to clearly think about whom you want to target when distributing content.

✦ **Object Level Compression:** Non-compressed objects are consolidated into streams for more efficient compression. You have choices for applying no compression (Off) or using Tags Only or Maximum (but there is no description in the Help file about what this means). You can reduce file sizes by selecting Tags only for Object Level Compression.

✦ **Auto-Rotate Pages:** You can have pages automatically or individually rotated during distillation. Choices from the pull-down menu include turning off rotation, rotating collectively by file, and rotating individually. When you select Collectively by File, Acrobat analyzes the text in the file and rotates pages based on the orientation of the majority of the text in the entire file. When you choose Individually, Acrobat rotates each page based on the majority of text on a given page. Selecting Off results in no page rotation.

✦ **Binding:** This setting relates to viewing pages in an Acrobat viewer with Continuous – Facing or Facing page layouts and with thumbnails when viewed aside each other. In addition the binding can affect other items like the direction of scrolling text across the screen and certain animated effects you add. By default, the binding is left-sided.

✦ **Resolution:** Settings for Resolution affect only vector objects and type in EPS files. The settings range between 72 and 4000 dpi. A handy Tool Tip appears when you click in the field box that shows the upper and lower limits of acceptable values. Lower resolution settings may create banding with gradients when files are printed. In practicality you'll notice no visual difference if you change the resolution around the default of 600. Setting the resolution to 2400 adds less than 3K to your file size.

✦ **All Pages/Pages From:** You can choose to create a PDF within a specified range of pages from a PostScript file that has been printed to disk from a document containing many pages. If one page is having trouble converting to PDF, you can eliminate it from distillation by choosing a specified page range. The default, All Pages, distills all pages in the PostScript file.

✦ **Embed thumbnails:** Thumbnails add about 3K per page to your PDF file. Thumbnails are helpful when you're editing PDF files in Acrobat or browsing PDF files onscreen. However, because they create larger files, you'll want to eliminate thumbnails when producing PDF files for Web use or sending your PDF files across the Internet for output to printing devices. If you're using Acrobat viewers 5.0 and greater, thumbnails are displayed on-the-fly regardless of whether they have been embedded. Any legacy PDFs created with older PDF formats are also displayed with thumbnails without embedding when viewed in later viewers.

✦ **Optimize for fast web view:** An optimized PDF file is smaller than one created without optimization. All files intended to be used for screen views, CD-ROM replication, and Web usage should all be optimized. Generally, almost any printing device also accepts optimized files. As a default, keep this option On. Acrobat optimizes files by eliminating repeating elements and supplying pointers to where the first occurrence of an object is found in the file. Optimization also prepares files for page-at-a-time downloading from Web servers. If byte-serving capability exists on a server, the optimized files download pages as they are viewed.

✦ **Default Page Size:** Setting page sizes in these field boxes only applies to distillation of EPS and PostScript files where page boundaries are not specified. Whatever you enter in the field boxes when distilling PostScript files is ignored if the page boundary is included in the file. If you want to trim a page size or create a larger page size for an EPS file, you can establish the dimensions in the field boxes for width and height. The Units pull-down menu enables you to choose from four different units of measure.

Images

You can manage compression and sampling of images better with Acrobat Distiller than with some other methods used to create PDFs. For example, Create PDF from File offers more limited sampling options than Distiller does. You have much control over how much compression is used and what methods of downsampling are used in the Images pane. Compression and sampling choices are available for three different image types: Color images, Grayscale, and Monochrome images.

Color images

The first category handles color images used in your original file. You have choices for the sampling method and the amount of compression you want to apply. These include

✦ **Downsample:** The Downsample pull-down menu offers choices for no sampling or three different sampling methods that include:

• **Off:** This turns off all compression for color images.

• **Bicubic Downsampling to:** A pull-down menu and two field boxes appear as your first choices in the Color Image section. Bicubic Downsampling is the default setting for all preset Adobe PDF Settings. Bicubic downsampling uses a weighted average to determine the resampled pixel color. The algorithm is much more mathematically intensive and, as a result, this method takes the longest time to complete distillation when files are downsampled. The upside is it produces the best image quality for continuous tone images. With this method as well as the other two choices for resampling images there are two field boxes where the amount of sampling is user defined. The values range between 9 and 2400 ppi. The *for images above* field box enables you to choose when an image is resampled. For example, in Figure 8-6, only images above 225 dpi are affected when distilled with this setting.

• **Average Downsampling to:** From the pull-down menu the item following the Off selection is Average Downsampling to. When you resample an image by downsampling, the average pixel value of a sample area is replaced with a pixel of the averaged color. The field boxes to the right of the sampling method are for user-determined sampling amounts, used in the same way as the preceding Bicubic method.

- **Subsampling to:** When Subsampling is specified, a pixel within the center of the sample area is chosen as the value applied to the sample area. Thus, downsampling noted previously, replaces pixels from averaged color values, whereas subsampling replaces pixels from a given color value. Of the two methods, subsampling significantly reduces the amount of time to resample the image. Because all that averaging is taking place with downsampling, the calculations are more extensive, thereby increasing the distillation time. Subsampling, however, may result in more problems in the printed PDF file. Unless you have a large single-color background, you are better off choosing Bicubic downsampling when printing to hard copy.

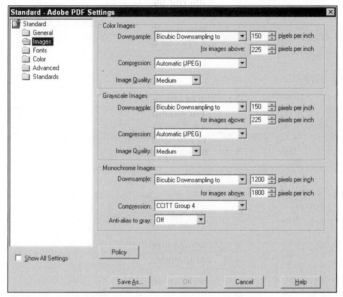

Figure 8-6: Distiller provides many more compression controls than some other PDF creators. In this dialog box, you make choices for the type of sampling and the amount of compression applied to images.

✦ **Compression:** The pull-down menu enables you to select from Automatic (JPEG), JPEG, ZIP, or Off., depending on the compatibility setting you use. When you select Automatic, Distiller examines each image and automatically determines which compression to use (that is, either ZIP or JPEG). If an image has large amounts of a common color value, ZIP compression is used. If an image consists of smooth transitions of color, such as a continuous tone photograph, JPEG compression is used. If you want to apply the same compression to all images, you can select either the JPEG or ZIP options. Doing so eliminates any decision making by Distiller about the type of compression to be applied. When you select Off, no compression is applied. You might want to downsample images as noted earlier with one of the downsampling options, but not want to apply compression to the images.

✦ **Image Quality:** After you select the compression type, you have one of five choices (also depending on compatibility) for the amount of compression applied. Maximum relates to less compression, whereas Minimum relates to high compression. For high-end prepress, use the Maximum or High choice from the pull-down menu. For desktop color printers, use Medium quality; and for Web, screen, or CD-ROM replication, use Low quality. The Minimum setting might be used in some cases with screen or Web graphics, but continuous tone photographs often appear visibly degraded. You might use this setting to transfer files quickly across the Internet for client approvals and then later use a higher setting for the final production documents.

Grayscale

All the choices you have for color images are identical for grayscale images. You can use different settings for color and grayscale images by toggling through all the options. When the final PDF is produced, the sampling and compression for your images are respectively applied from choices made for each image type.

Monochrome images

Monochrome images include only two color values — black and white. Photoshop line art is a monochrome image. This is not to be confused with line art as we define it with vector art applications. The sampling methods available to you for monochrome images are identical to those described for color images. Compression settings, however, are much different. In addition to Off for applying no compression, the options include

✦ **CCITT Group 3:** The International Coordinating Committee for Telephony and Telegraphy (CCITT) Group 3 compression is used by fax machines. The images are compressed in horizontal rows, one row at a time.

✦ **CCITT Group 4:** CCITT Group 4 is a general-purpose compression method that produces good compression for most types of bitmap images. This compression method is the default and typically the best method for bitmap images.

✦ **ZIP:** ZIP compression is more efficient than earlier versions of Acrobat that used LZW compression. ZIP achieves approximately 20 percent more compression. It should be used when large areas of a single color appear in an image.

✦ **Run Length:** The Run Length format is a lossless compression scheme particularly favorable to bitmap monochrome images. You can run tests yourself for the compression method that works best for you. Typically CCITT Group 4 handles most of your needs when compressing these images.

✦ **Anti-Alias to gray:** Bitmap images may appear pixelated onscreen or, in some cases, when printed. By using anti-aliasing, images are rendered with a smoother appearance. You can choose the amount of anti-aliasing from the pull-down menu. Choices are for 2, 4, and 8 bits that produce 4, 16, and 256 levels of gray, respectively. If you use anti-aliasing with scanned type, small point sizes may appear blurry, especially with higher gray levels.

✦ **Policy:** Click the Policy button and the Adobe PDF – Image Policy dialog box opens as shown in Figure 8-7. The options in the dialog box enable you to control a job determined from decisions you make about image resolution. From the pull-down menus below each resolution item you can select from Ignore, Warn and Continue, and Cancel Job. If a given image is below a resolution value you add to one of the three field boxes for a given image type, you can instruct Acrobat to honor the choice(s) you make from the menu selections. Ignore is the default and no result occurs if images fall below a certain resolution. Warn and Continue opens a warning dialog box, informs you that Distiller found an image below the resolution you specify in one of the field boxes, and continues producing the PDF. Cancel Job stops all distillation if an image is found below the resolution setting(s).

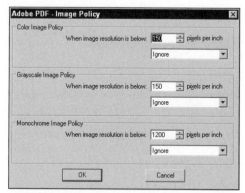

Figure 8-7: Adobe PDF – Image Policy enables you to set options for a job determined on decisions you make for image resolution.

Guidelines for sampling images

Acrobat handles sampling appropriate for your output needs as long as the image sampling is equal to or greater than the requirements for the output. If image resolution is lower than the output needs, then Distiller isn't able to upsample images to provide the necessary resolution. Even though Distiller can effectively downsample images, you should observe a few rules.

First, you should sample the resolution for all images in a layout or design at the highest output requirement. For example, if you intend to use prepress and commercial printing, then the image sample needs a resolution to support commercial printing. In this regard, you want to sample images in Photoshop at the required resolution. Don't rely on Distiller to downsample images during distillation. The time you save can add up if you're converting many files with high-resolution images. When you open the Adobe PDF Settings and select the Images pane, select Off for the sampling items.

You use the second rule when repurposing images. If you have a PostScript file that has been printed for a higher order of output, like the commercial printing discussed earlier in this chapter, then you don't need to create a second PostScript file for another output destination. Use the same PostScript file and select the sampling options appropriate for the output. Using this same example, if you now want to create a PDF for screen views, select Bicubic Downsampling to and set the resolution to 72 dpi.

Tip If you don't distill files in Acrobat Distiller to produce PDFs and you want to repurpose several documents, you can create Batch Sequences and use the PDF Optimizer to run a sequence on a collection of PDF documents. For more information on using the PDF Optimizer and creating Batch Sequences, see Chapter 14.

Fonts

The distinctive advantage of using the Portable Document Format is that it maintains file integrity across computers and across platforms. One of the greatest problems with file integrity is the handling of fonts. Fortunately, Distiller provides the ability to embed fonts within the PDF so the end user won't need font installations to view and print PDF files. The Fonts pane shown in Figure 8-8 offers options for setting font-embedding attributes during distillation.

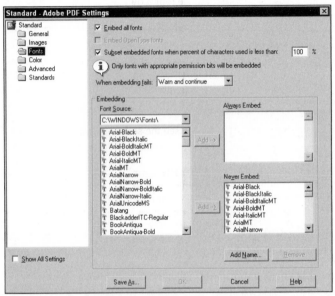

Figure 8-8: The Fonts item in Adobe PDF Settings displays the control over font embedding available to you during distillation.

Options in the Fonts pane include

✦ **Embed all fonts:** Unless you have a specific reason not to embed fonts, this option should always be enabled for file exchanges and printing. Circumstances for when not to embed fonts might be for where you want to reduce file sizes to the smallest possible size for Web hosting or if your documents will be exclusively in your organization and everyone has the fonts used.

Caution

Many different font developers exist, and the permissions for use of fonts from these developers vary considerably. To legally include font embedding in a PDF file, you need to know whether the developer provides the permission for inclusion. Adobe original fonts that are owned by Linotype-Hell, International Typeface Corporation, AGFA, AlphaOmega, Bigelow & Holmes, Fundicion Typografica Neufville, and Monotype Typography, Ltd., as well as those in the Adobe library, can be used for font embedding without written releases. Fonts with licensing restrictions often appear with an explanation of the limitations of use. If in doubt, you'll need to check with the developer or distributor to inquire as to whether you can legally distribute PDF files that include certain fonts. Failure to do so may result in a copyright violation.

✦ **Embed OpenType fonts:** If the box is active, check the box to embed all OpenType fonts. The box is active only when using Acrobat 7 compatibility.

✦ **Subset embedded fonts when percent of characters used is less than [ ]:** Some PDF producers provide you an opportunity to subset PostScript, OpenType, and TrueType fonts. The difference between the subsetting in Distiller as opposed to other producers is your ability to determine when a font is subset. With Distiller, you can specify when you want subsetting to occur. The subsetting percentage has to do with the percentage of *glyphs* (special renderings) in the font. If 100% is selected, Distiller includes all information necessary to draw all the glyphs in the font. Lower percentages determine what characters among the set are embedded. Type 3, TrueType, and CID fonts are always embedded regardless of what value is supplied. (For font format descriptions see Table 8-2 later in this chapter.)

When two or more PostScript files are converted to PDF with Acrobat Distiller using font subsetting, Distiller gives the resulting PDF only one font subset. The result is a more efficient PDF document and produces smaller file sizes, especially when combining several PostScript files to produce a single PDF.

Note

For information on concatenating PostScript files, see the section "Concatenating PostScript Files" at the end of this chapter.

✦ **When embedding fails:** This pull-down menu offers three choices. Choose Ignore to ignore a failed font being embedded, in which case distillation continues. The Warn and Continue option displays a warning and then continues distillation. Choose Cancel to cancel the distillation if a font embedding error occurs. When sending files off to service centers for imaging or when font substitution is not desired, use this latter option as your default. If the PDF is not produced, you won't inadvertently forget there was a problem with font embedding.

✦ **Embedding:** The left side of the dialog box lists all fonts available for embedding. From the pull-down menu you select from the different folders Distiller monitors for fonts. Distiller can monitor font locations on your computer. If you want to view the font list from another monitored folder, click the pull-down menu and select the folder. Regardless of what is listed in the Embedding list, Distiller can also embed fonts that were included in the PostScript file or all the folders listed for monitoring. The fonts to be embedded must be present in either the PostScript file or a monitored folder.

Note

Fonts that have license restrictions are shown in the Font Source list with a padlock icon. If you select the font, the restriction attributes are displayed in the Fonts pane. You cannot move locked fonts to the Always Embed list.

Cross-Reference

For information related to monitoring font folders, see the section "Identifying Font Locations" later in this chapter.

✦ **Always Embed:** A list of fonts for always embedding appears to the right of the Embedding list. You add fonts to this list by selecting them from the Embedding list and clicking the right-pointing chevron (double arrows). You can select multiple fonts by pressing the Ctrl (Windows) key or ⌘ (Macintosh) key and clicking all the fonts to be included. If the fonts are listed in a contiguous display, press Shift+click. After selecting the font(s), click the right-pointing chevron. A good use for the Always Embed list might be for a font that appears in your company logo. Regardless of the type of document you create, you may want to always include your corporate font set in all your documents to avoid any font substitution.

Note

The design of TrueType and OpenType fonts enables the type designer the ability to prevent font embedding. These fonts can be moved to the Always Embed list, but if they are designed without embedding permissions, they fail to embed in PDFs. Font embedding errors are reported in the log file, which you can view in a text editor. If a PDF is produced, you can choose File ➪ Document Properties ➪ Fonts to determine whether the font was embedded.

✦ **Never Embed:** This list operates the same way as the Always Embed list. You select fonts to be eliminated from the set of monitored fonts or fonts contained in a PostScript file. One use for this list might be to eliminate Courier, Times, Helvetica, and Symbol (the Base 13 fonts). Because they are usually burned into ROM chips on most PostScript devices, you rarely have a problem either viewing them or printing documents containing these fonts.

Note

The Base 14 fonts are sometimes referred to as the Base 13 + 1 fonts. The Base 13 fonts consist of Courier, Helvetica, Times, and Symbol. Courier, Helvetica, and Times include Roman, bold, italic, and bold italic, thus resulting in four fonts for each family. The extra font added to the base set is Zapf Dingbats. The fonts shipped with Acrobat 6 and 7 are no longer the Base 14 fonts that were shipped with earlier versions of Acrobat. Acrobat 6 ships with a new set of Base fonts that include AdobePiStd (a replacement for Zapf Dingbats), Courier, Symbol, AdobeSansMM, and Adobe SerifMM). Acrobat Distiller 6 and 7 does not embed the Base fonts.

✦ **Add Name:** You can add fonts to the Always Embed list or the Never Embed list by entering the font name in a separate dialog box. To add a font name, you must type the name in the dialog box precisely as the font is identified. When you click the Add Name button in the Fonts pane, the Add Font Name dialog box opens where you enter the name in the field box. Two radio buttons exist for determining where the font is added. Select either the Always Embed list or Never Embed list as needed. Click Done, and the font appears in the appropriate list.

✦ **Remove:** If you add a font name to either the Always Embed list or the Never Embed list, and you want to delete that name, select the font name to be deleted and click Remove. You can't remove fonts from the Embedding list. The only time Remove is enabled is when you select a font name in either the Always Embed list or Never Embed list.

Note

The priority used by Distiller to decide whether to embed a font in the PDF follows an order to resolve ambiguity. The Never Embed list is viewed by Distiller as having the highest order of priority. If you place a font in the Never Embed list, it is not to be embedded even though you may add the same font to the Always Embed list.

Font types

Any PDF author will tell you the continuing problem with file displays and printing as well as producing PDFs is in regard to font handling. People swear at times that they have enabled all the appropriate controls for font embedding and PDF file creation, yet the resulting PDF either displays or prints with font substitution. Gathering as much knowledge as you can with regard to font evolution, design, engineering, and proper use helps you understand how to overcome problems and provide solutions for your workflow. To gain a little more understanding, look at the font types, formats, and their characteristics:

✦ **Type 0:** Type 0 (zero) is a high-level composite font format that references multiple font descendents. Type 0 fonts use an OCF (Original Composite Font) format that was Adobe's first effort in attempting to implement a format for handling fonts with large character sets. A good example of a font using a large character set is Asian Language font types. Today, the OCF format is not supported.

✦ **Type 1:** By far the most popular PostScript font today is the Type 1 font. These are single-byte fonts handled well by Adobe Type Manager (Windows and Macintosh OS X) and all PostScript printers. Type 1 fonts use a specialized subset of the PostScript language, which is optimized for performance. For reliability, use of Type 1 fonts presents the fewest problems when embedding and printing to PostScript devices.

Note The one problem with Type 1 fonts is there isn't a means for flagging the font for *don't embed*. As a result, the end user can't determine font permissions for embedding Type 1 fonts. As of this writing Adobe is converting all its Type 1 fonts to OpenType fonts. OpenType fonts always have an extra bit to determine embedding rights. For more information on OpenType fonts, see "OpenType Font Format" later in this section.

✦ **Type 2:** Type 2 fonts offer compact character description procedures for outline fonts. They were designed to be used with the Compact Font Format (CFF). The CFF format is designed for font embedding and substitution with Acrobat PDFs.

✦ **Type 3:** Type 3 fonts are PostScript fonts that have often been used with some type-stylizing applications. These fonts can have special design attributes applied to the font such as shading, patterns, exploding 3-D displays, and so on. The fonts can't be used with ATM (Adobe Type Manager), and they often present problems when you're printing to PostScript devices. You should not use them when creating PDF files.

✦ **Type 4:** Type 4 was designed to create font characters from printer font cartridges for permanent storage on a printer's hard drive (usually attached by a SCSI port to the printer). PostScript Level 2 provided the same capability for Type 1 fonts and eventually made these font types obsolete.

✦ **Type 5:** This font type is similar to the Type 4 fonts but used the printer's ROM instead of the hard drive. PostScript Level 2 again made this format obsolete.

✦ **Type 32:** Type 32 fonts are used for downloading bitmap fonts to a PostScript interpreter's font cache. By downloading directly to the printer cache, space is saved in the printer's memory.

✦ **Type 42:** Type 42 fonts are generated from the printer driver for TrueType fonts. A PostScript wrapper is created for the font, making the rasterization and interpretation more efficient and accurate. Type 42 fonts work well with PDFs and printing to PostScript printers.

✦ **OpenType Font Format:** OpenType is a recent joint effort by Adobe Systems and Microsoft to provide a new generation of type font technology. OpenType makes no distinction between Type 1 and TrueType fonts. It acts as a *container* for both Type 1 and TrueType. OpenType doesn't care whether the font is Type 1 or TrueType; it uses the font inside the OpenType container accordingly. Font developers have a much easier way of porting font designs to a single format in production and mastering as well as across platforms. The OpenType format is supported with font embedding and distillation. Fonts eventually produced with this technology are as reliable as you find with Type 1 and Type 42 fonts. In addition OpenType offers a means for flagging the fonts for embedding permissions. To embed OpenType fonts in a PDF, use Distiller 7 and check the box for Embed OpenType fonts in the Fonts pane.

✦ **Compact Font Format:** CFF is similar to the Type 1 format but offers much more compact encoding and optimization. It was designed to support Type 2 fonts but can be used with other types. CFF can be embedded in PDFs with the PDF version 1.2 format and Acrobat 3.0 compatibility. Fonts supporting this format are converted by Distiller during distillation to CFF/Type 2 fonts and embedded in the PDF. When viewed onscreen or printed, they are converted back to Type 1, which provides support for ATM and printing with integrity.

✦ **CID-keyed Fonts:** This format was developed to take advantage of large character sets, particularly the Asian CJK (Chinese, Japanese, and Korean) fonts. The format is an extension of the Type 1 format and supports ATM and PostScript printing. Kerning and spacing for these character sets are better handled in the OpenType format. On the Macintosh you can find a utility called Make CID in the Distiller: Xtras folder. For Asian TrueType or Type 1 OCF formats, use the utility to convert the fonts to CID-keyed fonts. The first time Distiller launches with the Asian character set installed, you are prompted to convert any of these fonts found in monitored folders. If you want to manually convert the fonts you can double-click the application icon. On Windows, the Make CID application isn't available. Converted fonts can be copied across platforms, and Distiller running under Windows processes PostScript files created under Mac OS that have references to the character widths.

When distilling PostScript with Acrobat Distiller, font embedding and substitution are allowed as described in Table 8-1.

Table 8-1: Distiller Handling of Font Embedding and Subsetting According to Type Format

Font	Never Embed	Always Embed	Subset
Type 1	Yes	Yes	Yes
Type 2	No—Always embedded		No—Always subsetted
TrueType			
Type 42	Yes	Yes	No—Always subsetted
CIDFontType0	Yes	Yes	No—Always subsetted
CIDFontType1	No—Always embedded		No—Always subsetted
CIDFontType2	Yes	Yes	No—Always subsetted
OpenType*	Yes	Yes	No—Always subsetted

*OpenType is supported only with Distiller 5.0 and greater.

Color

Adobe has been working on developing standard color viewing and file tagging for color spaces for some time. Releases of the latest software products continue to support sophisticated color-handling methods. Latest releases of products such as Adobe Illustrator and Adobe Photoshop have color control options consistent with the new color-handling features initially introduced in Acrobat 5. When making choices for color handling, your first decision is whether to convert color. After your conversion choice, you move on to working spaces and profile assumptions. If you tag a file for conversion, what profiles do you want to embed in the document? Under the Color Management Policies settings, you choose control for many conditions for prepress operations as well as onscreen viewing. As you view the Color pane in the Adobe PDF Settings, examine each of the controls available for color handling (see Figure 8-9).

Tip A thorough coverage of color management is a complex subject and beyond the scope of this book. If you are confused about many issues discussed in this chapter or you want to work on developing a color-managed workflow, open any Acrobat viewer. Select the Search tool and click Search PDFs on the Internet. Add *color management* for the search criteria and select Match Exact word or phrase from the pull-down menu. Click the Search the Internet button. Many PDF documents are available on the Internet that define color management and discuss how to set up color-managed workflows. You can build a library of articles and essays on the subject and keep them readily available on your local computer.

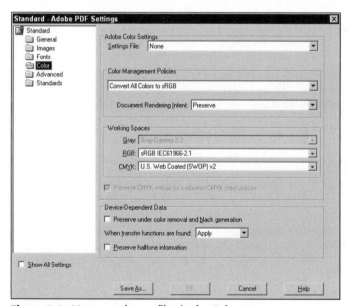

Figure 8-9: Manage color profiles in the Color pane.

Adobe Color Settings

Working with a color management system requires you to make some decisions about how the color is viewed on your computer monitor and on the final output medium. In some cases the monitor view and output medium view are the same, such as Acrobat viewer files onscreen and Web files. You make the first of your color decisions from among the choices in the pull-down menu for Settings File. The choices available to you include

✦ **Settings File:** When you select None from the pull-down menu, you can custom edit the Color Management Policies and Working Spaces choices. If you choose an option other than None, the Color Management Policies and Working Spaces options are grayed out. Other choices for Settings include prepress defaults, Photoshop emulation, defaults for Web graphics, and turning off color management. When color management and profile embedding is controlled by other programs such as Photoshop, leave the setting to None and turn off all color management for the choices discussed next.

Color Management Policies

If you select None from the Settings drop-down menu, the options for Color Management Policies and Intent are active. If you make any other choice from the menu, these items are grayed out. Choices for the Color Management Policies are different depending on what compatibility choice you select in the General pane of the Adobe PDF Settings dialog box. Acrobat 3.0 compatibility offers different options than the 4.0, 5.0, 6.0, and 7.0 compatibilities. As you look at the following policy choices, keep in mind the settings change according to the compatibility selection you made:

✦ **Leave Color Unchanged:** Enable this menu item if you presume all color handling in the PostScript file is defined for your specific needs. No color conversion occurs and device-dependent colors remain unchanged. When you send files to color-calibrated devices, you should use this option. The presumption is the device specifies all color handling and the file is not to be tagged for color management.

✦ **Tag Everything for Color Management:** When you choose Acrobat 3.0 compatibility or above, a color profile selected in the Working Spaces section is used to Tag Everything for Color Management, which embeds an ICC profile for the images, artwork, and text. The printed PDF file maintains the integrity of any documents containing embedded profiles; however, the view on your monitor screen assumes the color viewing space of the assumed profile selected respective to choices made in Working Spaces. When you choose Acrobat 3.0 compatibility, the option changes to Convert Everything for Color Management and no ICC profiles are embedded. Device-dependent color spaces for all color modes are converted to device-independent color spaces of CalRGB, CalGray, and Lab.

✦ **Tag Only Images for Color Management:** The same holds true as noted in the preceding entry except only raster images are tagged for color management according to the same compatibility options selected in the General pane. Text and vector objects remain unaffected.

✦ **Convert All Colors to sRGB:** Selecting this option converts all colors to sRGB. The RGB and CMYK color images are converted. When using Acrobat 3.0 compatibility, the RGB and CMYK images are converted to CalRGB (Calibrated RGB). Converting colors to sRGB is best used for screen and Web images. The file sizes are smaller and screen redraws appear faster. Grayscale images are unaffected by choices made for color tagging and conversion.

✦ **Convert All Colors to CMYK:** This option provides RGB and spot color conversion to CMYK. If your job is to be printed as process color, select the menu item.

Below the Color Management Policies pull-down menu is the Document Rendering Intent pull-down menu, which you use for the Intent for how color will be mapped between color spaces. Choices for Intent include

✦ **Preserve:** The first of the Intent choices is Preserve. Preserve involves no color compensation.

✦ **Perceptual:** Perceptual (Images) has to do with the mapping of pixels from one gamut to another. When you select this item, the image is mapped from the original pixels to the color gamut of the printer profile. All the out-of-gamut colors are remapped.

✦ **Saturation:** Saturation (Graphics) maintains relative saturation values. If a pixel is saturated and out of the color gamut of the printer, it is remapped preserving saturation but mapped to the closest color within the printer's gamut.

✦ **Absolute Colormetric:** This disables the white point matching when colors are converted. With no white point reference, you will notice a change in brightness values of all the remapped colors.

✦ **Relative Colormetric:** This preserves all color values within the printer's gamut. Out-of-gamut colors are converted to the same lightness values of colors within the printable gamut.

Working Spaces

Profile management for working spaces involves your decisions for embedding profiles for the color space while viewing your images onscreen. If a color space is defined for a given image and viewed on one monitor, theoretically it can be viewed the same on other monitors if the color profile is embedded in the image. Working space definitions are applied only to images tagged for color management. Either of the two tagging options, Tag Everything for Color Management or Tag Only Images for Color Management, must be selected in order for a working space to be defined:

✦ **Gray:** Selecting None from this menu prevents grayscale images from being converted. The Dot Gain choices affect the overall brightness of grayscale images. Lower values lighten the image whereas values above 20 percent display grayscale images darker. Gray Gamma choices might be used for images viewed between computer platforms. A Gray Gamma of 1.8 is suited for Macintosh viewing while the higher 2.2 Gamma is better suited for Windows.

✦ **RGB:** If you use a color calibration system or monitor profile, you can select the respective profile from this pull-down menu. Choices available to you depend on profiles installed on your computer. If you have created custom profiles from Adobe Photoshop and saved them, they are listed as menu options. Default RGB profiles from Photoshop appear here after Photoshop is installed on your computer. The default option is sRGB IEC61966-2.1. If in doubt, use this option. It is becoming an industry standard and generally good for matching color between display and color output devices.

✦ **CMYK:** CMYK profiles also appear according to those stored in the respective folder according to platform as mentioned in the preceding bullet. Profile tagging is uniquely applied to images according to the color mode of the image. Thus, the Gray options apply only to grayscale images. RGB choices are applied to only RGB images whereas the CMYK choices tag only CMYK images. When using CMYK output for prepress you may have a profile embedded in the CMYK images. You can select None for this setting while changing the Gray and RGB working spaces, which preserves the color for output while enabling you to tag the other color modes for screen views. It would be unlikely that you would use RGB and CMYK images together for prepress, but you could set up the Adobe PDF Settings for consistent display of files regardless of the color mode used.

CMYK color spaces

A single check box — Preserve CYMK values for calibrated CMYK color spaces — appears for this item. Unless you select Convert All Colors to CMYK in the Color Management Policies, the item is grayed out. Check the box when it's active and the CMYK color space is preserved when profile embedding has been applied.

Device-Dependent Data

All options available under the Device Dependent Data section are applied to images intended for prepress and printing. Whatever choices you make here have no effect on screen views:

✦ **Preserve under color removal and black generation:** If you made changes to under-color removal or black generation settings in Photoshop, these changes are preserved when the file is distilled. Disabling the check box eliminates any settings made in Photoshop.

✦ **When transfer functions are found:** If you embed transfer functions in Adobe Photoshop, you can preserve them by selecting Apply from the pull-down menu. If transfer functions have not been saved with your Photoshop file, it won't matter if Apply is used. Use Apply when you intentionally set them up in a Photoshop image and you have the settings confirmed by your printer. If you select Preserve, the transfer functions are preserved without applying them. You can eliminate transfer functions set in a file by selecting Remove from the pull-down menu. As a matter of default, if you don't use transfer functions or know what they are, select Remove from the pull-down menu. If you inadvertently save a Photoshop file as EPS and embed transfer functions, they are removed when the file gets distilled.

✦ **Preserve halftone information:** Preserving the halftone information does not disturb halftone frequencies embedded in documents, as well as custom angles, spot shapes, and functions specified. Depending on the service center you use, they may want to have you set halftone information in the PostScript file and preserve them in the PDF. For PostScript 3 devices, PDFs can be sent straight to the imagesetter and printed at the halftone frequency preserved in the file. Service centers using PostScript Level 2 RIPs won't care if the halftone frequency is preserved or not. They'll have to manually print the PDFs using the Print and Advanced Print Setup dialog boxes.

Advanced

Advanced settings enable you to make choices for other miscellaneous attributes. The controls listed in this dialog box greatly distinguish Acrobat Distiller from other PDF producers. When you select the Advanced pane in Adobe PDF Settings, the settings shown in Figure 8-10 appear.

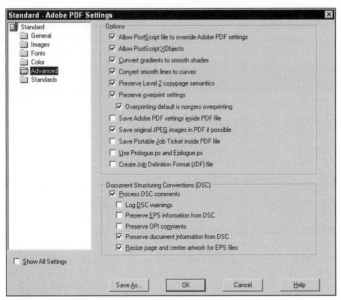

Figure 8-10: The Advanced Adobe PDF Settings offer a group of miscellaneous settings often not available with other PDF producers.

Advanced settings contain a variety of options for job ticketing, document structure, and other items not found in the previous panes. These include

✦ **Allow PostScript file to override Adobe PDF settings:** If you are certain the PostScript file you printed to disk has all the settings handled properly for output, enabling this option allows the PostScript file to supersede any changes you make in Adobe PDF Settings. Disabling the check box allows all Options specifications settings to take precedence.

✦ **Allow PostScript XObjects:** A PostScript XObject stores common information in a document, such as backgrounds, headers, footers, and so on. When PostScript XObjects are used, printing is faster, but requires more memory. If you disable the check box, XObjects won't be used and the memory burden is reduced.

✦ **Convert gradients to smooth shades:** This feature only works with Acrobat 4.0 compatibility and greater. Gradients are converted to smooth shades and appear much smoother when rendered on PostScript 3 devices. The appearance of the gradients is unaffected when viewed onscreen, but has noticeable differences when printing some files with more gray levels.

✦ **Preserve Level 2 copypage semantics:** This setting has to do with semantic differences between PostScript Level 2 and PostScript 3. If you are imaging to PostScript Level 2 devices, enable this option. If you're printing to PostScript 3 devices, disable this option. If you are sending files to an imaging center, ask the technicians which level of PostScript is used on their devices.

✦ **Preserve overprint settings:** Overprints manually applied in applications, such as illustration and layout programs, are preserved when you enable this option. Overprinting has an effect only when your files are color separated or possibly when you print composite color to proofing machines that display trapping problems from files printed as separations. If your workflow is consistent and you don't deviate between creating overprints and relying on a service center to perform them, then you could leave this item as a default for your high-end output needs. Enabling the check box has no effect on images where overprints are not present.

✦ **Overprinting default is nonzero overprinting:** When enabled, this option prevents objects with no color values specified as CMYK from knocking out other CMYK colors.

✦ **Save Adobe PDF settings inside PDF file:** This option embeds the Adobe PDF Settings used to produce the PDF inside the PDF document as a file attachment. Print shops can review the settings to diagnose problems that may have been produced during distillation. Open the Attachments pane to see the embedded file.

✦ **Save original JPEG images in PDF if possible:** Distiller decompresses JPEG files during distillation. If you select this option, the decompressed JPEG files are not recompressed by Distiller.

✦ **Save Portable Job Ticket inside PDF file:** Job tickets contain information about the original PostScript file and not the content of the PDF file. Information related to page sizes, page orientation, resolution, halftone frequencies, trapping information, and so on is some of what is contained in job tickets. When printing PDF files, enable this option. If you produce PDF files for screen, Web, or CD-ROM, you can eliminate job ticket information.

✦ **Use Prologue.ps and Epilogue.ps:** There are two files, named prologue.ps and epilogue.ps, located in the Documents and Settings\All Users\Documents\Adobe PDF \Data folder (Windows) or Users\Shared\Adobe PDF 6.0\Data folder (Macintosh) when you install Acrobat. In order to use the files, you must move them to the same folder as the Acrobat Distiller application, and both files must reside together in this location. The files contain PostScript code appended to a PDF file when it is created with Distiller. By default the files do not contain any data that affect distillation. They serve more as templates where you can write code to append data to the PDF. You use the prologue.ps file to append information to the PDF such as a note, cover page, or job ticket information. You use the epilogue.ps file to resolve PostScript procedure problems.

✦ **Create Job Definition Format (JDF) file:** This option creates a job ticket in XML. The job ticket contains information related to the file for use by print shops. For information about the contents of job tickets, see the "Save Portable Job Ticket inside PDF file" bullet later in this list.

Note

You can edit both of these files; however, you need to be familiar with the PostScript language to effectively change the files. When relocating the files, be certain to place a copy in the Distiller folder and leave the original in the Data folder, especially if you decide to edit either file. You can also use the files with watched folders, as explained a little later in this chapter. When using watched folders, place the prologue.ps and epilogue.ps files at the same directory level as the In and Out folders.

✦ **Convert smooth lines to curves:** Checking this box helps reduce file sizes significantly when creating PDFs from CAD drawing programs. Checking the box reduces the amount of control points used to build curves in CAD programs resulting in much smaller file sizes and much faster displays on your monitor. You can experience similar results on files where the Auto Trace tool was used in Adobe Illustrator.

✦ **Process DSC comments:** Document structuring comments (DSC) contain information about a PDF file. Items such as originating application, creation date, modification date, page orientation, and so on are all document-structuring comments. To maintain the DSC, enable this option. Because some important information such as page orientation and beginning and ending statements for the prologue.ps file are part of the document structure, you'll want to keep this item enabled as a default.

✦ **Log DSC warnings:** During distillation, if the processing of the document-structuring comments encounters an error, the error is noted in a log file. When you enable this check box, a log file is created. You can open the log file in a word processor or text editor to determine where the error occurred. Enable this option whenever document-structuring comments are processed.

✦ **Preserve EPS information from DSC:** This item is similar to the Process DSC comments option. If your file is an EPS file, enabling this check box preserves document-structuring comments.

✦ **Preserve OPI comments:** Open Press Interface (OPI) is a management tool used by many high-end imaging centers to control production. An OPI comment might include the replacement of high-resolution images for low-resolution FPO (for position only) files used in a layout program. OPI comments can include many different issues related to digital prepress such as image position on a page, crop area, sampling resolution, color bit depth, colors (in other words, CMYK, spot, and so on), overprint instructions, and more. If you're outputting to high-end imaging devices at service centers using OPI management, enable this option.

✦ **Preserve document information from DSC:** Document information items, discussed later in this book, include such things as title, subject, author, and keywords. Enabling this option preserves document information.

✦ **Resize page and center artwork for EPS files:** In earlier versions of Acrobat, distillation of a single-page EPS file, created from programs such as Adobe Illustrator, Macromedia FreeHand, or CorelDraw, used the EPS bounding box for the final page size. Many problems occurred when distilling EPS files directly as opposed to printed PostScript files. At times, a user would experience clipping and lose part of an image. With this option you have a choice between creating a PDF with the page dimensions equal to the artwork and having the artwork appear on the size of the original page you defined in your host application. When the check box is enabled, the page size is reduced to the size of the artwork, and the artwork is centered on the page. When the check box is disabled, the entire page appears consistent with the page size used in the host application.

Many of the controls available in the Advanced pane are explained when I discuss prepress and printing in Chapter 25. At this time, it is important to realize that Acrobat Distiller provides you with many more controls for setting attributes for PDF document creation and permits flexibility in designing PDF files for specific purposes. With all these toggles and check boxes, becoming confused and feeling overwhelmed is easy. Fortunately, Acrobat can help make this job a little easier for you. If you work in an office environment where a network administrator sets up all the controls for your PDF workflow, you can load preset custom Adobe PDF Settings. If you are the responsible party for creating the Adobe PDF Settings, you can create different custom settings, save them, and later load them from a menu option in Acrobat Distiller. Either way, you won't have to go back and reread this chapter every time you want to distill a file for another purpose.

Standards (Acrobat Professional only)

The Standards pane provides options for creating subsets of the PDF file in the form of PDF/X and PDF/A documents designed for printing and archiving, respectively. Click the Standards folder and select a Compliance Standard from the pull-down menu options. Although there are several options from which to choose, the categories are centralized around PDF/X and PDF/A.

Note   Standards options are only available when using PDF compatibilities less than version 6. If you use Acrobat capability 6 or 7, the Standards options are grayed out.

PDF/X

As explained earlier, PDF/X is a subset of the PDF format developed by an ISO (International Organization for Standardization) standards committee outside Adobe Systems. Adobe is a participant on the committee and supports the development and advances in PDF/X standards.

PDF/X has gained much acceptance among commercial printing companies for the purposes of creating files suitable for printing. PDF is a reliable format for any kind of electronic file exchanges. However, files developed for viewing in Acrobat viewers, Acrobat PDF forms, Web-hosted documents, and so on carry a lot of overhead not necessary for printing on commercial printing devices. The PDF/X compliance standard was developed to streamline documents by eliminating unnecessary data and optimizing files for print. The process of tailoring a PDF document for print by creating a PDF/X-compliant file does not necessarily reduce file size. In many cases, file sizes grow from a standard PDF to a PDF/X file.

The PDF/X options available to you in Acrobat Distiller produce either a PDF/X-1a:2002, PDF/X-1a:2003- or PDF/X-3:2002-, PDF/X-3:2003-compliant file. These file types are different versions of the PDF/X format. PDF/X-1a is designed to work well with both process and spot color, but no support is provided for color management or profile embedding. PDF/X-3 supports process and spot color and does support color-managed workflows and ICC (International Color Consortium) profile embedding.

Note   The PDF/X pane appears only in Acrobat Professional and is not available to Acrobat Standard users.

The two distinctions between the versions for PDFX-1a:2002, and PDF/X-1a:2003 have to do with versions of the same subset. With PDF/X-1a:2002 you have compatibility with Acrobat 4. With PDF/X-1a:2003 you have compatibility with Acrobat 5. The same applies to the version 2002 and version 2003 of the PDF/X-3 subset. If you select Acrobat compatibility for version 6 or 7 in the General pane, you lose the ability to select either PDF/X format.

When you use PDF/X during distillation you are checking the file for PDF/X compliance. If the file does not meet the PDF/X standard you select (that is, PDF/X-1a or PDF/X-3), you can halt the distillation process much like halting distillation when fonts don't embed properly. If a file meets PDF/X compliance, you have much greater assurance that your PDF document will print on almost any kind of commercial printing device.

You create PDF/X-compliant files with Acrobat Distiller or an authoring program that specifically addresses PDF/X compliance when exporting to PDF. InDesign CS is one application that supports PDF creation with delivery of a PDF/X-compliant file. Other PDF producers such as PDFMaker used with Microsoft Office applications, Microsoft Project, Microsoft Visio, and

Autodesk AutoCAD do not support PDF/X. If you want to print any of these files on commercial printing devices, print PostScript files and distill them with Acrobat Distiller and PDF/X enabled.

Cross-Reference For information about exporting PDF/X files from Adobe InDesign CS, see Chapter 7.

The options you have in the Standards pane in Acrobat Professional, shown in Figure 8-11, include the following:

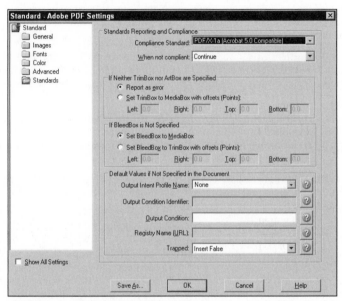

Figure 8-11: Click the Standards folder (Acrobat Professional only) to open the Standards pane.

✦ **Compliance Standard:** The pull-down menu contains options for all the PDF/X compliance versions, a setting for PDF/A compliance, and an option for None.

✦ **When not compliant:** Two menu choices are available from this pull-down menu. Select Continue to create the PDF file if the file does not meet PDF/X compliance. The PDF file is created and a log file is generated reporting problems. If you select Cancel Job, the PDF is not created and assures you of only producing files that meet the PDF/X standards.

✦ **Report as error:** Enabling this radio button reports the file noncompliant if a trim box or media box is missing on any page in the document.

✦ **Set TrimBox to MediaBox with offset (Points):** When the radio button is enabled, the trim box is calculated against the media box for offset distances if neither is specified in the PostScript file. The trim box is always equal to or smaller than the media box. Edit the field boxes for determining the offset amounts that are analyzed.

✦ **Set BleedBox to MediaBox:** Uses the media box values for the bleed box if no bleeds are specified in the PostScript file. In many layout authoring programs you have options for specifying bleed areas. If no bleeds are defined in the print dialog boxes, the media box values are used.

✦ **Set BleedBox to TrimBox with offsets (Points):** If the bleed box is not defined, the values specified in the field boxes are computed against the trim box.

✦ **Output Intent Profile Name:** If the file does not specify an output intent, such as SWOP coated for example, Distiller uses the intent you select from the pull-down menu. The field box is editable and you can type an output intent in the field box. If you don't require an output intent for the devices you use, select None. When the file is distilled and no intent was used when the PostScript file was printed, selecting None forces the job to fail compliance.

✦ **Output Condition Identifier:** This item is a reference name specified by the Output Intent Profile Name's registry. The name is automatically supplied for known Output Intent Profile Names. If a conditional identifier is used, then the parameter must be manually added.

✦ **Output Condition:** This field box is where you supply the intended output condition. The field value is not assessed for compliance. It is used by the service center for information purposes. If you leave the field blank, it has no effect on whether the job meets compliance.

✦ **Registry Name (URL):** This item is also informational. For certain profiles selected in the Output Intent Profile Name pull-down menu, you'll see a URL where more information is hosted on a Web site related to the profile.

✦ **Trapped:** Three options are available from the pull-down menu. PDF/X compliance requires that the Trapped state be analyzed for True or False. If you select Undefined, you are checking the file against trapping. If it does not specify a trapping state the file fails PDF/X compliance. Insert True checks for a trapped state. If no trapping was added to the file, the file fails compliance. Insert False checks for no trapping. If trapping is applied to the file, the file fails compliance when this item is selected.

✦ **Help:** The five icons to the right of the items in the Default Values if Not Specified in the Document area of the PDF/X pane offer help information. Click one of the icons and a pop-up menu opens with a definition for the respective option.

✦ **Save As:** The Save As button captures all the settings you make for the Adobe PDF Settings and opens a dialog box that defaults to the Settings folder. If you change any item in one of the preset options and click OK in the Adobe PDF Settings dialog box, the Save As dialog box opens automatically to prompt you to save the new settings to a new file. Provide a filename and click the Save button to create a new settings file.

PDF/A

Adobe Systems has been working with international standards committees toward a goal of ensuring you that the documents of today can be electronically read 10, 20, even 100 years from now. One of the fruitions of these labors is the PDF/A standard developed for archiving purposes.

PDF/A files contain essentials in terms of document structure. The necessary essentials include raster images, fonts (embedded), and vector objects. Code used in documents such as JavaScript is deemed a nonessential ingredient as well as any form of security. Therefore, you cannot create PDF/A files containing any scripts or encryption. In general you'll find PDF/A files are much leaner than other file standards such as PDF/X.

To select PDF/A from the Compliance Standard pull-down menu you need to select Acrobat 5 or earlier compatibility in the General pane. When you select PDF/A from the Compliance Standard pull-down menu the options in the PDF/A pane appear as shown in Figure 8-12.

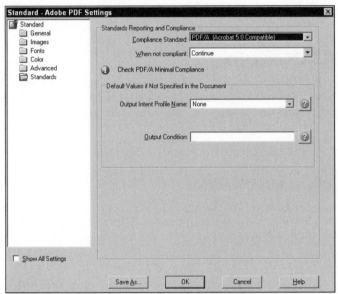

Figure 8-12: Select Acrobat 5 or earlier compatibility and select PDF/A (Acrobat 5.0 Compatible) from the Compliance Standard pull-down menu.

The few options you have include the same options for file handling when a file is not compliant as you have with PDF/X files. Under the Output Intent Profile Name pull-down menu are options for choosing the output intent like you see available in the Color pane. The Output Condition is a field box for user-supplied data.

Managing Adobe PDF Settings

If you select Cancel in any of the panes where settings are adjusted, you return to the Acrobat Distiller window. From the same Settings menu in Distiller (Windows) or top-level menu bar (Macintosh) select Add Adobe PDF Settings. The Add Adobe PDF Settings dialog box opens where you can load a settings file created by other users in your workflow or a settings file sent to you by a service provider. You can load settings files from any folder on your computer. When you add the file using the Add Adobe PDF Settings dialog box, the file is moved to a folder where Distiller retrieves the settings and lists them in the Default Settings pull-down menu.

Choose Settings ➪ Remove Adobe PDF Settings to open the Remove Adobe PDF Settings dialog box. The only settings you see displayed in the dialog box are custom settings files you added after your Acrobat installation. Select a file to remove and click Open. When you click Open, the file is discarded and doesn't appear in the Default Settings list in the Distiller window.

All additions and deletions for settings files can be accomplished through the menu commands. If you want to locate the folder where the settings files are located, look in C:\Documents and Settings\All Users\ Documents\Adobe PDF \Settings folder (Windows) or Library\Application Support\Adobe PDF \Settings folder (Macintosh).

Identifying Font Locations

Font embedding as described earlier in this chapter occurs when Adobe PDF Settings is enabled for font embedding and a font is contained in the PostScript file or loaded in the system with a utility such as Adobe Type Manager, Extensis Suitcase, or the system folder where fonts are accessed. If fonts reside neither in the PostScript file nor are loaded in your system, Distiller offers another method for locating fonts. Choose Settings ➪ Font Locations. The Acrobat Distiller – Font Locations dialog box opens, as shown in Figure 8-13.

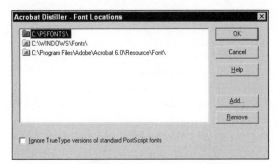

Figure 8-13: Distiller monitors fonts installed on your hard drive when the fonts appear in a list in the Acrobat Distiller – Font Locations dialog box.

In this dialog box you add folders of fonts that Distiller looks in when a font is neither contained in the PostScript file nor loaded in the system memory. Monitored font folders are listed in the window shown in Figure 8-13. To add a new folder, click the Add button. To remove a folder, select it in the list and click the Remove button.

A check box at the bottom of the dialog box enables you to resolve some problems that may occur when a TrueType font has the same name as a PostScript font. To eliminate embedding TrueType fonts with the same names as PostScript fonts, check the box at the bottom of the dialog box.

Creating Watched Folders

Watched folders enable you to automate distillation of PostScript files in a business or production environment. You can easily develop a PDF workflow by hosting a server on a network where Acrobat Distiller is continually running in the background and watching a folder or many folders for the introduction of new PostScript files. When Distiller encounters a new PostScript file, the file is distilled in the background while foreground applications are running. The resulting PDF files are automatically moved to another folder or directory, and the PostScript files are either preserved or deleted automatically.

Licensing restrictions

Before moving on to working with watched folders, please look over this section carefully and try to understand the proper use and authorization of working with watched folders on networks. Adobe Systems grants you license for working on a single computer when installing Acrobat. When you create PDFs on your computer you can distribute them to anyone who uses an Acrobat viewer. Therefore, the PDFs you create can legitimately be distributed to anyone who acquires the free Adobe Reader software.

Creating PDFs, whether locally or on a network, assumes you have complied with the proper licensing agreements for use of the Acrobat Distiller application. Ambiguity arises when using the Distiller application on networks with watched folders. If you set up a watched folder on a network where multiple users access the watched folders, you need a site license to use the Acrobat Distiller application, you need to have a licensed copy of Acrobat Standard or Professional for each user, or you can purchase Acrobat Distiller Server. Because Distiller is used by multiple users in this example, site licensing or individual purchases of the product is required.

Therefore, the licensing policies in this regard are related not to distribution, but rather, how the PDFs are created. As I move through the discussion on watched folders, keep in mind that when I make mention of using watched folders on networks, I'm assuming you are compliant with the proper licensing agreements.

Creating watched folders (Acrobat Professional only)

Watched folders can be individual folders, hard drive partitions, or dedicated hard drives. When you choose Settings ➪ Watched Folders, the Watched Folders dialog box opens, enabling you to establish preferences for the watched folders and distillation attributes.

The options available in the Watched Folders dialog box include the following:

✦ **Path:** The list window displays all folders identified as watched folders. The name of the watched folder appears in the list as well as the directory path. In Figure 8-14, notice the directory path is shown.

Figure 8-14: Watched folder preferences are established in the Acrobat Distiller – Watched Folders dialog box. When you open this dialog box a reminder for the licensing restrictions appears at the bottom.

✦ **Check watched folders every [ ] seconds:** This user-definable field accepts values between 1 and 9999 seconds. When Distiller monitors a watched folder, the folder is monitored according to the value entered in this field box.

✦ **PostScript file is:** Distiller automatically treats the PostScript file according to the options available in this pull-down menu. You can select the Deleted menu item, which deletes the PostScript file after distillation, or select Moved to "Out" folder, which moves the PostScript file to a folder entitled *Out*. If you intend to repurpose files for different uses, be certain to keep the PostScript file.

✦ **Delete output files older than [ ] days:** If you elect to keep the PostScript files in the Out folder, they can be deleted after the time interval specified in this field box. The acceptable range is between 1 and 999 days.

✦ **Add Folder:** To create a watched folder or add to the current list of watched folders, click the Add Folder button. A navigation dialog box opens. To add a folder to the watched folders list, the folder must first be created before you click the Add Folder button. Folders as well as partitions and drives can be added to your list. On a network, remote folders, partitions, and drives can also be added to the list. If you want to select a folder, browse your hard drive and select the folder name after clicking the Add Folder button. If you want to have the entire hard drive watched, select the drive designation (C:\, D:\, E:\, and so on in Windows or Macintosh HD, Hard Drive, and so on with a Macintosh) and click the OK button in the Browse For Folder dialog box.

✦ **Remove:** To delete watched folders, select the folder name in the watched folders list and click the Remove Folder button. If a folder is moved or deleted from your hard drive, the next time you launch Distiller, a warning dialog box opens notifying you that Distiller cannot find the watched folder(s). Removal of watched folders must occur in the Acrobat Distiller – Watched Folder dialog box. If you inadvertently deleted a watched folder on the desktop, you need to delete the folder name in the watched folders list. Return to your desktop and create a new folder; then return to the dialog box and add the new folder to the list.

✦ **Edit Security:** You can apply security to PDF files during distillation. Adding security during distillation is handy for multiple files created in PDF workflow environments. If you select the Acrobat 3.0 or 4.0 compatibility option in the current General pane, the security level is limited to 40-bit encryption. If you select Acrobat 5.0 compatibility in the General pane, 128-bit encryption is used, compatible with Acrobat 5.0 and higher. If you select Acrobat 6.0 or 7.0 compatibility, 128-bit encryption compatible with Acrobat 6 and above is used.

Cross-Reference

For more information on applying security to PDF documents, see Chapter 21.

✦ **Clear Security:** Select any one or all of the watched folders in the list and click Clear Security. The Security is removed from the folders.

✦ **Edit Settings:** The Edit Settings button becomes active when you select a watched folder name in the watched folders list. With a folder name selected in the list, click the Edit Settings button to open the Adobe PDF Settings dialog box. You can apply different settings to different watched folders. If, for example, you print PostScript files to disk and have them distilled for high-end output and Web page design, you will want compression and color modes distinctive for the output sources. You can set up two watched folders and have the same PostScript file distilled with the different settings. Editing settings here overrides Distiller's defaults and applies new options to the specific watched folder where the attributes are established.

✦ **Load Settings:** All the settings contained in the Settings folder are available for loading and applying to watched folders listed in the window. Click Load Settings to open the Settings folder.

✦ **Clear Settings:** This option removes any settings applied to a watched folder. If you leave the watched folder listed with no specific settings assigned to the watched folder, the current default Adobe PDF Settings are used.

PDF Workflow

Watched folders greatly help your PDF workflow and assist you in automating the smallest office environment to large offices with multiple networks and servers. When you install a site-licensed copy of Acrobat Distiller on a server, the burden of PDF creation is dedicated to the server and relieves individual workstations.

In identifying watched folders, you need only have the directory or folder created on a hard drive. After you identify the watched folder, Distiller automatically creates the other folders needed to execute distillation from watched folder files. The In folder created by Distiller is monitored. When a PostScript file is placed or written to the In folder, the distillation commences according to the interval you establish in the Watched Folder settings dialog box. Files can be placed into the In folder, or you can print to PostScript directly to the In folder from within an application.

Watched folders work well in cross-platform environments, too. In order to use a watched folder from one platform and have the distillation performed on another platform, you need to have the computers networked and have software installed that enables you to communicate between two or more computers on your network.

Working with Non-Roman Text

Acrobat provides great support for text created from character sets foreign to U.S. English and other Roman text alphabets. Eastern languages such as Russian, Ukrainian, and similar languages based on forms of Cyrillic characters require proper configuration for font access and keyboard layouts. After configuring and using the fonts in a layout application, be certain to embed the fonts in the PostScript file or have Distiller monitor the font's folder of the character set used. As is the case with any font embedded in the PDF, the document is displayed without font substitution. In Figure 8-15, I used a Cyrillic font in Microsoft Word. The file was printed to disk as PostScript and font embedding was used in Distiller's Adobe PDF Settings.

Здравствуйте
Меня зовут Тед

Figure 8-15: When fonts are properly configured from character sets foreign to Roman characters, the fonts can be embedded and viewed without font substitution.

Eastern language support is provided by Acrobat but requires much more in regard to configuration and proper installation of the Asian Language Support option (Windows) or the Asian Language Kit (Macintosh). As long as the language support respective to your platform is installed with the Acrobat installer, files can be printed as PostScript and embedded in the PDFs. Viewing PDFs with embedded Asian languages such as Traditional Chinese, Simplified Chinese, Japanese, and Korean (CJK) are displayed without font substitution.

When installing Acrobat for use with these languages, you need to use the custom installation and include the language support with the other Acrobat components. After the support is installed, font problems need to be resolved when you print to PostScript. PostScript fonts have fewer problems being embedded. TrueType fonts require special handling depending on the platform and type of fonts used. Special documentation for managing PostScript and TrueType fonts is included in the Acrobat documentation. For specific handling of Eastern Language support and TrueType fonts, review the documentation thoroughly before attempting to convert PostScript files to PDF.

Accessing Distiller

After all the controls have been established in the Adobe PDF Settings dialog boxes you're ready to use the Distiller application. Files used with Distiller need to be PostScript files printed to disk or EPS files. You can access the Distiller application several ways. These include

✦ **Open from Distiller:** Find the Distiller application on your hard drive and double-click the application icon to launch Distiller. When the Distiller application window opens, choose File ⇨ Open. Navigate to the file you want to convert to PDF and select it in the Acrobat Distiller – Open PostScript File dialog box. Select multiple files by using the Shift key to select a contiguous group of files or Ctrl/⌘ to select a non-contiguous group. If the Preferences have been set up to ask for a filename or ask to replace a PDF, a navigation dialog box opens where you supply filename and destination.

✦ **Drag and drop to the application icon:** Either the application icon or a shortcut (alias in the Dock on Macintosh OS X) of the application can be used for drag-and-drop distillation. In this regard you can drag multiple PostScript files, EPS files, or a combination of both to either icon. Release the mouse button when the files are over the icon and Distiller launches and subsequently converts the file(s) to PDF.

✦ **Drag to the application window:** You can drag and drop a single file or multiple files on the Distiller application window. Launch Distiller to open the application window. Select a single file or multiple files and release the mouse button. All files are converted as individual PDFs.

✦ **Launch Distiller from within Acrobat:** To open Distiller from within Acrobat choose Advanced ⇨ Acrobat Distiller. The Distiller application launches and opens in the foreground in front of the Acrobat window. Choose File ⇨ Open or use the drag-and-drop method to open the file.

✦ **Print to Adobe PDF printer:** From any authoring program, open the Print dialog box and select Adobe PDF. Execute the Print command and the file is distilled with the current default Adobe PDF Settings.

✦ **Use the Run command (Windows):** You can create PDFs with Distiller by accessing the Run command from the Windows status bar. Select Run and supply the directory path first for Distiller, then the path for the files to be converted. Syntax must be exact. Pathnames need to be contained within quotation marks and a space needs to separate the pathname for Distiller and the pathname for the file(s) to be converted. Filenames having spaces need to be contained within quotation marks. To distill multiple files enter the pathname and filename, and separate each file with commas. Inasmuch as Acrobat offers you this capability, you'll often find drag-and-drop methods much easier.

✦ **Exporting to PDF:** From many application programs, such as Microsoft Office, and illustration and layout programs as discussed in Chapters 5 and 6, Distiller is used to produce PDFs. When distillation is complete, the user is returned to the application document window.

✦ **Watched folders:** As described earlier in this chapter, copying a PostScript or EPS file to the In folder inside a watched folder prompts distillation at the interval specified in the Acrobat Distiller – Watched Folders dialog box. Distiller must be launched before distillation of files from watched folders occurs.

When Distiller is used in all the preceding circumstances other than the use of watched folders, the current Adobe PDF Settings selected in Distiller are used to produce the PDF. That is to say, if Distiller is launched and the Standard settings appear in the pull-down menu, the Standard settings are used to create the PDF. When using watched folders, the settings associated with the watched folder are used to produce the PDF. If no settings are assigned to the watched folder, the current default settings are used.

Concatenating PostScript Files

Suppose you have several documents that you want to convert to a single PDF file. All these documents can be of a single application type — for example, a group of Microsoft Excel spreadsheets. Or the documents may come from many different applications — for example, PageMaker, Microsoft Word, Microsoft Excel, QuarkXPress, and Photoshop. In either case, if you want to create a single PDF document from all those separate files, there are two ways to handle the task. You can use the Create Adobe PDF From Multiple Files command and select the various file types for conversion, or you can choose to let Distiller combine the files into a single PDF document.

Acrobat Distiller reads PostScript code and as such, Distiller can begin its job by looking at a PostScript file that includes instructions to concatenate, or join together, all PostScript files in a given directory. If you attempt to write this code from scratch, you'll need to be fluent in PostScript. For those of us with much more limited skills, Adobe has made performing the task easier.

When Acrobat is installed, a folder entitled Example Files includes two files with PostScript code that are used for concatenating distilled files into a single PDF file. The PostScript code is generic and needs to be edited in a text editor. You need to edit these files for the directory path and filenames or file directory for the files you want to distill.

Note The path for the two files is the same path where the epilogue.ps and prologue.ps files are found: Documents and Settings\All Users\Shared Documents\Adobe PDF 7.0\Example Files folder (Windows) or Library\Application Support\Adobe PDF \Example Files folder (Macintosh).

The RUNFILEX.PSRUNFILEX and RUNDIREX.TXTRUNDIREX files installed in the Example Files folder inside your Adobe PDF folder concatenate PostScript files — RUNFILEX.ps concatenates individual files, and RUNDIREX.txt combines all the files in a specified directory whose names include a common extension. These two files need to be edited individually.

Note RUNFILEXRUNFILEX.ps and RUNDIREX.txt have two different extensions. The idea is that the RUNFILEXRUNFILEX.ps file is distilled and only produces the PDF from the files listed in the code. When RUNFILEXRUNDIREX.txt is distilled, it also produces a PDF with files in the code. But if it has a .ps extension, the RUNDIREXRUNDIREX file is also distilled creating a blank page.

Combining files by name

The *Fil* in RUNFILEXRUNFILEX.ps is your first clue that this file is used for concatenating PostScript files by filename, each of which you identify in the PostScript code. When using this file, you must tell Distiller specifically which files (by exact name) are to be distilled. To edit the filename for distillation, open the RUNFILEXRUNFILEX.ps document in a text editor, as shown in Figure 8-16. If using a Macintosh, you can edit this file in TextEdit. In Windows, use Windows Notepad or WordPad.

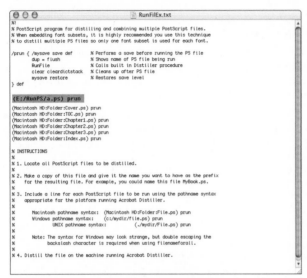

Figure 8-16: Open the file RUNFILEX.ps in a text editor such as Windows NotePad or WordPad (EditText on the Macintosh) to supply filenames for distilling in Acrobat Distiller.

When you open RUNFILEX.ps, the PostScript code containing instructions for concatenating files from user-supplied names appears. All lines of code beginning with a % symbol are comment lines that do not supply instructions to Distiller. These comments are provided to explain the procedures.

Tip   If you double-click the file on the desktop, it may open in Adobe Illustrator or Acrobat Distiller. To avoid problems when launching the file, to open it in a text editor, change the file extension to .txt. When you double-click the file, it opens in your default text editor.

RUNFILEX.ps in Windows

The syntax for directory paths in the PostScript code is different between Windows and the Macintosh, and on Windows varies somewhat from standard DOS syntax. When you open the RUNFILEX.ps file in Windows WordPad or another text editor, the sample lines of code show directory paths and filenames for Macintosh users. The comments below the code provide a guideline for proper syntax when using Windows. In Figure 8-17, notice the comment line for Windows pathname syntax located toward the bottom of the figure. In Windows, identify your drive as a standard drive letter — for example, C:. After the drive letter, use a forward slash instead of a backslash to separate the drive name from the directory name. Nesting occurs in Windows the way it does later in the Macintosh example, but be certain to use forward slashes to separate the folder names. The filename should include the name and extension as it was written.

When describing drive, directory, and filenames, case sensitivity is not an issue. Any of these identifiers can be either upper- or lowercase. In Figure 8-17, I used my E: drive and a directory labeled RunPS. Only the file a.ps is noted for distillation, as it is the only file identified in the code. Notice the filename was changed from RUNFILEX.ps to RUNFILEX.txt, as you can see in the title bar.

RUNFILEX.ps on the Macintosh

The same file and location is used on the Macintosh as observed in the previous section with Windows. When you open the RUNFILEX.ps in a text editor, the complete directory path, as described in the preceding section with Windows, needs to be supplied. In Figure 8-18, a description of a Macintosh directory path and filenames is shown.

It is critical to precisely code the directory path and filename(s) for Distiller to recognize the location and files to be distilled. The name of your volume (that is Macintosh HD, Hard Drive, and so on) would be the name you have provided for your hard drive. By default, many Macintosh hard drives are labeled Macintosh HD. If you have named your hard drive another name, enter it exactly as found on your desktop. After the hard drive name, enter a colon (:) followed by a folder name. Folders are not necessary, but it is recommended you save the files to a folder below the root of your hard drive. Folders can be nested as long as you follow the proper syntax (in other words, *Hard Drive:FolderA:FolderB:FolderC*, and so on). The last entry for each line of code is the filename.

In TextEdit or any other text editor, save your file as text-only. Save the file with a descriptive name — you needn't use the RUNFILEX.txt name of the original file. Be certain the file is a copy of the original, so you can return to the Examples folder and find this file again when needed.

In order to convert the named files in the RUNFILEX.ps file, you need to open the newly edited file in Acrobat Distiller. You can drag the file on top of the Distiller window on either platform or launch Distiller and choose File ⇨ Open. The instructions in the PostScript code direct Distiller to the files you listed for conversion to PDF.

Combining files in folders

The second file in the Examples folder used for concatenating PostScript files is RUNDIREX.txt. Whereas RUNFILEX.ps requires you to name all the PostScript files to be distilled, this file uses a wildcard character to distill all files with a common extension in a specified directory. The directory path for either the Mac or Windows uses the same syntax as illustrated previously; however, instead of filename(s), a wildcard character followed by the extension for the filenames is used. The wildcard is the standard asterisk (*), which is used to indicate all files with the same extension you specify in the line of code for the pathname.

In Figure 8-17, I specified my D: hard drive on my Windows computer and the ClientFolder directory. All the files with a .ps extension will be distilled by Acrobat Distiller. In this example for Windows, I used /PathName (D:/ClientFolder/*.ps). I then saved the file as MyFile.txt to the same ClientFolder directory.

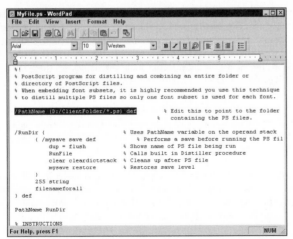

```
%!
% PostScript program for distilling and combining an entire folder or
% directory of PostScript files.
% When embedding font subsets, it is highly recommended you use this technique
% to distill multiple PS files so only one font subset is used for each font.

/PathName (D:/ClientFolder/*.ps) def        % Edit this to point to the folder
                                             %   containing the PS files.

/RunDir {                              % Uses PathName variable on the operand stack
      { /mysave save def               % Performs a save before running the PS fil
          dup = flush                  % Shows name of PS file being run
          RunFile                      % Calls built in Distiller procedure
          clear cleardictstack         % Cleans up after PS file
          mysave restore               % Restores save level
      }
      255 string
      filenameforall
} def

PathName RunDir

% INSTRUCTIONS
```

Figure 8-17: Following /*PathName* in the RUNDIREX.txt file, enter the path and *.extension* for all the files included in the distillation.

After you edit the RUNFILEX.ps or RUNDIREX.txt file, it becomes the file that you open in Acrobat Distiller. This file tells Distiller where to go and what files to convert to PDF. The file can be located in any directory on your hard drive because it instructs Distiller where to go to find the files for distillation. If the file is saved in the same folder where the files to be distilled are stored, it is important to provide a different extension for this filename from the extension of the files to be distilled when using RUNDIREX.txt. If you name the file MyFile.ps and include it in a directory with a number of files also having a .ps extension, the PostScript code file for combining the other files is included in the final PDF file.

When you run MyFile.txt (or whatever name you have supplied for the file), the page order occurs in the same order as an alphanumeric character set. To help simplify understanding how the page order is applied, view your files in a folder as a list. Be certain the order is not date, type, or anything other than listed by name. The order you view is the same page order as the resulting PDF.

In Figure 8-18, the top of the list begins the page order. In my example, the 0.ps file is the first page in the PDF file, followed by 2.ps, and so on. All eight pages are distilled if the RUNDIREX.txt file is used and includes all files ending in .ps in the ClientFolder directory.

Figure 8-18: PostScript files in a Windows directory are viewed as a list, with the files arranged by name.

Note

As you examine the list in Figure 8-18, notice that 44.ps is followed by 9.ps. If you want these files to be consecutively ordered, the filenaming has to follow some different rules. Both Distiller and your operating system arrange the files according to the characters in left-to-right (dictionary) order. If two files have the same first character, the second character is examined and the file placed in the list accordingly. In this example, Windows doesn't care about 49 being larger than 9. It looks at the 4 in 49 and sees it as a lower order than 9.

To rearrange your files in the order you want to have them appear in an Acrobat viewer, rename them before distillation, taking into consideration the first character is the highest order of priority. For this example, I renamed my files as illustrated in Figure 8-19. When the PDF file is produced, the page order matches my new order as viewed in the folder.

Tip

To combine files in a page order where the filenames are not listed in a folder in the order you want the pages to appear, you can use the Create PDF From Multiple Files command in Acrobat. You can add PostScript files to the Create PDF From Multiple Documents dialog box and order the .ps files as you want the page order to appear in the resulting PDF.

Cross-Reference

For more information on using Create PDF From Multiple Files, see Chapter 5.

Figure 8-19: I renamed the files in the ClientFolder directory by including a zero (0) in front of the single-digit filenames so the two-digit filenames would follow in numerical order.

Tip

Because Distiller and your operating system order alphanumeric characters the same, view your folder contents as a list before distilling the files. The list order you see is the same order of the page numbers in the final PDF document.

Combining PostScript files on networks

If you want to develop a PDF workflow and use a server to collect all your PDF files on a local area network, you need to follow some simple guidelines in order to produce PDF documents. Whereas files can be printed to disk on remote systems and drives that are cross-platform, Distiller can't follow cross-platform directory paths. Therefore, if you use RUNDIREX.txt and want to distill files in C:\MyFolder*.ps, Distiller running on a Macintosh isn't able to execute instructions for following cross-platform directory paths. This also applies to Windows users who may want to use a file describing directory paths on a Macintosh. Distiller can be used cross-platform to distill files on remote drives, and the RUNDIREX.txt file works between two computers running the same operating system. Using Distiller and RUNDIREX.txt on networks have the following capabilities and limitations:

✦ **Running Distiller across platforms:** Distiller can open PostScript files on local hard drives and across platforms. PDF files from distillation can be saved to local hard drives and across platforms. For example, using Distiller on a Macintosh, you can open a PostScript file on a PC and save it to either computer's hard drive.

✦ **RUNDIREX.txt across platforms:** RUNDIREX.txt cannot run across platforms where directory paths are specified for one platform while distilling on a different platform. For example, you can't open from a Macintosh the RUNDIREX.txt file that resides on a PC with directory paths specified for the PC. The alternative solution is to either run Distiller on the platform consistent with the path identity or set up watched folders where the RUNDIREX.txt file is introduced into a watched folder or create a virtual drive or hot folder and mount the drive/hot folder on both systems.

✦ **RUNDIREX.txt in a common platform:** Distiller can open the RUNDIREX.txt file that resides on one computer where the directory path includes files on another computer of the same platform. The RUNDIREX.txt file can be located on either computer, the destination of the PDF can be saved to either computer, and the path to find the .ps files can be on either computer.

Summary

✦ PostScript is a streamed language that can contain many different dialects and is often redundant in describing page elements for imaging. PDF is a much more efficient file format, as it is structured like a database that offers logical order and eliminates redundancy.

✦ When creating PostScript files, the preferred PPD to use is the Acrobat Distiller PPDs, or print to the Adobe PDF printer.

✦ Distiller Preferences enable you to establish settings for filenaming and overwriting.

✦ Acrobat Distiller has many Adobe PDF Settings enabling you to control font compression, image compression, color, high-end digital prepress output, PDF/X compliance, and PDF/A compliance. All Adobe PDF Settings are available to Acrobat Standard users except PDF/X and PDF/A compliance.

✦ The various PDF/X subsets are used for creating PDF-compliant files for commercial printing. PDF/A files are used for archival purposes.

✦ Additional font monitoring is established in the Distiller Settings menu for identifying different font locations on your computer.

✦ Watched folders enable you to create PDF workflows that automate the PDF creation process. Watched folders can be contained on local or remote storage systems in network environments. Use of watched folders with multiple-user access on a network requires strict compliance with Adobe's licensing agreements.

✦ Acrobat enables you to supply security passwords at the time of distillation. Security levels are applied consistent with PDF compatibility.

✦ Eastern language character sets and Asian text are supported font-embedding features as long as font formats and font management are properly configured.

✦ Access to Acrobat Distiller is supported from within Acrobat 7.0, by using shortcuts or aliases, printer drivers, and through a variety of drag-and-drop procedures.

✦ You can join PostScript files in a single PDF document by using either the RUNFILEX.ps or RUNDIREX.txt PostScript file installed on your computer during the Acrobat installation. RUNFILEX.ps concatenates files by filename, and RUNDIREX.txt concatenates all files within a folder that have the same extension.

✦   ✦   ✦

Editing PDFs

Saving and Versioning Files

To begin this section on editing PDF documents I'll start with saving files and exporting data. As you find in this chapter, Acrobat has Save tools and commands and supports exporting your PDF data in a variety of file formats. As you learned in Part II, files are not originally authored in Acrobat, but rather, they are converted to the PDF format. If you need to perform some major editing, it's always best to try to return to the original authoring application, make your edits, and then convert to PDF. In some cases however, you may not have an original authoring application document. In such circumstances, you may need to get the PDF data in a format that you can manipulate and edit in another program. Fortunately, Acrobat supports exporting to many different file formats that can be imported in other programs.

In addition to saving documents, you may find a need to create several versions of a file. If you plan on engaging in a review session, you may want to send several versions of a document to your review committee or share different versions in a workgroup. A nice new feature in Acrobat 7.0 is support for the Version Cue workspace, in which you can save different document versions just like you find with all Adobe Creative Suite programs.

In this chapter you learn how to save PDF documents, update edits, export data into other formats, and use the Version Cue workspace to save different versions of your PDF files.

Setting Up the Work Environment

The only tool used in this chapter is the Save tool, which appears in the default File toolbar. To return to default tools, open a context menu on the Toolbar Well and select Reset Toolbars or press Alt/Option+F8. The remaining tools used with this chapter are derived from menu commands.

Saving PDF Files

When you open a PDF document in any viewer, the Save tool in the File toolbar and the File ⇨ Save menu command are both grayed out.

When you open the File menu and look at Save As, you notice the menu command is active. After you edit a file through the use of tools or menu commands, the Save tool and Save menu command become active.

You can use the File ➪ Save As command at any time. As you edit PDF documents, they tend to become bulky and contain unnecessary information. To optimize a file and make it the smallest file size, choose File ➪ Save As and select the default PDF format for the file type. If you save to the same folder location with the same filename, Acrobat rewrites the file as you use Save As. You should plan on using Save As and rewriting your file after your last edits. Doing so assures you of creating a smaller, more optimized file.

Another factor affecting optimized files is ensuring the default preferences are set to file optimization when using the Save As command. Open the Preferences dialog box (Ctrl/⌘+K) and click General in the left pane. In the General preferences pane, be certain the check box is enabled for Save As optimizes for Fast Web View. Enabling this option ensures that your files are always optimized when you use Save As.

Exporting Data

By default, when you use either Save or Save As, the file type is a PDF document. Using Save offers you no other option for changing the file type; but when you select Save As, you can choose to export your PDF document in one of a number of different file formats. If you need to update a file or export data from PDF files, choose File ➪ Save As and choose a file format from the Save as type (Format on Macintosh) pull-down menu, as shown in Figure 9-1.

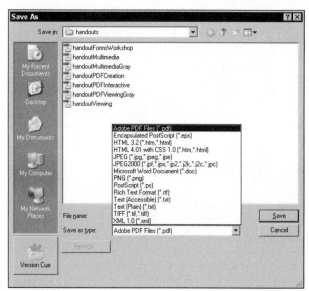

Figure 9-1: Choose File ➪ Save As and choose the file format to be saved from the Save as type pull-down menu.

Selecting all but the Adobe PDF Files (*.pdf) and Text (Accessible) (*.txt) formats provides user-definable options in the Settings dialog box for the respective file type. When you select any of the formats other than the preceding two, the Settings button becomes active. Click Settings and the Save As Settings dialog box opens. The various options change according to the file format selected from the Save as type pull-down menu (Windows) or Format (Mac) in the Save As dialog box.

Adobe PDF files (*.pdf)

By default the Acrobat PDF Files (*.pdf) format is selected in the Save as type (Windows) or Format (Macintosh) pull-down menu. Saving as PDF without changing the filename updates the existing PDF by overwriting it.

Note   The default PDF format is one of the many nice little changes you'll notice between Acrobat 7 and versions of Acrobat earlier than 6.0. In earlier versions the default file format was the last file format you selected in the Save as type pull-down menu. In Acrobat 6 and above the default always returns to PDF as the file format.

Encapsulated PostScript (*.eps) and PostScript (*.ps)

EPS files are saved as single page files. When multiple-page PDFs are saved to EPS, each page is saved as a new EPS document. PostScript files save the PDF to disk like you would print a file to disk as PostScript. PostScript files can then be re-distilled in Acrobat Distiller to convert back to PDF. You can also download PostScript files to PostScript printers through a downloading utility or a hot folder, which is used for sending files directly to the printer.

Many of the options for creating either an EPS file or a PostScript file are identical. You'll notice some differences as you travel through the many options found in the Save As Settings dialog box. Select either Encapsulated PostScript (*.eps) or PostScript (*.ps) from the Files of type (Format on Macintosh) pull-down menu and click the Settings button. The options appear in the Save As Settings dialog box. Shown in Figure 9-2 is the EPS Save As Settings dialog box.

General settings

On the left side of the Save As Settings dialog box are several categories for choices you make on the right side of the dialog box. The first of the categories is the General settings where you set some general attributes for the way an EPS or PostScript file is saved. These settings include

- ✦ **Defaults:** The Defaults button at the top of the dialog box returns all settings to the original defaults. You can access this button at any time as you travel through the various option categories in the list at the left side of the dialog box.

- ✦ **ASCII:** PostScript files are encoded as ASCII (American Standard Code for Information Interchange). ASCII files are larger than binary files, which is the second option for encoding selections. If you want to place an EPS file in another program for color separating, use the ASCII settings.

Cross-Reference   For information on color separating EPS files and Acrobat PDF, see Chapter 25.

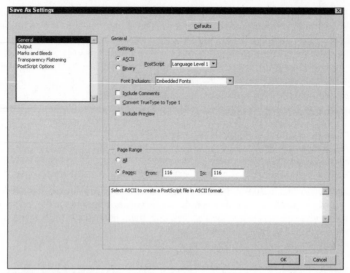

Figure 9-2: Select Encapsulated PostScript (*.eps) or PostScript (*.ps) from the Save as type (Format on Macintosh) pull-down menu. Click the Settings button to open the Save As Settings dialog box. In this figure, Save as Encapsulated PostScript (*.eps) was selected.

✦ **Binary:** Binary files are much smaller than ASCII files. Use binary encoding when the PostScript language level is 2 or 3.

✦ **PostScript:** Select the language levels from the pull-down menu choices. For ASCII encoding use Language Level 1 from the menu. For exporting EPS files to Adobe InDesign, you can use Language Level 2. If you're using Language Level 2 or 3, select binary encoding. Use PostScript 3 only when the output devices use PostScript 3 RIPs.

Note Users of previous versions of Acrobat had to either export PDF files to EPS, place PDFs in separating programs, or use third-party plug-ins to print color separations and print to high-end devices. These workarounds are all a part of the past. Acrobat Professional affords you almost all the printing controls you need for high-end printing. Forget about exporting EPS files if your only need is to print color separations or composites to high-end devices.

✦ **Font Inclusion:** You have three choices for font inclusion. Choose None to not embed fonts. Choose Embedded Fonts to keep the same fonts embedded in the PDF in the exported EPS file. Choose Embedded and Referenced Fonts to keep the PDF embedded fonts and fonts referenced from fonts loaded in your system. If you're using a font that is not embedded in the PDF document but is loaded as a system font, the font is embedded in the resulting PDF.

Cross-Reference For more information about font embedding and understanding font embedding limitations, see Chapter 8.

✦ **Include Comments:** When the check box is enabled, any comment notes are included in the resulting EPS or PostScript document. When the PostScript document is distilled in Acrobat Distiller, the comment notes are retained in the resulting PDF document.

✦ **Convert TrueType to Type 1:** Check the box to convert TrueType fonts to Type 1 fonts.

Cross-Reference

For more information on TrueType and Type 1 fonts, see Chapter 8.

✦ **Include Preview (EPS file exports only):** The preview is a screen view of the EPS file. If this check box is not enabled, the EPS file appears as a gray box when you place the file in another program. The data are all there, but you won't be able to see the EPS image. When this check box is enabled, a preview is embedded in the EPS file. Preview image formats are TIFF on Windows and PICT on the Macintosh.

✦ **Page Range:** You can export all pages by selecting the All radio button or entering the page numbers for a range of pages to be exported. EPS files are exported as individual files for each page and automatically numbered by Acrobat.

Output

Click the Output item in the list on the left side of the Save As Settings dialog box and the options change, as shown in Figure 9-3.

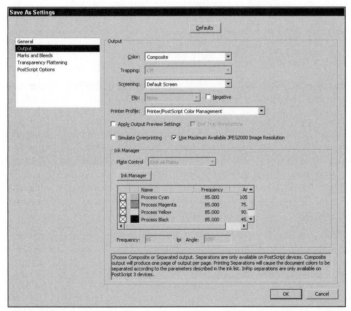

Figure 9-3: Select Output and the options change to attribute settings designed for printing and prepress.

Output options enable you to control prepress output attributes that include

✦ **Color:** The four choices for handling color in resulting EPS and PostScript file(s) are

- **Composite:** Use this option to export the file as a composite image. If the file is a four-color image, you can still import an EPS file in a separating program and print separations. The intent for Composite is for use with composite color printing and printing separations to non-Adobe PostScript devices. For PostScript files, composites can be downloaded directly to PostScript 2 and 3 devices.

- **Composite Gray:** If the files are grayscale, use Composite Gray.

- **Separations:** This option creates a DCS (Desktop Color Separation) file, and each color as well as a composite are exported as separate files. If pre-separating the EPS file(s), be certain you use a program such as Adobe InDesign that supports DCS files, or you can directly download each plate to your RIP. For PostScript files, the file is separated. When you download the PostScript file, all colors print on separate plates.

Cross-Reference For more information about DCS files, color separations, and RIPs, see Chapter 25.

- **In-RIP Separations:** This option only works on Adobe PostScript 3 RIPs. A composite color image is printed to the RIP and the RIP color separates the composite file.

✦ **Trapping:** In order to activate this pull-down menu you need to assign trap attributes in the Trap Presets dialog box accessed in the Print Production toolbar. When a trap preset is assigned, this option offers a choice for turning trapping off or on.

Cross-Reference To find out how to open the Trap Presets dialog box and assign a trap preset to a file, see Chapter 25.

✦ **Screening:** You make choices for screening from this pull-down menu. Unless you have some special need for embedding half-tone frequencies in the EPS file, leave the Screening set to Default Screen and handle all your frequency control at the RIP. For PostScript files, set the screening as desired before downloading the file.

✦ **Flip:** The single limitation in Acrobat for prepress and printing is the lack of emulsion control for composite prints. The Flip and Negative options are available only for Separations. If you want to save the EPS as Emulsion Down and Negative, select options from the Flip pull-down menu and select the Negative check box. For PostScript files, set the output to Emulsion Down and Negative only when using service centers controlling emulsion through authoring applications. Many centers want Positive, Emulsion Up files because the emulsion control is handled at the RIP.

✦ **Printer Profile:** You can embed a printer profile in the EPS file(s) from the available choices in the pull-down menu. If you want to eliminate color management, select the option at the top of the menu choices for Same As Source (No Color Management).

✦ **Apply Output Preview Settings:** Select this option to simulate the output of one device on another. This option simulates the output condition defined in the Output Preview dialog on the current output device.

✦ **Simulate Overprinting:** Overprints and knockouts can be soft-proofed onscreen for color-separated devices. The check box is grayed out unless you choose one of the separation items in the Color pull-down menu.

✦ **Use Maximum Available JPEG2000 Image Resolution:** For any raster images contained in the EPS file export, the file compression uses JPEG2000 at the maximum setting when this check box is enabled. If disabled, the original compression level at the time the PDF was created is used.

✦ **Emit Trap Annotations:** The check box is grayed out unless you save the file with one of the color separations options from the Color pull-down menu. If trapping annotations are to be eliminated, check the box.

✦ **Ink Manager:** Unchecking the box on the far left of each color plate eliminates the plate for separated files. Scroll the box to see any spot colors and you can select spot colors for conversion to CMYK color.

Marks and Bleeds

Select the Marks and Bleeds item in the list at the left of the Save As Settings dialog box and the options for adding printer's marks appear, as shown in Figure 9-4.

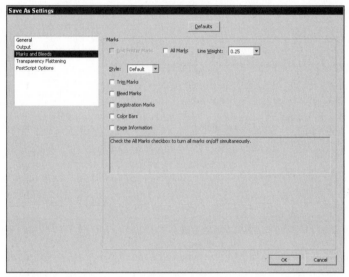

Figure 9-4: Select Marks and Bleeds to add printer's marks to the EPS/PS export.

The options include

✦ **Emit Printer Marks/All Marks:** You can select from Emit Printer Marks and All Marks in the first two check boxes. Selecting All Marks checks all the boxes below the Marks Style pull-down menu.

✦ **Line Weight:** From the pull-down menu select line weights for the printer's marks from 1/8, 1/4, and 1/2 inch choices.

✦ **Style:** You have choices for compatibility with authoring and illustration programs. Choose from different versions of InDesign, Illustrator, or QuarkXPress.

✦ **Marks:** The check boxes below the pull-down menu for style should be self-explanatory. You can include the marks desired by checking boxes individually. Only the checked items appear on the exported file.

Transparency Flattening

For anyone who's experienced difficulty with printing transparency on PostScript RIPs, you can choose to rasterize vector objects in EPS and PostScript files to eliminate printing problems on PostScript Level 2 devices and some PostScript 3 devices. Click Transparency Flattening in the Save As Settings dialog box and the options for controlling rasterization and flattening appear, as shown in Figure 9-5.

Note

Raster objects are pixel-based. Photos and scans you might edit in image-editing programs such as Adobe Photoshop are known as raster images. Vector objects are constructed with mathematical formulas describing the paths and contents of the objects in programs such as Adobe Illustrator and CorelDraw. The pixel-based raster objects are much easier than vector-based objects to print on PostScript and non-PostScript devices. Vector-based objects are more difficult to print than raster objects and can sometimes fail to print properly on non-PostScript devices. The process of converting vector objects to raster data is known as *rasterization*.

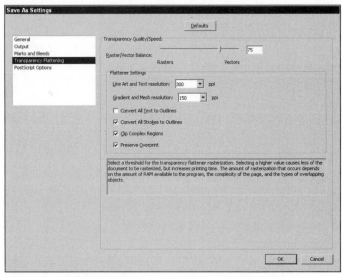

Figure 9-5: Select Transparency Flattening to make choices for rasterizing vector objects.

The Transparency Flattening options include

✦ **Transparency Quality/Speed:** This slider enables you to flatten vector objects in such a way that the true transparency in vector objects is rasterized and results in simulated transparency. You determine the level of rasterization by moving the slider left or right. Moving left rasterizes and flattens transparent objects. Moving right reduces rasterization and preserves more vector objects.

✦ **Rasterization Resolution:** Vector-based objects are device-dependent and carry with them no resolution values. Resolution is dependent on the resolution of the machine printing the vector data. Raster objects are device-independent, and a fixed resolution is embedded in the raster data. When rasterizing vector data, you assign the resolution to the resulting raster images. For type, you'll want much higher resolution on most printing devices. You can often gain acceptable results with lower resolutions for gradient objects. The options here let you assign resolutions individually for rasterizing type and gradients.

✦ **Convert All Text to Outlines:** All text in the EPS/PS is converted to outlines. As a standard operating procedure, you should avoid converting type to outlines. Converting type to outlines makes printing these files on PostScript RIPs more difficult. If you have a stubborn font that doesn't want to print you can use this option as a last resort.

✦ **Convert All Strokes to Outlines:** If stroke weights present problems with transparent objects, you can convert the strokes to outlines and simplify the transparency. The results, however, can be unpredictable and often you'll find the stroke weights thicker in the EPS/PS export than the original design.

✦ **Clip Complex Regions:** Depending on where you set the slider for Transparency Quality/Speed, you'll have distinct boundaries between raster and vector objects. When part of an object is rasterized and another part is a vector object, artifacts along the boundaries can appear. Checking this box reduces the stitching artifacts produced when vector objects are flattened and rasterized.

✦ **Preserve Overprint:** Any overprints assigned in the original document before conversion to PDF are preserved when the box is checked.

PostScript Options

Click the last item in the list for EPS/PS exports and the options shown in Figure 9-6 appear. The PostScript options offer you settings for embedded PostScript attributes in the EPS/PS file.

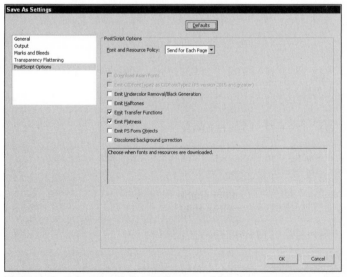

Figure 9-6: Select PostScript Options to add various PostScript printing attributes to the EPS/PostScript file(s).

The PostScript options include

✦ **Font and Resource Policy:** You determine how fonts download to a printer's RIP via three choices in the pull-down menu:

- **Send at Start:** The entire font sets for all pages are downloaded to the printer's RIP. The file prints faster than any of the other methods, but puts a memory burden on the printing device to hold all the font matrices in memory during printing.

- **Send by Range:** Fonts are downloaded from the first page where the fonts are used and stays in memory until the job is printed. The font downloading occurs as each font is found on a page that uses them. The job prints a little slower than when using the Send at Start option, but uses less memory initially as the job is printed.

- **Send for Each Page:** Fonts encountered on a page are downloaded to the RIP, then flushed as the next page is printed. The second page's fonts are then downloaded and flushed after printing, and so on. This method requires the least memory. Files print slower than when using either of the other two methods.

✦ **Download Asian Fonts:** Check this box if Asian fonts are in the document and not available on the RIP nor embedded in the document. If the fonts are embedded, you need not be concerned about checking this option.

✦ **Emit CIDFontType2 as CIDFontType2 (PS Version 2015 and greater):** Use this option to preserve hinting in the original font when printing. The options is available only for Language Level 3 output.

✦ **Emit Undercolor Removal/Black Generation:** GCR/UCR removal is only necessary if the original document contained assignments in the PostScript file converted to PDF. If you want to remove any embedded settings for handling the amount of black or compensating for black generation with different inks, check this box. If you don't know what any of this means, checking the box or not won't have an effect on your own personal documents.

✦ **Emit Halftones:** If a halftone frequency was embedded in the original file, you can eliminate it in the exported document. Unless you want to use embedded frequencies, leave the box checked in case you accidentally preserved a frequency in the original file for EPS files. When printing PostScript files to high-end devices, you'll want to assign frequencies at the time the PostScript file is created.

✦ **Emit Transfer Functions:** The same criteria as the preceding bullet apply to transfer functions. If you intend to use embedded transfer functions, leave the check box disabled. Otherwise, keep it checked as a default.

✦ **Emit Flatness:** Flatness settings applied in Photoshop, Illustrator, or other illustration programs are generally applied to clipping paths in images and on vector objects to ease the burden of printing complex objects. When checked, the flatness settings applied in the original authoring program are honored.

✦ **Emit PS Form Objects:** This option relates to PS Form XObjects. XObjects are used to create a description of multiple smaller objects repeated several times like patterns, brushes, backgrounds, and so on. Emitting the XObjects reduces the size of the print job; however, more memory is needed to RIP the file(s).

✦ **Discolored background correction:** If white backgrounds assume a discolored appearance, such as a yellow or gray tint, select this radio button to correct the discoloration.

Click OK in the Save As Settings dialog box and click Save in the Save As dialog box. The PDF is exported in EPS or PostScript format, containing all the attributes you described for all the options listed earlier.

Because printing in Acrobat Professional takes care of all the print controls you need, exporting EPS files for printing is a task you won't need to perform unless there's some strange problem that needs to be resolved in a file that won't print. A more practical use for exporting EPS files from Acrobat is if you need to import a PDF file in another program that does not support PDF, but does support EPS. In such cases you'll find it helpful to understand all the options you have available for EPS exports.

You have many advantages in creating PostScript files from Acrobat. Files can be re-distilled in Acrobat Distiller with PDF/X formats for printing and prepress, sometimes as a workaround for repurposing documents, and for downloading directly to PostScript Level 2 devices (PostScript 3 devices accept PDFs directly).

Cross-Reference For more information about PDF/X files, see Chapters 8 and 25.

HTML 3.2 (*.htm), HTML 4.01 with CSS 1.0 (*.htm), XML 1.0 (*.xml), and Text (Plain) (*.txt)

Options available for exporting PDFs to HTML files, HTML files with Cascading Style Sheets, Plain Text, and XML files all use the same attribute settings. Text is exported according to the encoding method you select and images are exported according to the format option you select. These settings are available when you select any one of the three file formats from the Save as type (Format on Macintosh) pull-down menu. Select a format and click the Settings button. The Save As *XXX* Settings dialog box opens as shown in Figure 9-7.

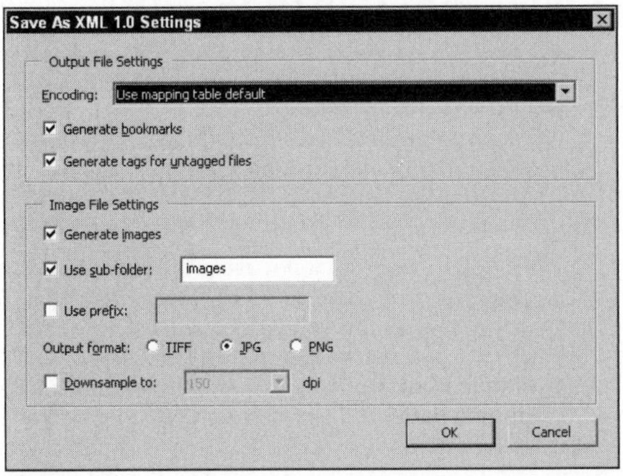

Figure 9-7: To set attributes for file exports for HTML, XML, or TXT files, select one of three file formats in the Save as type (Format on Macintosh) pull-down menu and click Settings. The dialog box is called Save As *XXX* Settings, where *XXX* is the format you selected.

The attribute settings are as follows:

✦ **Encoding:** Choose the encoding method from options for Unicode settings (UTF-8, UTF-16, or UCS-4), ISO-Latin-1, HTML/ASCII, or the default setting of Use mapping table default.

✦ **Generate bookmarks:** Generates Bookmark links to content for HTML or XML documents. Links are placed at the beginning of the resulting HTML or XML document.

✦ **Generate tags for untagged files:** Tags are temporarily created for file conversion for untagged documents. You need to select the check box for legacy untagged files or with files created with Acrobat 4 or in order to complete the conversion. The tags are temporary for the conversion to work and are not added to the PDF. If you do not select this for legacy PDFs, you will not get the conversion.

✦ **Generate images:** Enable this check box for images to be exported as separate files.

✦ **Use sub-folder:** Images are saved to a subfolder below the directory where the HTML files are created. The default name for the folder is *images*. In the field box you can change the folder name by editing the line of text.

✦ **Use prefix:** This option adds prefixes to image filenames. Check the box and supply the prefix text in the field box.

✦ **Output format:** Three options buttons enable you to determine the file format for the saved images. Choose from TIFF, JPG, or PNG.

✦ **Downsample to:** Images are downsampled to the setting selected from the pull-down menu. The settings are fixed with choices for 72, 96, 150, and 300 pixels per inch (ppi).

JPEG (*.jpg, .jpeg, .jpe), JPEG2000 (.jpf, *.ipx, *.jp2, *.j2k, *.j2c, .jpc), PNG (.png), and TIFF (*.tif, *.tiff)

You can export the PDF document as any one of the preceding image file formats. Each entire page, including text and images, is exported as a single image file. From the Settings dialog box you choose options for image compression and color management. The options settings for exporting image file formats are the same as the options used when importing images in Acrobat with the Create PDF From File or From Multiple Files commands discussed in Chapter 6.

Caution   When exporting PDF documents containing images, you cannot achieve a better resolution than the resolution in the source file. If you have, for example, a PDF document with a TIFF image where the image was originally sampled at 72 ppi, you cannot gain any resolution by saving the file from Acrobat as a TIFF file with 300-ppi resolution. The file is saved with the resolution you specify in the Save As *XXX* Settings dialog box, but image resolutions higher than source files are upsized with image interpolation. The results are often unusable and produce poor quality images. If you need image resolutions higher than the source images, you need to return to your scanner and scan images at higher resolutions. Recreate the original document and convert to PDF.

Cross-Reference   For a better understanding of image resolutions required for printing, see Chapter 25.

Microsoft Word Document (*.doc) and Rich Text Format (*.rtf)

You can also export PDF files to Microsoft Word format and Rich Text Format files (RTF). The conversion settings include choices for image handling and sampling. Unlike HTML and XML files, exports to Word and RTF embed the images in the exported text files when you choose to export images. Acrobat does not offer an option for exporting images apart from the text data.

Be aware that although you can export PDF documents directly to MS Word format, the integrity of your file all depends on how well you created the PDF. If the PDF was created without tags and through less desirable PDF-creation methods, the ultimate file you produce in Word or RTF format may not be suitable for editing and converting back to PDF. Inasmuch as tags are added during conversion to PDF, the tagged structure is not retained in the resulting file.

Cross-Reference For more information on programs supporting exports to PDF as structured and tagged files, see Chapter 6.

As a general rule you should keep native documents archived and return to them to perform any major editing tasks. As a workaround, you can use the export to Word and RTF formats for legacy files where no original documents are available. In some cases you'll need to perform some extensive editing in either your word processor or page layout program.

Clicking the Settings button in the Save As dialog box for exports to MS Word or RTF opens the Save As Settings dialog box. The settings are the same for RTF as for Word-formatted file exports (shown in Figure 9-8).

Figure 9-8: Select either MS Word or RTF for the file export and click the Settings button. The options in both dialog boxes are identical.

Settings for exporting to MS Word or RTF formats include

✦ **Include Comments:** Like EPS and PostScript files discussed earlier, Comment notes can be exported to Word or with RTF files. Select the box for Include Comments and the Comment notes are exported.

✦ **Retain Columns:** For documents containing a columnar layout, the structure is preserved in the exported document when this box is selected.

✦ **Retain Page Size and Margin:** This setting is particularly helpful when pages in MS Word are of non-standard size (US letter, US Legal, tabloid, and so on). Select this box when you have documents not conforming to standard page sizes.

✦ **Include Images:** You can extract image files from the PDF and embed them in the .doc or .rtf file in either of two formats. Select JPG or PNG for the image file format.

✦ **Use Colorspace:** You have choices for colorspaces from a pull-down menu. Choose from Determine Automatically in which case Acrobat determines using either grayscale or color, or select Grayscale or Color from the menu options.

✦ **Change Resolution:** Downsampling and resolution issues are the same as those noted when exporting PDF documents to image formats.

Cross-Reference
For more information on resolutions and sampling, see Chapter 9.

✦ **Generate tags for untagged files:** If you attempt to save an untagged document as either a .doc or .rtf file with the Generate tags for untagged files check box disabled, Acrobat prompts you in an alert dialog box to set the preference option. This check box must be enabled in order to export the file.

Text (Accessible) (*.txt)

Files are saved as text. For tagged PDF documents made accessible, all alternative text used to describe items like images and form fields that are contained in the document tags are converted to text. The alternate tags can be viewed in the Tags palette in Acrobat but won't necessarily appear in the document page. When you export PDFs as Accessible Text, the text is generated in the body of the document.

Saving Different Document Versions (Acrobat Professional and Adobe Creative Suite Only)

When you install Acrobat, the program is Version Cue ready. However, creating a Version Cue workspace and administering Version Cue files requires installation of the Adobe Creative Suite. This section applies to users who have Adobe Creative Suite installed. There are two versions of Adobe Creative Suite. The Adobe Creative Suite Standard edition includes Adobe Photoshop, Adobe Illustrator, Adobe InDesign and Version Cue. The Adobe Creative Suite Premium edition includes all the Standard programs along with Adobe GoLive and Adobe Acrobat Professional. Either version supports Version Cue management.

For saving different document versions, you use Adobe Version Cue. Version Cue is a file versioning system that is tightly integrated into all the Adobe Creative Suite applications and now supports Acrobat 7. Once enabled, the Version Cue file interface may be accessed from within all the standard file dialog boxes in Acrobat and all the CS Applications.

If you install Acrobat on one computer and another user on your network has installed either version of the Creative Suite, you can take advantage of saving and opening files in the Version Cue workspace. A key benefit of Version Cue is that it lets you set up projects that may be shared over a network. All files within these projects are version controlled, allowing all members of the team access to the very latest versions of each file. The versioning features also ensure that team members don't accidentally save changes over the top of other changes.

Using the Version Cue Workspace Administration utility (available only to Adobe Creative Suite users), you can control all aspects of Version Cue from an administration interface. This interface lets you create and edit the access properties for users and create and define properties for each project including which users have access and authentication and file locking.

Setting Up the Version Cue Workspace (Adobe Creative Suite users only)

Before Version Cue may be used, several steps are required to enable Version Cue for the various CS applications and Adobe Acrobat Professional and to turn the Version Cue system on.

Note   Version Cue was introduced with the introduction of the Creative Suite. If you purchased Acrobat 6 as part of the Creative Suite, Version Cue was not supported in Acrobat. You need to upgrade to Acrobat Professional version 7 in order to use Version Cue.

Enabling Version Cue and setting preferences (Adobe Creative Suite users only)

When Acrobat 7 is installed, the Version Cue client is also installed by default, but even though Version Cue is installed, it is not active until you turn it on.

Version Cue's existence is a bit ambiguous. Unlike executable applications contained in your Programs folder (Windows) or Applications folder (Macintosh) you need to access Version Cue through the Control Panel (Windows) or the System Preferences (Macintosh). To turn on Version Cue, double-click the Version Cue icon to open the Version Cue Preferences dialog box, shown in Figure 9-9. The icon is found in the Control Panel folder and appears as a control panel item denoted as Adobe Version Cue (Windows) or under the Other category on the Macintosh at the bottom of the System Preferences dialog box.

If you want Version Cue turned on automatically each time you start your computer, check the box for Turn Version Cue on When the Computer Starts.

The Workspace Access field offers menu options to make the workspace shared or private. The two options are This Workspace is Visible to Others and This Workspace is Private. To make the Version Cue workspace accessible to other users, leave the default at This Workspace is Visible to Others.

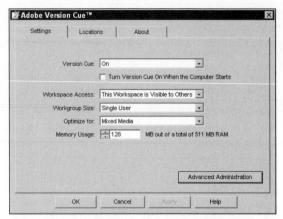

Figure 9-9: The Version Cue dialog box includes a pull-down menu where you can turn Version Cue On or Off.

The next three preference choices are used to optimize the workspace and to specify the type of files that you'll be versioning. The Workspace Size may be set to Single User, Small (2–4 People), Medium (5–10 People), or Large (10+ People). By specifying the workspace size, Version Cue can make more connections available so users don't have to wait as long to gain access to the files. The Optimize for field lets you select the type of media files you'll most often be saving. The options include Print Media, which are typically fewer in number, but much larger; Web Media, which includes a large number of smaller files; and Mixed Media.

The Memory Usage field lets you specify the amount of memory on your local hard drive or on a network hard drive that is available for Version Cue to use. Increasing this memory value enables you to retrieve files very quickly, but leaves less memory available on your hard drive.

Specifying workspace folders (Adobe Creative Suite users only)

When Version Cue is first enabled, two folders are created on your local system. One folder named Version Cue is located in the Documents folder on Macintosh systems or in the My Documents folder on Windows systems. This folder holds temporary working copies of the files that you are currently editing.

The other folders are located by default in a folder where the Creative Suite applications and Acrobat were installed. These folders, consisting of folders named Adobe Version Cue\data\ and Adobe Version Cue\backups\, hold the actual versioned files and are referenced in the Locations panel of the Version Cue Preferences dialog box, shown in Figure 9-10.

Caution   If you look at the files located in the Data and Backup folders, you won't be able to find any recognizable file formats. Do not manually move or edit any of these files or Version Cue won't work properly.

If you want to change the Data and Backups folder locations, you'll need to turn Version Cue off and click the Apply button before the Choose button in the Locations panel becomes active. Once active, you can click the Choose button to select a new directory location.

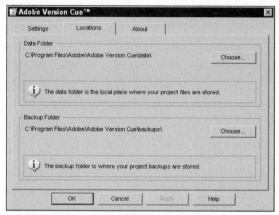

Figure 9-10: The Locations panel of the Version Cue Preferences dialog box displays the location of the versioned files.

Enabling Version Cue within Acrobat Professional (Acrobat and Creative Suite users)

In Acrobat, Version Cue is not available unless you visit the General preferences and select Enable Version Cue Workgroup File Management in the General pane. Other CS applications use various methods to enable Version Cue and some programs require you to quit the program and relaunch it before Version Cue is accessible. For a quick look at moving through the procedure for starting Version Cue, follow these steps.

STEPS: Setting Up Version Cue for Acrobat Professional

1. **Turn Version Cue on.** If you're not an Adobe CS user, you must have your computer connected to a network where Version Cue is enabled by an Adobe Creative Suite user. For the Creative Suite users, open the System Preferences dialog box for Macintosh systems or the Control Panel dialog box for Windows systems and double-click the Version Cue icon (Macintosh) or Adobe Version Cue application (Windows). In the Version Cue dialog box, open the Version Cue pull-down menu and select On. Leave the remaining settings at the defaults and click OK.

2. **Enable Version Cue for Acrobat.** Within Acrobat, choose Edit ➪ Preferences (Windows) or Acrobat ➪ Preferences (Macintosh). Click the General item in the list at the left side of the dialog box. Check the box at the bottom of the General pane where you see Enable Version Cue workgroup file management. Click OK in the Preferences dialog box.

3. **Open a PDF document.** Click the Open tool or press Ctrl/⌘+M and select a file to open. Open any PDF document you have handy.

4. **Open Version Cue projects.** Choose File ➪ Save As. In the Save As dialog box, a button appears for Version Cue. Click the button and the Save As dialog box changes as shown in Figure 9-11. In the Save As dialog box you'll see your local computer name and any servers if you have them mounted.

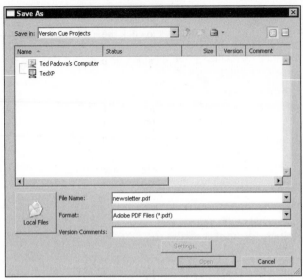

Figure 9-11: The Save As dialog box offers options for saving your document in a target Version Cue space.

Note In Figure 9-11 note the icon for Local Files. When you click the Version Cue button, the button changes to Local Files, and clicking Local Files changes the button back to Version Cue. If you want to save your document outside the Version Cue workspace, click Local Files to return to the Save As dialog box, where you can navigate your hard drive and select a target folder for saving the file.

5. **Cancel out of the Save As dialog box.** Don't attempt to save a new project yet until you review the remainder of this chapter.

Working with Version Cue files (Acrobat and Creative Suite users)

When Version Cue is turned on and enabled for Acrobat (or any other CS application), you can access the Version Cue workspace by clicking the Version Cue button that appears at the bottom of any file dialog box. In addition to the Save As dialog box shown in Figure 9-11, you'll find the same Version Cue button in Open dialog boxes.

If you open the File menu you can see two menu commands related to saving Version Cue projects. The Save As Version menu and Versions menu commands appear grayed out until you have a version of the active document saved in the Version Cue workspace. Opening a PDF document does not provide access to these menu commands until you use the Save As dialog box, click the Version Cue button, and save the file to a folder that Version Cue monitors.

Creating a Version Cue project (Adobe Creative Suite users only)

To manage your Version Cue workspace, you need to click the Advanced Administration button in the Version Cue dialog box. When you click the button your default Web browser opens with help information and tools to manage your Version Cue projects. The first Web page appearing in your Web browser is a log-on page.

In order to access the Version Cue administration, you need to supply a log-on name and password. When you first work with Version Cue, the default log-on and password are both *system*. Type **system** (lowercase) in the log-on field box and the password field box, click OK, and you are provided access to the Adobe Version Cue Workspace Administration page as shown in Figure 9-12.

You can change the administration password at any time, or you can password-protect individual projects. The administration and management for Version Cue appears on Web pages after you log on where you have four tabs from which to choose to handle your projects. These include

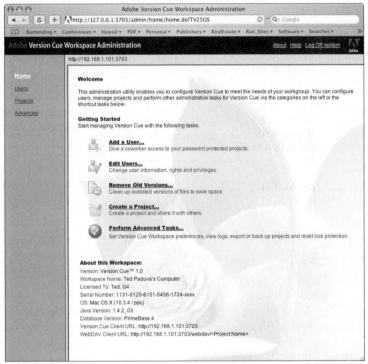

Figure 9-12: When you click Advanced Administration, enter **system** in the log-on and password field boxes, and click the log-on button to gain access to the administration settings.

✦ **Home:** By default the Home tab opens. The Home tab links to the following three options.

- **Users:** The Users tab offers options for managing the users added to your projects and lists all users working on the project in a list window. You can add a new user, delete an existing user, duplicate a user, and export a user list.

- **Projects:** The Projects tab is where you manage Version Cue projects and lists all active projects in a list window. You can create new projects, duplicate a project, back up a project, export a project, and delete a project in this pane.

- **Advanced:** The Advanced tab enables you to perform advanced tasks such as setting Version Cue preferences, importing Web workgroup server projects, exporting projects, performing maintenance tasks, and reviewing logging reports.

To create a new project, click the Create a Project link on the Home page or click the Projects link. You arrive at the New Project Web page where you can choose from creating a blank project, importing a project from a folder, importing a project from an ftp server, or importing a project from a WebDAV server. Click Blank and click the Next button to start a new project with an empty folder.

In the Create a Blank New Project pane you enter a name for your project and can assign permissions and comments. Click Next and you arrive at the Assigned Users pane. You can add new users in this pane and assign user privileges here. Click Save and the project is created as the Projects pane opens. Here you see a list of all active projects. In Figure 9-13 you can see three active projects in the Projects pane.

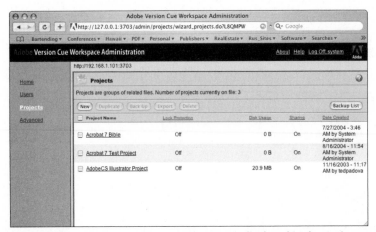

Figure 9-13: All active Version Cue projects are displayed in the Projects pane.

When you finish with the advanced administration click the Log Off: system link in the title bar. You are returned to the log-on page. At this point, quit your browser and you're ready to save projects to your Version Cue folders.

The number of options in the Advanced Administration panes may at first appear a bit overwhelming. However, to begin, try to create a simple blank project folder using this section as a guide. You can also open the Adobe Version Cue dialog box from the Control Panel (Windows) or System Preferences (Macintosh) and click the Help button. Ample help is offered with Version Cue and most of the questions you may have can be answered in the Help pages.

Saving Version Cue files (Acrobat and CS users)

When you save Version Cue files with the File ➪ Save command, the working copy is updated, but the actual versioned copy isn't updated until you use the File ➪ Save As or File ➪ Save a Version menu commands.

When you are ready to save a new version of the edited file to the Version Cue repository, choose File ➪ Save a Version. This command opens a simple dialog box, shown in Figure 9-14, where you can quickly type a Version comment and save the file. The version comment that you enter appears in the Version Cue file interface when you select the file.

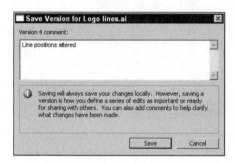

Figure 9-14: Choosing File ➪ Save a Version lets you enter comments for the file.

When you use File ➪ Save As, the Version Cue file interface opens. The Version Cue file interface includes fields for naming the file, selecting a Format, and entering Version Comments. If you elect to save the file using the same filename, then a warning dialog box asks whether you want to save these changes as a new version or you can elect to save the file using a new name.

Understanding states (Acrobat and CS users)

Each file that is saved is given a status that defines the state of the file. The available statuses include the following:

✦ **Available:** This status indicates that the file is available to be selected and edited.

✦ **Ready for Download:** This status indicates that the file is available to be copied to your local working file.

✦ **In Use By Me:** This status indicates that you are currently editing this file.

✦ **In Use By Me Elsewhere:** This status indicates that you are editing this file on a different computer.

✦ **In Use By User:** This status indicates that the file is currently being edited by another user. The user's name is listed.

✦ **Offline:** This status indicates that the file is unavailable because Version Cue has been turned off.

The status of a file opened using the Version Cue interface is displayed in the title bar of the document.

Adding files to a Version Cue project (Acrobat and CS users)

The File ➪ Save As and the File ➪ Save a Version menu commands may be used to add single files to a Version Cue project.

To add multiple files to a project, copy all the files into their correct folders of the working project file in the Version Cue folder located in the Documents folder on Macintosh or in the My Documents folder on Windows. For example, your Acrobat documents or other CS application files should be put in the Documents directory under the project folder. If you're using Adobe GoLive, place these files in the web-content and web-data folders.

With the files added to the working directory, select the Synchronize menu command from the Project Tools pull-down menu. This command copies all the files added to the working directory to the Version Cue repository where they are accessed by all users.

Working with the Versions command (Acrobat and CS users)

When a versioned file is opened in Acrobat or another CS application, you can gain access to the various versions by choosing File ➪ Versions. This command opens a dialog box, shown in Figure 9-15, where all the versions of the open file are listed along with their thumbnails, version numbers, and version comments.

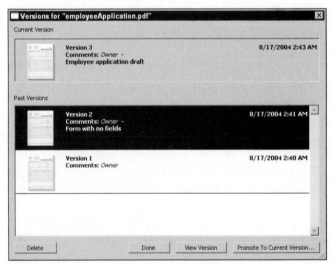

Figure 9-15: All the versions for an open file are accessible when you use the File ➪ Versions menu command.

Using this dialog box, you can select a version, delete a version, open a version, or promote a selected version to the Current Version. In Figure 9-15, note that Version 3 is promoted to the top level as the Current Version. When you open this document in Acrobat you see the Current Version appear in the Document pane. This particular file is an Acrobat PDF form. The promoted version has a watermark stamped as "draft." Version 2 is the form without form fields and without a watermark. Version 1 is the PDF form with form fields and without the watermark.

If you e-mail the example file as it appears in Figure 9-15 or send it for an e-mail review, the only version your recipients can view is the Current Version. You can collect comments, promote Version 1, edit the document, and save the file as a final document ready to distribute. To promote any version to the top level and make it the default view when it's opened in Acrobat, select any version and click the Promote To Current Version button. You can delete all other versions in a final file by selecting them and clicking the Delete button.

Caution

When you save versions, you add to the original file size. Using Version Cue does not save you any hard drive space for storing files. When you post documents on the Web, write to CD-ROMs, or distribute final files, be certain to delete all unnecessary versions. Doing so reduces your file size.

Summary

✦ Acrobat can save PDFs in a variety of different formats. Many formats have an elaborate number of options settings to set attributes for the saved files.

✦ Before you may use the Version Cue features, the Version Cue client must be turned on using the Version Cue Preferences dialog box, and Version Cue must be enabled for Acrobat and each CS application using their respective Preferences dialog boxes.

✦ The Version Cue file interface may be accessed using any of the file dialog boxes used to open, save, place, import, and export files.

✦ The Version Cue file interface lets you create new projects, search for files, sort files, view thumbnails, and view deleted files.

✦   ✦   ✦

Editing Text

Ideally you should always return to an original document when you want to make changes on PDF pages that were converted from an authoring application. With all of Acrobat's impressive features, it is not designed to be used as a page layout program. The options you have in Acrobat for text editing are limited to tweaks and minor corrections. Inasmuch as Acrobat 7 has greatly improved text editing on PDFs, returning to your authoring program, editing the pages, and converting them back to PDF is a preferred method.

For minor edits and for purposes of editing PDF files where original documents have been lost or are unavailable, Acrobat does provide you tools and means for text editing. As you look through this chapter realize that the pages ahead are intended to describe methods for minor corrections and text editing when you don't have an option for returning to an original document.

Setting Up the Text Editing Environment

For text editing, there are several toolbars that you'll want to make visible and dock in the Toolbar Well or float in the Document pane, depending on what is handier for you. Toolbars you need for text editing include

+ **Basic toolbar:** By default the Basic toolbar is loaded when you reset the toolbars. In the Basic toolbar you find the Select tool. You use this tool extensively when editing text in PDF documents. Be certain you reset the toolbars by opening a context menu on the Toolbar Well and selecting Reset Toolbars before loading the additional tools needed for text editing.

+ **Zoom tools:** For zooming in and out of the Document pane, use the Loupe, Pan and Zoom, and Dynamic Zoom tools. By default, the Zoom toolbar is docked in the Toolbar Well. You can expand the toolbar for easy access to any one of the Zoom tools by selecting the pull-down arrow adjacent to the Zoom In tool and choosing the Show Zoom Toolbar command. The toolbar expands in the Toolbar Well and makes all tools easily accessible.

+ **TouchUp toolbar:** The TouchUp toolbar contains the TouchUp Text tool used for editing short text passages, the TouchUp Object tool that permits you to move text blocks around a page, and the TouchUp Reading Order tool used for changing the reading order in accessible documents. Choose Tools ➪ Advanced Editing ➪ Show TouchUp Toolbar. Notice in Acrobat 7 you now have direct access to the TouchUp toolbar from the Tools menu without opening the Advanced Editing toolbar as was the case in Acrobat 6.

Cross-Reference

For more information on using the TouchUp Order tool and document accessibility, see Chapter 20.

✦ **Edit toolbar:** The Edit toolbar contains tools that duplicate some common menu commands such as Copy (used for copying selected text or an object), Undo, and Redo tools. You also find a tool for spell checking although checking spelling is limited to only comment notes and form fields. Dock the toolbars in the Toolbar Well using a context menu from the Toolbar Well and your toolbars should look something like Figure 10-1.

Note

If you need help at any time, you can click the Help button in the Toolbar Well to gain access to Acrobat Help. For an editing session, close the window to allow more room in the Document pane to display your pages.

Figure 10-1: Load all editing tools in the Toolbar Well before beginning your text editing session.

Using the TouchUp Text Tool

 For minor text edits, the TouchUp Text tool on the TouchUp toolbar enables you to edit text along single lines of copy and edit bodies of text. Before you attempt to change text passages on a PDF page, you need to keep a few things in mind. Some of the considerations include

✦ **Font embedding:** If you attempt to edit an embedded font, Acrobat prompts you in a dialog box to unembed the font. Text editing is only possible after a font is unembedded. Depending on the permissions granted by the font developer, some fonts can't be unembedded. If Acrobat informs you that font editing cannot occur, you need to make your changes in the original authoring document.

Cross-Reference

For more information on font embedding, see Chapter 8.

✦ **Tagged and untagged PDF documents:** If you want to edit a body of text, such as text with two or more lines, using a tagged file is best because the tagged documents retain more paragraph structure. When you edit tagged PDFs with document structure, the text blocks are divided into structured paragraphs. Editing one paragraph won't have an effect on the other paragraphs on a page. Untagged files appear in contiguous text blocks, which makes controlling text flow, indents and tabs, and paragraph structure difficult. Figure 10-2 shows text selected with the TouchUp Text tool in an untagged file. Figure 10-3 shows the same file created with tags. In a file created with tags, only single paragraphs can be selected with the TouchUp Text tool. In the untagged document, all text can be selected and remains a contiguous body of text.

Cross-Reference For more information on tagged and structured PDF documents, see Chapter 20. For information on creating tagged PDF files, see Chapter 7.

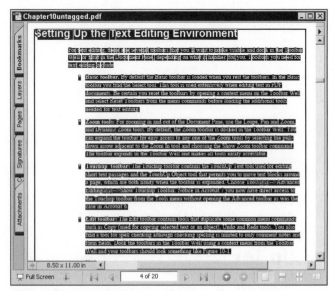

Figure 10-2: Untagged PDFs without any document structure are more difficult to edit because you lose some control over the text flow.

✦ **Property changes:** You can apply property changes for fonts, such as color, size, and other attributes, to text without unembedding the font.

Fortunately, Acrobat alerts you ahead of time if you attempt to edit a PDF document with embedded fonts and those fonts aren't installed on your computer. To edit fonts on a page, select the TouchUp Text tool, and click and drag over a body of text to be changed. Acrobat pauses momentarily as it surveys your installed fonts and the font embedded in the PDF document. Enter your changes and the selected text is replaced with the new text you typed.

You'll be able to see onscreen whether your text editing results in an acceptable appearance and the edits are properly applied. If the text scrambles and you lose total control over the document page, you need to either find the original authoring document or export text from Acrobat into a word processor or layout program to make the changes.

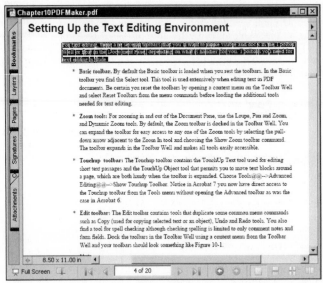

Figure 10-3: Tagged PDF files are structured into elements that are segmented and provide more control over editing single paragraphs without affecting the other paragraphs on a page.

Prepress

Editing text passages are fine for screen displays when the text flows in an acceptable manner. For high-end printing and prepress you might be able to successfully make changes and minor edits without experiencing printing problems. However, for any kind of paragraph editing you are best off returning to the authoring application. You might get away with some edits in Acrobat, but eventually they will catch up with you. If you do make a spelling error change or other minor text edit, be certain to re-embed the font (see "Changing text attributes" later in this chapter).

In addition to selecting the Properties menu command, a context menu opened from a TouchUp Text tool selection offers menu commands for insertion of special characters. Four choices are available to you when you open a context menu and select the Insert menu command. From the submenu you can choose

✦ **Line Break:** This choice adds a line break from the cursor insertion. This command is handy when creating new text on a page or when pasting text. Text lines may extend beyond the page width when creating new text or pasting text. You can create line breaks to keep text within a specific area of the page.

✦ **Soft Hyphen:** This choice adds a soft hyphen for text scrolling to a new line.

✦ **Non-Breaking Space:** To add spaces without line breaks, choose non-breaking space.

✦ **Em Dash:** To add an em dash (—) at the cursor insertion, choose em dash.

When text is selected and you insert a special character, the selected text is deleted and the new character is added. If you use special characters in untagged PDF files, the results may be less than desirable. Line breaks can flow text into following paragraphs and the text can overlap, making the page unreadable. If you encounter such problems and the edits are necessary to make your files more readable, you must return the file to the authoring program, make the edits, and recreate the PDF document.

Changing text attributes

You can make many text attribute changes without unembedding fonts. You can change colors, point sizes in lines of text, character and word spacing, and other similar text attributes, as well as make changes related to the document structure. You make all of these changes in the TouchUp Properties dialog box.

To edit text properties, select the characters, words, or paragraph(s) you want to change. Be certain the text is highlighted and open a context menu as shown in Figure 10-4. From the menu options, select Properties.

Figure 10-4: To change text properties, select the text to be changed with the TouchUp Text tool and select Properties from the menu options.

Cross-Reference

Two tools enable text selection—the TouchUp Text tool and the Select tool. Always use the TouchUp Text tool context menu when opening the TouchUp Properties dialog box. The Select tool context menu does not provide access to the TouchUp Properties dialog box. For information related to using the Select tool, see "Using the Select Tool" later in this chapter.

After you select Properties from the context menu, the TouchUp Properties dialog box opens as shown in Figure 10-5. The first two tabs relate to changing tags and document structure. Leave these alone for the moment and look at the third tab labeled Text. The properties contained on it relate to changing font attributes for the selected text.

Cross-Reference

For information on using the Content and Tag tabs, see Chapter 20.

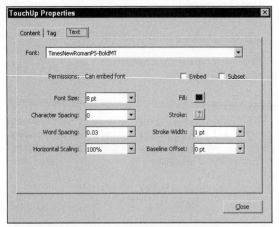

Figure 10-5: Select the Text tab in the TouchUp Properties dialog box to make changes to font attributes.

Items contained in the Text tab include

✦ **Font:** This pull-down menu contains a list of fonts for all the fonts loaded in your system and fonts embedded in the document. Keep in mind that just because a font is listed in the pull-down menu doesn't mean you can select the font. If the font is an embedded/subsetted font and you don't have a compatible font loaded in your system, Acrobat won't let you use that font. Fonts loaded in your system can be selected to replace fonts that are both embedded and not embedded.

Note   The font list in the pull-down menu shows a line dividing the list at the top of the menu. All fonts appearing above the line are embedded fonts in the document. All fonts below the line are fonts loaded in your system.

✦ **Permissions:** A message is displayed for font permissions. If the font can be embedded, the message is *Can embed font*. If the font cannot be embedded, the message reads *Cannot embed font*. Some fonts may not be embedded because of licensing restrictions from a font manufacturer.

✦ **Font Size:** You select preset font sizes from this pull-down menu. If the desired size is not listed among the menu choices, select the font size in the field box and type a new value to change the size.

✦ **Character Spacing:** You can move characters in a line of text closer together or farther apart. The values shown in the pull-down menu are measured in em spaces. Choose from the menu choices or type a value in the field box. Using negative (–) values moves the characters together.

✦ **Word Spacing:** This option controls the space between whole words. You make choices for distance the same way you do for the preceding character spacing option.

✦ **Horizontal Scaling:** Sizing of individual characters (narrower or wider) is set according to the percentage of the original size. Values above 100% scale characters larger than the original font. Values below 100% result in smaller characters.

✦ **Embed:** Check the box to embed the selected font.

✦ **Subset:** Check the box to subset the font.

Cross-Reference

For information on font embedding and subsetting, see Chapter 8.

Caution

In order to legally embed a font, you must own a copy of the font to be embedded and comply with the licensing restrictions of the font manufacturer. Be certain to review the licensing agreement that came with your fonts to be certain embedding the font(s) is permitted. Some manufacturers do not license fonts for embedding.

✦ **Fill:** The color swatch shows the default color of the selected font. Clicking the color swatch opens a pop-up menu as shown in Figure 10-6. You select preset colors from the palette. When you click Other Color the system color palette opens. You can create custom colors from the system color palette and apply them to the text fill.

Figure 10-6: Click the color swatch in the TouchUp Properties dialog box to open the pop-up menu used for making color selections.

Prepress

If you intend to print your PDFs for color separations, don't make color changes in Acrobat. The color space for the preset colors and custom colors is RGB. You can experience color-matching problems if you attempt to convert RGB or Spot files to CMYK. If color changes to text are needed, you have to return to the authoring application and make the color changes, and then recreate the PDF file. For more information on RGB, Spot, and Process color, see Chapter 25.

✦ **Stroke:** Stroking text creates outlines for the font characters. You can make the same color choices for strokes as you can for the character fills.

✦ **Stroke Width:** You change the weight (in points) of the stroke outlines by making choices in the pull-down menu or by typing values in the field box.

Tip

If you want to create outline text, select No color from the Fill Color pop-up menu and add a stroke color and width. When stroke fills are set to No color, the fills appear transparent and show the background color.

✦ **Baseline Offset:** You can raise or lower text above the baseline or below it. To move text up, enter positive values in the field box. To move text below the baseline, use negative values.

After making choices in the TouchUp Properties dialog box, click the Close button. The changes you make in the dialog box are reflected only on text you selected with the TouchUp Text tool.

Editing text on layers

You can edit text on layered PDF documents. When layer data are visible, you can use the TouchUp Text tool to select text and edit the properties as described in the section "Changing text attributes." If you have difficulty selecting text you can hide layers and select just the text on visible layers.

You can also select and edit text appearing on all visible layers. If text appears on all layers, the edits are applied to all layers. If text appears on a single layer, the text edits reflect changes only on the respective layer.

Engineering Engineers working in AutoCAD and Microsoft Visio can export drawings as layered files. When the PDF is opened in Acrobat, the layers created contain separate layer data. If you anticipate changing text, try to keep all the text on a single layer for a given drawing if it's practical. You can then hide layers and select all the text on the text layer. Make your edits and the changes are reflected only on the layer(s) that was edited.

Cross-Reference For more information on managing layers, see Chapter 19.

Adding new text to a document

You can also use the TouchUp Text tool to add a new line of text in a document. Select the TouchUp Text tool and press the Ctrl/Option key and then click the mouse button in the area you want to add new text. The New Text Font dialog box opens as shown in Figure 10-7.

Figure 10-7: Ctrl/Option+click on a document page when you have the TouchUp Text tool selected and the New Text Font dialog box opens. Select a font from the Font pull-down menu and select text alignment — Horizontal or Vertical — from the Mode pull-down menu.

From the Font pull-down menu you can select any font loaded in your system. Fonts appearing below the horizontal line in the menu represent the current fonts loaded in your system. Fonts above the line are the embedded fonts in your PDF document. For an embedded font to be usable, it needs to be unembedded and available in your system.

From the Mode pull-down menu you can select between Horizontal or Vertical alignment. Click OK in the dialog box and the cursor blinks at the location where you clicked the mouse button. The words "New Text" appear in a text field box. Type the text you want to add and open the TouchUp Properties dialog box by choosing Properties from a context menu. Select the check boxes for embedding and subsetting to embed the new text font in the document.

Tip Acrobat does not permit any edits on text where a font has been embedded and the font is not installed on your system. To resolve the problem, you can select the text, open the TouchUp Properties dialog box, and select a system font from the Font pull-down menu. After you change a font to one available to your system, you can make text edits.

Copying text with the TouchUp Text tool

The TouchUp Text tool is probably the last tool you want to use for copying text and pasting the text into other programs. I mention it here so you know what limitations you have in Acrobat for copying text with this tool. Inasmuch as the TouchUp Text tool enables you to copy multiple lines of text, you are limited to single paragraphs or short blocks of text.

To copy text with the TouchUp Text tool, click and drag the tool through the text block(s) you want to copy. The text is selected as you drag the mouse cursor. After making a selection, open a context menu and select Copy from the menu commands as shown in Figure 10-8. You can also choose Edit ➪ Copy.

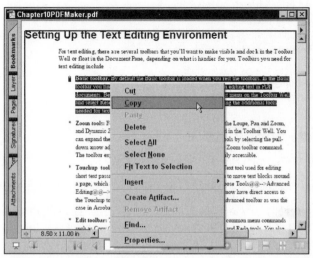

Figure 10-8: Select the TouchUp Text tool and drag through the text paragraphs you want to select.

Note Acrobat 6 and 7 enable you to select multiple lines of text with the TouchUp Text tool.

In Figure 10-8 the selected text block is the only block of text that you can select because the document is a tagged file and the individual paragraphs are structured into separate blocks. When you drag the cursor through a block of text the only text that you can select with this tool is the respective block. If you want to copy and paste additional text blocks you need to individually select the separate blocks and copy and paste them. Obviously, if you have pages of text, this tool isn't the tool of choice. Copying and pasting a single line or a single paragraph of text with the TouchUp Text tool achieves the same results as when using other tools for copying and pasting.

To paste text in a word processor or other application where pasting text is permitted, open the application and select the Paste command. Typically, you find Paste under the Edit menu. The text formatting of the pasted text is preserved if you copy text from tagged PDF documents.

Setting Text Editing Preferences

You have some options for preference choices when using tools for text editing. Using the TouchUp Text tool doesn't require you to make any preference changes. However, when using the Select tool you have some options in the General preferences settings. To open the Preferences dialog box, press Ctrl/⌘+K. When the Preferences dialog box opens click General in the left pane. At the top of the right pane under the Selection category are options that impact selecting text as shown in Figure 10-9.

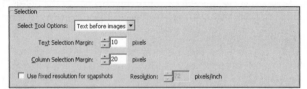

Figure 10-9: Open the Preferences dialog box and click General in the left pane. Under the Selection category are options for handling text selections.

Selecting the order of objects

The Select Tool Options pull-down menu shown in Figure 10-9 reflects the order that objects are selected (consider a text block as an object as you review this section). When you select the menu item *Images before text*, images are selected first when images and text occupy the same space on a page. You use the Select tool to click in an area and the selection is made according to the preference choice made in the Selection section of the General preferences. Selecting the *Text before images* reverses the order and, hence, text is selected before images when they both occupy the same space.

When I refer to occupying the same space, I'm talking about an image that may have a bounding box larger than the displayed image and text appears over the bounding box area, or when text is superimposed over an image.

Using the Hand tool for text selections

 If you're editing text on a page, you can choose to make text selections with the Hand tool instead of the Select tool or the TouchUp Text tool. You need to select the check box for Enable text selection for the Hand tool in the General preferences in order to select text with this tool.

With the Hand tool, you can move a page around in the Document pane or scroll pages when viewing pages in views other than Single Page view. If you move the cursor above any text, quickly drag the page around the Document pane to move the page. If you wait a moment, the cursor changes and any dragging you do selects text. If you accidentally select text when you wanted to move the page, deselect the text by clicking outside a text block.

Tip   If you find it awkward toggling back and forth between the Hand tool and the Select tool when preferences are enabled for text selections with the Hand tool, disable the preference setting. Use the Select tool and press the Esc key when you want to return to the Hand tool.

Caution   If you open the General preferences and the preference option for *Enable text selection for the hand tool* is grayed out, you need to make an adjustment in the Accessibility preferences. Click Accessibility in the left pane and remove the checkmark for *Always display keyboard selection cursor.* If this item is selected, the Hand tool preference options cannot be changed.

Using the Select Tool

Users of earlier versions of Acrobat will immediately notice the absence of the Select Text tool, the Select Table tool, and the Select Image tool. All three of these tools have been combined in the form of the Select tool to perform all three functions.

The Select tool is a much better choice than the TouchUp Text tool for selecting text to be copied from a PDF document and pasted in an editor especially if you have multiple text blocks to copy. With this tool you can select multiple blocks of text and text in columns. However, you cannot make text edits with the tool like you do with the TouchUp Text tool.

To select text with the Select tool, click and drag the tool through the text on a page you want to copy. If a single column appears on the page, click just before the first character to be selected and drag down to the last character. If you want to copy a single column in a two-column layout, click the Select tool at the beginning of the column to be selected and drag down to the end of the column. Be certain you don't click at the beginning of a text character or in the middle of a word. You need to click outside the space occupied by the text and then drag through the column. Acrobat won't copy the text in the adjacent column as long as you stay within the boundaries of the column you are selecting. Figure 10-10 shows text selected with the Select tool where only one column in a multiple-column layout is selected.

Note   The Column Select tool that was available in versions of Acrobat prior to 6.0 is no longer needed by Acrobat 6 and greater. The Select Text tool in Acrobat 6 and the Select tool in Acrobat 7 both permit column selections without the use of modifier keys or separate tools.

In conjunction with the Select tool, shortcut keys and mouse clicks provide several ways to make various text selections including

✦ **Select a word:** Double-click on a word, space, or character.

✦ **Select a line of text:** Triple-click anywhere on a line of text.

✦ **Select all text on a page:** Click four times (rapid successive clicks) to select all text on a page.

✦ **Select a column of text:** Click outside the text area and drag through the column.

✦ **Select a contiguous block of text:** Click and drag through the block of text or click the cursor at the beginning of the text to be selected, press Shift, and click at the end of the text block.

✦ **Stop text selection and revert to the Hand tool:** Press the Esc key.

✦ **Deselect text:** Click outside of the text selection or press Ctrl/⌘+Shift+A.

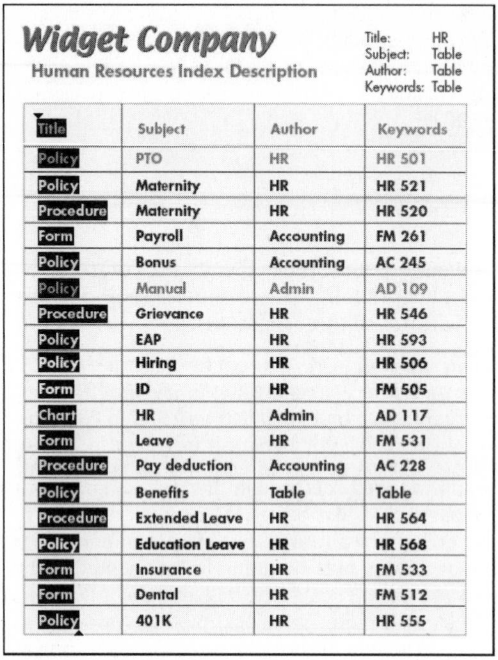

Widget Company

Human Resources Index Description

Title: HR
Subject: Table
Author: Table
Keywords: Table

Title	Subject	Author	Keywords
Policy	PTO	HR	HR 501
Policy	Maternity	HR	HR 521
Procedure	Maternity	HR	HR 520
Form	Payroll	Accounting	FM 261
Policy	Bonus	Accounting	AC 245
Policy	Manual	Admin	AD 109
Procedure	Grievance	HR	HR 546
Policy	EAP	HR	HR 593
Policy	Hiring	HR	HR 506
Form	ID	HR	FM 505
Chart	HR	Admin	AD 117
Form	Leave	HR	FM 531
Procedure	Pay deduction	Accounting	AC 228
Policy	Benefits	Table	Table
Procedure	Extended Leave	HR	HR 564
Policy	Education Leave	HR	HR 568
Form	Insurance	HR	FM 533
Form	Dental	HR	FM 512
Policy	401K	HR	HR 555

Figure 10-10: To select a column of text, use the Select tool and drag down the column length.

Depending on choices you make for copying text, text pasted in other programs can retain certain formatting attributes. Your options for what you copy are derived from menu choices when you select text with the Select tool and open a context menu. When you select text and move the cursor within the text selection, a text selection icon appears at the first line of selected text as shown in Figure 10-11.

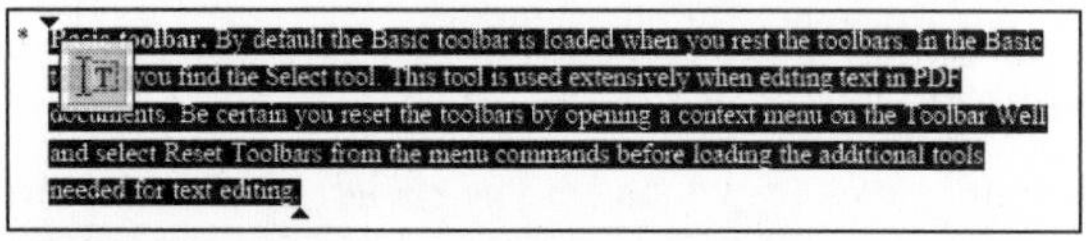

* olbar. By default the Basic toolbar is loaded when you rest the toolbars. In the Basic
you find the Select tool. This tool is used extensively when editing text in PDF
ents. Be certain you reset the toolbars by opening a context menu on the Toolbar Well
and select Reset Toolbars from the menu commands before loading the additional tools
needed for text editing.

Figure 10-11: A text selection icon appears at the beginning of the text selection.

Move the cursor over the text selection icon and a menu opens as shown in Figure 10-12. The menu does not open with a right-click (Windows) or Control+click (Macintosh). If you open a context menu using right-click (or Control+click on Macintosh), you see different menu options as shown in Figure 10-13.

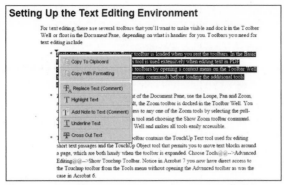

Figure 10-12: Move the cursor over the text selection icon and a menu opens.

The options shown in the context menu provide choices for marking text with a Highlight, Cross Out, Underline, Replace, and adding a note. These items are used for commenting on PDF files. You use the remaining options for copying and exporting text.

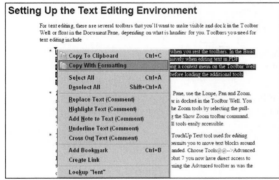

Figure 10-13: Open a context menu using right-click (Windows) or Control+click (Macintosh) and the menu options change.

Copying text

When you open a context menu on a non-structured document, you have a single menu command available for copying text to the system clipboard. If you open a tagged PDF document and then open a menu with the Select tool, an additional menu item is provided as shown in Figure 10-12. Use the Copy With Formatting command to copy text while preserving text and paragraph formatting. If the Copy With Formatting command is not available, your document is not tagged.

Cross-Reference   For information related to tagging PDF documents, see Chapter 20.

When you use either Copy to Clipboard or Copy With Formatting, you can paste the text into another document, a form field, or a Comment note.

Copying multiple pages of text

If you view PDF files in a Single Page view, you can drag through the text on the page in view to select it. However, if you want to copy text on multiple pages, you need to change the view to a Continuous Facing Pages view. Zoom out of the document so you can see several pages in the Document pane and drag through the text you want to copy. If you need to copy more pages than those in view, drag the cursor to the bottom of the Acrobat window. The document pages scroll to place more pages in view. Keep the mouse button pressed as the pages appear in view and release the mouse button on the last page you want to copy. In Figure 10-14 you can see a document in a Continuous view and text selected on multiple pages.

Figure 10-14: Click Continuous in the status bar and drag the Select tool through multiple pages to select the text.

To copy the text, select one of the Copy commands at the top of the context menu or choose Edit ⇨ Copy. If you want to copy formatted text, always use the context menu command.

Using the Select All command

If you have a need to select all the text on a page or throughout a PDF document, you can use the Select All menu command. Depending on the tool you use and the page view mode, text selections behave differently. You must first determine whether you want to select all the text on a page or all text in the document. When selecting text on a PDF page, be certain the page layout view is set to Single Page view. With the Select tool, click the cursor on any text block and choose Edit ➪ Select All or press Ctrl/⌘+A. All the text on a single page is selected. To copy the text you just selected, open a context menu and select Copy to Clipboard or Copy With Formatting. All the text is copied to the clipboard file and ready to paste into an editor.

If you want to select all text in a PDF document, change the page view to any one of the other three page views (Continuous, Continuous – Facing, or Facing). Click the cursor on any text block and use the same Select All menu command. Any one of these views permits you to select all the text in the document.

This method only works when you use the Select tool. If you select all text using the TouchUp Text tool, the selected text is confined to a bounding box. On any given page there can be one or more bounding boxes and using Select All only selects all text within a single bounding box. Regardless of which page layout view you choose, the TouchUp Text tool doesn't permit text selections across multiple pages.

Copying a file to the clipboard (Windows only)

Clicking the Select tool and choosing the Select All tool selects all text in a document. You can also accomplish the same task by choosing Edit ➪ Copy File to Clipboard. Open your word processor and you can paste the text into a new word processor document.

If you don't see the menu command, you don't have OLE (Object Linking and Embedding)–compliant applications installed on your computer. Microsoft's OLE is installed by default with Office applications on Windows. If the menu command does not appear, use the Select All menu command to achieve the same results.

Copying and pasting text in word processors is a better alternative for text editing than saving a file to RTF if the PDF was created as an untagged file. For tagged PDF documents, saving in RTF preserves much formatting, but may still be less desirable than copying and pasting text.

Cross-Reference   For a description of exporting to RTF, see Chapter 9.

Working with table data

You can copy and paste formatted text in columns and rows with the Select tool in word processors; however, precise column tabs and formatting can fall apart when you attempt to paste the text in programs like spreadsheets. If you use the Select tool to select text in a table and use Copy to Clipboard or Copy With Formatting, the data are pasted in a spreadsheet program in a single cell as shown in Figure 10-15. If you want to copy table data so the data spread to separate cells in a spreadsheet program from where the column and row breaks occur in Acrobat, you need to use another menu choice.

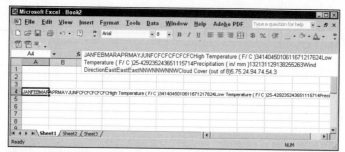

Figure 10-15: When you copy data with the Copy to Clipboard or Copy With Format commands, data pasted in a spreadsheet all fall into a single cell.

You can use several methods to select table data in Acrobat. With the Select tool, click and drag across the text just as you do when selecting text passages, move the cursor outside a table and marquee select the data, or simply click on a table with the Select tool. When you use a simple click method, look for your cursor to change its icon. You should see the cursor change to a cross-hair with a tiny graph in the lower-right corner. When the shape so changes, click to select the table. When you copy the table, use the Copy as Table menu command from the context menu shown in Figure 10-16.

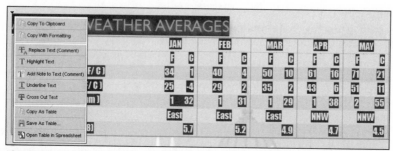

Figure 10-16: When tables are selected, the menu options change to support commands used with copying table data.

Once copied to the clipboard, you can paste the data in a spreadsheet program. Open your spreadsheet application and paste the data. The same data copied and pasted in Figure 10-14 is pasted in Microsoft Excel, shown in Figure 10-17, after using the Copy as Table method of copying the data.

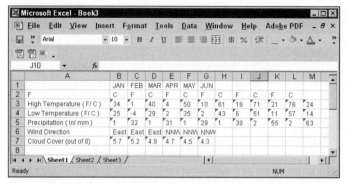

Figure 10-17: When pasting data in spreadsheet applications after using the Copy as Table command, the data are pasted into individual cells.

Saving data to a spreadsheet file

Another option you have for getting PDF data to a spreadsheet is to select the table data as described in the previous section, "Working with table data," and select Save as Table from the Select tool context menu. When you choose this command, the Acrobat Save As dialog box opens and offers you choices for saving your data in a variety of file formats. From the Save as Type (Windows) or Format (Macintosh) pull-down menu, select from

✦ **Comma Separated Values (*.csv):** CSV-compliant applications can open files saved in this format. Microsoft Excel recognizes CSV data, and you can open the files directly in Excel. If you use other applications recognizing the format, use CSV.

✦ **HTML 4.01 with CSS 1.0 (*.htm):** If you need to get table data to a Web page, you can save the data to HTML format.

✦ **Rich Text Format (*.rtf):** If you want to import data into programs such as word processors, accounting programs, and other applications that support RTF, save the file as RTF. If you want columns and rows of data without a table defined in the word processor, use the RTF format.

✦ **Text (Tab Delimited) (*.txt):** When you need to import data into a database management system (DBMS), export the data as tab delimited. Tab delimited tables import into programs like FileMaker Pro with data in separate fields and records.

✦ **Unicode Text (Tab Delimited) (*.txt):** If you use some foreign language kits, Unicode might be a better choice for your file exports. Select Unicode and import the data into applications supporting Unicode text data.

✦ **XML 1.0 (*.xml):** Acrobat supports exporting tables in Adobe XML format. XML data can be exchanged between many programs. If your workflow uses XML, save in this format.

✦ **XML Spreadsheet (*.xml):** This is an XML format defined by Microsoft. Use XML Spreadsheet when using XML data with spreadsheet applications like Microsoft Excel.

Click the Save button and the data are saved in the file format you select from the pull-down menu in the Save As dialog box.

Opening data in a spreadsheet

To make a direct link to Microsoft Excel select Open Table in Spreadsheet from the Select tool context menu. When you choose the menu command after selecting table text, Excel is launched and the data are pasted into cells.

Looking Up Definitions

Whether you're editing a PDF file or browsing documents, you can find the spelling and word definition for any text in an open document. This very nice little feature in Acrobat saves you time when looking up a definition. To employ the Look Up command from one of two context menus, use either the Hand tool or the Select tool and open a context menu over selected text. If using the Select tool, open the traditional context menu by right-clicking the mouse button (Windows) or Control+clicking (Macintosh). From the menu choices, select Lookup "..." The item appearing inside the quotation marks is your selected word. In Figure 10-18 you can see the context menu opened when the word *Procedure* was selected.

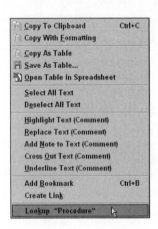

Figure 10-18: Select a word with the Select tool. Open a context menu (right-click or Control+click) and select Lookup "..." at the bottom of the menu.

After you make your selection, Acrobat launches the default Web browser and the browser takes you to the Dictionary.com Web site. The Web page opens on the word selected in the PDF document. You can check for spelling errors, word definitions, pronunciation, and browse through a thesaurus. If you have an account for the Web site, you can click on the audio button to hear an audio pronunciation through your computer speaker(s).

Currently Acrobat only supports U.S. English as a language. Regardless of whether you have a foreign language kit installed, Acrobat launches the Dictionary.com Web site.

Summary

✦ You use the TouchUp Text tool to make minor edits on PDF pages. You can use the tool to change font attributes, add new lines of text, and access a Properties dialog box where you can select fonts to embed and subset.

✦ The TouchUp Text tool is not well suited for copying and pasting text data into other programs. Text selections are limited and text formatting is lost when pasting text into other programs.

✦ The Select tool can select text on a page, across multiple pages, and all text in a document.

✦ When pasting text copied from a Select tool selection, the text data retains much integrity and can be edited with minimum character and paragraph reformatting.

✦ Text can be edited on visible layers. You can't select text on hidden layers with the Select All command. Edits made to text appearing on all layers result in changes on all layers. Edits made to text on a single layer result in changes on a single layer.

✦ You also use the Select tool to select table data. You can copy and paste tables in other applications and save the data to a number of different file formats.

✦   ✦   ✦

Editing Images and Objects

Images and objects, such as raster images from programs like Photoshop, vector images like those created in Adobe Illustrator, and text, can be edited in external editors and dynamically updated in a PDF document. The process involves launching the external editor from within Acrobat, making changes in the external editor, and saving the file. The file is treated like a link to the PDF where the edits are updated. Acrobat itself doesn't have any image editing tools, but you can use the external editors provided through companion programs to help out when you need to make modifications to objects in a PDF file.

Like text edits discussed in Chapter 10, image editing with Acrobat is intended to be a minor task for last-minute small changes. For major editing tasks, you should return to the original authoring program. In circumstances where you do not have an original document, you may need to extend the editing a little further by updating documents or exporting them for new layouts. In this chapter you learn how to handle images and objects for editing and exporting purposes.

Setting Up the Editing Environment

Tools used for working with images and objects are found in the Basic toolbar. The toolbar appears by default when you reset your toolbars. You also need the TouchUp toolbar, which opens from the Tools menu. To open the TouchUp toolbar, choose Tools ➪ Advanced Editing ➪ Show TouchUp Toolbar. Drag the separator bar on the toolbar to the Toolbar Well to dock it and you're ready to handle most image and object editing jobs.

Note   Toolbars are also accessed using a context menu on the Toolbar Well. However, the TouchUp toolbar is not available as a context menu command. In order to access TouchUp tools from the Toolbar Well context menu you need to open the Advanced Editing toolbar. The Advanced Editing toolbar is where you access the TouchUp tools. Because all you use in this chapter are the TouchUp tools, save yourself some space in the Toolbar Well and use just the TouchUp toolbar.

Selecting Images

Two tools in Acrobat enable you to copy images and objects. You can use the Select tool discussed in Chapter 10 to select images as well as text, and you also use the TouchUp Object tool to select images and objects. Objects can be vector-based artwork created in programs like Adobe Illustrator and blocks of text that Acrobat interprets as objects. Only the TouchUp Object tool can be used to select objects; therefore, you cannot use the Select tool unless the item is an image such as a Photoshop file contained in the PDF document.

The distinction between text as text and text as an object can easily be understood in what you see selected in the Document pane. If you drag the Select tool through text, the text becomes highlighted. When you see the text highlighted, realize that the text is selected as text. When you click a text block with the TouchUp Object tool, you'll see a bounding box (border) around the text block but the text itself is not highlighted. When you see this view, you can be assured the text is selected as an object. In Figure 11-1 you see text selected as text by dragging through it with the Select tool, and in Figure 11-2 you see multiple text blocks selected as objects when dragging through text with the TouchUp Object tool.

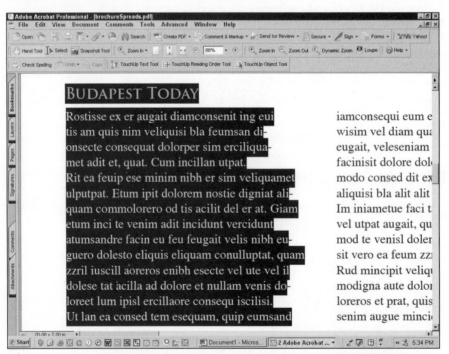

Figure 11-1: Text selected with the Select tool is selected as text and highlighted.

Each tool has different options and editing features associated with it. You use the Select tool, for example, when you want to select a photo image, copy it in Acrobat, and paste it in another program, but not paste it in another PDF document. When you select an image with the Select tool and copy it to the clipboard, the Paste command in the Edit menu remains grayed out. However, the Select tool permits you to save an image from within a PDF document to a separate file.

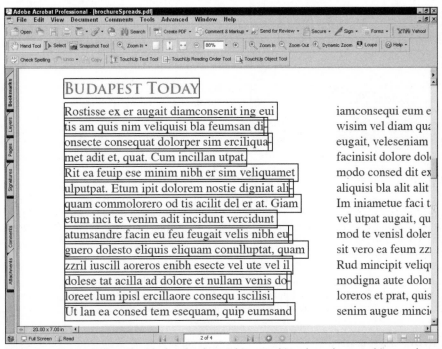

Figure 11-2: Text selected with the TouchUp Object tool is selected as an object and appears with a bounding box (border).

The TouchUp Object tool, on the other hand, permits you to copy an image in a PDF document and paste it back to the same document or another PDF document. All the paste operations remain in Acrobat, as you cannot copy with the TouchUp Object tool and paste an image or object into another program. Furthermore, you cannot save an image file using the TouchUp Object tool like when using the Select tool, but you can launch an external editor to edit either an image or object.

Using the Select tool

In Chapter 10 you used the Select tool to select text and tables. The third operation you can handle with this tool is selecting images. As was covered in Chapter 10, you have some preference choices for handling selections when using the Select tool. If your last visit to the General preferences was to set the selection option to select text before images, you need to return to the General preferences by pressing Ctrl/⌘+K and select the radio button for Select images before text.

Click an image and either left-click on the Copy Image to Clipboard button in the top-left corner or open a context menu by right-clicking (Windows) or Control+clicking (Macintosh) and select Copy Image to Clipboard, as shown in Figure 11-3.

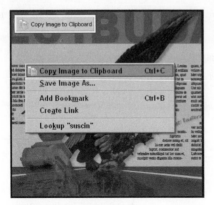

Figure 11-3: Choose the Select tool and click an image in a document. Either click the Copy Image to Clipboard button or open a context menu and select from several menu choices.

Pasting images

As I said earlier in this section, you cannot paste images copied with the Select tool in PDF documents. Copying with this tool is designed to permit you to copy to documents created in other programs. To easily transport an image to a document created in another program, the image you copy in Acrobat remains on the system clipboard while you switch programs and is ready to paste into another document.

 Caution   If you use professional layout and illustration programs designed for commercial printing, don't paste files in these applications. A preferred method is to save an image file from Acrobat and place or import the image in your design application.

Saving image files

From a context menu opened by right-clicking the mouse button (Windows) or Control+clicking (Macintosh) you can save an image file when using the Select tool. Select Save Image As (shown in Figure 11-3) and the Save Image As dialog box opens. From the Save as type (Windows) or Format (Macintosh) pull-down menu you have options for saving in one of two file formats. Choose the default Bitmap Image Files (*.bmp) or JPEG Image Files (.jpg) format.

Saving as a bitmap file saves the file without compression and data loss. However, bitmap files may not retain all the data in the image. If you have images with clipping paths or drop shadows, for example, the saved image can appear significantly degraded, as shown in Figure 11-4.

 Note   A clipping path is a mask like a cookie cutter that cuts out all the image data outside the path. Without the clipping path and drop shadow the image in Figure 11-3 would have a white background around the image instead of transparent space.

JPEG files retain all data integrity; however, the downside to saving as JPEG is that the files are compressed and you end up with data loss. If saving as a bitmap works well, use the .bmp file format when you can. As you can see in Figure 11-4, an image with a clipping path saved as a bitmap on the left is degraded compared to the correct detail shown in the JPEG export on the right.

Figure 11-4: Saving files with clipping paths in bitmap format can present problems with image quality. Saving the same file as a JPEG (right) preserves data integrity.

 Tip
If you're not certain whether a bmp file will be saved preserving all data integrity, you can select the image with the Select tool, copy the file to the clipboard, and from the Create PDF Task Button, select Create File from Clipboard. Acrobat creates a separate PDF document and the image you see appears exactly as when saving as a bmp file. If the file looks good, save the PDF or return to the image and select Save Image As from a context menu.

Using the TouchUp Object tool

 You use the TouchUp Object tool for selecting objects on a page. You select photo images, drawings and illustrations, and blocks of text with the tool.

The TouchUp Object tool copies images and objects and pastes them back into a PDF or other PDF documents you open in Acrobat. You can click an image or object or marquee several images and/or objects to select multiple items. Acrobat interprets any text you click on with the TouchUp Object tool as an object. Hence, you can edit the object in an external editor or move the object(s).

Cross-Reference
For information on external editing, see the section "Image and Object Editing" later in this chapter.

You can also use the TouchUp Object tool to move or nudge objects. Click on a single object or marquee a group of objects on a page, and then click and drag the selection to a new location. You are limited to moving objects on a single page. You can't select an object on one page and drag it to another PDF page. For moving objects to different pages you need to cut the selection, move to another page, and choose Edit ➪ Paste. If you want to nudge objects, create a selection with the TouchUp Object tool and press the arrow keys on your keyboard to move the object right, left, up, or down.

Note   If two or more images or objects are spaced apart and each object is selectable, you can click to select an object and Shift+click to select additional images/objects. If you have objects such as vector graphics where many paths are contained within the object or you have multiple overlapping objects, marquee the objects to be certain you select all you want to copy.

To copy and paste objects, including photo images, illustrations and vector objects, and text blocks, you use the TouchUp Object tool. To select a single object, click the object with the TouchUp Object tool. A keyline border shows the bounding box for the selected item. Open a context menu and you find menu options different from those available with the Select tool, as shown in Figure 11-5.

Figure 11-5: Select an image with the TouchUp Object tool and open a context menu. Select Copy from the menu choices to copy the selection.

From the menu command you have several commands related to handling images and objects. Select Copy to copy the image to the clipboard and select Cut to cut the image from the page and place it on the clipboard. From either choice you can then paste the data on another PDF page or into another PDF document.

Pasting images and objects

After copying with the TouchUp Object tool choose Edit ➪ Paste or use a context menu opened with the tool and select Paste. When pasting data the new image or object is pasted in the foreground. If you need to keep a stacking order intact, you need to carefully plan out copying and pasting images and objects. In more complex documents, it makes sense to return to the original authoring program as you do not have commands in Acrobat to paste in front, paste in back, and paste in place. These kinds of commands are found in design programs where you can easily control the stacking order of images and objects.

If you want to replace text, images, or objects on a page with a pasted block of text, an image, or an object, select the items you want to replace after copying the item you want to paste. Choose Edit ➪ Paste or use Paste from a context menu, and the pasted item replaces the selected items.

Deleting clips

The context menu opened with the TouchUp Object tool contains the Delete Clip menu command. You can delete a clipping path from an image or object that had the path applied in an image editor like Adobe Photoshop or an illustration program such as Adobe Illustrator. Deleting a path shows data outside the defined path. In Figure 11-6 you can see an image where a clipping path was created in Photoshop to hide edge artifacts as it appears in the PDF document on the left and after removing the clipping path on the right side of the figure.

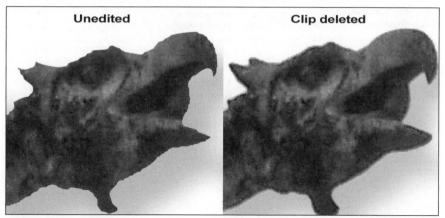

Figure 11-6: Selecting Delete Clip from a context menu removes clipping paths assigned to objects and images.

Image and Object Editing

As demonstrated in the first part of this chapter, Acrobat offers you methods for copying and pasting images, moving them around the page, and exporting them to files. However, changing the physical attributes of images and shapes is not something you can do in Acrobat. To modify certain appearances or attributes of raster and vector objects you need to use an external editor. When you launch an editor from a menu command in Acrobat, you can make changes to images, text, and shapes and save your edits in the external editor. These saves are then dynamically updated in the PDF document. Acrobat treats external editing like many programs that support file links. When you edit linked files, the links are updated in the program where they are imported.

To access an external editor you need to use the TouchUp Object tool. You cannot access external editors with any of the other selection tools.

TouchUp preferences

By default, Acrobat's external editors are Adobe Photoshop for image editing and Adobe Illustrator for object editing. When you install Acrobat, the installer locates these editors on your hard drive, if they are installed, and designates them as the default editors. If you install Photoshop and/or Illustrator after Acrobat, you need to instruct Acrobat where to look for the application files to use as your image/object editors.

Choose Edit ⇨ Preferences to open the Preferences dialog box. Click the TouchUp item on the left pane of the Preferences dialog box. In the right pane are two buttons, as shown in Figure 11-7. Click Choose Image Editor to open the Choose Image Editor dialog box. The dialog box enables you to navigate your hard drive and locate Adobe Photoshop. Select the Photoshop application icon and click Open.

For page and object editing, Adobe Illustrator is the default tool. If you need to locate Illustrator, click the Choose Page/Object Editor button. Find the Illustrator application on your hard drive and select it in the Choose Page/Object Editor dialog box. Click Open and Adobe Illustrator is enabled as your page/object editor.

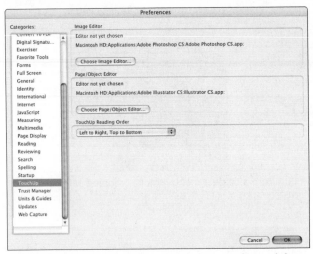

Figure 11-7: Select TouchUp in the preferences list and the Choose buttons appear on the right side of the dialog box. Click one of the buttons to navigate your hard drive and select the respective editor.

After identifying your editors, click OK in the Preferences dialog box. The choices you made are immediately available. If Acrobat loses contact with either program, you are prompted in a dialog box that external editing cannot be done. If you see warning dialog boxes open as you attempt to use an external editor, return to the Preferences and reestablish the connection to your editors.

Editing images in Adobe Photoshop

You launch Adobe Photoshop from Acrobat by selecting an image with the TouchUp Object tool and opening a context menu. From the menu commands, select Edit Image or press Control (Windows) or Option (Macintosh) and double-click. Depending on the speed of your computer and the amount of memory you have, Photoshop may take a few moments to launch. When the program opens, the image you selected is placed in a Photoshop document window.

You can change color modes and resolution, edit images for brightness and contrast, add effects, and just about anything else you can do in Photoshop to a single layer file. If you add type, add layers, or create transparency, you need to flatten all layers before saving the file. Layers added to a Photoshop file require you to use the Save As command to update the file. When using Save As, the file is not updated in the PDF document. Flattening layers enables you to use the Save command that updates the PDF document when the file is saved. In Figure 11-8, a file in Photoshop was edited for color changes. Note that the file contains transparency and appears as a single layer image. Because the file opened from Acrobat was a file on a single layer with transparency, all edits you make without creating additional layers enable you to still use the Save command.

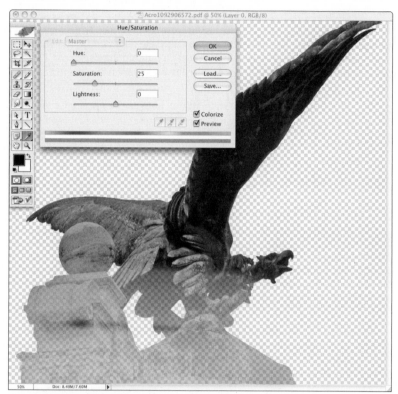

Figure 11-8: You edit files in your image editor and dynamically update the PDF from which they originated.

Photoshop updates the PDF document dynamically according to the edits you make with the Save command. If you add a layer to the file, you are prompted by Photoshop to Save As a new filename. Selecting Save As and writing to a new file disrupts the link. If you save in this manner, your PDF document won't update. If the file is saved without writing a new file, the updates are dynamically recorded in the PDF when you return to Acrobat.

Editing objects in Adobe Illustrator

Objects, for the purposes of discussing external object editing, can be vector objects such as illustrations created in Adobe Illustrator, CorelDraw, or Macromedia Freehand. Objects can also be text. Both vector objects and text are edited in Adobe Illustrator when you select Edit Object(s) from a context menu with the TouchUp Object tool.

To edit a single object, select the object with the TouchUp Object tool and open a context menu. The Edit Image command changes to Edit Object in the context menu. Select Edit

Object and Adobe Illustrator launches. Changes you make to the object are dynamically updated when you save the file just as the file saves discussed with image editing are updated. If selecting a single object on the PDF page is difficult, you can marquee a group of objects and select Edit Objects.

If no object is selected and you open a context menu with the TouchUp Object tool, the menu command changes to Edit Page. To easily access the Edit Page command, you can also open a context menu outside the page boundary. When you click outside the page area, the Edit Page command appears in the context menu. Select Edit Page and all objects are opened in Adobe Illustrator.

Be certain to not use the Save As command when editing objects. The procedures for saving files with object editing follow the same principles as described with image editing. Regardless of whether you edit a single object, multiple objects, or the entire page, the edits you make in Illustrator are only updated in the PDF document when you choose File ➪ Save.

Editing text in Adobe Illustrator

In some circumstances you may find editing text in an external editor to prove more satisfactory than editing text with the TouchUp Text tool. Editing text in Adobe Illustrator requires you to have embedded fonts loaded on your computer. Keep in mind that returning to an authoring application to apply major edits to documents is more advantageous than using the TouchUp Text tool. But, for those jobs where you don't have a document available and using the TouchUp Text tool just doesn't do the job, here's a little workaround you can try. I offer a disclaimer and tell you upfront that these methods may not always work, but I've found more often than not that you can successfully edit text in Illustrator for some minor edit jobs.

One problem you can face when editing text in Illustrator is the text blocks are likely to be broken up and lose their paragraph formatting attributes. You need to select the text, cut it from the page, and paste it back keeping the general size and position close to the original. You can then edit the text and choose File ➪ Save, to update the PDF document.

Using the Snapshot Tool

The Snapshot tool performs in some ways like the Graphics Select tool in earlier versions of Acrobat. You use this tool to create a marquee around any area on the document page. You can select text and graphics with the Snapshot tool. Select the tool from the Basic Toolbar and click and drag a marquee around the area to be selected. When you release the mouse button, Acrobat takes a snapshot of the area within the marquee and copies it to the clipboard. A dialog box opens to inform you the data have been copied to the clipboard.

After you click OK in the Alert dialog box, the marquee is still active on the document page. You can open a context menu where you have options for copying the data or printing the selection. In addition you can create a link to the snapshot by selecting Create Link in the context menu shown in Figure 11-9.

Cross-Reference   For more information on creating links from snapshots, see Chapter 15.

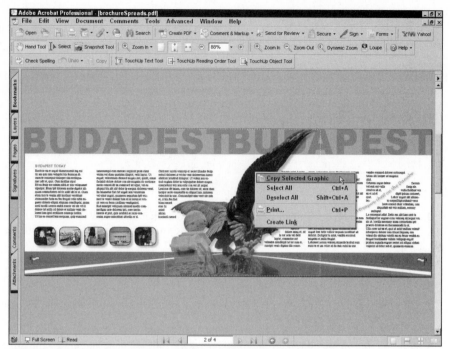

Figure 11-9: After you create a snapshot, the marquee remains active. Open a context menu to copy the data, print the selected area, or create a link.

Caution
Taking a snapshot of a page containing images and text or text only creates a bitmap of the selected area. All text is converted to a raster image. If you intend to preserve text and edit it later, don't use the Snapshot tool. The text is not editable from snapshot images.

The Snapshot tool provides paste functions equal to both the Select tool and the TouchUp Object tool. Once you take a snapshot you can paste the data back to the PDF document or to another application document. By default, the Snapshot tool places a copy of the snapshot on the clipboard and makes the clipboard data available to Acrobat. When you open a context menu on the snapshot and select Copy Selected Graphic, you can paste the data to other application documents.

Changing snapshot resolutions

New in Acrobat 7 is an option for changing image resolutions when copying data with the Snapshot tool. By default snapshot resolutions are 72 ppi (pixels per inch), which is sufficient for screen views at 100 percent. If you want to print files or zoom in to a document view above 100 percent, 72 ppi is not sufficient for rendering images that appear without obvious image degradation.

To understand how image resolutions affect image quality, try following these steps.

STEPS: Changing Snapshot Image Resolutions

1. **Change Preferences.** Open the Preferences dialog box by pressing Ctrl/⌘+K. Click General in the left pane and check the box for *Use fixed resolution for snapshots*. In the resolution text box, type **72** as shown in Figure 11-10.

Figure 11-10: Set the resolution for snapshots to 72 ppi.

2. **Take a snapshot.** Click the Snapshot tool in the Acrobat Toolbar Well. Drag a rectangle around the area you want to copy. When you release the mouse button the data are copied to the clipboard.

3. **Paste the data in an image editor.** Open an image editor such as Adobe Photoshop CS or Adobe Photoshop Elements. Paste the data in a new document window.

Cross-Reference

For information on pasting data in an image editor, see the next section "Pasting snapshot data in image editors" later in this chapter.

4. **Zoom in on the document.** Zoom to at least a 200 percent view and notice the quality of the image. You should see poor image quality especially if you copy any text. In Figure 11-11, the pasted data includes both image and text.

Figure 11-11: Zoom to a 200 percent view after pasting the data in an image editor.

5. **Change preferences.** Return to the Acrobat Preferences dialog box as described in Step 1. Change the image resolution to 300 ppi.

6. **Take a Snapshot.** Try to take a snapshot as described in Step 2 in the same area of the PDF document as you took the first snapshot.

7. **Paste the data.** Paste the new clipboard data in your image editor and zoom to the approximate same view as the first image you pasted in your image editor. Because the image resolution is much higher, the zoom will be much lower than a 200 percent view.

8. **Compare the two images.** Examine the second image you pasted at 300 ppi. You should see a noticeable difference in image quality. In Figure 11-12, compare the text with the text shown in Figure 11-11.

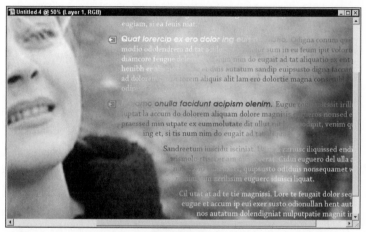

Figure 11-12: Paste the image copied at 300 ppi and compare the document with the first image pasted at 72 ppi.

Note that if you try to change resolution in your image editor to raise the resolution in a document, the results won't be as good as when you change the snapshot resolution in Acrobat. If you, for example, create a document from a 72 ppi image in your image editor and change the resolution to 300 ppi, the quality doesn't change and won't appear equal to a snapshot taken at 300 ppi.

Pasting snapshot data in image editors

Because you have control over image resolutions, taking snapshots is much preferred over copying data with the Select or Touchup Object tools. With snapshots you decide what image resolution you want before copying the data. The other tools offer you a fixed resolution of 72 ppi when copying data. If you use the TouchUp Object tool and the Edit Image menu command, the image opens at the resolution originally established before the file was converted to PDF.

If you want to extract images for repurposing documents or print images at sufficient resolution to render good quality, you might find taking snapshots and pasting data in an image editor to be the best solution if the images in the PDF were created at lower resolutions such as 72 ppi.

If you use Adobe Photoshop CS or Adobe Photoshop Elements, the clipboard data can be used to define the dimensions and resolution of new documents you create in either program. Take a snapshot and open your image editor. Select File ⇨ New and the New dialog box opens, as shown in the New dialog box for Photoshop CS in Figure 11-13.

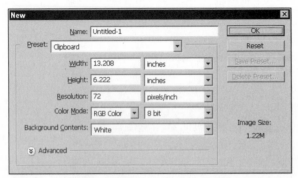

Figure 11-13: Take a snapshot and select File ⇨ New in your image editor. The file dimensions are derived from the clipboard data.

The Width and Height in the New dialog box may appear extraordinary when creating new documents from clipboard data. The dimensions are calculated at 72 ppi, which results in an oversized image. If you change the resolution to match the resolution set in the Acrobat General preferences for fixed resolution for snapshots, the file dimensions are reduced to match the actual dimensions of the snapshot. For example, if you set the resolution to 144 ppi and take a snapshot on a 2-inch-square area of a PDF page, the New document dialog box in your image editor displays 4 inches for the width and height at 72 ppi. If you change the resolution to 144 ppi in the New dialog box, the height and width reduce to 2 inches square.

If you use Adobe Photoshop Elements, you have an additional menu command that helps you create new image documents from clipboard data. Select File ⇨ New from Clipboard and the clipboard data opens in a new document window. The size and resolution are the same as when selecting File ⇨ New.

Exporting Images

If you need to completely overhaul a document and want to lay it out in an authoring program, you might want to copy and paste text into a word processor, format your text, save the file, and then import the text into a program best suited for layout design, such as Adobe InDesign CS. If your PDF document contains photo images, you need to export the images and add them to your layout. Having to individually export images with the Select Image tool would be tedious for a large layout project containing many images. Fortunately, Acrobat offers you a feature for exporting all images in a PDF with a single menu command.

Choose Advanced ⇨ Export All Images. The Export All Images As dialog box opens where you can make selections for filename, destination, and the format you want to use for the exported images. In the Export All Images As dialog box, open the pull-down menu for Save as type (Windows) or Format (Macintosh). Four format options are available from the menu choices — JPEG, PNG, TIFF, or JPEG2000. Select one of the format options and click the Settings button to assign file attributes to the exported images.

Cross-Reference   For more information on image file format definitions, see Chapter 6.

When you select JPEG for the file type and click the Settings button, the Export All Images As JPEG Settings dialog box opens as shown in Figure 11-14. The settings change according to the file type you select. Therefore, if you choose TIFF as a format, for example, you'll see changes for compression choices. The options for File Settings and Color Management are the same as those options discussed in Chapter 6. In addition to these settings, the Extraction item at the bottom of the dialog box enables you to eliminate certain files when the sizes are smaller than the size you choose from the pull-down menu.

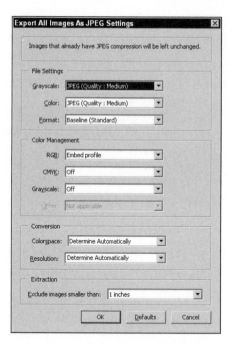

Figure 11-14: Make a choice for file format in the Export All Images As dialog box and click the Settings button. You choose options in the Export All Images As (file format) Settings dialog box for File Settings, Color Management, Colorspace Conversion, and eliminating image extractions falling below user-defined values.

From the pull-down menu you choose a preset option for an image's physical size. You might have icons or logos appearing on all pages constructed at .75-inch sizes. You can elect to exclude these images by selecting the 1.00 inches item in the pull-down menu. When you click OK in the Extract All Images As dialog box, all files above the size selected from the pull-down menu choice are saved as separate files in the specified format. If you want every image extracted, choose the No Limit item from the pull-down menu.

Summary

✦ You use the Select tool to select individual photo images on PDF pages. You can select only a single image with the tool. Selected images can be copied to the clipboard.

✦ You can convert images copied with the Select tool to PDF with the Create PDF tool, and you can paste them into authoring programs. You cannot paste the copied images on PDF pages.

✦ To select objects use the TouchUp Object tool. Objects include photo images, illustrative artwork, and text. Dragging a marquee enables you to select multiple objects. Pressing the Shift key and clicking an object toggles between adding or eliminating an object from a selection.

✦ You can paste objects and images copied with the TouchUp Object tool on PDF pages. You cannot paste them into authoring application documents.

✦ External editing is handled by selecting an image or an object and opening a context menu. From the menu options, select Edit Image/Object.

✦ The default image editor is Adobe Photoshop and the default object editor is Adobe Illustrator. Select editors in the Preferences dialog box by clicking the TouchUp item in the left list and clicking the Change button on the right side of the dialog box.

✦ You use the Snapshot tool to marquee an area on a page and select text, objects, and images within the selection marquee. Releasing the mouse button after you create a selection marquee copies the data within the marquee to the clipboard.

✦ Image resolutions for snapshots can be changed in the General preferences dialog box. Snapshots taken at higher resolutions result in much better image quality than image resolutions changed (upsized) in image editors.

✦ All images in a PDF can be exported as separate files with a single menu command. Choose Advanced ⇨ Export Images to open the Export All Images dialog box.

✦   ✦   ✦

Editing Pages

Chapters 9 and 10 covered editing content on PDF pages. Minor edits for text passages and images may be completed with the tools discussed in the two previous chapters. If you want to modify larger portions of a PDF document, then you'll want to know something about the tools Acrobat offers you for page editing. If you return to an authoring application and edit text, graphics, and layouts, you may want to update your PDF document according to the page edits made in other applications. Rather than recreate the entire PDF file, Acrobat enables you to selectively append, replace, delete, and extract pages in a PDF document.

In addition to the number of different page editing tools found in earlier versions of Acrobat, Acrobat Professional offers some impressive features for creating headers and footers and adding backgrounds and watermarks. This chapter covers the page-editing tools in Acrobat and the many features that can help you modify documents.

Setting Up the Page Editing Environment

For page-editing tasks, you need to use some viewing tools, advanced tools, and page editing tools. Move the cursor to the Toolbar Well and open a context menu. From the menu options select Reset Toolbars. If the How To pane is open, click the Hide button or press F4.

From the pull-down menu adjacent to the Zoom In tool, select Show Zoom Toolbar. When editing pages, zooming in and out with these tools is a frequent exercise. Open a context menu on the Toolbar Well and select Edit to open the Edit toolbar. Return again to the same context menu and select Rotate View to open the Rotate View toolbar and Advanced Editing to show the Advanced Editing toolbar. Dock the toolbars and the Toolbar Well should look something like Figure 12-1.

Working with Thumbnails

Thumbnails are mini-views of PDF pages that can be displayed in various zoom sizes.

To see the thumbnail view of pages in an open document, click the Pages tab to open the pane as shown in Figure 12-1. Thumbnail views are created on-the-fly when the pane is opened. Users of Acrobat 5 and below will remember the pane was referred to as *Thumbnails*. In Acrobat 6.0 viewers the name was changed to the Pages pane and remains the same in Acrobat 7.

Figure 12-1: Click the Pages tab to open the Pages pane where thumbnail views of the pages are created on-the-fly.

Navigating pages

The Pages pane can be used to navigate pages. Clicking a thumbnail takes you to the page associated with the thumbnail. The page opens in the Document pane at the currently established zoom view. You can zoom in or out of pages in the Pages pane by dragging the lower-right handle on the rectangle appearing inside the page thumbnail. The changing zoom levels are reflected in the zoom view in the Document pane. In Figure 12-2, a rectangle shows the current page view in the Document pane. Click on the handle in the lower-right corner and drag it into the center of the rectangle to zoom in on the page. Click and drag out to zoom out of the page.

The Pages pane and the Document pane are two separate compartments in the open PDF document. Clicking in the Pages pane activates the pane. Conversely, clicking in the Document pane activates the area where you view pages. Unfortunately, Acrobat does not highlight any part of either pane to inform you when a pane is active. So you just have to remember to click first in the area you want to be active.

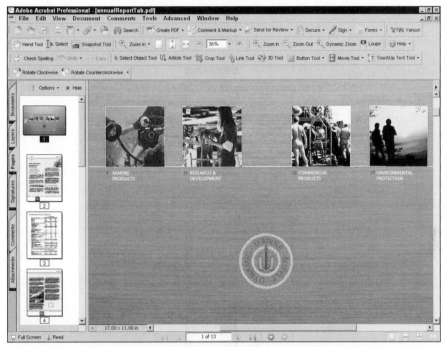

Figure 12-2: Thumbnails in the Pages pane are linked to the pages in the Document pane. Click a thumbnail to navigate to the page link. Drag the rectangle to zoom in or out of the page displayed in the Document pane.

If you press the Page Down key or down-arrow key while the Document pane is active, the pages in the Document pane scroll. As each page is scrolled, the Pages pane likewise scrolls pages and the respective page thumbnails are highlighted. When you click in the Pages pane, you experience a different behavior. Pressing the Page Down key scrolls several pages down only in the Pages pane. The respective pages in the Document pane are not scrolled. As you scroll through page thumbnails in the Pages pane, the Document pane remains fixed at its current view. The reason is that as you scroll in the Pages pane, thumbnails are not actually selected. The selected thumbnail is linked to the view in the Document pane.

With reference to thumbnails, the term *selection* needs a little definition. When you click a page thumbnail, the number appearing below the page icon is shown selected (highlighted), and the thumbnail is further highlighted with a keyline border around the icon. Likewise the respective page is placed in view in the Document pane. In essence there are two selection messages Acrobat communicates to you. If you press the down-arrow key on your keyboard, the number below the thumbnail remains highlighted and the respective page remains open in the Document pane. However, the keyline border moves to the next page down, indicating the current thumbnail selection in the Pages pane. In Figure 12-3, page 2 in a PDF document is selected and page 2 is open in the Document pane. When the down-arrow key is pressed, page 3 becomes selected in the Pages pane, while page 2 remains as the page viewed in the Document pane.

Figure 12-3: Click the cursor in the Pages pane to activate the pane, and then press the down-arrow key. The keyline border shows the page selection in the Pages pane, while the highlighted page number on the previous page shows what page is in view in the Document pane.

Tip

You can use the Pages pane and the Document pane to compare pages in a PDF document. If you insert a new page that is similar to an existing page in the PDF file, click the thumbnail of one page to open it in the Document pane. Use the arrow keys (up or down) to navigate to the inserted page. Enlarge the thumbnail view so you can clearly compare the thumbnail to the page in the Document pane. For information on enlarging views and inserting pages, see the next section on changing thumbnail sizes.

Changing thumbnail sizes

In Acrobat 6 and 7 you can reduce the size of pages to a mini thumbnail view and enlarge the size up to a maximum thumbnail view of about 300 percent. The support for increased thumbnail views in the Pages pane enables you to quickly find a page in a PDF document.

You reduce or enlarge page thumbnail size through menu commands. A context menu opened in the Pages pane or the pane pull-down menu includes the Enlarge Page Thumbnails and Reduce Page Thumbnails commands. Before using these commands, you should understand opening context menus.

If you click in the Pages pane on a page thumbnail and open a context menu, the Enlarge Page Thumbnails and Reduce Page Thumbnail commands are available as options in a menu that contains many different commands for page editing. If you click outside the page thumbnails, but still in the Pages pane, a different menu opens with fewer commands. However, the same menu commands for enlarging or reducing page thumbnails are still present. Likewise, the pull-down menu adjacent to Options at the top of the Pages pane offers the same commands. Regardless of which menu you use, you can enlarge or reduce page thumbnail views.

To enlarge the size of the page thumbnails, click the mouse button outside the page thumbnails in the Pages pane and open a context menu. Select Enlarge Page Thumbnails from the menu options as shown in Figure 12-4. Return to the menu and select the same menu command to enlarge again. Repeat the steps to zoom in to the desired view.

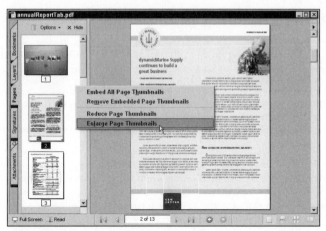

Figure 12-4: Open a context menu in the Pages pane and select Enlarge Page Thumbnails. Return to the context menu and repeat the steps several times to zoom in on a page thumbnail.

You'll notice that Acrobat makes no provision for selecting from among a number of preset zoom sizes. You need to return to the context menu or pull-down menu to successively increase or decrease page thumbnail views. If the zoom view in the Pages pane is larger than the pane width, click anywhere on the vertical bar on the right side of the pane and drag it to the right. The pane resizes horizontally to show more of the Pages pane while the Document pane is reduced in size. In Figure 12-5, I enlarged the thumbnail view through repeated steps for enlarging the thumbnails and widened the pane so the entire thumbnail could be viewed.

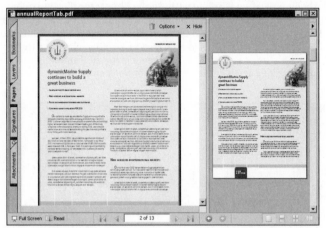

Figure 12-5: To size the Pages pane, click on the vertical bar on the right side of the pane and drag it to the right.

Embedding and unembedding thumbnails

Page thumbnails are created on the fly each time you open the Pages pane. In long documents, you may find your computer slowing down each time the Pages pane is opened and the thumbnails are recreated. If this proves to be a burden, you can choose to embed thumbnails when working with the Pages pane and avoid the delay caused by creating them.

Thumbnails add some overhead to your file. Each page thumbnail adds about 1K to the file size. Unless your files are to be viewed by users of earlier Acrobat viewers that don't support creating thumbnails on the fly, delete them as one of the final steps in your editing session.

To embed thumbnails, select the Embed All Page Thumbnails command from the pane Options menu or a context-sensitive menu. Thumbnails can also be created by batch-processing PDF files using a Batch Sequence or at the time of distillation when using Acrobat Distiller.

PDF Workflow   You can delete thumbnails from PDF documents either individually in Acrobat or by using the Advanced ⇨ Edit Batch Sequences command in Acrobat Professional. If your work environment is such that you do a lot of editing in Acrobat and often use thumbnails, you may want to create them during distillation. When thumbnails are embedded, screen refreshes for multiple edits in long documents are faster. After you finish editing jobs and want to post PDF files on the Web or create CD-ROMs, you can batch-process the files for optimization and delete the thumbnails. Run the Edit Batch Sequences command to optimize multiple files and remove thumbnails.

Cross-Reference   For information on creating and running Batch Sequences, see Chapter 14.

To unembed thumbnails, open a context menu on a page thumbnail and select Remove Embedded Page Thumbnails. All embedded page thumbnails are removed from the document. This step can be particularly helpful when working with Adobe Illustrator files including the most current version of Illustrator CS. When Illustrator embeds thumbnails a bitmap representation of the page is created as a thumbnail and displays poorly degraded, as you can see on the left side of Figure 12-6. After the thumbnail is removed in Acrobat, the page thumbnail appears as you see it on the right side of Figure 12-9. Whenever you see thumbnail images with a degraded view, always check to see whether the thumbnail is embedded.

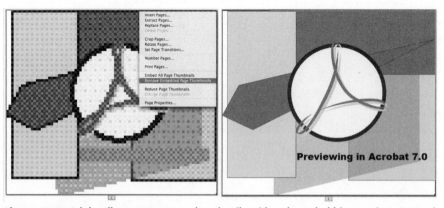

Figure 12-6: Adobe Illustrator exports thumbnails with a degraded bitmap view. Removing the thumbnail (shown right) improves the image quality.

Organizing Pages

The Pages pane offers you a wealth of opportunity for sorting pages and reorganizing them. You can move pages around, copy and paste pages when you want to duplicate them, delete pages, print selected pages within a document, and a host of other options specific to page management.

Reordering pages

Acrobat provides you with a marvelous slide sorter where you can shuffle pages and reorder them in a page sequence suited to your needs. With an opportunity to view page thumbnails in much larger views, you can easily see the content of text-only pages when no visible icons or graphics are present to distinguish differences in page content. Reorganizing pages in earlier versions of Acrobat was a little more difficult because of having to view text pages in small thumbnail views; however, now you can manage page order more easily by zooming in on pages to clearly view the content.

To rearrange pages in a PDF document, open the Pages pane to the full width of your monitor by dragging the right side of the pane to the far right of the Document pane. Open a context menu in the Pages pane and select Enlarge Page Thumbnails. Repeat the steps to enlarge the thumbnail views to a size that enables you to read text comfortably on the pages.

Click on a page and drag the page to a spot between the pages where you want to relocate the selected page. When you move a page around the Pages pane, a vertical bar appears where the page will be located. If the highlight bar is positioned in the area where you want to relocate a page, release the mouse button. Figure 12-7 shows page 3 selected. The page is moved to the area after page 13. Notice the vertical highlight bar appearing to the right side of page 13.

Tip   If you want to move pages between pages not in view in the Pages tab, move a page down or up and the pages scroll to reveal hidden pages. Keep the mouse button depressed until you find the location where you want to move a page.

To select multiple pages, click a page to select it. Hold down the Shift key and click another page. If you want to select a block of contiguous pages, click the first page to be selected, hold down the Shift key, and click the last page within the group. All pages between the two selected pages are included in the selection. For noncontiguous selections, hold down the Ctrl/Option key to individually add random pages to a selection. After you make your selection, click one of the selected pages and drag to a new location to reorder the pages.

Tip   For a super slide sorter, open the Pages pane and view thumbnails in a large size. Place the mouse cursor over the vertical bar to the right of the Pages pane and drag to the right of your monitor screen. Press the F8 and F9 keys to hide the menu bar and toolbars. Resize the viewing window to fit the screen size. You'll get as much real estate on your monitor as possible. Shuffling pages is much easier in Acrobat than in almost any other program.

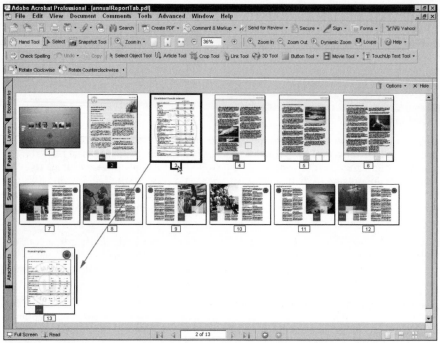

Figure 12-7: To move a page in a PDF document, click a thumbnail and drag it to the area where you want to relocate the page. When you see a vertical highlight bar appear in the desired location, release the mouse button.

Copying pages

You can copy and paste pages within a PDF document or from one open PDF document to another. To copy a page with thumbnails, hold down the Control/Option key as you drag a page to a new location in the same PDF file. Release the mouse button when you see the vertical highlight bar appear at the desired location. To copy a page from one PDF to another, open both PDF files and view them tiled either vertically or horizontally. The Pages pane must be in view on both PDF documents. Click and drag the thumbnail from one file to the Pages pane in the other document. The vertical highlight bar appears and the cursor changes, as shown in Figure 12-8. After the vertical bar is positioned at the desired location, release the mouse button, and the page drops into position.

Cross-Reference   To learn how to tile PDF documents, see Chapter 3.

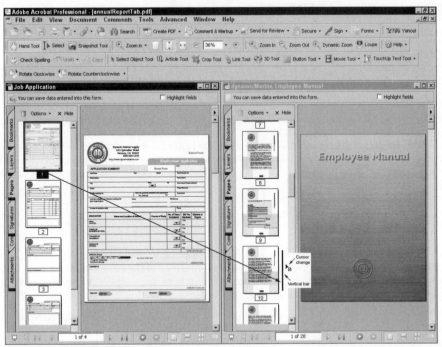

Figure 12-8: Dragging a thumbnail to a new location or copying between documents displays a vertical highlight bar where the page will be placed.

Removing pages

The previous example behaves like a copy-and-paste sequence. You can also create a cut-and-paste action whereby the page is deleted from one PDF document and copied to another. To remove a page and place it in another PDF file, hold the down Control/Option key and then click and drag the page to another Pages pane in another file. The page is deleted from the original file and copied to the second file.

Caution | Be certain not to confuse the shortcut keys. If Control/Option is used in the page thumbnails on one document with click and drag, the page is copied. If using the same keys between two documents, the page is deleted from the file of origin and copied to the destination file.

To delete a page with the Pages pane, use a context-sensitive menu or the pane Options pull-down menu. Select a single thumbnail or Shift+click to select multiple thumbnails in a contiguous order (Ctrl/⌘+click for a noncontiguous order), and select Delete Pages from the context menu. This command opens the Delete Pages dialog box, as shown in Figure 12-9.

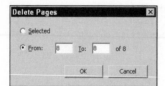

Figure 12-9: When you select Delete Pages from the Pages context menu, the Delete Pages dialog box opens. Click OK to delete the selected pages.

In the Delete Pages dialog box, by default the selected page is marked for deletion. You can make a change in the dialog box by selecting the From button and entering a contiguous page number range in the field box. The Selected radio button deletes all pages selected in the Pages pane. You can click and select pages in a contiguous or noncontiguous group. After you select the pages you want to delete, click OK. The selected pages are deleted from the document.

Modifying Pages

Users of earlier versions of Acrobat should pay special attention to the many options available from a context menu opened on a page thumbnail or in the pane Options menu. Certain commands formerly located in the Document menu in earlier versions of Acrobat have been moved to the Pages pane if they directly affect page editing.

In this context, *modifying pages* refers to the PDF page in its entirety and not individual page elements. Rather than look at changing single items on a page, such as text and graphics, this section examines some of the features for structuring pages as an extension of the commands found in the Pages pane. Page editing discussed here relates to the insertion, extraction, and replacement of PDF pages.

Before you go about creating a huge PDF document with links and buttons, understanding how Acrobat structures a page and related links is imperative. Bookmarks and other links are often created within a PDF document as user-defined navigation. Acrobat handles thumbnails and the link to the respective pages without user intervention. You have no control over the links from a thumbnail to respective pages.

For information on creating Bookmarks and links, see Chapter 17.

With regard to links and Bookmarks, think of Acrobat as having separate layers where the navigation items are placed and page content on the remaining layers. This use of the term *layers* is different than the Adobe PDF Layers that one might create from programs supporting layers and converting to PDF with Adobe PDF layers. In regard to a single-layer PDF document, where the background contains the page contents, the links appear as if on a second layer over the background. When viewing a PDF file, you don't see the navigation items independent of page content. This said, when you delete a page, all the links to the page are lost. Acrobat makes no provision to go to the page that follows a deleted page when links are deleted. Therefore, if you set up a Bookmark to page 4 and later delete page 4, the Bookmark has no place to go. Such links are commonly referred to as *dead links*.

When editing pages in Acrobat, you can choose to insert a page, delete a page, extract a page, and replace a page. If you understand the page structure, you'll know which option is right for your situation. You access each of the following options described by choices available in the Pages Options menu, by selecting commands from the Document menu, or by using a context-sensitive menu (as shown in Figure 12-10) while clicking a thumbnail in the Pages pane.

Caution   Using the menu commands for page editing is available only when you work with PDF documents that are not password protected prohibiting page editing. If you attempt to edit pages in a secure PDF document, Acrobat prompts you for a password. This behavior applies to all the options listed here.

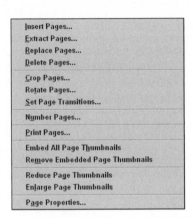

Figure 12-10: Move the cursor to a page thumbnail; click and open a context menu.

The page editing options include the following:

✦ **Insert Pages:** When you select this option, the Select File to Insert dialog box opens. Select a file to insert and click the Select button in the dialog box. The Insert Pages dialog box opens next, enabling you to choose the location for the insertion regardless of the current page viewed (see Figure 12-11). You can choose to insert a page either before or after the page in view, within a page range, or before or after the first or last page. Inserted pages do not affect any links in your document. All the pages shift left or right, depending on whether you select the Before or After option.

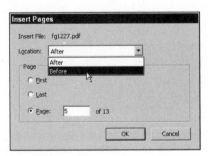

Figure 12-11: The Insert Pages dialog box enables you to locate the page that precedes or follows another page for the target location.

Appending Pages to PDF Documents

If you want to create a PDF document by combining multiple files that may have been created from multiple authors and multiple authoring programs, you can choose some alternatives in Acrobat that permit you to concatenate files to form a single PDF document.

When you use the Insert Pages command, the Select File to Insert dialog box enables you to select multiple files stored in a single folder. You can select multiple files by holding down the Shift key and clicking on the target files in a listed order from within a folder, or pressing the Ctrl/⌘ key to select files in a noncontiguous order.

However, when you use the Insert Pages command, the order the files are appended to the open PDF file does not follow the same file order you viewed in the list in the Select File to Insert dialog box. You have no control over rearranging the order or selecting additional files from within separate folders.

A much better alternative to use when appending pages is the Create PDF From Multiple Documents command. Select the Create PDF tool and open the pull-down menu. Select From Multiple Files to open the Create PDF from Multiple Documents dialog box. Note that you can start with no file open in the Document pane.

Click the Browse button to find the folder where files are located. In the Open dialog box, select a file or multiple files using the Shift or Ctrl/⌘ key to select a group of files. Click the Add button to add the files to the Create PDF from Multiple Files dialog box as shown in the figure.

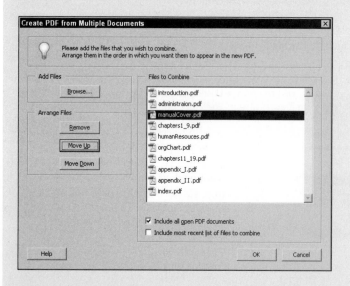

Add files to be concatenated in the Create PDF from Multiple Documents dialog box. If you need to add more files click the Browse button again. Search your hard drive or network server for another folder and add more files. When all the files are listed in the dialog box shown in the figure, select individual files and click the Move Up or Move Down buttons to rearrange the insertion order. Click OK and the files are concatenated to form a single PDF document. Choose File ➪ Save As and save the file to your hard drive.

✦ **Delete Pages:** When you delete a page, you delete not only its contents but also its links. If a Bookmark or other link is linked to a view in the deleted page, all links to the page become inoperable. When creating a presentation in Acrobat with multiple pages, you must exercise care when deleting pages to be certain no links are broken.

Select a single thumbnail or multiple thumbnails in the Pages pane. Pages can be selected in a contiguous or noncontiguous selection. Open a context menu or the Options pull-down menu and select the Delete Pages command. The Delete Pages dialog box opens where you can delete the selected pages by leaving the default Selected radio button active or by selecting a page range and clicking OK.

Acrobat opens a warning dialog box to confirm your choice. If you change your mind and want to keep the pages, click the Cancel button. To continue with the page deletion, click OK. (See Figure 12-8 earlier in the chapter.)

Tip

If you begin an editing session and work on files where you insert and delete pages frequently, you may find the confirmation dialog box annoying. To eliminate the dialog box opening every time you delete a page, open the Preferences dialog box (Ctrl/⌘+K). Click General in the left pane and select the box for Disable edit warnings in the right pane. When you return to the Document pane, all subsequent page deletions are performed without the warning dialog box opening. Be certain to exercise care when targeting pages for deletion if you are not using the edit warnings.

✦ **Extract Pages:** Extracting a page is like pulling out single or multiple pages and creating a new PDF file with them. Extracting pages has no effect on Bookmarks or links for the destination pages in the original document unless you delete pages when extracting them. All links are operable for pages among the extracted pages. For example, if you extract ten pages with Bookmarks to each page, all the Bookmarks within the extracted pages are functional in the new file. If you have a Bookmark to a page not part of the extraction, the link is not operational.

When you select the Extract Pages command, the Extract Pages dialog box opens as shown in Figure 12-12. You supply the page range in the From/To field boxes and check boxes exist for Delete Pages After Extracting and Extract Pages As Separate Files. You can select these two options individually or together when extracting pages.

When you select Extract Pages and you check the box for Delete Pages After Extracting, pages are extracted and deleted from the original file. The new pages open in the foreground as a single PDF document and remain unsaved until you use the Save or Save As command.

A new feature in Acrobat 7 is the Extract Pages as Separate Files option in the Extract Pages dialog box. Check this box to extract pages and save them to your hard drive instead of having them open in the Document pane. When you select the page range and click OK after checking the box to create separate files, a Browse For Folder dialog box opens, enabling you to select a target folder for the saved files. Check the box for Delete Pages After Extracting and pages are deleted from the original file after the new files are saved.

Figure 12-12: If you want to delete the pages extracted from the original file, check the box for Delete Pages After Extracting. Checking the box for Extract Pages As Separate Files saves each page as a separate PDF to your hard drive.

✦ **Replace Pages:** This option affects only the contents layer of a PDF page—the link layer is unaffected. If you have links going to or from the replaced page, all links or interactive content are preserved. When editing PDF documents where page contents need to be changed, redistilled, and inserted in the final document, always use the Replace Pages command.

Replace Pages is particularly helpful when recreating Acrobat PDF forms. If you create a form in an authoring program and add all the form fields in Acrobat, and then later decide you want to edit the appearance of the form, replacing the old design with a new design preserves the form fields.

You can click a single page thumbnail or select multiple pages in a contiguous order and open a context menu. Select Replace Pages to open the Select File With New Pages dialog box. Navigate to the file containing pages that are to replace pages in the open file, and click Select.

The Replace Pages dialog box opens. In the Original area of the dialog box shown in Figure 12-13, you select the page range in the open document for the target pages to be replaced. In the Replacement section of the Replace Pages dialog box, you select the first page number of the document selected in the Select Pages to Replace dialog box. The readout to the right of the field box automatically displays the range of pages that are targeted for replacement. At the bottom of each section, notice the filename listed for the open document and the selected document.

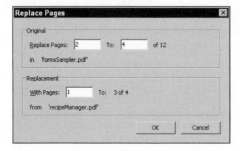

Figure 12-13: Specify the page range for the pages to be replaced in the first two field boxes. Enter the page number for the first page in the target file.

If you disabled the edit warnings, the pages are replaced according to the selection made in the Replace Pages dialog box. If the edit warnings are not disabled (in this case, the check box isn't selected in the General preferences dialog box), a confirmation dialog box opens. Click OK to replace the pages.

Tip

You can replace pages through drag-and-drop operations when viewing two documents in tiled views and when the Pages pane is opened for both documents. When you drag a page or a number of selected pages, move the cursor in the target document on top of the number below the thumbnail for the first page to be replaced. Rather than place the cursor between pages where the highlight bar is shown, be certain to drop the selection on top of the page number. The target page is highlighted in black when the cursor appears directly over the page number.

There are many ways you can approach page editing in Acrobat. Using the Pages pane helps you access menu commands quickly. You can also access the commands just discussed with the Pages pane collapsed by choosing the commands from the Document menu. In addition, you can open multiple documents, view them with horizontal or vertical tiling, and drag and drop pages to accomplish the same results. To help in understanding how page editing with tiled views is accomplished, try following these steps for a little practice:

STEPS: Editing pages with thumbnails

1. **Open two PDF documents where pages need to be arranged in a third document.** As an example for page editing, assume you have two files that need selected pages merged in a new, third file. Some of the pages need only to be copied to the new file and some pages need to be copied and deleted from the source document.

2. **Write a JavaScript.** Acrobat doesn't offer you a menu command for creating a new document, but you can use a JavaScript to create a file with a blank page. The routine is simple even if you haven't ever typed any JavaScript code. Open the JavaScript Debugger by pressing Ctrl/⌘+J. If any text appears in the window, click the trash icon at the bottom of the window. Enter the following code as shown in Figure 12-14:

```
app.newDoc();
```

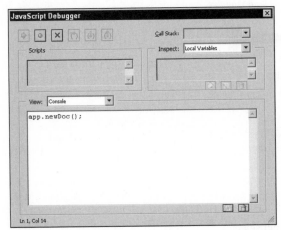

Figure 12-14: Open the JavaScript Debugger by pressing Ctrl/⌘+J. Delete any text in the window and type a new line of code.

3. **Create a new document.** With the cursor at the end of the line in the JavaScript Debugger, press the Enter key on the keyboard number pad. Be certain to press the number pad Enter key and not the Enter/Return key. A new blank document opens in the Document pane.

Note On notebook computers, use Control+Enter if a Num Pad Enter key is not available.

4. **Close the JavaScript Debugger.** Click the close box in the JavaScript Debugger window.

5. **Tile the page views.** Choose Window ➪ Tile ➪ Vertically (or Ctrl/⌘+Shift+L). Click the Pages pane in each file to open the panes. The two files you opened and the new file you created should appear similar to Figure 12-15.

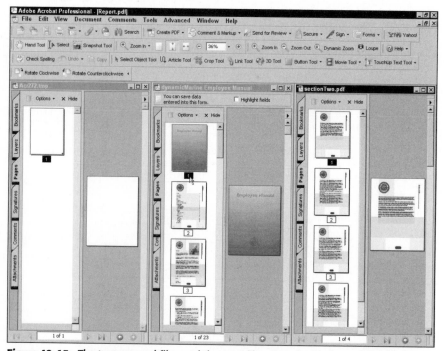

Figure 12-15: The two opened files and the new file created with the JavaScript appear with the Pages panes open.

6. **Replace a page.** The new document you created with the JavaScript contains a blank page. One of the cover pages in the opened files will be used as the cover in the new document. Select a page from one of the open document's Pages pane and drag the page to the top of *number 1* in the new document. When the page is targeted for replacement, the entire page is highlighted, as shown in Figure 12-16.

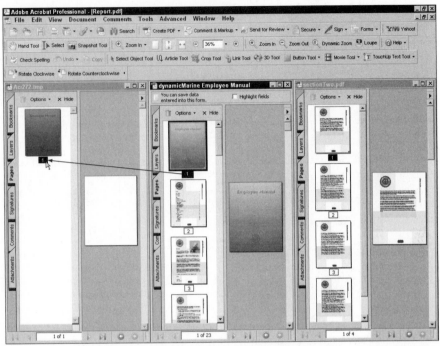

Figure 12-16: Drag a page thumbnail to the new document and place the cursor on top of the page number. The target page highlights.

7. **Insert pages.** Select a page in one of the open documents. Press the Ctrl/⌘ key and click on pages in a noncontiguous order. Release the modifier key and drag one of the selected pages below the title page in the new document. Wait until you see a highlight bar appearing below the page before releasing the mouse button.

8. **Extract pages with deletion.** Move to the second open file. In this document you copy pages to the new document while deleting them from the source document. Click on a contiguous or noncontiguous group of pages to select them. Press the Ctrl/Option key and drag the pages to the new document's Pages pane. Pages are inserted in the new file and deleted from the source document.

9. **Close the original source documents.** Click the close button or choose File ⇨ Close to close the documents. If you want to save the file where you extracted and deleted pages, save the document and close the file.

10. **Sort the pages.** Open the Pages pane by dragging the right side of the pane to the right side of the Acrobat window. Open a context menu and select Enlarge Page Thumbnails. Repeat the steps to enlarge pages until you have a comfortable view of the page content. Click and drag pages around the Pages pane to reorder the pages as shown in Figure 12-17.

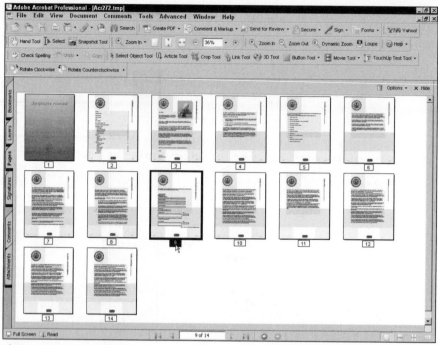

Figure 12-17: Open the Pages pane and move the pages to the desired order.

11. **Save the file.** Choose File ➪ Save As. Supply a filename and select a destination in the Save As dialog box. Click the Save button.

Save your work periodically if you have a major editing job. When you create a new file with a JavaScript, Acrobat supplies a temporary name, but the file is not actually saved to disk until you save the file. Save the file after a few edits; then repeat the Save command as you work on the file. When you finish the job, choose File ➪ Save As and rewrite the file. Page editing can add a lot of unnecessary data to a file during an editing job. When you rewrite the file, much of the redundancy is eliminated and the file size is reduced.

For information on rewriting files with the Save As command, see Chapter 9.

Cropping Pages

In the Advanced Editing toolbar, you find the Crop tool. Cropping pages in Acrobat is performed with the Crop tool, or Document ➪ Crop Pages, Tools ➪ Print Production ➪ Crop Pages, or by selecting a menu command from the Pages pane. You can select the Crop tool and draw a marquee in the document window to define the crop region, double-click on the Crop tool in the Advanced Editing toolbar, or select the Crop Pages command from a context menu or pane menu in the Pages pane. Regardless of which manner you select to crop pages, the Crop Pages dialog box opens, as shown in Figure 12-18.

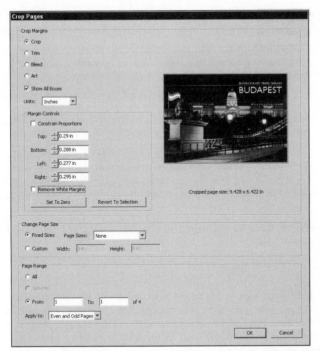

Figure 12-18: The Crop Pages dialog box displays a thumbnail image of the document page and offers options for crop margins and page ranges.

Tip   To quickly access the Crop Pages dialog box, double-click on the Crop tool.

If you don't use the Crop tool from the Advanced Editing toolbar, the Crop Pages dialog box opens with no crop zone specified. You can edit the margins numerically where a keyline border displays the crop area dynamically as you change the margins. When you use the Crop tool, open a rectangle marquee and move the mouse cursor inside the rectangle. The cursor changes to a selection arrow, indicating that you can double-click the mouse button to open the Crop Pages dialog box. The Crop Pages dialog box enables you to refine the page cropping. You can select from the following options:

✦ **Crop Margins:** Four radio button options are available. When you choose one of the options, the keyline border displaying the crop region changes color according to the option selected. The four options are

  • **Crop:** This is the default selection. It is shown with a black keyline for the cropped page when displayed or printed.

  • **Trim:** The trim box is shown with a green rectangle. Trim areas are usually determined by the printer's marks indicating the finished paper size. The paper trim is made inside the bleed box.

- **Bleed:** When you select the Bleed option, the keyline showing the crop area is blue. Bleeds allow colors to extend off the finished page size to account for paper trimming sizes.

  - **Art:** The art box is shown with a red rectangle. The art box size includes the entire bounding box for the page size.

✦ **Show All Boxes:** Displays the Crop, Trim, Bleed, and Art boxes.

✦ **Units:** From the pull-down menu select a unit of measure. The options include Points, Picas, Millimeters, Centimeters, and Inches.

✦ **Margin Controls:** Choices for margins are available for each side of the page. In the field boxes for each side, you can use the up or down arrows and watch a preview in the thumbnail at the top of the dialog box. As you press the up or down arrow, the margin line is displayed in the thumbnail. If you want to supply numeric values, enter them in the field boxes.

✦ **Constrain Proportions:** Check the box to keep proportions constrained. As you edit one text box in the Margin Controls, Acrobat supplies the same value in the remaining text boxes. For example, if you add one inch in the Top text box Acrobat adds one inch to the Bottom, Left, and Right text boxes.

Tip

To quickly adjust margins you can click in any field box and press the up and down arrow keys on your keyboard. The margins jump in increments according to the units selected from the Units pull-down menu. Press the Shift key and arrow keys and the margins jump to the next whole unit. For example, when inches are used for the units of measure, pressing Shift plus an arrow changes the amount in whole inches.

✦ **Remove White Margins:** Acrobat makes an effort to eliminate white space on the page outside any visible data. Acrobat's interpretation is confined to true white space. If a slight bit of gray appears as a border, it is not cropped.

✦ **Set to Zero:** This choice resets the crop margins to zero. If you change the dimensions with either of the preceding settings and want to regain the original dimensions of the crop boundary, click the Set to Zero button. From here you can redefine the margins. This button behaves much like a Reset button in other image editing programs.

✦ **Revert To Selection:** If you open a crop range and open the dialog box, and then change the margins or click the Set to Zero button, the crop rectangle is restored to the size it was when the dialog box was opened. That is, it's restored to the original crop area. The view displays the crop area within the current page. In other words, the thumbnail preview displays the entire page with the crop area indicated by a red rectangle.

✦ **Change Page Size:** You can change page sizes to standard fixed sizes by selecting options from the Page Sizes pull-down menu. You can also click the Custom radio button and the field boxes for Height and Width become active. Change values in the field boxes to create custom page sizes.

When defining new page sizes you can add to a page size to accommodate cropping to the page edge. Compare Figure 12-19 with Figure 12-18. In Figure 12-19, a custom page size was defined resulting in adding white space around the document. As you can see in the thumbnail view the page is larger than the same page used in Figure 12-18.

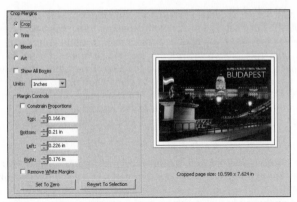

Figure 12-19: Set the page size dimensions to a larger size than the document and you can add white space around the page edge.

Tip If you want to see a larger view of what's happening on your PDF document while making adjustments in the Crop Pages dialog box, such as changing the page sizes, move the dialog box aside, and the background display in the Document pane dynamically updates to reflect many changes made in the Crop Pages dialog box.

✦ **Page Range:** Pages identified for cropping can be handled in the Page Range options. If All is selected, all pages in the PDF file are cropped according to the sizes you specify in the dialog box. You can target specific pages for cropping by entering values in the From and To field boxes. You select choices for Even and Odd Pages, Even Pages Only, and Odd Pages Only from the *Apply to* pull-down menu. The Selected option is available when you select page thumbnails in the Pages palette. If you select pages in the Pages palette, use the Document ➪ Crop Pages menu command. Using the Crop tool can deselect page thumbnails and the Selected option will appear grayed out when the Crop Pages dialog box opens.

Tip When creating PDFs for slide presentations or screen views, you may occasionally have an unwanted white border around the pages. This appearance may result from creating pages in layout or illustration programs when the image data doesn't precisely match the page size. To polish up the pages and eliminate any white lines, double-click the Crop tool or select the tool and double-click on the page. In the Crop Pages dialog box, select Remove White Margins and then select All for the page range. When the pages are cropped, the excess white lines are removed.

Cropping pages does not eliminate data from the PDF document regardless of whether you use the Save or Save As command. If you return to the Crop Pages dialog box either after cropping or after cropping and saving, reopen the file and select Set To Zero. The PDF page is restored to the original size.

Tip If you want to eliminate the excess data retained from the Crop tool, you can open the PDF in either Adobe Photoshop or Adobe Illustrator. Both programs honor the cropped regions of PDF files cropped in Acrobat. When you open a cropped page in either program, resave it as a PDF. Open the PDF in Acrobat. When you use the Crop tool and select the Set To Zero button, the page no longer has data remaining outside the page dimensions. The new file size saved from Photoshop or Illustrator is smaller due to elimination of the excess data. If you crop raster images such as photos, you can save the PDF in an image file format such as TIFF. After saving the file, use the Create PDF From File command and open the TIFF image in Acrobat. The cropped region is eliminated and the file size is reduced proportional to the cropped image size.

When you crop a page in Acrobat, the original data beyond the crop range is still contained in the PDF file. If you view a cropped page in the Document pane, you don't necessarily know that a page has been cropped unless you enable a preference setting to display the art, trim, and bleed boxes. Acrobat enables you to see the original page size through the display of a keyline color that matches the keyline border colors associated with the page display choices in the Crop Pages dialog box.

Press Ctrl/⌘+K to open the Preferences dialog box. In the left pane select Page Display and select the check box for Display art, trim, bleed boxes. Click OK and view a page that has been cropped. A keyline border displays at the edge of the crop choice you made in the Crop Pages dialog box.

In Figure 12-20, I cropped a page with Crop checked in the Crop Margins area of the Crop Pages dialog box. The original image is shown on the left and the cropped page is shown on the right. When the Preference choice is enabled for Display art, trim, and bleed boxes, the red keyline on the right side of the screen shows the original page size.

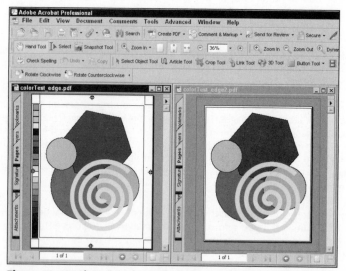

Figure 12-20: The original page is shown in the left window. The cropped image with the display for art, trim, and bleed boxes enabled in the Preferences dialog box shows the original page size with a red keyline border.

Rotating Pages

PDF documents can contain many pages with different page sizes. You can have a business card, a letter-sized page, a tabloid page, and a huge poster all contained in the same file. Depending on the authoring program of an original document and the way a PDF is created, you may experience problems with pages appearing rotated or inverted. Acrobat offers you tools to rotate pages for viewing and printing solutions to correct such appearance problems.

You rotate pages with the Document ➪ Rotate Pages menu command or in the Pages pane via context or Options menus. When you select Rotate Pages through any of these methods, the Rotate Pages dialog box opens. You choose the direction of rotation from a pull-down menu that enables you to rotate the page three different ways, as shown in Figure 12-21. Options in the Rotate Pages dialog box include

Note Rotate Pages is a menu command found in the menus discussed previously. When you rotate pages with a menu command, the pages are rotated and you can save the PDF with the new rotated appearances. You also have tools in the Rotate View toolbar used for Rotate(ing) View(s). When you use these tools to rotate a view, the page rotation is a temporary view and cannot be saved.

✦ **Direction:** Three choices appear from the Direction pull-down menu. Select from rotating pages clockwise 90 degrees, counterclockwise 90 degrees, or 180 degrees. Selecting clockwise or counterclockwise repeatedly rotates the page in 90 degree rotations.

✦ **Page Range:** Select All to rotate all pages in the PDF document.

✦ **Selection:** If you select page thumbnails in the Pages tab and select Rotate Pages from a context menu or by selecting Document ➪ Rotate Pages, the Rotate Pages dialog box offers you an option for rotating selected pages.

✦ **Pages:** Enter the page range you want to rotate in the From and To field boxes.

✦ **Rotate:** The pull-down menu for Rotate offers selections for Even and Odd Pages, Even Pages Only, or Odd Pages Only. The last pull-down menu offers choices for Portrait Pages, Landscape Pages, or Pages of Any Orientation.

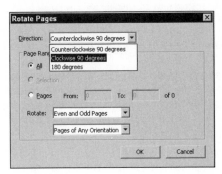

Figure 12-21: The Rotate Pages dialog box offers options for rotating pages in a range or by selecting even or odd pages. The Even/Odd choices can be helpful when printing to devices requiring page rotations for duplexing.

Rotating PDF elements

When you rotate a page, all page content is rotated. If you have any layers, visible or hidden, they are rotated. Acrobat provides no means for rotating individual layers.

If you create comments on a page and later rotate the page, the comment notes rotate at the point of origin, but the note displays are not rotated. For example, if you create a comment note in the top-left corner of a page and rotate the page 90 degrees counterclockwise, the note icon on the page is rotated, eventually ending up in the lower-left corner of the page. However, the open note is viewed at the default view with the note text in its original orientation.

Form fields behave differently than notes. If you create a form field containing text, the field and contents are rotated with the page.

Minimizing rotation problems

Among the major problems with PDF page rotation involves creating PDFs from layout programs. Layout programs such as Adobe InDesign or QuarkXPress enable you to transverse pages in the Print dialog box. This control is implemented for digital prepress and printing to high-end printing devices. In addition, many device PostScript Printer Description files (PPDs) used with high-end devices include transverse page options for page size selections.

For more information on commercial printing and PPDs, see Chapter 25.

As an example, a portrait page that prints transversed is rotated 90 degrees to conserve media on roll-fed devices. If you print files to disk as PostScript and distill the files in Acrobat Distiller, don't transverse the pages. When transversed pages are opened in Acrobat, even though the auto rotate feature is enabled during distillation, Acrobat interprets the page coordinates with a 90-degree rotation. The end result is a zero point (0,0) located in the lower-right corner of the page. This interpretation can lead to problems when you're trying to define x,y coordinates for JavaScripts, replacing pages, and copying and pasting data between documents.

If you set up a landscape page in a layout program, print the file as a portrait page with the horizontal width described in field boxes for custom page sizes. Print the file to disk and distill in Acrobat Distiller. The end product is a PDF that winds up with the proper page orientation and is interpreted by Acrobat with the zero point (0,0) located in the default lower-left corner.

Design and print professionals who seek to print files from PDFs can create the PDFs without transversing pages. When printing the PDFs for prepress, use the Acrobat Print dialog box to control printing and select device PPDs from within Acrobat. If you need to repurpose documents for Web or screen presentations, you can use the same file created for prepress without having to reprint and redistill the authoring document.

For more information on printing PostScript and using Acrobat Distiller, see Chapter 8.

Page Numbering

In Acrobat, page numbers appear in the status bar at the bottom of the Document pane and in the Pages pane. When you open the Go To Page dialog box (View ⇨ Go To ⇨ Page or Ctrl/⌘+Alt/Option+N) and enter a value in the status bar and press Enter/Return, you may find that the destination page does not correspond with the page number you supplied in the dialog box. This is because certain documents may be numbered in sections where front matter, such as a table of contents, foreword, preface, and other such items precede the page numbering in a document. This is particularly true of books, pamphlets, essays, journals, and similar documents using numbering schemes other than integers for the front matter.

Acrobat provides you a choice for how to view and access page numbers in a document. Open the Preferences dialog box (Ctrl/⌘+K) and click on Page Display in the left pane. In the right pane, select Use logical page numbers. When you want to jump to a page using the Go To Page dialog box or the status bar, the number you type takes you to the logical page number. Logical page numbers begin at the first page in a document and consider the first page number one regardless of what numbering scheme is used to number pages. A non-logical order considers the number of pages in Roman numbers in the document. If, for example, you have front matter with pages numbered with Roman numerals i through x, and page 1 is actually the eleventh page, disabling Use logical page numbers in the Page Display preferences requires you to type 20 in the Go To Page dialog box to arrive at page 10. When the check box is enabled, typing 10 in the Go To Page dialog box takes you to page 10.

In Figure 12-22, I opened a document and typed 10 in the status bar, and then pressed the Enter/Return key. The default setting in the Preferences dialog box was disabled for using logical page numbers. In the left window, page 10 is numbered page ix in the document, which is the actual tenth page in the file. I then enabled the preference setting for Use logical page numbers and again entered 10 in the status bar. After I pressed the Enter/Return key, the page numbered page 10 in the document opened. At the bottom of the Document pane the status bar reads: 10 (37 of 793). Page number 10 in this document is the thirty-seventh page in the file; therefore, 27 pages contain front matter using a numbering scheme different from the integers used for the body of the work.

You can change the way you view page numbers in the status bar and the way you seek out pages in a document via the Go To Page dialog box and the status bar. Acrobat provides several options for renumbering pages and saving the renumbered order. The options are available in the Page Numbering dialog box accessed from the Pages pane.

Open the Pages tab in the Navigation pane and open a context menu either from a page or from the pane pull-down menu. Select Number Pages from the menu options and the Page Numbering dialog box opens as shown in Figure 12-23.

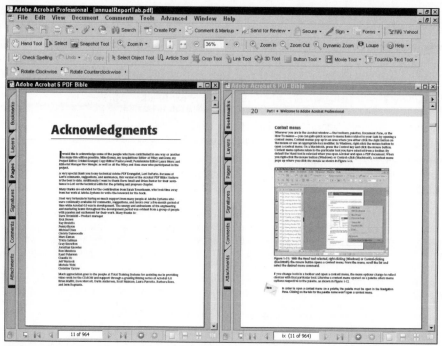

Figure 12-22: The left pane shows the tenth page in the document opened from an entry in the status bar when the Use logical page numbers preference setting is disabled. The right pane shows the page in the document numbered page 10 opened when the same action is invoked with the preference setting enabled.

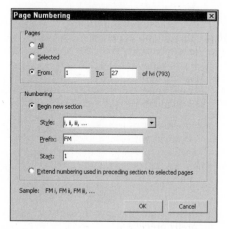

Figure 12-23: From a context menu opened on a page thumbnail in the Pages pane or from the Options pull-down menu, select Number Pages to open the Page Numbering dialog box.

The Page Numbering dialog box offers options for selecting a range of pages and renumbering them in sections or throughout the entire document. The choices available to you include

✦ **Pages:** This area of the dialog box asks you to specify the page range. If you want to renumber all pages with the same numbering scheme, select the All radio button. You might use this option when numbering pages numerically with integers.

   If you enable the radio button for Selected, only the pages selected in the Pages pane are affected. By default the Selected radio button is enabled if you click on a page or a page's thumbnail in the Pages pane and open the dialog box. If no page thumbnail is selected the default radio button selection is From.

   Enable the From radio button and supply a page range in the field boxes to select a page range numerically according to page position in the document. That is to say, pages 1 to 10 are interpreted as the first 10 pages in the file regardless of the page numbering scheme used before you open the dialog box. Perhaps you want to create a separate scheme for a document's front matter like the range specified in Figure 12-22. Specifying the scheme in the Numbering section of the dialog box renumbers the selection. Click OK to accept the changes. If you want to renumber another section, return to the dialog box and select a new section and new scheme. Repeat the process for all changes in page numbering according to different sections.

✦ **Numbering:** This portion of the dialog box offers you options for determining the page-numbering scheme you want to use. From the Style pull-down menu select a number style—the choices are shown in Figure 12-24.

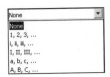

Figure 12-24: Select number styles from the Style pull-down menu.

   • **Style:** If None is selected, no page number is assigned to the page. The readout in the status bar would appear similar to this: (10 of 100). The numbers within the parentheses represent the original page number order preceded by a blank space where no number (None) is specified. If you want to add a prefix, you could add alphanumeric data to the Prefix field box and supply a prefix with no number. Using the same example, the readout would appear something like this: A000 (10 of 100), where A000 is the prefix and no number follows.

   The remaining options in the Style pull-down menu are specific choices for styles of page numbers. If you have front matter where you want to use Roman numerals, you can choose between the two styles shown in Figure 12-23. Alpha characters offer you options for uppercase or lowercase letters, and integers are also available. You can combine these options with special characters by typing data in the Prefix field box.

   • **Prefix:** Type any character, number, or combination of numbers and characters in the field box for a prefix value. The prefix precedes the numbering scheme defined in the Style pull-down menu.

- **Start:** The Start item is used to indicate the number a new section starts with. Typically you use 1 to start a new section, but you can begin sections with any number you want to type in the field box. Upon occasion you may have a document where page insertions might be added later. You can number pages in a section leaving room for new additions to be made later in another editing session.

✦ **Extend numbering used in preceding section to selected pages:** For this option you need to select a range of page thumbnails in the Pages pane, and then open the Page Numbering dialog box. Selecting the radio button and clicking OK removes the currently assigned numbers and extends the previous section. For example, you may have Appendix A numbered A-1 through A-10. You later decide to combine Appendix B with Appendix A. Appendix B might be numbered B-1 through B-10. To extend the previous B numbered pages, you select the page thumbnails in the Pages pane, open the dialog box and select this radio button. When you click OK, pages formerly numbered B-1 through B-10 are changed to A-11 through A-20.

Creating Headers and Footers

One of the most frequent questions I've had from readers over the past several years has been, "How can I number pages in a PDF file?" The page numbering previously discussed handles the structure of your PDF document and helps you navigate around pages, but once out of Acrobat and off to a desktop printer, all changes made to renumbering pages are not reflected in the printed output. Fortunately, Acrobat provides you methods for adding page numbers, time and date stamps, and text descriptions on pages that become part of the document content in the Add Headers and Footers dialog box. To add page numbers, a line of text, a date, or any combination of these, choose Document ➪ Add Headers & Footers. The Add Headers & Footers dialog box opens as shown in Figure 12-25. Two tabs appear in the top left of the dialog box. The default settings apply to document headers. Click the Footer tab to add a footer to the bottom of your pages.

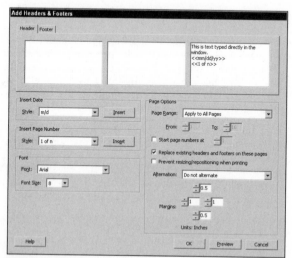

Figure 12-25: The default options are applied to document headers. Click on the Footer tab to select options for page footers.

You create page headers and footers in this dialog box. Options exist for adding a date stamp, a page number, and a custom text description. In Acrobat 6 the custom text is limited to a line of text you add in a field box. In Acrobat 7 you can type directly in the three list windows appearing at the top of the dialog box, copy and paste text, and cut text from a window and paste it into another window. Options for adding footers are identical to the settings provided for adding headers. Among your choices in the Add Headers & Footers dialog box are

✦ **List boxes:** I refer to the top section of the dialog box as *List boxes* to describe the area where you see three large white boxes. These three boxes are a display of the settings you make for adding the insertion items in the lower portion of the dialog box and/or that you type directly in the boxes.

Tip

As you add items to the list boxes, you can determine into which box the data are placed by clicking inside the box to select it. As you click an Insert button to add data, the data are added to the selected box. If you want to move data from one box to another, select the data, open a context menu, and select Cut or press Ctrl/⌘+X. Click in the box where you want to paste data, open a context menu, and select paste or press Ctrl/⌘+V.

✦ **Insert Date:** Down on the left side of the dialog box, the first item is the date style. From the pull-down menu you can select from twenty-three different styles. Selecting a style does not add the date to an upper window. You make a choice for the style and then click the Insert button adjacent to your style choice.

✦ **Insert Page Number:** Five different styles are available from the pull-down menu. Open the menu and make the style choice. In Figure 12-25 the 1of *n* style is used. When the pages are shown, each page is represented by the respective page number out of the total number of pages in the document. Regardless of the numbering system you use from the settings made in the Page Numbering dialog box, the *n* value calculates the total number of pages and represents the number with an integer.

✦ **Font:** All the system fonts available to you from your operating system are displayed in a pull-down menu. Select the down-pointing arrow and make your font choice. You can assign a different font to each line of text in the listed items in the upper boxes. After adding text from the Insert buttons in the lower portion of the dialog box, click on a line of text and make a font selection. If you use more than one font, select another line of text and choose another font.

✦ **Font Size:** Font sizes can be assigned individually to each line of text. If you want the Text to appear larger than the date or page number, select the item after clicking an Insert button and choose a font size from the pull-down menu. You select a font from preset point sizes. You cannot edit the field box to add a point size other than the preset sizes.

✦ **Page Options:** The items in the lower-right quadrant offer options for text position on the page and to which pages the text is applied in the document.

• **Page Range:** You choose between two options from the pull-down menu. If you select Apply to All Pages, the field boxes for From and To are not editable. The header, footer, or both are applied to all pages. If you select Apply to Page Range, the field boxes are editable and you specify in these boxes the page range where the header and/or footer text is applied. You can type values in each field box, click the up and down arrow keys to change page numbers, or select a field box and press the up or down arrow keys on your keyboard to change values. Acrobat knows how many pages your document contains before you open the Add Headers & Footers dialog box. If you attempt to add a page number exceeding the total number of pages in the PDF file, the field box value stops at the last page number in the document.

- **Start page numbers at:** Check the radio button and type a value in the field box for the page you want to start the renumbering.

- **Replace existing headers and footers on these pages:** If you change your mind after adding headers and/or footers, check the box and new data you type in the list windows replace the old data. If you want to erase all headers and footers, leave the three list windows blank, check this box, and click OK. The headers and footers are removed from the document.

- **Prevent resizing/repositioning when printing:** Check the box and the text is fixed to position when printing.

- **Alternation:** You have three choices in the pull-down menu for where the header, footer, or both are applied to pages. If you select Do not alternate, the data are added to all pages in the document. If you select either of the other two options, for Even Pages Only or Odd Pages Only, Acrobat adds data only to the respective even/odd pages in the document.

- **Margins:** The four Margins field boxes are editable. You can physically position a header or footer at any location on a page. If you add a header, the options relate to the top, left, and right field boxes. Footers relate to all but the top field box. Entering values in the lower field box has no effect on the position where the text is added when adding headers. If you use top = 5 inches, left = 3 inches, and select the left alignment radio button, the text is added 5 inches from the top and 3 inches from the left side.

- **Preview:** Before you close the dialog box, it's a good idea to preview the results of your choices. If you click OK in the dialog box and the data encroaches on the space where page content appears, you may need to alter the position of the header, footer, or both. When you click Preview, a page preview opens while the Add Headers & Footers dialog box remains open in the background. Preview your settings and click OK in the preview to return to the Add Headers & Footers dialog box. You can use the Preview button to make adjustments and preview the settings again. When all the options appear correct, click the OK button in the Add Headers & Footers dialog box.

When you open the Add Headers & Footers with a page displayed in the Document pane and attempt to add a header, footer, or both to a different page, you specify the page number in the Add Headers & Footers dialog box. If the target page is different than the page in view in the Document pane and you click on Preview, Acrobat intelligently shows you a preview of the target page.

Creating multiple headers and footers

You can add a header and footer to a page or range of pages in the Add Headers & Footers dialog box in a single session. Headers and footers can have different attributes assigned in a single session. When you add a header and select a font, font size, and add custom text, the attributes are associated with headers applied to the defined page range. When you click the Footer tab to create page footers, you can use different text, font styles, offset positions, and page ranges. Acrobat treats the header and footer as separate elements and, although you use the same dialog box with the same options, the settings are applied separately to the respective tab selections.

If you want to add a header, footer, or both to different pages with different fonts and styles, you need to reopen the Add Headers & Footers dialog box each time you change attributes. For example, if on page 1 you want the text aligned left for a header, you create the header for page 1 and adjust the margins. If you want page 2 aligned center, you create a new header with different attributes. If page 3 is treated differently, once again you return to the dialog box and select new options. Each time you open the Add Headers & Footers dialog box, all previous additions remain undisturbed as you add new page headers and footers to different pages.

Font handling

Fonts are automatically embedded when you use the Headers & Footers dialog box. The fonts become a permanent part of the document. However, you can select or edit the fonts on a page-by-page basis with the TouchUp Text tool. If, for some reason, you find your font not embedding in the document, you likely have a problem with the font. All fonts not embedded in a PDF are subject to font substitution. For some fonts substitution might not have much impact on the display, but with other fonts you can see radical differences. In Figure 12-26 you can see original fonts on the top and the font substitution displayed on the bottom. If you experience such problems, reinstall your fonts or use another font.

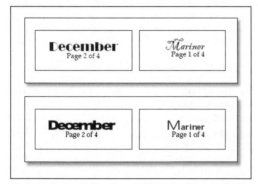

Figure 12-26: A header and footer were created in Windows XP. The top two boxes show the original font used in Windows. The two lower boxes show how Acrobat substituted the unembedded fonts when the file was opened in Acrobat on a Macintosh computer.

Headers and footers in layered PDF documents

You can add headers and footers to layered PDF documents. When you add a header, footer, or both to layered files, the data appears as if it resides on its own layer. A new layer is not created; however, if you hide all layers, the headers and footers are visible in the document. The header and footer are always displayed regardless of the choices you make in the Layers pane for viewing layers.

If you want to edit a block of text in a header or footer, you need to return to the Add Headers & Footers dialog box as the text is not editable using the TouchUp Text tool.

If you want to add headers or footers independently to different layers, you need to return to your authoring program or use an application capable of saving in PDF 1.5 format or above and supporting layers.

Cross-Reference For more information on editing layers, see Chapter 19. For more information on editing with the TouchUp Object tool and object editors, see Chapter 10.

Adding Watermarks and Backgrounds

In versions of Acrobat prior to version 6.0 you had to write JavaScripts to spawn pages from templates to create watermarks and backgrounds. In Acrobat 6 Add Watermark & Background enabled you to perform these functions without writing JavaScripts and the features have been improved in Acrobat 7.

Scaling Watermarks and Backgrounds

The scaling feature in the Add Watermark & Background dialog box is particularly helpful when you want to scale text. Text typed in the From text box in the Add Watermark & Background dialog box can be assigned a maximum point size of 72 points. If you want to type text and use it for a watermark such as stamping pages as *Draft*, 72 points may be too small to appear as a visible watermark on standard letter size pages — especially when viewed in a Fit Page view.

Here's a tip I received from my technical editor, Lori DeFurio. Add text in the From text field box. Click the Scale radio button and type a scale value in the field box. Press the Tab key and the preview shows the result in the Preview area. Change the value in the field box until the Preview displays as a suitable size.

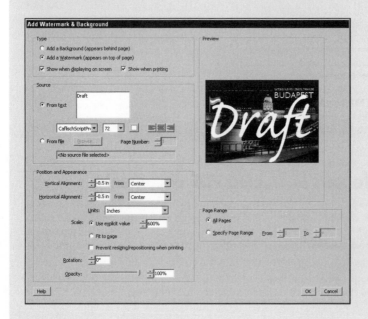

Cross-Reference For information related to writing JavaScripts and spawning pages from templates, see Chapter 29.

You add watermarks and backgrounds in the same dialog box, and the attributes for both items are identical. The distinction between a watermark and a background is that watermarks appear above all layers, and background data and backgrounds appear below all layers.

To add a watermark or background, choose Document ⇨ Add Watermark & Background. The Add Watermark & Background dialog box opens as shown in Figure 12-27. In this dialog box you make a selection for adding a watermark or a background, but not both in the same instance. The attributes after making the decision(s) are the same for both watermarks and backgrounds:

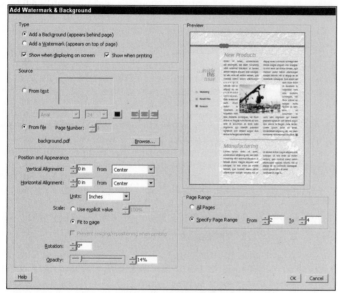

Figure 12-27: Choose Document ⇨ Add Watermark & Background to open the Add Watermark & Background dialog box.

✦ **Type:** The first two radio buttons in the dialog box offer you choices for adding a watermark or a background. If you select the radio button for Add a Background (appears behind page) and apply settings in the dialog box to add the background, you can come back to the radio button choices and select Add a Watermark (appears on top of page). After making a selection below the radio button choices, either a background or watermark is added to the page range selected in the dialog box. If you want both a watermark and a background, you need to add one or the other first, click OK, and then reopen the dialog box and add the other item.

✦ **Show when displaying on screen:** When the check box is enabled, the watermark/background are displayed on your monitor. Disabling the check box hides the elements from the screen view.

✦ **Show when printing:** You may have occasion to use a watermark on pages for messages that you communicate among workgroup members and later decide to print the file for distribution without the watermark (or background). If this is the case, you can hide the elements when printing the file by disabling the check box.

✦ **From text:** A new item added in Acrobat 7 is an editable box where you create custom text that can be used as either a watermark or a background. Click the radio button and type the text you want in the box.

✦ **Font attributes:** When you select the From text radio button, you choose a font currently active on your system, choose a font size from fixed options in a pull-down menu, and choose a text alignment represented by three icons for left, center, and right.

✦ **From file:** Click this radio button if you want to import a file. File types supported include PDF documents, BMP, and JPEG. Note that when this radio button is active the From text radio button is deactivated. You cannot import both text and a file at the same time. You can, however, import a background file, apply the settings by clicking OK, and then reopen the dialog box and type text for a watermark.

✦ **Browse:** Click the Browse button to locate a PDF file or image formatted file to import as a background or watermark. If you select a multi-page PDF document, you can select the source page that you want to import by supplying a number in the Page Number field box.

✦ **Page Number:** After selecting a file to import, select the page you want. You can toggle through the pages of a PDF document by changing the page number in the field box, clicking the arrows in the field box, or clicking in the field box and pressing the up and down arrow keys on your keyboard.

✦ **Vertical/Horizontal Alignment:** You use the Vertical and Horizontal Alignment field boxes to set the alignment for your background or watermark. Enter a value in the first field box (or click the up and down arrows to select a number) for each setting and from the alignment pull-down menu adjacent to the field boxes, select Top, Center, or Right.

Note   You can set vertical and horizontal alignments independently. In Figure 12-28 various combinations of vertical and horizontal alignment settings were applied to a 3-inch by 3-inch document imported as a background on an 8.5-inch by 11-inch page.

✦ **Units:** Choose from current units of measure defined in the Info pane or a Percentage of a page. When Units is selected, the Vertical and Horizontal Alignment field boxes permit you to type values in units of measure. When Percentage of a page is selected, you can increase or decrease the watermark/background data according to percentages of the page size.

✦ **Scale:** By default the scaling is set to 100%. Select the Use explicit value radio button and you can type values in the field box adjacent to this radio button. This measurement does not take into account the page size and scales the data used for a watermark or background according to the values you choose.

✦ **Fit to Page:** Scales the data to fit the page size.

✦ **Prevent resizing/repositioning when printing:** Locks the data in place so it prints the same as the screen view.

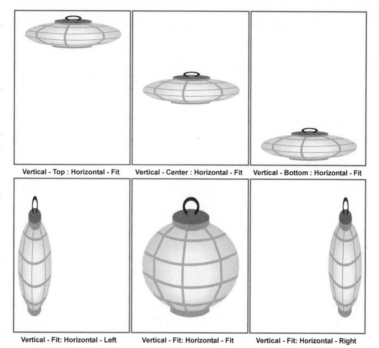

Vertical - Top : Horizontal - Fit   Vertical - Center : Horizontal - Fit   Vertical - Bottom : Horizontal - Fit

Vertical - Fit: Horizontal - Left   Vertical - Fit: Horizontal - Fit   Vertical - Fit: Horizontal - Right

Figure 12-28: The horizontal and vertical alignment options offer many different ways to display small images added to larger pages.

✦ **Rotation:** You can rotate backgrounds and watermarks in 1-degree increments. Edit the field box for the rotation angle desired.

✦ **Opacity:** You can apply opacity settings to raster and vector data contained used for a background or watermark. Move the slider to the left to add more transparency or type a number in the field box for the amount of transparency. In Figure 12-29, Fit to page was selected and the background was rotated. The figure on the right has an opacity adjustment.

✦ **Page Range:** Select All Pages to apply a watermark or background to all pages. Select Specify Page Range and use the From and To field boxes to restrict the watermark or background to selected pages within a page range by changing the values to only those pages on which you want to import the data.

Tip

Watermarks and backgrounds can be imported from multi-page PDF documents with different page sizes. If you routinely use logos, icons, symbols, and other such graphics in your workflow, you can create a library of images that all members in your workgroup can use. Create pages individually when you need to append pages to your library and use the Create PDF From File command. Add pages to the file and keep it handy when working on documents to which you need to apply watermarks and change backgrounds.

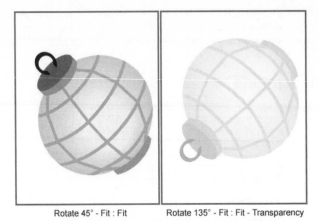

Rotate 45° - Fit : Fit   Rotate 135° - Fit : Fit - Transparency

Figure 12-29: The imported background was rotated
135 degrees on the left and 135 degrees on the right.
The image on the right has an opacity adjustment.

Deleting watermarks and backgrounds

If you click the OK button in the Add Watermark & Background dialog box, the data become a
permanent part of the document pages. You have one level of undo if you change your mind.
However, if you lose the Undo command or save the file, you cannot eliminate a watermark
or background after it has been added to the target pages. To be on the safe side, choose
File ➪ Save As and save your work to a new filename or save a version to your Version Cue
workspace. In the event you want to begin again, open the original file or promote the previous version to the current version and add new watermarks and backgrounds.

Cross-
Reference

For information on using Version Cue, see Chapter 9.

Tip

The text you add in the Watermark & Background dialog box is editable with the TouchUp
Text tool. If you want to delete a watermark or background comprised of text you add in the
From text box, use the TouchUp Object tool and delete the text object. If you need to edit it,
use the Text TouchUp tool.

Watermarks and backgrounds in layered files

You treat watermarks and backgrounds in layers the same as when you add headers and footers in layers. Watermarks and backgrounds are not applied to individual layers. In a layered
file, you add the watermark and/or background to the document as if it is on its own layer. If
you hide all layers, the watermark and/or background is visible on the document page(s). You
need to apply individual watermarks and backgrounds in an authoring program if you want to
show and hide them in the Layers pane.

Cross-
Reference

For more information on editing layers, see Chapter 19. For more information on editing with
the TouchUp Object tool and object editors, see Chapter 10.

Watermarks and backgrounds can be used in many different ways, especially with legacy files where you want to change content without returning to an authoring application. To demonstrate some of the flexibility of working with backgrounds for changing design appearances, follow these steps.

STEPS: Adding a background to a legacy PDF document

1. **Create a background file.** You can use scanned photos, textures created in a program such as Adobe Photoshop, vector art drawings from a program such as Adobe Illustrator, or any other document you convert to PDF, or use image files saved in an image file format such as BMP or JPEG.

2. **Open the destination file.** The file where you want to apply a new background needs to be opened in Adobe Acrobat. Open the file in the Document pane.

3. **Open the Add Watermark & Background dialog box.** Choose Document ➪ Add Watermark & Background.

4. **Select the background document.** Select the radio button for Add a Background (appears behind page). Select the From file radio button. Click the Browse button. In the Open dialog box select the document you want to use for your new background and click Open.

5. **Select the page range.** If you want the background applied to all pages, select the All Pages radio button. If you want to target a page range, enter the page range in the field boxes.

6. **Position the background.** If the background page size is the same page size as the destination pages, you can leave any settings for the alignment unchanged. If you have a smaller or larger page than the destination pages, select alignment options from the Scale options. You can check the display in the Preview as you make changes.

7. **Adjust transparency.** Move the slider for the Opacity item at the bottom of the Add Watermark & Background dialog box. Check the preview as you move the slider and rest it where you feel the right amount of transparency is applied so the background doesn't interfere with the foreground data.

8. **Apply the background.** Click OK in the dialog box to return to the Document pane. Your watermark or background should appear on the range of pages specified in the Add Watermark & Background dialog box.

Summary

✦ You can enlarge or reduce page thumbnails in size through successive menu commands in the Pages pane.

✦ You can open the Pages pane to full screen size where you can sort and reorder pages.

✦ Page thumbnails can be used to navigate pages and zoom in on pages.

✦ To copy pages in a PDF document and between PDF documents you can use page thumbnails.

✦ Page thumbnails are created on the fly when you open the Pages pane. If you want to speed up the screen refreshes when opening the Pages pane you can embed thumbnails from a menu option in the Pages pane and delete them after your editing sessions.

✦ Pages are inserted, deleted, extracted, and replaced through menu commands from the Pages pane context menu or the pane pull-down menu.

✦ You crop PDF pages with the Crop tool. When you crop a page, the page view is reduced to the crop region, but all the original data in terms of page size is still contained in the file. You can return to the Crop Page dialog box and undo crops even after a file has been saved.

✦ You can rotate PDF pages in 90- and 180-degree rotations via menu commands in the Rotate Pages dialog box.

✦ Enabling a preference setting for viewing logical pages helps you navigate to pages numbered with integers.

✦ Opening the Page Numbering dialog box from a context menu in the Pages pane enables you to renumber pages in a PDF file.

✦ To add page numbers to a PDF document use the Add Headers & Footers dialog box.

✦ You can add different headers and footers to different pages in a PDF document. Each time the content for headers and footers changes, you open the Add Headers & Footers dialog box, add the content, and specify the page range.

✦ Fonts added in headers and footers are automatically embedded in a PDF document. You can edit the fonts on a page-by-page basis with the TouchUp Text tool.

✦ To add watermarks and backgrounds to a document use the Add Watermark & Background dialog box. A watermark appears on top of all page data and a background appears behind all page data.

✦ After you save a PDF with a watermark and/or background, the data are embedded in the PDF document. You cannot return to the Add Watermark & Background dialog box to remove them.

✦   ✦   ✦

Scanning and OCR Conversion

✦ ✦ ✦ ✦

In This Chapter

Setting up the environment

Setting up a scanner

The basics of scanning

Scanning documents

Converting image scans to text

Correcting OCR errors

✦ ✦ ✦ ✦

Acrobat's Optical Character Recognition (OCR) feature can be used to perform two jobs. First you scan a document and convert it to a PDF file, and second you employ the Recognize Text Using OCR feature to convert the image file to rich text. Because scanning pages and converting to PDF is found under the Create PDF Task Button pull-down menu, you might think this chapter's information belongs back in Chapter 6 where the various methods of PDF creation were covered. The "Creating a PDF from a Scanner" section was added to this chapter because users typically scan from within Acrobat to convert scanned paper documents to searchable text. Accordingly, discussing scanning and OCR conversion together makes more sense.

When making a scan in either Acrobat Standard or Acrobat Professional you are not limited to scanning documents for text conversions. Acrobat enables you to scan photos and images that might have some other uses. Therefore, this chapter covers all the aspects of scanning from within Acrobat and using the Create PDF From Scanner command and the Recognize Text Using OCR command to perform OCR.

Setting Up the Scanning Work Environment

For scanning and Recognizing Text Using OCR tasks you need access to the TouchUp Text tool. First, reset the tools from a context menu opened from the Toolbar Well and choose Tools ➪ Advanced Editing ➪ Show TouchUp Toolbar. When the toolbar opens, dock it in the Toolbar Well.

During text recognition you may want to create several views that enable you to zoom in to see words requiring edits. Tools handy for displaying different views are found in the Zoom toolbar. Open the pull-down menu adjacent to the Zoom In tool and select Show Zoom Toolbar from the menu options. Dock the toolbar in the Toolbar Well.

Configuring Scanners

Before you can scan a page in Acrobat, you need to configure your scanner and be certain it functions properly. After you complete your installation of Acrobat, it should recognize your scanner immediately. If all the scanner hardware is in place and operational and Acrobat still does not recognize your scanner, the next step is to be certain the scanner's software is recognized by Acrobat. If Acrobat doesn't see your scanner, you may need to relocate software to another location on your hard drive or acquire a software update from your scanner manufacturer.

You get access to your scanner in Acrobat through one of two methods: TWAIN software or Acquire plug-ins.

TWAIN software

TWAIN (Technology With An Important Name) software is manufacturer-supplied and should be available on the CD-ROM you receive with your scanner. In Windows, the TWAIN files are stored in the \WINNT\twain_32 folder. When you install scanner software, the TWAIN driver should find the proper folder through the installer routine. On the Macintosh you'll find TWAIN resources in the System\Library\Image Capture\TWAIN Data Sources folder.

Many scanner manufacturers produce the equipment but use third-party developers to write the software. Adobe has certainly not tested the Scan plug-in with all scanner manufacturers and all software developers. Theoretically, the TWAIN software should work in all cases. If you have problems accessing your scanner from within Acrobat, but can perform scans in other applications, then you most likely have a problem with the TWAIN software. If this is the case, contact your scanner manufacturer and see whether it has an upgrade or whether you can get some technical support. In many cases, you can download upgrades for registered software on the Internet.

Adobe Photoshop plug-in software

Acrobat 7.0 supports Acquire plug-ins you use with Adobe Photoshop. More prevalent than TWAIN drivers, Photoshop plug-ins are available from just about every scanner manufacturer. If you use Adobe Photoshop, you may need to copy your Photoshop Acquire plug-in to your Acrobat plug-ins folder. On Windows, copy the Photoshop Acquire plug-in and open the Acrobat\plug_ins\PaperCapture folder and paste your Acquire plug-in.

Mac OS X requires you to expand the Acrobat 7.0 Professional or Acrobat Standard package in order to paste your Photoshop Acquire plug-in. To do so, follow these steps:

1. **Open your Acrobat 7.0 Professional folder and select (not double-click) Acrobat 7.0 Professional.**

2. **Control+click to open a context menu, and select Show Package Contents.**

   The Contents folder appears in the Acrobat 7.0 Professional folder.

3. **Double-click the Contents folder and double-click the Plug-ins folder that comes into view.**

4. **Double-click again to open the PaperCapture folder and drag your Photoshop Acquire plug-in into this folder.**

   When you close the folders, the package is restored.

Understanding Scanning Essentials

At this point you should have your scanner and Acrobat configured properly. Before I begin discussing how to use your scanner with Acrobat, take a moment to understand some of the essential issues to deal with in performing clean, accurate scans. A few items need to be discussed: the hardware and hardware-related issues; the types of scans to be produced; and understanding your scanner capabilities. A few moments here will save you much time in producing the best scans you can expect from your equipment.

Cross-Reference Preparing documents for scanning is discussed later in this chapter in the section "Preparing a document."

The first hardware issue to consider is your scanner. The single most important issue with scanner hardware is keeping the platen clean. If you have dust and dirt on the glass, these particles show up in your scans. Keep the platen clean, and use a lint-free cloth to clean the glass. If you use a solvent, always apply the solvent to the cloth and not the scanner glass.

Also in regards to your scanner, you should understand the technology used to manufacture the device. Flatbed consumer-grade scanners often use charge-coupled devices (CCDs), which are tiny little sensors placed along a horizontal plane in a number equal to the optical resolution of your scanner. Therefore, a 600-dpi scanner has 600 CCDs per inch. Each of these sensors picks up a pixel when the scanner pass is made. Where these sensors begin and end along the horizontal plane is important for you to know. If you experience some edge sharpness problems or degradation in your image at the edges, try placing the scanned source material a little farther from the edges of the scanner platen and toward the middle. When doing so, be certain to keep the material straight on the scanner bed.

Less expensive scanners that you can find today are CIS scanners. These scanners use contact image sensors instead of CCDs. They are well suited to scan text but you have to test the results to determine whether the scanner performs efficiently. In many cases, the low-cost CIS scanners can produce text scans that work well with Recognize Text Using OCR.

The second hardware item to consider is your computer. When performing scans, try to allocate as much memory as you can spare to Acrobat if your operating system allows memory allocations to programs. If you have multiple applications open simultaneously and subsequently experience crashes, then by all means, try using Acrobat alone when performing scans. Also related to your computer is virtual memory. Double-check the free space on your computer's hard drive before attempting to scan. Scans eat up memory fast, so be certain you have ample space before engaging in a scanning session. A scan of 300 pixels per inch (ppi) consumes about 24MB of hard drive space. You should plan on having three to five times that amount of free hard drive space for each page scanned at 300 ppi.

Preparing a document

Just as your scans can benefit from careful attention to your scanner, exercising a little care with the source material can help produce clean scans. Bits of dust, improperly aligned pages, poor contrast, and degraded originals affect your ability to create scans capable of being read without many errors by Recognize Text Using OCR. A little preparation before scanning saves you much time in trying to clean up poorly scanned images.

Photocopying originals

Sometimes you can improve image and text contrast by photocopying original documents. Try some experiments to test your results. Placing photocopies of large, bulky material on the scanner bed ultimately results in better scans than when using the original material.

Ensuring straight alignment

If you have documents with frayed edges or pages torn from a magazine, then you should trim the edges and make them parallel to the text on the page. Precise placement of pages on the scanner bed facilitates clean scans. Even though Acrobat has a recognition capability within a 14-degree rotation, the straighter the page, the better the results.

 Caution Be certain to observe copyright laws when scanning published material. If you scan text from books and magazines, you need to obtain permission from the publisher before using the material.

 Tip A method I use with all flatbed scanning is to place the source material in a jig I created from poster board. If a standard US Letter (8.5 by 11 inches) page is your source material, get a large piece of poster board that extends past the edges of the scanner lid on the sides and bottom. Use a T-square and align a standard-size page parallel to the top. Mark the edges for an 8.5 by 11 inch cutout in the center of the poster board. Cut out the marked area and use the waste as a lid on the poster board. You can tape the top so it opens much like your scanner lid. Use the cutout area as a template to place pages and ready them for scanning. Place the template under the scanner lid and preview a scan. If the preview is not straight, you can move the poster board because the edges extend beyond the scanner lid. When the preview appears straight, tape the poster board to the scanner. As you open the scanner lid, subsequently open the jig lid and place a page in the cutout area. Every scan you perform will have all the pages aligned precisely. The lid on the jig prevents the pages from rising in the cutout space and keeps them flat against the platen.

Try to remember the axiom "garbage in, garbage out" when you approach any kind of scanning. The better the source material, the better your scanned results. Exercise a little care in the beginning, and your Acrobat scanning sessions move along much faster.

Understanding Acrobat scan types

You can produce several different types of scans when converting to PDF from a scanner. Each of the scans you perform has different requirements and needs some special attention. Decisions related to image scans, color mode, text conversion, and so on need to be made when you open a Scan dialog box and set attributes for the type of scan you want.

Text recognition

If you scan directly into Acrobat, more often than not your requirements are for text and OCR scanning. Given the fact that PDF pages are usually created with layout, illustration, and photo-editing software, attempting to create PDF documents for final proofs by scanning them into Acrobat would be rare. If you create a page layout, scanning in Adobe Photoshop would be better than scanning in Acrobat because Photoshop enables you to enhance and optimize image quality immediately after each scan. The area Acrobat excels in is searching text documents. For this situation, you would use the Create PDF From Scanner command with the Recognize Text Using OCR box checked to recognize the text. When scanning text, you want to abide by the few simple rules that follow.

Image mode

Image modes range from 1-bit line art or black-and-white scans to 24-bit color. The higher the bit depth, the larger the file size. Text scans need only 1-bit line art mode for Acrobat to recognize text. If your scanner software has a line-art mode, use it to perform scans for text recognition.

Resolution

Resolution for text recognition needs to be high enough for good, clean scanning and tight pixels on the edges of characters, but not as high as you would need for output to high-end devices. As a general rule, you can scan normal body text at 300 dpi. Large text sizes can be sufficiently scanned at 200 dpi. For small text of 8 points or lower, you may want to raise the resolution higher than 300 dpi. In many cases, you need to run some tests for the target resolution for your particular type of scanner, software, and typical documents scanned. The maximum resolution supported by Acrobat is 600 dpi.

Grayscale scanning

Once again, scanning images is often the task of Photoshop. However, you may find grayscale scanning necessary or helpful when scanning for text recognition. The most important attribute of a scanned image for OCR software is a sharp contrast between the text and the background. If your line art scans aren't working out, try scanning in grayscale and applying contrast settings in your image-editing software before completing the scan. Many software applications provide controls for brightness and contrast settings. Most software displays previews of the adjustments you make, which greatly speeds up the entire process.

If you want to scan photographic images in grayscale, be certain to lower the resolution. Try 200 dpi or lower. You should plan on testing resolutions to achieve the lowest possible resolution that maintains a good quality image. If you scan grayscale images in Acrobat, they should be for screen view only. To create PDF files that ultimately are to be printed, you should use Photoshop and a layout or illustration application. Then distill the images with Acrobat Distiller or use an application such as Adobe InDesign that supports direct exports to PDF.

Color scanning

If you have color documents and want to recognize text from the pages, you might want to use a color mode if you can build up enough contrast during the scan. Large type of 12 points or higher in color images can be effectively recognized in 200 dpi scans.

Color images occupy the largest file sizes. For OCR conversion where retaining color is not required in the final output, converting color images to line art or grayscale saves considerable space on your hard drive. If you use an image editor like Adobe Photoshop and you have color images already scanned, you can run a Photoshop Action to automate the conversion of color to grayscale or line art. If existing scanned images are used for text recognition, you can use the Create PDF From Multiple Files command to convert to PDF and then use Recognize Text Using OCR to convert the image files to text.

Creating a PDF from a Scanner

To scan a page from within Acrobat, select the pull-down menu from the Create PDF Task Button and select From Scanner. When you perform a scan within Acrobat, the scanned image opens as a PDF document. You can choose to leave the scan as an image and save it as a PDF file. However, to do nothing more than scan images in Acrobat is less efficient than scanning images in Adobe Photoshop and saving the Photoshop scans as Photoshop PDF files. With

Acrobat you have no image editing tools for improving scan appearances, changing brightness values, performing color correction, and so on.

Create PDF From Scanner is only half of the equation related to scanning in Acrobat. The real power of using Acrobat for scanning images lies in its capability to convert scanned text into readable and searchable text with Create PDF From Scanner. Raw image files with no text are referred to in Acrobat terms as *Image Only* files. When you distill documents with Acrobat Distiller, create PDFs from files, or convert scanned pages with the Recognize Text Using OCR command, the files contain text that can be indexed, searched, and selected. These files are known in Acrobat terms as *Formatted Text & Graphics documents*. When a scan is acquired in Acrobat and the Recognize Text Using OCR box is not checked, the file opens as an Image Only PDF file.

In earlier versions of Acrobat the OCR feature was named Paper Capture. This tool's features were based on the OCR functionality found in Acrobat Capture 2. Acrobat Capture is a standalone product designed for industrial-strength scanning and marketed as a separate product by Adobe Systems. Starting with Acrobat 6, the feature set in Recognize Text Using OCR is based on features found in Acrobat Capture 3. Among the changes are renaming PDF Normal to Formatted Text & Graphics PDF and using new terminology to describe the types of image formats created with Recognize Text Using OCR. PDF Normal is an old term *retired* with the introduction of Acrobat Capture 3.0 and is not present in any of the current documentation.

Cross-Reference For information on PDF Normal Image and newer terms used to define the Recognize Text formats, see the section "Using Recognize Text Using OCR" later in this chapter.

After you verify proper configuration for both your scanner and computer hardware and prepare your document, the rest of the scanning process is easy. To scan an image, open the pull-down menu from the Create PDF Task Button and select From Scanner. The Create PDF From Scanner dialog box opens, as shown in Figure 13-1.

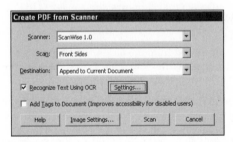

Figure 13-1: The Create PDF From Scanner dialog box opens after you select Create PDF From Scanner.

Look over the options in the Create PDF From Scanner dialog box. You need to make a few choices here before you convert a scan to searchable text.

✦ **Scanner:** If you have several Acquire plug-ins or TWAIN scanner drivers loaded on your system, they all appear in the pull-down menu after installation. Open the pull-down menu and make a choice for the scanner you want to use.

✦ **Scan:** Options are available for single-sided or double-sided scanning. Choose Front Sides for single-sided scanning and Both Sides for double-sided scanning. When you select Both Sides, a dialog box opens after the first scan and prompts you to select the next page as either the front side of the next page or the back side of the current page.

✦ **Destination:** You can access the From Scanner menu command without a PDF opened in the Document pane. If no file is open when the Create PDF From Scanner dialog box opens, the only selection for the destination is to create a New Document. If a file is open in the Document pane and you want the scan to open in a separate document, be certain to select New Document from the pull-down menu. If a file is open and you want to append the scan to the open document, select Append to Current Document.

✦ **Recognize Text Using OCR:** Selecting this option performs a scan and OCR conversion without a need to access a separate menu command. To the right of the check box is a Settings button. Click Settings to change the OCR language, PDF Output Style, and scan resolution.

✦ **Add Tags to Document (Improves accessibility for disabled users):** Creates an accessible document with tags.

Cross-Reference
For more information on working with accessible documents, see Chapter 20.

✦ **Image Settings:** Click this button to open the Image Settings dialog box where you define attributes for the scans you acquire in Acrobat.

When you click the Image Settings button in the Create PDF From Scanner dialog box, the Image Settings dialog box opens as shown in Figure 13-2.

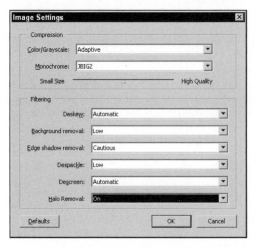

Figure 13-2: The Image Settings dialog box provides options for setting attributes for scanning images

In this dialog box you make some choices regarding the images scanned into Acrobat. They include

✦ **Compression:** For color/grayscale images choose from Adaptive or JPEG for file compression. JPEG files result in smaller file sizes, but you experience data loss. In many cases the data loss may have no effect on appearance or Acrobat's ability to recognize text. If you do experience problems, try using Adaptive compression.

Monochrome images are compressed with three different compression schemes depending on the choice made from the pull-down menu. JBIG2 is a JPEG compression scheme with little data loss. You also have Adaptive like that used for color/grayscale images and CCITT Group 4, which is a common compression used by fax machines.

When applying compression to images, try the defaults (Adaptive for color/grayscale and JBIG2 for monochrome) first. If your scans are presenting with visual problems or Acrobat has difficulty in recognizing text, experiment with the other settings.

You can adjust the quality slider for the amount of compression applied to the scans. As you move the slider left, the file size is smaller but the image quality is reduced. Move the slider toward Higher if you experience problems with text recognition.

✦ **Deskew:** Acrobat automatically straightens crooked scans when Deskew is set to automatic. To turn off the deskewing, select Off from the pull-down menu.

✦ **Background removal:** Removes background data. Use this option and choose from Low, Medium, High, or Off from menu choices. When text has drop shadows or original paper copies show dust and dirt, play with the amount settings to sharpen the text.

✦ **Edge shadow removal:** If you want to scan in grayscale or color mode, Acrobat can eliminate levels of gray where shadows appear around type. For cleaner text scans, enable this option. Note that you need to have crisp, clean originals to see much of a difference between scanning with the option enabled versus disabled. Two settings are used for Cautious and Aggressive as well as Off. Use Aggressive for more removal.

✦ **Despeckle:** This item and descreen are particularly helpful when scanning documents that have been printed and subject to moiré patterns (a condition common when scanning printed documents) or when scanning documents with dust and dirt.

✦ **Descreen:** Use Descreen like Despeckle mentioned previously when scanning printed documents and screened type.

✦ **Halo Removal:** Artifacts creating halo effects around type can be cleaned up by setting this option to On.

Many of the settings in the Create PDF From Scanner dialog box need to be tested in your own workflow, especially the Image Settings items and when you scan to create searchable documents. There's no substitute for testing. Change settings and test the results when capturing pages. With a little practice, you can easily determine what settings work best in your workflow.

Creating Workflow Solutions

Scanning individual pages for limited use can easily be handled by the methods described previously. As you scan documents, you need to attend to feeding papers under the scanner lid and manually clicking buttons to continue scanning. If you need to convert large numbers of pages to digital content, you may want to explore other solutions. Depending on how much money you want to spend, you may want to invest in a commercial-grade scanner with a document feeder.

Some scanners support automatic document feeders. If your workflow demands scanning volumes of papers, acquiring a good scanner with an automatic document feeder is a great advantage. When you scan in Acrobat, scanned pages are successively appended to a PDF. Therefore, you can leave a stack of papers in the scanner feeder and leave it unattended. Scanning can be performed automatically overnight. When you return to your computer, the PDF file is complete with recognized text and ready for saving to your hard disk. The only downside to this operation is that if your computer crashes, you lose everything because Acrobat won't save your PDF on the fly as new pages are appended.

A more expensive solution, but not out of the question for workflows needing automated means of capturing pages, is to purchase Adobe's stand-alone product, Adobe Acrobat Capture. Combined with a scanner and document feeder, the conversion of scanned images to text is handled in a single operation. You have other solutions from third-party vendors that support industrial-strength scanning and OCR conversion with the capability of converting the final file to PDF format.

Users in government and educational workflows seeking to scan volumes of text for document accessibility will find purchasing auto document feeding scanners and Adobe Acrobat Capture, or other software capable of batch scanning and OCR conversion, to be a much more effective means for converting publications and documents to accessible PDFs. Some hardware screen readers use proprietary software to read TIFF image files for document accessibility. Acrobat PDF is a much better solution over TIFF images and proprietary formats, as once converted to PDF, the document content is searchable and much smaller. If scanning textbooks and government papers is your task, PDF is a much better file format for document accessibility.

Using Recognize Text Using OCR

After you either scan pages into Acrobat (when not using the Recognize Text Using OCR item) or open images as a PDF file by using the Create PDF From File command, you can convert the page to text through an OCR conversion. Acrobat's OCR utility is Recognize Text Using OCR. To perform an OCR conversion on a file open in the Document pane, choose Document ➪ Recognize Text Using OCR ➪ Start. The Recognize Text dialog box opens as shown in Figure 13-3. Before beginning a conversion, you might want to review the settings in the Recognize Text dialog box. You can change the default settings for different options associated with the OCR conversion.

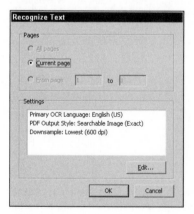

Figure 13-3: Choose Document ➪ Recognize Text Using OCR ➪ Start to open the Recognize Text dialog box.

The first series of options in the Recognize Text dialog box offers you a page range for converting pages. Select all pages, the current page only, or a specified page range. In the scrollable window you can see the default settings currently applied for your conversion session. If you want to make further option choices, click the Edit button in the Recognize Text dialog box. The Recognize Text - Settings dialog box opens as shown in Figure 13-4.

Figure 13-4: Click the Edit button in the Recognize Text dialog box to open the Recognize Text - Settings dialog box. In this dialog box you make options choices for the conversion attributes.

Attribute choices available in the Recognize Text - Settings dialog box include:

✦ **Primary OCR Language:** By default, Acrobat installs 16 language dictionaries available for OCR. If you scan documents from any of the supported languages, select the appropriate language in the pull-down menu in the Recognize Text - Settings dialog box.

✦ **PDF Output Style:** The three choices in this drop-down menu are

  • **Searchable Image (Exact):** This option keeps the image scan in the foreground with text placed in the background. The appearance of the scanned image does not change. Text is added on a hidden layer that gives you the capability of creating indexes and performing searches. Use this option when you don't want to change a document's appearance, but you do want to be able to search the text of that document. Something on the order of a legal document or a certificate might be an example of such a document.

  • **Searchable Image (Compact):** Text is also placed behind the original image, preserving the integrity of the original documents. The image scan is compressed to reduce file size. Some of the quality of the original scan is lost.

  • **Formatted Text & Graphics:** The bitmapped image is discarded and replaced with searchable text and graphics. If there is an instance where the OCR engine does not have confidence, the original bitmap is left in place and the best guess is placed behind, mimicking the "Searchable Image" style.

Note See the "PDF Image versus PDF Formatted Text & Graphics" sidebar in this chapter for more detail on the differences among the PDF Output Styles.

✦ **Downsample Images:** This option enables you to downsample images or keep them at the original scanned resolution. If None is selected, no downsampling is applied to images. The remaining options offer downsampling values at 600 dots per inch (dpi), 300 dpi, 150 dpi, and 72 dpi.

Cross-Reference For more information on image sampling, see Chapter 8.

After making your option choices in the Recognize Text - Settings dialog box, click OK to return to the Recognize Text dialog box. Your new settings are displayed in the scrollable window. These settings become a new default and remain in effect until you revisit the Recognize Text - Settings dialog box and make changes. Click OK in the dialog box and your pages are processed. Depending on the number of pages and the complexity of the document, you may need to wait before Recognize Text Using OCR finishes the conversion.

PDF Image Versus PDF Formatted Text & Graphics

When you search OCR pages with either Searchable Image (Exact) or Searchable Image (Compact), the pages are image files with searchable text. The original file is an image file produced from your scan designed to be viewed as an original, unaltered document. This option enables you to electronically archive documents for legal purposes or when unaltered originals need to be preserved.

When you convert a document with Recognize Text Using OCR, the OCR conversion places text behind the scan. The intent is for you to be able to archive files and search them either through using the Search pane to search files on your hard disk or by searching an index where these documents have been catalogued.

The text behind PDF Image is not editable with Acrobat. However, Adobe Acrobat Capture 3.0 does have tools to edit text in a PDF Image file. If Recognize Text Using OCR misinterprets a word, you cannot make corrections to the text. The text is selectable, and you can copy the text and paste it into a word processor or text editor. If you want to examine the OCR suspects, paste the text into a word processor and review the document. Or buy a copy of Adobe Acrobat Capture 3.0 to do the edits from within the PDF file.

To copy text from a PDF Image format select the Select tool. Click the cursor anywhere in the text and choose Edit ➪ Select All (Ctrl/⌘+A). Open a context menu and select Copy File to Clipboard. Open a word processor and choose Edit ➪ Paste. You may find the number of suspects to be too many to be usable. If you want to improve the OCR conversion, return to the Create PDF From Scanner dialog box and rescan the file with a higher resolution or different scanning mode.

PDF Formatted Text & Graphics files (previously referred to as PDF Normal in Acrobat 5 and earlier) are scanned documents converted to text. When you select Formatted Text & Graphics in the Recognize Text dialog box, the file conversion is made to a PDF Formatted Text & Graphics document. Recognize Text reads the bitmap configuration of words and converts them to text. This text can be edited and altered on a page. When you make text corrections, you see the changes reflected on the document page.

When capturing pages, be certain to view the options and know the difference between capturing pages as PDF Scanned Image and PDF Formatted Text & Graphics.

The Recognize Text dialog box remains open during the conversion and a display of the progress flashes by as various procedures are employed. When the conversion is finished, the dialog box closes. As a conversion from image file to text is made, Recognize Text Using OCR analyzes the document and compares its interpretation of words to its dictionary. When the process finds a word where the interpretation doesn't quite match a word contained in the dictionary, it marks the word as a *suspect*. Your next task is to view the suspect words and make edits for all the words misunderstood by Recognize Text Using OCR.

Editing OCR Suspects

A *suspect* word is one that Recognize Text interprets differently from the closest match found in the Recognize Text dictionary. The word is suspect because it may or may not be a correct interpretation. You might have proper names, industry terminology, abbreviations, and so on that Recognize Text marks as suspects. Simply because the word(s) is marked as a suspect doesn't necessarily require changing the word. Therefore, when you review suspects, you have two choices: Either change the word to a correct spelling or inform Acrobat to leave it as is and move to the next suspect.

After the Recognize Text dialog box disappears, the converted page(s) doesn't appear any different from before you began the OCR conversion. In order to see any words that may have been misinterpreted during the conversions, you need to access a menu command and tell Acrobat you want to view the suspect words. You have two choices in the Recognize Text Using OCR submenu.

Note In order to correct OCR suspects in Acrobat, you need to convert pages with the Formatted Text & Graphics PDF Output Style.

If you choose Document ⇨ Recognize Text Using OCR ⇨ Find First OCR Suspect, Acrobat shows the first word that it interprets as a suspect, which means the interpretation of Recognize Text did not exactly match a word in its dictionary. The suspect word is high-lighted with a black border.

If you choose Document ⇨ Recognize Text ⇨ Find All OCR Suspects, all the suspect words are highlighted with a red border across all pages converted. At a glance you can see the number of suspects that need to be reviewed.

To begin editing suspect words, choose Document ⇨ Recognize Text ⇨ Find First OCR Suspect. Acrobat highlights the first suspect word and shows a bounding box for the para-graph where the suspect word resides as shown in Figure 13-5. When the Find Element dialog box opens, make a choice for accepting the word and moving to the next suspect. If the word needs to be edited, edit the suspect with the TouchUp Text tool. (The TouchUp Text tool is automatically selected when you open the Find Elements dialog box.) If you accept the word, the bitmap image is discarded.

Tip When examining suspect words you should plan on zooming in to the suspects. If you prefer to view a page in a zoomed out view, select the Loupe tool to zoom in on suspect words. You can keep the page view in a smaller view while zooming in on suspects with the Loupe tool.

To leave a word unedited, you can choose either Find Next or Accept and Find. If the OCR engine recognized a graphic (like a signature) as text you can also select "Not Text" to return it to the original bitmap image. If you choose Find Next, the bitmap image of the text stays in place and the text behind the bitmap stays as is. When you click the Accept and Find button, the bitmap is thrown away and the word behind the bitmap is promoted to the text location. As you work with the text corrections, realize that you have two layers. The bitmap is the scanned image and Recognize Text created the text below the scanned image. Therefore, as you edit the text corrections you can choose to throw away the bitmap image on top of the text layer or choose to preserve it. To make a correction, edit a suspect word and click Accept and Find. The new text you edited is promoted to the text layer while the bitmap is thrown away.

PDF Workflow If you want to develop a workflow in an office environment, you may want to have several machines perform the function of scanning documents and have other computers perform OCR functions. You can scan images in software such as Adobe Photoshop and save your files in either an image format or as Photoshop PDFs. The scans can be routed to other work-stations used for the OCR conversion.

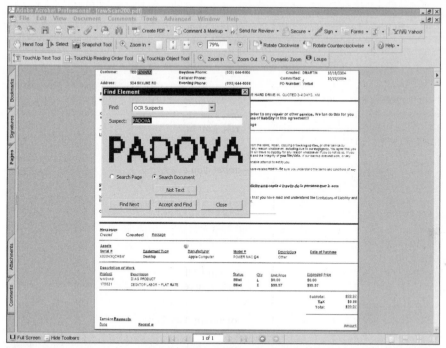

Figure 13-5: Choose Document ⇨ Recognize Text ⇨ Find First OCR Suspect to open the Find Element dialog box where the suspect word appears. You can choose to accept the word and move to the next suspect, or click Next to move to the next suspect.

When you begin a new Acrobat session and want to scan many pages with Recognize Text Using OCR, scanning one or two pages representative of the pages you want to convert and examining the number of suspects in your sample scan is a good idea. If the suspects outnumber the number of correct interpretations, editing the suspect words could take you more time than typing the document in a word processor. At some point the ratio between the number of suspects to correct words can make capturing pages more of a burden than providing you a solution.

If the number of suspect words is extraordinary, you may want to scan another few pages using different settings. For example, increase the image resolution or scan in a different color mode. Change the attributes in the Create PDF From Scanner dialog box or adjust settings in your Acquire plug-in to produce scans more suitable for capturing pages. Run Recognize Text Using OCR and examine the suspects. When a scan results in fewer suspects, you can then go about scanning the remaining pages. In Figure 13-6, I scanned a page at 200 ppi and converted the page with Recognize Text Using OCR. After viewing the number of suspects, I decided to scan the page again with a higher resolution. The results of my OCR suspects with a higher resolution were significantly reduced, as you can see in Figure 13-7.

A graph will display the tonal range of the data to be captured. Graphs can be an extra bonus and helpful when a visual diagram of the tonal ranges shows any drop off or clipping. Graphs are accompanied by controls you can make to change the data to be acquired to capture selected tonal ranges.

Advanced color contral:

Intuitive dialog boxes displaying a color wheel and adjustment provisions for hues and saturation will minimize the time needed in Photoshop for color correction.

Densitometer:

A densitometer for measuring brightness values in composite and separate channels can alleviate guesswork for brightness, contrast, white limit, black limit and color correction.

Color Matching and ICC Profile Management:

'Manyscanners, even some low end models will offer profiles for the devices and also enable you to choose monitor profiles, RGB and in some cases CMYK profiles. Once you set up profiles in Photoshop, you can choose the profiles from within the scanner software. This ability enables you to work toward a total Color Management Model from input to output.

Sharpening:

Sharpening and Unsharp Masking is provided by some vendors that enable the sharpening of the image to be performed on-the-fly during the scan. With more sophisticated software, unsharp masking controls may offer more options than Photoshop's filters.

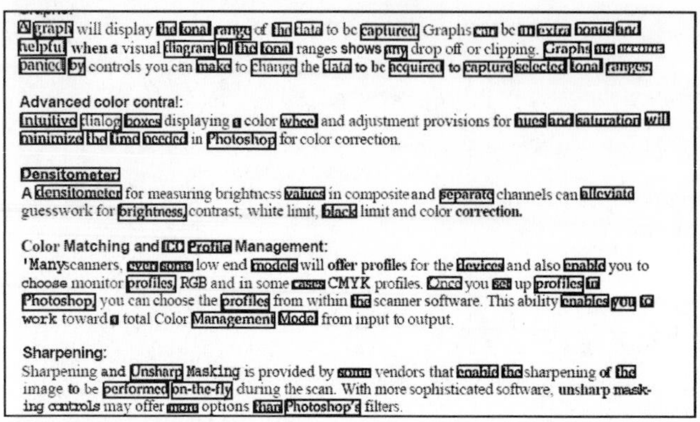

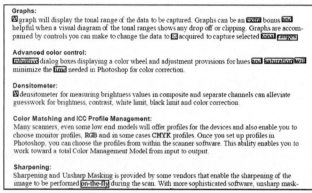

Figure 13-6: I scanned a page using Create PDF From Scanner and converted it with Recognize Text Using OCR. After I chose Document ➪ Recognize Text ➪ Find All OCR Suspects, I determined that the number of suspects made this job too difficult to edit in Acrobat.

Graphs:

A graph will display the tonal range of the data to be captured. Graphs can be an extra bonus and helpful when a visual diagram of the tonal ranges shows any drop off or clipping. Graphs are accompanied by controls you can make to change the data to be acquired to capture selected tonal ranges.

Advanced color control:

Intuitive dialog boxes displaying a color wheel and adjustment provisions for hues and saturation will minimize the time needed in Photoshop for color correction.

Densitometer:

A densitometer for measuring brightness values in composite and separate channels can alleviate guesswork for brightness, contrast, white limit, black limit and color correction.

Color Matching and ICC Profile Management:

Many scanners, even some low end models will offer profiles for the devices and also enable you to choose monitor profiles, RGB and in some cases CMYK profiles. Once you set up profiles in Photoshop, you can choose the profiles from within the scanner software. This ability enables you to work toward a total Color Management Model from input to output.

Sharpening:

Sharpening and Unsharp Masking is provided by some vendors that enable the sharpening of the image to be performed on-the-fly during the scan. With more sophisticated software, unsharp mask-

Figure 13-7: I scanned the same page from Figure 13-6 at a higher resolution and converted it again. Fewer suspects were found and the job of correcting the suspects was more manageable.

Summary

✦ Creating a PDF From Scanner uses TWAIN drivers or Adobe Photoshop Acquire plug-ins.

✦ Properly preparing the scanner and documents for scanning in Acrobat improves the quality of the scans. The scanner platen should be clean, the documents should be straight, and the contrast should be sharp.

✦ When scanning images in Acrobat, use the scanning software to establish resolution, image mode, and brightness controls before scanning. Test your results thoroughly to create a formula that works well for the type of documents you scan.

✦ Workflow automation can be greatly improved by purchasing Adobe's stand-alone product Adobe Acrobat Capture. When using Adobe Acrobat Capture with a scanner supporting a document feeder, the scanning and capturing can be performed with unattended operation.

✦ Acrobat Capture is a stand-alone application for optical character recognition used for converting scanned images into editable text.

✦ Text can be converted and saved as a PDF Formatted Text & Graphics, where you can edit text and change the appearance of the original scan. Text can be converted with Optical Character Recognition and saved using the Searchable Image option, which preserves the original document appearance and adds a text layer behind the image.

✦ OCR suspects are marked when Recognize Text Using OCR does not find an exact word match in its dictionary. Text editing is performed with the TouchUp Text tool on PDF Formatted Text & Graphics documents.

✦   ✦   ✦

Repurposing PDF Documents

PDF documents designed for one purpose, such as for prepress and printing, might need to be repurposed for other output intent such as Web hosting or for copying to CD-ROMs. Rather than going back to the original authoring program and recreating PDFs for each purpose, you can use tools in Acrobat that enable you to downsample file sizes and strip unnecessary content. The resulting documents can then be more efficiently viewed on Web sites or exchanged via e-mail.

In this chapter you learn how to repurpose PDF documents using some Acrobat tools and methods for downsizing file sizes and eliminating content unnecessary for other viewing purposes. In addition, you take a look at automating tasks by creating batch sequences.

Setting Up the Environment

For the purpose of downsizing files and optimizing them for other output circumstances, you don't need to access any special tools. The menu commands offer all the means for repurposing files. Therefore, set up your Acrobat work environment by opening a context menu and selecting Reset Toolbars from the menu options.

Reducing File Sizes

Reducing file sizes often occurs with downsampling images — that is to say, reducing the image resolution of all raster images or compressing images with higher compression options. In addition, you can reduce file sizes by eliminating redundant backgrounds; eliminating objects such as form fields, comments, Bookmarks, and destinations; unembedding fonts; and/or compressing the document structure. You can handle file-size reductions at the time of PDF creation when you control file compression, image sampling, and font embedding for designing PDFs for a specific output purpose. However, if you create PDFs for one purpose such as commercial printing and later want to host the same file on a Web site, you need to either create a new PDF document specific for the new purpose or use Acrobat tools to create smaller file sizes more suited for other output purposes. Fortunately, several means are available to you for squeezing file sizes down and optimizing PDFs for multiple purposes.

Cross-Reference For more information on understanding terms such as *downsampling* and *resampling,* see Chapter 8.

Downsizing cropped images

If you scan a document in Acrobat using the Create PDF From Scanner command, the scanned image is sampled according to settings you apply when scanning pages. After a scan opens in Acrobat you may have a need to crop the scan using tools in Acrobat.

When you use the Crop tool in Acrobat, the cropped image data remain in the file; data are not eliminated. To reduce file sizes when cropping images, choose the File ➪ Save As menu command and save as a TIFF file. After saving the file, open it in Acrobat to convert back to PDF. The result is a document where the cropped area is completely eliminated from the file. Choose File ➪ Save As and overwrite the file to optimize it.

Cross-Reference For more information on cropping PDF documents, see Chapter 12.

Using the Reduce File Size command

In both Acrobat Professional and Acrobat Standard you have a menu command enabling you to reduce file sizes. Open a document and choose File ➪ Reduce File Size. The Reduce File Size dialog box opens as shown in Figure 14-1.

Figure 14-1: Choose File ➪ Reduce File Size to open the Reduce File Size dialog box, where you select options for Acrobat version compatibility.

In the Reduce File Size dialog box you have four options from the pull-down menu for selecting Acrobat compatibility. The default is Acrobat 5 compatibility. If your PDF documents are to be viewed by Acrobat users of version 5 or later, choose the Acrobat 5 compatibility. If all users are using Acrobat 6 or 7 viewers, use Acrobat 6 or 7 compatibility, respectively. Although Acrobat 4 compatibility is an option, there is little need to use the menu choice as Acrobat 4 users can view your Acrobat 5 files without problems if you don't introduce things such as JavaScripts that work only in Acrobat 5 or greater viewers. For simply reducing file sizes, Acrobat 5 compatibility should work fine for all users of earlier versions of Acrobat.

Caution If you want to use many of the new features available in Adobe Reader 7, such as enabling documents for commenting and markup, you must use Acrobat 7 compatibility. For more information on using Adobe Reader with usage rights enabled, see Chapter 4. For information on commenting, see Chapter 15.

After you make the menu selection and click OK, the Save As dialog box opens. Provide a file-name and save the file to disk. As a matter of practice it's a good idea to write a new file to disk in case the file reduction fails and you need to return to the original file to try another method of file reduction.

Using PDF Optimizer (Acrobat Professional only)

In addition to the Reduce File Size command, you can use the PDF Optimizer in Acrobat Professional to reduce file sizes through downsampling images and a variety of other settings that offer options for eliminating unnecessary data. The Reduce File Size command doesn't provide user-definable settings for what data are affected during file reductions. With PDF Optimizer you make the choices from a number of different settings in the PDF Optimizer dialog box for what data are affected during optimization. The PDF Optimizer also offers you an option for analyzing a file so you can see what part of the PDF document occupies higher percentages of memory.

Auditing space usage

The first step you want to perform when optimizing files with the PDF Optimizer is to analyze a file so you can see what content occupies the larger amounts of memory. Analyzing a document and using the PDF Optimizer is handled in the PDF Optimizer dialog box that opens when you choose Advanced ➪ PDF Optimizer. The PDF Optimizer appears as shown in Figure 14-2.

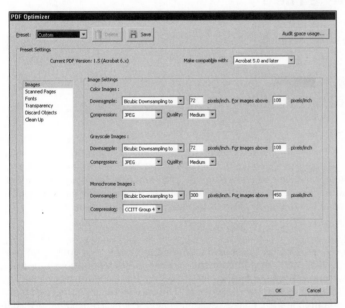

Figure 14-2: Choose Advanced ➪ PDF Optimizer to open the PDF Optimizer dialog box. To analyze a file for the space usage, click the Audit space usage button at the top of the dialog box.

Click the button labeled Audit space usage. Depending on the size and complexity of the document, the analysis can take a little time. When the analysis completes, the dialog box shown in Figure 14-3 opens.

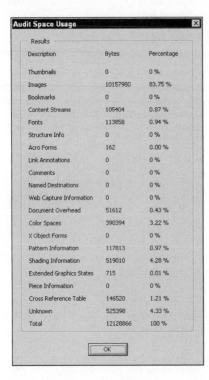

Figure 14-3: After the analysis is completed, the Audit Space Usage dialog box opens, where space usage according to different objects/elements is reported as a percentage of the total space.

In the example shown in the preceding figure, notice most of the document space is used for images (83.75 percent). If the image resolution in this document is higher than images suited for screen viewing at 72 pixels per inch (ppi), then downsampling the images by reducing resolution would compact the file and make it significantly smaller. If you have documents designed for print and want to repurpose the documents for Web viewing, image downsampling is likely to be one of the things you'll want to adjust in the PDF Optimizer.

Optimizing files

Using the PDF Optimizer, you control a number of different attributes that contribute to a document's structure and content. By adjusting the number of different options found in the PDF Optimizer dialog box you have the opportunity to produce documents much smaller than when using the Reduce File size menu command. The options found in the PDF Optimizer include Preset, Make compatible with, Images, Scanned pages, Fonts, Transparency, Discard Objects, and Clean Up, all discussed in the following sections.

Preset

This item appears first in the PDF Optimizer, but it's the last setting you address. When you open the PDF Optimizer, the default is Standard appearing in the pull-down menu. Select

Custom or make changes to any setting and the Save button becomes active. When you click Save, Acrobat prompts you to save your new settings as a preset. After saving, the name you define for the preset is added to the pull-down menu. When you return to the PDF Optimizer in another Acrobat session, you can select from the number of different presets and click the OK button to optimize files with the same settings defined for the respective preset.

If you want to clear a preset from the pull-down menu, select a preset in the menu and click the Delete button.

Make compatible with

From a pull-down menu you select Acrobat compatibility levels. You can make your optimized document compatible with Acrobat 4, 5, 6, and 7. When the need arises to serve users with earlier compatibility files, change the menu command to the desired compatibility level. By default, Acrobat 5 is selected in the menu. If you change from Acrobat 5 to Acrobat 6 or 7, some other attribute settings in the PDF Optimizer change to reflect choices supported by newer versions of Acrobat.

Images

To reduce file size with the PDF Optimizer, use the first set of options found in the left pane; the default Images pane appears as shown in Figure 14-2. You can make choices for downsampling color, grayscale, and bitmap images by typing values in the field boxes for the sampling amounts desired. To the right of the downsampling amount, another field box is used to identify images that are downsampled. This box instructs Acrobat to look for any image above the setting defined in the field box and downsamples the file to the amount supplied in the first field box.

The Images pane offers choices for the downsampling method. The default method is Bicubic Downsampling. Leave the choice for Bicubic Downsampling at the default selection. To learn more about the other methods and what they mean, see Chapter 8.

The Compression pull-down menu offers choices for Retain existing, JPEG, JPEG2000 (an additional setting available when Acrobat 6 and 7 compatibility is selected), and Zip compression. The Retain existing setting honors the original compression used when the PDF was created.

For more information on the JPEG, JPEG2000, and Zip file formats, see Chapter 5.

For either form of JPEG compression you have additional choices for the amount of compression from the Quality pull-down menu. If you choose a JPEG compression and use Minimum for the Quality choice, your images may appear severely degraded. As a general rule, Medium quality results in satisfactory image quality for Web hosting. If you try one setting and the images look too degraded you can return to the original file and apply a different Quality setting; then examine the results.

JPEG compression is a lossy compression scheme, which means that files are compressed with data loss. For Acrobat 4 and 5 compatibility, Zip offers a good choice when you want to maximize image quality. When using Acrobat 6 and 7 compatibility, you can select JPEG2000 for a better compression result and select Lossless from the Quality pull-down menu, which will save all the image data.

Scanned Pages

Click on Scanned Pages in the left pane and the right pane changes, offering options for handling scanned pages. The settings in this pane are intended to handle legacy documents where similar settings were not included in Create PDF From Scanner. If you use Acrobat 7 to scan documents you have the same options available in the Image Settings dialog box opened from the Create PDF From Scanner dialog box.

Cross-Reference   For more information related to the settings in the Scanned Pages pane, see Chapter 13.

Fonts

Fonts won't always appear in a list in the Fonts pane when you click the word Fonts in the PDF Optimizer. Only fonts that are available for unembedding are listed. On the left side of the Fonts pane, fonts are listed that can be unembedded. If no fonts appear in the list, you can move on to the Transparency settings. If fonts are listed in the box in the left side of the pane, select the fonts to unembed and click the Move button adjacent to the right chevron.

In the right box are fonts listed for unembedding. If you want to keep the font embedded, select it in the right box and click the Move button adjacent to the left chevron. To select multiple fonts in either window, press Shift+click to select a list in a contiguous group, or press Ctrl/⌘+click to select fonts in a non-contiguous group.

Transparency

Transparent images and objects can be flattened in Acrobat 7 for all PDF documents created in Acrobat 5 and greater. If you select Acrobat 4 compatibility, transparency is automatically flattened because Acrobat 4 compatibility does not support transparency. When you select all other compatibility versions, you have options for flattening the transparency.

Cross-Reference   For information on using transparency-flattening settings, see Chapter 25.

Discard Objects

Discarding items such as comments, form actions, JavaScript actions, cross references, and thumbnails affects document functionality as you might suspect. If the respective items are eliminated, any PDF interactivity created with these items is also eliminated. If you know that one or any group of these items won't have an effect on the way the repurposed document is viewed or printed, enable the check boxes for the items you want to remove.

Clean Up

Click on Clean Up in the left pane and you find a list of items checked by default that can be used safely without affecting the functionality of your document. Settings such as removing invalid Bookmarks, links, and destinations won't affect the document viewing but removing the unnecessary items helps reduce file size. As a matter of practice, leave the options in this pane at the defaults.

After you make your preferred settings in the PDF Optimizer click the Save button if you want to save the settings as a new preset or click the OK button to start the optimization process.

Redistilling Files

Creating a PostScript file from a PDF document and redistilling with Acrobat Distiller with different Adobe PDF options is something that may not always work. It all depends on the fonts embedded in the file and whether you have fonts installed on your system that are not embedded in a PDF. In other words, it doesn't always work, but in many cases it's usually best to try if using the Reduce File Size or PDF Optimizer doesn't produce a sufficiently smaller file for your output consideration.

Figure 14-4 is a document containing many form fields. If you use the PDF Optimizer to down-sample the document, minimal file reduction is achieved unless you eliminate all the form fields. In its present form, the file size is 5.2MB.

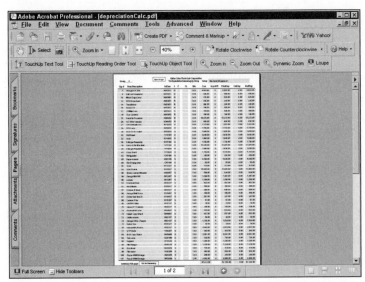

Figure 14-4: One of the 13 pages in a PDF file at 5.2MB is shown with all the form fields populated with data.

Before I discuss downsizing a file, I make a few assumptions when using the redistilling down-sampling method. The first assumption is that after the data are added to the document, the form fields are no longer needed. Second, the final document, complete with the data, is then used for e-mailing, hosting on a hard drive or network server, or hosting on a Web site for users to review. If changes are to be made, the original file is kept stored on a drive for editing purposes. With these assumptions in mind, the task at hand is to keep the data in the file while finding the most efficient means for downsizing the original 5.2MB file.

Because neither the Reduce File Size command nor the PDF Optimizer does the job, the next option is to choose File ➪ Save As and save the file as a PostScript file. After it's in PostScript, open Acrobat Distiller and select an Adobe PDF Setting for the output desired.

Cross-Reference

For information on creating PostScript files from PDF documents, using Acrobat Distiller, and making choices for Adobe PDF Settings, see Chapter 8.

When you print a PostScript file to disk and redistill the file, the form fields are eliminated from the document; however, the form field data are stamped down on the background and all data originally supplied in form fields remain part of the newly created PDF with Acrobat Distiller. In the earlier example where the original file size was 5.2MB, the file optimized with the PDF Optimizer reduced the file size to 3.45MB. The file printed to disk and redistilled in Acrobat Distiller produced a file of 63KB.

Tip

If you have interactive elements in a document such as Bookmarks, form fields, destinations, and so on and want to preserve the interactive elements when redistilling PDFs, realize that all such items are lost in the new file created with Acrobat Distiller. To regain Bookmarks, form fields, and so on, open the original file in Acrobat. Choose Document ➪ Replace Pages. Locate the new file created with Acrobat Distiller in the Select File With New Pages dialog box and replace all pages in the file. Choose File ➪ Save As to write a new optimized file to disk. The new file uses the optimized pages and the old file's interactive elements. You'll see a little increase in the file size due to the interactive elements, but the overall file size will be much smaller in your new file compared to the original file.

Once again, be aware that redistilling files is not always successful; however, in more circumstances than not, I've found the procedure described in this section to be successful when file reduction cannot be successfully accomplished via other means.

Cross-Reference

You can also eliminate form fields while retaining the form data to reduce file sizes by using one of several different plug-ins you can purchase from third-party manufacturers. For a comprehensive list of third-party plug-ins, demonstration versions of the software, and a description for each third-party product, log on to www.pdfstore.com and visit the Planet PDF store. For information related to using Acrobat plug-ins, see Chapter 2.

Batch Processing PDF Files

If you have multiple files that need to be refined for distribution on network servers, Web sites, or CD-ROM, then you'll want to create a batch sequence. *Batch sequences* are a defined series of commands in a specific order that can be run on multiple files. You create the batch sequence from a list of executable functions and determine the commands and order of the sequence.

Batch sequences help you automate tasks in Acrobat that might otherwise take considerable time to manually apply a common set of commands on many different files. After you develop one or more sequences, you can run the sequence(s) on selected PDF files, a folder of PDF files, or multiple folders of PDF files.

Tasks such as setting opening views of PDF documents, adding document descriptions, adding page numbers, or running the PDF Optimizer can be applied to multiple files you might want to distribute on CD-ROM or on Web sites. Before distributing files you can run a batch sequence as a final step in your production workflow to be sure all files have common attributes.

Creating a batch sequence

To create a new sequence, choose Advanced ➪ Batch Processing. The Batch Sequences dialog box opens as shown in Figure 14-5. The dialog box lists several sequences predefined for you when you install Acrobat. From the list in the dialog box you can run a sequence, edit one of the listed sequences, rename a sequence, or delete any one or more sequences from the list. The first button in the dialog box is used to create a new sequence where you choose what commands you want to run from a list in other dialog boxes.

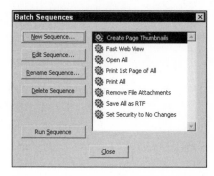

Figure 14-5: Choose Advanced ➪ Batch Processing to open the Batch Sequences dialog box.

Click New Sequence and the Name Sequence dialog box shown in Figure 14-6 opens. The first step in creating a batch sequence is to provide a name for the sequence. The name supplied in the dialog box ultimately is added to the list in the Batch Sequence window. When you want to run the sequence you can open the Batch Sequences dialog box, select any one of the sequences you added to the list, and click the Run Sequence button.

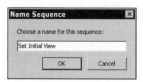

Figure 14-6: The first step in creating a new sequence is naming the sequence. You add the names of new sequences to the list in the Batch Sequences dialog box.

Type a name in the field box and click OK. The next dialog box that opens is the Batch Edit Sequence - Set Initial View dialog box shown in Figure 14-7. Three items are listed in the dialog box. The next step (the Batch Sequence dialog box actually lists this step as the first step in creating a sequence) is to click the Select Commands button. After you make choices for the commands added to the sequence, you are returned to this dialog box to make choices for items 2 and 3 where you identify the input location of files and the destination (output) location.

The Edit Sequence dialog box opens where you make choices for the commands added to your new sequence. From the scrollable list on the left side of the dialog box, select a command and click the Add button to move the command to the right side of the dialog box.

If you want more than one set of commands applied to your sequence, select a command and click the Add button; then select additional commands and click Add. In this example I added commands for setting the Initial View and adding a document Description as shown in Figure 14-8.

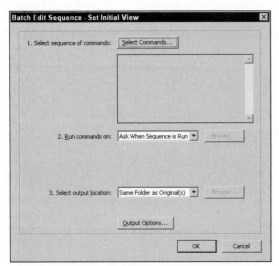

Figure 14-7: The Batch Edit Sequence - Set Initial View dialog box opens after you provide a name for a new sequence. Click the Select Commands button to choose the commands executed in the sequence.

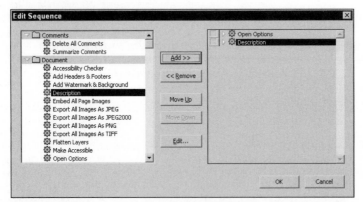

Figure 14-8: Select a command in the left window and click the Add button. Continue adding commands that you want run as part of your new sequence.

After the commands are added to the right window, you can make attribute choices for each command. From those commands in the right window, either select the command or double-click on the name to open dialog boxes where you make attribute choices. In Figure 14-9 I adjusted the Set Open Options dialog box to open PDF files in a Page Only view and Fit Page View with the Document Title displayed.

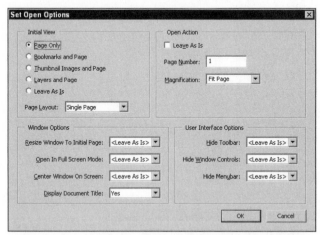

Figure 14-9: Initial View options are selected in the Set Open Options dialog box. To open the dialog box, double-click on the command in the right window in the Edit Sequence dialog box.

The settings applied for the Initial View are applied globally to files when you run the sequence. In some cases you'll want to supply data when each file is processed in a sequence to add unique settings for individual files. For example, the document Description fields for Subject and Author might be consistent among a group of PDF documents in a single folder; however, the Title and Keywords fields are unique for each file processed. In this example you can double-click on the Description item to open the Document Summary dialog box and add the common data to the fields that remain consistent across all PDFs processed when the sequence is run. In Figure 14-10 the common data are supplied in the Subject and Author fields while the Title and Keywords fields are left blank.

In order to supply data individually to each file processed in the sequence, you need to set a flag in the Edit Sequence dialog box so each file pauses during processing and the Document Summary dialog box opens where you add the unique data. After adding the common data, exit the Document Summary dialog box to return to the Edit Batch Sequence dialog box. Click in the square adjacent to the command name to display a mini menu icon. This toggle sets the flag for Acrobat to pause on each file processed for user-supplied data. When you add the data and click OK, Acrobat continues running the sequence and pauses at the next file processed where you again add data and click OK, and so on. You can also see each attribute setting for any command by clicking the right-pointing arrow to open the settings list associated with a command and review the settings. This feature is particularly helpful if you create a sequence and in some later Acrobat session want to review the settings before you run the sequence. In Figure 14-11 you can see the flag set for the Description command and the list of attributes assigned to the command in the expanded list.

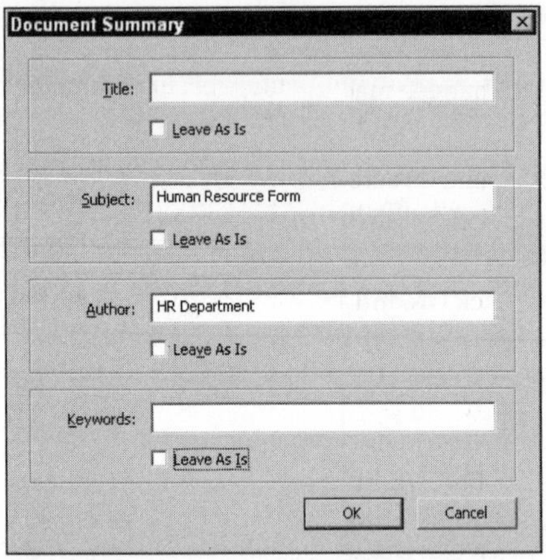

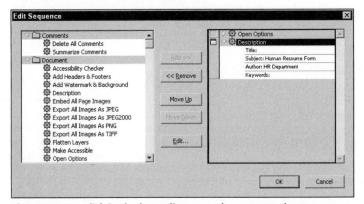

Figure 14-10: Add the data that are common in the PDFs processed when the sequence is run, and leave the fields requiring unique data blank.

Figure 14-11: Click in the box adjacent to the command name to set the flag to pause processing where user-supplied data are added to a command. To review the attribute choices, open a list by clicking the right-pointing arrow.

After adding all commands that you want to execute in a sequence, click OK and you are returned to the Edit Batch Sequence dialog box. The remaining items to contend with are choices you make for selecting the location of the files to be processed and where the processed files are to be saved. The default for item 2 (Run commands on) is Ask When Sequence is Run. This option prompts you as you run each new sequence to select files or folders in a dialog box. If you have a predetermined location of files you can choose other options such as Selected Files, Selected Folders, or run the sequence on files open in Acrobat at the time you choose to run the sequence. If you intend to use the sequence many times in other Acrobat sessions, leave the default choice at Ask When Sequence is Run. This way you'll be prompted to identify files or folders as you run a sequence.

The output for files can be a Specific Folder, the Same Folder as Original(s) processed in the sequence, or you can choose to be prompted when the sequence is run. In addition, a menu choice is available if you don't want to save the changes made. This choice is made for files processed from among the open files in Acrobat.

If you choose to write the processed files to the same directory where the original files reside, you can set up Output Options for adding a prefix or suffix to filenames so the original files won't be overwritten.

When you set all the attributes for a sequence, click OK and the new sequence is added to the list in the Batch Sequences dialog box.

Setting output options

When you click the Output Options button in the Batch Edit Sequence dialog box, you'll find choices for filenaming and output formats as well as file optimization. Select the Output Options check box when you create a new sequence in the Batch Edit Sequence dialog box and the Output Options dialog box opens, as shown in Figure 14-12.

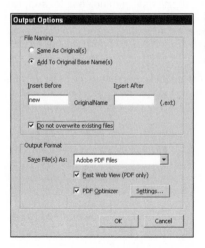

Figure 14-12: Output Options offer you choices for naming the processed files as well as saving in different formats and optimizing files with the PDF Optimizer.

You can add a suffix or prefix to filenames by clicking the Add To Original Base Name(s) button and editing the field boxes for Insert Before and Insert After. If you enter data in the Insert After field box the data are added before the filename extension. Selecting the box for Do not overwrite existing files ensures you that you won't inadvertently overwrite the original files.

The Save File(s) As pull-down menu offers choices for the file formats to be exported. The default is Adobe PDF. If you want to save files in text formats (Word, RTF, text only, and so on), you can make the choice for the text format from the pull-down menu options. Additionally, PostScript, EPS, image formats, HTML, and XML formats are available. You'll note that the Save As options in the Output Format Save File(s) pull-down menu offers the same options as when you choose the File ➪ Save As command. The one option not available to you when saving files with a batch sequence is saving to your Version Cue workspace.

For more information on using Version Cue, see Chapter 9.

Tip   If you want to optimize a number of files in a batch sequence, create a new sequence and add Save Optimized As to your sequence list in the Edit Sequence dialog box. After adding the sequence, double-click on it in the right pane and the PDF Optimizer opens. Select a preset or set the attributes in the PDF Optimizer. Click OK and run the sequence on a folder of files.

Running sequences

Presuming you created a sequence and added the new sequence, you can open the Batch Sequence dialog box by choosing Advanced ➪ Batch Processing and selecting the sequence you want to run. Click the Run Sequence button in the Batch Sequence dialog box and the Run Sequence Confirmation dialog box opens. A list of commands appears in the dialog box where you can review the settings for each command by clicking the right-pointing arrow to display the settings as discussed earlier in this chapter. If all the settings are appropriate for the sequence you want to run, click OK and the Select Files to Process dialog box opens. You can select a file or a contiguous or non-contiguous group of files by using the Shift plus click or Ctrl/⌘+Shift and click a folder, or a group of folders for processing. Click the Select button, and the sequence runs. If you created a sequence to toggle open a dialog box for supplying unique data for each file, the dialog boxes open. Make changes in any dialog boxes, click the OK buttons, and the sequence continues. Files are saved according to the choices you made in the Output Options dialog box or the choice made from the Select output location pull-down menu in the Batch Edit Sequence dialog box.

After running a sequence, examine the files to ensure all files are created with the options you expect them to have. If there are any errors and you saved the new set of files without overwriting the original set, you can edit the sequence and run the edited version on the original files.

Editing sequences

If you create a sequence for one purpose and want to modify the sequence for another processing venture, you can edit the attributes of a command, add new commands, or delete commands from the original sequence. To edit a sequence, choose Advanced ➪ Batch Processing. In the Batch Sequences dialog box select the sequence you want to edit and click the Edit Sequence button. The Edit Batch Sequences dialog box opens.

In order to edit the commands, add new commands, or delete commands, you first need to click the Select Commands button. The Edit Sequence dialog box opens where you can add new commands, or edit existing commands, following the information in the earlier section on creating sequences.

If you want to delete a sequence and all the commands associated with the sequence, click the Delete Sequence button in the Batch Sequences dialog box. This action removes the sequence from the list. If you delete commands in the Edit Sequence dialog box and keep a modified version of a sequence listed in the Batch Sequences dialog box, you may want to rename a sequence to more closely relate to the modified version. Click the Rename Sequence button in the Batch Sequence dialog box and edit the name in the Name Sequence dialog box.

Creating custom sequences

The batch sequences you create are chosen from the list of commands in the Edit Sequence dialog box. If you want to add a command that doesn't exist in the list in the Edit Sequence dialog box, you can create custom sequences from commands you add with JavaScripts.

JavaScripts offer you an infinite number of possibilities for automating commands and sequences applied to a group of PDF documents. As an example, suppose you want to add a Stamp comment to an assorted collection of PDFs designed to be documents in draft form. After the files have been stamped with a Draft icon from the Stamp comment, you disperse the documents, collect feedback, and use another batch sequence to delete all comments from the documents. The sequence for deleting comments is a preset installed with Acrobat. Adding Stamp comments, however, is something you need to do with a JavaScript. To see how you handle adding a JavaScript to a batch sequence, and in particular, adding a Stamp comment to a collection of PDF files, follow these steps:

STEPS: Creating a JavaScript Batch Sequence

1. **Create a new batch sequence.** Choose Advanced ➪ Batch Processing. In the Batch Sequences dialog box, select New Sequence. When the Name Sequence dialog box opens, type a name for the sequence. In this example I use Add Stamp. Click OK.

2. **Select Execute JavaScript and add it to the list of sequences to be executed.** In the Batch Edit Sequence dialog box, click on Select Commands to open the Edit Sequence dialog box. In the Edit Sequence dialog box, select Execute JavaScript from the list on the left and click the Add button to move the command to the right window.

3. **Add the JavaScript code to execute the action.** Select the command in the right pane and click the Edit button(or double-click on the command). The JavaScript Editor dialog box opens. In the JavaScript Editor, type the following code (Note: The same code is shown as it should appear in the JavaScript Editor in Figure 14-13):

```
/* Add a Stamp to Page 1 in a File */
var annot = this.addAnnot
({
   page:0,
   type: "Stamp",
   name: "Draft",
   popupOpen: false,
   rect: [400, 725, 580, 760],
contents: "This is a draft document",
AP: "Draft"
})
```

Note The coordinates for the position of the note are set for a standard US Letter size page (8.5 × 11 inches, portrait view). If you run the sequence on documents with different size pages or orientation, the results may not show the stamp on a page.

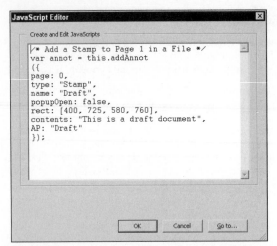

Figure 14-13: Type the code in the JavaScript Editor dialog box.

4. **Save the JavaScript.** Click OK in the JavaScript Editor dialog box. Click OK in the Edit Sequence dialog box to return to the Edit Batch Sequence dialog box. The script is saved when you exit the JavaScript Editor dialog box.

5. **Set the Output Options.** Leave Run commands on at the default for Ask When Sequence is Run. In the Select output location pull-down menu, select the option you want to use for the saved files location. If you want to be prompted at the time the sequence is run, select Ask When Sequence is Run. Click OK in the Edit Batch Sequence dialog box and the sequence is added to the list of Batch Sequences.

6. **Run the sequence.** Select the Add Stamp sequence in the Batch Sequences dialog box and click on Run Sequence. (Note if you closed the Batch Sequences dialog box after the last step, choose Advanced ➪ Batch Processing to reopen the dialog box.)

7. **Examine the results.** Select a single file to process when the Select Files to Process dialog box opens. You should see a Stamp comment in the top-right corner of the document page. Double-click the Stamp icon to open the pop-up note window and observe the note contents as shown in Figure 14-14.

Cross-Reference   For more information on creating stamps and using pop-up note windows, see Chapter 16.

The preceding steps create a Stamp comment (Line 2) at the coordinates (Line 8) — note that the page size where the stamps are added is a standard US Letter 8.5 × 11 inches in portrait view. The note pop-up window is closed by default (Line 7), and the content of the note pop-up is *This is a draft document* (Line 9). You can change the position of the note by editing the coordinates in Line 8, change the contents in Line 9, or change the stamp type in Line 10. The code can be easily modified or you can copy and paste the code in the JavaScript Editor if you want to create other similar sequences.

Cross-Reference   For more information on writing JavaScripts, see Chapter 29.

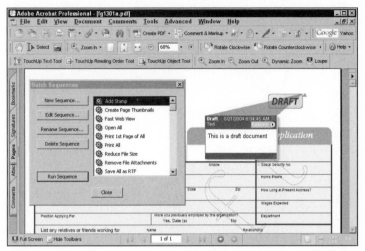

Figure 14-14: The Stamp comment is added to the first page of all documents processed with the Add Stamp routine created in the JavaScript Editor.

Summary

✦ File sizes can be reduced with the Reduce File Size menu command. If you're cropping image files in Acrobat, save the cropped image to an image format; then open the file in Acrobat to convert back to PDF.

✦ The PDF Optimizer is used to reduce file sizes and eliminate unnecessary data in PDF files. PDF Optimizer can often reduce file sizes more than when using the Reduce File Size command.

✦ Selecting options in the Discard Objects pane in the PDF Optimizer other than the default options can interfere with the PDF functionality. Care must be exercised in selecting options to prevent potential problems.

✦ In some cases, saving a PDF file to disk and redistilling with Acrobat Distiller can reduce file sizes. Redistillation can be used to stamp down data fields when form fields are no longer required.

✦ Batch sequences help you automate processing multiple PDF documents. From a standard set of sequence options you can create batch sequences for a limited number of actions. When custom options are needed, you can add JavaScripts for processing files with custom settings.

✦   ✦   ✦

PDF Interactivity

Review and Markup

Adobe Acrobat is the perfect tool for workgroup collaboration. With sophisticated tool sets and a number of menu options, Acrobat provides you the ability to comment and mark up PDF documents and share your annotations with users dynamically on Web sites or through file exchanges on servers or via e-mail. For example, you can mark up documents, send your comments to a group of colleagues, ask for return comments, and track the review history. Where PDF documents may be too large to efficiently exchange files in e-mails, you can export comments to smaller data files or summarize them and create new PDF documents from comment summaries that can be sent to members of your workgroup. You can compare documents for changes, for comment status, and for errors and omissions. And now in Acrobat 7.0 Professional, you can add usage rights to documents so Adobe Reader users can participate in reviews.

The review and comment tools and methods in Acrobat are extraordinary in number. Because Acrobat provides all these great tools doesn't necessarily mean you'll use all of them in your daily work activities. The best way to decide what tools work best for you and your colleagues is to review this chapter thoroughly and pick and choose the tools you favor and the features in review and markup that work best in your environment. In this chapter you learn how to use all the comment tools, and compare documents for reviewing purposes.

All the tools and features discussed in this chapter are related to workflow environments. Regardless of what industry you work in, the many features related to review and comment and comparing documents can be applied to virtually all environments with two or more individuals collaborating on common projects.

This chapter deals exclusively with non-layered PDF documents. Comments can be added to layered PDF documents. For a description of how Acrobat treats comments applied to layered PDFs, see Chapter 19.

Setting Up the Review and Comment Environment

You may be a user who adds comments infrequently with a few comment tools located in the Commenting toolbar, and you may not have much need for the Drawing Markup tools. However, to decide what tools work best in your workflow, you might want to add all the toolbars for review and markup to the Toolbar Well and look over all the tools available in your viewer.

To set up the review and comment work environment, open a context menu on the Toolbar Well and select Commenting. Return to the menu and select Drawing Markups (Acrobat Professional only). Finally, select the Properties bar from the context menu.

Some of the tools in the Commenting and Drawing Markup toolbars contain pull-down menus where other tools are found. At the bottom of the menu is a command to expand the toolbar. On the Commenting toolbar, open a pull-down menu by clicking on the down arrow adjacent to the Highlighter tool to show the Highlighting toolbar and select Show Highlighting Toolbar. Open similar toolbars by clicking on down arrows and selecting the Expand This Button command for Attach a File as a Comment, and the Drawing Toolbar within the Line tool. Open a context menu on the Toolbar Well and select Dock All Toolbars. After docking toolbars, your Toolbar Well should look similar to Figure 15-1.

Figure 15-1: To begin a review and comment session, add commenting tools and expand toolbars.

Notice that the tools are grouped together in logical collections. In a real-world scenario you might only use tools from a single group and not need to load all the tools in the Toolbar Well. If you work on a small monitor, you can see how expanding all the tools and the Comments pane can eat up a lot of screen real estate very quickly. If the view of your pages in the Document pane is too small to comfortably annotate files, close the less frequently used tools to open up more space in the Document pane.

Cross-Reference   Additional comment tools include the Measuring tools. These tools are often used with engineering and CAD drawings. For more information about the Measuring tools, see Chapter 19.

Setting Commenting Preferences

Acrobat provides an elaborate set of preference options that enable you to control comment views and behavior. As you draw comments on PDF pages you may see pop-up windows, connector lines across a page, changes in page views, and a host of other strange behaviors that might confuse you. Before you begin a commenting session, you should familiarize yourself with the comment preferences and plan to return to the preference settings several times to completely understand how you control comment behavior in Acrobat.

Open the preference settings by pressing Ctrl/⌘+K or choosing Edit ➪ Preferences (Windows) or Acrobat ➪ Preferences (Macintosh). In the left pane select Commenting. In the right pane you'll see a long list of preference settings as shown in Figure 15-2. Take a moment to review these settings before you begin a commenting session.

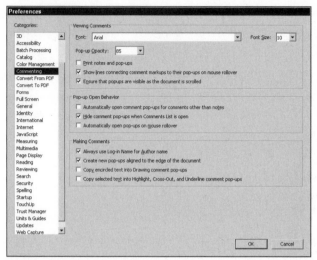

Figure 15-2: Open the Comment Preferences by pressing Ctrl/⌘+K or choosing Edit ➪ Preferences. When the Preferences dialog box opens, select Commenting in the left pane.

- ✦ **Font:** The comment tools are used to mark up text and create icons, symbols, and graphic objects on pages. Most of the comment tools have associated pop-up notes where you type remarks in a note window. By default the font used for the note text is Arial. To change the font, select another font from the pull-down menu. All fonts loaded in your system are available from the menu choices. The fonts you use are not embedded in the file. If you exchange PDFs containing comment notes with other users, the fonts default to another user's preference settings.

- ✦ **Font Size:** Font point sizes range from 4 points to 144 points. You can type a number between these values in the field box or select one from the preset point sizes from the pull-down menu. Changing font size applies to note popup windows you see on your computer. If you change font size and share the file with other users, fonts appear in sizes set by individual user preferences.

- ✦ **Pop-up Opacity:** A pop-up note background color is white. At 100 percent opacity the note is opaque and hides underlying page data. You can change the opacity of pop-up notes for a transparent view so the background data can be seen when a pop-up note window is open. You adjust the level of transparency by typing a value in the field box or selecting one from the preset choices in the pull-down menu. The default is 85 percent.

- ✦ **Print notes and pop-ups:** Enabling this check box prints the pop-up note contents for all pop-up note windows regardless of whether they are opened or collapsed.

✦ **Show lines connecting comment markups to their pop-ups on mouse rollover:** When you roll the mouse pointer over a comment markup (such as highlighting or a note icon), the shaded connector line between the comment and the open pop-up window appears (see Figure 15-3).

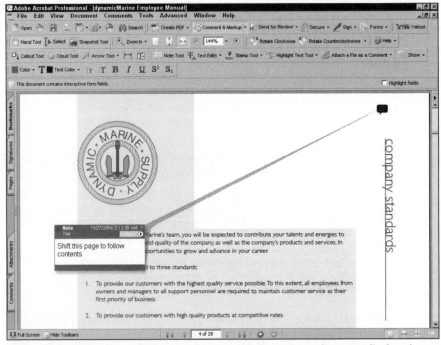

Figure 15-3: When the preference setting is enabled, connector lines are displayed on a mouseover between the comment and the associated note window.

✦ **Ensure that pop-ups are visible as the document is scrolled:** If a comment note extends beyond one page in a continuous page view, the note is visible when scrolling pages.

✦ **Automatically open comment pop-ups for comments other than notes:** As you create comments with drawing tools, the Text Box tool, or Pencil tool, the pop-up note windows are collapsed by default. If you want a pop-up note window opened and ready to accept type when creating comments with these tools, check the box.

✦ **Hide comment pop-ups when Comments List is opened:** The Comments List is contained in the Comments pane. When you open the Comments pane, the list shows expanded comment notes with the content displayed in the pane. To hide the pop-ups in the Document pane when the Comments pane is opened, enable the check box. If you set this item as a default, you can expand comments in the Comments pane by clicking icons to see the content of the pop-ups.

✦ **Automatically open pop-ups on mouse rollover:** Pop-up note windows can be opened or closed. Double-clicking a collapsed pop-up note window opens the window. If you want to have a pop-up note window open automatically as the cursor is placed over a comment icon, select this check box.

✦ **Always use Log-in Name for Author name:** Another set of preferences appears when you click on Identity in the left pane. The Login Name specified in the Identity preferences is used for the author name on all comments when this check box is enabled. If you are a single user on a workstation, setting the Identity preferences and enabling this check box saves you time creating comments when you want to add your name as the author name.

✦ **Create new pop-ups aligned to the edge of the document:** By default the top-left corner of a pop-up note window is aligned to the top-left corner of the comment icon. If you enable this check box, no matter where you create the note icon, the pop-up notes are aligned to the right edge of the document.

✦ **Copy encircled text into Drawing comment pop-ups:** When proofreading a document and using the Text Edit tools you might strike through text, highlight text, or mark it for replacement, or you may use drawing tools to encircle passages of text. When you select the text to be edited or encircle text with a drawing tool, the text selection is automatically added to the note pop-up window when this option is selected. You might use this option to show the author of the PDF document how the old text appears and follow up with your recommendations to change the text. In essence, the PDF author can see a before/after comparison.

✦ **Copy selected text into Highlight, Cross-Out, and Underline comment pop-ups:** This enables the text selected with tools in the Highlighting toolbar to automatically appear in the pop-up note window.

As you can see, there are many different preference settings. How you want to view comments and the methods used for review and comment is influenced by the options you set in the Commenting preferences. Take some time to play with these settings as you use the tools discussed in this chapter.

Using Commenting Tools

Users of either Acrobat Professional or Acrobat Standard can access the Commenting tools. Acrobat refers to these tools simply as Commenting tools; however, there are two other sets of commenting tools that include Drawing Markup and Measuring tools.

The Commenting tools are intended for use by anyone reviewing and marking up documents. Much like you might use a highlighter on paper documents, the commenting tools enable you to electronically comment and mark up PDF documents. A variety of tools with different icon symbols offer you an extensive library of tools that can help you facilitate a review process.

Most comment tools, among any group, have a symbol or icon that appears where the comment is created. They also have a note pop-up window where you add text to clarify a meaning associated with the mark you add to a document. These pop-up note windows have identical attributes. How you manage note pop-ups and change the properties works the same regardless of the comment mark you create, with the exception of the Callout and Text Box tools. I first explain how to use the Note tool in this section. All the features described for the Note tool are the same as when handling note pop-up windows for all the comment tools that accommodate note pop-ups.

Using the Note tool

 The Note tool is the most common commenting tool used in Acrobat. To create a comment note, select the Note tool in the Commenting toolbar and drag open a note window. When you release the mouse button, the note pop-up aligns to the top-left corner of the note icon.

Tip   You can also add notes to a page via menu commands. To add a note to a page, choose Comments ⇨ Add a Note or select the Hand tool and open a context menu on a page. From the menu choices, select Add Note.

Alternately, you can click without dragging. When you release the mouse button, a pop-up note window is created at a fixed size according to your monitor resolution. The higher you set your monitor resolution the smaller the pop-up note window appears. On an 800×600 display, the window size defaults to 360×266 pixels. In Figure 15-4, I drew a comment note with the Note tool in the center of the page. On the left side of the page, I clicked the Note tool. Notice the center note is aligned with the note icon whereas the icon on the left is linked to the note pop-up on the far right side of the page.

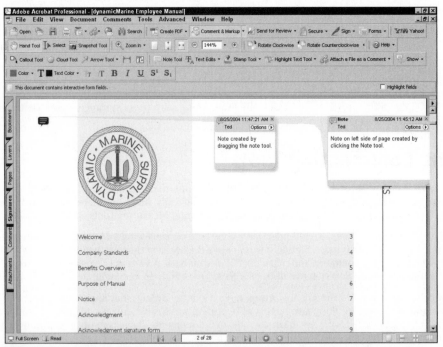

Figure 15-4: When clicking and dragging the Note tool, the pop-up note aligns to the top-left corner of the note icon. When clicking with the Note tool, a pop-up window is created at a fixed size away from the icon.

To add text to the pop-up note, begin typing. Acrobat places an I-beam cursor inside the pop-up note window immediately after creating the note. For font selection and font sizing, you need to address the Comment preference settings discussed earlier in this chapter.

Managing notes

The color of a note pop-up and the note icon is yellow by default. At the top of the note pop-up the title bar is colored yellow and the area where you add the contents is white. The title bar contains information supplied by Acrobat that includes the subject of the note, the author, and the date and time the note is created. You can move a note pop-up independently of the note icon by clicking and dragging the title bar.

Cross-Reference

The Subject of a note by default is titled *Note*. The default Author name is derived from either your computer log-on name or your Identity depending on how your preferences are established. For information on how to change the Subject and Author in the title bar, see "Note tool properties" later in this chapter.

You delete note pop-up windows and note icons either by selecting the note icon and pressing the Delete/Backspace or Del key on your keyboard or through a context menu selection. If you use a keystroke to delete a note, you must be certain to select the icon; then press the Delete/Backspace or Del key. Selecting the title bar in a note pop-up and using the same keys won't delete the note.

To resize a note pop-up window grab the lower-right corner of the window and drag in or out to resize smaller or larger, respectively. Note pop-ups containing more text that can be viewed in the current window size use elevator bars so you can scroll the window much like you would use when viewing pages in the Document pane. Only vertical elevator bars are shown in the pop-up windows. As you type text in the window, text wraps to the horizontal width, thereby eliminating a need for horizontal scroll bars. As you size a note pop-up window horizontally, the text rewraps to conform to the horizontal width.

You open context menus from either the note icon or the note pop-up window. When opening a context menu from the note pop-up window, you have two choices: open the context menu from the title bar or open the context menu from inside the note window (below the title bar). Depending on where you open the context menu, the menu selections are different. Opening a context menu from the title bar or from the note icon shows identical menu options. You can also use the Options menu to open the same menu as when opening a context menu inside the note window. Click the right-pointing arrow adjacent to Options and the menu opens.

In Figure 15-5, I opened a context menu from the title bar on a pop-up note window. The menu options are the same as if I had opened the context menu from the note icon. In Figure 15-6, I opened the context menu from inside the note pop-up window. Depending on edits you make in the note window and whether you have text selected, menu options change. In Figure 15-7, text was edited in the note window that adds the Undo command to the context menu. Additionally, text is selected that adds several other commands for cut, copy, and adding the selected text to a dictionary. In both menus you can select Delete Comment to remove the note pop-up menu and the note icon.

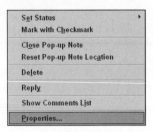

Figure 15-5: This context menu is opened from the note pop-up window title bar. From the menu options select Delete Comment to remove the note icon and the note pop-up menu.

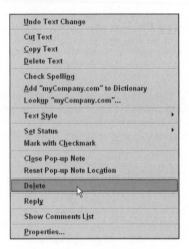

Figure 15-6: When you open a context menu from the note pop-up window below the title bar, menu options change. If you select text in the note window, additional commands are added to the context menu.

The context menus are similar and most commands existing in the smaller menu are the same as those found in the larger menu. If two notes are selected, additional menu commands appear in a context menu. From menu options you have a command to Group notes.

To group notes together, you need to select the Hand tool and Ctrl/Command+click each note icon to include in a selection. From a context menu opened on any note title icon and select Group. If you open the Comments list by clicking on the Comments tab, you see the note icon change for grouped notes as shown in Figure 15-7.

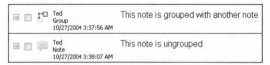

Figure 15-7: Grouped notes appear in the Comments list with a different icon than ungrouped notes.

In Figure 15-6 you see a long list of menu commands. Let's take a look at these commands; the same commands found in the context menu shown in Figure 15-5 operate the same way.

✦ **Undo Text Change:** When you type text in the pop-up menu and delete it, you can select the Undo Text Change command to regain your text. Deleting a comment note can also be undone. However, because deleting a comment note eliminates an opportunity to open a context menu from the note pop-up window, you need to choose Edit ➪ Undo. If text was added to a pop-up note window and you delete the note, choosing Edit ➪ Undo returns the note and the text in the note pop-up window.

✦ **Redo Text Change:** If you type a block of text and select Undo, you can later select Redo and bring the text back.

✦ **Cut Text/Copy Text:** These items work as you might assume from using any text editor or word processor. The commands relate to typing text in the note pop-up window. You can also highlight text and use key modifiers (Ctrl/⌘+C for Copy; Ctrl/⌘+X for Cut; Ctrl/⌘+V for Paste).

✦ **Delete Text:** Select text and choose Delete Text. The selected text is deleted.

✦ **Check Spelling:** When you select Check Spelling in the note pop-up menu the Check Spelling dialog box opens, as shown in Figure 15-8. When the dialog box opens, click the Start button and Acrobat checks the spelling for all the text typed in the note pop-up. When Acrobat finds a word it thinks is misspelled, the word is highlighted and a list of suggestions that closely match the spelling are shown in the lower window. Select a word with the correct spelling and click the Change button.

Figure 15-8: Select Check Spelling from a context menu and the Check Spelling dialog box opens. Click Start and Acrobat checks the spelling for the note pop-up contents. You can choose a replacement for the misspelled word(s) from a list of suggestions in the dialog box.

✦ **Add "........." to Dictionary:** Select text and the selected text appears within the quote marks. When you choose the menu command the selected text is added to your custom dictionary used when spell checking. If the word already exists in your custom dictionary, the menu command appears as Remove "..." from Dictionary.

✦ **Remove "..." from Dictionary:** This menu item is active only when you have a word selected in the note pop-up window and that note is contained in your custom dictionary. It's a nifty little feature in Acrobat 7.0. Because Acrobat automatically spell-checks text you type in the comment note pop-up window by matching your words to those found in its dictionary, words not found by Acrobat as a match in its dictionary are underlined in red with a wavy line like you might see in programs such as Microsoft

Word. If you want to have Acrobat flag you whenever you type a specific word, remove that word from the dictionary. Then Acrobat displays the word with a red underline each time you use it.

When would you use this feature? Assume for a moment that you want to use a generic reference to users as opposed to a masculine or feminine reference. Highlight the word *he* or *she* and open a context menu from the note pop-up window. Select Remove "*he*" from Dictionary. Each time you type the word *he*, Acrobat underlines the word because it can't find a match in the dictionary. When you review your notes, you might substitute *s/he* for the word *he*.

✦ **Look Up "...":** The default menu command is *Look Up Definition*. When a word is selected, the menu command changes to Look Up *selected word*. For example, if you select a word like *reply*, the menu command changes to Look Up "reply." Select the menu command and your Web browser launches and the Dictionary.com Web site opens in your Web browser where the word is searched and a definition is displayed on the Web page.

Cross-Reference

For more information on looking up a definition and the Dictionary.com Web site, see Chapter 10.

✦ **Text Style:** From a submenu select from (Bold/Italic/Underline/Superscript/Subscript/Clear Formatting). Select any one of the formatting options to apply to selected text. You can combine format changes by selecting text and a format option, and then return to the context menu and select another option, and so on.

✦ **Set Status:** You as a PDF author may share a document for review with others. As comments are collected you may decide to determine a status for comments among your workgroup. You may want to mark a comment as *Accepted, Rejected,* or *Cancelled,* or mark a comment thread as *Completed.* You select these options from the submenu that appears when you select the Set Status command. By default, a status is set to *None* when you begin a session. A second submenu appears for Migration where you have choices for None, Not Confirmed, and Confirmed.

✦ **Mark with Checkmark:** Whereas the Set Status items are communicated to others, a check mark you add to a comment is for your own purposes. You can mark a comment as checked to denote any comments that need attention, or that are completed and require no further annotation. Check marks are visible in the Comments pane and can be toggled on or off in the pane as well as the context menu. Check marks can be added to comments with or without your participation in a review session. You can choose to have your comments sorted by those with checkmarks and those comments without check marks.

✦ **Close Pop-up Note:** Closes the note pop-up window.

✦ **Reset Pop-up Note Location:** If you move a note pop-up window, selecting this menu command returns the note pop-up to the default position.

✦ **Delete:** Deletes the comment pop-up note and the note icon.

✦ **Reply:** When participating in a review, you select the Reply command to reply to comments made from other users. A new window opens in which you type a reply message. From the pop-up bar you can review a thread and click the Reply button to send your comments to others via e-mail, to a network server, or to a Web-hosted server.

Cross-Reference

For more information on comment reviews, see Chapter 16.

✦ **Show Comments List:** Selecting this item opens the Comments pane. Any comments in the open document are expanded in a list view in the Comments pane. When the Comments pane is open, this option toggles to Hide Comments List.

✦ **Properties:** Opens the Properties dialog box.

✦ **Text Style:** From this submenu, choose Bold, Underline, Superscript, Subscript, or a command to Create Formatting. You apply text styles to selected words in the Note popup window.

Note tool properties

Each comment created from either the Commenting tools or the Drawing Markup tools has properties that you can change in a properties dialog box. Properties changes are generally applied to note pop-up windows and icon shapes for a particular tool. In addition, a variety of properties are specific to different tools that offer you many options for viewing and displaying comments and tracking the history of the comments made on a document.

With respect to note pop-ups and those properties assigned to the Note tool, you have choices for changing the default color, opacity, author name, and a few other options. Keep in mind that not all property changes are contained in the properties dialog box. Attributes such as font selection and point sizes are globally applied to note pop-ups in the Comment preferences.

Cross-Reference

For information about Commenting preferences, see "Setting Commenting Preferences" at the beginning of this chapter.

You open the properties dialog box from a context menu. Be certain to place the cursor on a pop-up note title bar or the note icon before opening a context menu. Select Properties from the menu choices and the Note Properties dialog box shown in Figure 15-9 opens.

Note

When you create a comment with any of the Comment tools, the Hand tool is automatically selected when you release the mouse button. You can select a comment mark/icon or pop-up note with the Hand tool or the Select Object tool. You can use either tool to open a context menu where you can select Properties from the menu options. However, other menu items vary between the two context menus. For information regarding menu options from context menus opened with the Select Object tool, see the discussion on Drawing Markup tools later in this chapter.

Tip

To keep a comment tool selected without returning to the Hand tool after creating a comment, check the box in the Properties bar for Keep tool selected.

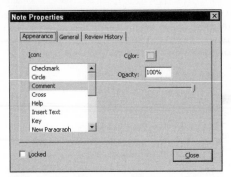

Figure 15-9: Open a context menu from a pop-up note title bar and select Properties.

The Note Properties dialog box contains three tabs. Select a tab and make choices for the items contained in the dialog box. For pop-up note properties the items you can change include the following:

✦ **Appearance:** Options in the Appearance tab relate to the note icon appearances and the pop-up note window appearance.

• **Icon:** From the scrollable list select an item that changes the Note icon appearance. Selections you make in this list are dynamic and change the appearance of the icon in the Document pane as you click on a name in the list. If you move the Note Properties dialog box out of the view of the note icon, you can see the appearance changes as you make selections in the list. Fifteen different icons are available to choose from, as shown in Figure 15-10.

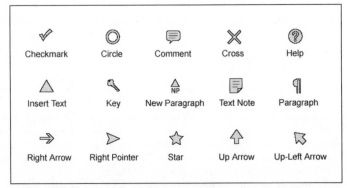

Figure 15-10: You select icon shapes from the Icon list in the Appearance tab in the Note Properties dialog box. You can choose from 15 different shapes.

- **Color:** Click the color swatch to open the pop-up color palette shown in Figure 15-11. You select preset colors from the swatches in the palette. You add custom colors by selecting the Other Color item in the palette, which opens the system color palette. In the system color palette, make color choices and the new custom color is applied to the note.

Figure 15-11: Click the color swatch to select from preset colors or select Other Color to open the system color palette where you select custom colors.

Changing color in the Appearance properties affects both the color of the note icon and the pop-up note title bar. If you mark up and review documents in workgroups, different colors assigned to different participants can help you ascertain at a glance which participant made a given comment.

- **Opacity:** Global opacity settings are applied in the Comment Preferences dialog box. You can override the default opacity setting in the Appearance properties for any given note pop-up window.

- **Locked:** Select the Locked check box to lock a note. When notes are locked, the position of the note icon is fixed to the Document pane and cannot be moved when you leave the Note Properties dialog box. All other options in the Note Properties dialog box are grayed out, preventing you from making any further attribute changes. If you lock a note, you can move the pop-up window and resize it. The note contents however, are locked and no changes to the text in the pop-up note window can be made. If you want to make changes to the properties or the pop-up note contents, return to the Note Properties dialog box and uncheck the Locked check box.

✦ **General:** Click the General tab to make changes for items appearing in the note pop-up title bar. Two editable fields are available as shown in Figure 15-12. The changes you make in the Author and Subject fields are dynamic and are reflected in the Document pane when you edit a field and tab to the next field. You can see the changes you make here before leaving the Note Properties dialog box.

- **Author:** The Author name is supplied by default according to how you set your Comment preferences. If you use the Identity preferences, the Author name is supplied from the information added in the Identity preferences (see "Setting Commenting Preferences" earlier in this chapter). If you don't use Identity for the Author title, the name is derived from your computer log-on name. You might see names like Owner, Administrator, or a specific name you used in setting up your operating system.

  If you want to change the Author name and override the preferences, select the General tab and edit the Author name. The name edited in the General preferences is applied to the selected note. All other notes are left undisturbed.

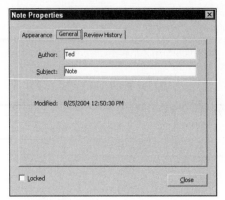

Figure 15-12: Make changes to the Author name and the pop-up note Subject in the General preferences.

- **Subject:** By default, the Subject of a note is titled *Note* appearing in the top-left corner of the pop-up note title bar. You can change the subject in the General properties by typing text in the Subject line. You can add long text descriptions for the Subject; however, the text remains on a single line in the pop-up note properties dialog box. Text won't scroll to a second line. The amount of text shown for the Subject field relates to the horizontal width of the note window. As you expand the width, more text is visible in the title bar if you add a long Subject name. As you size down the width, text is clipped to accommodate the note size.

- **Modified:** This item is informational and supplied automatically by Acrobat from your system clock. The field is not editable. The readout displays the date and time the note was modified.

✦ **Review History:** The Review History lists all comment and status changes in a scrollable list. The list is informational and not editable.

Cross-Reference   For more information on review history, Chapter 16.

After making changes in the Note Properties dialog box, click the Close button to apply the changes. Clicking on the close box or pressing the Esc key also applies the changes you make in the Note properties dialog box.

Tip   The Properties dialog boxes for all Comment tools are dynamic and enable you to work in the Document pane or the dialog box when the dialog is open. Make adjustments to properties and move the dialog box out of the way of your view of an object you edit. The updates are made when you tab out of fields in the dialog box. You have complete access to menu commands and other tools while the Properties dialog box remains open.

Using the Properties bar

If you set up your work environment to view the Properties bar while working in a review session, you can address several properties options from it. Options for note color, icon type, and fixed opacity changes in 20% increments are accessible without opening the Properties dialog box.

As shown in Figure 15-13, from a pull-down menu on the Properties bar, you can select the different note icons when the Note tool is selected. Clicking the color swatch opens the same color selection pop-up window as it does in the Properties dialog box. The checkerboard to the right of the icon menu is the opacity selection. Click the down arrow to see a list of preset opacity choices.

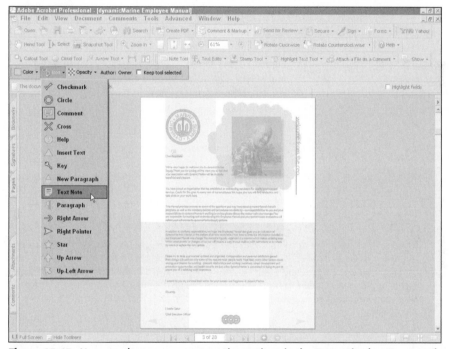

Figure 15-13: You can change some properties options in the Properties bar. To open the toolbar, open a context menu on the Toolbar Well and select Properties bar.

Notice the Author name appears in the Properties bar; however, the name is not editable and you need to open the Properties dialog box to make an author name change. The last item in the Properties bar is a check box. Click this box if you want to keep the Note tool selected. Disabling the check box causes the Hand tool to be selected each time a note is created. When you select a different comment tool from either the basic Commenting toolbar or the Advanced Commenting toolbar, the Properties bar changes to reflect choices available for the selected tool.

Tip   With some tools you see a *More* button on the Properties bar. Clicking on More opens the Properties dialog box.

Adding a note to a page

You can add notes to a page either inside a page in the Document pane or outside the page boundary. Use the Note tool to add notes or add a note while browsing pages with the Hand tool selected. Open a context menu with the Hand tool and the menu options include Add Note, as shown in Figure 15-14.

The new note is added at the cursor position. You can use the Hand tool to browse pages by selecting the Next Page and Previous Page context menu commands and add a note when you want to comment on a page without changing tools.

The Add Note command is also available from the Comments menu. Choose Comments ➪ Add a Note and the note is added to the center of the page.

Figure 15-14: Open a context menu with the Hand tool and select Add Note from the menu options. The note is added at the cursor position.

Tip   If you're proofreading a document and you think terms might be expressed better using different words and you want to find word definitions or access a thesaurus, open a context menu with the Hand tool and select Add Note. Type a word in the note pop-up window and highlight the word. Open a context menu from the highlighted word and select LookUp. The Dictionary.com Web site opens in your Web browser, with the word definition on the open Web page.

Working with the Text Edits tools

The Text Edits tools can be acquired from several menu locations. When you load the Commenting toolbar, the Text Edits tools are all located in a pull-down menu adjacent to the Indicate Text Edits tool in the toolbar. Open the Comment & Markup Task Button pull-down menu and choose Commenting Tools ➪ Indicate Text Edits Tool from a submenu. You can also choose Tools ➪ Commenting ➪ Text Edits ➪ Indicate Text Edits Tool and see the tools in a submenu. Another way to access the tools is by choosing Comments ➪ Text Edits ➪ Indicate Text Edits Tool and select the tools from another submenu. All of these menus offer you a set of tools, shown in Figure 15-15, used for marking text with comments. These tools can be used for any kind of review session; however, they were designed to be used for comments that you want to export to source documents that originated in programs such as Microsoft Word and Autodesk AutoCAD. To export comments to MS Word you need to be running Acrobat on Windows XP using Microsoft Office XP.

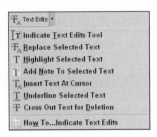

Figure 15-15: The Text Edits tools appear in several pull-down menus.

To use the tools, you first select either the Select tool or the Indicate Text Edits tool and click or select text in the Document pane. If you select the Indicate Text Edits tool, a dialog box opens as shown in Figure 15-16. Note that when you first open the Text Edits pull-down menu from any menu command or the Indicate Text Edits tool, all the tools are grayed out and inaccessible. You first need to use the Indicate Text Edits tool to select text or select text with the select tool, and then the other tools become active.

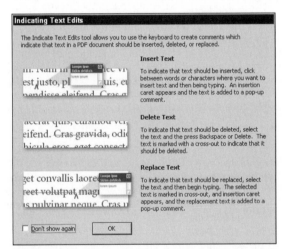

Figure 15-16: When you first start to use the Text Edits tools, a dialog box opens providing you information on using the tools. You can dismiss the dialog box from future editing sessions by selecting the Don't Show Again check box.

As you move to text you want to mark, drag the cursor to highlight text to be annotated. When text is selected, return to the Indicate Text Edits tool and open the pull-down menu. Select one of the Text Edits tools shown in Figure 15-15.

✦ **Indicate Text Edits:** You'll notice the Indicate Text Edits tool looks like the Select tool. In actuality, Acrobat selects the Select tool when you make this menu choice. The procedure for adding any text edit is to first select this menu command or select the Select tool. You move the cursor to the document page and either click or click and drag through a block of text. Once the cursor appears inside a text block or text is selected, you then use one of the other menu commands to mark the text for commenting.

Note　All the tools below the Indicate Text Edit tool are grayed out unless you either select this menu command or select the Select tool and click or click and drag in a text block. Selecting either option without a cursor insertion on the document page or without highlighting text does not enable any of the Text Edit tools.

✦ **Replace Selected Text:** Use this tool to mark text for replacement. The line appears similar to the Cross Out Text for Deletion mark, but the caret at the end of the mark distinguishes this tool from the aforementioned one. A note pop-up window opens where you can add comments. The note contents do not include the text marked for replacement.

✦ **Highlight Selected Text:** This tool works like the Highlight tool and similar to a yellow highlighter you might use on paper documents. Select the Highlight tool and drag across a block of text. The text is highlighted and a note pop-up window enables you to add comments.

✦ **Add Note to Selected Text:** Select a word, a paragraph, or a body of text. When you release the mouse button a note pop-up window opens in which you add a comment. Selecting the text does not include the selected text in the pop-up note.

✦ **Insert Text At Cursor:** Select the menu command and move the cursor to the document page. The cursor appearance changes to an I-beam, informing you that text can be selected. Rather than selecting text, most often you'll find clicking the cursor at a specific location to be the method used with this tool. The intent is to suggest to a reviewer that text needs to be inserted at the cursor position. When you click on a document page, a caret is marked on the page at the insertion location and a note pop-up window opens. Type the text to be inserted in the note pop-up.

✦ **Underline Selected Text:** Use this tool to underline the selected text. A note pop-up window opens where you can add comments.

✦ **Cross Out Text for Deletion:** Select text and the text mark appears as a strikethrough. The symbol is used to mark text that needs to be deleted. A note pop-up window opens where you can add comments.

✦ **How To . . . Indicate Text Edits:** The How To pane opens with the Text Edits help page in view.

Notice that the item for Insert Text At Cursor is not among the menu selections. In order to open a context menu with choices for text edits, you need to select at least one character in a text block. Clicking the cursor without selecting text won't produce the same context menu choices.

Highlighting tools

Adjacent to the Stamp tool in the Commenting toolbar is the Highlighter Text tool. From the pull-down menu you find the Cross-Out Text tool and the Underline Text tool. These tools perform the same functions as their counterparts found among the Text Edits tools. Use these tools when marking documents for comment reviews in Acrobat and where you don't have a need to export the comments made with these tools to MS Word or AutoCAD.

Differences Between Text Edit and Highlighting Tools

You may wonder why Acrobat offers you two toolbars with what appears to be identical tools performing the same functions. Although the appearances of the markups you make on PDF documents are the same for the Highlighting tools as the respective Text Edit tools, they are intended for different purposes.

When you make edits with the Text Edit tools, you can export comments directly to Microsoft Word (Windows XP and Word 2002 only) and Autodesk AutoCAD. If you export the Text Edit comments to Word and accept changes, Word treats the comments as though you had created them in Word. For example, marking text for deletion and accepting changes deletes the marked text.

Although you can use the Text Edit tools to mark up PDFs not intended for export to Word, the intent for using the tools is when working between Word or AutoCAD and Acrobat. If you use either the Text Edit tools or the Highlighting tools on PDFs for comments designed for use in Acrobat, there is no difference between the markups.

Note that exporting comments to Word documents from comments made with the Text Edit tools is only available in Acrobat Professional.

Using the Stamp tool

The Stamp tool is part of the Commenting tools, but it differs greatly from the other tools found in the Commenting toolbar. Rather than mark data on a PDF page and add notes to the marks, Stamps enable you to apply icons of your own choosing to express statements about a document's status or add custom icons and symbols for communicating messages. Stamps offer you a wide range of flexibility for marking documents similar to analog stamps you might use for stamping approvals, drafts, confidentiality, and so on. You can use one of a number of different icons supplied by Acrobat when you install the program, or you can create your own custom icons tailored to your workflow or company needs.

 Cross-Reference All the features related to the Stamp tool, including creating your own custom stamps, are treated in Adobe Reader the same as Acrobat Standard and Acrobat Professional when PDFs contain usage rights for Adobe Reader. To learn more about usage rights with Adobe Reader, see Chapter 3.

Whether you use a preset stamp provided by Acrobat or create a custom stamp, each stamp has an associated note pop-up window where you add comments. You select stamps from menu options in the Stamp pull-down menu where stamps are organized by categories. Add a stamp to a page by clicking the Stamp tool after selecting a stamp from a category; or you can click and drag the Stamp tool to size the icon. After creating a stamp, you access Stamp properties by opening a context menu and selecting Properties.

Selecting stamps

Using a stamp begins with selecting from among many different stamp images found in submenus from the Stamp tool pull-down menu. Click the down-pointing arrow and the first three menu commands list categories for stamps installed with Acrobat. Selecting one of these three menu items opens a submenu where you select specific stamps from the respective category, as shown in Figure 15-17.

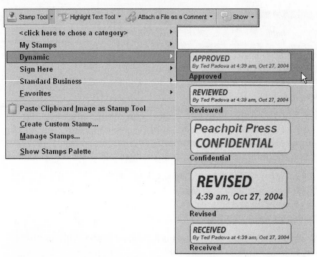

Figure 15-17: Select the pull-down menu from the Stamp tool and select a Stamp category. Select a subcategory and slide the mouse over to the Stamp name. Release the mouse button and the selection becomes the new default stamp.

Adding a stamp to a page

The stamp name you select in the menu becomes the new default stamp. When you click the Stamp tool or click and drag open a rectangle with the Stamp tool, the default stamp is added to the document page. Stamps are created by default with the pop-up note window collapsed unless you enable the Comment preferences for *Automatically open comment pop-ups for comments other than notes*. To open the pop-up note window, double-click the mouse button on the stamp image. The pop-up note opens and appears the same as other pop-up note windows for other Comment tools.

If you want to resize a stamp after creating it on a page, select the Hand tool and click the stamp icon to select it. Move the cursor to a corner handle, shown in Figure 15-18, and drag in or out to resize the stamp.

> **Note**   Stamps are always proportionately sized when you drag any one of the corner handles. You don't need to drag handles with a modifier key to proportionately size the image.

Acrobat offers you an assortment of stamps you can select from the category submenus in the Stamp tool pull-down menu. These stamps are created for general office uses and you'll find many common stamp types among the sets. The three categories of stamps and their respective types and icons are shown in Figure 15-19.

You should think of these stamps as a starter set and use them for some traditional office markups when the need arises. The real power of stamps, however, lies in creating custom stamps where you can use virtually any illustration or photo image.

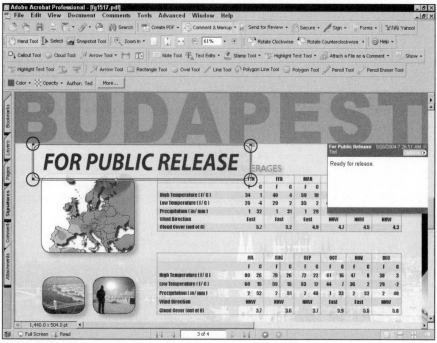

Figure 15-18: To resize a stamp, select the Hand tool and click the stamp icon. Drag a corner handle on the selection marquee and drag in or out to size the icon.

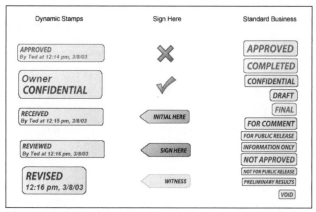

Figure 15-19: Choose stamps from three categories. The stamps installed with Acrobat are general office stamps used in many traditional workflows.

Resizing Stamps

The stamps you find installed by Acrobat are all vector art images created in Adobe Illustrator. When you resize vector art images, the display quality remains the same no matter how large you size the stamp.

When creating custom stamps you can use a program like Adobe Illustrator and use vector art for your stamp design. You can also create custom stamps from Photoshop files. These files, however, are raster art. If you size raster artwork above a 100% actual view size, you can see distortion in your stamp image.

If you plan on using photographs or other artwork created in Adobe Photoshop, be certain to anticipate the largest size you might need to size up a stamp icon. When you view a Photoshop image created at 72 ppi (pixels per inch), the largest size you can see on your monitor without distortion is a 100% actual size view. If you size the stamp up 200% or more you'll notice image degradation and the image is likely to display jagged edges.

If you anticipate sizing stamps up to a 400% view, for example, create your stamps from Photoshop images at 288 ppi. This calculation is determined by taking 72 ppi and multiplying times 4 (72 X 4 = 288). Hence, when you size the stamp up to 400%, the actual size view is 72 ppi. As size increases, resolution decreases.

If you plan your work and anticipate the size you might use for custom stamps created from Photoshop files, you can avoid any display problems when viewing files in Acrobat. The sizing issues only have to do with physically sizing a stamp image containing raster artwork. If you use zoom tools in Acrobat, the stamps appear at the same size no matter what zoom level you view a document page.

Stamp properties

You change stamp properties in the Stamp Properties dialog box. You have the same options in the Stamp Properties as those found in the Note Properties dialog box with one exception. In the Note Properties dialog box you make choices for the icon appearance from a list in the dialog box. Because stamps have appearances determined before you create the stamp, no options are available for changing properties for the stamp image. The color options in the Stamp Properties dialog box apply to comment notes and not the stamp images. Opacity settings, however, can be applied to the stamp image.

If you want to change the appearance of a stamp, you need to delete the stamp and create a new stamp after selecting the category and stamp name from the category submenu. You delete stamps by opening a context menu and selecting Delete, or selecting the stamp icon and pressing the Backspace/Delete or Del key.

Creating custom stamps

You add custom stamps from the Stamp tool pull-down menu. Click the down arrow on the menu and select Create Custom Stamp or choose Tools ➪ Commenting ➪ Stamps ➪ Create Custom Stamp, or from the Comment & Markup Task Button choose Commenting Tools ➪ Stamps ➪ Create Custom Stamp. The Select Image for Custom Stamp dialog box opens. Click the Browse button in the dialog box and select a file to import. The Select Image for Custom Stamp dialog box displays a thumbnail preview for your new stamp as shown in Figure 15-20.

Figure 15-20: Select Create Custom Stamp from the Stamp tool pull-down menu. Click Browse and select an image to use for your new custom stamp.

When you first create a custom stamp in any Acrobat viewer, the Select Image for Create Stamp dialog box is empty. The scroll window is used for PDF documents that have multiple pages. Only one stamp image can be selected in the dialog box to add to your stamp library.

Among the different file formats supported for creating custom stamps, you find the following listed in the Open dialog box appearing after you click the Browse button:

✦ **PDF:** All PDF documents can be used for Stamp icons; however, only single pages can be imported as a stamp. PDFs containing transparency are supported. Any PDF document imported as a custom stamp can have opacity applied in the Stamp Properties dialog box.

✦ **Autodesk AutoCAD:** AutoCAD drawings can be selected for use as a custom stamp. When you select an AutoCAD .dwg file, the file is converted to PDF and added to the Select Image for Custom Stamp dialog box.

✦ **BMP (Bitmap):** You can import 1-bit line art to 24-bit color images saved as BMP as a custom stamp. You can adjust BMP files for opacity in the Stamp Properties dialog box.

✦ **Compuserve GIF:** GIF files, including transparent GIFs, are supported. You can adjust GIF files for opacity in the Stamp Properties dialog box.

✦ **HTML:** Documents you convert with the From Web Page command or the Create PDF from Web Page tool can be converted to PDF and added as a custom stamp.

✦ **JPEG/JPEG2000:** JPEG files are supported with the same options as GIFs and BMP files mentioned earlier.

✦ **Microsoft Access/Office/Project/Publisher/Visio:** All Microsoft products supporting the PDFMaker are converted to PDF and can be added as custom stamps.

✦ **PCX:** PCX files are supported. The file attributes are the same as those found with BMP and GIF mentioned earlier.

✦ **PICT (Macintosh only):** PICT (Picture Format) files from Mac OS can be imported. The attributes are the same as those applied to BMP and GIF images.

✦ **PNG:** PNG files and files saved as interlaced PNG are supported. Interlacing is not applied to the image once imported in Acrobat. The file attributes are the same as those found with BMP and GIF mentioned earlier.

✦ **PostScript/EPS:** PostScript files you might use to distill with Acrobat Distiller and files saved as EPS can be converted to PDF and used as custom stamps.

✦ **TIFF:** TIFF files are supported. The file attributes are the same as those found with BMP and GIF mentioned earlier.

Cross-Reference
For more information on converting all the file types listed here to PDF, see Chapter 7.

Note
Although several file formats are supported for importing layered files, the layers are flattened when imported as custom stamps. Transparency is preserved with these file types, but you can't have stamps applied to different layers in Acrobat.

Cross-Reference
For information regarding comments and layered PDFs, see Chapter 17.

After selecting one of the supported file types, click the Select button in the Open dialog box. Acrobat returns you to the Select Image for Custom Stamp dialog box where you can see a preview of the image imported as your new stamp. In Figure 15-20, I used a PDF saved from Adobe Illustrator CS for a new stamp.

The last step in creating a new stamp is to supply a name for the category and stamp. When you click OK in the Select Image for Custom Stamp dialog box the Create Custom Stamp dialog box opens as shown in Figure 15-21. Type text in the Category field box for a new Category name. If you have several categories added to your stamps files, the names appear listed in the Category pull-down menu. You can select a menu item and the stamp is added to that category. When you first visit the Create Custom Stamp dialog box, the text in the Category field box reads *<click here to choose a category>*. Highlight the text and type a name for your first category.

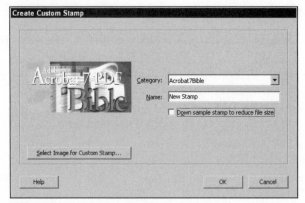

Figure 15-21: Type a name for the Category and a name for the stamp in the Name field box.

The Name field box defaults at *New Stamp.* Delete the text and type a more descriptive name for your new stamp. As you add stamps, you can add new stamps to the same category. When you have multiple custom stamps within a category, the category name is added to the Stamp tool pull-down menu and a submenu lists all the stamp names for that category.

The check box for *Downsample stamp to reduce file size* is checked by default. If you want to size image resolution down, leave the check box enabled. If you want to preserve the original resolution, remove the check mark.

Cross-Reference

For more information on the effects of resizing stamps without sufficient resolution, see the sidebar "Resizing Stamps" earlier in this chapter.

If you decide to change your mind or want to alter the stamp image, click the *Select Image for Custom Stamp* button and the Select Image for Custom Stamp dialog box reopens. You can click the Browse button and select a new image for the custom stamp.

When finished setting attributes for the category name, the stamp name, and the image downsampling, click OK and the category and stamp are added to your Stamps pull-down menu as shown in Figure 15-22. In this example I used Acrobat7Bible as a new category name and added a single stamp to the category that I named BibleCover. Notice in Figure 15-22 the name of the stamp appears below the stamp icon.

Figure 15-22: After creating a custom stamp, the category is added to the Stamp pull-down menu and a submenu displays all custom stamps added to the category.

To use the stamp, open the Stamp tool pull-down menu and select your category name. Acrobat automatically adds the category to the menu. Select the stamp name from the submenu and your new stamp is loaded in the Stamp tool. Click or click and drag with the Stamp tool and the new stamp is added to the document page. If you want to adjust properties such as opacity, open a context menu and choose your options. If you want to add a note, double-click the stamp icon and a pop-up note is opened.

Tip

If you aren't in a review and markup session and you don't have the Commenting tools open, you can apply a stamp from the top-level menus. Open the Commenting & Markup Task Button pull-down menu and choose Commenting Tools ⇨ Stamps ⇨ Create Custom Stamp. The submenu lists your custom stamp categories. Select a category and select a stamp from another submenu.

Appending stamps to a new category

After creating a custom stamp and adding a new category, the next time you open the Create Custom Stamp dialog box you have a choice for adding a new category or appending a new stamp to your existing category. When you open the Create Custom Stamp dialog box, open the pull-down menu for Category and select your stamp category to add a stamp to the same category. If you want to create another category, type a new name in the Category field box. Follow the procedures in the preceding section for adding a stamp.

You can also append stamps by using page templates. In earlier versions of Acrobat, you created a custom stamp by creating a PDF document, making a page template of a page, and supplying the category name in the Document Properties dialog box. When you create a custom stamp in Acrobat 6 or 7, Acrobat creates a PDF file, adds a page template, and supplies the category name in the Description pane in the Document Properties dialog box. This series of events is transparent to you when creating custom stamps in Acrobat viewers 6.0 and above.

If you want to add a number of stamp icons to an existing library you can open the PDF file and use the Create PDF From File or Insert Pages command to insert pages. Navigate to all newly inserted pages and choose Advanced ⇨ Forms ⇨ Page Templates. Add a page template for each appended image. When finished, save the file. When you return to the Stamp tool, you can import the newly appended stamps.

Cross-Reference   For more information on creating page templates, see Chapter 29.

Creating dynamic stamps (Acrobat Professional only)

Among the stamp categories you find in the Stamp pull-down menu is the Dynamic category. Dynamic stamps use a JavaScript to retrieve identity and operating system information from your computer and place the results in a field box. These stamps are dynamic because the data changes according to changes made to your identify preferences and system information such as the time and date.

The first thing you want to check out is your Identity preferences. Open the Preferences dialog box (Ctrl/⌘+K) and click Identity in the left pane. The right pane changes to display the options shown in Figure 15-23.

Type text in the field boxes to fill in your personal identity information.

Identity	
Login Name:	Owner
Name:	Ted Padova
Title:	Author
Organization Name:	Wiley Publishing
Organizational Unit:	Manuscript Development
Email Address:	ted@west.net

Your identity information is used with comments, reviews, and digital signatures. Information entered here is secure and not transmitted beyond this application without your knowledge.

Figure 15-23: Open the Preferences dialog box and click Identity to access the Identity preferences. Fill in the field boxes with your unique identifying information.

Finding the dynamic stamps files

The best way to create your own dynamic custom stamp is to copy a script and paste it into your own custom stamp design. Unless you know a lot about programming JavaScript, this method will work well for you. In order to copy an existing script, you need to locate the files containing scripts.

Acrobat keeps the default stamps files nested in folders in a specific location. Depending on your operating system, the directory path is different. On Windows open the ENU folder inside the Stamps folder using the following directory path: C:\Program Files\Adobe\Acrobat 7.0\ Acrobat\plug_ins\Annotations\Stamps\ENU.

On the Macintosh you need to open the Applications folder on your boot drive. Select Adobe Acrobat 7.0 Professional and open a context menu (Control+click). From the menu choices select Show Package Contents. A single folder appears named Contents. Open the Contents folder and open the Plug-ins folder. Search for Comments.acroplugin and open the folder. Find the Stamps folder and open it. You'll arrive at the ENU folder. Open ENU and you see the six default stamps files.

On either system you find Dynamic.pdf appearing inside the ENU folder. To keep this file accessible for future editing sessions where you might want to create custom dynamic stamps, copy the file to another location on your hard drive you can easily find. To follow the steps in the next session, copy and paste this file to a convenient folder location.

Creating a custom dynamic stamp

To completely understand the process for creating dynamic custom stamps, try working through the steps in this section. You should have a copy of the Dynamic stamps in a convenient location on your hard drive and you need to be in Acrobat Professional to follow the steps. You should also have a document compatible with the file types listed in the section "Creating Custom Stamps" earlier in this chapter. For your stamp design, use a document you create in Adobe Illustrator, Adobe Photoshop, or other program that you use and export the file to PDF.

STEPS: Creating custom dynamic stamps (Acrobat Pro only)

1. **Open the Dynamic.pdf document containing dynamic stamp designs.** Open the file you copied from the ENU folder and saved to another location.

2. **Copy a form field.** Press R on your keyboard to access the Select Object tool (note you must have *Use single key accelerators to access tools* checked in the General preferences pane). There are six pages in the Dynamic.pdf file. You can scroll pages and select any field. When you select the Select Object tool, the fields appear on the page as shown in Figure 15-24. Click on a field and choose Edit ⇨ Copy.

3. **Paste the field into your custom stamp design.** Close the Dynamic.pdf file by clicking on the close button or press Ctrl/⌘+W. Open your stamp design in Acrobat. Be certain the Select Object tool is active and choose Edit ⇨ Paste. You can click and drag the field box to the desired location. Choose File ⇨ Save As and save your file, overwriting the previous save to optimize the file. In Figure 15-25, I pasted a field copied from the Revised dynamic stamp.

Cross-Reference   For information on using Save As and overwriting PDF files, see Chapter 9.

Figure 15-24: Select the Select Object tool and click on a field on one of the six pages in the Dynamic.pdf file.

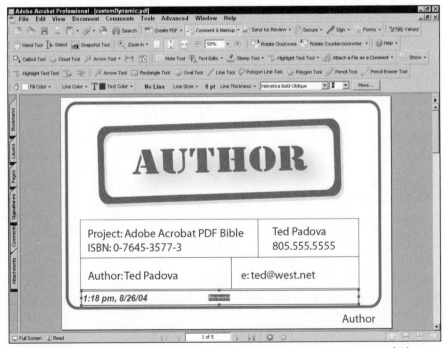

Figure 15-25: Paste the field copied from a Dynamic stamp into your custom design.

4. **Add a category name for your stamps.** Unlike creating custom stamps from menu commands where you add a category and stamp name from within Acrobat, your dynamic stamps need to be copied to the Stamps\ENU folder. The name for the category is derived from the Document Title. To add a Document Title, choose File ➪ Document Properties. Click on the Description tab and type a name in the Title field you want to use for your category name as shown in Figure 15-26. Save your edits and quit Acrobat.

Cross-Reference

To learn more about Document Descriptions, see Chapter 5.

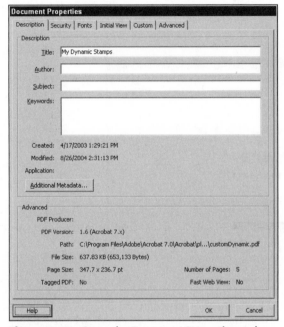

Figure 15-26: Open the Document Properties and type a name for your category in the Title field of the Document Description.

5. **Copy the PDF file to the Stamps\ENU folder.** Copy the PDF file to the proper folder. On Windows open the ENU folder inside the Stamps folder using the following directory path: C:\Program Files\Adobe\Acrobat 7.0\Acrobat\plug_ins\Annotations\ Stamps\ENU.

On the Macintosh open the Contents folder after expanding the application package and open the Comments.acroplugin\Stamps \ENU folder.

Copy the PDF file to the ENU folder.

Note

The name of your PDF document is incidental as the Category name is supplied from the Document Title information.

6. **Add a name for your stamp.** Once your PDF file is copied to the correct folder, the category appears in the Stamp pull-down menu. You can edit the name for your stamp in the Create Custom Stamp dialog box. To open the dialog box, launch Acrobat and select Manage Stamps from the Stamp tool pull-down menu. The Manage Custom Stamps dialog box opens as shown in Figure 15-27. Select the stamp listed under your new category and click Edit. In the Name field edit the stamp name as you want it to appear in your new category submenu. Click OK and you are returned to the Manage Custom Stamps dialog box. Click OK again and you're ready to use the new dynamic custom stamp.

Note You are not required to have a document open in the Document pane while adding and editing custom stamps.

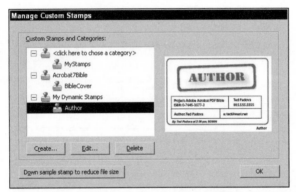

Figure 15-27: Select a stamp to edit and click the Edit button.

7. **Use your new dynamic custom stamp.** Open a PDF file and select your new stamp from the Stamps pull-down menu. The cursor is loaded with the stamp when you select the stamp in the submenu. Click in the document and you should see the text field containing information derived from the text field script, as shown in Figure 15-28.

Managing stamps

Acrobat offers you various options for handling stamps and making them easily accessible. The menu commands below the stamp categories in the Stamp tool pull-down menu offer menu choices for managing stamps where you can create new stamps, edit stamps, and append and delete them. To open the Manage Custom Stamps dialog box, select Manage Stamps from the Stamp tool pull-down menu.

Dynamic data

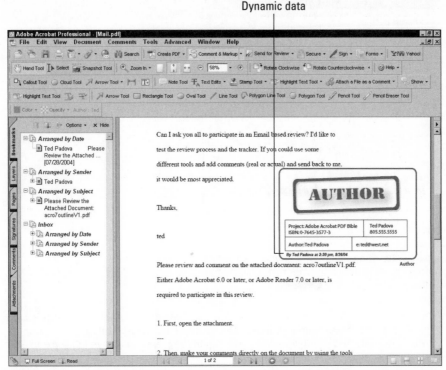

Figure 15-28: Your custom stamp is dynamic and retrieves data from your Identity preferences and your system clock.

Click the Create button shown in Figure 15-27 to create new stamps. Select a stamp in the list and click Edit to edit the name, category, or change the stamp icon. Click on a category in the list and click Edit to edit a category name. Select a Category or stamp in the list and click Delete to delete the respective category or stamp.

If you use several stamps during an editing session, you can open a window and select stamps from all categories. Select Show Stamps Palette from the Stamp Tool pull-down menu. A Stamps window opens. At the top of the window is a pull-down menu listing all categories including your custom stamps categories as shown in Figure 15-29. Select a category and the stamps for that category are placed in view in the window. Click a stamp in the window and drag to the Document pane to add a stamp to a document page.

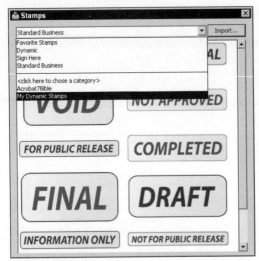

Figure 15-29: The pull-down menu in the Stamps window lists all stamp categories including custom stamps.

At the bottom of the Stamp tool pull-down menu is a command for adding favorite stamps to the menu. Select a stamp from a submenu and choose Favorites ⇨ Add Current Stamp to Favorites. The selected stamp appears at the top of the menu, as shown in Figure 15-30.

Figure 15-30: Favorite stamps are added to the top of the Stamp tool pull-down menu.

If you want to add more stamps to your favorites, follow the same procedures and new stamp names are added to the menu. If you want to delete a stamp from the favorite list, you must first select the stamp and make it active in the Stamp tool. Return to the Stamp tool pull-down menu and choose Favorites ⇨ Remove Current Stamp From Favorites.

Paste Clipboard Image as Stamp

 In previous versions of Acrobat the Paste Clipboard Image tool was found in the Attach toolbar. In Acrobat 7 the tool was replaced by a menu command and now appears in the Stamps tool pull-down menu as Paste Clipboard Image as Stamp.

To use the Paste Clipboard Image as Stamp menu command, you first copy image data in any application or use the Snapshot tool in Acrobat to copy data. Note that copying text with the TouchUp Text tool, TouchUp Object tool, or the Select tool won't paste back as a stamp. The image data are copied to the clipboard. Whatever image data you can copy to the clipboard can be used as a stamp comment. As a comment, you have all the options for properties changes and review tracking. Keep in mind that pasting with this tool is much different from pasting data using menu and context menu commands.

Cross-Reference For more information about pasting data on PDF pages, see Chapters 10 and 11.

In Figure 15-31 I copied an object and selected the Paste Clipboard Image as Stamp from the Stamp tool pull-down menu. To paste the clipboard data as a new comment move the tool to the document page and click the mouse button. The image is pasted as a comment. You can then double-click on the image with the Hand tool to open a pop-up note and add a description for the message you want to communicate.

Tip Once you create a Stamp comment using the Paste Clipboard Image as Stamp command, you can create a custom stamp from the pasted data. This is a fast way to create a stamp without having to convert another document to PDF.

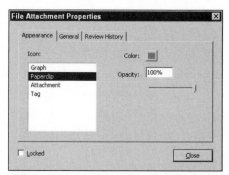

Figure 15-31: To use the Paste Clipboard Image as Stamp menu command, copy an image to the clipboard in an authoring program and click the tool on a page. The clipboard data becomes a comment where you can double-click on the image to open a comment note pop-up.

Note The Paste Clipboard Image as Stamp command is available in Adobe Reader when a PDF is enabled with Adobe Reader usage rights. Using the menu command is the only way you can introduce new image data on a PDF document using Adobe Reader.

Tip

Once you copy data to the clipboard you can use the keyboard shortcut Ctrl/⌘+V and the clipboard data are pasted as a new stamp.

Pasting PDF images and text

If you want to copy part of a PDF document page that includes an image, text, or both an image and text, you can use the Snapshot tool to create a comment from an image. This task can be particularly helpful if you want to comment about integrating data between PDF documents or suggest moving data between pages.

To copy an area on a PDF page, select the Snapshot tool. Marquee the area you want to include as your comment image. The selection you create can include text and images. Acrobat takes a snapshot and places the selection on the clipboard.

Navigate to another PDF file or another page and select Paste Clipboard Image as Stamp from the Stamps pull-down menu. Click in the area you want to paste the image as a comment. If you want to add text in a pop-up note to amplify your message, add text to the note. In Figure 15-32 I copied a block of text in a document and pasted the text with the Paste Clipboard Image as Stamp menu command on another page. The note adds a short message to the comment.

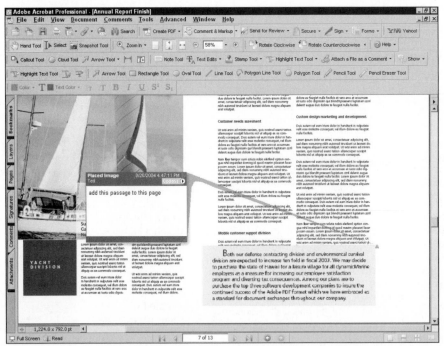

Figure 15-32: A passage of text was copied with the Snapshot tool and pasted using the Paste Clipboard Image as Stamp command where a comment note clarified the message.

Inasmuch as the Select tool, the TouchUp Object tool, and the TouchUp Text tool can all copy data, none of the tools support Paste Clipboard Image as Stamp. The only tool within Acrobat you can use with the Paste Clipboard Image as Stamp command is the Snapshot tool. For more information about using the Select tool, TouchUp Object tool, and TouchUp text tool, see Chapters 10 and 11.

Stamp Properties for Placed Image

Properties options when you create a stamp from the Paste Clipboard Image as Stamp command are the same properties options found with the Stamp tool. By default the Subject field in the General properties is titled *Placed Image*. The field is editable and you can type a new subject if desired. In the Appearance tab, you have choices for Color and Opacity. The color selections made from the color swatch pop-up menu relate to colors used for the pop-up notes. The pasted image itself does not change color. The Opacity settings enable you to add transparency to the image.

If the Paste Clipboard Image as Stamp command is grayed out, you don't have an image copied to the clipboard. To verify content on the clipboard, open the Create PDF Task Button pull-down menu. If the From Clipboard Image menu item is grayed out, no data exist on the clipboard.

Using the Attach tools

File attachments enable you to attach any document file on your hard drive, a recorded sound, or a pasted image to an open PDF file. When you attach files, the file is embedded in the PDF document. Embedding a file provides other users the capability to view attachments on other computers and across platforms. At first it may appear as though the attachment is a link. However, if you transport the PDF document to another computer and open the attachment, the embedded file opens in the host application. Users on other computers need the original authoring application to view the embedded file. You can add file attachments in Acrobat Standard and Acrobat Professional. You can also add file attachments in Adobe Reader when PDFs have been created with usage rights for Adobe Reader.

There are two methods available to you when attaching files. You can use the Commenting toolbar and attach a file as a comment or use the Attach a File menu command from the Document menu. When files are attached using the Attach a File as a Comment, the PDF does not need to be enabled with usage rights for Adobe Reader users to extract the file. Additionally, when Attach a File as a Comment is used, the file attachments show up in any comment summary you create in Acrobat.

When using the Attach a File menu command, any Adobe Reader user in version 7.0 and above can extract the file attachment without the file enabled with usage rights. Note that attaching files using either method provides Adobe Reader users access to the file attachments.

For more information on adding usage rights to PDFs for Adobe Reader, see Chapter 3.

To attach a file to a PDF document, select Document ➪ Attach a File. The Add Attachment dialog box opens where you can navigate your hard drive, locate a file to attach, select the file and click the Open button. The file is attached to the open document and all users of all Acrobat viewers version 7.0 and greater can extract the attachment.

Tip   You select tools for using Attach a File and Attach a File as a Comment from the File toolbar. Open the pull-down menu on the Attach a File tool adjacent to the Organizer tool and select from Attach a File or Attach a File as a Comment menu commands.

To use the Attach File as a Comment tool, select the tool and click in the Document pane. The Select file to Attach dialog box opens, in which you navigate to a file and select it for the attachment. Any file on your computer can be used as a file attachment. Select a file and click Select. The File Attachment Properties dialog box opens with the Appearance tab in view as shown in Figure 15-33.

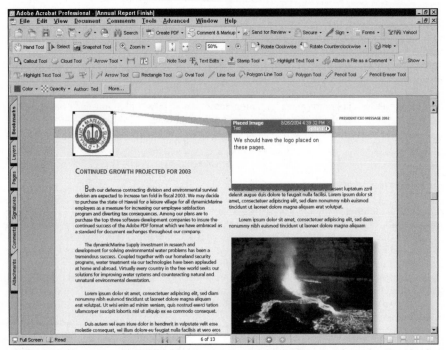

Figure 15-33: In the Appearance properties pane, the icon list provides selections for four different attachment icons and a choice for color and opacity.

The Appearance properties for file attachments offer you choices for icon appearances to represent file attachments. Choose from one of the four icon choices shown in Figure 15-31. By default the Paperclip icon is used.

By default the name of the file attachment is placed in the Description field box in the General tab. You can edit the Description field, but leaving it at the default keeps you informed of what file is attached to the document. Figure 15-34 shows the General tab with the description noted as the name of the attached file.

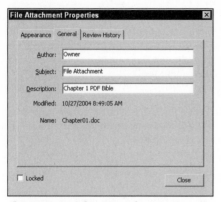

Figure 15-34: The General properties offer choices for author name, subject, and a description of the attached file.

If you place the cursor over a file attachment icon, a Tool Tip displays the attached filename, and the time and date the attachment was made. The name shown in the Tool Tip is related to the Description field in the General properties. As a matter of practice it's best to leave the descriptions at the default to be clear about what files are attached to documents.

Attach File as Comment does not support an associated pop-up note. Double-clicking an attachment icon opens a dialog box where you are asked whether you want to open the file. Click Open in the dialog box to open the attachment or Don't Open to not open the file. If you click Open and the file is a file type other than PDF, the authoring application is launched and the file opened by the program that created it.

Note   You must have the original authoring application to open file attachments when the attachments are other than PDF.

You can use PDF documents like a security wrapper for any file you want to exchange with colleagues and coworkers. Use the Attach File as Comment tool and attach one or more files to a PDF document. Secure the PDF with Password Security and use the Email tool to send the file to members of your workgroup. You can protect the document with password security and prevent unauthorized users from opening your PDF or extracting attached files. In this regard you can use Acrobat to secure any document you create from any authoring program.

Cross-Reference   For more information on using Password Security, see Chapter 21. For more information about using the Email tool, see Chapter 22.

File attachments are embedded in PDFs, and double-clicking on the Attach File as a Comment icon provides you access to the file. If you want to save an embedded file to disk without opening the file, open a context menu and select Save Embedded File to Disk. Acrobat opens a dialog box where you can navigate your hard drive and designate a location for the file to be saved to. Neither opening a file nor saving the embedded file to disk removes the file attachment. If you want to delete a file attachment, open a context menu on the attachment icon and select Delete or select the icon and press Delete or the Del key.

Record Audio Comment tool

 Sound comments are recorded from within the PDF document or from prerecorded sounds saved in .WAV (Windows) or .AIFF or .WAV (Macintosh). For recording a sound, you must have a microphone connected to your computer. The resulting sound file is embedded in the PDF when you use the Record Audio Comment tool.

Attaching prerecorded sounds

Select the Record Audio Comment tool and click on a PDF page. The Sound Recorder (Windows shown in Figure 15-35) or Record Sound (Macintosh shown in Figure 15-36) dialog box opens. Click on Browse (Windows) or Choose (Macintosh).

Figure 15-35: To select a sound file to attach to the PDF (Windows), click the Browse button.

Figure 15-36: To select a sound file to attach to the PDF (Macintosh), click the Choose button.

The Select Sound File dialog box opens after you click Browse (Windows) or Choose (Macintosh). Navigate your hard drive and find a sound file to attach to the document. Select the sound file and click the Select button. Acrobat returns you to the Sound Recorder (Windows) or Record Sound (Macintosh) dialog box. At this point you can play the sound or click OK to embed the sound in the PDF. Click the right-pointing arrow (Windows) or Play (Macintosh) and you can verify the sound before importing it. After you click OK the Sound Attachment Properties dialog box opens.

After the sound file has been embedded in the PDF document you can play the sound by opening a context menu on the Record Audio Comment icon and selecting Play File.

Recording sounds

Click the mouse button with the Record Audio Comment tool to open the Sound Recorder (Windows) or Record Sound (Macintosh) dialog box. Click the record button and speak into the microphone connected to your computer. When you've finished recording the sound, click OK (Windows) or Stop (Macintosh). The Sound Attachment Properties dialog box opens immediately after you stop the recording. The General properties are shown (Windows) in Figure 15-37 or Appearance properties (Macintosh) in Figure 15-38.

When you close the Sound Attachment Properties dialog box, the sound can be played like imported sounds. Open a context menu and select Play File (or double-click on the Record Audio Comment icon). Because the sound becomes part of the PDF document, you can transport the PDF across platforms without having to include a sound file link. All sound files are audible on either platform once imported into PDFs.

Cross-Reference

For more information on importing sound files, see Chapters 18 and 23.

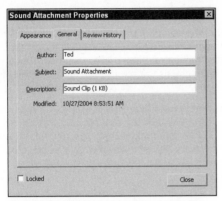

Figure 15-37: After you stop a recording, the Sound Attachment Properties dialog box opens (Windows).

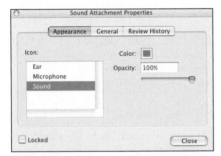

Figure 15-38: After you stop a recording, the Sound Attachment Properties dialog box opens (Macintosh).

Sound Attachment Properties

Properties for sound comments are made available in the same manner as with other comments. Open a context menu and select Properties to open the Sound Attachment Properties dialog box. The Sound Attachment Properties dialog box, shown in Figure 15-35, offers selections for adding a text description and editing the author name. By default, the Description field shows the file size of the sound clip. You can change the description by typing in the field box. All descriptions are also viewed in the Attachments tab. (See "Using the Attachments tab" later in this chapter).

The Appearance properties offer you options for three different icon appearances. The color swatch and opacity adjustment are used to change color for the icon.

Using the Attachments tab

A new addition to Acrobat 7 is the Attachments tab docked in the Navigation pane by default. When you click the Attachments tab the pane opens horizontally like the Comments tab. The Attachments pane includes a list of file attachments contained in a document that were attached with either the Attach a File or the Attach File as Comment tool. File attachments such as sound comments are not listed in the pane.

Depending on what tool is used to attach a file, you see a different description in the Location in document column as shown in Figure 15-39. In Figure 15-39 the first file listed in the Attachments tab was added using the Attach a File as a Comment tool. The second file shown in the list was added using the Attach a File command. The two different type of attachments include

✦ Attach File as Comment (shows the page where it was attached)

✦ Document ⇨ Attach a File (shows "Attachments tab" as the location)

Figure 15-39: Click the Attachments tab to open the Attachments pane where a list of all file attachments appear when added with either the Attach a File as Comment tool or the Attach a File menu command.

At the top of the Attachments pane you find tools for the following:

✦ **Open:** Click an attachment listed in the pane and click Open. The attachment opens in the program that created the document.

✦ **Save:** Select an attachment and click Save to save the file to disk. Attachments are contained within PDF files and not accessible to authoring programs unless you open the file by using the Open tool or double-click on an attachment icon. Clicking the Save tool extracts the attachment and saves the extracted file to disk. (Note: Extraction does not delete the file attachment from the PDF.)

✦ **Add:** Add is the only tool accessible when an attachment is not selected in the pane. Click Add to open the Add Attachment dialog box where you can attach additional files. As new files are added as attachments, they are listed dynamically in the Attachment pane.

✦ **Delete:** Click an attachment and click the Delete tool to remove the attachment from the host document.

✦ **Search:** Clicking the Search tool opens the Search pane. You enter search criteria in the Search pane and click the Search Attachments button. Your Acrobat viewer searches all attached PDF files and the current active document.

Tip If you inadvertently delete an attachment, you can choose Edit➪Undo and bring the attachment back. If you delete several attachments, you can select Undo several times and bring back each deleted attachment.

Cross-Reference For more information on using Acrobat Search, see Chapter 5.

From the Options pull-down menu in the pane or from a context menu opened on a selected attachment you have additional choices from menu selections. Click the down-pointing arrow adjacent to Options or open a context menu and the menu appears as shown in Figure 15-40.

Figure 15-40: The Options menu and context menu opened from selected attachments offer the same menu commands.

The menu commands for Open Attachment, Save Attachment, Add Attachment, Delete Attachment, and Search Attachments perform the same functions as their tool counterparts. The remaining two menu commands include Edit Description and Show attachments by default. Select Edit Description and a dialog box opens where you change the Description as you would edit a Description in the File Attachment Properties dialog box.

Select Show attachments by default and the Attachments pane opens each time you open the current document. Selecting this option is document specific and you need to save the file after making the menu choice. This menu item is the same as selecting the Attachments Panel and Page option in the Show pull-down menu in the Initial View pane for the Document Properties.

Cross-Reference For more information on setting Initial Views, see Chapter 4.

Using Drawing Markup and Drawing Tools

Drawing Markup tools offer you a range of different tools that can be used with technical drawings, manuals, brochures, design pieces, as well as routine office memos and other such documents. These tools deviate from the standard highlighter and text edit tools in that they tend to be used as graphic enhancements for communicating messages. If you're an engineer or technical writer you may be inclined to use all the tools. If you're a business professional you may pick and choose certain tools you favor when reviewing and marking up documents. At the least, Acrobat provides a tool for just about any user in any environment when it comes to review and markup.

The Drawing tools can be viewed in two toolbars. Actually, one toolbar is an expansion of the Drawing Markup toolbar. You first open the Drawing Markup toolbar containing the Callout tool, Cloud tool, Arrow tool, Dimension tool, and the Text Box tool. From the Arrow tool pull-down menu you can select Show Drawing Toolbar and the Drawing tools appear in a separate toolbar. Hence, you have Drawing Markup tools and Drawing tools.

Callout tool

The Callout tool is used to note attention to an object, block of text, image, or other element on a page where you want to focus comments about a specific item. Notice in Figure 15-41 the Callout in the upper-right corner of the figure.

Cloud tool

The Cloud tool is used like the Polygon Line tool where you click, release the mouse button, and move the cursor, click, and move the cursor again, and continue until you draw a polygon shape. Return to the point of origin and release the mouse button and Acrobat closes the path. The paths appear as a cloud shape. The shape can be filled and stroked. In Figure 15-41 a shape was drawn with the Cloud tool, and an opacity of 25 percent was applied so the underlying area could be viewed with transparency.

Dimension tool

You use the Dimension tool to mark or comment about the distance between two points. The mark is drawn with two lines at right angles to the distance line as shown in Figure 15-41. After you draw a line you can reshape it, changing the angle or the length of the two lines at right angles or the distance line.

Text Box tool

You use the Text Box tool for creating large blocks of text. You have more control over fonts, text attributes, and flexibility with the Text Box tool than when using a Note comment. Notice in Figure 15-41 text in the Text Box and the options available in the Properties bar at the bottom of the Toolbar Well. As text is selected in the Text Box, you have an abundant number of font attribute choices in the Properties bar.

In the Text Box Properties dialog box you can change opacity for text boxes, background colors, and line styles for borders. The remaining options are similar to properties for other comment tools.

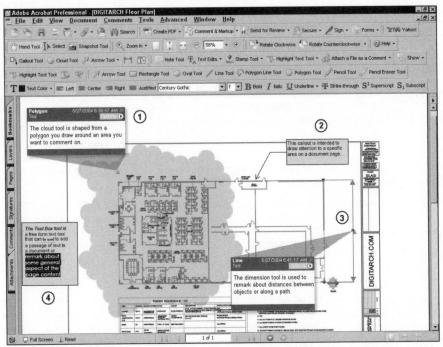

Figure 15-41: Markups shown are the 1) Cloud tool, 2) Callout tool, 3) Dimension tool, and 4) Text Box tool.

Drawing tools

The Line tools are used for creating straight lines. You might use Line tools with or without arrowheads to illustrate points of interest, point out where background elements need to be moved, point to an object, or similar kinds of notations. These tools include

✦   **Arrow tool:** The Arrow tool can be used with arrowheads, although applying arrowheads is a matter of user preference. You can draw straight lines on a 360-degree axis.

✦   **Line tool:** The Line tool can have the same attributes assigned as the preceding Arrow tool, making them indistinguishable from each other. The intent is for the Arrow tool to provide you with a line for arrowheads while the Line tool remains without arrowheads. When marking up a document and using both line tools you don't need to keep addressing the Line Properties dialog box each time you want to toggle on or off arrowheads. It's a matter of user preference, though, as you can choose to add or eliminate arrowheads from either tool.

✦ **Rectangle tool:** Use this tool to draw rectangle or square shapes. To keep the object constrained to a square, hold down the Shift key as you click and drag.

✦ **Oval tool:** Using this tool involves the same process as the Rectangle tool for constraining objects to circles. Oval shapes are drawn without adding the Shift key.

✦ **Polygon tool:** Use the same sequence of clicking and moving as described earlier for the Cloud tool. When you release the mouse button back at the point of origin, the shape closes with flat edges instead of semi-circles like the Cloud tool.

✦ **Polygon Line tool:** The Polygon Line tool also creates straight lines, but the lines are connected as you click the cursor to move in another direction. When you finish drawing a shape or lines with angles, double-click the mouse button to complete the line.

✦ **Pencil tool:** You use the Pencil tool to draw freeform lines. Whereas all the line tools draw straight lines, you use the Pencil tool for marking a page by drawing with a pencil, as you would with pencil and paper. The properties for pencil markings include choices for line weights, line colors, and line opacity settings.

Pencil comments are one contiguous line. If you stop drawing by releasing the mouse button, click, and drag again, a new comment is added to the document.

✦ **Pencil Eraser tool:** The Pencil Eraser tool erases lines drawn with the Pencil tool. Lines drawn with other tools cannot be erased with this tool. When you draw a line with the Pencil tool and erase part of the line, the remaining portion of a Pencil comment is interpreted as a single comment. Broken lines where you may have several smaller lines remaining after erasing part of a Pencil comment are considered part of the same comment.

A note pop-up is associated with the entire group of Drawing tools. You can access tool properties by opening a context menu on a mark drawn with any tool. In the Properties dialog box for the respective tool, you can change stroke and fill colors and opacities. For strokes, you can change line weights. Like other comment tools you also have available in the Properties dialog box General attributes options and Review History options.

Drawing tools and context menus

When you use any of the Drawing tools to create a mark on a page, releasing the mouse button automatically selects the Hand tool. You can use either the Hand tool or the Select Object tool to open a context menu. The context menu options appear different depending on what tool you use to select the comment. In Figure 15-42, a context menu is opened on a line with the Hand tool.

One difference you find with menu options in the Drawing tools as opposed to other comment tools is the Flip Line command. Flip Line is available only for the Arrow tool and the Line tool. When you select Flip Line, the line is flipped horizontally.

Cross-Reference
For more information on the context menu commands, see the section "Managing Notes" earlier in this chapter.

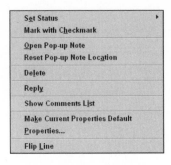

Figure 15-42: Menu options from a context menu opened with the Hand tool offer choices similar to those found in context menus opened from Commenting tools and note pop-up windows.

After comments have been created you may want to manage comments by aligning, sizing, cutting, copying, and pasting them. These options are available when you use the Select Object tool as shown in Figure 15-43. When you use the Hand tool you can select only a single comment. When using the Select Object tool you can select all the comments on a page or select a group of objects. Open a context menu and you can apply changes to all selected objects. This feature is particularly helpful when you want to align Drawing tool comments.

Alignment options are the same for Drawing tools as they are for form fields and buttons. For a detailed description of the submenu selections of the menus shown in Figure 15-43, see Chapter 27.

Figure 15-43: Open a context menu with the Select Object tool for menu options suited for managing multiple comments.

When comments share common properties options, you can use the Select Object tool to select the Properties dialog box for multiple comments. If you attempt to select objects where the properties options are different for the comments — for example, objects created with the Line tool and objects created with the Cloud tool — the Properties dialog box offers only property changes that are common between the comments.

Line tool properties

With either the Hand tool or the Select Object tool, click a Line tool comment and open a context menu. Alternatively, you can open the Line Properties dialog box by selecting a comment with the Select Object tool and clicking the More button in the Properties dialog box or double-clicking with the Select Object tool on a line. From the menu options select Properties. If you have more than one comment selected when you use the Select Object tool, the Line Properties dialog box opens as shown in Figure 15-44.

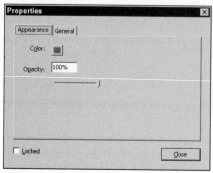

Figure 15-44: If you use the Select Object tool and have selected several Drawing tool icons, the Line Properties dialog box displays two tabs where you can change common attributes.

The Line Properties dialog box opens with two tabs accessible for changing line attributes. If you use the Hand tool or select a single comment with the Select Object tool, the third tab, Review History, is accessible. Review History is displayed only for individual comments. The Appearance tab includes the following options:

For information related to reviews and review history, see Chapter 16.

✦ **Start:** From the pull-down menu you select an arrowhead for the beginning of a line as shown in Figure 15-45. The default is None for no arrowhead.

✦ **End:** This is the same as the preceding option but applied to the end of the line. The pull-down menu choices are the same as for Start.

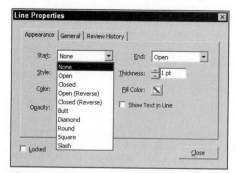

Figure 15-45: Open the pull-down menu for either the Start or End and select an arrowhead from the menu options.

✦ **Style:** From this pull-down menu you have choices for drawing solid lines and six differ-ent dashed lines.

✦ **Thickness:** Select a line weight from 0 to 12 points. Click the arrows or type a value in the field box.

✦ **Color:** Represents the stroke color. You make color choices from the pop-up swatch palette the same way you do with the Note tools.

✦ **Fill Color:** Represents the Fill color. For Drawing tools that enable you to apply a fill, you choose a color from the color swatch pop-up menu.

✦ **Show Text in Line:** When you check the box, text in the pop-up note appears within the line itself. You can use this option with the Arrow and Line tools. In Figure 15-46 the Arrow tool was used to draw a line and the box was checked in the Arrow tool proper-ties for Show Text in Line.

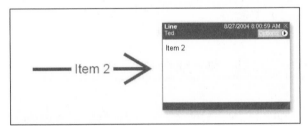

Figure 15-46: When Show Text in Line is selected in the Properties dialog box, text appears within a line created with the Arrow and Line tools.

✦ **Opacity:** Opacity is applied to both the stroke and fill colors. Move the slider the same as you do when adjusting opacity in the Note Properties dialog box.

✦ **Locked:** When Locked is selected, the line cannot be moved. Unlock a line to move it on the page.

The choices you make for arrowheads are available from either the Properties dialog box or the Properties bar. Not all choices are the same between the two items. In Figure 15-47 you can see the choices available from the Properties bar and the Properties dialog box.

Figure 15-47 shows arrowheads applied to a single end. You can combine different shapes in the same line with a start and end selection.

The Style pull-down menu offers you choices for a line style. The default is Solid, as shown in Figure 15-47. The remaining line styles are dashed lines. Select from Dashed 1 through Dashed 6 for a different style as shown in Figure 15-48.

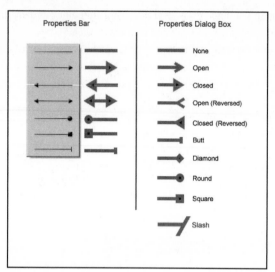

Figure 15-47: The Properties dialog box offers more selections for arrowheads.

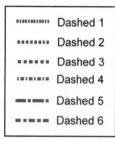

Figure 15-48: Six different dashed line styles are displayed in the Style pull-down menu. The default is Solid, whereas the remaining six styles are dashed lines.

The other two tabs in the Properties dialog box are the same as those you find when using the Note tool. A Subject line is included in the General properties tab just like with the Note tool. The default name for the Subject is Line when you're using the Line tool. The default name changes according to the tool used to create the shape.

Managing line comments

To move drawing objects, align them, or reshape them, you need to select an object with the Hand tool. If you experience difficulty selecting a line it may be because the Enable text selection for the Hand tool preference option is selected. If selecting drawing tool objects is awkward, open the Preferences dialog box (Ctrl/⌘+K) and select General in the left pane. Disable the check box for Enable text selection for the Hand tool.

Tip If you want to keep the Hand tool preferences set to select text with the tool and you have difficulty selecting markups, open the Comments tab and click a comment to select it.

Cross-Reference For more information on using the Hand tool for text selections, see Chapter 10.

Click an object and handles appear either at the ends of lines or at each end of line segments around polygon objects (see Figure 15-49). You can drag any handle in or out to resize or reshape objects. To move an object, click on a line or a fill color and drag the shape.

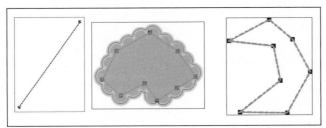

Figure 15-49: To reshape objects, select the Hand tool and click on a handle (square shape on a line) and drag to change the shape.

Drawing tools comments can be copied, cut, pasted, deleted, aligned, distributed, and sized. Use the Select Object tool and open a context menu while one or more objects are selected. Choose a menu command for the operation desired.

Tip When selecting objects with the Select Object tool you can draw a marquee through objects to select them. You don't need to completely surround comments within a marquee to select them.

Using the Show Menu

You can adjust several settings for comments and comment pop-up notes in the Show tool contained in the Commenting toolbar. Options for the pull-down menu are also found in the Comments pane. Open the pull-down menu to see the menu commands shown in Figure 15-50.

From the menu selections, you have the following choices:

✦ **Commenting Toolbar:** Use this command to show or hide the Commenting toolbar. When you hide the Commenting toolbar, the Show tool moves into the Drawing Markups toolbar if both toolbars are visible when you hide the Commenting toolbar.

✦ **Drawing Markups Toolbar:** Use this command to show or hide the Drawing Markups toolbar. If the Commenting toolbar is hidden and you hide the Drawing Markups toolbar, the Show tool disappears from the Toolbar Well. The menu appears on the Drawing Markups toolbar when the Commenting toolbar is hidden.

✦ **Show Comments List:** Select this command to open the Comments pane. You can also open the Comments pane by clicking the Comments tab.

Figure 15-50: The Show tool pull-down menu offers commands for working with comments and comment note pop-ups.

✦ **Hide All Comments:** Selecting the command opens a warning dialog box indicating that all replies in a review will be hidden. Click OK in the warning dialog box and all comments are hidden from view, but still attached to the document. Return to the menu and the command changes to Show All Comments.

✦ **Show by Type:** You can selectively show comments by type. Choices from the submenu include Notes, Drawing Markups, Text Editing Markups, Stamps, and Attachments. You can select multiple types by returning to the submenu and making additional selections. For example, if you want to show Notes, Stamps, and Attachments while hiding Drawing Markups and Text Editing Markups, select Notes, return to the menu, and select Stamps. Notes remains selected when you make the second selection. Return again and select Attachments and all three types remain in view while the other types remain hidden from view.

✦ **Show by Reviewer:** You can choose to show comments by one or more reviewers for documents retrieved from a review session. The method of selecting multiple reviewers follows the same behavior as with Show by Type.

✦ **Show by Status:** Also used with review sessions, you can show comments by selected Review status and by Migration status.

Cross-Reference

For information on Status assignment, see "Using the Comments pane" later in this chapter. For information on the Migration options, see Chapter 16.

✦ **Show Checked State:** You can check comments for your own personal use. Comments are either Checked or Unchecked in the Comments pane. From the submenu options you can choose to show all checked comments, unchecked comments, or both.

✦ **Open All Pop-ups:** Opens all pop-up notes.

✦ **Close All Pop-ups:** Closes all pop-up notes.

✦ **Show Connector Lines:** When the mouse cursor appears over a comment, connector lines are shown from the comment to the comment note. If you don't want to show the connector lines, select this command. By default, connector lines are shown.

✦ **Align New Pop-ups by Default:** By default, comment notes are aligned to the right side of the document page. When this menu item is checked, the comment notes appear aligned together on top of each other. Removing the check mark from this option causes note pop-ups to align with the note icon.

✦ **Comment Preferences:** Opens the Preferences dialog box and selects Commenting in the left pane.

Using the Comments Menu

In Acrobat 7 you have a menu dedicated to commands related to commenting. Open the Comments menu shown in Figure 15-51 and you find several commands redundant with the Show pull-down menu and a single command not available in other menus.

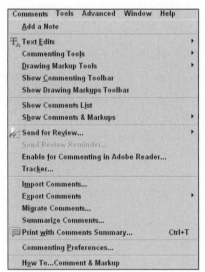

Figure 15-51: The Comments menu lists all the commands you might use for comment and review.

All the commands, with the exception of the Enable for Commenting in Adobe Reader command, in the Comments menu appear in menus from other tools and in the Comments pane. When you want to enable PDF documents for Adobe Reader users, select this command and the Save As dialog box opens as shown in Figure 15-52.

Figure 15-52: Select Enable for Commenting in Adobe Reader and the Save As dialog box opens.

The Save As dialog box opens to permit you to save a copy of the original PDF document with usage rights for Adobe Reader users. Your original file remains unaffected when you use the Save As dialog box. Note that from the Save as type (Windows) or Format (Macintosh) pull-down menu the only acceptable format is Adobe PDF.

When a file has been deployed with usage rights for Adobe Reader users, the Reader user has access to all the commenting tools you have available in Acrobat Professional with just a few limitations on some options choices. For example, the Text Edits tools are available to Adobe Reader and Acrobat Standard users, but exporting Text Edits to Microsoft Word or Autodesk AutoCAD is not permitted. In Figure 15-53 a document was saved with usage rights and opened in Adobe Reader.

Adobe Reader users also have the option for saving updates on a document that has been enabled with usage rights. In addition the Attachments pane shows tools available to Reader users when working with file attachments.

Cross-Reference   For more information on commenting in Adobe Reader, see Chapter 3.

Another item appearing in the Comments menu is the How To Comment & Markup command. Although you can access this menu item from the Help pull-down menu, the command does not exist with any other commenting tool. Select the menu item and the How To pane opens with category links to help information related to commenting.

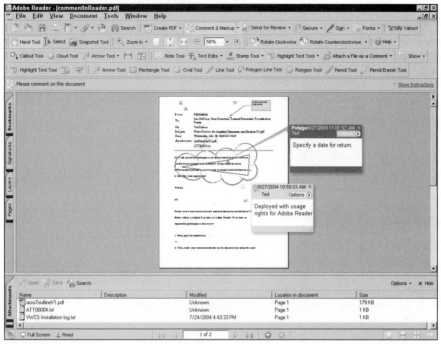

Figure 15-53: When documents have been enabled for commenting in Adobe Reader, all the comment tools are available to the Reader user.

Using the Comments Pane

The Comments pane conveniently contains many tools and options for managing comments. By default the Comments pane opens horizontally across the bottom of the Acrobat window like the Attachments pane and lists all the comments created in a PDF document. If you toggle views between several PDF files, the Comments pane dynamically updates the list of comments to reflect comments on the file active in the Document pane.

Depending on the size of your monitor, you'll find that viewing the pane occupies substantial space in the Acrobat window. If you're working on a small monitor, the amount of room left over for viewing pages, after loading toolbars in the Toolbar Well and expanding the Comment pane, can be very skimpy. Fortunately, you can view the pane docked in the Navigation pane and control the size by dragging the horizontal separator bar at the top of the pane down to reduce size.

You also have a choice for floating the pane by undocking it from the Navigation pane and resizing the pane. To undock the Comments pane, click on the tab and drag it to the Document pane as shown in Figure 15-54. You can resize the pane by dragging the lower-right corner in or out to reduce or expand the size.

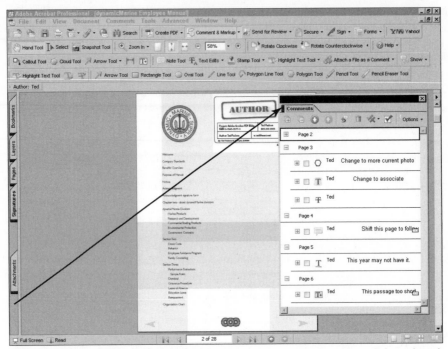

Figure 15-54: To undock the Comments pane from the Navigation pane, click on the tab and drag it to the Document pane. Drag the lower-right corner in or out to resize the pane.

Either way you choose to view the Comments pane, you'll find using it to be a great asset when reviewing documents and participating in review sessions. At first it may be a struggle to find the right size and location for the pane, but with a little practice you'll find the many tools contained in the pane much easier to access than using menu commands.

Viewing comments

The Comments pane lists all the comments contained in the active document. By default the comments are listed by page. In a multi-page document, you'll see Page 1, Page 2, Page 3, and so on displayed in the list on the left side of the pane.

You can view the list of comments expanded or collapsed. In Figure 15-55 you see the list expanded. Expanded lists show comments in a hierarchy like Bookmarks are shown in the Bookmarks pane. You can expand individual pages that contain comments by clicking on the plus (+) symbol (Windows) or the right-pointing arrow (Macintosh). To expand all comments, click the Expand All button in the Comments pane toolbar shown in Figure 15-55. Conversely, you can collapse all comments by clicking the Collapse All button. Note that in Figure 15-55 the minus (–) symbol shows the Collapse All tool but the text is not shown because of a lower resolution monitor view.

Figure 15-55: Comments are ordered in a hierarchical list. By default comments are viewed nested in a page order. The first three pages are expanded while the individual comments remain collapsed.

Comments are listed in a hierarchical order. If you have several comments on a page and you click on the icon to the left of the comment to expand the page comments, you see the Comment icon, author, and content of a note pop-up. You can further expand each comment in the expanded list by clicking on the plus (+) symbol (Windows) or right-pointing arrow (Macintosh). When further expanded, the comment subject and the creation date are displayed in the pane.

Sorting comments

Also shown in Figure 15-55 is the pull-down menu for Sort By. You can change the default Page sorting to any of the following:

✦ **Type:** Comments are sorted together by the type of comment contained on pages. All Note comments appear together, highlight comments together, stamps together, and so on.

✦ **Page:** The default. Comments are listed together successively by page.

✦ **Author:** If a document has comments from several different authors, the comments are listed by author and sorted in an alphabetical order by author name.

✦ **Date:** The creation date is the sort order with the most recent date appearing first in the list.

✦ **Color:** Comments are sorted according to the color settings made in the comment Properties dialog boxes.

✦ **Checkmark Status:** You can check a comment for your own personal method of flagging a comment. Checking comments might be made for you to alert yourself to review comments, perhaps mark them for deletion, or to spend more time in a later editing session reviewing the comments made by others. The choice for what the check mark signals is a personal choice. When you view comments according to Checkmark Status, all unchecked Comments (Unmarked) are listed first followed by comments marked with a check mark.

✦ **Status by Person:** The menu option includes a submenu where you can select an author. Select an author name from the submenu and comments are sorted with the comments for the selected author appearing first. The unchecked comments are listed next by author name. You must have Status set on at least one comment to activate this command.

Navigating comments

The up and down arrows in the Comments toolbar enable you to move back and forth between comments. Click the down-pointing arrow to move to the next comment in the list. Click the up-pointing arrow to navigate to a previous comment. The arrow tools are grayed out when comments are collapsed. In order to use the tools you need to have one or more groups of comments expanded and have a comment selected.

Double-clicking a comment in the list takes you to the page where the comment appears. When you double-click the comment in the Comments pane, an associated pop-up note also opens.

Searching comments

You can search the contents of comment pop-up notes. To find a word in a pop-up note, select the Search comments tool. Enter the search criteria and click Search Comments. You can also open the full or generic Search pane and select the Include Comments check box. The Search pane offers you the same search options used for searching open PDF documents. You can match case, search for whole words only, and other search criteria. The results of your search, however, return words found in the document as well as words found in comment pop-up notes.

When a word is found in a comment pop-up note, the page where the note appears opens and the pop-up note opens with the found word highlighted.

Cross-Reference For more information on using the Search pane, see Chapter 5.

Printing comments

The Print Comments tool does more than print the comments in a document to your printer. When you select the Print Comments tool, a pull-down menu opens where you can choose from two menu options. These menu commands include the following:

✦ **Print Comments Summary:** Use this command to create a summary page as a new PDF file and print the summarized comments to your default printer. The comment summary is a temporary file that Acrobat creates while you print the summarized comments. After completing the print job the summary is deleted by Acrobat.

✦ **Create PDF of Comments Summary:** Use this command to create a new PDF document that summarizes the comments in your document, rather than print a file to your printer. You can save this file and keep it around to review a summary of the comments. This document is created with the Summarize Comments option called "Document and comments with sequence numbers on separate pages."

From each of the menu commands, Acrobat defaults to "Document and comments with sequence numbers on separate pages." If you want to print pages with comments configured with different settings use the File ➪ Print with Comments Summary menu command.

Cross-Reference For details in regard to working with comment summaries, see the section "Creating Comment Summaries" later in this chapter.

Deleting comments

 In addition to the context menus used when creating comments, you can delete them from within the Comments pane. Select a comment in the pane and click on the Trash icon to delete the selected comment. After deleting a comment you have one level of undo available to you. If you change your mind after deleting a comment, choose Edit ➪ Undo. You can also undo selecting multiple comments and clicking on the Trash icon. Choose Edit ➪ Undo successively if you change your mind after deleting multiple comments. In the event you lose the Undo command, you need to choose File ➪ Revert to bring back the comment. Be certain to update your PDF file after reviewing any comment deletions. The Revert command reverts to the last saved version of the file.

Marking comments

The Mark the current comment with a checkmark tool is used to flag comments for a special purpose. You can select a comment in the Comments list in the pane and select the tool to check mark the current selection. You can also apply check marks to comments by clicking in the open check mark box when a comment is expanded. Between the expand/collapse icon and the comment icon is a check box. Click the box to check mark a comment. When viewing an expanded comments list, you do not need to select comments in order to mark the check boxes.

Setting comment status

Marking a comment with a check mark, described in the preceding section, is a method for you to keep track of comments for your own purposes. The Set the comment status tool is used to mark a comment's current status that is intended for use in comment reviews and when shared with other users. From the tool pull-down menu you have two subcategories for marking the status of a comment. Under Review you have five choices: None, Accepted, Rejected, Cancelled, and Completed. Under Migration you have three choices: None, Not Confirmed, and Confirmed.

When you mark comments for status and view the comments sorted according to Status by Person, the comments are sorted according to the status groups. For the Review categories, beginning with Rejected, comments are listed for an author for all rejected comments appearing first in the list. Next the same author's Completed comments are listed, followed by Cancelled. Comments marked as None are listed last for each author. (In other words, the order is Rejected, Completed, Cancelled, Accepted, None.)

Cross-Reference For more information on using the status marks in review sessions, see Chapter 16.

Editing comment pop-up notes

A very handy feature available to you when viewing comments in an expanded list is the ability to edit note pop-up text. Rather than navigating to each page containing a comment and opening the associated note pop-up window to make your edits, you can delete, change, or modify text listed in the Comments pane.

When you select the note pop-up text in the Comments pane, the note pop-up window opens in the Document pane. As you make changes in the Comments pane, changes are dynamically reflected in the pop-up note window. If you edit text in the pop-up note window, the text edits are reflected in the Comments pane. To enable the dynamic viewing between the pop-up notes and the Comments pane, be certain to disable the check box in the Comment preferences for *Hide comment pop-ups when Comments List is open.*

Exporting and Importing Comments

If you ask a colleague to comment on a document, you can bypass the e-mail and browser-based reviews by having a reviewer export comments and e-mail the exported file to you. When you export comments from a PDF document the data are exported as an FDF or XFDF file. The data file results in much smaller file sizes than PDF documents and can easily be imported back into the original PDF or copy of the original PDF document.

To export comments from a PDF document, choose Comments ⇨ Export Comments. From a submenu you have three options. Select from To Word, To AutoCAD, and To File.

Exporting comments to Microsoft Word

If you create PDFs from Microsoft Word and use comments in Word and Acrobat, it may be easier to export comments directly back to your Word document. In order to take advantage of this feature you must be running Windows XP Service Pack 1 or above and you must be using Word 2002 or above. The feature is not supported on Macintosh OS X, nor in Windows 2000.

Be certain to use the Export Comments to Word feature on files that are not changed while importing or exporting comments. If you edit a Word document after creating the PDF file, or you edit the PDF document by inserting, deleting, or performing other page-editing functions, the import/export operations may not work properly.

Comments that are exported from Acrobat to a Word document appear as comment bubbles in Word. Marking text for deletion and insertion are also supported in Word and will appear as integrated comments in the word text

You can either start this process from within Acrobat with Export Comments To Word, or you can start this process from within MS Word with Import Comments from Acrobat under the Acrobat Comments menu. In both cases the Import Comments from Acrobat dialog box is launched. If you start from MS Word, the Word file is filled in and the PDF file is blank. If you start from Acrobat, the PDF file is filled in and the MS Word file is blank.

To export comments to a Word document from Acrobat, choose from one of several menu commands, such as, Comments ⇨ Export Comments ⇨ To Word, or use the Comments pane Options pull-down menu and select Export Comments To Word.

To import the exported comments in a Word document, in Word 2002 on Windows XP open the Word file that you converted to PDF. In Word choose Acrobat Comments ➪ Import Comments from Acrobat. The Import Comments from Adobe Acrobat dialog box opens. You can select the comments you want to import and choose from All Comments, All Comments with Checkmarks, and Text edits only: Insertions and Deletions. For a specific set of comments, select Custom Set and choose the filter options to filter the comments.

Cross-Reference
For information on comment filtering, see the section "Filtering Comments" later in this chapter.

If you import text edit comments, Word prompts you for confirmation as each comment is imported. Be certain to track changes in Word or you won't see the dialog box appear. As you are prompted to accept changes, you can choose to apply changes or discard them as the comments are imported.

Exporting comments to AutoCAD

You can export comments to an Autodesk AutoCAD file. The menu options and process are very similar to exporting comments to Microsoft Word. You need the original source document in order to export the comments to the .dwg file.

Exporting comments to files

When you export comments to a file the Export Comments dialog box opens. The dialog box behaves similarly to a Save As dialog box where you select a destination folder, provide a filename, and click a Save button. Acrobat provides a default name by using the PDF filename with an .fdf extension. You can use the default name or change the name in the File Name field box. From the Save as Type (Windows) or Format (Macintosh) pull-down menu you can select between FDF formatted files and XFDF (XML-based FDF file). The default is FDF.

Click Save in the Export Comments dialog box. The resulting file can be exported to a user who has the same PDF document from which the FDF file was created. If you receive an FDF file and want to load the comments, choose Comments ➪ Import Comments. The Import Comments dialog box opens. Navigate to the location where the data file is located and select it. Click the Select button and the comments are imported into the open PDF document. Note: You have three file format options — not only FDF and XFDF for export, but also PDF. If someone sends you not just the comments but the whole PDF with the comments, you can import those comments directly to your version without having to export them from your reviewer's copy and then import into your copy.

When you import comments in a PDF document, all the comments are imported in the exact location where they were originally created. If you delete a page in a PDF file and import comments, Acrobat ignores comments where it can't find matching pages. Note pop-ups and icons are matched with the way they appear in the file from which the comments were exported.

Exporting selected comments

You can select comments and choose to export only the selected comments to an FDF file. Open the Comments pane and select comments according to the sort order listed in the

Comments pane. The default is by page. Select a page in the list and open the Options pull-down menu from the Comments pane toolbar. Select Export Selected Comments from the menu options as shown in Figure 15-56.

Figure 15-56: Select comments in the Comments pane and select Export Selected Comments from the Options pull-down menu. In the Export Comments dialog box, provide a filename and click the Save button.

The Export Comments dialog box opens. Navigate your hard drive to find the folder where you want to save the FDF or XFDF file, provide a name for the file, and click the Save button.

Tip   When exporting all comments leave the filename for the FDF or XFDF exported file at the default provided by Acrobat. When exporting Selected Comments, be certain to edit the filename. By default, Acrobat uses the same name. If you elect to export all comments and then want to export selected comments, you might mistakenly overwrite files with the same filename. By getting into a habit of being consistent when naming files, you'll prevent potential mistakes.

Filtering Comments

You can further enhance the features available to you for review and markup, exporting and importing comments, and viewing comments in the Comments pane, by filtering comments in groups. Filtering comments temporarily hides comments you don't want to use at the moment. You can choose to display all comments by an author, a date, a reviewer, selected types of comments, and a range of other criteria. When comments are filtered, exporting comments or creating comment summaries (explained in the next section) is applied only to those comments currently viewed. Any hidden comments are excluded from the task at hand.

You manage the comment filter via the Show pull-down menu. The options in the Show pull-down menu in the Toolbar Well are identical to the menu options in the Show tool pull-down menu in the Comments pane.

Cross-Reference   To understand more about the Show menu options, see the section "Using the Show menu" earlier in this chapter.

Tip   If you know ahead of time that you want to export edits back to Microsoft Word, you can mark only those comments received from reviewers that you intend to export to Word. When the review session is completed, choose Show ➪ Hide All Comments. Open the menu again and choose Show by Type ➪ Text Editing Markups. Return to the menu and choose Show by Checked State ➪ Checked. Export the comments, and only the Text Edit comments with the items you checked during the review are exported to Word.

The remaining menu options include non-filtering menu choices such as opening/closing note pop-ups, showing connector lines, aligning icons and pop-up notes, and accessing the Comment preferences. You can also make these menu selections from other tools and menus as described earlier in this chapter.

Creating Comment Summaries

If you create an extensive review from many participants over a period of time, the number of comments may become too many to comfortably manage in the Comments pane or on the document pages. Or you may have a need to create a comment summary you want to distribute to users after filtering out comments that you don't want included in a summary. Furthermore, you may want to print a hard copy of comments that show the PDF pages with connector lines to a summary description. You can accomplish all these tasks and more when you create comment summaries.

To create a comment summary, you need to have a PDF document open in the Document pane and comments in view in the Comments pane. The pane can be open or collapsed. Comments can be filtered according to the sorts and filtering you want to apply, but at least one comment with the criteria must exist for a summary report to contain comment information.

If the Comments pane is collapsed, you create a comment summary by opening the Comment & Markup Task Button pull-down menu and select Summarize Comments. If the Comments pane is open, you can choose the menu command from the Options menu.

When you select Summarize Comments from either menu command, the Summarize Options dialog box opens, as shown in Figure 15-57.

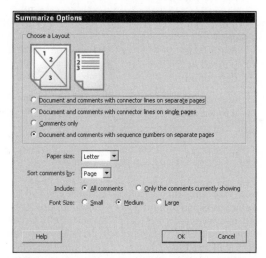

Figure 15-57: Select Summarize Comments from the Comments menu or a context menu in the Comments pane to open the Summarize Options dialog box.

The first four radio buttons in the dialog box offer you choices for the way the summary pages are created and the page layout view, which may contain single page views or Continuous – Facing Pages views. The resulting summaries are created as separate PDF documents.

Choices for creating a comment summary in the Summarize Options dialog box include

✦ **Document and comments with connector lines on separate pages:** This option creates a comment summary with each summary page aside the respective document page with connector lines from each comment on a page to the summarized item in a new summary. When the summary is created, Acrobat automatically switches to a Continuous – Facing Pages layout as shown in Figure 15-58.

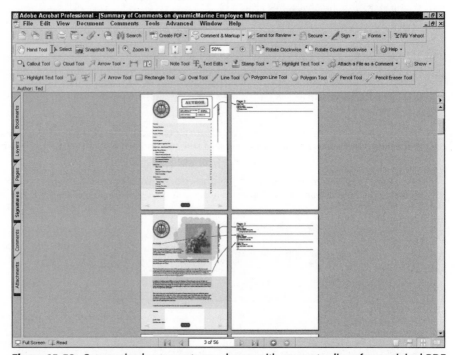

Figure 15-58: Summarized comments are shown with connector lines from original PDF pages and comments. Summary pages are created for each page in the PDF.

✦ **Document and comments with connector lines on single pages:** The summary is similar to the preceding option; however, the PDF document and the summary are created together on a single landscape page as shown in Figure 15-59. The size of the paper is determined by the setting specified in the Paper size drop-down menu. One advantage for this summary view compared to the preceding summary is the comments, connector lines, and summary data require a little less room on your monitor to view the original file and the summary information. Furthermore, if you export summaries for other users, the summarized information and original file are assembled together in a single document.

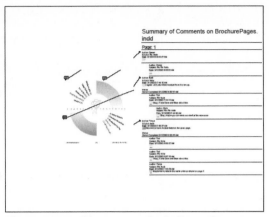

Figure 15-59: This summary is similar to the one created in the preceding figure, but the PDF page and summary are created on new pages in a single document.

✦ **Comments only:** This summary option is similar to summaries created in earlier versions of Acrobat. Only the summarized data are assembled together on single pages. The comment summaries are shown in a hierarchy according to the sort order you select in this dialog box. In Figure 15-60 the sort order is shown with comments sorted by Page. The page layout is a single page view.

✦ **Document and comments with sequence numbers on separate pages:** Summaries are created similarly to the method described in the preceding bullet, but with the addition of sequence numbers assigned to each comment according to the sort order and the order in which the comments were created. The page layout view is Continuous – Facing Pages, which shows the comments with sequence numbers and the resulting summary in the opposing page view.

✦ **Paper size:** From the pull-down menu select a paper size according to the sizes available for your selected printer.

✦ **Sort comments by:** From the pull-down menu you can choose from four different options. The default is a sort according to Page. If you want another sort order, choose from Author, Type, or Date from the pull-down menu options. The sort order selected in the Summarize Options dialog box supercedes the sort order selected in the Comments pane.

✦ **Include:** All comments summarizes all comments on the PDF pages regardless of whether the comments are in view or hidden. The Only the comments currently showing option creates a comment summary from the comments visible in the Comments pane.

✦ **Font Size:** Applies to the font used in the comment summary description on the newly created pages. Depending on the size selected, the summary pages may be fewer (Small) or more pages (Large). The point size for small is 7.5 points, for medium 10 points, and for large 13.33 points.

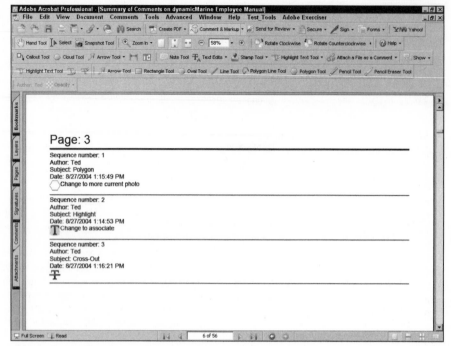

Figure 15-60: The summary of comments is created as single pages in a hierarchical order according to the specified sort order.

Comment summaries are particularly useful when sending PDF documents to Adobe Reader users. Although Reader users can see comments you create in a PDF document, they cannot create comment summaries. You can create a summary for a Reader user and append the new document to the existing PDF file, then send the file to other members in your workgroup.

Comparing Documents (Acrobat Professional)

If you set up a review for users to provide feedback on a document, you may incorporate recommended changes in a file. As you work on modifying files, you may end up with several documents in different development stages. If you aren't quite certain which document contains your finished edits, you may have a need to compare files to check for the most recent updates. Acrobat's Compare Documents feature (Acrobat Pro Only) provides you a method for analyzing two files and reporting all differences between them.

To compare two documents choose Document ➪ Compare Documents. The Compare Documents dialog box opens. You can open the dialog box without any file open in the Document pane or open both files to compare and then select the menu command. In Figure 15-61 I have two files titled graph.pdf and grapha.pdf. Because these two files have similar names, I'm not certain which document contains revisions. Therefore, the documents are selected for comparison to check the differences.

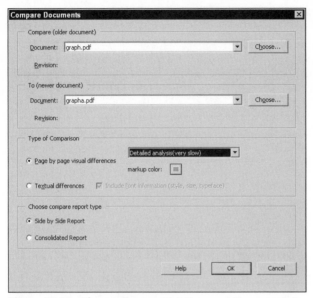

Figure 15-61: Choose Document ⇨ Compare Documents to open the Compare Documents dialog box.

The Compare Documents dialog box contains the following options:

✦ **Document:** The first two items are used to identify the documents for comparison. If no files are open in the Document pane, click the Choose button and select a file in the Open dialog box that appears. Click the second Choose button and open a second file. If you have the two documents to be compared open in the Document pane before opening the Compare Documents dialog box, the pull-down menus show you both open files. Select one file in the top pull-down menu and the second file in the next pull-down menu.

✦ **Page by page visual differences:** Three options are available from pull-down menu choices. Depending on which item you choose, the reports are more or less detailed and the speed in which the documents are compared relate to how much detail you want to analyze. A detailed analysis takes more time than the other two options. Choose from Detailed analysis, Normal analysis, and Coarse analysis from the menu. Small visual differences between documents are reported when choosing the Detailed analysis (very slow) option. The resulting report shows differences in very small graphics. The Coarse analysis ignores small graphics that may appear on one document or another, and the Normal option falls somewhere in between the other two.

✦ **Textual differences:** Selecting this radio button deselects the preceding radio button selection. Use this option if your only interest is in comparing text in the document while ignoring graphics and the layout or reading order. If you want to compare fonts between documents, select the Include font information (style, size, typeface) check box. This option is very handy for reviews where you have moved chunks of text around in a document, but have not really changed the words. It's good for legal documents, chapters, articles, and so on.

✦ **Markup color:** A report is created with markups. You can choose what color is used for the markups by clicking on the color swatch and selecting a preset color or a custom color.

✦ **Choose compare report type:** After comparing two files, Acrobat creates a report. The type of report can be either a Side by Side Report with the two documents displayed in a Continuous – Facing Page layout and comparison marks showing the differences, or a Consolidated Report where differences are marked with comment notes in a single PDF document. Choose the report type and click OK.

Acrobat compares the documents according to the attributes selected in the Compare Documents dialog box. When the comparison is finished, the report is created according to the report type selected in the Compare Documents dialog box.

Summary

✦ Acrobat provides an extensive set of Comment preferences. Before beginning any review session you should review the preference settings by choosing Edit ⇨ Preferences and clicking on Commenting in the left pane.

✦ Two toolbars exist with commenting tools — the Commenting toolbar and the Drawing Markups toolbar.

✦ Most comments created in Acrobat have associated note pop-up windows where you can type comments.

✦ You access comment properties by opening context menus from a note icon or pop-up note title bar.

✦ You can create custom stamps in Acrobat from a variety of different file formats.

✦ The Comments pane lists all comments in a PDF document. Additional tools are available in the Comments pane where you can mark status changes in comments, check comment status, and filter comments.

✦ You can enable usage rights for Adobe Reader users to participate in comment reviews from Acrobat Professional.

✦ Comments can be filtered and sorted to isolate authors, types, dates, and other criteria. When exporting comments, only the sorted comments in view in the Comments pane are exported.

✦ Comments exported from a document can be imported into a matching PDF file, a Word file, and an AutoCAD file.

✦ When exporting comments from Acrobat as a file, the comment data are saved as FDF or XFDF and result in smaller file sizes.

✦ Comment summaries are displayed in one of four different report styles. When a summary is created it can be sorted upon creation and saved as a separate PDF file.

✦ The Compare Documents command enables you to locate differences for text and images between two PDF documents. Reports are generated with comments describing found differences.

✦   ✦   ✦

Working with Review Sessions

Throughout this book the use of PDFs on the Web is addressed. As I discussed in Chapter 7, you can download selected Web pages or entire Web sites and have all the HTML pages converted to PDF. In Acrobat 6 and 7 you can convert media, animation, and sound to PDFs with the animated pages appearing the same in Acrobat viewers as when you see them on Web sites.

Coming ahead in Chapter 24, I talk about eBooks and downloading books as Digital Editions; in Chapter 27 I talk about submitting form data; and in other chapters you find similar discussions on Acrobat PDFs hosted online. In short, the Web plays a major role with much of your Acrobat activity.

This chapter builds on information covered in Chapter 15 where I discussed using the commenting tools, menus, and Comments pane and combines that information with yet another means related to the Web. In this chapter I cover commenting through e-mail–based reviews & approvals, and browser-based reviews.

Setting Up the Commenting for Reviews Environment

Commenting in review sessions requires use of the same tools discussed in Chapter 15. If you haven't read over Chapter 15 take a moment to look over loading commenting tools and opening the Comments pane. The tools you need to follow along in this chapter are the Commenting tools, Drawing Markups tools, Drawing tools, and Properties bar. Load these tools as was explained in Chapter 15.

Creating an E-mail–Based Review

The abundant number of comment tools, properties, and menu commands would be nothing more than overkill if all you want to do is add some comments on PDF pages for your own use. Acrobat is designed with much more sophistication when it comes to commenting, and the tools provided to you are intended to help you share comments in workgroups.

Comment and review among workgroups is handled in two ways. You can set up an e-mail–based review and exchange comments with your coworkers and colleagues where PDFs and data are exchanged through e-mail, or you can set up a browser-based review where comments are uploaded and downloaded by participants to a network or Web server in the review process. In Acrobat 6 browser-based reviews were limited to Acrobat running under Windows. In Acrobat 7 browser-based reviews are supported as equally on the Macintosh as they are on Windows.

Adobe's Acrobat team wanted to make it almost seamless for any user to not only start a review session but participate in a review session. And now with the ability to enable documents with usage rights for Adobe Reader users, anyone with the free Adobe Reader software can participate in a review.

Cross-Reference   For more information on adding usage rights to PDFs, see Chapters 3 and 15.

Initiating an e-mail review

An e-mail–based review is a method for you, the PDF author, to share a document that needs input from other members of a workgroup, such as a proposal or draft document, with other users and ask them to make comments for feedback. As comments are submitted from other users, you can track comments from others and make decisions for how the comments are treated. Decisions such as accepting or rejecting comments are part of this process. The comment exchanges between you and your workgroup members are handled through e-mail exchanges.

When you send a file for review, an FDF (Forms Data Format) file, which includes a copy of your original PDF as well as information to ensure the review will return to you, is sent to users in an e-mail list. When a recipient receives the e-mail inviting him or her to review your document, the attachment to the e-mail is an FDF packaged with the PDF document. The recipients open the e-mail attachment in Acrobat and make comments. When a reviewer finishes commenting, the reviewer sends the data back to the PDF author. The data sent from the reviewers are also sent as FDF files, but the PDF document is not sent along with the comment data for files in excess of a file size you can specify in the Reviewing Preferences. If you start with a large PDF file, the comment exchanges require much less data transfers as the comment data are typically much smaller than original PDF files.

Note   Before initiating a review, be certain to add your e-mail address in the Identity preferences. If you don't add the Identity preferences Acrobat prompts you in a dialog box and opens the Identity preferences for you. You can't proceed until you fill in the preference text boxes. Open the Preferences dialog box and select Identity. Add your personal identity information including your e-mail address. The e-mail address supplied in the Identity preferences is used when e-mailing PDFs from within Acrobat.

To understand how to start an e-mail–based review, follow these steps:

STEPS: Initiating an e-mail–based review

1. **Open a document in Acrobat Professional.** Opening a document is optional as you can begin a review without a document open in the Document pane. In this example, I start with a document open in Acrobat Professional. If using Acrobat Standard, you can

initiate an e-mail–based review, but you cannot enable the document with usage rights for Adobe Reader users. If using Acrobat Professional you have an option for enabling the document for Reader users to participate in your review.

2. **Initiate the review.** If you want to make a comment on your document you can do so, but you need to be certain to save all your updates. After saving the file, select Send by Email for Review from the Send for Review Task Button in the Tasks toolbar. The Send by Email for Review: Step 1 of 3 dialog box opens as shown in Figure 16-1. This is the first of three dialog boxes appearing when you initiate a review.

By default documents active in the Document pane are specified in the field box in the dialog box. If you change your mind or you start a review without a document open in Acrobat, click the Browse button and browse your hard drive to locate a file.

Note   You can also access the same menu command by choosing Comments ⇨ Send for Review ⇨ Send by Email for Review or also by choosing File ⇨ Send for Review ⇨ Send by Email for Review. Each of the commands opens the same dialog box to initiate the review.

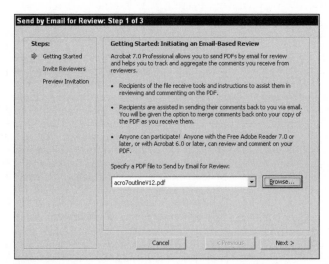

Figure 16-1: To start a review session, open the PDF to be used for the review and choose File ⇨ Send for Review ⇨ Send by Email for Review. The Send by Email for Review dialog box opens containing instructions for starting a review.

3. **Invite reviewers.** After identifying the file to send out for review, click the Next button to open the Send by Email for Review: Step 2 of 3 pane, as shown in Figure 16-2. The Address Book window will contain a list of recipients for your review. Type in the e-mail addresses for the people you want to participate in the review or click Address Book to launch your e-mail address book to select reviewers to invite.

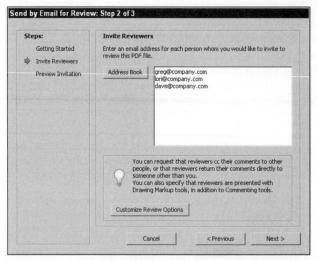

Figure 16-2: Add e-mail addresses for the review participants.

4. **Enable the PDF for Adobe Reader usage rights.** Click the Customize Review Options button to open the Review Options dialog box shown in Figure 16-3. If you want the Drawing Markup tools accessed by Acrobat Standard and Adobe Reader users, check the box for Display Drawing Markup Tools for this Review. If you want Adobe Reader users to participate in the review, check the box for Also allow users of Free Adobe Reader 7.0 to participate in this review. Click OK and you return to the Step 2 pane. Additionally, you can specify who will receive the review comments; the default is the e-mail address you specified in the Identity properties. However, you can add additional names or change it to a name of a co-worker or administrator. For more information on working with an Address Book in review sessions, see the sidebar at the end of these steps.

Note   In Figure 16-3 you can see a light bulb in the dialog box. Whenever you see this image, be certain to read the text warning aside the image. This is particularly important when enabling PDFs with Adobe Reader usage rights. Some features on PDFs are lost when the files are enabled with usage rights. For example, if you send a form out for review and enable the document with usage rights, all form fields are lost to both Acrobat and Adobe Reader users.

5. **Preview the invitation.** Click Next and you arrive at the Send by Email for Review: Step 3 of 3 pane as shown in Figure 16-4. This pane displays a preview of the e-mail message you are about to send to reviewers. You can edit the Invitation Message Subject or Invitation Message by typing in the respective window. Click Send Invitation when the preview appears as you like to start the e-mail process.

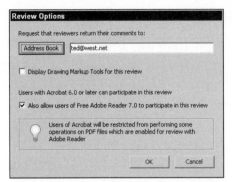

Figure 16-3: Open the Review Options dialog box and add options for using Drawing tools and Adobe Reader usage rights.

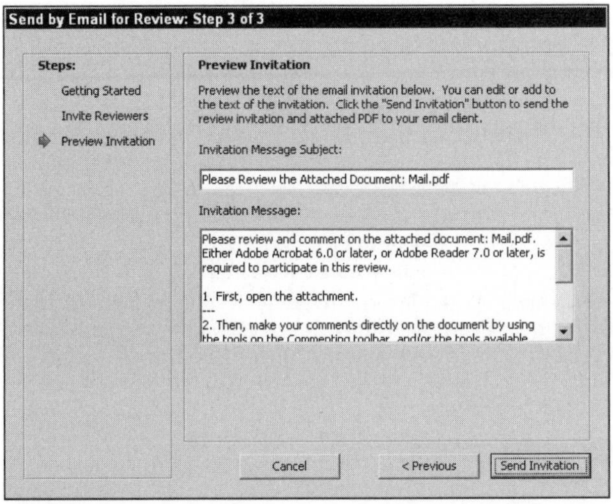

Figure 16-4: Preview the message to be sent to reviewers.

6. **Send the invitation.** If your default e-mail program does not immediately send the invitation to reviewers, open your default e-mail program and click the Send (or Send/Receive) button to commence the e-mail initiation. In Figure 16-5 an invitation is displayed in Microsoft Outlook showing the recipients in the To field, the Subject of the e-mail, and a file attachment in the Attach field. The message is derived from the Send by Email For Review dialog box. Note that before initiating a send, you can still edit the message. Click the Send (or Send/Receive) button and the e-mail and attachment are sent to the reviewers.

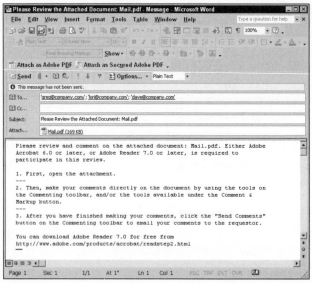

Figure 16-5: If your default e-mail program does not send the message, open the program and click the Send (or Send/Receive) button.

Managing an Address Book for Review Sessions

When you open the Address Book from the Invite Reviewers section, shown in Figure 16-2, or from the Review Options dialog box shown in Figure 16-3, several options are available to manage addresses that you can use in future review sessions. The Address Book shown in the figure offers the following:

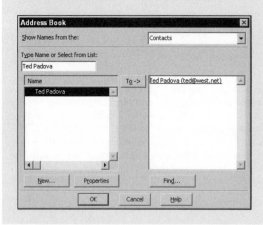

✦ **Show Names from the:** Choices appear from a pull-down menu. If using Microsoft Outlook the choices are Outlook Address Book and Contacts. You can choose to use either your e-mail program's address book or a contact list you create in Acrobat.

✦ **Type Name or Select from List:** Type a name to be added to your recipients list or select a name from the left list window.

✦ **To:** Click a name in the Name list and click the To-> button to copy the name to the To list window. All addresses you list in the right window are added to a review session when you click the OK button.

✦ **New:** Your e-mail program's contact identity form opens where you add identifying information for a new contact. To add contacts, complete the information in the window that's shown in the figure.

✦ **Properties:** Select a name in the Name list and click Properties to open the contact identifying information where you can edit the fields.

✦ **Find:** Click Find to search for a contact.

After entering e-mail addresses in your Address Book you can return to the Address Book each time you create a new review and select participants from the list of e-mail addresses.

Participating in a review

Participants in a review include you, the PDF author and review initiator, and the people you select as reviewers. In your role, you field all comments from reviewers. If you use the e-mail–based review to send comments back to users, Acrobat does permit you to reply to users' comments. A review session is designed for a single set of responses; however, if you want, you can exchange comments back and forth between you and the reviewers.

Before you begin a review, be certain to save any edits made on the PDF. If you insert pages, delete pages, or perform a number of other edits without saving, the comments retrieved from others will appear out of place and make it difficult to understand where comments are made from the reviewers. Also, be certain to keep the original PDF in the same folder. If you decide to move the PDF to another folder, be certain to keep track of the location where the PDF resides. As you update comments, Acrobat needs to keep track of the directory path where the original PDF can be found. If Acrobat can't find the PDF, you are prompted to search for it.

During a review period you and your recipients use tools in Acrobat designed for use with e-mail reviews. When starting an e-mail review, the first time you access the Send by Email for Review menu command, the FDF file with the PDF copy are sent to recipients. All subsequent comment exchanges between you and reviewers are handled with other tools. Be certain to not return to the command if you decide to respond to user comments. Doing so sends another FDF wrapper with the embedded PDF. If PDF files are large in file size the redundancy in sending the original PDF burdens users by having to download larger files when retrieving their e-mails.

Avoiding Problems with E-mail Reviews

It is critical to understand what data are exchanged during an e-mail review. When you begin a review and select the Send by Email for Review command, an FDF *wrapper* embeds a PDF document in the e-mail attachment. The PDF document is received by other participants who then add comments to the PDF document.

When the review participants send responses back to the PDF author, only FDF data may be sent without an embedded PDF document. If a participant wants to add a reviewer and the participant sends the FDF data to a user who has not been invited to participate in a review, the new participant won't be able to open the FDF file because it includes only the comments and *not* the original PDF document.

If recipients want to invite additional users (on the authority of the review initiator) the *unwrapped* PDF needs to be distributed to other users. If you want to send the FDF data, you need to send the FDF file *and* the PDF document to users who have not been invited for participation from the PDF author.

If you receive additional comments during a review, an FDF data file is sent to you. Double-clicking the FDF data file opens the PDF document you originally sent (or started with) if you haven't deleted the file or changed the directory path. When working with e-mail reviews it's important to understand that two files exist. If you experience problems trying to open an FDF file in Acrobat you either don't have the PDF on your hard drive or Acrobat lost the connection to the file.

An author who wants to invite new users to participate in a review must make the invitation with the proper menu command. You add additional users to a review by opening the Tracker (Send for Review ⇨ Tracker or Comments ⇨ Tracker or Comments pane Options ⇨ Tracker) and selecting Invite Additional Reviewers from the Manage pull-down menu. When you select this command, the PDF is contained in the FDF wrapper and sent to new users.

Recipient participation

A recipient receiving your e-mail with the FDF attachment can open the attachment from the attachment folder or from directly within the e-mail message. Double-clicking the file attachment launches Acrobat and loads the PDF in the Document pane.

Note   When a recipient sees the file attachment in an e-mail message, the file appears as an FDF file. Although instructions are provided in the e-mail message on how to open the file, some users may become confused about the file received when they see the FDF extension on the filename. You may need to help users understand that although the file reads as an FDF file, the user can double-click the file attachment to open the wrapped PDF document.

Reviewers make comments with any of the comment tools discussed earlier in this chapter. After a reviewer completes a review session, the reviewer clicks the Send Comments button in the Commenting toolbar as shown in Figure 16-6.

When the reviewer sends a response to the PDF author, the PDF author's e-mail address is automatically supplied in the To field in the e-mail program. The reviewer clicks Send and the FDF data are sent back to the PDF author.

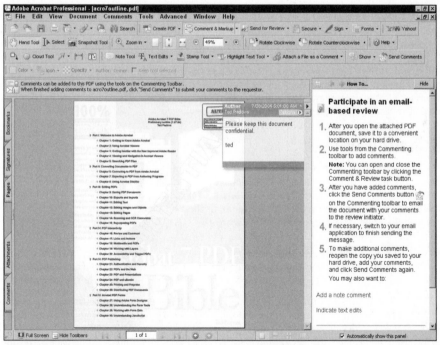

Figure 16-6: A reviewer clicks the Send Comments button in either the Commenting toolbar or the Comments menu after making comments to send back to the review initiator.

Author participation

As comments are submitted from reviewers, you'll want to track reviews and decide to mark them for a status. If you want to reply to the recipients you can elect to send a reply to recipient comments; however, in many cases you'll want to make corrections and start a new review session. If you send a reply, each comment is treated like a separate thread in Acrobat. Rather than your having to select different tools to make responses scattered around a document page, Acrobat keeps each thread nestled together to make following a thread easier. Replies are contained in Note pop-up windows. If you want to reply to a comment, open a context menu on the note pop-up and select Reply or select the comment in the Comments pane and click the Reply button.

Updating comments

You send a file to recipients for review. The reviewers then send comments back to you. Your original document needs updating to reflect the new additions added by other reviewers. When you receive an e-mail attachment, the data are submitted to you in FDF format that contains all the comment information. Only a single PDF resides on your computer. If you want to merge the data sent by other reviewers with your existing PDF document, double-click the file attachment sent back to you. Acrobat updates the original PDF document with the new comments.

Asking new reviewers to participate

You may begin a review and later decide you want to add new users to participate in the review. You can add new reviewers to a review at any time. To add a reviewer, open the Tracker from the Comments menu, the Comments & Markup Task Button, or the Options pull-down in the Comments pane. The Tracker opens in a separate window. From the Manage pull-down menu, select Invite More Reviewers. The same dialog box opens as when you initiate a review. Add the recipient's e-mail address and any additional message in the Invitation Message window and click OK.

Using the Tracker

The Tracker is a separate window that opens on top of the Acrobat window where you find menu commands to help manage e-mail–based reviews and browser-based reviews. To open the Tracker, select Tracker from the Comment & Markup Task Button, choose Comments ➪ Tracker, or from the Options pull-down menu in the Comments pane select Tracker. All three menu items open the Tracker shown in Figure 16-7.

Viewing documents in the Tracker

The left pane in the Tracker lists all documents you have in review. From the list, select a filename and click the Open tool in the Tracker. The respective file opens in the Document pane.

Three categories appear in the left pane. All reviews you initiate are listed in the My Reviews list. Expand the list to see reviews by filename. The Participant Reviews contain all reviews sent to you by another review initiator. Offline comments include browser-based reviews where you have saved files for offline commenting. (See "Sharing Comments online" later in this chapter.)

Figure 16-7: The Tracker is a pane that provides menu commands for helping you manage e-mail– and browser-based reviews.

When a document is viewed in an expanded list, you can select additional menu commands by opening a context menu from a file in the list. The menu commands include

✦ **Open:** Opens the selected file the same as clicking the Open tool.

✦ **Email All Reviewers:** Select this option and your default e-mail application is opened with the To field populated with all review participants. Type a message and click the Send button and you can send a message to the reviewers.

✦ **Send Review Reminder:** This option also launches your default e-mail application with the To field populated with the addresses of the review participants. An automated message appears in the message window to remind reviewers to comment on the document in review. This option is only available to review initiators and does not appear in a context menu when selecting a file in the Participant Reviews context menus.

✦ **Invite Additional Reviewers:** Also launches your default e-mail application with an automated message to invite other reviewers. The selected PDF file used for initiating the original review is added as a file attachment.

✦ **Remove:** Removes the selected file from the review category the same as clicking the Remove tool.

✦ **Send To Folder:** From the submenu you can create a new folder that is added to the menu. When you return to the Send To Folder command, the submenu shows a list of folders where you can nest reviews to organize the documents in a hierarchical order.

Expand/Collapse

Click the Expand tool to expand a list. On Windows a collapsed list is marked with a plus (+) symbol. On the Macintosh a collapsed list is marked with a right-pointing arrowhead. If a list is collapsed, the Expand button is active. If a list is already expanded, the Expand button is grayed out.

Click the Collapse tool when a list is expanded. Collapsing lists can help you manage more reviews in the list.

Expand and Collapse appears active for any one of the three groups when you select that group. For example, selecting Participant Reviews when the list is expanded activates the Collapse tool. Selecting a file in the expanded list from any category displays the name of the PDF document used in the review, the date the review was sent, and a list of participants that were invited to the review in the right pane.

Services

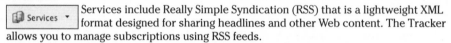 Services include Really Simple Syndication (RSS) that is a lightweight XML format designed for sharing headlines and other Web content. The Tracker allows you to manage subscriptions using RSS feeds.

Select from the first two menu commands for additional services. The first command is Subscribe. Select Subscribe and a dialog box opens where you type a URL to subscribe to an online service. In Figure 16-8 you can see news services listed in the Tracker window. These services were subscribed to using the Subscribe command in the Services pull-down menu. As shown in Figure 16-7, the Tracker can be used as a news subscription service. Additional services can include news broadcast services, music channels, and any other service using the RSS feed.

The second command is Search for Additional Services. The Search for Acrobat Services dialog box opens and lists additional services if they are available. If nothing appears in the dialog box, no additional services are available for the respective review.

New Folder

Click New Folder to create a new folder where you can organize review documents in nested folders. This tool performs the same action as the submenu command available when you open a context menu from a selected review document.

Remove

Select a document in one of the category lists and click Remove to eliminate the document from the Tracker window. Use this tool when you complete a review as an initiator, participant, or when performing offline reviews.

Manage

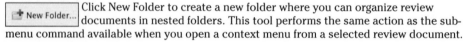 The Manage tool contains a pull-down menu with menu options for managing reviews. Three menu commands appear that are the same as some of the menu commands found when you open a context menu. Choose from Email All Reviewers, Send Review Reminder, or Invite Additional Reviewers. These options are described in the earlier section "Viewing documents in the Tracker."

The Tracker is described here in the section related to e-mail–based reviews; however, the Tracker is used for all review types. Whether you send e-mail–based reviews or work with browser-based reviews, the Tracker window is something you'll use frequently.

Note   Online commenting cannot be performed by Adobe Reader users when files have been enabled using usage rights for Acrobat Professional. In order for Adobe Reader users to particiapate in browser–based reviews, a PDF document needs to be enabled with usage rights using Adobe Live Cycle Reader Extensions Server (ARES).

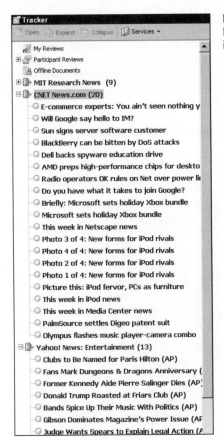

Figure 16-8: After subscribing to an RSS subscription servic e, services are listed in the Tracker window.

Using Browser-Based Reviews

In order to share comments online or on network servers, you must use a Web browser and you must have Acrobat installed on your computer. The fundamental structure of comment sharing requires a PDF document to be present at a location on a network server or URL where workgroup members have access. As comments are added to the PDF file, the data are stored in individual FDF (Form Data File) files. The associated FDF data can be viewed and shared among users. An individual may delete or amend his/her own data, but won't be able to delete the data submitted by other users. The commenting tools for Send and Receive Comments are added to the Commenting toolbar when PDFs are viewed within a Web browser, as shown in Figure 16-9. These tools enable you to upload and download the FDF data that are shared among workgroup members.

Setting reviewer preferences

Regardless of whether you elect to share comments on Web servers or on a local area network, you need to configure Acrobat properly for online commenting. To set up the configuration, choose Edit ➪ Preferences and click Reviewing in the left pane in the Preferences dialog box. The Reviewing preferences appear in the right pane as shown in Figure 16-10. The first item to address is the Server Type, which you choose from the pull-down menu.

Figure 16-9: Commenting tools are loaded in a Web browser when viewing PDFs online in browser-based reviews.

On Windows you have choices for Custom, Database, Network Folder, None, Web Discussions, and WebDAV. All options other than Network Folder and None require assistance from your system administrator. In order to properly configure a server, your network administrator can obtain assistance from Adobe help documents hosted online at Adobe's Web site. Special documents designed for configuring Web servers are made available to users. If you want to configure a WebDAV server for example, log on to http://support.adobe.com/devsup/devsup.nsf/main.html. The Adobe Solutions Network provides instructions on configurations for WebDAV servers. If you use other server types, you can search the Adobe Solutions Network by clicking the Search button on the Adobe Home page.

The Macintosh is supported for browser-based reviews in Acrobat 7 and you need to set preferences like you do in Windows when you first start working with browser-based reviews. The options available to you when opening the Server Type pull-down menu include Custom, Network, None, and WebDAV. Note that Database and Web Discussions are not available on Macintosh.

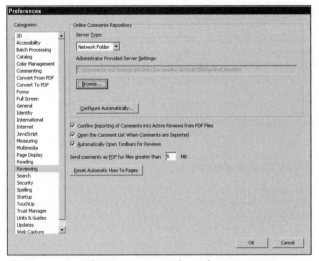

Figure 16-10: Select a server type from the Server Type pull-down menu in the Reviewing preferences.

Other options in the Reviewing preferences include

✦ **Configure Automatically:** Your system administrator can make available comment repositories. When they are available, clicking this button opens an auto configuration dialog box where you can select a configuration for a particular review session.

✦ **Confirm Importing of Comments into Active Reviews from PDF Files:** When enabled, an alert dialog box opens to confirm importing comments when you open the online document in a Web browser.

✦ **Open the Comment List When Comments are Imported:** The Comments pane opens when comments are imported in the document.

✦ **Automatically Open Toolbars for Reviews:** The Commenting and Markup toolbars are automatically opened when you open the review document in your Web browser.

✦ **Send comments as FDF for files greater than:** Prior to version 7.0 of Acrobat all comments were exchanged using FDF data only. In Acrobat 7, the PDF document and FDF data are sent to the server. By default, if the file size is less than 10MB, the PDF and FDF data are exchanged. If you want just FDF data used in the exchanges for files lower than a certain size, edit the text box to the desired value. For example, entering 2 in the text box sends just FDF data for PDFs above 2MB.

✦ **Reset Automatic How To Pages:** Resets the help pages in the How To window to default views.

Comments on local area networks

Configuration for sharing comments on local servers requires no special assistance from network administrators. You can create a folder or directory on a server and identify the folder containing documents shared among users. For network collaboration, select the Network Folder menu command in the Reviewing preferences. A Browse button directly below the Server Type pull-down menu enables you to navigate your server and find the file or folder to be used for collaboration. If you change server settings, you'll need to return to the preferences. However, if you add PDFs to a folder where sharing comments is targeted, you can leave the preferences alone and select different files for sharing comments.

Uploading a document for review

In order to use online commenting on a network or server, you have to properly copy the document to the target destination. Copying the file to a server is handled within Acrobat. Open either the Comment menu or the File menu and choose Send for Review ⇨ Upload for Browser-Based Review. The Initiate an Online Review: Step 1 of 4 dialog box opens. You select a file to upload and toggle through the panes much like you select files for e-mail–based reviews. When you arrive at the last pane you complete the upload with an invitation to users to participate in the review. The process ends much like e-mail–based reviews where recipients receive an e-mail notifying them of the invitation. The e-mail received by recipients contains FDF data which includes information about the initiator and the URL to the review location.

Sharing comments

After the configuration has been set up in Acrobat, open your Web browser and navigate to the location where the PDF file used for sharing is located. Be certain to use the most recent versions of either Microsoft Internet Explorer, Netscape, or Apple's Safari.

You can use any of the comment tools among the tool groups in the Acrobat Toolbar Well that appears inside the browser window. For access to additional toolbars, open a context menu on the Toolbar Well and select the toolbars you want to use. After adding a comment, click Send and Receive Comments on the Commenting toolbar. All comments you make are uploaded to the server and comments from other users are downloaded to the document in review.

Caution   If you create a comment and quit your browser or you navigate to another page before uploading new comments, Acrobat automatically uploads the comments for you. This feature is handy, but it can also create problems if you have any second thoughts about sending a comment. Before you create a comment, be certain to think it out and add only those remarks you intend to submit to avoid inadvertently sending the wrong comments.

To delete a comment, you can use a context menu from either the Comments palette where the comments are displayed or select the comment in the Document pane and select Delete from the menu commands. When the context menu opens, select Delete. You can also address properties by opening a context menu. If you want to change author name or select a different icon for the comment appearance, options are available in the comment properties. If you want to use the Stamp tool, all the stamps accessible from Acrobat are also available from within the Web browser. In addition, the Text Edit tools, the drawing tools, and so on are all available inside your browser window.

Working offline

Acrobat also offers you an opportunity to work offline when sharing comments on any kind of server. You may be temporarily away from an Internet connection or network connection and want to organize comments and later submit them. To work offline, click the Save and Work Offline button on the Commenting toolbar shown in Figure 16-11.

Figure 16-11: Click Save and Work Offline to save the PDF locally on your hard drive.

The Save and Work Offline dialog box opens where you can save a copy of the PDF file to your local hard drive. The PDF file immediately opens in Acrobat with the How To window displaying information about participating in a browser-based review. Additionally, the document is listed in the Tracker window in the Offline Documents category.

You can make comments on the document, and when you're ready to re-synch with the online server, select Go Back Online from the Commenting toolbar as shown in Figure 16-12.

Figure 16-12: When working offline, the Go Back Online tool is loaded in the Commenting toolbar. Click Go Back Online and the online version of the PDF opens in your Web browser.

The online version of the PDF opens in your Web browser with your comments visible. To upload your comments to the server, click the Send and Receive Comments tool shown in Figure 16-13.

Figure 16-13: Click the Send and Receive Comments tool in the Web browser to upload comments that you added in an offline session.

Summary

✦ You can initiate e-mail reviews in Acrobat and participate in reviews in either Acrobat Standard or Acrobat Professional. For Adobe Reader participation, documents need to be enabled with usage rights from Adobe LiveCycle Reader Extensions Server.

✦ The Tracker lists all documents in review from e-mail–based reviews, browser-based reviews and documents in review that are offline. The Tracker contains several tools to help manage your document reviews. Additionally, you can manage RSS (Really Simple Syndication) feeds.

✦ Online commenting first requires you to identify the location where a PDF is stored for workgroup commenting. Open the Preferences dialog box and select Reviewing. Choose the type of connection from the pull-down menu for Server Type.

✦ Online comments can be made directly online inside a Web browser or offline in Acrobat Professional or Acrobat Standard. After making comments you need to log on to your server and select the Send and Receive Comments tool to upload and download comments. The comments are sent as FDF data.

✦   ✦   ✦

Links and Actions

One of the truly great features Adobe Acrobat offers is the ability to create interactive documents containing hot links that invoke many different actions. Acrobat provides you with many tools and methods for making your PDFs come alive, and Acrobat helps you refine documents for user navigation and interactivity. Regardless of whether you post PDFs on Web servers, communicate via e-mail, replicate CD-ROMs, or work with documents on local network servers, Acrobat offers tools and features that help you create dynamic documents.

In this chapter you learn how to create links with a variety of Acrobat tools and learn some of the differences between several methods for linking views. With links originating from various elements such as Bookmarks, page actions, links, and destinations, you have a number of action tools that provide you with an almost limitless opportunity for handling views and relationships between documents. This chapter covers creating hot links and all the different actions you can associate with links.

Setting Up the Links and Actions Environment

Online review and comment was the subject of the previous chapter. If you have read this book in a linear fashion, all the tools used in review and comment might be docked in your Toolbar Well. Because these tools take up so much room, you'll want to eliminate them and reset the toolbar. From a context menu, select Reset Toolbars to return to defaults.

Tools used for creating links come from the Advanced Editing tools and the Forms tools. To set up the environment for working with links and actions, open the Advanced Editing tools by opening a context menu on the Toolbar Well. Return to the context menu and open the Properties bar. Choose Tools ➪ Advanced Editing ➪ Show Forms Toolbar. Open a context menu on the Toolbar Well and select Dock all Toolbars.

Note Acrobat Form tools are available only in Acrobat Professional.

Working with Bookmarks

If you use programs that support exporting to PDF with structure, you can add Bookmarks automatically at the time PDF files are created. Programs such as Microsoft Word, Microsoft Excel, Microsoft PowerPoint, Microsoft Visio, Autodesk AutoCAD, Adobe PageMaker, Adobe InDesign, Adobe FrameMaker, and QuarkXPress support Bookmark creation from style sheets when you use export tools in the authoring programs. Ideally, in a workflow environment where these programs are used, creating Bookmarks from authoring applications when permitted by the program and when the Bookmark action relates to page views is advantageous. In other programs, or when editing PDFs with Bookmarks, you may need to reassign Bookmark actions, order Bookmarks in a hierarchy, or create additional Bookmarks.

Cross-Reference   For more information regarding Bookmark exports from authoring programs, see Chapter 7.

The most common Bookmark action in Acrobat is navigating page views. Whereas analog Bookmarks mark pages, the electronic Bookmarks in a PDF document enable you to navigate to different pages and different zoom views. You can capture various page views and zoom in on images, text, tables, and so on in Acrobat as Bookmark destinations. In a broader sense, you can use Bookmarks to invoke actions such as opening/closing files, opening secondary files, executing menu commands, submitting forms, playing sounds and movies, executing JavaScripts, and a host of other related actions.

Creating Bookmarks

As long as you understand the sequence of steps, creating Bookmarks is an easy task. Creating a Bookmark is like capturing a snapshot. The process involves navigating to the page and view you want to capture and then creating the Bookmark. Therefore, if you want to capture page 13 of a document in a Fit Page view, you navigate to page 13, click on the Fit Page tool, and then create the Bookmark.

You create Bookmarks from several options. When the page view is in place, open the Options menu in the Bookmarks pane and select New Bookmark. You can also open a context menu on a page and select Add Bookmark from the menu options. In Figure 17-1 the Bookmark Options menu is shown on the left and a context menu is shown on the right. Note that Figure 17-1 is used for illustration purposes — only one context menu can be opened at one time.

Click on the Bookmarks tab to access the Options menu for Bookmarks. Using a context menu, you can create a Bookmark when the Navigation pane is collapsed. When you create a Bookmark from a context menu while the pane is collapsed, the Navigation pane opens and the Bookmarks pane is placed in view.

If you open the Options menu without selecting a Bookmark in the Bookmarks pane, the menu options appear as shown in Figure 17-1. However, if you first select a Bookmark and then open the Options menu, the menu commands change to menu commands shown in Figure 17-2.

You have fewer menu options when selecting a Bookmark in the Bookmarks pane and opening a context menu than when opening the Options pull-down menu. In Figure 17-3, a context menu was opened from a selected Bookmark.

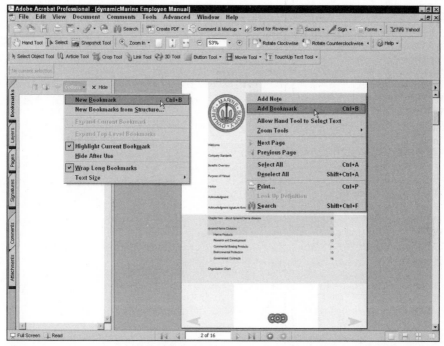

Figure 17-1: To create a Bookmark, navigate to the desired page view and select New Bookmark from the Options pull-down menu in the Bookmarks pane (left). You can also open a context menu when the Hand tool is selected and choose Add Bookmark from the menu (right).

Note By default the items *Paste under Selected Bookmark* and *Paste after Selected Bookmark* are grayed out. You need to select Cut from the menu options to make the two Paste commands become active.

You can also use shortcut keys to create a Bookmark when the Bookmarks pane is either opened or closed. Press Ctrl/⌘+B on your keyboard to create a Bookmark. In all of these methods, a Bookmark defaults to the name *Untitled*. Acrobat highlights the *Untitled* Bookmark name after the Bookmark is created. You type a name and press the Enter or Return key when finished typing.

On pages where text on the pages corresponds to names you want to use for Bookmarks, Acrobat helps simplify the naming process. Select the Select tool and highlight the text you want to use as your Bookmark name. From a context menu, select Add Bookmark. The Bookmark is created and the highlighted text is used as the Bookmark name. Figure 17-4 illustrates the stages of creating a Bookmark in this manner: 1) the page view is in place; 2) text is selected on the page and a context menu opened; 3) Add Bookmark is selected from the menu options; and 4) the Bookmark is created using the selected text for the Bookmark name. Using the Options menu or modifier keys for creating a Bookmark while text is selected creates the Bookmark in the same manner.

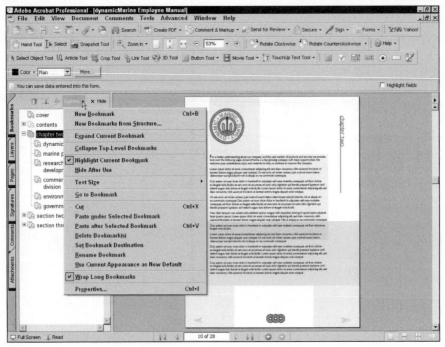

Figure 17-2: If you select a Bookmark in the Bookmarks pane and then open the Options menu, the menu offers additional commands as compared to opening the menu without selecting a Bookmark.

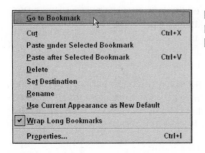

Figure 17-3: If you select a Bookmark in the Bookmarks pane, the context menu is as shown here.

Managing Bookmarks

Bookmarks created in a document appear in the Bookmarks pane in the order they are created, regardless of the page order. For example, if you create a Bookmark on page 15, and then create another on page 12, the Bookmarks are listed with page 15 before page 12 in the Bookmarks pane. At times you may want to have the Bookmarks list displayed according to page order. Additionally, Bookmarks may appear more organized if they are nested in groups. If you have a category and a list of items to fit within that category, you may want to create a hierarchy that expands or collapses. Fortunately, Acrobat enables you to change the order of Bookmarks without recreating them. Additionally, you can categorize the Bookmarks into groups.

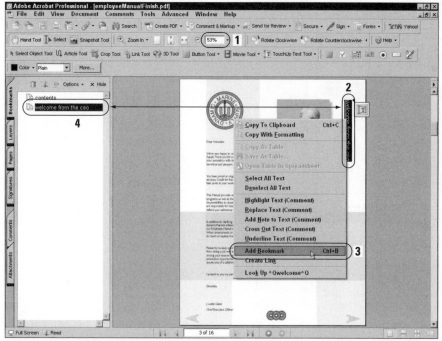

Figure 17-4: To automatically name a Bookmark, select text with the Select tool and create the Bookmark.

To reorder a Bookmark, select either the page icon or Bookmark name in the list and drag it up or down and left or right. A triangle with a dotted line appears when you drag a Bookmark, as shown in Figure 17-5. To nest a child Bookmark below a parent Bookmark, drag straight up. The triangle and line show you the target area for the Bookmark. In Figure 17-5 the first Bookmark is targeted for a child Bookmark (dragging straight up). The second Bookmark highlighted is targeted for a parent Bookmark (dragging up and to the left).

If you have a parent Bookmark with several child Bookmarks nested below it, you can move the parent to a new location. Drag the parent Bookmark and all child Bookmarks below it move with the parent. If you want to remove a child Bookmark from a nest, click and drag the Bookmark to the left and either down or up to the location desired.

In addition to moving Bookmarks, you can cut and paste them. Select a parent or child Bookmark and from a context menu or the Bookmark pane Options menu and select Paste under Selected Bookmark or Paste after Selected Bookmark. When you choose Paste under Selected Bookmark the cut Bookmark(s) is pasted as a child Bookmark under the selected Bookmark. Pasting after a selected Bookmark pastes the cut Bookmark(s) after the selected parent and all child Bookmarks.

Multiple nesting is also available with Bookmark organization. A Bookmark can be subordinate to another Bookmark that is itself nested under a parent Bookmark. To subordinate a Bookmark under a child Bookmark, use the same method as described previously for creating the first order of children. As you drag right and up slightly, you can nest Bookmarks at several levels.

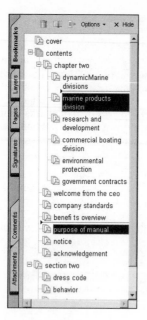

Figure 17-5: The triangle indicates where a Bookmark is to be reordered.

You can also relocate multiple Bookmarks at one time. To select several Bookmarks, Shift+click each Bookmark in a group. As you hold down the Shift key, you can add more Bookmarks to the selection. If you click one Bookmark at the top or bottom of a list and Shift+click, all Bookmarks between are selected. For a non-contiguous selection, Ctrl/⌘+click. Once selected, drag the Bookmarks to a new location in the list. Their order remains the same as it was before the move.

By default, new Bookmarks appear at the end of a Bookmark list. If you want to place a Bookmark within a series of Bookmarks, select the Bookmark you want the new Bookmark to follow. When you select New Bookmark from the Bookmarks Options menu, from a context menu, or press Ctrl/⌘+B, the new Bookmark is created at the same level after the one you selected.

Tip   If you have a file you use as a template that contains bookmarks and you want to add your template to another PDF file, open the file without bookmarks. Select Insert Pages from the Document menu. Select the template file containing bookmarks and insert the file in the open document. The pages as well as bookmarks are in your document.

Renaming Bookmarks

If you create a Bookmark and want to change the Bookmark name, select the Bookmark to be edited from the Bookmarks pane. From the Options menu, select Rename. Acrobat highlights the name in the Bookmarks pane. Type a new name and press the Return or Enter key on your keyboard to finish editing the Bookmark name. You can also click the cursor anywhere in the Document pane to finish editing the name.

You can also rename Bookmarks by clicking on a Bookmark name and clicking again on the Bookmark. You can also use a context menu, but be certain you first select the Bookmark; then open a context menu to select the menu option for Rename. When you click on a Bookmark, you go to the associated Bookmark view. Clicking a second time informs Acrobat you want to edit the name. To select the text, click and drag across the part of the name you want to edit or press Ctrl/⌘+A to select all text. When you type a new name, the selected text is deleted and replaced with the new text you type.

Structured Bookmarks

Structured Bookmarks retain document structure in files generated from Microsoft Word, Web page captures, and programs supporting PDF creation with tags. You can use structured Bookmarks to navigate PDF pages, reorganize the pages, and delete pages. If you create PDFs without tags, you can add structure to a document by choosing Advanced ⇨ Accessibility ⇨ Add Tags to Document. After you have a structured document and you create Bookmarks, more options are available to you. For example, moving a Bookmark in the Bookmarks pane only moves the Bookmark; the page associated with the Bookmark is unaffected. When you move a structured Bookmark, the page associated with the Bookmark is moved. The same holds true for Bookmark deletions, extractions, and printing.

Depending on whether you have a Bookmark or a structured Bookmark, context and the Options menu commands appear different. When you open a context menu from a standard Bookmark, the menu commands appear as shown in Figure 17-3. When you open a context menu from a structured Bookmark, the menu commands are as they appear in Figure 17-6. Notice the items that relate to Print Pages, Delete Pages, and Extract pages that are available when you open a context menu from a structured Bookmark.

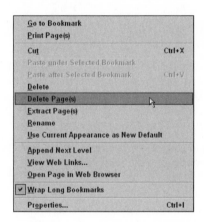

Figure 17-6: These menu commands are available when you open a structured Bookmark context menu.

When you create a Bookmark, the destination for the Bookmark is a link to a page view. In the context menu for standard Bookmarks, you see the menu command for Set Destination. You can navigate to a new page and select this command to change the Bookmark link to a new view. With structured Bookmarks, you capture the page structure (a page view, a table, a head, and so on). In the context menu be certain to select Delete and not Delete Page(s) if you want to delete a Bookmark. The Delete command deletes just the Bookmark. Delete Page(s) deletes the Bookmark and the page associated with the Bookmark.

Bookmark appearances

Both Bookmarks and structured Bookmarks contain menu options for Use Current Appearance as New Default. This menu choice is like a Bookmark style sheet where you first select the appearance of the Bookmark in terms of font style and color; then you select this menu option to set the attributes as a new default. For example, change the Bookmark to small text, italicized, in red; then open a context menu and select Use Current Appearance as New Default. All subsequent Bookmarks you create use the same style until you change the default.

The Wrap Long Bookmarks option from either menu creates a word wrap for the Bookmark name in the Bookmarks pane. By default a Bookmark appears on a single line. When you move the cursor to a Bookmark with a name longer than the pane width, a Tool Tip displays the complete Bookmark name across the page as shown in Figure 17-7. When you select Wrap Long Bookmarks, the Bookmark names appear as shown in Figure 17-8.

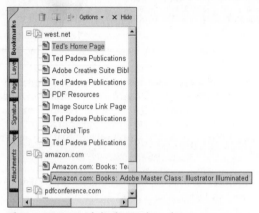

Figure 17-7: By default, Bookmark names are shown in a single line of text cut off at the end of the Bookmark pane. When the name is longer than the pane width, a Tool Tip shows the complete name extended beyond the pane width.

Figure 17-8: When Wrap Long Bookmarks is selected, Bookmark names are wrapped to the pane width and shown in multiple lines of text.

If you open the Options menu you have more choices for how the Bookmarks appear in the pane. In Figures 17-7 and 17-8, Bookmarks are expanded. The minus (–) symbol (a down-pointing arrow on Macintosh) shows all nested child Bookmarks below it. Click on the symbol and the Bookmark collapses to hide all child Bookmarks below the parent. If you want to show all top-level Bookmarks expanded, select Expand Top-Level Bookmarks from the Options pull-down menu. To collapse the Bookmark list, select Collapse Top-Level Bookmarks from the same menu. The latter menu command is dynamic and is only accessible in the menu if you have first expanded Bookmarks.

Select Hide After Use from the Options menu if you want to hide the Bookmarks pane after you select a Bookmark. To change text sizes, make selections from the Options pull-down menu. Select Size and choose from one of the three submenu items for Small, Medium, or Large point sizes.

Bookmark properties

The Options pull-down menu offers you choices for text sizes. For other text attribute changes you need to use the Bookmark Properties dialog box. Select Properties from a context menu and the Bookmark Properties dialog box shown in Figure 17-9 opens.

Figure 17-9: The Bookmarks Properties dialog box opens when you open a context menu from either a standard Bookmark or a structured Bookmark.

You select type styles from the Style pull-down menu. Select from Plain, Bold, Italic, or Bold & Italic. Clicking the Color swatch opens the color pop-up window where you select preset colors or custom colors. You can capture changes from these style options when you select the Use Current Appearance as New Default menu command previously discussed.

The Actions tab enables you to change Bookmark actions. By default the Bookmark action is set to open a view within the active PDF document. You can assign many other actions to Bookmarks in the Actions properties.

Cross-Reference

For assigning Bookmark actions, see the section "Working with the Link Tool" later in this chapter.

Setting Bookmark opening views

If you create Bookmarks in a document and want the document to open with the Bookmarks pane open, you can save the PDF document in a manner where the Bookmarks pane opens in the Navigation pane each time the PDF is opened.

Choose File ➪ Document Properties or press Ctrl/⌘+D to open the Document Properties dialog box. Click the Initial View tab. From the Show pull-down menu select Bookmarks Panel and Page. Save the file after making the properties change. The next time you open the document, the Bookmarks pane opens.

Cross-Reference

For more information on setting Initial Views, see Chapter 4.

The width of the Bookmarks pane is a user default specific to Acrobat on the end user's computer and not the file you save. If you open the Bookmarks pane to a wider view than the default, each time you open a PDF with the Bookmarks in view, the Bookmarks pane is opened at the width you last adjusted. If you save the file with the Initial View showing Bookmarks and pages, Acrobat does not take into consideration your Bookmarks pane width. Other users who open your files see the Bookmarks pane sized to their personal pane width default sizes. This default is made from the last time a user adjusted the pane size.

Working with Articles

Acrobat offers a feature to link text blocks together for easy navigation through columns of text. User-specified ranges of text can be linked together, thereby forming an article. Articles help a user navigate through a PDF file, enabling the user to read logical sequences of paragraphs throughout a document. Working with articles is particularly helpful when you view PDF files on the World Wide Web. PDF files can be downloaded a page at a time in a Web browser. If you have a column or group of paragraphs of text that begins on page 1 and continues on page 54, an article thread can assist a reader in jumping from page 1 to page 54 without his or her having to download the remaining pages in the document.

Viewing and navigating articles

You need to know a few basics on navigating through an article in a PDF. To determine whether articles exist, choose View ➪ Navigation Tabs ➪ Articles. A pane opens with tabs for Articles and Destinations, as shown in Figure 17-10.

Tip   If you want to move the Articles pane to the Navigation pane, click the tab and drag it to the top of the Navigation pane. The Articles pane can remain in the Navigation pane for all subsequent Acrobat sessions as long as you leave it docked in the pane when you quit Acrobat.

The Articles tab displays any articles existing in the PDF file in the pane list. If you select the Article tool from the Acrobat toolbar, the article definition boundaries are shown. In Figure 17-10, the Article tool is selected. The defined article is contained within a rectangular box with an identifier at the top of the box. In this example, 1-1 indicates that this is article number 1 and box number 1. If the article is continued on another page, the subsequent boxes read 1-2, 1-3, 1-4, and so on, indicating they are continuations of the same article thread. If you create a second article, the article begins with numbers 2-1, indicating the second article in the document and the first box of the second article.

Article properties

The article properties are contained in a dialog box that opens immediately after you create an article or double-click an article with the Article tool. The Properties dialog box shown in Figure 17-11 is informational. When you view Article Properties, information supplied at the time the article was created is displayed for four data fields. The Title, Subject, Author, and Keywords fields are the same as those found in the Document Information dialog box. Inasmuch as the data for these fields are identical to that found in document information, Acrobat Search does not take advantage of the article properties information. Properties are designed to help you find information about an article before you jump to the page where the article is contained. All the fields are editable when you open the Article Properties dialog box.

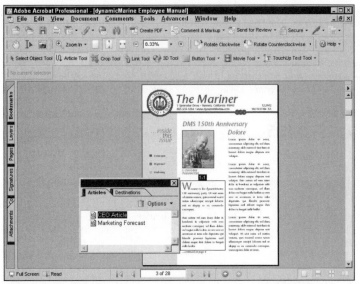

Figure 17-10: To determine whether articles exist in a document, open the Articles Navigation tab.

Figure 17-11: The Article Properties dialog box displays user-supplied information for Title, Subject, Author, and Keywords fields. These fields are not searchable with Acrobat Search.

Viewing articles

Articles are viewed at the maximum view established in the Preferences dialog box. When you view an article, you select the Hand tool and click on an article thread. The screen view jumps to the maximum view assigned in the Page Display Preferences. By default the zoom is set to an 800% view. In most situations this view is much larger than needed for comfortable viewing. Choose Edit ➪ Preferences and click Page Display in the left pane. From the Max Fit Visible Zoom pull-down menu select a zoom view comfortable for reading on your monitor.

After you establish the zoom, open the Articles pane by choosing View ➪ Navigation Tabs ➪ Articles. The Articles pane can remain open as an individual pane, or you can drag it to the Navigation pane and dock the pane. The pane pull-down menu in the Articles pane offers only one option. If you select Hide After Use from the pane pull-down menu, the pane disappears when you view an article. If you want to have the pane remain open, but want more viewing area in the document, dock the pane in the Navigation pane.

Double-click an article to jump to the first view in the thread. Acrobat places the top-left corner where the article begins in view. You immediately see a right-pointing arrow blink on the left side of the first line of text. Once an article is in view, select the Hand tool and position the cursor over the article. The cursor changes to a Hand tool icon with an arrow pointing down. As you read articles, the cursor changes according to the direction Acrobat takes you when you're reading an article. For example, if you're viewing a column up instead of down, the cursor changes to inform you which direction you're going. The different cursor views are shown in Figure 17-12.

A B C   **Figure 17-12:** When you view articles, different cursors inform you ahead of time the direction you need to navigate.

You can use several keyboard shortcuts to help you navigate with the Article tool. The cursor changes according to the following modifier keys:

✦ **Click:** The first click zooms to the Max Fit Visible preference setting. Click the cursor again to continue reading down a column. Click at the end of an article box, and the view takes you to the beginning of the next column.

✦ **Shift+click:** Moves backward or up a column.

✦ **Control+click or Option+click:** Moves to the beginning of the article.

✦ **Return or Enter:** Moves forward down the column or to the top of the next column.

✦ **Shift+Return or Shift+Enter:** Moves up or to the previous column.

Defining articles

You define articles by drawing rectangular boxes around the text you want to include as part of your article thread. While you're using the Article tool, the rectangular boxes are visible. When the tool is not active, the rectangular boxes are invisible.

Click and drag open a rectangle surrounding the column where you want to begin a new article. When you release the mouse button, the rectangular box displays on the page. At each corner and side of the article box are handles that you can grab and move to reshape the box. Notice that the lower-right corner of the article box contains a plus (+) symbol. When you finish your edits, deselect the Article tool to exit edit mode. You can return to edit mode and add more columns after reselecting the Article tool. Click the aforementioned plus symbol to let Acrobat know you want to extend the article thread (see the later section, "Combining articles" for more on extended article threads).

Tip   You can create article threads at the time the PDF file is either exported or distilled with Acrobat Distiller. Many layout applications support creating articles prior to exporting to PDF. In some cases you may want to have a single article thread used to help user navigation through your document. To practice, identify an article in one of the programs discussed in Chapter 6 and then export to PDF either through the program's export feature or by printing to PostScript and later distilling in Acrobat Distiller.

Ending an article thread

When you reach the end of the article, Acrobat needs to know you want to finish creating the thread. To end an article thread, press Return, Enter, or Esc. Acrobat prompts you with a dialog box in which you supply the Title, Subject, Author, and Keywords fields for the article properties. This dialog box appears immediately after you define an article. Supplying the information at the time the dialog box opens is a good idea because then you won't need to worry about returning to the Article Properties dialog box for last-minute cleanup.

Deleting articles

You might want to delete a portion of an article thread or an entire article. To delete either, select the Article tool and click an article box. Press the Backspace (Delete) key on your keyboard or open a context menu and select Delete from the menu options. A dialog box (simply titled Adobe Acrobat) opens providing options for deleting the currently selected box or the entire article. Or to delete the entire article from within the Article tab, select the Article and click the 'trash can icon,' or open a context menu and select Delete.

If you select the Box button in the Adobe Acrobat dialog box, the deletion eliminates the article box within the article thread you selected when you pressed the Backspace (Delete) key on the keyboard. Clicking the Article button deletes all boxes in the thread across all pages in the document.

Combining articles

At times you may want to join two articles to create a single article. To join two articles, you must first have them defined in the PDF document. Move to the last column of the first article and click the plus symbol in the last box. This click loads the Article tool. Next, move to the beginning of the article to be joined to the first article and Ctrl+click or Option+click inside the first box. While you press the shortcut keys, the cursor icon changes, as illustrated in Figure 17-13.

Figure 17-13: When you press the Ctrl or Option key while clicking the mouse button, the cursor changes to an icon, informing you that the selected articles are to be joined.

The numbering at the top of each box in the second article changes after the articles are joined. For example, if you have two articles, the first numbered 1-1, 1-2, 1-3, and the second article numbered 2-1, 2-2, the new numbering for the second article changes to 1-4 and 1-5. Article 2 takes on the attributes of Article 1 and assumes the next order of the article boxes. In addition, the properties identified in the second article are lost. Because the continuation of the thread is from Article 1, all attributes for Article 1 supersede those of Article 2. You can select multiple articles join them all together in a single article following the same steps.

Tip When combining two articles, always start with the article containing the attributes to be retained. For example, in the preceding case, to retain the attributes of Article 2, select the plus symbol at the end of the last column in article 2 and click. Ctrl+click or Option+click in the first box for article 1. When the two articles are combined, the attributes of article 2 are retained.

Working with the Link Tool

You use the Link tool to create links from a rectangle drawn with the tool to other pages, other documents, and a host of other link actions you can define in the Link Properties dialog box. The area within a link rectangle is the hot spot for invoking a link action. Links used with tools like Bookmarks and Form Field buttons have the same attribute choices for the actions associated with the objects created with the respective tools.

When creating links with the Link tool, you encounter two dialog boxes used to establish link actions. For link actions used in opening a view, opening a secondary document, or opening a Web page, the action choices are contained in the Create Link dialog box that opens when you click and drag open a link rectangle and release the mouse button. If you want to assign different link actions, you create a custom link and make attribute choices in the Link Properties dialog box. The Create Link dialog box requires you to make all option choices in the dialog box before you can access any commands in the Document pane. The dialog box is static, which means you need to cancel out of the dialog box or click OK to use menus, shortcut keys, or select objects on a page in the Document pane. When you work with the Link Properties dialog box you can access tools and menu commands, and select items such as buttons and other links on pages while the dialog box remains open.

Linking to views

Select the Link tool and click and drag open a rectangle on a page where you want the link placed. When you release the mouse button, the Create Link dialog box opens as shown in Figure 17-14. In the Create Link dialog box you make one of four radio button selections. The first three radio buttons enable you to specify link attributes in the Create Link dialog box. If you select the fourth radio button and click OK, the Link Properties dialog box opens where you select different actions for the link behavior.

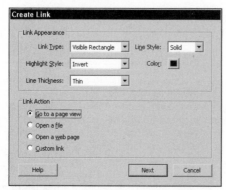

Figure 17-14: The Create Link dialog box is static which means you need to dismiss the dialog box before you can access tools, menu commands, or keyboard shortcuts.

The first three radio button choices offer you options for selecting a page view or a file to open. Options shown in the Create Link dialog box include

✦ **Go to a page view:** Use this option to link to a page in the open document or create a cross-document link that opens a page in another document. When you click the Next button, the Create Go to View dialog box opens as shown in Figure 17-15. While the dialog box remains open you have access to menu commands and tools. Navigate to a page in the open document or click the Open tool, open a second file, navigate to the desired page, and click Set Link.

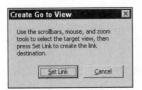

Figure 17-15: Navigate to a page in the open document or another document and click Set Link to complete the link action.

✦ **Open a file:** Select this option if you want to open a PDF document or any file from another authoring program. When you click the Next button, the Select File to Open dialog box opens and allows you to select any file on your system. If you select a file other than files that can be opened in Acrobat, you (or your customer) must have the native authoring program installed in order to click on the link and open the file. If you select a PDF document, you link to the Initial View in the secondary document.

✦ **Open a web page:** When you select this radio button, the Edit URL field is enabled. You type a URL in the Edit URL field to link to a PDF hosted on a Web site. When you add a URL, be certain to supply the complete Web address, including *http://www*. After you add a URL, the address becomes a new default. Each time you create a new link, the last URL added to the Edit URL field box is inherited and appears in the field box.

✦ **Custom Link:** Custom Link in and of itself contains no properties. You select this radio button if you want to set a different action for a link. If you select Custom Link and click the OK button, the Link Properties dialog box opens.

Tip

If you want to link from text on a PDF page, select the Select tool and highlight the text you want to use for a link button. Open a context menu and select Create Link. The Create Link dialog box opens with the same attribute choices found in the Create Link dialog box generated from the Link tool, with the exception of the Custom Link option. If you want to edit text attributes such as text color after a link has been created, select the TouchUp Text tool and highlight the text. Open a context menu and select Attributes. Change the text color to a color that clearly indicates to a user that a link is present. For example, blue text amidst black text communicates to a user that clicking on the blue texts invokes a link action.

Cross-Reference

For more information on using the Select tool, see Chapters 10 and 11.

Editing a link action

If you create a link using any one of the first three radio buttons in the Create Link dialog box and later want to edit the link, you are not returned to the Create Link dialog box. The Create Link dialog box opens only after you first use the Link tool to create a link.

To change a link action, use either the Link tool or the Select tool. Double-click the mouse button with either tool to open the Link Properties. If you select the Hand tool and click on a link, the link action is employed.

Link appearance properties

The link appearance applies to the rectangle drawn when you drag the Link tool on a page in the Document pane. Default appearances are established from the last appearance settings made for the link properties. To change properties you have two choices. You can use the Properties bar (described in "Setting Up the Editing Environment" at the beginning of this chapter) or the Link Properties dialog box.

When using the Properties bar, you make changes to link appearances for the items contained across the bar as shown in Figure 17-16. The choices in the Properties bar include

Figure 17-16: Select a link with the Link tool or the Select tool to enable the options in the Properties bar.

✦ **Color:** The Color pop-up window opens when you click on the square at the far left side of the Properties bar. Choices for color apply to strokes only and the options are the same as you find when changing colors in Note properties.

Cross-Reference

For more information on changing Note properties, see Chapter 14.

✦ **Line Style:** You have choices from the pull-down menu for No Line, Solid, Dashed, and Underline. No lines might be used when you have a graphic image or text on a page and a link is apparent to a user. If text appears blue and underlined is one condition where you might use No Line for the line style.

✦ **Line Thickness:** The default shown in Figure 17-16 is 1 pt. You have choices for Thin, Medium, or Thick that translate to 1 pt, 2 pts, or 3 pts, respectively. The line weight you choose appears in the Properties bar. If you select No Line, 0 pt appears listed in the Properties bar.

✦ **Highlight Style:** Use this option to display highlights when the mouse button is pressed. When you select the Hand tool and click on a link, the highlight is shown within the link rectangle while the mouse button is pressed. You can choose from No Highlight, Invert, Outline, and Inset.

✦ **More:** Clicking the More button opens the Link Properties dialog box the same as when using a context menu command.

Link properties

To open the Link Properties dialog box, you can open a context menu and select Properties; double-click on a link with the Link tool or the Select tool; select a link and press the Enter or Return key; or, with a link selected, click the More button in the Properties bar. Opening context menus with the tools described previously performs two actions. A right-click in Windows or Control+click in Macintosh selects the link and opens the Link Properties dialog box. As you move the mouse cursor over a link with the Link tool or the Select tool, the link rectangle is highlighted in black with red handles. When you select the link, the highlight changes to red. Right-clicking (Control+clicking on the Macintosh) selects the rectangle and opens a context menu.

When the Link Properties dialog box opens, you have options nested in two tabs: the Appearance tab and the Actions tab. By default the Appearance tab is placed in view, as shown in Figure 17-17.

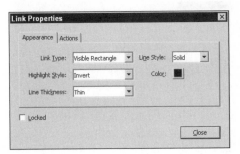

Figure 17-17: Two tabs exist in the Link Properties dialog box where you select appearance and actions options.

The same options offered in the Properties bar for appearance settings are available in the Appearance tab with the addition of a check box for Locked. If you enable Locked, the link rectangle is locked to position on the document page and cannot be moved; however, when you select the Hand tool and click on a locked link, the action associated with the link still executes. Locking a link also disables all option choices in the Properties bar and the Link Properties dialog box for that link. If you need to change properties for a locked link, open the Appearance tab and disable Locked.

Notice the dialog box uses a Close button instead of an OK button. Changes you make for either appearance settings or assigning action items are dynamic. The changes you make are immediately reflected in the Document pane. You can leave the Link Properties dialog box open while you create additional links and change properties and/or actions for each new link created. When finished editing links, use the Close button, check the box in the top-right corner, or press the Esc key. There is no Cancel button in the dialog box. If you make a change to a link's properties and want to revert to the same properties assigned when the dialog box was opened, you must physically revert to those changes before closing the Link Properties dialog box.

Link actions properties

Click on the Actions tab to assign an action to a link. The default link action is Execute a menu item as shown in Figure 17-18 (the top item in the Actions list). After you create a link with another action type, the new action becomes the default.

The process of creating links to page views differs depending on whether you're working in the Create Link or Link Properties dialog box. With the Create Link dialog box you need to specify a page number and click OK. The Create Link dialog box doesn't offer you a preview of the page link. When you open the Link Properties dialog box to reassign a page link, you can navigate pages while the dialog box is open. Find the page you want to link to, click the Edit button, type the viewed page number in the dialog box, and click the Close button in the Link Properties.

Tip

If you want to emulate the behavior more closely associated with earlier versions of Acrobat, create a link with the Link tool and select Custom link in the Create Link dialog box. Click OK and the Link Properties dialog box opens. Navigate to the page you want to assign the link action and click Add. When the action is listed in the Actions window, select it and click Edit. Type the page number in view and click Close. In this sequence, you see a preview of the page before you assign the link rather than trying to remember what page number to type in the Create Link dialog box.

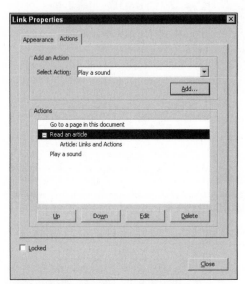

Figure 17-18: Click the Actions tab to open the options settings for link actions.

The Select Action pull-down menu offers a number of link actions you can assign to a link. You can select an action and repeat a selection for a different action to nest action types that are executed in the order displayed in the Actions window. In Figure 17-18, three separate actions are associated with the same link. When you select the link with the Hand tool, a page opens, the article thread zooms to the Max Fit Visible Zoom established in the Preferences dialog box, and a sound plays. From the pull-down menu, you can choose action types such as the following.

Go to a page view

You add the action and the Create Go to View dialog box opens. Navigate to a page in an open document or a secondary document and click Set Link.

Users of Acrobat 6 will notice the absence of the Go to page in another document action. Because you can go to pages in other documents with the Go to a page view action, the Go to page in another document action is unnecessary.

After you create a link to another document and open the Link Properties dialog box you see the action referred to as Go to a page in another document as shown in Figure 17-19. Although the menu command is not available in the Select Action pull-down menu, Acrobat records the link action in the link properties as a Go to page in another document.

Figure 17-19: Links to pages in other documents are recorded by Acrobat as a Go to page in another document link.

Note   Acrobat 7 eliminated another action type related to page viewing. Acrobat 6 offered a link to a Snapshot view. Acrobat 7 no longer supports this action type. To link to different views, use the Go to page view action, zoom to the view you want, and click Set Link.

Execute a menu item

You can use almost all the menu commands in Acrobat as link actions. If you want to open a file, convert to PDF, open or collapse panes in the Navigation pane, show or hide toolbars, or use any other menu command, you can use the Execute a menu item action from the Select Action pull-down menu.

On Windows the Menu Item Selection dialog box opens in which the top-level menu commands are nestled together, as shown in Figure 17-20. In the dialog box, select a menu and scroll down the menu items to select an item. Figure 17-20 shows the Tools ⇨ Basic ⇨ Snapshot Tool menu command.

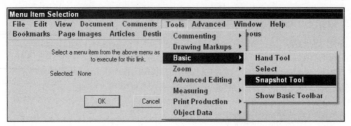

Figure 17-20: Select menu commands from the Menu Item Selection dialog box when using the Execute a menu item action type.

On the Macintosh, the Menu Item dialog box opens as shown in Figure 17-21. The dialog box is informational and instructs you to select menu commands from the top-level menus. While the dialog box remains open, select a menu and a menu command, as you normally would while editing in Acrobat. The menu selection you choose is set for the link destination.

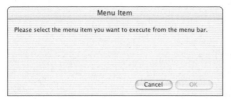

Figure 17-21: When you choose Execute a menu item on the Macintosh, the Menu Item dialog box informs you to make menu selections from the menu bar at the top of the Acrobat window.

Import form data

When you select the Import form data option and click Add, the Select File Containing Form Data dialog box opens. Select the file containing the form data you want to import and click the Select button. Imported form data are from files saved in FDF format that are exported from PDF documents. When you click the Select button, the data matching identical form fields are imported. Using Import form data limits you to importing data saved only in FDF format. If you use the Execute Menu Item action, data can be imported when saved as FDF, XFDF, XML, XFD, and TXT. Note that you must have at least one form field on the page for this to work.

Open a file

You use Open a file to open any file on your computer. When you select the action type and click the Add button, the Open dialog box opens. Browse your hard drive and select the file you want to open. If the file is other than a PDF file, you (or your customer) need to have the authoring application that created the file installed on your computer in order to execute the link action. Creating the link does not require you to have any external programs installed on your computer.

Open a Web Link

The Open a Web Link option enables you to associate a link action to a Web address. Web links can be contained in PDF documents locally on your computer or within a PDF page where the PDF is hosted on a Web server. If a Web link is contained locally in a PDF document, selecting the link launches the browser configured with Acrobat and establishes a URL connection. Acrobat remains open in the background while the Web browser appears in the foreground. Always use the complete URL to identify a Web address.

When you specify a URL in the Edit URL dialog box that opens after you click the Add button in the Link Properties, you can add custom viewing in the URL address for the way you want to open a PDF document. For example, if you want to view a page other than the opening page you can add to the URL a request for opening any page number. To open a specific page, enter this text:

http://www.mycompany.com/myDoc.pdf#page=3

In this example the file myDoc.pdf opens on page 3 in the Web browser. In addition to opening a specific page you can add other viewing parameters such as zoom levels, page modes such as viewing layers or Bookmarks, opening named destinations, and other viewing options.

For more information on setting viewing options with Web links, see Chapter 20.

Play a sound

You can create a button to play a sound in a PDF document. When you select the Play a sound action and click the Add button, the Select Sound File dialog box opens where you locate a sound file on your hard drive and import the sound. Acrobat pauses a moment while the sound is converted to a format usable in Acrobat viewers. After it's imported in the PDF, the sound can be played across platforms. When the link button is selected, the sound plays. Sounds imported with the Play a Sound action and those added with the Record Audio Comment tool support only Acrobat 5 media. If you use the Sound tool you can choose to import either Acrobat 5– or Acrobat 6–compatible sounds.

For importing sounds with the Sound Attach tool, see Chapter 15. For information on using Acrobat 5– and Acrobat 6–compatible sound and media see Chapter 18.

Notice the Advanced Editing toolbar contains a Sound tool. You can use the Sound tool to import sounds. In addition, you can use the Record Audio Comment tool to import sound files. Playing sounds from any of these tools is identical. The Sound tool and the Record Audio Comment tool are limited to adding sounds on a page where a user needs to click or double-click a button to play the sound. The link action is more versatile as you can add sounds with nested link actions, page actions, and form fields. Sound files are supported from files saved as AIFF or WAV.

For information on using the Sound tool, see Chapter 18, and for information on using the Attach Sound tool, see Chapter 15.

Play media (Acrobat 5–compatible)

To select the Play Media action type, a media file must be present in the PDF file. If there is no media file present, you are prompted with a dialog box. You import media clips with the Movie tool and at least one movie file needs to be present before you can create a link with the Play Media action type. After a movie is contained in a PDF file, create a link and select the action type. After you click Add, the Play Media (Acrobat 5 Compatible) dialog box opens. If you have several media clips in the PDF document, the Select Media pull-down menu lists all the clips by filename. Select a file and choose from one of four action types in the Select Operation pull-down menu shown in Figure 17-22. You may choose to play a movie, stop a movie, pause a movie during the play, or have it resume after it has been paused.

Figure 17-22: When the Play Media (Acrobat 5 Compatible) dialog box opens, select a media clip from the Select Media pull-down menu and select the play option from the Select Operation pull-down menu.

Play media (Acrobat 6 and later compatible)

Playing Acrobat 6–compatible media clips requires you to first import a movie (or import a sound). When you import a movie with the Movie tool or import a sound with the Sound tool you have a choice for importing the media as an Acrobat 5– or Acrobat 6–compatible file. Acrobat 6 allows you to embed Acrobat 6–compatible media in the PDF document. All previous versions of Acrobat treated movie files as links. When you transport PDFs with Acrobat 5–compatible movie files you need to send the movie file along with the PDF whereas Acrobat 6–compatible files offer you a choice for importing the movie and embedding the file in the PDF document.

After you have imported a media clip with the Movie tool as an embedded file or a file link, select the Play Media (Acrobat 6 and Later Compatible) action and click the Add button. The Play Media (Acrobat 6 and Later Compatible) dialog box opens as shown in Figure 17-23. The operations available with Acrobat 6–compatible imports are the same as those used with Acrobat 5–compatible imports, with the exception of being able to add a Custom JavaScript and Play from beginning.

Figure 17-23: In addition to offering the same operations available with Acrobat 5–compatible imports, Acrobat 6 compatibility provides an option for adding a custom JavaScript.

To add a JavaScript, select Custom JavaScript from the Operation to Perform pull-down menu and click the Specify JavaScript button. Other dialog boxes open for specifying a rendition if you choose to do so and the JavaScript Editor dialog box opens where you write a custom JavaScript.

You can use media clips saved in a variety of formats compatible with Acrobat 5 or the newer formats supported with Acrobat 6. When you use the Play Media (Acrobat 6 and Later Compatible) action type, the file you select does not require Acrobat 6 compatibility for newer file types per se. However, Acrobat 6 compatibility enables you to embed files and use custom JavaScripts, and provides support for newer compression schemes.

When you use Acrobat 6 compatibility, be aware that users of earlier versions of Acrobat won't be able to use your PDF documents. If you need to work with users of older versions of Acrobat viewers, be certain to use Acrobat 5 compatibility.

Cross-Reference For more information on Acrobat 6–compatible file formats, see Chapter 18.

Read an article

When you select Read an article as the action type for a link, the Select Article dialog box opens when you click the Add button. If no articles are present in the PDF document, you receive a dialog box alerting you that there are no articles present and you can't use this link action. When articles are present, select the article you want to associate with the link from the listed articles in the Select Article dialog box. When you select the link in the navigation mode, Acrobat opens the page where the first box in the article appears. Additionally, the cursor changes to the Article icon that enables you to continue reading the selected article.

Reset a form

The Reset a form link action relates to PDF documents with form fields. When a form is filled out, you can reset the form to remove all data contained in the form fields. Acrobat provides an opportunity to clear the data from all fields or from selected fields you identify individually. A Reset a form dialog box opens, enabling you to select the fields to clear.

Cross-Reference For more information on resetting forms, see Chapter 25.

Run a JavaScript

JavaScript adds great opportunity for making PDF documents interactive and dynamic. You can add JavaScripts to link button actions as well as form fields. When you select Run a JavaScript and click the Add button, the JavaScript Editor dialog box opens. You type the code in the dialog box, or copy and paste code from a text editor to the JavaScript Editor. Click OK to commit the JavaScript.

Set layer visibility

For PDF documents containing layers, you first create the layer view you want in the Layers pane. Open the Layers pane and show the layers you want displayed when a user clicks on the link. In Figure 17-24, one layer (Layout) is hidden as shown in the Layers pane. When you use the Set layer visibility action type, the layer view at the time you create the link is what is shown to the user when he or she clicks the link. This behavior works similarly to Bookmarks in which you place in view in the Document pane your resultant view, and then create the Bookmark. Layer visibility works the same. Set the visibility you want, and then set the link.

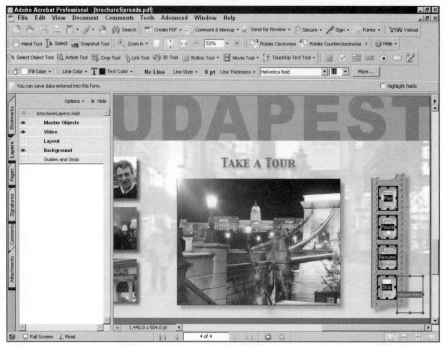

Figure 17-24: When using the Set layer visibility action type, you first show the layer view you want to display to assign it to the link action.

After setting your layer view for the display when the user clicks the link, create a link and click the Custom Link button. Select Set layer visibility from the Actions pull-down menu and a dialog box opens, informing you the current layer state has been captured, as shown in Figure 17-25.

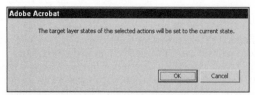

Figure 17-25: When you add the Set layer visibility action type, a dialog box opens, informing you the layer state has been captured.

When you return to the Document pane, open the Layer pane Options menu and select Reset to Initial Visibility. This command resets the layer visibility to the default view. Presumably, your layer state is set to a different view when you create a link; therefore, the view should appear different when you reset the layers to initial visibility. In this example, all layers are set back to initial visibility where the Layout layer is on and the Video layer is off (see Figure 17-26).

The link rectangle appears in the lower-right corner, as shown in Figure 17-24. (Note: The button is accessible from all layers.) When I click the link button the opening Layout layer, shown in Figure 17-24, is turned off and the Video layer in Figure 17-26 is turned on and appears in the Document pane.

Cross-Reference
For more information on layer visibility, see Chapter 19.

Show/hide a field

The Show/hide a field action enables the user to allow selected form fields to be visible or hidden. Forms can be created to display and hide form fields for help menus, informational items, protecting data, and so on. You can make a hidden field visible by opening the Show/Hide Field dialog box and selecting the Hide radio button. Within this dialog box the options for both hiding and showing fields are enabled through radio buttons.

Cross-Reference
For more information on working with Acrobat PDF forms, see Part VI.

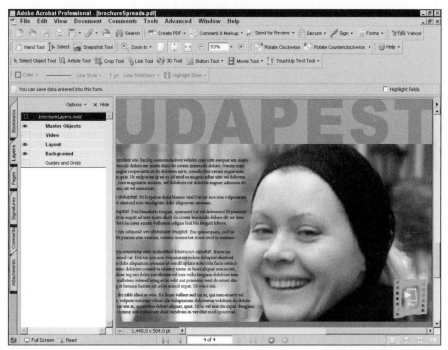

Figure 17-26: From the Layers pane Options menu select Reset to Initial Visibility. When you click the link button, the layer visibility changes to the state established when the link was created.

Submit a form

Form and comment data contained in PDF documents can be transported on the World Wide Web. When a user completes a form, the data can be submitted to a URL as a Form Data File (FDF), HTML, or XML data. Additionally, the entire PDF can be submitted. The PDF author can then collect and process the data. Using form and comment data with Web servers has some requirements you need to work out with the ISP hosting your Web site. If you use forms on PDF Web pages, include a button that submits data after the user completes the form. Using the Submit a form action enables you to identify the URL where the data are submitted and determine which data type is exported from the PDF document. If comment data are to be submitted, a check box enabling comment delivery appears in the dialog box.

Cross-Reference   For more information on submitting PDF forms to Web servers, see Chapter 27.

Managing links

Acrobat 7 provides many menu options for link management. You can copy/paste, align, and distribute links and more through the use of a context menu. If you need to apply these editing tasks to multiple links, select the Select tool and click and drag through the links you want to manage. If you attempt to use the Link tool, you can select only a single link.

After selecting a link with the Link tool or selecting multiple links with the Select tool, open a context menu as shown in Figure 17-27. The context menu offers several menu categories with submenu items used for managing links. The menu items include

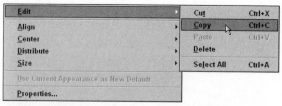

Figure 17-27: Select a single link with the Link tool or multiple links with the Select tool and open a context menu. Select a menu category and select from the submenu items the command you want to use.

✦ **Edit:** The Edit menu contains several items in a submenu for cut/copy/paste, as are accessible in the top-level Edit menu. You can delete a link or group of links by selecting Delete.

   • **Select All:** Select All deserves some special comment. When you select a link with the Link tool or choose Edit ➪ Select All, all links are selected on a page. If you click on a link with the Select tool and choose Select All from the Edit submenu, all objects selectable with the Select tool are selected on the page. For example, if you have links and form fields, Select All selects all links and form fields on the target page. If you want to edit the links for deletion, alignment, copying, and so on, be certain to click on the Link tool and then use Edit ➪ Select All.

✦ **Align:** You can align multiple links Left, Right, Top, Bottom, and along the vertical and horizontal centers. Choose the respective submenu command for the alignment option of your choice.

✦ **Distribute:** If you have a row or column of links and you want to position them equidistant from each other, choose the Distribute command and select from either Vertically or Horizontally. Vertically distributes a column and Horizontally distributes a row of link objects.

✦ **Size:** As you create link rectangles, the rectangle size may differ from among a series of links you add to a page. To resize links on a given page to the same size, select one of the links with the Link tool. Using a context menu select "Select All," move the Link tool to the target size link rectangle, and open a context menu. (The target link rectangle is displayed with a red keyline and red handles while the other rectangles in the selected group are highlighted blue.) Select from the submenu Height, Width, or Both. The selected link rectangles are resized to the size of the target link.

✦ **Properties:** Use this option to open the Link Properties dialog box. If you select more than one link rectangle, the link actions shows Varies in the action list if the link actions are different from among the selected links. You can apply common appearance settings to all selected links or you can edit actions if the actions are all the same among the selected links.

STEPS: Creating links

To gain a little experience with creating and manipulating links, try practicing on any PDF document you have on your hard drive following these steps:

1. **Open a PDF document.** For this example, I use a PDF file containing a contents page. I want to create links from the contents headings on the contents page to the respective pages in the PDF document.

2. **Create a link from text.** Click the Select tool and click and drag through a word or line of text. Open a context menu and select Create Link, as shown in Figure 17-28.

3. **Set the link action.** The link needs to open another page in the same document. In this example, I set the Appearance attributes to Invisible Rectangle and the Link Action to "Go to a page view" and click the Next button in the Create Link dialog box. The Create Go to View dialog box opens. Navigate to the target page by clicking the Next or Previous Page tools in the status bar. When the desired view is in place in the Document pane, click Set Link.

4. **Create additional links.** Add additional links. If you use an example similar to this one for linking from a contents page, create links for the remaining text on the page. Repeat the previous steps for adding links and set the appearance properties to the same values.

Tip

If you forget to set link appearances when creating the links, you can change appearances on a group of links with common properties. Use the Link tool and select all the links from a context menu. In the Properties bar select No Line from the Line Style pull-down menu.

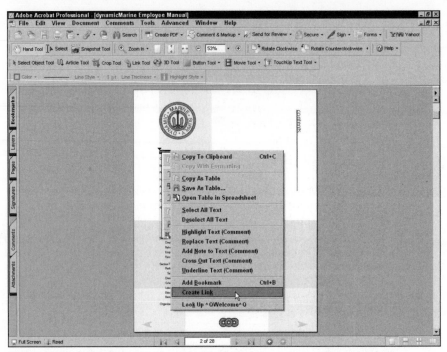

Figure 17-28: Select text with the Select tool. Open a context menu and select Create Link.

5. **Link to a file.** The last item on my contents page requires the user to open a second file. For this example I need to create a link that opens another PDF document. Select text with the Select tool on the text where you want to click to open a secondary file and select Create Link from a context menu. Set the Appearance attributes and click the Next button. When the Create Go to View dialog box opens, click the Open tool and open a secondary file. Navigate to the desired page and click Set Link. Notice the Create Go to View dialog box remains open as you open files and navigate pages.

6. **Edit properties.** Click on the Select Object tool and double-click on the link rectangle. Click the Actions tab and select Go to page in another document. Click the Edit button shown in Figure 17-29.

7. **Change open preferences.** The Go to page in another document dialog box opens as shown in Figure 17-30. In this dialog box you make choices for the window opening preferences. From the Open in pull-down menu select New Window to keep the current document open as the linked file opens in a new window. Click OK to return to the Link Properties. Click Close to return to the Document pane.

8. **Click on the link to open a file.** Select the Hand tool and click on the link to open the second file. The current document stays open in the background as the new file opens.

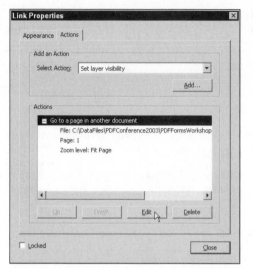

Figure 17-29: Select Go to a page in another document and click Edit.

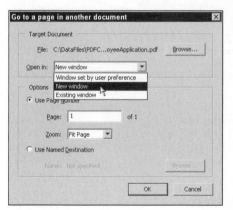

Figure 17-30: Select New Window to open the linked file in a new window.

This example shows you how to create interactive documents by linking back and forth between files while controlling the document open options. As you practice creating links, try to understand some of the differences between using the Create Link dialog box and the Link Properties dialog box so you know when to use one set of options versus another.

Working with Page Properties

A Page Action is like a link button that invokes an action when a page is opened or closed in the Document pane. You don't have to click on anything because the trigger for executing the action type is handled by Acrobat when the page opens or closes. All the action types you have available with links are the same actions that are associated with Page Actions.

To create a Page Action, open the Pages pane. Select a page with the Hand tool and open a context menu. From the menu options select Page Properties. The Page Properties dialog box opens with two sets of properties types available. The default page properties options are contained in the tab for Tab Order, but these settings don't have anything to do with setting a Page Action, so I'll skip them for the moment.

Cross-
Reference   For information related to setting Tab Orders, see Chapter 27.

It is the second tab in the Page Properties dialog box that is used for setting Page Actions. Click on the Actions tab shown in Figure 17-31, and the options for defining actions to page behavior are displayed. Two areas are used for applying a Page Action to any page in a PDF document. You first select the Trigger for either Page Open or Page Close and then select the action from the Select Action pull-down menu. The options in this menu are the same as you have available with link actions.

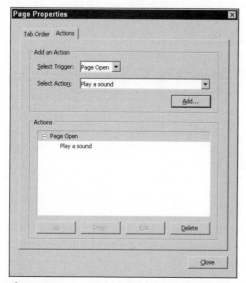

Figure 17-31: Open the Page Properties dialog box from a context menu on a page thumbnail. Click on the Actions tab to open the Page Actions options settings.

Page Actions help you make your PDF documents more automated. You might select a sound to play when a file opens, as shown in Figure 17-31. You may want to set layer visibility, play a movie, or execute a menu item. Of all the options available for action types, with Page Actions you have the addition of an infinite number of choices when running JavaScripts. You might want to run a script that analyzes the Acrobat viewer version when a user opens a PDF document and alerts the user that Acrobat 6 is needed to properly view your document if the user opens the file in a viewer version earlier than Acrobat 6. This example and many more options are available to you when running JavaScripts from Page Actions.

Cross-Reference To see examples of JavaScripts that analyze Acrobat viewer versions and viewer types, see Chapter 29.

Creating Destinations

A destination is a specific location in a document. Whereas a Bookmark and a link may link to page 5 in a file, a destination links to the location where page 5 resides. If you delete page 5, Bookmarks and links have no place to go and the links are often referred to as *dead links*. If you delete page 5 where a destination has been created, the destination remains at the same location — that is, following page 4 and preceding page 6. Furthermore, if you insert a page after page 4, the Bookmarks and links are linked to page 6. All pages shift to make room for a new page, but the links from Bookmarks and links remain fixed on a specific page. With destinations, if you insert a page after page 4, the destination takes you to the new page 5.

You can also use destinations when you want to use JavaScripts for creating pop-up menus, creating smart forms, and adding other interactive features.

It all sounds pretty nifty but there's a downside to using named destinations. Adding many destinations in a PDF document adds a lot of overhead to the file size. Destinations can make a PDF bulky and slow if they are used extensively. Destinations should not be thought of as a substitute for Bookmarks and links, but rather, a complement to creating interactive documents when other methods don't support the same features.

Destination tools

You create, organize, and display destinations within the Destinations pane. To open the pane, choose View ⇨ Navigation Tabs ⇨ Destinations. If you want to use the Destinations pane frequently in an Acrobat session, you can drag the tab away from the pane and place it in the Navigation pane. As a tab in the Navigation pane it is visible and easily accessible until you remove it by dragging it out of the pane.

The pane contains a few icons and a pull-down menu as shown in Figure 17-32. In addition to the pane tools, context menus offer several menu options. You create, edit, and manage all destinations through this pane. The options include

   ✦ **Destinations list (A):** When you create destinations, they are listed in the pane.

   ✦ **Name (B):** Name in the pane is a button. When you click the button, the destinations are sorted alphabetically according to name.

   ✦ **Scan Document (C):** Click the icon appearing first in the pane to scan the open document for any existing destinations. Destinations don't dynamically appear when you open a PDF. You must first scan the document to see them listed in the pane. From the Options pull-down menu the Scan Document menu command performs the same action. Another option for scanning a document is to open a context menu away from destination names.

   ✦ **New Destination (D):** You use the Adobe icon and a context menu option to create new destinations. You create a destination by first navigating to the page and view, and then creating the destination, much like you create Bookmarks.

A   B   C D E F G

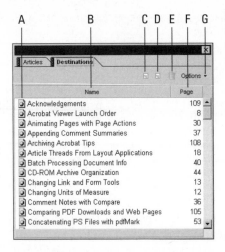

Figure 17-32: Open the Destinations pane by choosing View ➪ Navigation Tabs ➪ Destinations. Several icons and a list of destinations appear in the pane.

✦ **Delete (E):** You can use the Trash can icon in the pane, as well as a menu command available when opening a context menu on a selected destination, to delete the destination.

✦ **Page (F):** Page is also a button. When you click it, the destinations are sorted according to page number and tab order on the page.

✦ **Options pull-down menu (G):** Like pull-down menus in other Acrobat panes, this menu offers additional commands. With destinations, the pane menu commands include Scan Document, New Destination, Sort by Name, and Sort by Page.

If you select a destination name and open a context menu, the choices are as follows:

✦ **Go to Destination:** The first menu choice is Go to Destination, as shown in Figure 17-33. Keep in mind this context menu offers this option only when you open the menu when a destination is selected. When you invoke the command, Acrobat opens the destination page.

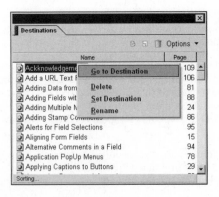

Figure 17-33: When named destinations have been created, selecting a destination and opening a context menu offers the same menu commands as found in the Options pull-down menu.

✦ **Delete:** Select a destination and select either the Trash can icon or the menu command to remove the destination from the document.

✦ **Set Destination:** If the current destination view is not what you want, navigate to the desired page and click on Set Destination. The destination is modified to open the current view when the destination is selected.

✦ **Rename:** You can change a destination name from any of those names listed in the pane. Select a destination name and select Rename. The text for the destination name is highlighted enabling you to edit the name.

You can also create destinations from within the Go to page in another document dialog box. When creating links and editing the Go to a page view action, open the Go to page in another document dialog box. At the bottom of the dialog box is a radio button for Use Named Destination, as shown in Figure 17-34. You need to first create a destination and then select the radio button in the dialog box to link to the destination.

Figure 17-34: Select Use Named Destination to link to a destination.

Creating a pop-up menu

You can use destinations to create a pop-up menu on a page that displays menu options for navigating to other pages. To create a pop-up menu that links to other pages, you create destinations and then add some JavaScript to a link or button field. When a user selects a menu item, the page destination opens in the Document pane.

To create a pop-up menu with named destinations, open a PDF document containing several pages. Begin by creating a destination for each menu item you want to display in a pop-up menu. Navigate to a page and set the zoom view using the Zoom tool or Zoom toolbar.

Cross-Reference

See the section *Creating a JavaScript link action* later in this chapter for an example on creating popup menus.

Creating the destination links

Open the Destinations pane by choosing View ➪ Navigation Tabs ➪ Destinations. Scan the document for destinations by clicking the Scan Document tool in the pane.

If the page and view are set, click the Create new destination button in the Destinations pane. Creating a Destination is like capturing a view. After creating a Destination, you need to name the destination in the Destinations pane. The default name is Untitled. Start typing after you create a destination and the Untitled text is replaced with the text you type. If you type and Acrobat does not accept the text, select the Untitled name and select Rename from a context menu. Continue navigating to new pages and zoom views and create new destinations.

When you finish adding new destinations, your Destinations pane should appear similar to Figure 17-35. In Figure 17-35 the destinations are sorted by name. You can also sort destinations by page number by clicking the Page button in the pane.

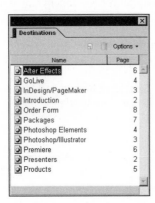

Figure 17-35: After you add destinations, the Destinations pane displays the names you used when creating each new destination. The destinations are sorted by name in the list. To sort the list by page number, click the Page button in the Destinations pane.

Creating a JavaScript link action

After you have finished adding new destinations, you need to do a little programming. If you haven't used the JavaScript Editor, don't panic. These steps are no more complicated than following a few simple directions.

Cross-Reference   For a better understanding of using JavaScript and the script created here, see Chapter 29.

Select the Link tool and click and drag open a link rectangle. Ideally, having some text or an icon on the page indicating that a button or link is present is best. Without getting into button faces and icons, you can also simply use a keyline border to show where the link appears on the page. In the Create Link dialog box select Custom link and click OK. The Link Properties dialog box opens with the Actions tab in view. From the Select Action pull-down menu, select Run a JavaScript.

Click Add and the JavaScript Editor opens. In the JavaScript Editor, type the following code:

```
1. var c = app.popUpMenu
2. (["category_1", "item_1", "item_2", "item_3"],
3. ["category_1", "item_1", "item_2", "item_3"],
4. ["category_1", "item_1", "item_2", "item_3"]);
5. this.gotoNamedDest(c);
```

In the script, the first line of code sets a variable c for a pop-up menu. Regardless of what your destinations are named or the contents of your PDF, copy this line of code exactly as you see it into your JavaScript Editor.

Lines 2 to 4 contain the categories and submenu commands that link to the destinations you created. Here's where you need to modify your code. Where you see "category_x" replace the name with a category title of your choosing. You might want to use names such as Personnel, Administration, and Finance, or you may use category names such as Designs, Illustrations, and Photos, or any other combination of names that relate to the categories you want to use. Notice that line 2 begins with an open parenthesis — (—followed by a left bracket — [. These characters are important to include in your code.

Continuing with the data, in lines 2 through 4 are three item numbers contained in quotes and separated by commas. These names need to be the same as your destination names. Type the destination names exactly, including letter case, as you created them in your Destinations pane. The order in which you add the names is unimportant. Also notice that after the last destination name and quote mark, no comma is inserted. Lines 2 and 3 end with a comma and line 4 ends with a semicolon. These characters are also important to type just as you see them in the sample code.

Line 5, the final line of code, is the instruction to take the user to the destination selected from the menu options. Type this line exactly as you see it into your JavaScript Editor. Click OK in the JavaScript Editor and click Close in the Link Properties dialog box. Select the Hand tool and click the link. You should see a pop-up menu similar to Figure 17-36. In this example, I included six items in the first category by adding more destination names in quote marks. In Figure 17-37 you can see the code that produced the pop-up menu in Figure 17-36.

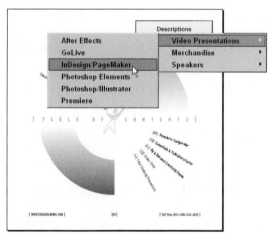

Figure 17-36: If the pop-up menu was created properly, you should see submenu items listed when selecting a category.

Note   To modify JavaScript code, select the Link tool and double-click the link. In the Link Properties dialog box select the item denoted as Run a JavaScript in the Actions list and click the Edit button. The JavaScript edit dialog box opens where you can make changes to the code.

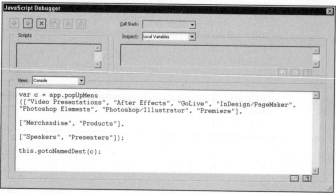

Figure 17-37: In the JavaScript Editor, I added the script that produced the pop-up menu shown in Figure 17-36. Select a name from the submenu and Acrobat should open the page associated with the destination. Check your work to be certain all menu items open the respective destinations. If you encounter an error, double-check the spelling and letter case for the destination name and the code you typed in the JavaScript Editor.

In this example, destinations are used to navigate pages in a PDF document via a pop-up menu. If the design of your PDF documents better suits pop-up menus, you have many options when using JavaScripts. You can also create pop-up menus with JavaScripts that open other PDF documents, specific pages in other PDF documents, and that execute many different menu commands.

Cross-Reference   For an example of a pop-up menu that opens secondary PDF documents, see Chapter 29.

Working with Buttons (Acrobat Professional)

In the previous section you saw how to use the Link tool to navigate pages and open files. When links are created, you need some kind of icon or text that lets a user know that a link button exists. If you add links on a page in empty white space with no border keyline, users won't know where or when to click on a link button. If you want to use images or icons for button appearances, you can use another form of link tool with the Button Tool that supports importing icons.

Using form fields instead of links has some advantages. You can add image icons to button fields, use rollover effects, copy and paste fields across multiple pages, and you have all the same action types accessible as those used with Bookmarks, links, and page actions.

Cross-Reference   The discussion of button fields in this chapter is limited to creating button fields with actions similar to those discussed in this chapter when creating link actions. For a more thorough discussion on using form fields in Acrobat, see Part VI.

Creating a button field

The Button tool is on the Forms toolbar. If you don't have the Forms toolbar open, choose Tools ➪ Advanced Editing ➪ Show Forms Toolbar. Dock the toolbar in the Toolbar Well. The Button tool appears on the left side of the Forms toolbar. Select the tool and click and drag open a rectangle.

To access the Button Properties dialog box click the More button in the Properties bar or double-click on the field. By default Acrobat automatically names the field for you beginning with Button1, then Button2 for the next button you create, then Button3, and so on. When you open the Properties dialog box you can change the field name in the General tab. Highlight the default name and type a new name. In this example I want to create some navigation buttons. The name of the button I'll use is goNext, as shown in Figure 17-38.

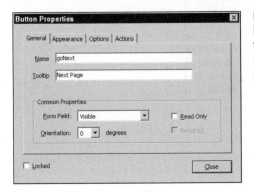

Figure 17-38: Double-click on the button field or click the More button on the Properties bar to open the Button Properties dialog box. Click on General and type a name for the button field.

Button faces are handled in the Options tab. Click the Options tab and select Icon Only from the Layout pull-down menu. Click the Choose Icon button and the Select Icon dialog box opens. From this dialog box you need to access yet another dialog box by clicking the Browse button. The Open dialog box opens where you can navigate your hard drive and select a file to import as your button face. Any file format compatible with the Create PDF from File tool is acceptable. Select a filename in the Open dialog box and click Select. Acrobat returns you to the Select Icon dialog box where you can see a preview of the imported file as shown in Figure 17-39.

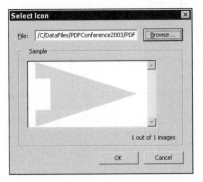

Figure 17-39: The Select Icon dialog box displays a thumbnail preview of the imported file. Click OK to return to the Button Properties dialog box.

If the preview looks like the file you want to use as a button face, click OK to return to the Button Properties dialog box. Click the Actions tab where you assign the action type associated with your button. In this dialog box you make a choice for the trigger action. The default is Mouse Up, which means when the mouse button is released the action executes. Leave the Select Trigger menu option at the default and open the Select Action pull-down menu.

Select Execute a menu item from the pull-down menu. On Windows the Menu Item Selection dialog box opens. On the Macintosh make a menu item selection from the top-level menu bar. Choose View ⇨ Go To ⇨ Next Page. Click OK and click Close in the Button Properties dialog box.

Now repeat the preceding steps to create a second navigation button.

To move a button field, select either the Button tool or the Select tool. In the example here, two buttons are created to provide navigation back and forth between pages. If you want to move the two buttons together, you need to use the Select tool. Drag the buttons to an area on the page where you can easily click the buttons to navigate pages.

Duplicating buttons

At this point, the obvious advantage of using a button field over a link is when you need some image contained within the link button. Another advantage for using button fields over links is the ability to duplicate button fields across pages. The hard part is finished after you create the fields and add the button faces. The next step is to duplicate buttons so you don't have to copy/paste them on each page.

With the button fields in place, select the Select tool and click and drag through both fields. Be certain to click and drag outside the first field so as not to select it while dragging. When both fields are selected, open a context menu and select Duplicate.

When you release the mouse button, the Duplicate field dialog box opens as shown in Figure 17-40. In the dialog box select the page range for the duplicated fields. If you created fields on the first page, enter **2** in the first field box and enter the last page number in the second field box. Click OK and the fields with the same field properties are duplicated across the specified pages.

Figure 17-40: Enter the page range in the Duplicate Fields dialog box and click OK. The fields are duplicated on the pages you specified.

Click the buttons to navigate pages. Notice that each button appears in the same relative position on each page.

The important thing to remember as you work with Bookmarks, links, Page Actions, destinations, and fields is that each is designed for different purposes. Although you can create the same results with one method or another, at times you'll favor one method over the others for a particular editing assignment. Acrobat offers many tools and features for creating dynamic interactive documents, often limited only by your imagination. The more time you invest in learning all that Acrobat affords you, the more impressive results you'll produce.

Summary

✦ You can name, organize, and create Bookmarks with different appearance properties. You can move, reassign, and delete standard Bookmarks without affecting page content. When you delete or move structured Bookmarks, the respective pages are deleted or moved.

✦ Bookmarks support actions the same as found when creating link actions. Actions enable you to view pages, open documents, create Web links, and write JavaScripts and other types of commands that act as hypertext links.

✦ Article threads enable viewers to follow passages of text in a logical reading order.

✦ Links support many different actions from page navigation to running JavaScripts. Links can be copied and pasted and the link properties are retained in the pasted objects. Links cannot be duplicated across PDF pages and links do not support content files with colors or images.

✦ Acrobat supports opening user-defined pages in external PDF documents via link actions.

✦ You select link properties in the Create Link dialog box, from a context menu command, or by double-clicking on a link. All link actions are changed in the Link Properties dialog box.

✦ You make links from text by selecting text with the Select tool and selecting Create Link from a context menu.

✦ All the actions assigned to links can also be assigned to page actions. Page actions are established in the Page Properties dialog box accessed by opening a context menu on a page thumbnail and selecting Properties.

✦ Page actions are invoked when a page opens or a page closes.

✦ Destinations are similar to Bookmarks. Destinations do not support actions. Destinations tend to make file sizes larger than when using Bookmarks and links.

✦ You can use destinations, together with a JavaScript, to create pop-up menus.

✦ You can assign form field buttons different button faces from external files.

✦ Form fields can be duplicated across multiple pages. Duplicated fields are placed on all pages in the same relative position as from where they were duplicated.

✦ ✦ ✦

Multimedia and PDFs

Acrobat offers you a wide range of possibilities with animation, motion, and sound. You can import sound files in PDFs, import movie files, convert Web pages with Flash animation, convert PowerPoint files with motion objects, and create animation by writing JavaScript routines. With the exception of writing JavaScripts, you create animation and sound in other applications and import them in PDF documents.

Movie files and sounds added with the Sound tool are available only in Acrobat Professional. Acrobat Standard does not have these tools and you have no way of adjusting properties for movie and sound files with Acrobat Standard. However, after you've added movie and sound files in Acrobat Professional, all Acrobat viewers, including Adobe Reader, can play the movies and sounds.

In this chapter you learn how to create animation and sound, import multimedia files into PDF documents, and create some motion effects by writing JavaScripts in Acrobat Professional.

Setting Up the Multimedia Environment

You import sound and video files with the Movie and/or Sound tools available from the Advanced Editing toolbar. To open the toolbar, select Tools ⇨ Show Advanced Editing Toolbar or open a context menu on the Toolbar Well and select Advanced Editing. When the toolbar opens, right-click to open a context menu from the Toolbar Well and select Dock All Toolbars.

The Movie tool is shown in the Advanced Editing toolbar by default. When working with sounds and movie clips, you'll want to use the Sound tool as well as the Movie tool. From the pull-down menu adjacent to the Movie tool, select Expand This Button. The Sound tool and the Movie tool both become visible.

Working with Sound Files

You import sounds in Acrobat in one of two ways. You can use the Record Audio Comment tool and record or import a sound in the form of a comment. Once recorded, the sound is embedded in Acrobat and not accessible for importing via an action. The other method of handling sound in PDF documents is to import sounds from files saved on your hard drive. By importing sounds you can invoke a sound with various action types — for example, using a page action to play a sound when the user opens or closes a page or clicks a button or link field.

 Cross-Reference For information on using the Record Audio Comment tool and setting action types, see Chapter 15. For more information on action types, see Chapter 17.

You import sound files with the Sound tool found on the Advanced Editing toolbar. Be certain to understand the difference between creating an audio comment and importing a sound with the Sound tool. Using the Record Audio Comment tool enables you to record a sound or import a sound file from your hard drive. Using the Sound tool enables you to import a sound from a file saved in a format compatible for importing sounds, but does not offer you an option for recording a sound. Before you can use the Sound tool, you need to either acquire or edit sounds and save them to a file format recognized by Acrobat.

Creating sound files

If you are so inclined, you can purchase a commercial application for editing sound and saving recordings that Acrobat can recognize. If recording sounds is an infrequent task and does not warrant the purchase of expensive commercial software, you can find sound recording applications as shareware and in the public domain that can satisfy almost any need you have for using sounds on PDF documents.

Web sites change frequently, so you may need to do a search for public domain and shareware applications for your computer platform. As of this writing you can find sound-editing programs at `www.freewarefiles.com` (Windows) or `www.macupdate.com` (Macintosh). You can find applications that enable you to record sounds and save them in formats acceptable to the platform you use that can then be recognized by Acrobat. The most common of the file types recognized by Acrobat is .wav for Windows and .aiff for Macintosh.

 Note You can import video and sound files that are compatible with Apple QuickTime, Flash Player, Windows Built-In Player, RealOne, and Windows Media Player. Windows media files need to be converted to QuickTime if you're importing a Windows Media file on a Mac. Windows needs a QuickTime installation in order to import QuickTime files on Windows. Sound files saved as .wav and .aiff can be imported in Acrobat running on either platform.

Be certain you have a microphone properly connected to your computer according to your computer's user manual. Launch the sound-editing application you downloaded from a Web site or use a commercial application if you have one available. Most programs offer you a record button similar in appearance to a tape recorder or VCR. Click the Record button and speak into the microphone. When finished recording, click the Stop button. Depending on the application, you may be prompted in a dialog box to save the file or you may see a window where you can further edit the sound as shown in Figure 18-1.

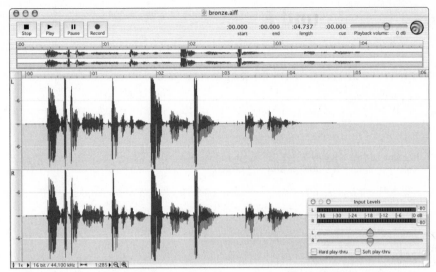

Figure 18-1: To record sounds and save the sound to a file available for importing in Acrobat, use a sound-editing program.

If a dialog box does not prompt you to save the recording, select Save or Save As from a menu option. Typically the commands are under the File menu, but these may vary depending on the program you use. When you save the file, be certain to save in a format acceptable to Acrobat. A .wav (Windows) or .aiff (Macintosh) file format can be imported in Acrobat, but be careful of any file compression applied to the file when saved. You may need to test various compression options in order to find a format that Acrobat can recognize. After choosing the format, supply a name for the file with the proper extension as shown in Figure 18-2.

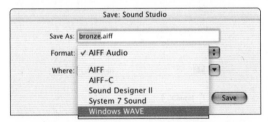

Figure 18-2: After editing a sound, save the file in either .aiff (Macintosh) or .wav (Windows).

Adding sounds to page actions

A sound might be added to a Page Open or a Page Close action to provide informational instructions to complete a form, play a music score, or other similar function. In order to add a sound to a page action, you must have the sound file saved to disk as described in the preceding section. To add a sound to a page action, follow these steps:

Note   Acrobat Standard does support importing sounds on page actions, Bookmarks, and with links. Although you have no Sound tool in Acrobat Standard, you can use an action to import sounds.

STEPS: Adding sounds to page actions

1. **Open the Page Properties.** Be certain your sound file is available in a directory on your hard drive and click on the Pages tab in the Navigation pane. From a context menu opened on the page where you want the sound to play, select Page Properties. The Page Properties dialog box opens.

2. **Set the action trigger.** Click the Actions tab and select either Page Open or Page Close from the Select Trigger pull-down menu.

3. **Set the action type.** Open the pull-down menu for Select Action and select Play a sound from the menu options, as shown in Figure 18-3.

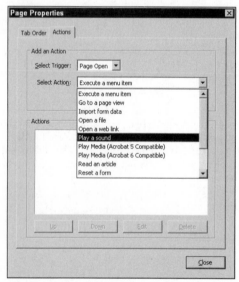

Figure 18-3: Select Play a sound from the Select Action pull-down menu.

Note   By default, the Select a sound menu item in the Select Action pull-down menu may not be in view. Scroll the menu down to show the command.

4. **Add the action to the page trigger.** Click the Add button in the Page Properties dialog box to add the sound to your PDF.

5. **Select the sound file.** The Select Sound File dialog box opens. Navigate your hard drive to find the sound to import, select it, and click the Select button. After importing the sound, click Close in the Page Properties dialog box.

Note   Acrobat may pause momentarily. The sound file imported in Acrobat is converted during the import. When a sound is imported in a PDF file, the sound can then be played across platforms. Therefore, a .wav file can be played on a Macintosh computer and an .aiff file can be played on a Windows computer.

6. **Save the file.** Choose File ➪ Save As and rewrite the file to disk. Close the file and reopen it to test the page action.

After you save the PDF file and reopen it, the sound is played. You can also test the sound by scrolling a page in the PDF file and returning to the page where the sound was imported. The action is dynamic and the sound plays before you save the PDF file.

Adding sounds to form field actions

Of the mouse behavior types, you may find that Mouse Enter, On Focus, or On Blur behaviors work equally as well as using a Mouse Up or Mouse Down trigger. As an example, you might have a descriptive message display when the user places the cursor over a button field and before he or she clicks the mouse. Or you may want to invoke a sound when the user tabs out of a field as a reminder to verify data entry in a PDF form. In these situations and similar uses, the sound is played from a mouse behavior related to a data or button field. To understand how to use sound actions with data fields, follow these steps:

Note   Acrobat Standard does not support Forms tools. You can substitute a button field for a link with Acrobat Standard and import sounds on a link action.

STEPS: Adding sounds to form fields

1. **Open a PDF document with form fields.** In Figure 18-4, I use a form with several check boxes. I want to create a sound when the user places the cursor over one of the check boxes or tabs to the field.

2. **Open the field properties.** Select the Select Object tool in the Advanced Editing toolbar and double-click on the field you want to edit. If no fields exist in your document, create a check box field. The field type properties dialog box opens, which in this case is the Check Box Properties dialog box.

Cross-Reference   For more information on creating form fields, see Chapter 27.

3. **Select the mouse trigger.** In the Check Box Properties dialog box click the Actions tab and select Mouse Enter as the Select Trigger.

4. **Add a sound to the field.** Open the Select Action pull-down menu and select Play a sound.

5. **Select the sound file.** Click the Add button to open the Select Sound File dialog box. Select the file to import and click the Select button.

6. **Close the Check Box Properties dialog box.** Check to be certain the mouse trigger is set to Mouse Enter. Click Close in the Check Box Properties dialog box.

7. **Test the sound.** Place the mouse cursor over the check box where you added the sound. (Note: To play the sound by tabbing to the field, use the On Focus mouse trigger.)

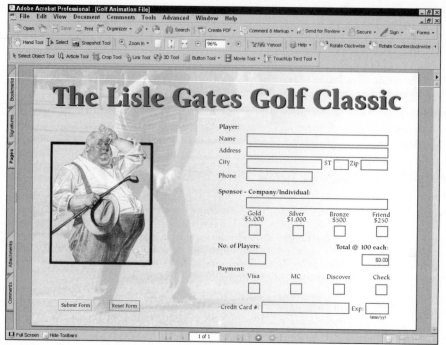

Figure 18-4: Four check boxes are to be configured to play a sound on a Mouse Enter trigger.

When the mouse enters one of the check boxes, the respective sound plays. The sound plays completely even if the cursor leaves the field. Sounds added to forms either for page actions or field actions can be played from any Acrobat viewer.

Tip
A sound continues to play to completion. If you want to stop the sound while editing a document, select the Select Object tool or press the R key on your keyboard to activate the Select Object tool. (Note: You need to enable Use single-key accelerators to access tools in the General Preferences to use key modifiers to select tools.)

Using the Sound tool

Importing sounds with page actions, form fields, links, bookmarks, and so on limits your import options to fewer file formats and limits the attributes you can assign to the imported file. In essence, you import the file and play the sound. Not much else is available when you use the Select Action command. Another method for importing sound files in PDF documents is using the Sound tool. When you use the Sound tool to import sounds, your options are much greater for the kinds of files you can import and attributes you can assign to the imported sounds.

To import a sound with the Sound tool, select the tool from the Advanced Editing toolbar and just double-click on a document page or drag open a rectangle on a document page. The area contained within the rectangle becomes a trigger to play the sound. When you release the mouse button, the Add Sound dialog box opens as shown in Figure 18-5.

Tip   You can manage sound and movie links similarly to links and form fields where context menu options enable you to size, align, copy, paste, and distribute fields. You can access these menu commands when you select sound and movie links in a group together with links and form fields.

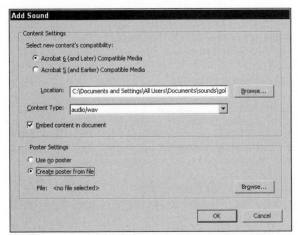

Figure 18-5: When you use the Sound tool, the Add Sound properties offer you many different file format import options and attribute choices and playing sounds.

You set the attributes for sound imports when you initially use the Sound tool. After specifying choices in the Add Sound dialog box, you can access the Multimedia Properties dialog box by opening a context menu. Your first stop is the Add Sound dialog box where the options include

✦ **Compatibility:** From the radio button choices you decide whether the sound import is Acrobat 6 (and Later) or Acrobat 5 (and Earlier) compatible. If you select Acrobat 5 (and Earlier) compatible, the format options are limited to .wav and .aiff formats. If you use Acrobat 6 (and Later) Compatible Media, the sound may not play with earlier Acrobat viewers depending on the file types you import and attributes assigned to the sound.

✦ **Browse:** Click the Browse button to locate the sound you want to import.

✦ **Content Type:** By default the type of the file you import is listed automatically in the field box. By clicking the down arrow you can open a pull-down menu where all compatible file formats are listed. A total of 27 different file formats are supported including newer MPEG4 and several MIDI formats. When you import files, let Acrobat interpret the file format and leave the format unchanged. If you select a sound for which Acrobat does not know the Content Type, Acrobat prompts you to click in a dialog box to select a content type.

✦ **Embed content in document:** Using Acrobat 5 compatibility automatically embeds sound files. If you use Acrobat 6 compatibility you can choose to link the sound file to the PDF or embed the sound in the PDF document. If you disable the check box for not embedding the file, you need to send the sound file to a user as well as the PDF in order for other users to play the sound.

✦ **Poster Settings:** If you select Acrobat 5 (and Earlier) this option is not available. The rectangle you create appears similar to a button field. If you leave the default at Use no poster, then the rectangle is invisible when the Hand tool is selected. A user can click anywhere within the rectangle boundary to play the sound. If you select Create poster from file, you can fit a graphic to the rectangle; for example, using button faces for form field buttons. You click the Browse button to select the file you want to use for the poster. You can choose any file type that is compatible when using the Create PDF From File command. If the file type is other than PDF, Acrobat converts the file to PDF as it imports the image. If you're using a multi-page PDF document for the poster, the first page in the PDF document is used for the poster.

Cross-Reference   For information on creating button faces, see Chapter 17.

Click OK after selecting options in the Add Sound dialog box. When you return to the document page, the rectangle is visible. You assign additional properties when you open the sound properties from a context menu. When the properties dialog box opens, the title of the dialog box is Multimedia Properties if Acrobat 6 (or Later) and Movie Properties if Acrobat 5 (or Earlier).

Acrobat 5–compatible Movie (Sound) Properties

If you're using an Acrobat 5-compatible sound import, the Movie Properties dialog box opens when you select Properties from a context menu opened from the sound rectangle. As shown in Figure 18-6, the dialog box contains three tabs used for selecting more options than were available in the Add Sound dialog box.

Tip   When you use either the Sound tool or the Movie tool and create a sound or movie field, the first dialog box that opens is the Add Sound or Add Movie dialog box. While selecting options in the dialog box, you have no opportunity to select objects on the document page or use menu commands. However, after you create a sound or movie field and open the Properties dialog box, working with it is similar to working with Link Properties and Form Field Properties windows where you can access both objects on the page and menu commands. When editing properties for sound and movie files, you don't need to close the Properties window to select and edit additional fields.

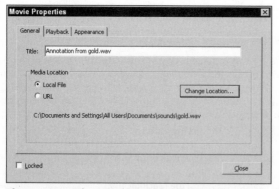

Figure 18-6: When working with Acrobat 5 (and Earlier) media, to open the Movie Properties dialog box, use the Sound tool, the Movie tool, or the Select Object tool and select Properties from a context menu.

General Properties

The default properties are the General Movie Properties. In this dialog box you make selections for

✦ **Title:** By default the title of the sound clip is the filename. Edit the title name in the field box to change the title.

✦ **Media location:** Local files are stored locally on your hard drive. Although the sound file is embedded in the PDF, you can change the sound to another file by clicking the Change Location button. Click the button and the Select Multimedia File dialog box opens. Select another file and click the Select button and the sound is changed to another file. If you select URL, another dialog box opens asking you to specify a URL where a file is located. If importing sounds, you need to add the sound filename as part of the URL when using Acrobat 5 compatibility. When you deselect the option to embed the file with Acrobat 6 compatibility, the directory path is all you need to address in the line where the URL is specified.

Playback

The Playback tab offers options settings for playing sound clips and movies as shown in Figure 18-7:

Figure 18-7: Click on Playback to set options for playing sounds.

✦ **Show player controls:** A control palette opens when a sound is played if this check box is enabled. In the control palette you have a button to play/pause and a slider. Click and drag the slider to move forward or backward in the sound file.

✦ **Use floating window:** With sounds, the sound file is fixed to a location. With video clips you can select the Use floating window option to float a video clip in a window centered in the Acrobat window. If you select floating window for a sound file, the player control opens in a floating toolbar. In Figure 18-8 you can see the difference between using a floating window or disabling a floating window when showing player controls. On the left is the player control with Use floating window disabled. On the right the same sound clip is played with the Use floating window check box enabled. In both examples, the Show player controls check box was enabled.

Note   Viewing floating windows in Full Screen mode on the Macintosh was problematic in Acrobat 6. In Acrobat 7 the problem has been fixed and floating windows now display correct behavior the same on Macintosh as they do on Windows.

Figure 18-8: When Show player controls is checked, the control appears below the sound import (left). When Use floating window is checked, the player controls open in a floating toolbar (right).

✦ **Size:** For sound imports, the Size pull-down menu and field box are disabled. These options relate to sizing video clips, explained in the "Playback" section later in this chapter.

✦ **Play:** From the pull-down menu you can choose to play a sound Once; play a sound once and Keep the player open; Loop through the sound and continue playing it over and over again; and play Forward and backward, which provides an interesting way of hearing your voice played backward. This latter option is best used for video clips without sound.

Appearance

Many of the options for appearance settings are the same as those found for link and form field appearances. Click on the Appearance tab and make choices for the appearance of the rectangle border and the contents of the rectangle as shown in Figure 18-9.

Figure 18-9: Click on the Appearance tab to change border colors and the poster image.

✦ **Type:** From the Type pull-down menu select from Visible Rectangle or Invisible Rectangle. If Invisible Rectangle is selected, the following options for Width, Style, and Color are grayed out.

✦ **Width:** The same three choices for link and form field rectangle widths of Thin, Medium, and Thick are listed in the pull-down menu.

✦ **Style:** Two choices appear for either setting the rectangle to a solid line or a dashed line.

✦ **Color:** You can choose from the same color options you have available for links and form fields by clicking on the color swatch and selecting either preset or custom colors.

✦ **Option:** The Option pull-down menu applies to movie files. If you select Put in Document from the pull-down menu when using a sound file, the menu defaults back to Don't Show. With sound files you cannot show a poster image because the sound contains no graphic data.

✦ **Colors:** The Colors pull-down menu and field box are disabled for sound files.

✦ **Locked:** The Locked check box is accessible from all tabs. When you select the Locked check box the sound rectangle is locked to position on the document page and the attributes are locked. If you want to make any edits on the Movie Properties dialog box, you first need to uncheck the Locked item.

Acrobat 6–compatible Multimedia (Sound) Properties

If you elect to use Acrobat 6 compatibility, the options in the Add Sound dialog box are the same as discussed in the "Using the Sound tool" section earlier in this chapter. After you create a sound import and select Properties from a context menu, a different set of property options appear in the Multimedia Properties dialog box. In Figure 18-10 the Multimedia Properties dialog box shows the default Settings tab options.

Figure 18-10: Select Properties from a context menu to open the Multimedia Properties dialog box for Acrobat 6–compatible sounds.

Settings

The Settings tab offers options for labels and renditions. By default the Settings tab is placed in view when you open the Multimedia Properties. As you can see in Figure 18-11, the Appearance tab is consistent with the Movie Properties dialog box, but the other two tabs offer options much different from those found with Acrobat 5–compatible sound files:

✦ **Annotation Title:** Add a title for the sound in this field. The title supplied here can be different from the filename.

✦ **Alternate Text:** When creating accessible files for vision- and motion-challenged users, you can add alternate text that can be read by screen-reading software.

Cross-Reference

For more information on creating accessible PDFs, see Chapter 20.

✦ **Renditions:** A good number of options available when editing renditions apply to movie clips. For information on setting rendition options for sound files, see the section "Adding a rendition" later in this chapter for movie files.

Appearance

The Appearance tab (shown in Figure 18-11) in the Multimedia Properties dialog box offers options similar to those found in the Movie Properties for defining the attributes of a rectangle border for Type, Width, Style, and Color. In addition to these settings, other options include

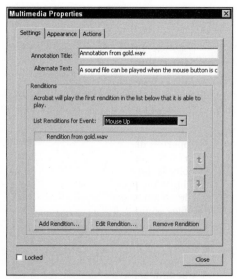

Figure 18-11: The Appearance tab offers options for setting the field rectangle appearance and a button to access the Change Poster Options dialog box.

✦ **Annotation is hidden from view:** The annotation added to the field box in the Settings tab is visible by default. To hide the annotation, enable this check box.

✦ **Change Poster Option:** Options for the poster image are similar to those used with Acrobat 5–compatible files. The settings appear in a dialog box, shown in Figure 18-12, as opposed to a pull-down menu described earlier. When you click the button for Change Poster Option, you'll find a few differences among the choices. The three options include

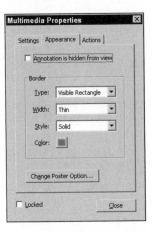

Figure 18-12: When you click the Change Poster Options button, a dialog box opens, offering three choices for poster displays.

- **Use no poster:** This choice is the same as selecting Don't Show in the Movie Properties dialog box. No poster is shown in the sound field.

- **Retrieve poster from movie:** Also a similar choice as you find in the Movie Properties dialog box. With sound files a dialog box opens informing you that no support for a poster is retrievable from sound files. For movie files the poster is retrieved from the first frame in the movie file.

- **Create poster from file:** The Movie Properties dialog box used with Acrobat 5–compatible files offers you an option for Retrieve From Movie as the third choice in the pull-down menu. This choice is the same as the preceding option and pulls the first frame in the movie clip as the poster image. With Acrobat 6 compatibility the Create poster from file option enables you to use a PDF or file compatible with the Create PDF From File command as the poster image. To add a poster from a file, click the Browse button and select the file you want to import.

Actions

The Actions tab offers you options for setting an action on mouse triggers much like you apply actions to links, Bookmarks, page actions, and form fields. Options from the Select Trigger pull-down menu differ slightly from those you select for links, Bookmarks, page actions, and form fields (see Figure 18-3 earlier in this chapter). Some of the triggers are available only to movie clips whereas others work with both sounds and movie files. The options in the Actions tab include

✦ **Select Trigger:** Open the pull-down menu and you see the trigger actions shown in Figure 18-3.

Cross-Reference

For more information on selecting trigger options, see Chapter 17.

- **Mouse Up:** This trigger belongs to both sound and video clips. The behavior is identical to the same trigger used for other items such as page actions, links, and buttons where actions are applied.

- **Page Visible:** A current page active in the Document pane can be different than page visibility. When using Continuous page layout, Facing Pages, or Continuous – Facing Pages, you can have one page active while other pages are visible in the Document pane. When this trigger is selected, the media clip plays dependent on page visibility and not necessarily the current page. This trigger is only available with video clips.

- **Page Invisible:** If a page is not visible in the Document pane, the media clip can be played on an action such as a button, link, or Bookmark. This trigger is available only with video clips.

- **Page Enter:** Also available only with video clips, this trigger is like setting a page action. When the page becomes the current page, the video plays.

- **Page Exit:** The opposite of the preceding option. When you scroll to another page, only video clips play.

- **Mouse Down:** When the mouse button is pressed down, the trigger is invoked. This trigger is available to both sound and video clips.

- **Mouse Enter:** When the mouse cursor enters the focus rectangle either sound or video clips play.

- **Mouse Exit:** Opposite of the preceding option where the sound or video plays when the mouse cursor exits the focus rectangle.

- **On Receive Focus:** For video clips only, this trigger is like the On Focus mouse trigger used with form field buttons. Pressing the Tab key activates the focus rectangle and the video clip plays.

- **On Lose Focus:** The opposite of the preceding option and like the On Blur mouse trigger where a video clip plays when you tab out of the movie field.

✦ **Select Action:** From the Select Action pull-down menu you can select any action type that is also available to links, fields, Bookmarks, and page actions.

Cross-Reference

For more information on Select Action options, see Chapter 17.

✦ **Add:** When you select an action, click the Add button to add the action to the Actions list window.

✦ **Actions:** The Actions list window shows all the trigger options and actions assigned to the sound or video clip. You can add multiple actions with different triggers and view all the additions in the Actions list.

✦ **Up/Down:** The buttons at the bottom of the Actions tab enable you to reorder multiple actions. Select an item in the Actions list and click the Up or Down button to move the selected action before or after other items in the list. When the actions are invoked, the play is in the order shown in the Actions list.

✦ **Edit:** Select an item in the Actions list and click the Edit button to edit action item attributes. If you select a sound or video file in the Actions list and click the Edit button, the Play Media (Acrobat 6 and Later Compatible) dialog box opens as shown in Figure 18-13. From the pull-down menu you make choices for changing the play options. Notice you also have an option for writing a custom JavaScript.

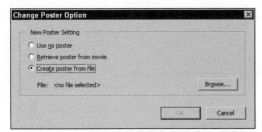

Figure 18-13: When you select Edit in the Actions tab for media files, the Play Media (Acrobat 6 Compatible) dialog box opens. Make choices in the dialog box for play options you want to change.

✦ **Delete:** If you want to delete an item in the Actions list, select the item to be removed and click the Delete button.

✦ **Locked:** The Locked check box offers the same option as discussed earlier in the Movie Properties "Appearance" section.

Creating Movie Files

Like the sound files discussed earlier in this chapter, video files require that you create video clips in other authoring programs. No tools or features are contained in Acrobat for editing movies. However, after you create video clips in authoring applications you have the wealth of import options and play opportunities similar to those used with sound files.

Video editing at the high end is handled by sophisticated software like Final Cut Pro, Adobe Premiere, Adobe After Effects, and other similar professional programs designed to offer you limitless choices for editing video and audio channels. On the low end, you have some impressive features in programs that cost very little. For Windows, Adobe's new product, Adobe Photoshop Album, is a low-cost editing program designed to take your still images and video clips and create PDF presentations. On the professional side you can add still photos and sound clips to create presentations and demonstration projects. For personal use you can create entertaining presentations and videos for family and friends. The great advantage of using Photoshop Album for either purpose is that the program exports direct to PDF along with JavaScripts that allow the PDFs to be viewed in Full Screen mode with various player options.

For Macintosh users, Apple's own iMovie is a free application shipping with System X that produces QuickTime movies. You don't have the export options that Photoshop Album does, but iMovie offers many more features for video editing than Photoshop Album. iMovie supports PDF imports as well as still photos and video clips. If you happen to be a cross-platform user, the combination of using both programs offers you a sophisticated editing environment where you can produce PDF presentations and displays for just about any purpose.

Cross-Reference
Discussion in this chapter is related to multimedia authoring and working with video and sound in PDF documents. For additional information related to creating presentations and other application support for various kinds of animation, see Chapter 21.

Note
You have many options for video and sound editing programs and different users will favor one application over another. I mention Adobe Photoshop Album in this chapter because Photoshop Album is optimized for direct export to PDF. I mention Apple Computer's iApplications because they ship free with the operating system. If you use other applications for creating video clips, look at the section "Importing Movies" where importing video in PDF files is covered for you to determine whether Acrobat supports the programs you use.

Using Photoshop Album (Windows)

Although not a feature in Acrobat, the PDF support provided by Adobe Photoshop Album makes it worthwhile to talk about in a book on Acrobat especially with features available in Adobe Reader related to Photoshop Album files. For less than $50 U.S. retail, Photoshop Album was designed for working with Acrobat. With easy-to-follow, step-by-step instructions for video creation and export to PDF, anyone not using professional video authoring applications will find Photoshop Album a favorite tool.

Cross-Reference
For information on Adobe Reader and Photoshop Album, see Chapter 3.

When you launch Photoshop Album, an easy-to-use help screen opens as a default. From the tabs shown in Figure 18-14 you select options for acquiring photos (Get Photos) and editing images with tools for cropping, image brightness, red-eye removal, and color saturation. After editing, select the images behind the Quick Guide window and click on the Create tab.

Figure 18-14: Photoshop Album opens with a Quick Guide window where you import photos and/or video clips, edit images, and create an album package.

Photoshop Album offers several ways to package your creations. Choose from one of the options in the Quick Guide made available after you click on the Create tab shown in Figure 18-15. Among some of your choices are exporting to a slide show, a greeting card, a calendar, or a photo album. If you use video imports, some of the layout options aren't available for exporting to PDF. If an option is not available, Photoshop Album warns you ahead of time.

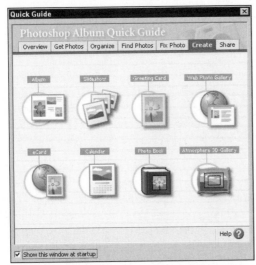

Figure 18-15: When you click on the Create tab, several package options are made available. Select from the thumbnails in the Quick Guide and the Workspace dialog box opens.

After selecting your package option, the Workspace dialog box opens. You can examine the images/videos in the Workspace to ensure all photos are selected for export. Click on the Start Creations Wizard and a step-by-step Creations Wizard dialog box opens, as shown in Figure 18-16. You simply click the Next buttons and make the edits you want for layout style, titles, transitions, music, and number of images per page.

Click the Next button until you arrive at Step 5 shown in Figure 18-16. The export options are shown on the right side of the Creations Wizard. Click the Save as PDF button and the Save as PDF dialog box opens. You have options for Optimize for Viewing Onscreen, Optimize for Printing, or Use Full Resolution. Click OK in the dialog box and the Export PDF As dialog box opens. Find a location on your hard drive where you want the file saved and click the Save button. The Photoshop Album document is exported to PDF.

When you open the file in Acrobat, the file opens in Full Screen view. Depending on the options you selected when you exported the file, you may have a control palette open in the Full Screen view window as shown in Figure 18-17. The Photoshop Album document plays through completion and returns you to edit mode after the last slide is viewed.

Cross-Reference   For more information on Full Screen views, see Chapter 21.

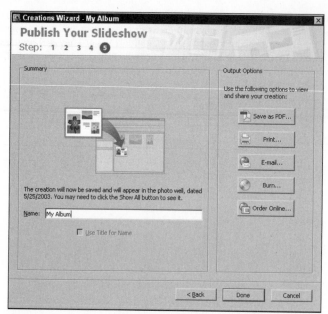

Figure 18-16: Photoshop Album walks you through five steps to produce your creation with easy-to-follow instructions.

Figure 18-17: The PDF exported from Photoshop Album opens in Full Screen view in Acrobat.

The animation, controls, and buttons contained in the PDF exported from Photoshop Album are made possible with JavaScripts. Photoshop Album creates the JavaScripts and exports them in the PDF document. If you want to edit the JavaScript, you can edit the document-level scripts or the button actions. In Figure 18-18 you can see some of the code added to the PDF from Photoshop Album.

 Cross-Reference For more information on writing and editing JavaScripts, see Chapter 29.

```
JavaScript Editor                                                    X
 Create and Edit JavaScripts
  var haveSVG = typeof alternatePresentations != 'undefined' &&
          alternatePresentations['Slideshow.svg'] != null;

  var playButton;
  var closeButton;
  var upgradeButton;
  var pluginButton;
  var playMsg;
  var pluginMsg;
  var upgradeMsg;
  var itv,timeout;
  var doc = this;

  if( typeof doAutostart == 'undefined' )
          doAutostart = false;

  function hideAllButtons()
  {

                                        OK      Cancel      Go to...
```

Figure 18-18: Photoshop Album creates JavaScripts during the export to PDF. You can edit the JavaScripts in the JavaScript Editor in Acrobat.

Exporting to PDF from Photoshop Album is a complete PDF package. The files you create in Photoshop Album don't provide you options for saving video clips you can import in Acrobat with the Movie tool. If you want to use a PDF exported from Photoshop Album as part of a larger presentation, you can use button links to open and close files while in Full Screen mode.

Cross-Reference For more information on creating link actions while viewing PDFs in Full Screen mode, see the section "Creating Play Buttons" later in this chapter, and see Chapter 23.

Using iMovie (Macintosh)

When QuickTime movies are needed for importing into PDFs with the Movie tool, Macintosh users can create some impressive video clips with Apple Computer's iApplications. iMovie ships free with System X and together with the companion products of iTunes, iPhoto, and iDVD you have an elaborate editing environment for adding sounds and video to PDF documents and writing your creations to DVDs.

Windows users need to install QuickTime as the Acrobat 7 installer does not install the QuickTime player. QuickTime is part of the System X operating system files on the Macintosh so no additional installation is necessary. Once QuickTime is installed, users of either Windows or Macintosh operating systems can import QuickTime videos in PDF files. When using iMovie for video creation, you can export the source document to a QuickTime format. Be certain to regularly check Apple Computer's Web site at www.apple.com for upgrades. QuickTime is constantly being upgraded and you'll want to use the most recent version.

Like Photoshop Album, iMovie enables you to import video clips and still images. iMovie also offers you options for importing sounds, creating transitions and effects, and adding titles. You start by creating a new project and adding video and/or movie clips to the Clips pane as shown in Figure 18-19. Choose File ➪ Import to select multiple files to add to the Clips pane. From the Clips pane, drag files to the timeline at the bottom of the window.

Figure 18-19: Start iMovie by importing still photos and/or video clips in the Clips pane.

You add transitions, effects, titles, and sounds to the timeline by clicking the Trans button and dragging effects to the timeline as in the example shown in Figure 18-20. You can control zooms, speed, and volume by moving sliders below the timeline. After assembling the movie clip, click the Play movie button represented by a right-pointing arrow below the display window. When the preview looks like the final video you want to produce, choose File ➪ Export. In the iMovie:Export dialog box are options for file format and compression. Play with some different settings to determine the best compression and quality that work for your presentations.

The file you save from iMovie is a QuickTime .mov file. The resulting file can be imported in Acrobat. iMovie offers you a little more flexibility for sizing movie files and moving them around PDF documents. However, if a Photoshop Album package works for your presentation, you can import the QuickTime movie in Photoshop Album and create a PDF file as described in the previous section "Using Photoshop Album (Windows)."

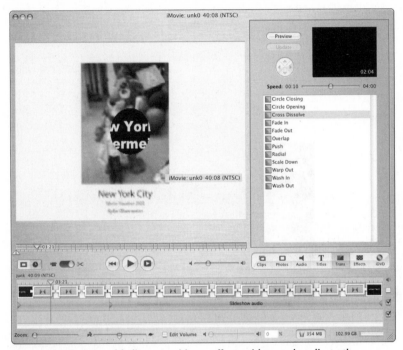

Figure 18-20: You add clips, transitions, effects, titles, and audio to the timeline by clicking on the items and dragging them to the timeline. Click on the right-pointing arrow to preview the movie before exporting.

Importing Movies

You use the Movie tool in the Advanced Editing toolbar to import movies. To import a movie, you create a movie link in the same way you create a link with the Sound tool. Select the Movie tool from the Toolbar Well and double-click the mouse button or click and drag open a rectangle. When you release the mouse button, the Add Movie dialog box opens as shown in Figure 18-21.

Select the compatibility you want to use and click the Browse button to locate the movie to import. Import a movie file by clicking Select and click OK in the Add Movie dialog box. The movie is imported with the movie frame selected.

Tip   In Acrobat 6 or 7, when you double-click the mouse button or click and drag open a rectangle, the movie frame defaults to the size to which the video was compressed. If you want to size the frame up or down, press the Shift key and drag one of the four handles with the Movie tool or the Select Object tool to reshape the rectangle. Be aware that if you size up the movie frame from the default size, the video will look distorted when played.

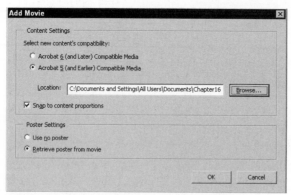

Figure 18-21: The Add Movie dialog box offers you options for selecting the content compatibility for either Acrobat 5 (or Earlier) compatible media or Acrobat 6 (and Later) compatible media.

Acrobat 5–compatible movies

Figure 18-21 shows the Add Movie dialog box options for Acrobat 5–compatible movies. You have options for selecting either Acrobat 5 or Acrobat 6 compatibility like you do with sound imports. When you select the Acrobat 5 (and Earlier) Compatible Media radio button, the dialog box reduces in size and displays only the options available when using Acrobat 5 or earlier compatibility.

Add Movie

You make choices in the Add Movie dialog box when you first create a movie field. After creating the field, you can make changes and select attributes in the Movie Properties dialog box that are similar to the Sound properties choices. In the Add Movie dialog box, you select from the following:

✦ **Compatibility:** Click on the compatibility for either Acrobat 5 or Acrobat 6 Compatible Media. If you select Acrobat 5 compatibility the movie clips cannot be embedded in the PDF file. Therefore, you need to send the PDF and the movie file to other users or host both on a Web site in order for users to view the movies. If using Acrobat 6–compatible media and embedding movie clips in a PDF, Acrobat users with viewers earlier than Acrobat 6 won't be able to see your movie files.

✦ **Location:** On local drives, the location of the movie file is added to the Location field box. When you first import a movie, identify the movie in the Add Movie dialog box and leave the Location at the default. After you create the movie rectangle, you can change the location to a URL for Web-hosted documents in the Movie Properties dialog box.

✦ **Snap to content proportions:** When enabled, the movie remains proportional as you drag open a rectangle, preventing distortion when the movie is played. The media file's original dimensions are preserved no matter how large you draw the rectangle.

✦ **Poster Settings:** Select the Use no poster option to show a blank video frame. Select the Retrieve poster from movie option to show the first movie frame in the movie rectangle when the movie is not playing.

Acrobat 5 Movie Properties

After you import a movie with Acrobat 5 compatibility, you can make further attribute choices in the Movie Properties dialog box. Select either the Movie tool or the Select Object tool and open a context menu. From the menu options, select Properties. The Movie Properties dialog box opens as shown in Figure 18-22.

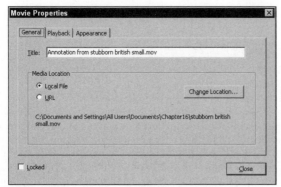

Figure 18-22: The General Movie Properties are identical to the Sound Properties.

General

Notice that options in the General tab are identical to the Sound Properties. For further definition of the options refer to the section "Using the Sound Tool" earlier in this chapter.

If you want to link the movie to a URL location, select the URL radio button. The Enter URL dialog box opens where you add the URL. Be certain to include the complete URL address, beginning with *http://*.

Note   If you move a movie file on your hard drive to another location, the path to the file is broken and the movie won't play. To reset the directory path, click the Browse button, find the movie file, and click Select in the Select Movie File dialog box.

Playback

Playback options are also identical to the options found with Sound files. The pull-down menu for Size is accessible for movie files only. From the menu options you make choices for the size of the video frames during playback as shown in Figure 18-23. If you choose a size above the Default (1x) size, the video may be distorted when played.

If you choose Full Screen from the menu choices, the video plays at the largest possible size on your monitor in a separate window. However, the video playback does not change the view to Full Screen mode.

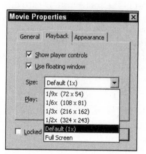

Figure 18-23: Playback options are identical to the Sound properties with the exception of the Size options. Choose the playback size from the menu choices.

Options for showing the player controls and using a floating window are handled a little differently than when enabling the same options for sound files. The player controls are fixed at the bottom of the video clip for viewing movies either with or without a floating window. Also, rather than the player control being affected when you use the floating window option, the movie is shown in a floating window. In Figure 18-24 you can see the video frame playing with the player controls visible at the default size of the video. In Figure 18-25 the player controls are enabled as well as floating window.

Appearance

Appearance options are also the same as those discussed for Sound properties. In the Appearance options, you have access to showing the movie poster in the file when the movie is still and not playing. If you choose to Put the Poster in the Document, you can also make choices for the color display of 8-bit (256 colors) or 24-bit (millions of colors).

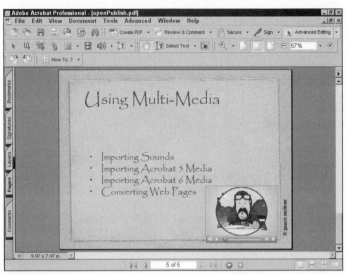

Figure 18-24: Player controls are enabled and the floating window option is disabled.

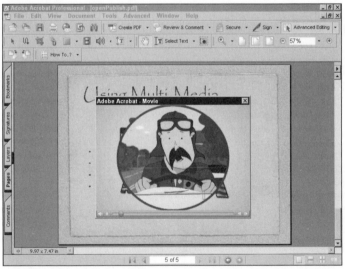

Figure 18-25: Player controls are enabled and the floating window option is enabled.

Acrobat 6–compatible movies

If you decide to use Acrobat 6 compatibility, you need to do it when you use the Movie tool to draw the field. If you create a movie field and specify Acrobat 5 compatibility, then change your mind and want to use Acrobat 6 compatibility, you need to delete the first movie field by clicking on it with the Movie tool or the Select Object tool. Press the Backspace/Delete key on your keyboard or open a context menu and choose Edit ➪ Delete. Double-click the mouse button with the Movie tool and select Acrobat 6 compatibility and the dialog box changes to reflect the Acrobat 6–compatible options as shown in Figure 18-26.

Add Movie

Select Acrobat 6 (or Later) Compatible Media and you'll notice the dialog box expands to offer more options than when you use Acrobat 5–compatible files. The settings are the same as those discussed in the section "Acrobat 6–Compatible Multimedia (Sound) Properties." When adding movies you have options for the poster view in a still frame while the movie is not playing. Select from Use no poster, Retrieve poster from movie, or Create poster from file. These options are the same for sounds with the exception of the Retrieve poster from movie. Whereas sound files produce an error when you make this menu choice, movie files retrieve the first frame in the video for the poster image.

After making choices in the Add Movie dialog box, access more options in the Multimedia Properties dialog box. Click OK after selecting the Acrobat 6–compatible settings. Open a context menu with either the Movie tool or the Select Object tool and choose Properties from the menu options.

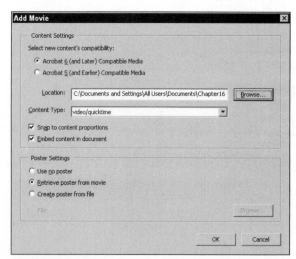

Figure 18-26: Select the Movie tool and draw a rectangle or double-click in the Document pane. In the Add Movie dialog box, select Acrobat 6 (or Later) Compatible Media.

Acrobat 6 Multimedia Properties

The Multimedia Properties dialog box shown in Figure 18-27 contains the same options found when you open Acrobat 6–compatible sound files properties. The first stop is the Settings tab, where you see options for annotation text and alternate text. The items below the text fields contain options for renditions. Because I didn't cover renditions earlier in the sounds discussion, I address the options you have for adding renditions here.

Understanding renditions

When you import a sound or video, the rendition of the clip is assigned to a Mouse Up trigger and plays according to the properties you enable for the play options. By default imported sounds and videos have a single default rendition. When using Acrobat 6–compatible media options, you have an opportunity to add different renditions to the same media clip or multiple media clips. For example, you may have a rendition that plays full screen from a large file and you may want to add an alternate clip of a duplicate movie with a smaller file size. If hosting the media on a Web site you can assign what media clip is downloaded to a user's computer based on the end user's connection speed. The movie field remains the same, but the attributes contain two different renditions for the same field.

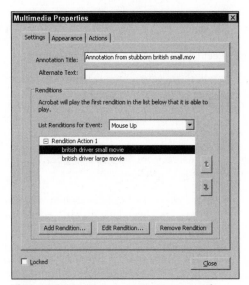

Figure 18-27: Open a context menu and select Properties to open the Multimedia Properties dialog box.

You have options for editing existing renditions after importing a media clip or you can add new renditions to an imported file. When you add new renditions they are listed in the Settings tab in the Multimedia Properties dialog box.

Adding a rendition

By default a rendition is listed in the lower window in the Settings properties. To add a rendition, click the Add Rendition button. A pull-down menu opens where you make choices for one of the following:

✦ **Using a File:** For local files select Using a File. The Select Multimedia File dialog box opens where you navigate your hard drive and select the file to use. This option might be used to select a duplicate file smaller or larger in size than the original rendition.

✦ **Using a URL:** If you want files downloaded from Web sites, select Using a URL. The Add a New Rendition Using a URL dialog box opens where you add the URL address for where the file is located. When you add the URL, a pull-down menu opens where you can select the content type for the media format.

✦ **By Copying an Existing Rendition:** If you want to use the same rendition as one listed in the Settings list window for the purpose of duplicating the rendition and providing alternate attributes, select By Copying an Existing Rendition. The Copy Rendition dialog box opens where you select the rendition to copy from a pull-down menu. The new Rendition is not actually *copied*, but rather points to another file and adds about 4K to your file size.

Select any one of the three options and click the Edit button to open the Rendition Settings dialog box.

Editing a rendition

You can choose to edit an existing rendition or edit the new rendition you added to the media file (see the preceding section). If you want to edit an existing rendition, click the Edit Rendition button from the Settings properties. If you've added a new rendition, it now appears in the list window, so you can select it and click the Edit button. In either case, the Renditions Settings dialog box opens, as shown in Figure 18-28.

Cross-Reference   There are a considerable number of options in the Renditions Settings dialog box. For more information on editing Renditions, refer to the Acrobat Help document.

A considerable number of options are available in the various tabs of the Rendition Settings dialog box. By default the dialog box opens at the Media Settings tab. The various tabs and choices you have include

✦ **Media Settings:** Make choices from the Media Settings tab for the rendition name, the media location and content type, and the rendition for alternate text, and choose from the Allow Temp File pull-down menu for various options related to accessibility. If the media is to be made accessible to JavaScript, be certain to check the box for enabling JavaScript.

✦ **Playback Settings:** Click the Playback Settings tab to make choices for the player window visibility, volume settings, showing player controls, continuous looping, or times played. In the list at the bottom of the Playback Settings tab, click the Add button to add the type of media players you want users to use for playing the media. You have an option for enabling all players and a setting for the preferred player.

✦ **Playback Location:** Make choices on this tab for where the media is played, such as in the document, floating window, or full screen. If you select floating window, you have many different choices for document size and position.

✦ **System Requirements:** From a pull-down menu you have choices for connection speeds. If you want a particular rendition to be downloaded for all users with 384K connections or greater, you can make the choice in this dialog box. In addition you have choices for screen displays, captions, subtitles, and language.

✦ **Playback Requirements:** Based on options you selected in the other settings tabs, a list is displayed in the last settings tab. Each item has a check box for enabling a required condition. Check all the boxes for those items you want to make a required function.

Click OK in the Rendition Settings dialog box when you're finished setting the options in the various settings tabs. If you need to add another rendition with some alternate options to the last rendition you edited, copy the rendition and make the necessary edits. You can list as many different renditions as you like to provide much flexibility for your viewer audience and the systems they use.

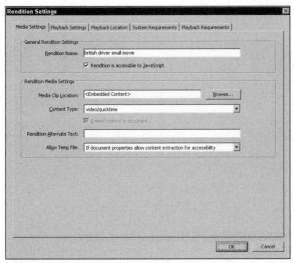

Figure 18-28: Select a rendition and click the Edit button. The Rendition Settings dialog box opens.

Appearance

The Appearance tab in the Multimedia Properties dialog box offers the same options as those you find when editing Sound Properties. Options are available for poster display in the Change Poster Option dialog box when you click the Change Poster Option button shown in Figure 18-29. The poster options are the same as those available as discussed in the "Acrobat 6–Compatible Media (Sound) Properties" section described earlier in this chapter.

Actions

The Actions tab also offers the same choices as those available with sound files for adding an action to the media clip. You can choose an action from the Select Action pull-down menu the same as when using action types with Acrobat 5 media.

Figure 18-29: Click the Change Poster Option button to change the poster image.

Creating Play Buttons

As I explain in Chapter 21, you can create presentations from programs such as Microsoft PowerPoint where animated effects from PowerPoint appear in PDF documents in Full Screen mode. You can add media clips to a presentation while showing slides in Full Screen mode and set up some buttons to play, pause, and stop the media clips.

Cross-Reference   For more information on converting PowerPoint files to PDF, see Chapter 23.

To understand how play buttons are added to a PDF document, follow these steps:

STEPS: Adding play buttons to PDF documents

1. Open a PDF document in Acrobat Professional. Note that Acrobat Standard does not support importing media, therefore, the following steps can only be performed in Acrobat Professional. Use a PDF document converted from PowerPoint or any other PDF you want to use with imported media.

2. Select the Movie tool and double-click on the document page where you want to import the media. The Add Movie dialog box opens.

3. Select Acrobat 6 (and Later) Compatible Media.

4. Click Browse and locate the file you want to import. Select the file in the Select Movie File dialog box and click Select.

5. You are returned to the Add Movie dialog box. Click OK and the movie is imported.

6. Using either the Movie tool or the Select Object tool, open a context menu and select Properties. The Rendition Settings dialog box opens.

7. Click the Playback Location tab and select Floating Window from the Playback Location pull-down menu as shown in Figure 18-30. Click OK and you return to the Document pane.

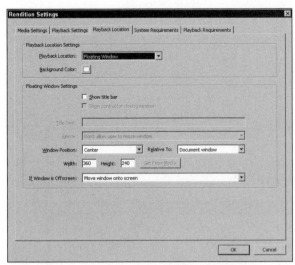

Figure 18-30: Set the Playback Location to Floating Window.

8. Select the Button tool and create a button on the page by dragging open a rectangle.

9. Name the button in the General tab in the Button Properties dialog box. Click the Options tab and type **Play** in the Label text box. Click the Actions tab and open the Select Actions pull-down menu. Select Play Media (Acrobat 6 and Later Compatible) from the menu options.

10. Click Add in the Button Properties dialog box and the Play Media (Acrobat 6 and Later Compatible) opens as shown in Figure 18-31.

11. Select Play and click OK.

12. Add additional buttons for stopping, pausing and resuming the play by following steps 8 through 11. Be certain to change the name for the button and type descriptive names for the labels.

13. Press Control/Command+L to set the viewing mode to Full Screen.

14. Click the buttons and the media plays, stops, pauses and resumes according to the buttons you click. In Figure 18-32, three play buttons were added to the PDF document. The media opens in a floating window in Full Screen mode.

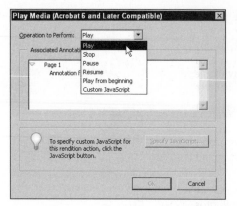

Figure 18-31: When you select the Play Media (Acrobat 6 and Later Compatible) option from the Select Action pull-down menu, a dialog box opens where you make choices for the play action from a pull-down menu.

Figure 18-32: The presentation viewed in Full Screen mode shows the video clip displayed in a floating window. Because no controls are visible in the window, the play buttons at the bottom of the window control the media play.

Tip

When using a floating window the movie field size is of no importance to the video clip played in the floating window. Create a movie field and size it down to a half an inch or lower and move it to any location on the document page. When the movie plays in a floating window the window is positioned according to the attributes you assign to the playback location.

Cross-Reference

For more information on creating button fields, see Chapters 27. For more information on Full Screen mode and button actions, see Chapter 23.

Summary

✦ Sound files can be imported with either Acrobat 5 or Acrobat 6 compatibility. Acrobat 5–compatible sound imports can be used with earlier Acrobat viewers. Acrobat 6–compatible sounds are only available to Acrobat 6 or later viewers. Acrobat 6 compatibility offers more options for attribute settings and file format compatibility.

✦ You can add sounds to page actions, links, bookmarks, and form fields or by using the Sound tool.

✦ Importing sounds on actions or with the Sound tool requires you to have access to a sound file. You create and save sound files from sound-editing programs. A number of sound editing programs are available as freeware or shareware on the Internet.

✦ You edit movie files in multimedia authoring programs. Among low-cost alternatives for creating movie files are Adobe Photoshop Album (Windows) and Apple Computer's iMovie. You save Photoshop Album files direct to PDF. You save iMovie files in QuickTime format and import them in PDFs with the Movie tool.

✦ Movie and sound files can have several renditions. Renditions offer you many options for assigning attributes to sound and media clips as well as providing end users with alternatives for downloading different versions of the same file.

✦ You can create button fields to play, pause, and stop movies in Full Screen mode without showing the player controls.

✦ You can embed Acrobat 6–compatible media files in PDF documents. Acrobat 6–compatible media files offer much more support for importing different file formats.

✦ A poster is a still image that shows inside a sound or movie field. Posters for movie fields can be retrieved from a movie. Posters for sound and movie fields can be created from files including all file formats supported by the Create PDF From File menu command.

✦ You can add animation to PDF documents with JavaScripts.

✦ Although capturing different animation formats from Web pages is functional in Acrobat, PDFs with animation cannot be imported as button faces, watermarks, or backgrounds. No animated GIF support is provided by Acrobat 7.

✦ ✦ ✦

Working with Layers

Layers are an integral part of many professional imaging applications and specialized technical programs, such as AutoCAD and Microsoft Visio. In Acrobat 6 and 7 you can view native layered documents and toggle on and off different layer views.

With the introduction of the Adobe Creative Suite, support for Adobe PDF layers has been integrated in Adobe Illustrator CS and Adobe InDesign CS. As we advance in time and software development, more applications are supporting exports to PDF with layer data.

Design and creative, scientific, and engineering professionals can find many uses for communicating ideas and concepts with layered documents. To help simplify viewing layered documents, you can add interactive buttons for guiding users through various layer views. In this chapter you learn about what constitutes a PDF with layers, how to manage them, and how to create links to different layer views.

Setting Up the Work Environment

Viewing layers requires no special set of toolbars — the tools you need are dependent on what you intend to do with a PDF containing layers when you begin editing. If, for example, you intend to review and comment layered documents, you'll open the Commenting tools. In this chapter adding links to layer views and using the Measuring tools is explained. To prepare for this, you need to open the Advanced Editing toolbar and the Measuring toolbar, and it's also a good idea to open the Properties bar. Additionally, if you add buttons to show and hide layer views you might want to open the Forms toolbar. For this toolbar access choose Tools ➪ Advanced Editing ➪ Show Forms Toolbar. Users of Acrobat Standard can use the Link tool from the Advanced Editing toolbar, but Standard doesn't support use of the Measuring tools or the Forms tools.

As explained later in this chapter, the Measuring tools offer you options for annotating measurements. For some commenting issues, you may want to open the Commenting toolbar. Another option you may find helpful is a grid. To set up the grid, you might want to determine the distances for major and minor grid lines. These settings are available in the Preferences dialog box. Select Units and Guides in the left pane in the Preferences dialog box and define the grid height and width values as well as the offset and subdivisions.

After opening the toolbars, dock them in the Toolbar Well; your work environment should look like Figure 19-1. The following figure shows grid lines turned on so you can see how they are displayed in the Document pane. For the remaining figures in the chapter the gridlines are off to make it easier to see objects drawn with the Measuring tools. You can easily toggle grid lines on and off by choosing View ➪ Grid or pressing Ctrl/⌘+U.

Cross-Reference   For information on opening toolbars and docking them in the Toolbar Well, see Chapter 1.

Figure 19-1: Open the Advanced Editing toolbar, the Measuring toolbar, the Properties bar, and the Forms toolbar, and dock the toolbars in the Toolbar Well.

Understanding Layers

Acrobat Professional supports the creation of layered documents from several authoring programs. Among the programs supporting the PDFMaker are Microsoft Visio, Microsoft Project, and Autodesk AutoCAD. In regard to exporting to PDF with Adobe PDF layers, you can use Adobe Illustrator CS and Adobe InDesign CS. Other Creative Suite programs such as Adobe GoLive CS and Adobe Photoshop CS in the first release of the Adobe Creative Suite do not support layered PDFs. When layers are created in these programs, the document can be converted to PDF with Adobe PDF layers and viewed in all Acrobat viewers 6.0 and above with the layers intact. The creation of Adobe PDF layers requires Acrobat Professional; however, after the PDF creation, layers can be viewed in any Acrobat 6.0 or greater viewer, including Adobe Reader.

There are two important points to understand when creating layered PDF files. First, you must begin with an authoring program that supports layers — programs such as Adobe Photoshop, Adobe Illustrator, Adobe PageMaker, Adobe InDesign, CorelDraw, and Macromedia Freehand are some of the popular imaging programs that support layers. Second, the authoring application must export to the PDF 1.5 format or above (Acrobat 6 compatibility or greater). Just because the authoring program supports layers is no guarantee that your resultant PDF will contain layers.

If you use a program that enables you to create and save layered documents and the program does not currently export to Acrobat 6 or greater compatibility, log on to your software manufacturer's Web site and see whether a new version of the program is available and whether the latest release exports to PDF v1.5 or v1.6.

Layer Visibility

When you open a layered document in Acrobat and the Layers palette is open in the Navigation pane, you see a list of all the layers contained in the document and an eye icon adjacent to each layer name when the respective layer is in view. A layer's visibility is either on or off as shown in the Layers palette.

Initial visibility is determined from the visibility shown in the original authoring program when the PDF is created. In Figure 19-2 you see a layered document with three layers visible as indicated by the eye icons in the Layers palette. The remaining layers in the document are hidden and the hidden state is expressed in the Layers palette by the absence of an eye icon adjacent to the layer names.

Figure 19-2: The initial visibility of layers in this file shows three layers in view as indicated by the eye icons and the remaining layers hidden.

Setting initial visibility

The initial layer visibility is the default view of visible layers when you open a PDF document. The layers in view when you open a layered PDF document are determined from the visibility of the layers in view in the original authoring application. If layers are hidden in the authoring application, the Initial View in Acrobat viewers shows the same layers hidden as well. The Initial View or *state* is the same view displayed in the authoring application at the time of PDF creation. As you browse a file in an Acrobat viewer and turn on and off different layer views, you may want to return to the initial state. You return to the default view with the Reset Initial Visibility menu command in the Options pull-down menu in the Layers palette, as shown in Figure 19-3. Select this command to return to the layer views you saw when you first opened the PDF document.

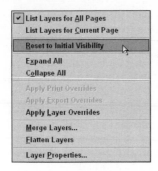

Figure 19-3: To return to the default layer visibility, open the Options pull-down menu in the Layers palette and select Reset to Initial Visibility.

Showing/hiding layers

You show and hide individual layers by clicking on the eye icon in the Layers palette. When the eye icon is hidden, the respective layer is hidden. If you want to display a hidden layer, click in the box adjacent to a layer name; the eye icon appears, and the layer is made visible in the Document pane.

At times you may have pages in a PDF with different layers associated with different pages. If you want to display all layers on the page in view in the Document pane while hiding layers on other pages in your document, select List Layers for Current Page in the Options pull-down menu. All layers not contained on the page in view in the Document pane are hidden. If the same layer spans more than one page and you select this menu command, the layer is made visible only when the layer is contained on the active page.

When you change layer visibility in the Layers palette and save the PDF document, the layer visibility is not recorded when you save the file. When you open a file after saving with a different layer view, you are still returned to the initial visibility from your first editing session. To create a new default Initial View, you need to change the Layer properties.

Initial Views

You can open the Layers palette when the PDF is opened in the Document pane by setting the Initial View in the Document Properties. Choose File ➪ Document Properties and select Initial View in the left pane. From the Show pull-down menu, select Layers Panel and Page. Save the PDF document. When you reopen the file the Layers palette is expanded to show the layers.

Cross-Reference

For more information on Initial Views, see Chapter 3.

You'll also notice a "slice of cake" icon in the lower-left corner of a PDF document containing layers. Click the icon and the Document Status dialog box opens. If you want to open the Document Status dialog box at any time when a file is open, click on the slice of cake icon in the lower-left corner of the status bar and the Document Status dialog box opens as shown in Figure 19-4. The dialog box informs you that the document contains layers and not all layers may be visible when the file is displayed in the Document pane. This dialog box is more like a help item to inform users that they need to use the Layers palette to show and hide layers. As you first begin working in Acrobat, you may want to have the Document Status dialog box open. After a while though, it will be an annoyance. To eliminate the Document Status dialog box appearing when you open layered files, open the Preferences dialog box by pressing Control/Command+K. Click Startup in the Left pane and remove the check mark for Documents with Layers. Click OK in the Preferences dialog box and the next time you open a layered document the Document Status dialog box wont open.

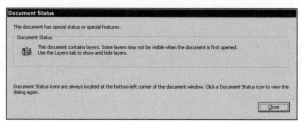

Figure 19-4: Click the Document Status icon to open the Document Status dialog box. The dialog box informs users that the open document contains layers and the Layers palette may be needed to view hidden layers.

Layer Properties

Layer properties are specific to each layer. To open the Layer Properties dialog box, you must have a layer selected in the Layers palette. Click on a layer name and open a context menu (or choose Options ➪ Layer Properties). The context menu contains two menu options — one for Show Layer and the other for Properties (unless it is a locked layer, in which case Properties is the only option). Select Properties to open the Layer Properties dialog box, as shown in Figure 19-5.

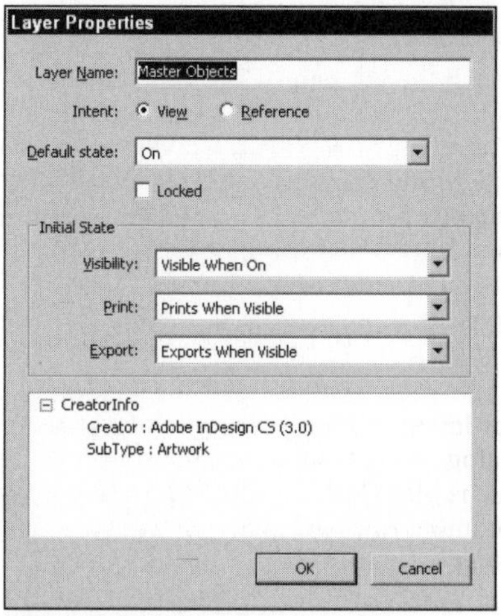

Figure 19-5: To open the Layer Properties dialog box, select a layer in the Layers palette, open a context menu, and select Properties from the menu options.

You adjust layer properties for individual layers only. Acrobat does not permit you to select multiple layers. If you need to make changes in visibility for several layers, you must open the Layer Properties dialog box independently for each layer. When you open the Layer Properties dialog box, the layer name appears in the dialog box for the respective layer contained in the Layers pane. Two radio buttons exist for the Intent. By default you see View selected, which is normal viewing mode. Select View to allow the layer to be turned on or off. If you click Reference, the remaining items in the dialog box are disabled and the eye icon in the Layers tab disappears. All layer attribute choices are disabled and the behavior is similar to locking a layer. You use Reference, you keep the layer on at all times, which permits editing layer properties. When a layer is set to the Reference Intent, the layer name appears in italics.

Changing the default state

The Default state pull-down menu contains menu options for either On or Off. The menu choice you make here determines the layer visibility when a file is opened. If you want to change the default state, select On or Off from the pull-down menu. When you click OK in the Layer Properties dialog box and save the PDF document, the default visibility changes according to the views you set in the Layer Properties.

Locking visibility

When you select the Locked check box, you lock the layer visibility (either on or off). A lock icon appears in the Layers tab and prevents you from turning the visibility on or off from the tab. You need to return to the Properties dialog box and disable the check box to return visibility control to the Layers tab.

Changing the initial state

Initial State settings include Layer Visibility, Print, and Export. The default state described previously enables you to determine whether a layer is visible or hidden when a PDF document opens. To apply the individual settings for layer states, you enable a preference setting. Open the Preferences dialog box and select Startup in the left pane. Check the box for Allow layer state to be set by user information. When this preference option is enabled, the layer state options chosen from the Initial State pull-down menus override the layer visibility set from the Default State pull-down menu. For example, if the default state is set to On and the preference item is deselected, the PDF opens with the layer visible. If you enable the preference settings and select Always Visible from the Visibility pull-down menu, the layer is always visible regardless of whether you have the default state On or Off.

The options for initial states include

✦ **Visibility:** Three choices are available from this pull-down menu. They include Visible When On, Never Visible, and Always Visible. The first option displays a layer according to whether you have the eye icon visible in the Layers palette. When toggled on, the layer is visible. When toggled off, the layer is hidden. Never Visible hides the layer data regardless of whether the default state is on or off. Always Visible always shows the layer.

✦ **Print:** You may have a watermark or message that you want to eliminate or display on a printed page. The three choices, Prints When Visible, Never Prints, and Always Prints, are similar to the options for visibility. Printing a layer does not require the layer to be in view in the Document pane at the time you print the file if Always Prints is selected.

✦ **Export:** This setting applies to exporting PDF documents back into authoring programs using a Save As command and selecting a file format compatible with your intended authoring program. Export provides you the same three options when exporting layer data as are available for printing. You can eliminate layers exported by selecting Never Exports or hide or show a layer and choose Exports When Visible. Likewise, you can choose to always export a layer regardless of the visibility and print settings by selecting Always Exports.

Cross-Reference

For information on exporting PDF data back to authoring programs, see Chapter 9.

The window at the bottom of the dialog box displays information according to the initial state(s) you select from the pull-down menu. When you open the Properties dialog box you can see, at a glance, the options for each initial state. At the bottom of the scrollable list is information related to the authoring document that was exported to PDF. By default when the initial state is set to Visible When On, you see no view information in the window at the bottom of the Properties dialog box. Change the Visibility to Never Visible or Always Visible. Click OK and when you opened the Layers Properties dialog box, a new category labeled *View* appears at the bottom of the window. Below the category name you see ViewState: ON or ViewState: OFF depending on the respective visibility choice you made after changing the initial state.

Tip

A good real-world condition for setting a layer state to be visible when printing is when you want to use a watermark or stamp on printed copies. If you want the watermark or stamp to be hidden when viewing the PDF in Acrobat set the layer visibility for Print to *Prints When Visible*. If you distribute the document and want all users to print a watermark or some symbol, secure the document with Acrobat security and other users wont be able to avoid printing the file without the mark.

Overriding defaults

In your original authoring program you can create PDF documents with layers that aren't visible in the Layers palette. You can also hide layers in the Default State or the Initial State pull-down menus. If you change defaults to hide layers in the Layers palette, you can change layer visibility in the Options menu. If the Options menu shows a menu item for overriding a layer state grayed out, the menu choice is not available. To change the options you need to return to the Layer Properties dialog box.

Open the Options pull-down menu to see the three options for overriding defaults. They include

✦ **Apply Print Overrides:** When selected, this option overrides any options you made for not printing layers. When you select this menu item in the Options palette, when you print the PDF all the layers are printed.

✦ **Apply Export Overrides:** When selected, this option overrides any options you made for exporting layer data. When you select this option, all layer data are exported.

✦ **Apply Layer Overrides:** Layer Overrides relates to the layer visibility. When this option is enabled, all layers are visible in the Document pane, but the individual layer visibility options are no longer available to you. You cannot click on an eye icon for hiding a layer when the override is enabled. To individually show or hide a layer you need to deselect the Apply Layer Overrides menu option and use the Layers palette for showing/hiding layers.

Managing layers

You can edit layers in that you can name, merge, and flatten them. However, you cannot rearrange layers in Acrobat. To rename a layer, select the layer in the Layers palette and click a second time on the layer name. The layer name is highlighted. Begin typing, and the text you type replaces the highlighted text. You can click and drag across a layer name and edit a portion of the text much like you might change names in Bookmarks. You can also edit layer names in the Layer Properties dialog box. If you are changing properties and decide you also want to change a layer name, select the name in the Layer Name field in the Layer Properties dialog box and edit the name.

Merging layers

You can merge layers whether they are visible or hidden. All layer merging takes place in the Merge Layers dialog box and is available only to users of Acrobat Professional. To open the dialog box select Merge Layers from the Options pull-down menu in the Layers palette. The Merge Layers dialog box opens as shown in Figure 19-6.

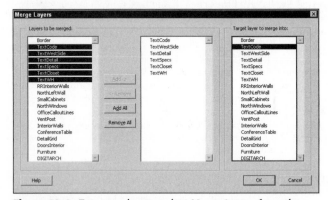

Figure 19-6: To merge layers, select Merge Layers from the Options pull-down menu. The Merge Layers dialog box opens where all layers (visible and hidden) are listed in the Layers to be merged column.

Regardless of whether a layer is visible or hidden, the list in the *Layers to be merged* column on the left side of the dialog box lists all layers in the document in a scrollable window. You can merge visible layers with hidden layers. To merge layers, select the layers to be merged into a single layer from the list on the left and click the Add button. You can select multiple layers by holding down the Shift key for a contiguous selection or by using the Ctrl key (Windows) or ⌘ key (Macintosh) to randomly select layer names in a noncontiguous group.

When the layers to be merged are visible in the center column, select the target layer in the *Target layer to merge into:* column. The name you select here is the name listed in the Layers palette and contains all the data from the other layers. The properties associated with the target layer become the properties in the merged layer. After you merge layers, all previous layer names are removed from the Layers palette.

When adding layers to the list in the center of the dialog box (add list), you can move the target layer to the add list or elect to not move the target layer to the list. For example, if you have Text as a target layer where you want to merge Text02 and Text03 together with Text, you can add Text to the center window or not add Text to the list. When you select Text as the target layer and click OK, Text01 and Text 02 are added to Text regardless of whether Text was added to the center column.

Tip   If you want to merge a group of layers to a new layer name, you can edit the name of one of the layers to be merged in the Layers palette. Click, and click again on the layer name in the Layers palette to edit the layer name. Open the Merge Layers dialog box and merge the desired layers to the new target layer name.

Flattening layers

Users of Acrobat Professional can flatten a group of layers or all layers in a PDF document into a single layer. Neither the merging layers option discussed earlier nor the flattening layers option is available to Acrobat Standard users. You may want to flatten layers to simplify printing a document, exchange a PDF with users of an Acrobat viewer earlier than version 6, or reduce the file size. When layers are flattened, the layer visibility is taken into account. If you have four layers and two layers are visible, the flattened PDF document results as a combination of the visible layers only. Be certain about what layer data you want to remain visible before selecting the Options menu and choosing Flatten Layers, as you won't be able to undo the operation and regain the data that was discarded from the hidden layers.

Using Measuring Tools

Although using the Measuring tools is not specific to PDF documents containing layers, it can be a great help to users creating engineering drawings and CAD documents for measuring distances and surface area in layered documents. Therefore, I included the use of these tools along with layers. Keep in mind that you can use these tools in any PDF document you open in Acrobat regardless of whether layers are present. Measuring tools, however, are not available in Acrobat Standard. This complete section on using the Measuring tools is relevant only to Acrobat Professional users.

The three tools available to you in the Measuring toolbar include

✦   **Distance tool:** You use the Distance tool to measure linear distances between two x,y coordinates on a document page. To use the tool, click and release the mouse button. Move the cursor to a different location and click again. The measurement is calculated when you make the second click and can be recorded in a comment note.

✦   **Perimeter tool:** You use the Perimeter tool to measure the outside perimeter of any angle or polygon object. To use the tool, click and release the mouse button. Move the cursor and click again. Repeat the steps to continue along a path (right angle, triangle, or polygon). When finished, make the last click and keep the mouse stationary. Click a second time when you see a small circle appear aside the cursor. The second click on the destination point informs Acrobat you're finished measuring. As each segment is drawn, the Distance Tool dialog box opens where measurement information is reported.

✦ 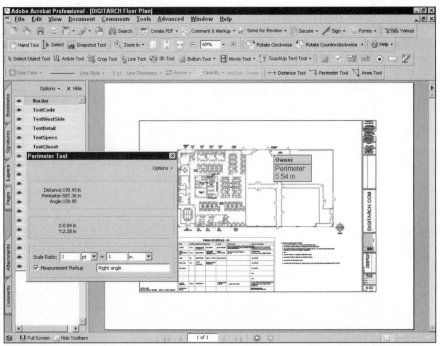 **Area tool:** You use the Area tool with any polygon object (three or more sides) to measure the surface area contained within the perimeter. When using the tool you need to draw line segments and return to the point of origin to close the path. Acrobat Professional informs you when you reach the point of origin by adding a small circle to the cursor. When you use the Area tool, the circle appears only when you reach the point of origin. After you click at the point of origin, the surface area is calculated within the path you draw.

Measuring surface area

Click the mouse button and move to another location with any measurement tool. If you use the Distance tool, click the mouse button at the destination; using the Perimeter or Area tool, move the mouse and click the next coordinate. For the Perimeter tool where you measure an angle or two sides of an object, click at the destination and click again to end the measurement. For area measurements continue clicking and moving the mouse until you end up at the point of origin. Click the mouse when you see a small circle at the lower-right side of the cursor. When you finish a measurement the tool's properties dialog box opens. In Figure 19-7 the Perimeter Tool dialog box displays information about a perimeter measurement.

Figure 19-7: The Perimeter Tool properties dialog box reports information related to a perimeter measurement.

The dialog box offers several attribute options from pull-down menus and field boxes. The options include

✦ **Scale Ratio:** Choose a value for the first field box that equals a particular unit of measure you select from the pull-down menus. For example, if you want to scale a drawing at a 5:1 ratio, enter 5 in the first field box and 1 in the second field box.

✦ **Measurement Markup:** The measurement data and a comment can be contained in a comment note. The comment for the note is derived from the text you type in the Measurement Markup field box. Check the box and type a line of text. The assessment of the measurement is also reported in the comment note. Acrobat automatically supplies this value.

The Options menu offers the following menu commands:

✦ **Show Details:** When Show Details is not selected you see just the measurement coordinates. When this option is selected, the dialog box expands to show x,y coordinates, Scale Ratio information, and the Measurement Markup comment.

✦ **Show Rulers:** Select the menu command to show/hide rulers.

✦ **Snap to Content:** When you place the cursor above a line on a drawing a small square snaps to the line when you have Snap to Content checked. Uncheck the item and no square appears below the cursor. This item is similar to lines drawn when snapping to a grid.

✦ **Ortho:** When you select this option, your ability to draw is constrained to 90-degree angles.

✦ **Export Measurement Markup to Excel:** All measurement data that was recorded as a comment (that is, the Measurement Markup option was selected) are exported as a .csv file compatible with Microsoft Excel. When you select this menu command, the Export Measurement Markup dialog box opens where you type a filename and navigate to a destination folder.

✦ **Preferences:** Select Preferences and the Preferences dialog box opens with the Measuring pane in view. You can set some defaults such as Snap to Content or Use Scale and Units from Document.

Changing markup appearances

Use the Properties bar to change appearance attributes for the lines you draw with the Measurement tools. You can change line color, line width, assign arrowheads, and set transparency with the Properties bar shown in Figure 19-8. In order to open the Properties dialog box you need to switch from a measurement tool to the Hand tool. Select the measurement line and open a context menu. Select Properties from the context menu. Additionally, when you use the Properties bar, you also need to select a measurement line with the Hand tool.

Figure 19-8: Select a line with the Hand tool and use the Properties bar to adjust appearances for markups created with the Measurement tools.

Comments, measurements, and layers

When you add measurement lines on layered documents and open pop-up notes, the lines and notes are visible on any layer in the document. When you hide all layers, the lines and pop-up notes are still visible.

If you have text that appears on all layers, you can edit the text regardless of what layer is visible. For example, adding a header to a document and selecting the TouchUp Text tool to change the text properties is one condition where the text is visible on all layers. Regardless of what layers are in view, you can edit the text; the changes are reflected in all layer views.

Cross-Reference   For information on using the TouchUp Text tool, see Chapter 10.

If you want objects in terms of PDF content to appear on separate layers, you need to return to your authoring application and create the objects on specific layers. Objects and data created in Acrobat cannot become a part of individual layers or toggled on and off in the Layers palette.

Creating Visibility Buttons

You may have a document in which you want to create navigation buttons to help a user easily navigate through different layer views. Inasmuch as the Document Status dialog box informs users how to view layers, having some buttons that link to different layer views can help users understand the document structure and quickly navigate different views.

Creating buttons to layer visibility is much like creating Bookmarks. You first establish the view you want to be as the destination view of a link action and then create the link button. Figure 19-9 shows a document displayed in the Navigation pane at the layer initial visibility.

Cross-Reference   For more information on creating form fields, see Chapters 25 and 26.

Figure 19-9: The open document is viewed at the default layer visibility with the Layers palette open.

To create the view that you want to display when a user clicks on a button, use the Layers palette to toggle on or off different views to create the layer visibility you want as the final result of the link action. Then create a button using the Button tool. Select the Actions tab in the Button Properties dialog box and select Set layer visibility from the Select Action pull-down menu. In Figure 19-10 you can see the new visibility in the Layers palette; the Video layer is visible as well as the Master Objects and Background layers. This view is different from the Initial View shown in Figure 19-9. After setting the view, create a button field and select Set layer visibility in the Select Action pull-down menu as shown in Figure 19-11.

Figure 19-10: Use the Layers palette to set the visibility for the resultant view.

Cross-Reference   You can also assign layer visibility to links, Bookmarks, and page actions. For more information on showing visibility and assigning actions, see Chapter 17.

After clicking the Close button, you can select the Options pull-down menu and choose Reset to Initial Visibility to return to the default view. You can select the Hand tool and click the button to see the new view displayed in the Document pane.

The most difficult part of the process is to keep in mind that you first need to set the visibility you want as the result of clicking the button. After you create a few buttons, the process becomes second nature and creating links to layer visibility will become as easy as creating Bookmarks.

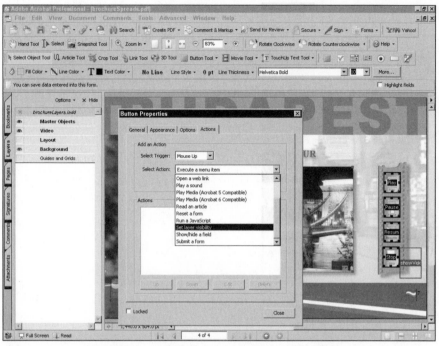

Figure 19-11: Select Set layer visibility from the Select Action pull-down menu of the Button Properties dialog box. The link action captures the current view.

Summary

✦ The PDF 1.5 and above formats support layers from authoring applications that are capable of creating layered files and exporting with Acrobat 6 or greater compatibility.

✦ You can view and hide individual layers in Acrobat. The initial visibility for what layers are in view and what layers are hidden is determined at the time the PDF is created.

✦ Saving files after showing and hiding layers does not change initial visibility. You change initial visibility in the Layer Properties dialog box, where you toggle layers on and off.

✦ You change layer states for visibility, printing, and exporting data in the Layer properties. Layers can be printed or exported without visibility.

✦ You merge and flatten layers using menu commands from the Options pull-down menu in the Layers palette.

✦ Measuring tools enable you to measure distances, perimeters, and surface area. Distances and area are displayed in the Measurement Tools dialog box and distances can be recorded in comment notes.

✦ Measurements can be exported to Microsoft Excel.

✦ Measuring distances to scale is available by selecting options for scale values and units of measure in the Measurement Tools dialog box.

✦ You can create link buttons to display different layer visibility. To create a link action to a view, you first create the desired view in the Layers palette and then set the link action in the Link or Button Properties dialog box.

✦   ✦   ✦

Accessibility and Tagged PDF Files

Adobe Acrobat 7 is compliant with United States federal code regulating document accessibility for vision- and motion-challenged persons. This means that screen readers can intelligently interpret the PDFs you create; in other words, PDF files can be read aloud in a reading order like a sighted person would read a document. Through an extensive set of keyboard shortcuts available in Acrobat, almost anyone with vision or motion challenges can share your documents and read them.

In order for a document to be accessible, you must use authoring applications capable of delivering a document's structure to Acrobat. Hence, you need to know something about the internal structure of documents and what programs to use to create the structure required by Acrobat to make a document accessible. Not all the content in a document travels through the PDF creation process with information necessary to make a document completely accessible. Therefore you need to perform some work in Acrobat to either add accessibility or to polish up a document for delivery to a screen reader in a form that makes sense to the user. In this chapter I cover how to make documents accessible from authoring programs, as well as how to use Acrobat tools to make existing documents accessible.

Setting Up the Work Environment

The essential tools for working with document accessibility include the Tags tab, Content tab, and Order tab. To view the Tags tab, choose View ⇨ Navigation Tabs ⇨ Tags. The Tags tab opens in a palette nested with the Content and Order tabs and the Fields tab. Click the Tags tab and drag it away from the palette to undock it. Continue dragging the tab to the Navigation pane to dock it among the other tabs in the "'free" or "open'" region below the Pages tab and above the Attachments tab. Drag the Content and Order tabs and dock them in the Navigation pane. Click the close box in the top-right corner of the palette to close the palette containing the Fields tab.

The TouchUP toolbar is important not only for editing text and objects, but the new TouchUp Order tool was specifically designed to work with reading order on accessible documents. Be certain to load the TouchUp toolbar. Open a context menu on the Toolbar Well and select Advanced Editing. From the pull-down menu adjacent to the TouchUp Text tool, select Show TouchUp Toolbar. To dock the toolbars, select Dock All Toolbars from a context menu opened from the Toolbar Well.

Creating Accessible Documents

The terms *document accessibility, structure,* and *tagged PDFs* may be a mystery to you. If the term *accessibility* is new, then you need to begin with an understanding of what accessible documents are before working with them. After you know more about document accessibility, you can move forward to look at how to create an accessible document, and then look at how you can edit accessible documents. Therefore, the three areas to work with are understanding accessibility, creating accessible documents from authoring programs, and finally, working with accessible documents in Acrobat.

Understanding accessibility

Sighted people can view a document on the computer or read a printed page and easily discern the difference between titles, subtitles, columns, graphic images, graphic elements, and so on. With regard to Acrobat PDFs, you can easily see the difference between background designs, button links, Bookmarks, animation, and form fields, and you typically see visual clues to know where buttons and fields exist.

With regard to screen-reading devices, which depend on software to generate audio output from an Acrobat PDF file, the software readers aren't intelligent enough to distinguish differences based on visual clues. For example, a screen reader may interpret a three-columned document as one continuous column and read the text from left to right across all three columns row by row. Obviously the output is useless to the end user working with a screen reader. Screen readers interpret headings, subheadings, and tables the same as body copy, and they offer no distinction in the structure unless the screen reader software has some clue that these items are different from the body text.

Screen Readers

I use the term *screen reader* extensively in this chapter. When I use this term, I'm referring to tools created by third parties to read open documents aloud in Acrobat and other programs or from files in various formats saved to disk.

Screen readers range in price from $99 to over $1,000. The advantage of using third-party products with Acrobat PDF files is that they can read aloud single words as well as spell out words character by character. Through keyboard controls, users choose reading rates, audio output levels, voices, and navigation.

Screen readers are typically software programs installed on either Mac OS or Windows. More programs support Windows than Macintosh operating systems, but developers have been increasing support for both platforms. In past years, PDF documents were not supported by many developers. Today, much more support exists for reading PDF documents with the Adobe Reader software.

For a complete list of screen readers that have been tested with Acrobat, log on to Adobe's Web site at: http://access.adobe.com. From Adobe's Web page you'll find URL links to vendor sites as well as general information about accessibility.

Some authoring programs provide you an opportunity when creating the PDF file to retain the underlying structure of a document in the resulting PDF file. With a series of tags and retention of the document structure, screen readers use alternate text to make distinctions in the document much like the visual user would interpret a page. The document flow, alternate text for graphic elements, distinctions between headings, and so on, can all be managed in Acrobat when the internal document structural tree is included in the PDF export. When files are not exported with the document structure, you can use Acrobat commands to add structure to PDFs. In order to make it possible for people with screen readers to navigate your PDF documents correctly, the underlying structure must be present.

To gain more of a grasp on what I mean by terms like *structure* and *tagged PDF files*, a definition is warranted. PDF files fall into three categories when we are talking about a document's structure. The categories include

✦ **Unstructured PDF files:** Unstructured PDF documents cannot be interpreted by screen readers with complete document integrity. For example, when you export the PDF to other formats such as a Rich Text Format (RTF), the basic paragraph structure is preserved, but tables, lists, and some text formatting are lost. Another kind of repurposing for PDF files is the ability to view them on handheld devices and various-sized monitors with text reflows. Unstructured documents, however, cannot be reflowed on screens.

> **Cross-Reference**
>
> For more information on reflowing text, see Chapter 4.

✦ **Structured PDF files:** Structured PDF files can be read by screen readers, but the reliability is much less than the next category of tagged PDF documents. When you export structured PDF files to other formats, more structural content is preserved, but tables and lists can be lost. Additionally, structured documents, like the unstructured documents discussed previously, do not support text reflows for different-sized devices.

✦ **Tagged PDF files:** Tagged PDFs contain both the document structure and a hierarchical structure tree where all the internal structure about the document's content is interpreted. Tagged PDFs have the highest reliability when you're repurposing files for screen reader output and saving files in other formats such as RTF, HTML, XHTML, and XML. In addition, tagged PDF files support text reflow for viewing on different-sized screens and accommodate any zoom level on a monitor.

> **Cross-Reference**
>
> For more information on document reflow, see Chapter 4. For more information on exporting PDF content, see Chapter 9. For more on document structure, see "Understanding Structure" in this chapter.

The goal for you when creating PDF documents for accessibility is to be certain you use PDF documents that are not only structured, but also tagged PDFs. After you create tagged PDFs you can work with the structure tree and modify the contents for optimum use. In terms of making Acrobat PDFs accessible, you must consider several criteria to optimize files for effective handling by screen readers. These include

✦ **Assessing accessibility:** Fortunately, Acrobat provides tools for determining whether a PDF file is an accessible document. As a first order of business you should plan on assessing a file for accessibility. If you work with legacy files or files that are created from authoring programs that don't support the export of the document structure, be certain to make the document accessible before beginning an editing session.

Cross-Reference

For adding accessibility to PDF files from within Acrobat see the section "Making existing PDFs accessible" later in this chapter.

✦ **Logical reading order:** The text should follow a logical flow. You need to properly define column text in terms of the path that a screen reader follows (that is, down one column; then begin at the top of the second column, and so on). You should also mark headings and subheadings for distinction.

✦ **Alternative text descriptions for image and graphic elements:** Those familiar with HTML know that you can code an HTML document with alternate tags so users with text-only browsers can understand the structure of Web pages. The same principle for accessible documents applies. Alternate text needs to be inserted so the screen reader can interpret graphic elements.

✦ **Form field descriptions:** Form fields need to be described with text to inform a user with a screen reader that a form field is present.

✦ **Field tab order:** Setting the logical tab order for fields on a form is important for the visual user. With screen readers it is essential. The logical tab order for fields should be strictly followed.

✦ **Document security:** If documents are secured with Acrobat security, you must use 128-bit encryption compatible with Acrobat 5 and above. If you use compatibility less than Acrobat 5 or 40-bit encryption, the PDF is rendered inaccessible.

✦ **Links and interactivity:** Use form fields for link buttons with descriptions so the user knows that another destination or a link action is invoked if he or she selects the field.

✦ **Document language:** Screen readers typically deliver accessible documents in only one language. To protect your documents against inoperability with new releases, specify a document language when creating accessible PDFs. Document language specification is also important when using tools in Acrobat for checking accessibility.

Cross-Reference

For more information on field tab order, see Chapter 27. For more information on document security, see Chapter 21. For more information on links and interactivity see Chapter 17.

Adding accessibility in authoring applications

Not all authoring programs currently support accessibility. This phenomenon may change with new upgrades to software, so what is said today may change tomorrow. As of this writing the programs offering the best support for document accessibility include Microsoft Word version 2000 or higher, Adobe PageMaker 7.0 or higher, and Adobe InDesign 2.0 or higher. If you use other authoring applications, you do have the option to make documents accessible with Acrobat Standard and Acrobat Professional.

When converting Microsoft Word files to PDF, be certain to use the PDFMaker in the Word toolbar or from the Acrobat menu. Set up the conversion settings for enabling accessibility and reflow with tagged PDF documents. This option is available in the Settings tab in the Acrobat PDFMaker dialog box. Select the "Enable accessibility and reflow with Tagged PDF" check box.

Cross-Reference

For more on creating PDF files with accessibility and tags from Microsoft Office applications, see Chapter 7.

When creating documents with text, images, charts, diagrams, and so on, using a professional layout program often works better than a word processor. Adobe InDesign CS is an ideal tool for creating layouts that you need to make accessible. When you design a document for accessibility, be precise about how you add elements on each page. The order in which you lay out documents can have an effect on the order of the exported structure. For example, adding a block of text, and then importing an image may result in the text appearing first in the structure tree and the image following the text even if you move the elements so the image appears first on the page. The only way to observe the results of how the document structure ultimately converts to PDF is to practice and examine the tags structure tree in Acrobat versus your layouts. You can develop a workflow that minimizes the work in Acrobat to properly create the structure needed for optimum performance when read by a screen reader.

Tip   If you arrange objects in an authoring program like Adobe InDesign and the reading order is not following the viewing order, you can cut either text or images and paste them back into the document. If, for example, an image should be first in the structure tree followed by text, but the order is reversed when you examine the tags in Acrobat, cut the text block and paste it back into the document in InDesign. Recreate the PDF and you'll find the order changed according to the order that the elements were last placed on the page. This method is not always a precise solution for reordering elements, but can often be used to resolve problems.

Making existing PDFs accessible

If you have PDF documents either from legacy files or from files converted from authoring applications that do not support exports to PDF with tags, you can use Acrobat commands to add structure to the document and make the files accessible. The first step is checking a document for accessibility. If the document contains no tags, then you can add tags in Acrobat Standard or Acrobat Professional.

Performing a Quick Check

To determine whether a document is accessible, you can perform a Quick Check. In Acrobat Standard or Acrobat Professional choose Advanced ➪ Accessibility ➪ Quick Check. In Adobe Reader, choose Document ➪ Accessibility Quick Check. This method of checking the PDF is a quick analysis to determine whether tags exist in the file. When the check is completed, a dialog box opens informing you of the accessibility status. If the document is not accessible, the dialog box message states that the document is not structured and reading problems may occur.

Note   Document accessibility can be checked in Adobe Reader. Making a document accessible, however, requires Acrobat Standard or Acrobat Professional.

Performing a Full Check (Acrobat Professional only)

Acrobat Professional offers you a more sophisticated analysis where more file attributes are checked and a report is created either in a file, or by adding comments to the open PDF document, or both. To use the Full Check option, follow these steps:

STEPS: Checking accessibility in Acrobat Professional

1. **Choose Advanced ⇨ Accessibility ⇨ Full Check.** The Accessibility Full Check dialog box shown in Figure 20-1 opens.

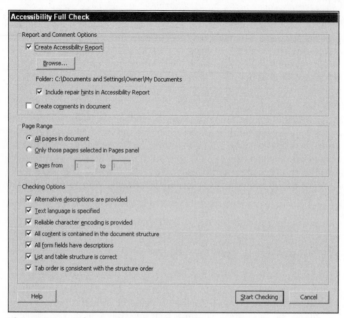

Figure 20-1: When you run a Full Check in Acrobat Professional, you can choose options for what content to check.

2. **Check the box for Create Accessibility Report and Create comments in document.** Checking these boxes creates a report and adds comment notes in the document pertaining to the results of the analysis. All errors found during the check are reported in comment notes.

3. **Select the Checking Options for the items you want to check.** Enable the check boxes in this section for items you want to check. In this example I selected all the check boxes.

4. **Click the Browse button.** Identify the location for the report file if you want a report saved to an HTML file, which you can view in the (search/help) panel.

5. **When you set all the attributes, click Start Checking.** Acrobat opens a dialog box similar to Figure 20-2, reporting the findings.

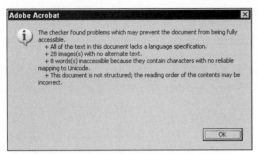

Figure 20-2: After running the Full Check, the findings are reported in a dialog box.

After completing the check, the How To pane opens and displays a more detailed report as shown in Figure 20-3.

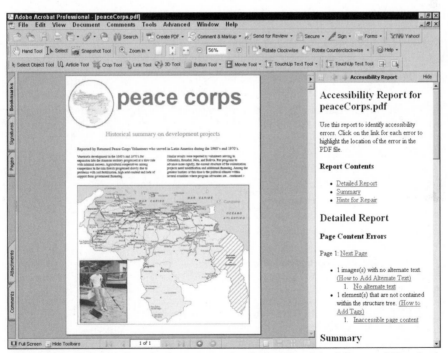

Figure 20-3: The How To pane shows you a detailed report of the full accessibility check findings.

An Accessibility report is also saved to your hard drive in HTML format. If you click the Browse button in the Accessibility Full Check dialog box you can target a location for the saved report. By default the report is saved to your My Documents folder (Windows) or your Documents folder (Macintosh). Open your Web browser and select File Open. Navigate to the folder where the report is found and open the file. The report is displayed in the browser window, as shown in Figure 20-4.

Figure 20-4: Open the report in your Web browser.

The links in the HTML document link directly to the PDF file and highlight the item associated with the link. Click a link in your Web browser and the PDF file opens in the foreground with the respective item highlighted as shown in Figure 20-5. You can correct problems by clicking links in the Web browser and correcting the problems in the PDF document.

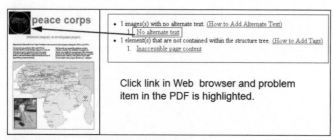

Figure 20-5: Click a link in the Web browser and the referenced item in the PDF is highlighted.

Adding accessibility

Keep in mind you are always best served by adding accessibility at the time a PDF document is created from authoring programs supporting exports to PDF with accessibility and tags. If you have files where either returning to the authoring program is impractical or the authoring program is incapable of exporting to PDF as tagged files, choose Advanced ➪ Accessibility ➪ Add Tags to Document. Or from the Tags tab in the Navigation pane, select Add Tags to

Document from the Options pull-down menu. Immediately after you select the menu command from either Acrobat Standard or Acrobat Professional, a slider bar opens displaying Acrobat's progress in adding tags to the document. After completion, no confirmation dialog box opens to report the status. If problems were encountered while adding the tags, a dialog box opens, reporting the problems found.

After adding the tags you can return to the Quick Check or Full Check menu command and check the document for accessibility.

If a file has tags and you choose Advanced ➪ Accessibility ➪ Add Tags to Document, Acrobat opens a dialog box informing you that the file already has tags. Adding tags is not permitted using the menu command. If you are unhappy with the current tagging, you can remove all tags from the document, and then reapply with this method. To remove all tags, open the Tags tab in the Navigation pane. Select the topmost tag (typically labeled "Tags") and click the Trash can icon or select Delete Tag from the Options pull-down menu.

Understanding Structure

To understand more clearly the need for creating accessibility and adding tags to a document, look at Figure 20-6 as an example. This document contains several items that need attention to make the file accessible and comprehensible when read by a screen reader.

Figure 20-6: A document with images, illustrations, and text in multiple columns needs to have the structure modified for proper reading by a screen reader.

In Figure 20-4 the items of importance in regard to accessibility include the following:

1. **The first element on the page is a logo.** A screen reader won't interpret the logo unless you add some alternate text to the document describing the object. Adjacent to the logo on the right side is text that a screen reader can read after you make the document accessible. If the text does not read properly, the two lines of text need to be modified for the proper interpretation by the screen reader.

2. **The two lines of text are in a single column.** These lines should be read in logical order without any problems. They are shown here to illustrate the difference between the two lines and the two columns following.

3. **The text is blocked in two columns.** Unless the structure is established for the screen reader to read down one column before moving to the second column, the screen reader defaults at a left-to-right reading order, reading across both columns.

4. **Item four is a large map.** Alternate text for the illustration is needed for the screen reader to explain what graphic appears on the page.

5. **Item five is an inset photo.** The alternate text for the map can describe the photo or the photo can have an alternate text description. Either way, you need to create the alternate text for the screen reader to fully interpret the graphics.

When you export to PDF from authoring programs with tags, the structure of the document for the blocks of text in logical reading orders is preserved. In the example in Figure 20-4, the single and double-column text is typically not a problem when the file is read by a screen reader. Images, however, need some form of manual editing. Even the best source exporting with tags wouldn't be able to describe the visual elements in the layout. These are subjective items that need a description.

If using a program such as Microsoft Word, you can add alternate text in Word before the file is exported to PDF. In other applications you need to create the alternate text in Acrobat.

Using the Tags palette

When you export a document from an authoring program with tags or use the Add Tags to Document menu command, a *structure tree* is created in the PDF file. The structure tree is a hierarchical order of the elements contained in the file. Elements may be in the form of heads, subheads, body text, figures, tables, annotations, and other items identified as separate individual structural elements. The hierarchy contains a nested order of the elements with parent/child relationships. A heading, for example, may have a subhead. The heading in this case is a parent element with the subheading a child element.

When a document contains tags, you view the tag elements and the structure tree in the Tags tab. Open the Tags tab and click on the top item. By default you see an icon labeled Tags with a plus (+) (Windows) or right-pointing arrow (Macintosh) symbol adjacent to it. Click the symbol and you open the tree at one level. Other child elements are nested below.

The Tags palette may have an extensive list of elements depending on your document length and complexity. If you want to edit an element or find it in the document, you need some help from Acrobat to find out exactly what tag in the Tags palette is related to what element on a given page. The help comes in the form of a menu command in the Tags palette. Click the down-pointing arrow adjacent to Options in the Tags palette and select Highlight Content from the menu options as shown in Figure 20-7.

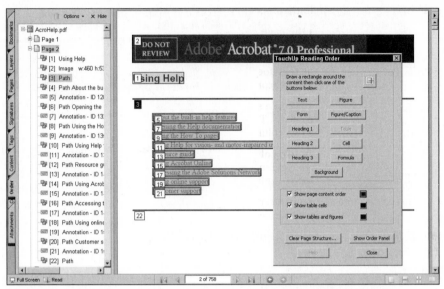

Figure 20-7: Open the Tags palette Options menu and select Highlight Content.

When you return to the structure tree, the items you select are highlighted on the respective elements on pages in the Document pane. Click an element and Acrobat navigates to the page where the content is located. The object is highlighted with a keyline border as shown in Figure 20-5.

Adding alternate text

In the example in Figure 20-3, the logo appearing at the top of the page is an image file. When a screen reader reads the document, no specific instructions are contained in the document to interpret this image. As an option, you can create alternate text so a visually challenged person knows a graphic element exists on the page. To add alternate text in a tagged PDF document, follow these steps:

STEPS: Adding alternate text to tagged elements

1. **Open a tagged PDF file.** Or add tags to a document. Open the Tags tab in the Navigation pane. Note: If you didn't set up the working environment as described in the beginning of the chapter, choose View ➪ Navigation Tabs ➪ Tags to open the Tags tab.

2. **Open the structure tree.** Click the Tags Root icon to the left of the text. On Windows a plus (+) symbol appears adjacent to the text. On the Macintosh, a right-pointing arrow appears next to the text. Clicking the icon opens the tags tree.

3. **Select Highlight Content.** If you haven't selected the menu command for highlighting content, open the Options palette in the Tags tab and select Highlight Content.

4. **Find the element for which the alternate text is to be added.** In this example, the figure below the second paragraph (<P>) was selected. When you click the Figure tag, the logo at the top-left corner of the page highlights. Alternately, you can also select the TouchUp Object tool, click an object on the page, and select Find Tag From Selection from the Tags palette Options pull-down menu.

5. **Open the element's properties.** Select the TouchUp Object tool from the TouchUp toolbar you opened earlier. If you do not have this toolbar opened, choose Tools ➪ Advanced Editing ➪ Show TouchUp Toolbar. Click the element and open a context menu. Select Properties from the menu options.

6. **Add alternate text.** Click the Tags tab. Add a title for the tag by typing a title in the Title field box. The title is not necessary for, nor read by the screen reader. Add the text you want the screen reader to read out loud in the Alternate Text field. Select the pull-down menu for Language and select a language. The edits made in this example are shown in Figure 20-8.

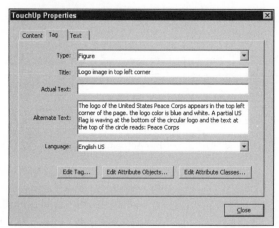

Figure 20-8: Fill in the fields for a title and alternate text, and select a language in the TouchUp Properties dialog box.

7. **Close the TouchUp Properties dialog box.** Click Close in the TouchUp Properties dialog box.

Using the Content tab

The Content tab contains a hierarchical list of the objects in the PDF file. Objects are listed in the order in which they appear on the page, similar to the logical structure tree in the Tags palette. In the Content tab click open the structure tree as shown in Figure 20-9. Click on an object and move it up or down to change the order of the objects.

The Content tab can be helpful when you want to navigate to and highlight a content item listed in the tab. Click an item such as a text item or figure and the page appears in the Document pane with the respective item selected. One thing to note when navigating to content items in the Content tab is that links to the content don't work when you select Document Reflow. When Reflow is enabled, content items are not shown in the Document pane with highlights.

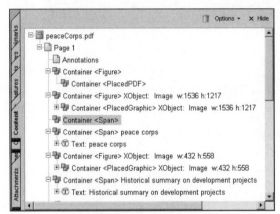

Figure 20-9: Click objects and drag up or down to reorder the objects in the Content pane.

In addition to physically reordering objects, a number of menu commands are available from the Options pull-down menu. Among the menu commands is an option to create a New Container. Notice in Figure 20-7 all the tags are nested within containers. You can select a tag and select New Container to add alternate text to any area in the document.

Using the Order tab

You use the Order tab to correct reading order problems. After you create a tagged PDF document, Acrobat infers the reading order from the document structure. You may need to change the order for text and images to create a more logical flow in the document.

You use the Order tab in conjunction with the TouchUp Reading Order tool. Select the tool and open the Order tab. Acrobat lists the reading order of the elements according to page as shown in Figure 20-8. To reorder the elements or regions, click and drag a tag up or down to change the reading order. Each tagged object is numbered on a page indicating the order the tags are read. From the Touchup Reading Order dialog box you can change the attributes of tags and renumber them to change the reading order. Figure 20-10 shows the tagged elements and the reading order defined by numbers adjacent to each tagged object.

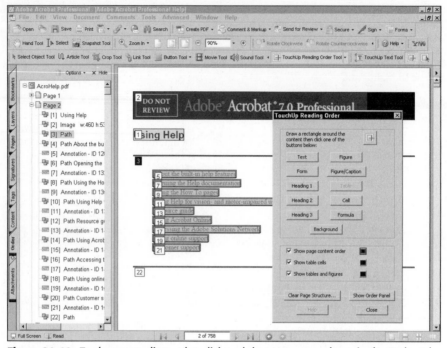

Figure 20-10: To change reading order, click and drag tags up or down in the Order tab.

Checking accessible tags

You can check your work easily in Acrobat by having Acrobat read the document. Choose View ➪ Read Out Loud ➪ Read This Page Only. The default text-to-speech voice installed on your computer reads the text as a screen reader would interpret it. If you prepare files for screen readers, you can use Acrobat's built-in reading engine to read aloud the text in the document and the alternate tags you add to the file.

Although the Read Out Loud menu command is not intended to replace screen readers, the feature in all Acrobat viewers offers you a good means for checking files that meet accessible standards.

Tip   You can save PDF files as accessible text. Select File ➪ Save As and select Text (Accessible).txt from the Save as Type (Windows) or Format (Macintosh) pull-down menu. The saved text is saved in the same reading order as when you read a document out loud.

Cross-Reference   For more information on Read Out Loud and controlling voices and reading speeds, see Chapter 4.

In addition to using Acrobat's built-in function for reading documents aloud, you can acquire a low-cost plug-in from a third-party developer without purchasing a screen reader. PDFAloud, marketed by textHELP Systems (www.texthelp.com), is more robust than Acrobat's Read Out Loud command. With PDFAloud you can read text a word, sentence, or paragraph at a time. The plug-in also offers you synchronized colored highlighting while the text is read.

Viewing Accessible Documents

Some accessibility requirements extend beyond text-to-speech reading. Individuals with assistive devices for visual impairments can view documents when text is zoomed and when text color significantly contrasts with background colors. You can modify the display of documents on your screen by adjusting preferences for Accessibility in the Preferences dialog box, or you can customize viewing by choosing Advanced ➪ Accessibility ➪ Setup Assistant, which opens the Accessibility Setup Assistant dialog box, shown in Figure 20-11.

You make attribute choices in a pane and click the Next button to advance through the Accessibility Setup Assistant. You can make choices for color displays, text smoothing, zoom displays, reading orders, and page delivery by moving through the panes. When you finish, these selections will be set in the Accessibility Preferences for you.

Figure 20-11: The Accessibility Setup Assistant contains options for screen displays and reading orders.

Summary

✦ Screen readers can interpret accessible PDF files and create audio output for people with vision and motion challenges.

✦ Adobe PDFMaker for Microsoft products, including Word, Excel, Visio, and so on; Adobe PageMaker 7 and higher; and Adobe InDesign 2.0 and higher are capable of creating tagged and accessible PDF forms.

✦ You can add tags to PDF documents from a menu command within Acrobat Standard and Acrobat Professional.

✦ You check files for accessibility with the Quick Check command in Adobe Reader, Acrobat Standard, and Acrobat Professional or with a Full Check in Acrobat Professional.

✦ Tagged documents contain a structure tree. Elements in the tree locate respective elements in the document if you enable the Highlight Content menu command.

✦ You can add alternate text to elements in Acrobat by addressing the element's properties.

✦ You can make text and background color changes in the Accessibility Preferences dialog box or via the Accessibility Setup Assistant.

✦   ✦   ✦

PDF Publishing

Authentication and Security

A crobat PDF documents can be secured using a host of different security methods and encryption tools to prevent unauthorized users from opening files and changing documents. Acrobat Security combined with digital signatures enables you to protect data and secure files for just about any purpose. There's much to learn about using Acrobat Security and digital signatures, and it's important to know what levels of security are available to you and what kinds of security you can apply in many different circumstances. This chapter covers a broad description of security and digitally signing PDF documents and the methods you use to protect files against unauthorized viewing and editing.

Setting Up the Work Environment

You add security to a PDF document through menu commands and the Secure Task button that appears in the Tasks toolbar when you return to the default view. If all you want to do is add security to PDFs, you can open a context menu and select Reset Toolbars from the menu options.

If you want to add digital signature fields on a form where users can digitally sign documents, you need to use the Forms tools or use a document created in Adobe Designer that contains signature fields. Documents can be signed without using signature fields, but when you want to add a field for signing the document, you'll want to work on a form created in Adobe Designer with signature fields or have the Form tools available in Acrobat Professional.

For the examples in this chapter, open the Tools menu and choose Advanced Editing ⇨ Show Forms Toolbar. In addition to the Forms tools, add the Properties bar by opening a context menu on the Toolbar Well and selecting Properties Bar from the menu. After the toolbars open, dock them in the Toolbar Well.

Cross-Reference For information on creating signature fields, see Chapters 26 and 27.

Note   Use of the Forms tools is available only in Acrobat Professional, however, Acrobat Standard users can create digital signatures and and signature fields. Adobe Designer is available only on Windows. The preferred method for adding signature fields is with Designer. Therefore, Windows users should look at working in Designer for adding Signature fields and security. Macintosh users need to add signature fields in Acrobat Professional.

Restricting the Opening and Editing of Files

Acrobat security comes in many different forms, allowing you to secure PDF files against user viewing and/or editing in many ways based on the level of security you assign to a PDF document. However, depending on what level of security you apply to a file, the document may or may not be able to be opened by users of earlier versions of Acrobat. Therefore, when you add security, knowing your audience and what versions of Acrobat they are using to view files is critical.

Methods of security available in Acrobat include three types of restrictions. You can secure a file against opening and editing using Password Security at different levels of encryption, you can secure files using public key certificates, or if your organization is using Adobe LiveCycle Policy Server you can apply security policies from here. You should think of the first method (Password Security) as security you might apply globally to PDFs when you want the public to have a password to open your PDFs or you want to restrict certain Acrobat features, such as content editing or printing. In this regard you secure documents for what is referred to as *unknown* users. You can further delineate securing individual files into two categories. You can secure documents by applying security settings that you select via options in security windows, or you can create a security policy in which the same level of security and encryption attributes are applied to documents each time you secure files.

Think of the second method (Certificate Security) as restrictions you want to apply for a selected group of people, or what are referred to as *known* users. You might want to restrict opening documents or PDF editing for a group of co-workers, colleagues, or individuals with whom you have direct communication. This method requires the use of digital IDs and public key certificates. This form of security also uses a security policy you create from public key certificates derived from user's digital IDs.

The third method (Adobe Policy Server) is not covered in this book. Please see the Acrobat Help Guide for more details or information. Adobe Policy Server enables you to apply server-based security policies to PDF documents. One of the great benefits for using a policy server is that you can encrypt documents for limited time use.

Keep in mind that Security Policies can be used with either Password Security or Certificate Security.

The discussion on Acrobat Security starts with the first method of applying security for a more global environment for unknown users. Later in this chapter encryption using a security policy with public key certificates for known users is covered along with digital signatures.

Using password security

To secure an open document, choose File ➪ Document Properties. Click the Security tab in the Document Properties dialog box. Notice the Security Method pull-down menu. Four options are listed in the menu for different security methods. The default selection is No Security. Open the pull-down menu and select Password Security. The Password Security–Settings dialog box shown in Figure 21-1 opens. Depending on which compatibility option you select from the Compatibility pull-down menu, the bottom of the dialog box activates additional options or removes options. In Figure 21-1 you can see that when choosing Acrobat 7 compatibility, all options are available in the dialog box. If you select an earlier version, like Acrobat 3 compatibility, some options are grayed out, such as two of the options in the Select Document Components to Encrypt section.

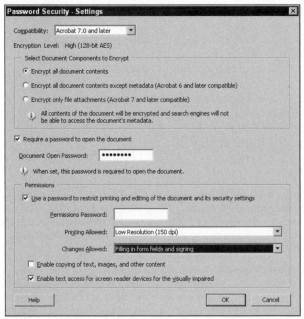

Figure 21-1: Depending on what level of compatibility you choose, the options available for Password Security will change.

Creating a Policy for Adding Security

If you've used earlier versions of Acrobat, accessing the Document Properties dialog box is something you are probably familiar with. It's a fast and easy way for adding document security and it's okay when you have a single document you want to secure and never again want to secure additional documents with the same permissions and restrictions. In Acrobat 7, Adobe Systems has made securing PDF documents much easier when you want to routinely secure PDF files using the same permissions settings. The preferred method for securing files in Acrobat 7 is to create a *Security Policy*.

To create a security policy you use the Secure Task button pull — down menu and select *Secure This Document* or select *Manage Security Policies* from the same menu. Either choice opens a dialog box where you create a new policy. You step through a New Security Policy wizard where you make choices for the security method you want to use and make choices for the permissions you want to assign to a document.

Once you create the policy, you can easily apply the same policy when you want to secure additional documents without the need to select the different permissions options each time you apply security. For more detail information on creating and using security policies, see "Using a security policy" later in this chapter.

You add Password Security via this dialog box any time you want to restrict users from opening a file and/or making changes to the content. Users must know the password you add in this dialog box in order to open a file and/or make changes. The options available to you include

✦ **Compatibility:** The options from this pull-down menu include Acrobat 3, Acrobat 5, Acrobat 6, and Acrobat 7 compatibility. If you select Acrobat 7 compatibility and save the PDF document, users need an Acrobat 7 viewer or greater to open the file. The same holds true when saving with Acrobat 5 or 6 compatibility for users who have Acrobat viewers lower than version 5 or 6.

✦ **Encryption level:** Below the Compatibility pull-down menu Acrobat informs you what level of encryption is applied to the document based on the compatibility choice made in the pull-down menu. If you select Acrobat 3 from the Compatibility pull-down menu, the encryption level is 40-bit encryption. Acrobat 5 and Acrobat 6 compatibility are encrypted with 128-bit RC4 encryption. Acrobat 7 supports 128-bit AES. All the higher encryption levels offer you more options for restricting printing and editing.

✦ **Encrypt all document contents:** This option applies encryption to all document contents.

✦ **Encrypt all document contents except metadata (Acrobat 6 and later compatible):** Use this option to apply encryption to all document contents except document metadata. As the item name implies, this level of security is compatible with Acrobat 6 and later. This is a good selection if you want to have the metadata in your secure documents available for a search engine.

✦ **Encrypt only file attachments (Acrobat 7 and later compatible):** Use this option to encrypt file attachments but not the PDF document. This option is only compatible with Acrobat 7 and above. You might use this when sending an eEnvelope where you want to encrypt only files attached to the envelope. This prevents anyone from editing your files.

For more information on encrypting eEnvelopes, see the section "Using Secure PDF Delivery" later in this chapter.

Encrypting only file attachments is a nifty new feature in Acrobat 7. As an example for using this feature, you might have a document such as a memo you want to distribute to all employees. Attached to the memo you might have a financial report, draft company policy document, or some other file you want to have reviewed by management personnel only. All company personnel can see the memo, but only those who have a security password can open the file attachments.

✦ **Require a password to open the document:** Select this check box if you want a user to supply a password to open the PDF document. After selecting the check box, the field box for Document Open Password becomes active and you can add a password. Before you exit the dialog box, Acrobat prompts you in another dialog box to confirm the password. Note: if you select 'Encrypt only file attachments (Acrobat 7 and compatible) you must enter a password to be able to open the attachment(s).

✦ **Use a password to restrict printing and editing of the document and its security settings:** Select this check box if you want to restrict permissions from the items active in the Permissions area of the dialog box. You can use this with or without a Document Open Password.

✦ **Permissions Password:** Fill in the field box with a password. If you also have a Document Open Password, the passwords must be different. Acrobat opens a dialog box and informs you to make different password choices if you attempt to use the same password for opening the file and setting permissions.

✦ **Printing Allowed:** If you use Acrobat 3 compatibility, the options are available to either enable printing or disallow printing. The choices are None and High Resolution. Even though the choice reads High Resolution, the result simply enables users to print your file. With Acrobat 5, 6, and 7 compatibility, you have a third choice for enabling printing at a lower resolution (150 dpi). If you select Low Resolution (150 dpi) from the menu options, users are restricted to printing the file at the lower resolution. This choice is typically something you might use for files intended for digital prepress and high-end printing, eBooks or eContent, or to protect your content from being printed and then re-scanned.

✦ **Changes Allowed:** From this pull-down menu you make choices for the kinds of changes you allow users to perform on the document. Acrobat 3 compatibility offers you four choices; Acrobat 5, 6, and 7 compatibility offers you five choices. These options include

  • **None:** This option prevents a user from any kind of editing and content extraction.

  • **Inserting, deleting, and rotating pages:** This option is not available when using Acrobat 3 compatibility. Users are permitted to insert, delete, and rotate pages. If you create PDFs for eBooks, allowing users to rotate pages can be helpful when they view PDFs on tablets and portable devices.

  • **Page layout, filling in forms, and signing existing signature fields (Acrobat 3 only):** Select this option to enable users to extract pages, insert pages, and also perform actions on form fields.

  • **Filling in form fields and signing existing signature fields:** If you create Acrobat forms and want users to be able to fill in the form fields and digitally sign documents, enable this check box. Forms are useless to users without the ability to fill in the form fields.

  • **Commenting, filling in form fields, and signing existing signature fields:** You might use this option in a review process where you want to have users comment on a design but you don't want them to make changes to your file. You can secure the document against editing, but allow commenting and form field filling in and signing. When you enable form filling in with this option or the Filling in form fields and signing existing signature fields option, users are restricted against changing your form design and cannot make edits other than filling in the fields. A good example of using this option might be having your customers fill out a form, and also add comments to describe their selections.

  • **Any except extracting pages:** With this option, all the permissions are available to users except extracting pages from the document and creating separate PDFs from selected pages.

✦ **Enable copying of text, images, and other content and access for the visually impaired:** This option is available when selecting Acrobat 3.0 and later. If you restrict permissions for any of the previous pull-down menu options, users aren't allowed to copy data. You can add permission for content copying by enabling this check box. Enable copying of text, images, and other content: The setting above was replaced with two settings in Acrobat 5.0 and higher security. This setting restricts the user from copying information from your PDF.

✦ **Enable text access for screen reader devices for the visually impaired:** This option is available for all versions except Acrobat 3 compatibility. As a matter of practice, checking this box is always a good idea. If you check this box, you can restrict all editing features while permitting users with screen reading devices the ability to read your files. If the check box is not enabled, screen readers and other devices designed for accessibility are not able to read the PDF document and all the options for using the View ⇨ Read Out Loud menu command are grayed out. Furthermore, users can index your files with Acrobat Professional by using Acrobat Catalog when this check box is enabled, regardless of the other items you prevent users from accessing.

Cross-Reference For more information on screen readers and accessibility, see Chapter 20. For more information on creating index files, see Chapter 5.

After you make choices for the password permissions, click OK, click OK again in the Document Properties dialog box, and then save your file to apply the security. If you close the document without saving, the security settings are not applied.

Using a security policy

Security policies are settings you save that are later used when securing documents — similar to creating style sheets in word processors or layout programs. The three different options for creating a security policy are

✦ **Use passwords:** This option is the same as applying a password to a document via the Document Properties Security pane. The difference between applying password security in the Password Security – Settings dialog box shown in Figure 21-1 and adding a security policy is that the latter is more efficient when you're applying the same security settings repeatedly to multiple documents. If you use the Password Security – Settings dialog box you need to set options each time you secure a document by selecting check boxes and making choices from pull-down menus. When you use a security policy, the options you choose are captured and saved as part of the policy; you just use the policy each time you want to encrypt documents with the same settings.

Understanding Password Encryption

When you encrypt a file with password security, it's important to understand that tools exist that can be used to decrypt files. Just about anything that can be encrypted using a password can be broken given enough time with the right tools. Software applications used for decryption run through cycles combining different characters to arrive at the right combination that accesses the encrypted file.

If you use a three-character password, the amount of time to break your password by a sophisticated decryption tool might be a matter of a few hours. As you add characters to the password, the decryption tool requires more time to explore all combinations of characters. If you add 10 to 12 characters to a password, the most sophisticated tools on the fastest computers can take decades of constant running to come up with the right combination of characters to break a password.

As a matter of practice when assigning permissions for sensitive material, always use no fewer than eight characters to secure a file. Adobe Systems has provided a sophisticated tool that enables you to protect your content if you observe a few simple rules.

✦ **Use public key certificates:** Use this option to share files with users who have a public certificate. These certificates include ones you've added to your Trusted Identities list, or by searching directories you have access to. You can create a policy that applies different permissions to different users. Using this policy ensures that every document is encrypted with the same settings for the recipients.

✦ **Use the Adobe Policy Server:** If you have access to an Adobe LiveCycle Policy Server, you can create a security policy that is enforced by connecting to the Adobe Policy Server. PDF documents and attachments can be secured for a selected group of users or for a period of time you determine when creating the policy. When a policy changes or expires on the server, the documents tied to the policy respect these changes as well.

To make the process of creating a security policy a little more clear, try the following steps to create a policy using password security.

STEPS: Creating a password security policy

1. **Open the Managing Security Policies dialog box.** You open the Managing Securities Policy dialog box by selecting Manage Security Policies from the Secure Task Button pull-down menu. You can access the dialog box with or without a file open in the Document pane.

2. **Create a new policy.** In the Managing Security Policies dialog box, click the New button to open the New Security Policy dialog box as shown in Figure 21-2. You have three options from which to choose. The default is Use passwords as shown in Figure 21-2. Leave the default settings as is and click the Next button. The *Use the Adobe Policy Server* is grayed out if you don't have access to an Adobe LiveCycle Policy Server.

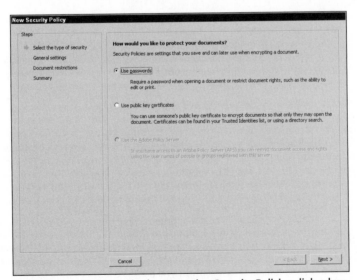

Figure 21-2: Click New in the Managing Security Policies dialog box to open the New Security Policy dialog box.

3. **Add a name and description for the new policy.** Type a Policy name and Description in the respective field boxes in the General Settings panel of the New Security Policy dialog box as shown in Figure 21-3. Select the box for Save passwords with the policy. The name and description you add in the second pane appears when you access the Managing Security Policies dialog box. Try to add information in the field boxes that describe the settings you use when creating the policy.

Note   If you want to periodically change passwords, leave the check box unchecked. Each time you use the policy, Acrobat prompts you for a new password.

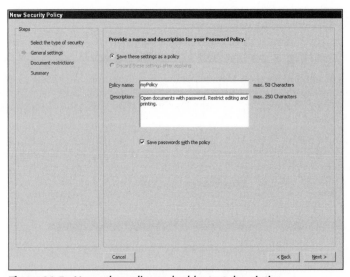

Figure 21-3: Name the policy and add a text description.

4. **Add the security settings.** Click Next, and you arrive at the Document restrictions panel of the New Security Policy dialog box, shown in Figure 21-4. This is the same dialog box you see in the Password Security – Settings dialog box. Here you set the attributes for the security to be applied when using the policy. In my example, I selected Acrobat 6 compatibility; enabled the *Require Password to open the document* checkbox; checked the box for *Use permissions password is required to restrict editing of security settings*; added a password; selected *None* from the Print allowed pull-down menu; set the Changes allowed pull-down menu to *None*; and checked the last check box in the dialog box.

5. **Review the policy.** Click Next, and the last pane (Summary) appears with a Finish button. Click Finish to create the policy. You are returned to the Managing Security Policies dialog box where your new policy is listed in the policy list window, as shown in Figure 21-5. Notice that the name and description you added when creating the policy now appear in the Name and Comment columns. Additionally you see a description of the policy details and encryption components for the policy you created. If creating multiple policies, select a policy name in the top window and the policy details and encryption components in the lower half of the dialog box change to reflect attributes for the selected policy. Click the Close button to return to the Document pane.

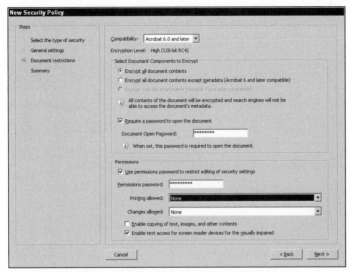

Figure 21-4: Make your security settings choices in the Document restrictions panel of the New Security Policy dialog box.

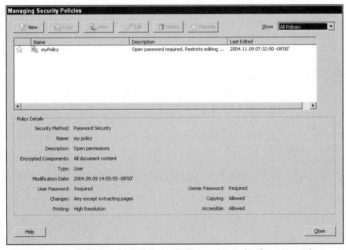

Figure 21-5: The Name and Description appear in the Managing Security Policies dialog box under the Name and Description columns.

6. **Select a Policy to Apply.** If you work with documents where you need to add different permissions depending on the document content and the users with whom you want to distribute your files, you'll want to add additional policies each designed with different permissions. As you add additional policies, you can choose what policy you want to use to secure a document. To use a policy, open a PDF document and select Secure This Document from the Secure Task Button pull-down menu. The Select a Policy to

Apply dialog box opens as shown in Figure 21-6. This dialog box is similar to the Managing Security Policies dialog box. Select your policy and click the Apply button; the security is applied with the permissions options you set when you created the policy. After applying the policy you need to save the PDF file to complete the encryption process.

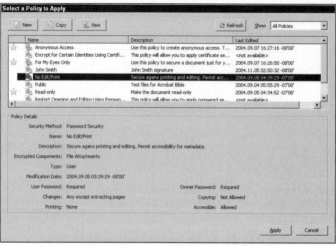

Figure 21-6: Select the policy you want to use for securing a document and click the Apply button.

Managing security policies

You can add several policies using different permissions settings. Each time you create a new policy appears in the Select a Policy to Apply dialog box. Each time you want to secure documents with the same settings, open the Select a Policy to Apply dialog box and select a policy from the list. Click the Apply button and the open document is secured with the settings created from the selected policy.

A nice feature is the ability to tag some of your policies as Favorites. Favorites will appear in the Secure Task Button pull-down menu so you don't have to open the Select a Policy to Apply dialog box. As you add security policies you can choose whether or not to list policies as Favorites in the Secure Task Button pull-down menu. By default new policies are added as Favorites and appear at the top of the menu. Select a policy and click the Favorite button in the Managing Security Policies dialog box to hide the policy from the Favorite list. Select and click the policy again and click Favorite and the policy returns to the Secure pull-down menu in the Secure Task Button. As shown in Figure 21-7, two policies appear with a star icon adjacent to the policy name and two policies appear without the icon. To hide a policy name from the Secure Task Button pull-down menu, select a policy and click the Favorite button to remove the star icon. If a policy appears without the icon adjacent to the policy name, select the policy and click the Favorite button to add the icon and thereby add the policy to the Secure Task Button pull-down menu.

To delete a policy, click a policy name and click the Delete button. You can also edit a policy by selecting it and clicking the Edit button.

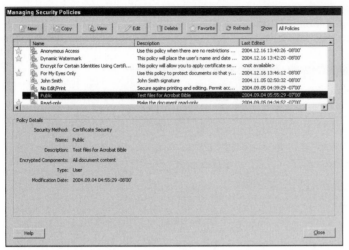

Figure 21-7: Select a policy and click the Favorite button. The icon indicates that the policy name is listed as a Favorite in the Secure Task Button pull-down menu.

Understanding Digital IDs

A digital ID is a file that you create in Acrobat or acquire from a third-party signature provider. Your ID, also known as a *credential* or *profile*, is password protected and used to electronically sign or certify documents. Before you can digitally sign a document you need to create or acquire your own personal ID.

Digital IDs have two components important to understand — your personal or private digital ID and your public certificate. When you create a digital ID with Acrobat you are creating your private ID and your public certificate. The public certificate is a file you share with other users so they can encrypt files that they send to you. In order to open such encrypted files you need to supply the password used when you created your Digital ID.

As a matter of understanding the security involved when using digital signatures, realize that, unless you choose to save a password when you create a policy, every time you want to sign a document, you need to supply your password. Therefore, anyone having access to your computer cannot sign or certify a document on your behalf unless the user has your password. When a file is encrypted using your public certificate, the file is opened only when you supply your password. Again, anyone having access to your computer cannot open a document encrypted with your public certificate unless that user has access to your password. Private digital signature IDs are used to sign and decrypt documents. Public Certificates are used to encrypt documents and validate signatures.

As mentioned earlier each digital ID has two components — the private ID and the public certificate. The private ID can be used to either digitally sign a PDF or to decrypt documents encrypted with the public certificate, and conversely, the public certificate can be used to encrypt documents or to validate digital signatures.

Digital IDs can be created in Acrobat or acquired from other parties. They can then be accessed locally from your computer or from a remote server. For a quick look at the options available when working with Digital IDs and public certificates, select Advanced ⇨ Security Settings and the Security Settings dialog box shown in Figure 21-8 opens. This dialog box is used to manage and create digital IDs; and configure servers which can locate public certificate directories; time stamp digital IDs; or Adobe Policy Servers. As shown in the dialog box, the options you have for working with Digital IDs and configuring server access include

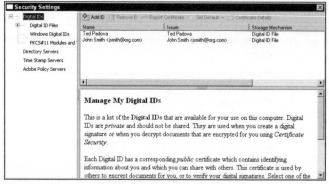

Figure 21-8: Open the Security Settings dialog box to create new Digital IDs and manage your existing IDs.

- ✦ **Digital IDs.** There are three types of IDs available that include:

  - • **Digital ID Files.** Available on Windows and Macintosh, this form of ID is similar to what you had available in earlier versions of Acrobat when using Acrobat Certificate Security. You can select 'Add ID'(which opens the Add Digital ID dialog box to find an existing Digital ID, create a new Acrobat Self-Sign Certificate, or get a 3rd party certificate.

  - • **Windows Digital IDs.** This ID is available only on Windows. The ID is installed in the Windows Certificate Store where it is also available to other Windows applications. This Digital ID is protected by your Windows logon password.

  - • **PKCS#11 Modules and Tokens.** PKCS#11 encryption is used on hardware devices such as smart cards. You acquire the module from your device manufacturer.

- ✦ **Directory servers.** This option is used to enable you to locate specific digital ID certificates from network servers for encrypting documents using Certificate Security. Directory servers can be added by importing a configuration supplied by a System Administrator, or by entering the parameters required to configure the server.

- ✦ **Time Stamp Servers.** This option is used if you will be adding time stamps to documents. Like Directory Servers, Time Stamp Servers are added by importing a configuration from a system administrator or by adding parameters required to configure the server.

- ✦ **Adobe Policy Servers.** Adobe LiveCycle Policy Server (http://www.adobe.com/products/server/policy/main.html) is a web server-based security solution provided by Adobe Systems that provides dynamic control over PDF documents. Policies created with Acrobat or Adobe Policy Server are stored on the server and can be refreshed from the server. Once you've configured an Adobe Policy Server, all polices maintained on this server are available to you. You must log into Adobe Policy Server to use these policies. This option also requires access to a URL provided by a System Administrator and adding the server to your list of Adobe Policy Servers.

Using Third-Party Signature Handlers

Digital signature handlers, tokens, biometrics, hardware solutions, and other similar products are available from third-party providers and offer you many different options for securing PDF documents depending on the product and manufacturer. To find information on acquiring third-party products for signature handling, take a look at a new area on Adobe's Web site at `http://partners.adobe.com/security` . On the Adobe Web pages you find links to digital signature and document control vendors worldwide.

If you use Acrobat for languages other than US English, go to your local Web page and logo on to Adobe's Web site. You might use, for example, a URL like `http://www.adobe.com.fr/security` for a French language document page. This page will include a link to security partners supporting the localized products..

When you create a digital ID in Acrobat by choosing Advanced ➪ Security Settings, the Security Settings dialog box opens. Select Digital IDs and select Add ID from the buttons at the top of the Security Settings dialog box, which opens the Add Digital ID dialog box. The third button option in this dialog box opens your Web browser and takes you to Adobe's Web site where a listing of the Adobe partners appears. Click a link on this Web page to go to an Adobe partner offering signature handlers for US English and many other languages.

Creating a personal digital ID

Acrobat offers you two different menu options for creating a digital ID and creating a digital ID appearance. You access dialog boxes for digital ID creation, appearance settings, and ID profile management in the following areas:

✦ **Security Preferences:** You use the Security Preferences to create digital ID appearances for your personal digital IDs. If you want to add a logo, analog signature, symbol, or some text to an ID, you can do so by using the appearance settings available by pressing Ctrl/⌘+K. Select Security in the left pane and the window on the right side of the dialog box lists all your currently configured signatures. You can select a signature profile or add a new appearance in this dialog box by clicking the New button shown in Figure 21-9.

✦ **Advanced Preferences:** If you have an ID configured, the ID appears listed in the Appearance list in the Security Preferences dialog box. Select an ID and click Advanced Preferences to open another dialog box where a number of options exist for verifying signatures; creating them; and on Windows, settings for Windows Integration. A number of different options exist in three tabs (Windows) or one tab (Macintosh). For a detailed description of each item consult the Acrobat Help document.

Note   If you have not created a digital ID yet, you will not see anything listed in this box, but you still can create appearances that can later be used with a digital ID.

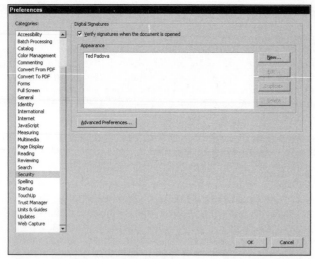

Figure 21-9: Choose Edit ⇨ Preferences (Acrobat ⇨ Preferences on the Macintosh) or press Ctrl/⌘+K and click Security in the left pane to display digital ID appearance options.

To understand how to create a digital ID, and use the Preferences dialog box to create an appearance follow these steps:

STEPS: Creating a digital ID and appearance

1. **Open the Security Settings dialog box.** Click Advanced ⇨ Security Settings The Security Settings dialog box shown earlier in this chapter in Figure 21-8 opens.

2. **Create a Self-Signed ID.** Select Digital IDs from the left panel. Click Add ID in the Security Settings dialog box. The Add Digital ID dialog box opens as shown in Figure 21-10. Select the *Create a Self-Signed Digital ID* and click Next. The next pane in the Add Digital ID dialog box (Windows only) is informational. Read the information and click Next again to open the third pane.

3. **Choose where you want to store the ID (Windows only).** Click New PKCS#12 Digital ID file. Note: Macintosh users don't see this pane or the previous pane.

4. **Add Identity Information.** The next pane opens with text boxes for you to supply identity information. If you added Identity information in the Identity preferences, the information is transposed to the pane shown in Figure 21-11. If you want to use special characters, non-Roman languages or non-ASCII check the box for Enable Unicode Support. Notice in Figure 21-11 an ampersand is used.

5. **Add a Password.** Click Next and the next pane shows you a directory location where your ID will be saved and asks you to supply a password and confirm the password. Leave the target directory location at the default and type a password in the Password text box and type the password again in the Confirm Password text box.

6. **Close the Security Settings dialog box.** Click Finish in the Add Digital ID dialog box and you return to the Security Settings dialog box. Click the close button (top right corner Windows or top left corner Macintosh).

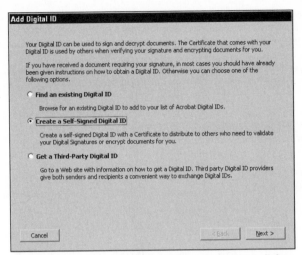

Figure 21-10: Click Add ID in the Security Settings dialog box and the Add Digital ID dialog box opens.

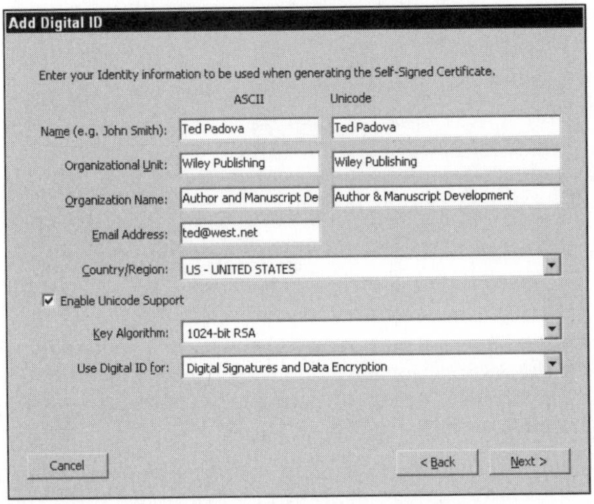

Figure 21-11: Add identity information if all fields are not completed in your Identity preferences.

7. **Configure the signature appearance.** Open the Security Preferences dialog box (Edit ⇨ Preferences ⇨ Security) Click the New button in the Security Preferences dialog box to open the Configure Signature Appearance dialog box shown in Figure 21-12. Type a title in the Title text box at the top of the Configure Signature Appearance dialog box.

8. **Add a graphic for the signature appearance.** If you have a graphic you want to use as a signature appearance, click the Imported graphic radio button and then click the File button. A Select Picture dialog box opens containing a Browse button. Click Browse and locate the file you want to use for the appearance. Select the file in the Browse dialog box and click the Select button. Click OK in the Select Picture dialog box to return to the Configure Signature Appearance dialog box. The imported graphic appears as you see in Figure 21-12. Click OK in the Preferences dialog box and your ID is ready to use.

Figure 21-12: Look over the signature appearance in the Preview window and type a title in the Title text box.

Managing multiple IDs

If you create several IDs used for different purposes, you may have a need to remove old IDs and add new IDs. In the Security Settings you have options for assigning attributes to your IDs, adding new IDs, and removing IDs. Choose Advanced ➪ Security Settings to open the dialog box shown earlier in this chapter in Figure 21-8.

Click an ID in the Name column to select it and click the Remove ID button to delete an ID. You also have options in the Security Settings dialog box for Exporting Certificates, Setting an ID among a list to a default ID, and viewing certificate details.

Using a signature field

To sign a document containing a signature field, click on the field with the Hand tool. If your document is not certified, the Document Is Not Certified dialog box opens offering you choices for certifying the document or signing the document. For more information on creating a Certified Document see later in this chapter "Certifying Documents" secion. Click the Continue Signing button. The Apply Digital Signature – Digital ID Selection dialog box opens if your persistence option is set to prompt you for which digital ID to use. If you're prompted for which ID to use, select the ID name in the dialog box shown in Figure 21-13.

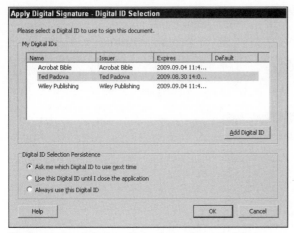

Figure 21-13: Select an ID to sign a document from the list.

Select the ID you want to use and click OK. The next dialog box that opens is the Apply Signature to Document dialog box shown in Figure 21-14. Make selections from the options available from pull-down menus and type options information in the field boxes. Click either Sign and Save As to save a copy of the signed document or Sign and Save to sign the document and update it.

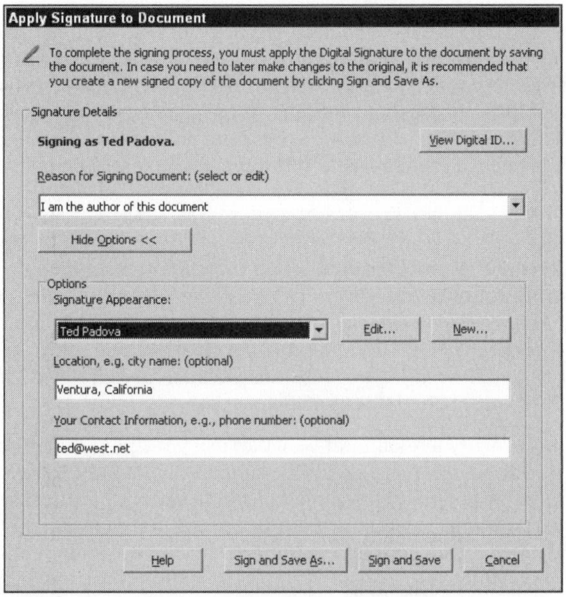

Figure 21-14: Select options and click Sign and Save As or Sign and Save to sign the document.

Creating a signature field when signing a document

 If no signature field appears on a document, you can sign a document by accessing Sign this Document from the Sign Task Button pull-down menu. This method of signing prompts you to marquee an area on a page where you want to create a signature field in the Sign Document dialog box shown in Figure 21-15. Click *Create a new signature field to sign*.

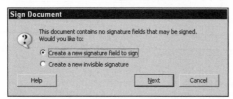

Figure 21-15: Select Sign this Document from the Sign Task Button pull-down menu. The Sign Document dialog box opens.

Click Next to continue and the next pane informs you that the Digital Signature field tool has been selected for you and you need to create the field on the page. Click OK and create a rectangle on the page where you want the signature to appear. When you release the mouse button the Apply Digital Signature - Digital ID Selection dialog box opens. You move through the same dialog boxes and have the same options described previously in the "Using a signature field" section. The difference lies in the fact that you need to create a signature field when you sign a document using this method.

Note

The Sign Document dialog box also offers you an option for creating a new invisible signature. When you select this option and click the Next button, you select your digital ID and sign the document without creating a signature field. When the field has been created, you don't have a way to select the field on the page because it's invisible. These signatures do, however, appear in the Signatures palette where you can view the signature attributes and verify the signatures. (See the section "Validating Signatures" later in this chapter for more information.)

Certifying documents

When you save an Adobe PDF document as certified, you attest to its contents and specify the types of changes that are permitted for the document to remain certified. You might think of certification like a notary seal. This certification can be made visible on the document or invisible, and during the certification process the document is also marked with permissions restricting editing functions. You determine editing permissions via several pull-down menu options when you choose File ➪ Save as Certified Document.

For the individual user who wants to certify a document, you can use your personal digital ID to sign a document when using the File ➪ Save As Certified Document command. However, if you work in a corporate environment or you need the highest level of security for certifying documents you'll want to acquire a digital ID from a Certified Document Services partner. Certified Document Services (CDS) provide a service to automatically certify documents from a trusted authority, ensuring the highest level of document integrity and verification because the user's digital credentials must be stored on a secure USB key device, and they must be issued by a WebTrust certified authority. Recipients of your certified document do not require any additional software or configuration to be able to validate your signature. When a recipient opens your document that was certified using a CDS partner, the document is authenticated over the Internet from the partner's Web site.

Using Certified Document Services (CDS)

When you save a file as a certified document you are not encrypting the file nor adding any type of security. Ultimately, certified documents lock out some editing features, but end users can alter the settings you choose to disallow. To do so requires a user to clear the document certificate and render the file uncertified. You can prevent users from editing PDF content as long as the document remains a certified document. If a user clears the document certification and edits the file, there is no way to get back the original certification and the PDF author always knows whether a document has had the certification altered. However, you do have an option to lock a certifying signature to prevent users from deleting the certification when you save as a certified document.

When you select the Save as Certified Document menu command, the Save as Certified Document dialog box opens. Click OK to use a digital ID you have already created, or select Get Digital ID from Adobe Partner to sign up with a Certified Document Services (CDS) partner if you plan to distribute your document to a wide audience and you want to ensure they can verify its authenticity. Once you've acquired a digital ID from a CDS or choose not to use this service, you can click the 'Don't Show Again' box to by-pass this dialog box in the future.

Click the OK button and the Save as Certified Document – Choose Allowable Actions dialog box opens, as shown in Figure 21-16. In this dialog box you make choices for what editing is allowable after you save the file. The choices available from the Allowed Actions pull-down menu are Disallow any changes to the document, Only allow form fill-in actions on this document, or Only allow commenting and form fill-in actions on this document.

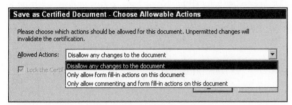

Figure 21-16: Make a choice for the edits you want to permit from choices available in the Allowed Actions pull-down menu and click Next to move to the next dialog box.

Select one of the three options and click Next. The Save as Certified Document – Select Visibility dialog box opens, as shown in Figure 21-17. In this dialog box you make a choice for whether you want to Show Certification on document or Do not show Certification on document. Select a radio button and click the Next button.

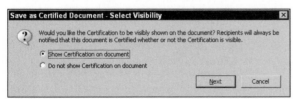

Figure 21-17: Choose whether or not to show the certificate on the document and click the Next button.

If you choose to show the certification on the document, Acrobat opens a dialog box instructing you to click and drag open a signature field where the certification will appear on the document page. Click OK and use your mouse to drag out a marquee area for the certification. The Apply Digital Signature – Digital ID Selection dialog box opens allowing you to select your digital ID and sign the document using the same dialog box you use when signing fields or signing documents (described earlier in the section "Signing a document").

If you choose Do not show Certification on document and click the Next button, you arrive at the Apply Digital Signature – Digital ID Selection dialog box to select your digital ID and continue signing the document. This method works the same as choosing the Create a new invisible signature.

If you select either *Only allow form fill-in actions on this document* or *Only allow commenting and form fill-in actions on this document* the Save as Certified Document – Warnings dialog box similar to the one shown in Figure 21-18 appears when your document contains some sort of interactivity such as layers, links to URLs, or JavaScripts. After you click Next, you will see the Save as Certified Document – Select Visibility dialog box shown earlier in Figure 21-16. The Save as Certified Document – Warnings dialog box informs you that the security could be compromised if you continue signing because of certain elements that may be included in your document such as layers, display settings and other items that appear listed in the dialog box. Acrobat informs you that to obtain greater security you should remove the items suggested in the list window.

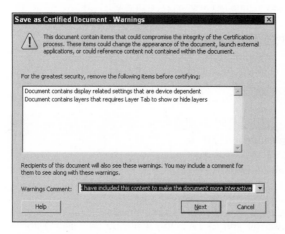

Figure 21-18: If you select *Only allow form fill-in actions on this document* or *Only allow commenting and form fill-in actions on this document* in the Save as Certified Document – Choose Allowable Actions dialog box, warnings are listed that may compromise your security. This dialog box only appears when you have some form of interactivity such as layers, links to URLs, or JavaScripts.

If you want to continue signing, you can select the default message (shown in Figure 21-18) or you can create your own message. If you want to include the content and add the warning comment, leave the default *I have included this content to make the document more interactive*, or create your own message.

The certified document signature is listed in the Signatures palette as shown in Figure 21-19. Click the Signatures tab to open the palette and you can see the signature applied for certified document as 'Author Signature' and if there are other digital signatures they are listed as "Recipient Signatures."

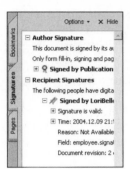

Figure 21-19: The certified document signature appears in the Signatures pane as *Author Signature* and other digital signatures appear as *Recipient Signatures*.

Using Trusted Identities and Certificate Security

Trusted Identities are added to the Trusted Identities Manager dialog box. The list of Trusted Identities is like an address book where you can add contacts and set certificate properties. You can maintain a contact list of Trusted Identities from people with whom you will do business. Each user listed in Trusted Identities can be used to validate digital signatures and encrypt PDF documents for these users. The Trusted Identities Manager additionally permits you to set levels of trust from the users listed in the contact list.

Using certificate encryption

Encryption using certificates is a means for you to add security for a selected group of users. The advantage of using certificates is you can control the permissions settings individually for each user in the same PDF document. For example, you may want to allow one user to view your document, but restrict printing. For another user you may want to disallow editing, but enable printing. For a third user you may want to allow editing and printing. All these permissions can be set for each user in the same PDF document using the Certificate Security Settings dialog box.

To encrypt a file using certificates, you need access to the public certificate. You can either search for the public certificates which may be located on a network server, or you can collect the public certificates for each user and load them into your Trusted Identities list. Keep in mind, the Trusted Identities Manager is like an address book and merely is a convenient location for where you can store contact and certificate information for users you frequently work with. During encryption you can specify permissions settings individually for each user.

Exporting public certificates

Public certificates are used for validating signatures on documents received and encrypting files which you plan to share. For another user to validate your signature or encrypt a file unique to your profile you need to export your public certificate and share it with other users. Your public certificate does not compromise your password settings or ability to secure your own files. Public certificates are generated from your profile, but do not send along your password to other users.

Note   Companies using directory servers to host public certificates do not need to export certificates.

Understanding Encryption, Validation and the Trusted Identities Manager

In the Manage Trusted Identities dialog box there are two drop-down menus: Contacts and Certificates. Items listed in the menus do not have to match. You can have certificates in the list that are not in the Contacts. From the Display pull-down menu you can select either Contacts or Certificates and you can *Add Contacts or Certificates* respective to the menu item you select.

In order to encrypt documents you do *not* have to have a public certificate in your Trusted Identities. For example, a company may have a corporate level security solution in which each employee is issued a certificate that is stored on a network server.. You can search certificates on your company's LDAP (Lightweight Directory Access Protocol) server to find someone you want to encrypt for and just use their certificate without adding the certificate to your list of Trusted Identities.

To validate a signature, you do not have to have the public certificate in your Trusted Identities if you've already established a trust with a parent in the chain of trust. For example, you can create a Class 1 certificate for a security partner. So the chain might be Your Company, Inc. ⇨ Partner Class 1 ⇨ Your Name.

You can then *trust* Your Company, Inc. (the root) and therefore everybody under that chain is automatically trusted by you so you don't need any individual's certificate in your local Trusted Identities for validation. However, if you want to give any user a different trust setting than the trust settings used by the parent, then you do need to add the individual's certificate to your Trusted Identities.

Does an individual need to send you a public certificate? The answer is no, not if the user sends you a file signed with his/her certificate. You can always get the public certificate from a file sent to you.

To acquire a public certificate from a signed document, open a context menu on the signature and select Properties. In the Signature Properties dialog box, click the Show Certificate button. The Certificate Viewer dialog box opens. Click the Export button and you are prompted to save the certificate as a file or email the certificate.

The entire range of possibilities regarding using digital IDs, signing documents, and authenticating signed or certified documents is a very complex subject. In an effort to break it down to a more simplified view, the detail in this chapter assumes you are working in an environment where you are not using a corporate-wide security solution and you're using the self-sign methods of security. If you want the highest levels of security and the most efficient means for securing documents I encourage you to carefully review the Acrobat Help document and explore all the security information on web pages hosted by Adobe Systems.

To export a public certificate you need to start with a digital ID you have already created. Choose Advanced ⇨ Security Settings. The dialog box shown earlier in Figure 21-8 opens. If you have more than one ID listed in the dialog box, select the ID you want to use and click the Export Certificate button. The Data Exchange File – Export Options dialog box opens as shown in Figure 21-20.

Figure 21-20: When exporting your certificate, you can choose to save the public certificate as a file or e-mail the certificate to another user.

In this dialog box you make a choice for saving your public certificate to disk or e-mailing the certificate directly to another user. If you elect Save the data to a file, you can later attach it to an e-mail message and send it to users as needed. If you select the Email the data to someone radio button and click the Next button, the Compose Email dialog box opens where you add the recipient's e-mail address. Enter an e-mail address and click the Email button and the data file is attached to a new e-mail message. Acrobat supplies a default message in the e-mail note for you providing instructions for the recipient, but you can edit if desired.

Trusted identity preferences

At some time before or after compiling a list of certificates from other users, you'll want to visit the Trust Manager Preferences. The permissions settings you assign to individual users don't cover handling file extractions or multimedia. For determining how these items are handled you need to choose options in the Trust Manager Preferences. A document is said to be trusted if it's added to the list of trusted documents and authors. If a document is not trusted, you are prompted to add the document to this list when you try to play a media clip in which the permission is set to Prompt. If you decide to add a certified document to the list, both the document and the author's certificate are added to the list. All documents certified by this author are trusted.

To set attributes for Trusted documents, choose Edit ➪ Preferences (Windows) or Acrobat ➪ Preferences (Macintosh). Select Trust Manager in the left pane when the Preferences dialog box opens as shown in Figure 21-21.

In this dialog box you determine whether you can open file attachments and how multimedia operations are handled. In the list of multimedia operations, select the items individually and choose the permission setting from the pull-down menu. For example, if you wanted to restrict multimedia playback to only using QuickTime, you would select all permissions lines except QuickTime and select Never from the pull-down menu. If you want to have permission to use any of the listed applications to view multimedia, be certain either Always or Prompt is selected for each item. By default, all five applications are set to Always.

Note   The list of multimedia players is derived from installed players on your system. If you do not see one of the options listed in Figure 21-19, you do not have the player installed or you may be using a version not compatible with Acrobat 6 or later. If you want to restrict viewing to additional players, install them and verify that the player you want to use appears in the Preferences dialog box.

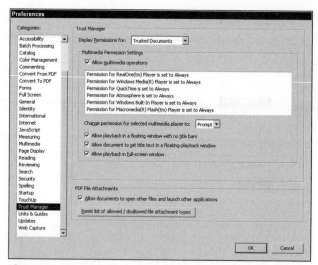

Figure 21-21: Select Trust Manager in the left pane to display the preference settings for handling multimedia and file attachments in documents.

The three check box options at the bottom of the dialog box determine how media clips are viewed onscreen. You can choose from a display in floating windows, displaying the title text in floating windows, and allowing the playback in a full-screen window. The settings in the Trusted Manager Preferences are intended more for the restrictions you want to employ to correspond with the way you want media files to be viewed on your system. Keep in mind that these settings have to do with trust on *your* system and are not specific to any given document.

Click OK in the Preferences dialog box and you're ready to move on to loading recipients for either validating signatures or encrypting files for certain identities.

Requesting contacts

If you want to add a contact and/or certificate to your list of Trusted Identities, select Advanced ➪ Trusted Identities to open the Trusted Identities dialog box. Click the Request Contact button and the Email a Request dialog box opens. You add your name, email address and any contact information you want to supply in the text boxes in the Email a Request dialog box. Click the Next button to open the Compose Email dialog box. In this dialog box, you add the recipient email address. A default subject and message appears in the Compose Email dialog box informing the recipient you are requesting a copy of the individual's certificate. Click the Email button and the request is emailed to the recipient. Note, you may need to open your default email program and click the Send or Send/Receive button to initiate a send.

When a copy of a certificate is emailed back to you, the file appears in a message window as a file attachment. Double click the attachment and the certificate is automatically added to your list of Trusted Identities.

Managing Trusted Identities

After you collect public certificates, you need to load the certificates into your Trusted Identities list To load certificates, choose Advanced ➪ Trusted Identities. The dialog box shown in Figure 21-22 opens

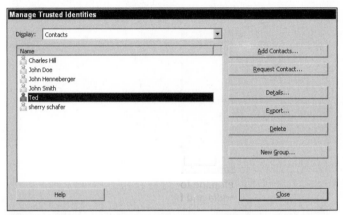

Figure 21-22: You use the Manage Trusted Identities dialog box to add identities from public certificates you collect from other users.

To add a recipient, click the Add Contacts button. The Choose Contact to Import dialog box shown in Figure 21-23 opens where you can browse your hard drive or network server to locate certificates from other users. When adding identities collected by other users, click the Browse button. The Locate Certificate File dialog box opens where you navigate your hard drive and locate certificates to add to a recipient list. Click Open and the recipient's name appears in the top window of the Choose Contacts to Import dialog box. Select the name of the added contact and click the Import button to add the certificate to the identities list. You use the Search button to search through network servers configured in your Directory Servers.

Add the certificate and return to the Manage Trusted Identities dialog box and continue adding new certificates to your list of recipients.

Setting certificate security permissions

With the new features in Acrobat 7, the one thing to keep in mind is that when you have circumstances that require you to repeat document security for the same set of users or when encrypting documents with the same set of permissions, you'll always want to set up a security policy. In those instances where you intend to secure a document using certificates one time only, you can set permissions without creating a policy. To help simplify the process, this section refers to setting up permissions using certificates for a one-time use.

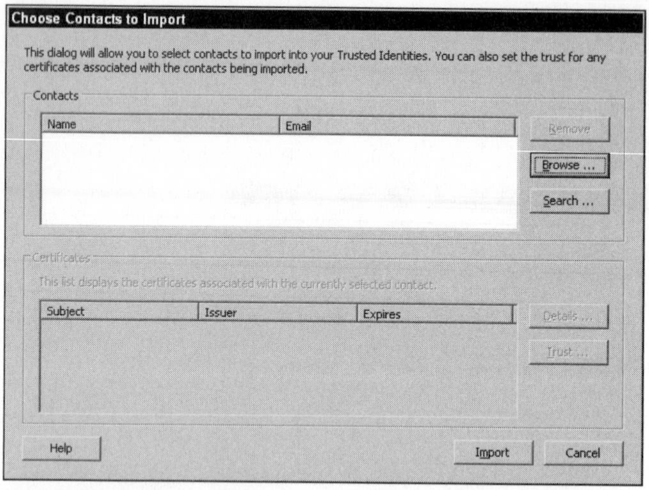

Figure 21-23: Use the Choose Contacts to Import dialog box to add new recipient identities.

To secure a document using Certificate Security, open the Document Properties dialog box (File ➪ Document Properties). Click the Security tab and select Certificate Security from the Security Method pull-down menu. The Certificate Security Settings dialog opens. The General settings panel offers you the choice to save your settings as a policy or discard the settings after applying the security. In addition you have options for what you want to encrypt such as the document only or the document and file attachments and the type of encryption you want to apply. In Figure 21-24 you can see the options in the General settings pane.

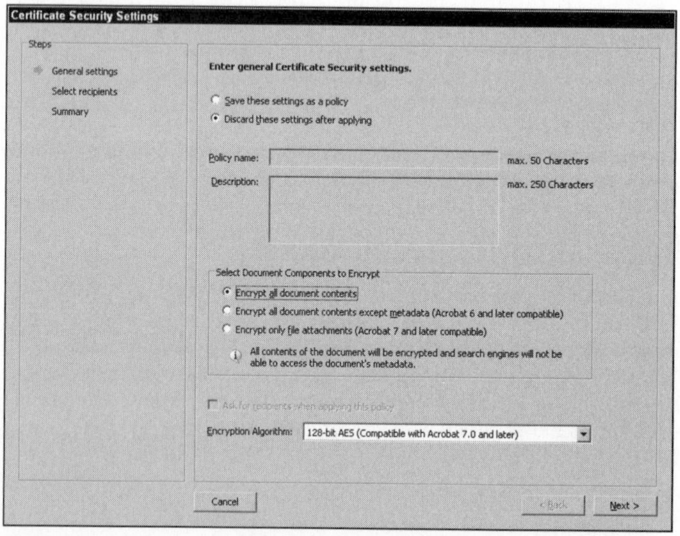

Figure 21-24: Select Certificate Security from the Security Method pull-down menu in the Security tab from the Document Properties dialog box to open the Certificate Security Settings dialog box.

Click Next and the Document Security –Digital ID Selection dialog box opens. Select the digital ID you want to use and click OK. You return to the Select Recipients panel in the Certificate Security Settings dialog box as shown in Figure 21-25. This panel is used to add recipients from your Trusted Identities list or from searching a network server. The first recipient added is your Digital ID. In the event you want to open the document, you'll need your ID and password to open the file. As a default, your ID is always added to the list.

In Figure 21-25 several recipients appear in the list.

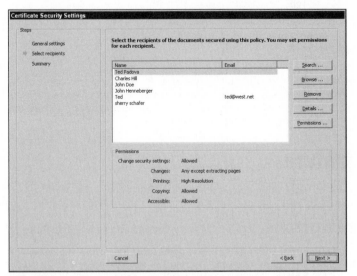

Figure 21-25: After adding your digital ID you are returned to the Certificate Security Settings dialog box where the Select recipients panel opens. In this example, I have added 5 recipients in addition to the author.

Click the Search button to add recipients to the list. You can search all the directories configured, or deselect the check box and select Trusted Identities from the drop-down list. Select one or many (using shift click or control-click). Alternatively, you can Browse your hard drive and select files to add to your list of recipients.

Select a recipient in the list and click the Permissions button. The Acrobat Security dialog box opens to inform you that not all third party products support the settings. The dialog box is informational. Read over the information and click OK. The Permissions Settings dialog box shown in Figure 21-26 opens where you set permissions for the selected user. Select the permissions options you want to apply and click OK.

The great strength for using Certificate Security is that all the recipients in your list can be assigned unique permissions. For example, you can prohibit printing for one user, allow low resolution printing for another user and high resolution printing for a third user. In addition you can protect against a number of different editing options. All of these permissions settings are applied to individual recipients in the same PDF document. Each user needs to open the file using his/her own digital ID and password.

Figure 21-26: Select the permissions you want to assign to the selected user and click OK.

To complete the Certificate Security, click the Next button and the Summary panel opens. A summary for your policy is listed in the panel. If you want to make any changes click the Back button. To accept the settings you made click Finish. Save the file and all the permissions assignments to your recipients are encrypted in the document.

Validating Signatures

Digital signatures would be of no value unless you could confirm that a document was signed by the individual claiming to have signed the document. For confirmation purposes you use menu commands and options to validate signatures. There are several options you have when validating signatures and all depends on different circumstances which include:

✦ If you have established trust with a parent, you don't need the certificate listed in your Trusted Identities. See the "Understanding Encryption, Validation, and the Trusted Identities Manager" sidebar earlier in this chapter. When you open a signed PDF from another person using a third-party security partner certificate, the signature appears as *Unknown*. Select Properties from a context menu you open on the signature,. In the Signature Properties dialog box, click *Verify Signature*. The signature appears valid without adding to your Trusted Identities. If you want to change the level of trust, you can add the certificate to your Trusted Identities and set the trust in the Manage Trusted Identities dialog box. See the "Managing Trusted Identities" section earlier in this chapter.

✦ If you open a document where a user has self-signed a document and hasn't used a third-party security partner, and you know the document has been sent to you by the PDF author, you can retrieve the certificate from the document without needing the individual to send you the certificate. You might receive files from members of your workgroup where you are confident the document you receive comes from the individual who signed it. In this case, you can open a context menu on the signature, select Properties and click the Show Certificate button in the Signature Properties dialog box. The Certificate Viewer dialog box opens. Click the Trust tab and click the button for Add to Trusted Identities. The certificate is added to your Trusted Identities where you can set the level of trust and use the certificate to validate signatures.

✦ If you open a document from an anonymous user or one where you question the document authenticity, you can request a certificate. You add the certificate you receive from a PDF author to your Trusted Identities and you can choose to set the level of trust following the same steps outlined in the section "Managing Trusted Identities" earlier in this chapter.

To validate a signature you use the Sign Task Button, or the Signatures pane. Choose either Validate All Signatures in Document from either the Sign Task Button pull-down menu or from the Options menu in the Signatures pane. To validate a single signature, select that signature from the Signatures pane or hover over the signature in the Document pane. Open a context menu and select Validate Signature.

When you open a signed document and view signatures in the Signatures palette, an icon with a question mark may be displayed adjacent to the signature(s). In addition you'll notice the text below the signature icon often states that the signature validity is unknown. This occurs when the user has not been added to your Trusted Identities list. See the list of options at the beginning of this section.

Note   Contained in the Security Preferences is a check box for *Verify signatures when the document is opened*. If the check box is enabled, the signatures in the document are validated when the document opens. In this case, you do not need to manually access a menu command to validate a signature. You do, however, still need to have a trusted certificate from the individual who signed the document in order to validate upon opening the file. If using external certificate authority, you need to have an active Internet connection to your service to verify signatures. If this box is unchecked you must manually validate your signatures. Be aware that if your document has many pages, Acrobat may not validate signatures automatically upon opening the document. This behavior prevents a document from slowing down during open time. If you find documents not certifying signatures at open time, manually review the signatures in the Signatures pane and use the Validate Signature command in the Options pull-down menu.

When you validate a signature, Acrobat opens a dialog box reporting the validation status. If the public certificate is loaded and the validation is true, a dialog box opens reporting the certificate is valid.

If you get UNKNOWN, this certificate is not in your Trusted Identities. Select the Signature Properties button. From the Summary tab select Show Certificate. From the Trust tab select your Trust Settings and select Add to Trusted Identities. The Import Contact Settings appears where you determine which Trust Settings you desire. Select OK in the Certificate Viewer window. You are returned to Signature Properties. Select Verify Signature. This signature will now be Valid. Select Close to return to the Document pane.

You can view the signature properties by clicking the Signature Properties button to display the Signature Properties dialog box which reports all the properties of the certificate, including the reason for signing, the e-mail address of the person signing the document, and the certificate fingerprint. The Signatures palette reflects a valid signature as shown in Figure 21-27.

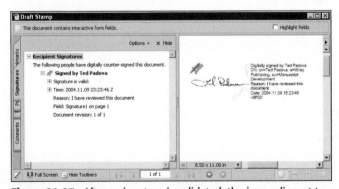

Figure 21-27: After a signature is validated, the icon adjacent to the signature name changes to a pen and check mark, and the status is reported as valid.

Using Secure PDF Delivery

Working with file attachments has been greatly improved in Acrobat and Adobe Reader in the latest version. You can create eEnvelopes containing file attachments and secure the PDF and file attachment(s) against unauthorized access. Users of Acrobat or the free Adobe Reader software with access rights can open the PDFs and extract the file attachment(s).

To understand how files are attached in a Secure PDF Delivery workflow, follow these steps:

STEPS: Creating a secure eEnvelope

1. **Open the Creating Secure eEnvelope dialog box.** Open the Secure task button pull-down menu and select Secure PDF Delivery. Note that you do not need to have a document open in Acrobat.

2. **Choose files to include.** The Choose the files to enclose panel in the Creating Secure eEnvelope dialog box opens as shown in Figure 21-28. Click the Add File to Send button and the Choose the files to enclose dialog box opens. Navigate your hard drive, select the file you want to include, and click Open.

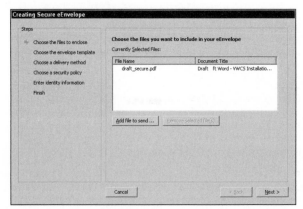

Figure 21-28: Click Add file to send and locate the file to add to your eEnvelope.

3. **Select a template.** Click Next and the *Choose the envelope template* panel opens. You can select from preinstalled templates or click the Browse button to locate a PDF file you want to use for your template. Select a preinstalled template from the list shown in Figure 21-29 and click Next.

Note You have templates available for date stamping the envelope and signing the envelope. Choose from template2.pdf to date stamp an envelope and choose template3.pdf to open a template with a digital signature field. All templates have field boxes where you can add addressee information.

4. **Choose a delivery method.** The next panel that opens is the *Choose a delivery method* panel. You have two choices for delivering your eEnvelope. Choose from options for saving the envelope or emailing it from the two radio button options. To see your envelope in Acrobat, select *Complete the eEnvelope manually*. Click the Next button to deliver the eEnvelope to the option selected here.

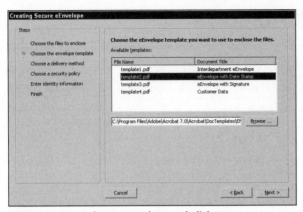

Figure 21-29: Select a template and click Next.

5. **Choose a security policy to apply.** To show all policies you created, click the *Show all policies* radio button as shown in Figure 21-30. Select a policy in the list and click Next.

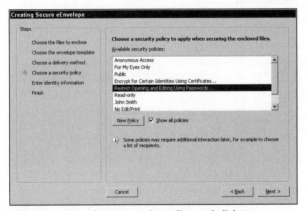

Figure 21-30: Select a security policy and click Next.

6. **Enter identity information.** The next pane asks for identity information similar to the identity information you add in the Add Digital ID dialog box in Figure 21-11 shown earlier in this chapter. Complete the fields if necessary, with your personal identity information and click Next.

7. **The Finish panel displays your settings.** If you are satisfied, click the Finish button. If your security policy requires interaction (like setting the password, or identifying your recipients) you will be prompted to set these values. and the eEnvelope opens in the Acrobat Document pane and the Attachments pane is opened to show you the file attachment as shown in Figure 21-31. You can save the file and email it later or make edits on the envelope and click the Email tool to email the file.

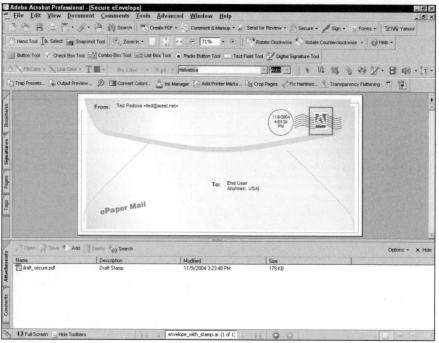

Figure 21-31: Click Finish and the eEnvelope opens in the Document pane with the Attachments pane open.

Summary

✦ PDF documents can be secured with built-in Acrobat Self-Signed Security and security handlers acquired from third-party developers. Files can be secured from users opening documents, editing documents, or for both.

✦ Different levels of security can prevent users of Acrobat viewers earlier than version 6 from opening files. It is important to know your user audience and what version of Acrobat viewers they use before securing files.

✦ To digitally sign a document you need to create a digital ID. You create and manage digital IDs via several menu commands and menu options found in the Secure Task Button pull-down menu.

✦ You can apply appearance settings to your signatures in the form of scanned documents, icons, and symbols from files saved as PDF or other file formats compatible with the Create PDF From File command. You add signature appearances via the Security Preferences dialog box.

✦ You can digitally sign a document by using an existing signature field or by selecting a menu command where you are prompted to create a signature field.

✦ You can certify a document using your signature by selecting a menu command to certify the document..

✦ Trusted Identities are a list of digital ID certificates from people you share information with. You can export your public certificate to a file or attach your public certificate to an e-mail message from within Acrobat. When other users have your public certificate, they can validate your signature or encrypt documents for your use.

✦ You can encrypt files for a group of users by using their public certificates stored as Trusted Identities. A single PDF document can be secured for different users and with different permissions for each user.

✦ Envelopes are designed for Acrobat and Adobe Reader users to receive file attachements. Using eEnvelopes gives you an easy method for securing file attachments.

✦   ✦   ✦

PDFs and the Web

Throughout this book I address using PDFs on the Web. As I discussed in Chapter 6, you can download selected Web pages or entire Web sites and have all the HTML pages converted to PDF. In Acrobat 6 and 7 you can convert media, animation, and sound to PDFs with the animated pages appearing the same in Acrobat viewers as when you see them on Web sites.

In Chapter 15, I discussed comments and in Chapter 16 I covered online reviews. Coming ahead in Chapter 24, I talk about eBooks and downloading books as Digital Editions. In Chapter 27 I talk about submitting form data, and in other chapters you find similar discussions on Acrobat PDFs hosted online. In short, the Web plays a major role with much of your Acrobat activity. In this chapter I cover more about using PDFs online for viewing in Web browsers, linking to PDF views on Web sites, and creating PDFs with different Web tools.

Setting Up the Environment

To accomplish the tasks in this chapter, you use other authoring applications and set preferences for Acrobat viewers to accommodate viewing PDFs in Web browsers. When creating links and form fields in PDFs designed for Web viewing, you need to open several toolbars.

Open the Advanced Editing toolbar from the Toolbar Well. Choose Tools ⇨ Show Forms Toolbar to open the Forms toolbar. When creating form fields and links, the Properties bar can be helpful. To open the Properties bar, open a context menu on the Toolbar Well and select Properties Bar.

When the toolbars are opened, open a context menu on the Toolbar Well and select Dock All Toolbars. If the space available in the Document pane is too small for comfortable editing, you can collapse toolbars by hiding toolbar labels. Right-click in the Toolbar Well and select Show Button Labels ⇨ No Labels. For clarity in this chapter I keep the tool labels in view.

When the tools are docked in the Toolbar Well they should look something like Figure 22-1.

Figure 22-1: Open the Advanced Editing tools, the Forms tools, and the Properties bar.

When viewing PDFs in Web browsers, you may need additional tools depending on what you do in Acrobat sessions related to viewing PDFs on the Web. As you need additional tools when viewing PDFs in a browser window, you can open toolbars through the same context menu opened from the Toolbar Well in the browser window. Rather than setting up the work environment ahead of time with these additional tools, leave the tools used for viewing PDFs online hidden until you need them during a Web-viewing session.

Viewing PDFs in Web Browsers

You open a PDF in a Web browser the same way you open a file to view an HTML document. You specify a URL and filename to view the PDF directly in the browser or click on a Web link from within a PDF document to open a URL where a PDF is hosted. For example, logging on to `www.provider.com/file.pdf` results in the display of the PDF page inside the browser window. This type of viewing is referred to as inline viewing, an example of which appears in Figure 22-2.

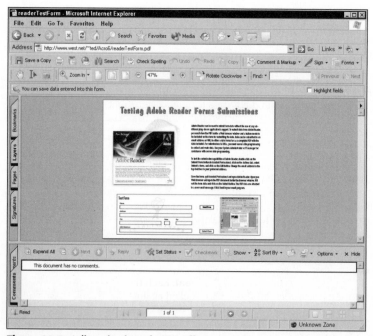

Figure 22-2: Inline viewing of PDFs offers you access to many Acrobat tools that you access from the Toolbar Well the same as when viewing PDFs in Acrobat.

In Figure 22-2 toolbars are open and docked in the Toolbar Well, and the Comments pane is open. You have access to tools, commands, and preference settings while viewing PDFs online or locally from your hard drive directly in a browser window. You open toolbars in Web browsers the same way you open them in Acrobat: selecting them from a context menu opened from the Toolbar Well.

By default, all Web-hosted PDFs are opened inside your browser. From the browser application you can save a PDF document to your hard drive by choosing File ➪ Save As. The Acrobat 6 issues that prevented Macintosh users from viewing PDFs with Apple's Safari and Microsoft Internet Explorer have been resolved in Acrobat 7.

If you prefer to open Web-hosted PDFs in Acrobat, you need to adjust preferences in Acrobat.

Setting Web-viewing preferences

Preference options provide you choices for viewing PDFs inside your Web browser as an inline view or viewing Web-hosted PDFs inside Acrobat the same as you would view locally hosted PDF documents. To change preferences, choose Edit ➪ Preferences. In the Preferences dialog box, select Internet in the left pane. The viewing preferences appear in the right pane as shown in Figure 22-3.

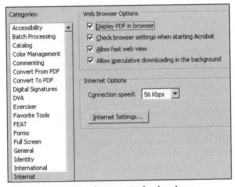

Figure 22-3: To change Web viewing preferences, open the Preferences dialog box and select Internet in the left pane.

Options for handling PDFs on Web sites with Acrobat viewers include the following:

✦ **Display PDF in browser:** The check box is enabled by default, and PDFs viewed on Web sites are displayed as inline views in browser applications. If you disable the check box, PDFs are displayed in Acrobat viewers. The default Acrobat viewer installed on your computer opens if no viewer is currently open and the target document is shown in the Acrobat viewer Document pane.

✦ **Check browser settings when starting Acrobat:** Each time you launch an Acrobat viewer, your default browser settings are checked against the viewer application. If your default browser is not configured to use the Acrobat viewer, a dialog box opens asking whether you want to set the configuration to use Acrobat with the default Web browser.

✦ **Allow fast web view:** This option speeds up viewing PDFs on Web servers. When this option is enabled, a single page is downloaded to your computer and shown according to how you set your preferences — in the browser window or in an Acrobat viewer window. As you scroll pages in a PDF document, each new page downloads when the page is loaded in the Document pane. If you deselect the check box, the entire PDF document is downloaded to your computer before the first page appears in the browser window or the Acrobat Document pane.

✦ **Allow speculative downloading in the background:** If you select the preceding Allow fast web view option, and want to continue downloading multiple page PDF documents, check this box. As you view a page, the remaining pages continue to download until the complete PDF is downloaded from a Web site.

✦ **Connection Speed:** Select the speed of your Internet connection from the pull-down menu choices. This setting applies to viewing Web pages, but also influences the speed selection for viewing multimedia.

✦ **Internet Settings:** If you click the Internet Settings button, the Internet Properties dialog box opens. In the Internet Properties dialog box you can make choices for configuring your Internet connection, choosing default applications for e-mail, making security settings choices, setting privacy attributes, and other such system-level configurations.

Working with Web links

Web links to PDFs hosted on Web sites occur from within HTML documents and from within PDF files. If using an HTML editor like Adobe GoLive CS or Macromedia Dreamweaver, or writing HTML code, you create Web links the same as you link to Web pages. A PDF Web link in HTML might look like `http://www.mycompany.com/brochure.pdf` — where the link is made to the PDF instead of a document that ends with an .htm or .html extension.

Web addresses contained in the text of a PDF document can be hot links to URLs where PDFs are hosted. In order for links from text to be functional, the complete URL address must be supplied in the text, including http://. Text in PDF documents with complete URL addresses are converted to Web links via a menu command. To create Web links from text in PDF documents, choose Advanced ➪ Links ➪ Create from URLs in Document. Acrobat opens the Create Web Links dialog box shown in Figure 22-4. In the dialog box you make decisions for the pages where the links are created. Select All to create Web links from all pages in the PDF. The From button enables you to supply page ranges in the two field boxes.

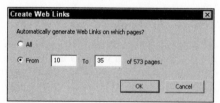

Figure 22-4: The Create Web Links dialog box enables you to target pages for creating Web links.

Acrobat can also globally remove Web links from all pages or a specified page range. To remove Web links, choose Advanced ➪ Links ➪ Remove All Links From Document. The same options are available in the Remove Web Links dialog box as those found in the Create Web Links dialog box.

Tip   You can only create Web links from text that has been properly identified in the text of the PDF file or in a text field. If you need to add a Web link, you can easily create the text in Acrobat without having to return to the authoring program. Select the TouchUp Text tool from the Advanced Editing toolbar. Hold down the Ctrl key (Option key on Macintosh) and click. The text cursor blinks where you click and is ready for you to add new type on the page. Another option is you can also add text in a header or footer and then apply the text to a range of pages or all pages in your document (select Document ➪ Add Headers & Footers). Type the URL for the Web link wherever you decide to add the text URL and deselect the text by selecting the Hand tool; then click in the Document pane. Choose Advanced ➪ Links ➪ Create from URLs in Document. Acrobat creates the Web link from the URL you added to the document. You can also create a text field using Acrobat Professional. Add URL to the text field and use the same menu command to create a link.

Web links in the Organizer

The Organizer behaves like a Web browser bookmark repository when you're creating links to URLs. You first view a PDF document as an inline view in your Web browser and access the Organizer tool in the Acrobat Toolbar Well within the browser window. The URL for the current viewed document in the Web browser is captured when you add the URL to a collection. After quitting your Web browser, you can access the URL from within Acrobat and the Organizer collections. Opening a document within a collection launches your Web browser and takes you to the URL where the PDF is located. The PDF is then opened inside the browser window if your viewing preferences remain at the defaults.

Cross-Reference   For more information on using the Organizer, see Chapter 4.

Adding Web links to multiple pages

You may have documents that need Web links created across multiple pages. An example might be a document that has been repurposed from an original design that was created for output to prepress, and then later downsampled and hosted on a Web site. In the original design you might have a Web link on the cover page, but for the Web-hosted document you may want to create a Web link to an order form or your home page on each page in the brochure document. Where the same URL is specified on each page and the location of the Web link is the same on every page, you can create the Web links in Acrobat after the PDF has been sampled for Web display. The following steps outline a procedure for creating Web links on multiple pages for similar designs or legacy files that don't have Web addresses added in the original authoring application document before a PDF has been created:

Cross-Reference   For information related to repurposing documents and downsampling, see Chapter 14.

STEPS: Creating Web links on multiple PDF pages

1. **Add a header/footer to a multi-page PDF document.** Open the file where the Web links are to be added and choose Document ➪ Add Headers & Footers. In the Add Headers & Footers dialog box, create a header or footer and set the type size, the alignment, and the offset distance desired. In this example I added a footer (center aligned), used Arial 8-point text, and set the bottom offset to 40 points as shown in Figure 22-5. Note: Be certain to add the complete URL in the box. Note: All URL Web links require you to use *http://* or *https://* preceding the domain name.

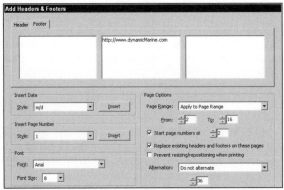

Figure 22-5: Click on the Header or Footer tab in the dialog box and add the URL text in one of the three windows at the top of the dialog box. Select a font, font size, and offset distance; then click the Insert button.

2. **Preview the header/footer.** Click the Preview button in the Add Headers & Footers dialog box. A preview of the text placement is shown in the Preview dialog box as illustrated in Figure 22-6.

3. **Create URL links.** Choose Advanced ➪ Links ➪ Create from URLs in Document. Select the All radio button in the Create Web Links dialog box and click OK. When you return to the Document pane and place the Hand tool cursor over a Web link, a Tool Tip shows the URL, as shown in Figure 22-7.

Tip   If you want Web links to appear rotated along the left or right side of your PDF document, choose Document ➪ Rotate Pages. Add a header or footer as described in the preceding steps and create the Web links described in Step 3. Choose Document ➪ Rotate Pages and select the rotation option that turns the pages back to the original view. Save the document, and the Web links are positioned vertically on each page.

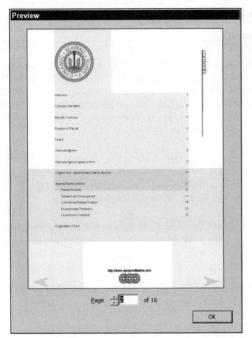

Figure 22-6: Click the Preview button before leaving the Add Headers & Footers dialog box to see how the text is placed on a page.

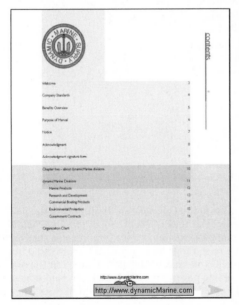

Figure 22-7: When you select the Hand tool and place the cursor over a Web link, the URL appears in a Tool Tip.

Adding Web links from form fields (Acrobat Professional only)

The disadvantage you have when using the Add Headers and Footers dialog box is that you have limited control of setting font attributes when specifying type. For example, if you want your Web links to appear in a different color to make it a little more clear to a user that a Web link exists, you don't have the options for specifying font colors when creating headers and footers. To add more flexibility when assigning font attributes you can use form fields and set the font attributes in the form-field appearance properties.

Note Form tools are not available in Acrobat Standard. If using the Link tool in Acrobat Standard, you do not have options for duplicating links across all pages. You would need to copy/paste links on each page. For Acrobat Standard users your best option is to set type in an original authoring program or use the Add Headers & Footers dialog box.

To create Web links from form fields, select the Text Field tool in the Forms toolbar. Create a form field rectangle at the location on a page where you want the link to appear. By default the Text Field Properties dialog box opens. Click on the Appearance tab, select the font type, size, and color as shown in Figure 22-8. Click on the General tab and check the box for Read Only.

Click the Options tab and type the URL in the Default Value text box. Click Close to close the Text Field Properties dialog box.

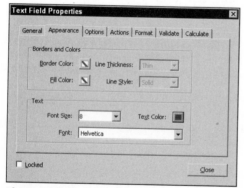

Figure 22-8: Set the Appearance properties and click Close in the Text Field Properties dialog box.

The URL is derived from the Default Value in the Options tab. To duplicate the field on the remaining pages in your document, select the Select Object tool or the Text Field tool and click on the field to select it. Open a context menu and select Duplicate. In the Duplicate Field dialog box either select All or enter the page range by selecting the From radio button and supplying the From and To page ranges. If you create the field on page 1 in the document and want to duplicate the field on the remaining pages, enter 2 in the From field box and the last page number in the To field box. In Figure 22-9, I duplicated a field from page 2 to page 12.

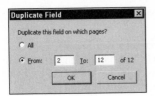

Figure 22-9: Enter the page range in the Duplicate Field dialog box to duplicate the field across the pages where you want the URL link to appear.

As a final step, choose Advanced ⇨ Links ⇨ Create from URLs in Document. Add the page range for all form fields including the first field you created. A link rectangle is placed over the form field rectangle with a link to the URL specified within the text field.

For more information on creating form fields, see Chapter 27.

Viewing Web links

Depending on how you have your Internet preferences set for Web-browser options, clicking on a URL link in Acrobat or in your Web browser either displays the PDF in the browser window or in an Acrobat viewer window. If the link is made to an HTML page, and the preferences are set to view the Web link in an Acrobat viewer, the Web page is converted to PDF with Web Capture. If you're using Adobe Reader, the PDF is displayed in the Web browser regardless of how you set your viewing preferences because Adobe Reader cannot convert Web pages to PDF.

For more information on Web capture, see Chapter 5.

Another way to view URL links is by pressing the Ctrl/Option key when clicking on a link. If the preference settings are enabled for viewing links in a Web browser, using the modifier key displays the link in your Acrobat viewer and vice versa.

When the cursor appears over a URL link you may see one of two icons in the Tool Tip. When you see a *W*, clicking the link opens the linked destination in your Web browser. When you see a plus (+) icon and click, the Web page at the URL address is converted to PDF with Web capture.

Controlling links to view behavior

By default, when you click on a URL link to a PDF document, whether from within your Web browser or from within Acrobat, the resulting view takes you to the same view established in your Initial View properties. Therefore, if your Initial View properties are set to Page Only, Single Page, Fit Page, and Page number 1, the PDF document opens in the Web browser according to these settings the same as you would view the file in Acrobat.

The links you create to open different documents and different pages in a PDF file are often unusable when you're viewing PDFs in Web browsers. A link, for example, that opens a secondary PDF won't work in a Web browser unless you modify the link properties and link to the URL where the destination document resides. The Web browser needs URL links to open secondary files. Inasmuch as you may have all links working well for CD-ROM distribution, the links need to have some adjustments made before you can host the PDF documents with useable links on Web servers.

As an example, suppose you want to open page 2 in a PDF file on a Web server. You create a link in one document, direct the link to the URL where the PDF is hosted, and instruct the Web browser or Acrobat viewer to open page 2. To create the link, use either the Link tool or a form field button and enter the following code in an Open Web Link action:

```
http://www.west.net/~ted/pdf/manual.pdf#page=2
```

In this example, the #page=2 text following the PDF filename is the trigger to open page 2. In addition to accessing user-specified pages, you can control viewing behavior for page layouts, page views, zooms, linking to destinations, and a host of other attributes you assign to the Open Web Link action. Some examples of the code to use following the PDF document name in URL links include the following:

✦ **Zoom changes:** #zoom=50, #zoom=125, #zoom=200

✦ **Fit Page view:** #view=Fit

✦ **Destinations:** #nameddest=Section1

✦ **Open Bookmarks palette:** #pagemode=bookmarks

✦ **Open Pages palette:** #pagemode=thumbs

✦ **Collapsing palettes:** #pagemode=none

✦ **Combining viewing options:** #page=3&pagemode=bookmarks&zoom=125

The preceding are some examples for controlling view options when opening PDFs in Web browsers. For each item be aware that you need to use the complete URL address and add one of these options following the location where the PDF document is hosted. Using the page mode example, the complete open action URL might look like http://www.mycompany.com/file.pdf#pagemode=bookmarks.

Creating PDFs from Web Browsers (Windows)

Acrobat on Windows with Microsoft Internet Explorer offers more features than when using other browsers or operating systems. Of the advantages found with Explorer running under Windows is the ease of converting HTML pages to PDF. Acrobat adds the Adobe PDF toolbar and Convert Current Web Page To An Adobe PDF File button to Internet Explorer 5.01 and later, which allow you to convert the currently displayed Web page to an Adobe PDF file, or convert and perform an activity in one easy operation. When you install Acrobat 7.0 Standard or Professional, the Adobe PDF toolbar is installed. From this toolbar you can select "Adobe PDF Explorer Bar" to open an explorer pane on the left of the browser window. In this pane you can click the Convert button, which converts the current Web page to an Adobe PDF file, as shown in Figure 22-10. Clicking the down-pointing arrow adjacent to the tool opens a menu with options for converting and printing Web pages.

Figure 22-10: The Adobe PDF toolbar is installed in Microsoft Internet Explorer's menu bar when Acrobat is installed on Windows. Click the down-pointing arrow adjacent to the tool on the right side of the Internet Explorer window to open a pull-down menu allowing you to convert or open the Adobe PDF Explorer Bar (shown at the left of the screen).

To convert the Web page in view in the Internet Explorer window, click on the Convert current web page to an Adobe PDF file tool; the Convert Web Page to Adobe PDF dialog box opens. Navigate to the desired location on your hard drive and click the Save button. The Web page is saved to disk much like when you use the Create PDF from Web Page tool in Acrobat.

Using the Convert current web page to an Adobe PDF file menu commands

If you want to open a Web page in Internet Explorer and convert the Web page to PDF as an appended page to an existing PDF, open the pull-down menu of the Adobe PDF toolbar. From the menu options, choose Add Web Page to Existing PDF. The Add Web Page to Existing Adobe PDF dialog box opens where you select the file to receive the page conversion as an appended page. All pages appended to documents are added after the document's last page. Click Save in the dialog box after selecting a PDF file stored on your hard drive. The current page in view in Internet Explorer is converted to PDF and added to the selected file.

When you append pages, the file that you select for adding as a new page does not open in Acrobat. The new page is appended to the selected file and the file is updated without intervention from Acrobat.

Another menu command available from the Convert current web page to an Adobe PDF file tool pull-down menu is the Print Web Page command. Rather than using the print engine supplied with Internet Explorer, you can print Web pages using Acrobat's Print command and dialog box. Options for page scaling, printing as image, and other choices available from the Acrobat Print dialog box are made available when you choose the Print Web Page command. When you select Print Web Page, the Web page is first converted to PDF and the Print dialog box opens after PDF conversion.

Other menu commands exist for converting Web pages and attaching the converted page to an e-mail message in your default e-mail application, sending the converted PDF for an e-mail review, and accessing preference settings.

Cross-
Reference

For information on sending files for reviews, see Chapter 16.

Using the Adobe PDF Explorer Bar

Another menu option available from the pull-down menu adjacent to the Convert current web page to an Adobe PDF file button is the Adobe PDF Explorer Bar. Select the menu item and the Adobe PDF Explorer window opens on the left side of the Internet Explorer window. The view appears similar to Windows Explorer where you can easily navigate your hard drive to find PDF and HTML documents, as shown in Figure 22-11.

Figure 22-11: Open the Convert current web page to an Adobe PDF file button and select Adobe PDF Explorer Bar from the menu options. The Adobe PDF Explorer Bar opens on the left side of the Internet Explorer window.

The tools visible at the top of the Explorer Bar offer the same options as when using the menu commands described earlier in this chapter for converting Web pages to PDF and appending pages. In the Explorer Bar you can easily navigate your hard drive to find the file you want to append to and make your selection in the Adobe PDF Explorer Bar by clicking on the target file.

If you want to open a PDF document in Microsoft Internet Explorer, select the PDF in the Adobe PDF Explorer Bar and double-click on the file to open in MSIE. You might use this feature to participate in an online review where the PDF document needs to be viewed in a Web browser to share online comments while you work offline on adding comments before uploading them.

Cross-Reference
For more information on online commenting, see Chapter 16.

Alternatives for users of other browsers

The ability to create a PDF from a Web page within Microsoft Internet Explorer is a convenience feature added with Acrobat running in Microsoft Windows. However, you are not disadvantaged in any way if you don't use Explorer or other operating systems for Web page to PDF conversion. You get the same results by selecting the Create PDF From Web Page tool or Create PDF Task Button menu command.

Cross-Reference
For more information on converting Web pages to PDF, see Chapter 5.

Creating PDFs in Outlook or Outlook Express (Windows)

Yet another means of simplifying workflows for PDF conversion is available to users of Outlook or Outlook Express running under Windows. Once again, you can create PDFs with other methods, so users of other mail clients are not disadvantaged other than the loss of convenient one-click operations.

After you install Acrobat, the Acrobat tools are installed in Microsoft Outlook or Outlook Express. The tools and an Adobe PDF menu appear in Outlook/Outlook Express, as shown in Figure 22-12.

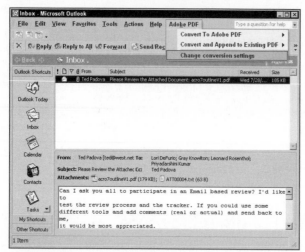

Figure 22-12: Adobe PDF tools are installed in Microsoft Outlook and Microsoft Outlook Express.

With the exception of the menu item for changing conversion settings in the Adobe PDF menu, the menu commands and the three tools on the top-left side of the Outlook window perform the same actions. The tools include the following:

For information on changing conversion settings, see Chapter 7.

✦ **Convert selected messages to Adobe PDF:** Select a message(s) in Outlook or Outlook Express and click to convert the message to a PDF document. The Save Adobe PDF File As dialog box opens enabling you to select a target folder for the converted document.

✦ **Convert selected folder to Adobe PDF:** To create an e-mail archive of a folder, click this tool. The converted documents appear in a single PDF file.

✦ **Convert and append selected messages to an existing Adobe PDF:** Click this tool when you want to append messages to a PDF document.

When you convert an e-mail message containing attachments, the attached files are added to the converted PDF document. Open the Attachments pane and you can see a list of file attachments if they were attached to the original message.

For information on working with file attachments, see Chapter 15.

Summary

✦ PDFs can be viewed inside Web browser windows. When viewed as inline views in Web browsers, Acrobat toolbars and menu options are contained within the browser window.

✦ Although Adobe PDFs can be viewed in many different Web browsers, Windows users will find more functionality when using Microsoft Internet Explorer.

✦ You change preferences settings for Web viewing PDFs in Windows in the Acrobat viewer Preferences dialog box.

✦ To make links from text in PDFs, choose Advanced ➪ Links ➪ Create from URLs in document. In order to create a link with the menu command, the complete URL address needs to be contained in the text, including http:// (or https://).

✦ To create multiple identical Web links across several pages, use the Add Headers & Footers dialog box. Type a URL as a header or footer and use the Create from URLs in document menu command to add Web links.

✦ By modifying code in the Open Web Link Action properties you can control opening views and override Initial View defaults. Add the code following the URL link to adjust page views, zooms, page modes, and so on.

✦ With Microsoft Internet Explorer running under Windows, you can convert, print, and append Web pages from within the Web browser by using tools and menu commands.

✦ The Adobe PDF Explorer window enables you to navigate your hard drive and select files for appending the page in view in the Internet Explorer window to the selected file.

✦ You can handle PDF conversion directly in Microsoft Outlook Express running under Windows. File formats compatible with the Create PDF commands are converted to PDF and attached to an e-mail message in one step.

✦　　✦　　✦

PDFs and Presentations

Among the many uses for Acrobat PDF files is for presentations. Acrobat does not provide the robust features for creating title slides, importing many different file formats in an open PDF document, or creating handouts such as those found in dedicated slide-authoring programs such as Microsoft PowerPoint. However, if you're willing to put in a little work in either designing a slide presentation in a layout program or converting a slide show from PowerPoint to PDF, you can explore many other opportunities in Acrobat for making slide presentations dynamic and suitable for any kind of audience through the use of file linking, JavaScripts, and other interactive elements. In this chapter you learn some helpful methods in producing PDF documents suited for presentations.

Setting Up the Work Environment

Interactivity is one element you'll want to add to documents designed for presentations. For adding interactive buttons and fields, open the Advanced Editing toolbar from a context menu on the Toolbar Well. Open the Forms toolbar by choosing Tools ⇨ Advanced Editing ⇨ Show Forms Toolbar. When using the Advanced Editing tools or the Forms tools, you'll find the Properties bar a valuable asset. To open the toolbar, open a context menu from the Toolbar Well and select Properties Bar. After opening the toolbars, open a context menu on the Toolbar Well and select Dock All Toolbars.

If you're familiar with the toolbar icons and don't need the tool labels, select Edit Preferences to open a context menu on the Toolbar Well. Select Show Button Labels and then select Default Labels from the submenu to hide the labels on the toolbars. For the figures in this chapter, the toolbar labels are displayed.

After setting up your work environment, the Acrobat widow should appear similar to Figure 23-1. In the figure I selected the Button tool to view the Properties bar expanded across the Document pane.

Figure 23-1: Open the Advanced Editing toolbar, Forms toolbar, and Properties bar and dock them in the Toolbar Well.

Creating Presentation Documents

The first step in creating presentations for viewing in Acrobat is making a decision for what authoring program you want to use. To convert either Microsoft PowerPoint or Apple's Keynote you can use the authoring application file to PDF. In regard to using PowerPoint, you'll want to determine whether the PDF conversion is worthwhile. If the slide presentation you create is designed to discuss Adobe Acrobat, showing the slides in Acrobat makes sense. If the presentation is designed for another topic, you need to determine whether displaying the presentation is more beneficial in an Acrobat viewer or displayed directly in PowerPoint.

If PowerPoint or another slide application program is not a tool you use and you prefer other authoring applications, conversion to PDF for showing slides in an Acrobat viewer makes a lot of sense. Obviously, PDFs offer you more functionality when showing slide presentations than the original authoring applications. Ideally, the best authoring applications to create a slide presentation, if you don't use dedicated slide authoring programs, is a layout program such as Adobe PageMaker, Adobe InDesign, Adobe FrameMaker, or QuarkXPress. These programs offer you the ability to create documents with multiple pages and assign different backgrounds to pages via master pages. In addition, some programs offer you the ability to create text blocks on master pages so the text placement, font sizes, and paragraph properties are identical on each page.

Converting PowerPoint slides to PDF

Microsoft PowerPoint files are converted to PDF similar to the way you convert other Microsoft Office files. The Adobe PDFMaker tool is installed in PowerPoint just as you find with Word, Excel, Visio, Project, and Access. The new version of Adobe Acrobat contains a self-healing feature that enables you to install Microsoft Office after you install Acrobat. The PDFMaker tools are then installed with Acrobat's self-healing feature.

Cross-Reference   For more information on conversion to PDF with the PDFMaker tool and Microsoft Office applications, see Chapter 7.

From the Adobe PDF menu, choose Change Conversion Settings as shown in Figure 23-2 to open the Acrobat PDFMaker dialog box. Select the Adobe PDF Settings you want to use for your file conversion. For presentations, the Standard Adobe PDF Settings should work sufficiently for showing slides on screens and overheads as well as printing handouts for your audience. If you want to change the compatibility settings, click the Advanced Settings button and you can custom-design Distiller Job Options.

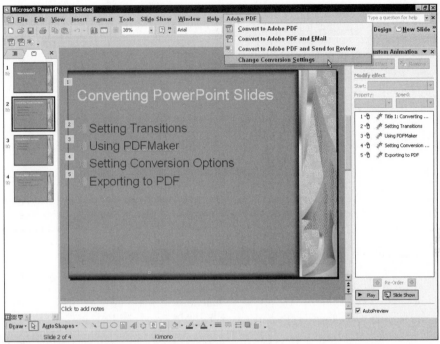

Figure 23-2: The PDFMaker toolbar and the Adobe PDF menu are installed in PowerPoint with the Acrobat installation.

Cross-Reference
For more information on changing Adobe PDF settings and using Acrobat Distiller, see Chapter 7.

As with the other Office applications discussed in Chapter 7, you click on the Convert to Adobe PDF tool in the PowerPoint toolbar to convert the slides to a PDF file.

If you want to create notes for your audience, then you need to set up PowerPoint properly for printing Notes pages. Choose File ➪ Print in PowerPoint. In the Print dialog box select the item you want to print. In this example, I chose Notes Pages as shown in Figure 23-3. Make the choice for your printer from the Name pull-down menu. Because you'll want the file set up for conversion to PDF, select the Adobe PDF printer. At the bottom of the dialog box, make choices for printing a keyline border (Frame slides), scaling if so desired, and including comments if you want to have any PowerPoint comments included in the resulting PDF.

Click Print when finished setting the attributes; the PDF is created. If you elect to view the file immediately in Acrobat, the converted slides appear in the Acrobat viewer Document pane. The document you end up with contains a slide in the top half of the pages and empty white space on the bottom of each page. If you want to add lines and any graphic elements after the PDF conversion, you can handle these edits in Acrobat.

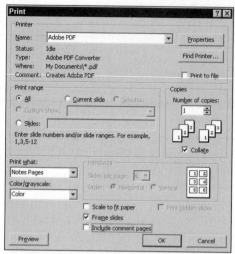

Figure 23-3: Select Adobe PDF as your target printer and choose Notes Pages from the pull-down menu choices for Print what.

To add a graphic and lines for the note takers, create a single-page PDF document in any authoring application that supports graphic imports and conversion to PDF. In this example I used Adobe Illustrator CS and added a logo and some lines at the bottom half of a standard US Letter size page, as shown in Figure 23-4.

After it's converted to PDF, open the slide show in Acrobat and choose Document ➪ Add Watermark & Background.

The PowerPoint conversion created pages with an opaque background; therefore, the tool to use is a Watermark that appears on top of the background data. In the Add Watermark & Background dialog box, I selected Add a Watermark so the new page is positioned on top of the slides as shown in Figure 23-4. Because I used Adobe Illustrator, all white space outside the graphic object and lines remains transparent and doesn't interfere with the view of the slides.

Cross-Reference   For more information on adding watermarks and backgrounds to PDFs, see Chapter 12.

Be certain All Pages is selected for the Page Range and click OK in the Add Watermark & Background dialog box. The file in Acrobat is updated to include the new data introduced with the Add Watermark & Background options as shown in Figure 23-5. After adding the data, you can send the file, along with your slide presentation, to a conference promoter for duplication and be confident all file links and fonts are contained in the document.

Note   Keep in mind that you end up with two files. One file is created as a PDF from PowerPoint for the presentation, whereas the other file is created for handout notes.

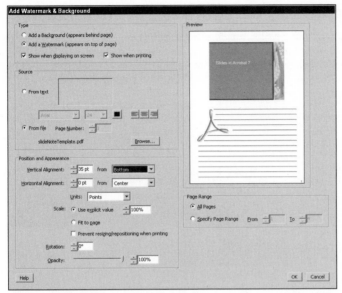

Figure 23-4: I added a Watermark by selecting the radio button for Add a Watermark and clicking the Browse button. I selected my Adobe Illustrator file saved as a PDF and opened it in the Add Watermark & Background dialog box.

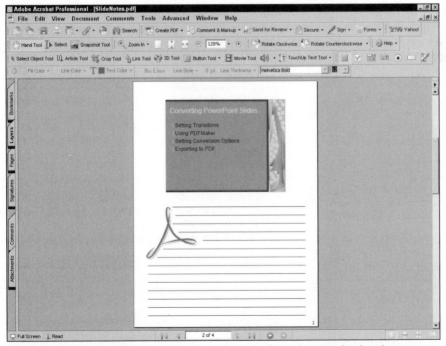

Figure 23-5: The final PDF document is ready to duplicate for attendee handouts.

Converting Apple Keynote slides to PDF (Macintosh)

A nice addition to Apple Computer's lineup of software is Keynote. Keynote is a dedicated slide presentation authoring application that offers a robust authoring environment offering simplicity and ease in creating slide shows. The charting features in Keynote are easy to use with intuitive palettes for editing chart types and data as shown in Figure 23-6.

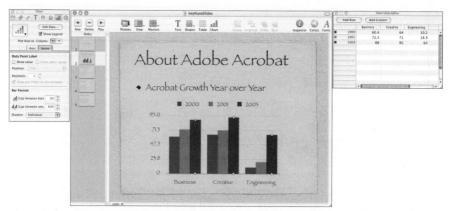

Figure 23-6: Keynote provides many attractive templates and supports charting with easy-to-use palettes for selecting chart types and editing data.

Keynote supports file imports for many image formats, video and sound, and PDF imports that can be sized and scaled. The templates installed with the program are attractive and well designed. After creating a slide show in Keynote, choose File ➪ Export. A dialog box drops down from the application menu bar where you are offered format options for exporting to QuickTime, PowerPoint, or PDF formats as shown in Figure 23-7. To export directly to PDF format, select the PDF radio button and click Next. Locate the folder where you want the PDF file saved and click the Export button.

If you want to create a PDF for handout notes, choose File ➪ Print Slides. From the pull-down menu below the Presets pull-down menus, select Keynote. Select Adobe PDF to create the PDF file using the Adobe PDF settings options. As described in converting PowerPoint presentations to PDF, the Standard preset works well for slide presentations. Select Slides with Notes and make choices as desired from the set of Options shown in Figure 23-8.

As is the case with any application on Mac OS X, you also have an option to create a PDF document by clicking the Save As PDF button. For PDF creation, you'll find writing PDFs to the Adobe PDF printer to be a better choice. When using the Adobe PDF printer you have choices for selecting the Adobe PDF settings. The Save As PDF option in the Mac OS X print dialog box offers a fixed set of options to create PDF files.

In addition to the PDF creation from Keynote documents, you can export to PowerPoint. If you are sending Keynote files to Windows users who want to edit slides, you can send an exported PowerPoint document to workgroup members who finalize your slide presentation in PowerPoint. For comments and review, your best choice is converting to PDF and starting an e-mail–based review or a browser-based commenting session.

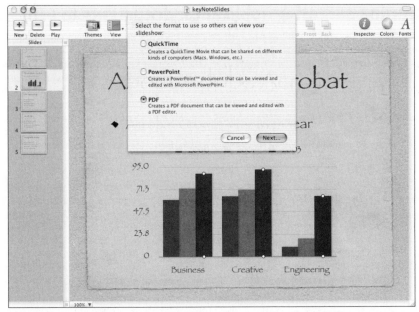

Figure 23-7: To save Keynote slide presentations to PDF, choose File ⇨ Export. Select the PDF radio button and click Next. Locate a folder where the file is to be saved and click the Export button.

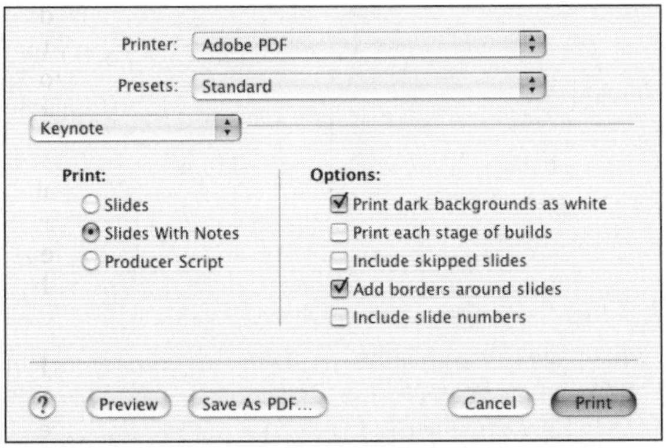

Figure 23-8: Select Keynote from the pull-down menu in the Print dialog box to open the options settings for printing the Keynote slides with notes.

Converting authoring application documents to PDF

Many creative professionals use layout programs for a variety of purposes, including slide presentations. If you use QuarkXPress, Adobe InDesign, Adobe PageMaker, or Adobe FrameMaker for creating a slide presentation, you can export your documents to PDF via the same methods used for PDF exports when preparing files for print. For creating notes and handouts, you can create master pages in any one of the applications with the graphics, lines, and style you want to use for the note appearances and import the PDF document into the layout application. Each of the aforementioned programs supports PDF imports.

Cross-Reference   For more information on converting layout program documents to PDF, see Chapter 7.

Depending on the program you use, you can set up either master pages with graphic place-holders or place and size PDF pages individually. In a program such as Adobe InDesign CS, creating Note pages is a snap. You begin by creating a master page with the design you want to use for the note handouts. On the master page add graphic elements such as the lines, text, logo, or other data. Next, create a rectangle with the Rectangle Frame tool. In this example the slide pages need to be sized down to 75%; therefore, I created the rectangle and used the Transformation palette to size the rectangle to 75% to accommodate the PDF slide pages.

After creating the template, I added pages to the document and assigned the template to each page. When it came time to import the slide file, I chose File ⇨ Place. In the Place dialog box, be certain to select Show Import Options. When the check box is enabled, InDesign opens the Place PDF dialog box, where you determine what page is placed. After clicking OK in the Place dialog box with the Show Import Options check box enabled, the Place PDF dialog box opens as shown in Figure 23-9.

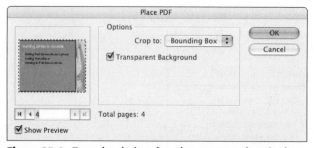

Figure 23-9: To make choices for what page to place in the InDesign file, be certain to enable Show Import Options in the Place dialog box. After clicking OK in the Place dialog box, the Place PDF dialog box opens where you can scroll pages to place the page of choice.

In the Show Import Options dialog box, click on the left- or right-pointing arrows to scroll pages. Select a page and click OK. Click the cursor in the area where the rectangle frame was drawn on the master page and the PDF page is placed and sized to the exact fit, including scaling. When the page is placed as shown in Figure 23-10, move to the next InDesign page and place the next PDF page.

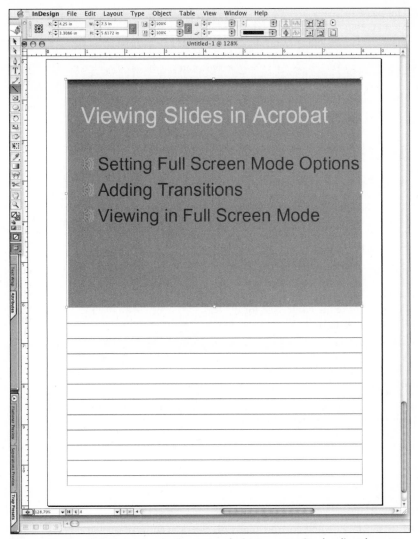

Figure 23-10: Click the cursor in the rectangle frame area after loading the page to be placed, and the PDF page drops into the frame at the size, scaling, and location prescribed on the master page.

A nice feature in InDesign is that each time you visit the Place PDF dialog box for placing the next page, the last placed page is the new default in the dialog box. Therefore, all you need to remember is to click the Next Page arrow to place the next successive page. This feature helps you avoid confusion about what page needs to follow the previous placed page.

Although InDesign happens to be my personal preference for creating a slide presentation when using a layout program, you can create similar workflows with other programs. Take advantage of the master page options in your layout program and find the simplest method for getting the PDF pages sized and placed on individual pages.

After completing PDF page imports, convert the file to PDF; you can be certain that all font embedding, image links, and a reduced file size is preserved in the resulting PDF file. You can send off the document to a conference promoter or a workgroup for commenting; the recipients won't need your original file, fonts, or links to view and print the handouts.

Using Layers with Presentations

Layers add another dimension when creating slide presentations. Using layers and toggling on and off layer views can simulate the power of presentation programs, with text popping up as you cover topics in a presentation. To create presentations using layers you need support for two essential ingredients. First, the authoring program you use needs to support layers. Second, the authoring program needs to support writing to the PDF 1.5 or greater format while preserving the layers.

You can view layers in several ways. A simple approach is to use the Link tool and create a link to set a new layer visibility. After discussing one topic, click the Link tool to show the next line of text while either hiding the previous line or showing the previous line of text with another color or tint of the color used for the text so the topic you discuss at the moment appears with visual emphasis.

When you navigate to a second page, you can use a page action to return to the default layer visibility state. Set either a Page Open or a Page Close action for Set layer visibility and collapse the layers. Thus, each time you show the slide presentation, the layers return to the default you want to use when addressing a new audience.

In Figure 23-11, I created a slide presentation with layers. The bullets at the bottom of the slide trigger layer visibility. The last line of text is the current topic being discussed. The four lines of text above the last line are subjects already discussed. Each bullet contains a link that shows a new layer state. When the page opens, a page action hides all the text below the slide title.

Cross-Reference   For information on showing and hiding layers and changing layer states, see Chapter 19.

One thing to remember when creating files with layers in authoring programs is to set the layer visibility in the original authoring program to the visibility you want to appear in the Acrobat PDF document before conversion to PDF. In the earlier example, all layers were hidden before the file was converted to PDF except the Background, Logo, and HeadType layers. The link buttons were added to show the text from the hidden layers created in the original authoring application.

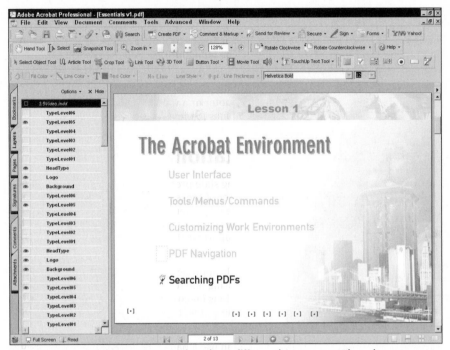

Figure 23-11: Link buttons are used to show different layer states. When the page opens, a page action sets the layer state to the Initial View.

Editing Slides in Acrobat

Invariably, you will need to edit slides after PDF creation and after adding all the interactive elements in the final PDF presentation. You may be speaking at a conference or seminar and find out at the last minute that one topic or another won't fit your assigned session or that someone asks you to cover another topic. Or you may have everything well prepared and need to do a little tweak on rewording a topic, moving a graphic, or introducing a new graphic. Rather than returning to the authoring program, you can make these minor edits in Acrobat.

For text editing, be certain that all fonts are loaded before opening Acrobat. If you open Acrobat first and load a font using a utility such as Adobe Type Manager (Windows) or Extensis Suitcase, the font isn't recognized by Acrobat until you quit the program and re-launch it after loading the font. When transferring files to laptop computers for presentations, be certain you have all the needed fonts installed on the computer and the tool you use to handle font management.

Tip   For a super font-management tool, log on to `www.extensis.com` and download Suitcase for either the Macintosh or Windows. You can try out the software for 30 days without buying the product. After assessing the product for your use, you can purchase Suitcase online and obtain the serial number to continue use. Suitcase does a superb job on both Macintosh OS X and Windows 2000 and XP.

Editing text

As an example for editing text in PDF documents, take a look at Figure 23-12. The title of the slide has two blocks of text. One text block is a drop shadow and the other text block appears in a color above the drop shadow. In order to edit the text, the two different lines need to be separated so you can use the TouchUp Text tool to edit each line of text. In this example, I used the TouchUp Object tool to move the top line of the title text down toward the bottom of the page.

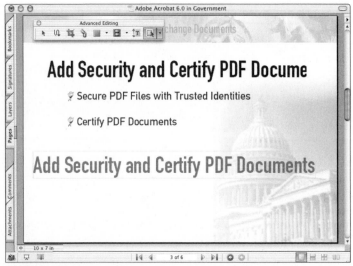

Figure 23-12: The original title text appeared at the top of the slide. Using the TouchUp Object tool, I moved the top line of text to the bottom of the slide.

After the text is moved and is easily accessed, select the TouchUp Text tool and click in a line of text. Press the Ctrl/⌘+A keys to select all the text in the line and type the new line of text. In this example I changed the entire line of text and repeated the steps for each line used as the slide title. When you complete the text edit, select the TouchUp Object tool to move the text to position. To nudge a line of text press the arrow keys on your keyboard. The finished edit in this example appears in Figure 23-13.

As you make text edits in a file you'll find that text blocks may have some structural problems, and editing a line of text and moving it around the slide won't always be easy. You may need to cut a line of text and use Ctrl/Option+click with the TouchUp Text tool and paste the line of text into a new text block. You can then select the TouchUp Object tool and move the text around the page as a single line of text apart from the paragraph from which it was copied.

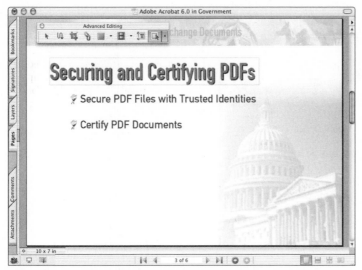

Figure 23-13: Edit text with the TouchUp Text tool and move the text back to position with the TouchUp Object tool.

Copying/pasting text and images

Continuing with the example slide discussed in the preceding section, I need to add a third line of text for another topic. In this case I need to duplicate a line of text and the graphic beside the subheads. To duplicate the objects, select the TouchUp Object tool and drag through the objects to select them. Choose Edit ➪ Copy. While the objects are selected, you can't paste them back into the document. First, click outside the selection to deselect everything; then choose Edit ➪ Paste.

In this example, I place the pasted objects in the center of the page. To move the objects to a precise location, press Ctrl/⌘+R to show rulers. Drag the ruler guides to mark the alignment for the pasted objects; then drag the objects to position with the TouchUp Object tool as shown in Figure 23-14.

As a final step, edit the text line with the TouchUp Text tool. Choose File ➪ Save As and overwrite the file to optimize it.

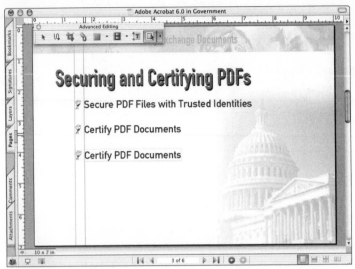

Figure 23-14: After pasting the objects, show the rulers and drag guidelines for positioning the pasted objects. Drag to position with the TouchUp Object tool.

Adding Page Transitions

Page transitions are available in both Edit mode and Full Screen mode in Acrobat. You can set page transitions for all pages in a file or from selected pages in the Pages palette. You can batch-process files and apply transitions on a group of documents with a batch command.

Cross-Reference   For more information on creating batch sequences, see Chapter 14.

To set transitions on all pages or a specified range of pages in a document while remaining in Edit mode (as opposed to Full Screen mode), choose Document ➪ Set Page Transitions. If you want to set transitions for pages in a noncontiguous order, open the Pages palette and Ctrl/⌘+click on the individual pages where you want page transitions. After making the page selections, choose Document ➪ Set Page Transitions. The Set Transitions dialog box opens as shown in Figure 23-15.

Note   You can also set Page Transitions by right-clicking (Windows) or Control+clicking (Macintosh) on a page thumbnail and selecting Set Page Transitions to open the Set Transitions dialog box. Also, select the Options pull-down menu in the Pages palette and select Set Page Transitions to open the same dialog box.

Figure 23-15: The Set Transitions dialog box offers you a wide range of choices for transition effects you can apply to pages while viewing documents in Edit mode.

From the Effect pull-down menu you select the transition effect to be applied for the pages selected either in the dialog box or from the range of pages selected in the Pages palette. Acrobat offers you a total of 40 different choices. One choice is to set no transition, with the remaining 39 choices being different effects.

If you enable Auto Flip, pages are scrolled at an automatic interval according to the number of seconds you select from the pull-down menu below the Auto Flip check box. Choices for the interval are between 1 and 32,767 seconds. You can select fixed interval options or type a value within the acceptable range. If you want to manually scroll pages, leave the check box disabled.

If you don't select pages in the Pages tab, use the Set Transitions dialog box to apply transitions to All pages in document, or specify a page range in a contiguous order by clicking on the Pages range and typing in the page From and To field boxes. When you select pages in the Pages tab, the Pages selected in the Pages panel check box becomes active by default and the transitions are applied to the selected pages.

After setting the effects and page range, click OK and transitions are applied to the pages when you scroll pages in Edit mode.

Although it isn't necessary with all the new features in Acrobat 7, you can apply page transitions in authoring applications prior to PDF conversion. If you happen to have an old Acrobat 3 installer CD you'll find a folder on the CD titled Transitions. The Transitions folder contains EPS files with PostScript code to create transitions when pages are scrolled in Edit mode. If you use a layout application to create your slide presentations, place one of the EPS transition effects on a master page in your layout program and convert to PDF. The transitions are applied to all the pages as you scroll through the document. If you elect to use this method, you don't have the flexibility for quickly changing transition effects. The one advantage is that any user of older versions of Acrobat can create PDF documents with transitions by using this method.

Using Full Screen Views

Full Screen mode offers you many different viewing options when you want to show a slide presentation where viewing in Edit mode is not necessary. If your presentation requires a discussion of Acrobat and you want to access tools and menu commands, working in Edit mode is the most obvious choice. When you use Full Screen mode, the menu bar and tools are hidden from view, but the viewing options and alternatives for showing slides in Acrobat are much greater.

Setting Full Screen preferences

The first task in working with Full Screen mode is to set up the environment for showing slides by setting the Full Screen preferences. Choose Edit ➪ Preferences (Acrobat ➪ Preferences on the Macintosh) or press Ctrl/⌘+K. In the left pane, select Full Screen and the preference choices appear as shown in Figure 23-16.

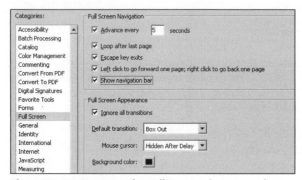

Figure 23-16: To set up the Full Screen view, open the Preferences dialog box and click on Full Screen in the left panel.

The preference choices include

✦ **Advance every:** If you enable the check box, the slide presentation automatically scrolls pages at the interval specified in the field box adjacent to the check box. The values permitted for the interval are between 1 and 60 seconds.

✦ **Loop after last page:** Using this option and the preceding setting for auto advancing, you can set up a kiosk and have the slide presentation continue with auto repetition. After the last page is viewed, the presentation begins again, showing the first page and continuing in an infinite loop.

✦ **Escape key exists:** Entering the Full Screen mode is handled by setting the Initial View options or pressing Ctrl/⌘+L. If you want to exit Full Screen view you can press the Esc key when this check box is enabled. Be certain to leave the check box at the default switch. If you disable the check box, you need to remember to use Ctrl/⌘+L to exit Full Screen view.

✦ **Left click to go forward one page; right click to go back one page:** When this check box is enabled, you can navigate pages with mouse clicks. For both Windows and Macintosh users who use a two-button mouse, clicking on the left or right button navigates pages in the respective direction.

✦ **Show navigation bar:** This feature is new in Acrobat 7. When the check box is enabled, icons appear in the lower-left corner of the screen permitting you to go to the previous slide or next slide, or exit Full Screen mode. In Figure 23-17 the three arrow icons are visible when this preference choice is checked.

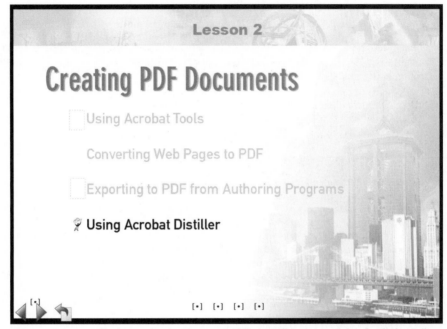

Figure 23-17: To display navigation buttons while in Full Screen mode, check the Full Screen preference choice for Show navigation bar.

✦ **Ignore all transitions:** If you set transitions while in Edit mode and want to eliminate the transition effects while in Full Screen view, enable this check box.

✦ **Default transition:** From the pull-down menu you have choices for 1 of 39 different transition effects. If you apply a transition in the Full Screen preferences, all pages use the same transition. Selecting Random from the menu choices offers you effects that change randomly as you move through slide pages. If you want to use specific transitions that change for selected pages, set the transitions from the Document ➪ Set Page Transitions menu command before opening the Preferences dialog box. Disable Ignore all transitions and the effects you choose for page transitions applied to selected pages in the Pages palette are used when you enter Full Screen mode.

✦ **Mouse cursor:** You have three choices from the pull-down menu for the mouse cursor display while viewing slides in Full Screen mode. You can choose from Always Visible, Always Hidden, or Hidden After Delay. The Hidden After Delay menu choice shows the cursor position when you scroll pages, and then hides it after a short delay (usually a two- to three-second delay).

✦ **Background color:** Click on the color swatch and the preset color palette opens where you can make choices for the background color. The background color appears outside the slide pages on all pages that do not fit precisely within the monitor frame. If you want to use a custom color, click on Other Color at the bottom of the palette and select a custom color from your system palette.

After setting the Preferences, you can enter Full Screen mode by pressing Ctrl/⌘+L. If you want your PDF document to always open in Full Screen view, open the Document Properties dialog box (File ⇨ Document Properties) and click on Initial View. Enable the check box in the Window Options for Open in Full Screen mode. Save the file and each time it opens, the document starts in Full Screen mode.

Cross-Reference   For more information on setting the Initial View options, see Chapter 3.

Scrolling pages

To advance through slides when in Full Screen mode you can use the preference setting to scroll pages with mouse clicks. If the preference choice for *Left click to go forward one page; right click to go back one page* is disabled, you scroll pages with keystrokes. Press the Page Down or Page Up keys to move forward and backward through slides. In addition, you can use the up or left arrow keys to move backward and the down or right arrow keys to move forward. Use the Home key to move to the first page and the End key to move to the last page. If you want to move to a specific page without leaving Full Screen mode, press Shift+Ctrl/⌘+N and the Go to Page dialog box opens. Enter the page number to open in the field box and click OK.

Using PowerPoint effects

PDF documents have never been more dynamic than the support for Power Point effects and animation that were introduced in Acrobat 6 and continue in Acrobat 7. With all the new animation and multimedia support, you can view motion in PDF documents in new ways. It stands to reason, therefore, that support for moving text, flying bullets, and motion objects created in Microsoft PowerPoint are now viewed in Acrobat as you might see them in PowerPoint.

If you start in PowerPoint and add animation to slides such as Entrance, Emphasis, Exit, or Motion Paths, and create a PDF document with PDFMaker, the effects are shown in Acrobat when the PDF is viewed in Full Screen mode. In Figure 23-18, I created a slide presentation in PowerPoint and applied motion paths to text on slides.

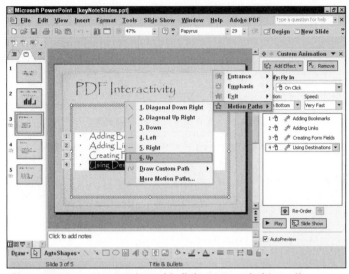

Figure 23-18: In PowerPoint, add all the type and object effects you want to display in the PDF document and convert to PDF with PDFMaker. View the PDF document in Full Screen mode and the animation is shown in Acrobat according to the effects applied in PowerPoint.

After converting the PowerPoint document to PDF, open the Preferences dialog box in Acrobat and disable the Ignore all transitions check box. If you enable the check box, the slides are shown as a flat file with all the text on a slide in view as you scroll pages. When the check box is disabled, the slide begins with the slide title in view. As you scroll pages, the animation shows the text on the slide with the motion applied in PowerPoint.

Tip

If you want to apply page transitions after converting a PowerPoint slide to PDF with the motion objects defined, leave the Ignore all transitions check box disabled in the Preferences dialog box. In Edit mode choose Document ⇨ Set Page Transitions. Select the transition effect you want to show in Full Screen mode and click OK. If you want different transitions applied to different pages, select the pages in the Pages palette and apply transition effects to specific pages, then open the Set Transitions dialog box, select Pages selected in Pages panel, and click OK. When you view the PDF in Full Screen mode, the slides are viewed with transitions along the PowerPoint motion effects.

Creating interactivity in Full Screen mode

You may have a slide presentation that does not require access to Acrobat menus and tools, but you want to show cross-document links. Perhaps you have a presentation about a company's financial status, economic growth, or projected growth and you want to show a financial spreadsheet, another PDF document, or a scanned image of a memo or report. The slide show created in PowerPoint with the motion objects and viewing in Full Screen view is what you want, but you also want the flexibility for opening other files without leaving Full Screen mode.

Creating links and buttons for cross-document linking

If you want to open a secondary document while in Full Screen mode, you can create links or form field buttons to secondary files. When you click on the link, the link action is invoked. If opening a secondary file, the file link opens in Full Screen mode. After viewing the file, press Ctrl/⌘+W to close the file and return to the last slide view, also in Full Screen mode.

To set up a file link, create a link or form field button and select Open a file in the Select Action pull-down menu. Click the Add button and select the file to open. When the Specify Open Preference dialog box opens, select New window as shown in Figure 23-19. Click OK and click the Close button. When you view the file in Full Screen mode and click the button, the secondary file opens in Full Screen mode, leaving the slide presentation open in Acrobat.

Figure 23-19: Select New window in the Specify Open Preference dialog box. When you click on the link, the secondary file opens in Full Screen mode.

The same behavior exists with other link actions. You can create a URL link to display a Web site while in Full Screen mode by using the Open a web link action. Click on the link and your Web browser opens at the specified URL. When you quit the Web browser, you are returned to the slide presentation in Full Screen mode. If you use PowerPoint effects, the effects are not disturbed.

Cross-Reference   To learn more about setting link actions, see Chapter 17.

Using interactive devices

Another interactivity tool that you can use with Full Screen view is a remote control device. For about $50 to $75 US, you can purchase a handheld remote control. The control comes in two parts. The control device has two buttons used for moving forward and backward in the slide presentation. The companion unit is plugged into a USB port on your laptop or desktop computer. You open the slide presentation in Full Screen view and click the left or right button to navigate slides while you walk across a stage. Some devices also have a button for cursor control. You can remotely move the cursor on a slide and click a button that opens a secondary file, Web link, or other action associated with the button or link.

When using remote devices, be certain to set your Full Screen preferences to *Left click to go forward one page; right click to go back one page*. The USB devices have two buttons enabling you to move backward and forward through your slide presentation. When the check boxes are enabled, the back and forward buttons on the handheld device are supported.

Summary

✦ You convert PowerPoint slides to PDF with the PDFMaker tool.

✦ To create note handouts from PowerPoint, use the Print dialog box and print the file to the Adobe PDF printer after making the attribute choices in the Print dialog box for the type of handouts you want to create.

✦ Apple Keynote slides can be exported to PDF and PowerPoint formats. Keynote offers Macintosh users a robust slide creation program with easy, intuitive palettes and tools.

✦ You can use layout programs to create slide presentations. For creating handout notes, set up a master page with objects and elements to be added to each page. Import the PDF slide presentation and convert to PDF to distribute handouts.

✦ Layered PDFs add additional viewing options in slide presentations. To create layered PDFs you need to use programs supporting layers and exporting to the PDF 1.5 or above format.

✦ Minor edits can be effectively made in Acrobat without returning to an authoring program. For last-minute changes, use the TouchUp Text tool to edit text and the TouchUp Object tool to move text, and copy and paste text and objects.

✦ You apply page transitions to pages individually using the Document ➪ Set Page Transitions command. To apply different transitions to different pages, select pages in the Pages palette and adjust the transitions in the Set Transitions dialog box.

✦ When using Full Screen mode, open the Preferences dialog box and select Full Screen. Make choices for options used in Full Screen viewing and click OK.

✦ Full Screen views support file linking with link and button actions, Microsoft PowerPoint animation, and transitions applied to pages with either the Full Screen preferences or the Set Page Transitions command.

✦ ✦ ✦

PDFs and eBooks

The promise of eBooks has been a roller coaster ride for users, providers, and would-be authors in recent years. The fall of some important content providers, coupled with some not-so-impressive display mechanisms, has slowed down an industry that many thought had a lot of promise. Notwithstanding hardware-display mechanisms and user acceptability, the software used to secure eBooks and make them accessible to every potential consumer was not as robust as viewing documents in Acrobat viewers.

With the introduction of Acrobat 6, Adobe Systems waved good-bye to the Adobe eBook Reader software and offered users, content providers, and content authors a much more attractive means of creation, protection, and delivery of eBooks. In Acrobat 7 the eBook branding has changed to Digital Editions, but the development and delivery for eBooks remains the same in Acrobat 7 as was introduced in Acrobat 6. Built into the Acrobat viewers, including Adobe Reader, Acrobat Standard, and Acrobat Professional, is Digital Editions' support for borrowing, purchasing, managing, and reading eBooks with a few new tools, making the reading process easier. In this chapter you take a look at how to set up an account to acquire eBooks and how to read and manage them in Acrobat.

Setting Up the eBook Work Environment

The eBooks Task Button has been eliminated in all Acrobat viewers. Accessing Digital Editions is all handled in menu commands. There are no special tools to load for acquiring or reading eBooks. From the Toolbar Well open a context menu and select Reset Toolbars. The default tools are sufficient for following along in this chapter.

Setting Up an Account

When you install Acrobat you are provided an option for setting up an Activator Account for handling eBook borrowing and purchasing. If you elect to postpone activation you can set up an account at any time by choosing Advanced ➪ Digital Editions ➪ Adobe Digital Media Store. In Adobe Reader select File ➪ Digital Editions ➪ Digital Media Store.

Your default Web browser launches, and the activation page on Adobe's Web site appears in your browser window. If you have an existing account you can click a button for Activate and your account is updated to include the eBook activation. If you haven't set up an account you are provided options for activating an account with Adobe Systems. Supply a user name and password, and you are taken to the activation page where you click Activate to create your account with your new user name and password. Activating an account either with Adobe Systems or Microsoft.Net is done without any fees for services.

To activate additional accounts choose Advanced ➪ Digital Editions ➪ Authorize Devices. You Web browser again takes you to Adobe's Web site where you can sign up for Microsoft.Net services.

Activating multiple devices

If you have an account on one computer and want to open eBooks on another computer, you need to activate all devices. Follow the same steps noted previously for "Setting Up an Account" and log on to Adobe's Web site. Follow the onscreen information for activating your second device and you're ready to view and manage eBooks on your other computer(s). If you have a handheld device such as a Palm Pilot, you need to activate your account on it. To activate a Palm device, place the unit in its synchronization cradle and choose Advanced ➪ Digital Editions ➪ Authorize Devices. On the Adobe Web site, click the Activate Palm OS Device button.

You must activate your account before you can download eBooks designed to be used with Acrobat viewers. If you attempt to download an eBook without activating your account, Adobe's Web site and activation page opens in your Web browser where you follow the same steps mentioned earlier for "Setting Up an Account" to create an account. You can receive eBooks from other users who send you content via e-mails or downloads. If the file is encrypted with Adobe DRM (Digital Rights Management), again you are required to create an account and comply with the purchase requirements before gaining access to the content.

Adobe Content Server 3

You handle the default Digital Rights Management (DRM) for eBooks viewed with Acrobat viewers with Adobe's server-side software. The Adobe Content Server 3 enterprise solution is designed for content providers to encrypt and manage electronic content with the highest levels of security. End users need not be concerned with the product. Your task is the acquisition of content encrypted with the Adobe Content Server 3 product.

Note Adobe partners such as FileOpen Systems, Authentica, SealedMedia, and DocuRights offer third-party solutions that legally use the Adobe Reader technology.

For enterprises, however, your mission is to protect against unauthorized distribution of your products. With the Adobe Content Server 3 product or other third-party solutions you can protect documents and distribute them to users meeting your requirements for distribution. If a user exchanges your content with another user who has not obtained permission to access the content, the user is directed to the Web site where he or she can purchase the product. Enterprises interested in finding out more about the Adobe Content Server 3 product can log on to www.adobe.com/products/contentserver.

Acquiring eBooks

After setting up your activation account, you're ready to download eBooks and store them in your Digital Editions library — a feature built into all Acrobat viewers. You can test the activation and eBook download procedures by downloading sample eBooks free of charge from Adobe's Web site.

To download an eBook, choose Advanced ⇨ Digital Editions ⇨ Adobe Digital Media Store. Your Web browser launches and takes you to the Adobe eBook Mall. On the Web page you find helpful information about purchasing eBooks and some sample books you can download for free. From a pull-down menu you can select the country where you live and download eBooks in other languages. The default location is for USA and Canadian users.

Click on a book to download, and a progress bar displays the download progress. When the download completes, you are prompted in a dialog box whether you want to read the downloaded book. Click OK and the book opens in your Acrobat viewer as shown in Figure 24-1.

Figure 24-1: If you click OK in the dialog box asking whether you want to read a downloaded eBook, the eBook opens in the Document pane.

If you select No when asked whether you want to read an eBook, the downloaded material is stored in My Digital Editions. Depending on the borrowing time frame, you can read the book at any time by opening your Digital Editions and double-clicking on the book you want to read. My Digital Editions stores all downloaded eBooks and any other PDF documents you want to organize and store in an easily accessible and organized manner. For Adobe Reader users the My Digital Editions bookshelf is ideal for storing all documents, For Acrobat users the Organizer is a much better solution for document storage.

Cross-Reference   For information on using the Organizer, see Chapter 4.

To open My Digital Editions, choose Advanced ➪ Digital Editions ➪ My Digital Editions. The Digital Editions opens as a floating window on top of the Document pane as shown in Figure 24-2.

Figure 24-2: To view, organize, and read eBooks, open My Digital Editions and view all content stored in your personal library.

Acquiring eBooks in PDF format is not limited to downloads from the Adobe Systems Web site. When you log on to the Adobe eBook Mall, Adobe partner Web sites and third-party links take you to other Web sites hosting eBooks. In addition, you can browse the Internet and download eBooks from content providers using the Adobe Content Server 3 software or other third-party solutions for eBook management and distribution.

Managing eBooks

eBooks are managed in the My Digital Editions window shown in Figure 24-2. Downloading an eBook automatically adds the eBook to My Digital Editions with the most recent download appearing first in the default thumbnail list. In the Digital Editions window you have several tools and commands to help you organize books, acquire new content, and create category listings for storing books according to preset or custom topics. The options contained in the My Digital Editions window include

✦ **Add File:** The first button at the top-left corner of the My Digital Editions window enables you to add any PDF document to the Digital Editions. Click the Add button and a dialog box opens where you navigate your hard drive and select a document to add to the list. Click the Add File button and the new acquisition is placed at the first position on the left side of the current thumbnail.

✦ **Adobe Digital Media Store:** Click this button and you are returned to the Adobe Web site eBook Mall in your Web browser.

✦ **Category views:** The default is All. From the pull-down menu you select which category you want to view on the Digital Editions. Each eBook can be categorized with one of the preset categories created when you installed Acrobat or a custom category you create in the My Digital Editions window.

✦ **Views:** The two icons adjacent to the pull-down menu offer viewing options in the library. By default, thumbnail views are shown in the list. Thumbnails are created from the first page in a document. If you select the second icon, you have a detail view listing the Title, Author, Date Last Accessed, and Category. By clicking on the heading you can sort your eBooks by any one of these four options.

✦ **Read:** To read a book you can double-click on one of the books in the list or select an eBook and click the Read button. When you read a book, it opens in the Acrobat Document pane and the Digital Editions window is hidden. To reopen the window, choose Advanced ⇨ Digital Editions ⇨ My Digital Editions.

✦ **Email:** If the eBook contains a URL for the Digital Edition retailer, and the permissions allow you to *share* with others, you will be able to e-mail it. Select Email and the selected file is attached to a new e-mail message. If e-mailing Digital Editions does not include sharing rights, a dialog box opens informing you that you cannot e-mail the document,

✦ **Save a Copy:** Click Save a Copy and save a duplicate of a selected eBook. Be certain to click on the book you want to copy before clicking the Save button.

✦ **Actions:** Actions opens a menu with the same menu options found when opening a context menu on an edition.

✦ **Backup:** Click Backup to back up copies of your editions. For more information on Backup see "Backing up eBooks" later in this chapter.

✦ **Send to Mobile Device:** This button works only when you install Adobe software for handheld devices. Click this button if you have installed software to read PDFs on handheld devices and want to copy a document to your handheld device. You must first activate your device for eBooks as described earlier in this chapter before copying an eBook to the device.

✦ **Summary window:** The window in the lower-left corner of the Digital Editions lists information relative to a selected document. Some information is derived from the Document Summary of the PDF file, and other information may include total pages in the book, filename, ISBN number, publisher, and so on.

✦ **Category:** There are two category lists. You apply a category by selecting a document and opening the pull-down menu for one of the categories. The document is assigned to one or two different categories. If you make selections from both pull-down menus the book is categorized for two categories and appears when books are sorted for either category. When you return to the category views at the top of the window and select a category, only those documents specified for the respective category are shown in either the thumbnail list or the alphabetical list.

✦ **Time-out:** If you borrow an eBook a tiny clock icon appears in the top-right corner of the borrowed eBook. Such books are borrowed for a limited-time use. After reading a borrowed book, click on the clock icon and the Document Expiration dialog box opens, as shown in Figure 24-3. You can view the information about the lending period or choose to return the book. If you select Return to Lender, the book is eliminated from your Digital Editions. If you click OK, the book remains in your library until you return it, delete it, or refresh the Digital Editions.

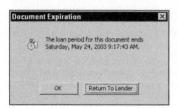

Figure 24-3: Click on a clock icon on a book in My Digital Editions and the Document Expiration dialog box opens. Click OK to keep the book on the Digital Editions or click Return to Lender to eliminate the book from the Digital Editions.

Categorizing documents

The term *documents* is used here to globally refer to both PDF documents you add to the Digital Editions and eBooks you acquire. Acrobat enables you to add both eBooks you download from content providers and PDF documents you add from files on your hard drive to the Digital Editions. If you want to view all eBooks, open the pull-down menu for the category views and select All eBooks. Likewise, if you want to open all documents (as opposed to only your eBooks), select All Documents from the pull-down menu. In addition, you'll notice the separate listings for categories such as Fiction, History, Mystery, and so on.

You also find an option for All Subscription Issues in the pull-down menu at the top of the window. A new Adobe Preview Book Club is sponsored by Adobe. Log on to the Adobe Digital Media Store and you can find information for subscribing to periodicals.

When you download an eBook it may have a category associated with the book and fall into one of the category listings. If you want to reorganize an eBook or document from one category to another, select the thumbnail for the item to be reorganized, and open the Category1 pull-down menu. Make the category selection from the list of menu items while the item is selected in the thumbnail list or when viewing the books in a list view.

If you want to create a new category, open the pull-down menu for the category views at the top of the window and select Edit Categories. The Digital Editions Categories dialog box opens as shown in Figure 24-4. Type a new category name and click the Add button. The new category listing is added to the pull-down menu and also added to the Category1 and Category2 pull-down menus. To place a book in the new category, select it in the Digital Editions and open either the Category1 or Category2 pull-down menu. Select the new category name, and the book is categorized according to the new listing.

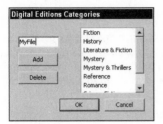

Figure 24-4: To create a new category, select Edit Categories from the category views pull-down menu. Add a name to the field box and click the Add button in the Digital Editions Categories dialog box.

Using a context menu

You can manage eBooks through menu commands available by opening a context menu on the Digital Editions. Open a context menu from an eBook and the following commands are available to you:

✦ **Read:** Selecting the Read command results in the same action as double-clicking on a book. The document opens in the Document pane.

✦ **Remove:** Selecting this menu option deletes the currently selected item from the Digital Editions. You can delete only a single book at a time.

✦ **Email:** When you select this menu choice and the publisher has given permission to enable e-mailing of the document, the Document Email Options dialog box opens. You have two choices available in the dialog box. Select the Mail a copy of the document as an attachment radio button or the Mail a link to a Web site where the recipient can obtain a copy of the document radio button. If you choose the first option, the entire eBook is attached to a new e-mail message in your default e-mail application. If you choose the second option, your e-mail application opens with a URL link to where the recipient can download the eBook. For either choice you can add to the message window in your e-mail application and specify recipient address(s) and copies of the message. If you e-mail a copy of a document secured with the Adobe Content Server 3 software, the recipient is instructed on how to purchase and activate the content.

✦ **Save a Copy:** This menu option is the same as clicking the Save a Copy button in the Digital Editions toolbar.

✦ **Check for New Issues:** If you subscribe to a service that publishes new issues, you can check for newer issues of a particular publication.

✦ **Subscription Preferences:** This option opens a dialog box where you set preferences for subscription services.

✦ **Visit Subscription Web Site:** Use this option to launch your default Web browser and navigate to the subscription Web site where you obtained the eContent.

✦ **Send to Mobile Device:** This menu option performs the same operation as clicking the Send to Mobile Device button.

✦ **Return to Lender:** This option is the same as clicking on the clock icon and selecting the Return to Lender button.

Backing up eBooks

In the lower-right corner of the Digital Editions is a button you can use to back up your books. Click Backup and the Backup and Restore Digital Editions dialog box opens. If you have content you purchased and other content that's hard to replace, you'll want to copy your books to another source. You can copy to a server, another computer on your network, another hard drive attached to your computer, or an external media storage device.

In the Backup and Restore Digital Editions dialog box, select Backup and choose the categories you want to back up from the pull-down menu. For backing up all eBooks, leave the default menu choice at All. If you added comments to books, you can choose to back up your comments by selecting the check box for Include user comments and markup, as shown in Figure 24-5.

Figure 24-5: Make choices for what categories to back up and whether to include comments and markups in your backup. Click OK and the Browse for Folder dialog box opens.

Click OK in the dialog box and the Browse for Folder dialog box opens where you can navigate to the destination where all the eBooks are saved. In the Browse for Folder dialog box, a button offers you an option for creating a new folder. Create a folder and click OK, and all your books are backed up to the device selected in the Browse for Folder dialog box.

Copying eBooks to Handheld Devices

To copy files to a handheld device such as a Palm Pilot, you need to download the Adobe Reader for Palm OS software. Visit Adobe's Web site at `www.adobe.com/products/acrobat/readermain.html`. Click the Get Acrobat Reader for Palm OS button on the Adobe Reader page and follow the directions to download the Adobe Reader software on your Palm OS device.

Note   Be certain to upgrade to an Acrobat viewer 6.0 or greater and Palm OS 3.0 or greater.

After Adobe Reader is installed on your handheld, you need to activate your device for downloading eBooks. Open Acrobat and choose Advanced ➪ Digital Editions ➪ Authorize Devices. If you've already set up an account, you'll see the Adobe DRM Activator Web page with a button for activating a Palm OS device. Click the button to activate your Palm device.

After activation, open Acrobat and select My Digital Editions from the eBooks Task Button pull-down menu. The button for Send to Mobile Device is added to the Digital Editions toolbar when you install the Adobe Reader for Palm OS software. If you haven't downloaded an eBook to your Digital Editions for copying to your Palm device, you need to first download the eBook and store it on your Digital Editions. When the book appears in the Digital Editions, select it and click the Send to Mobile Device button. A dialog box opens with instructions on how to prepare the file for copying to the mobile device as shown in Figure 24-6.

Figure 24-6: To copy an eBook to a mobile device, select the book to be copied in the Digital Editions and click the Send to Mobile Device button.

In the Transfer to mobile device dialog box, click Prepare. Acrobat prepares the file for delivery to the mobile device by restructuring the document. A progress bar shows the status of preparation and eventually you'll see the Adobe Reader for Palm OS dialog box open with your file added to the Files to Transfer list. If you want to add files stored on your computer to be copied to your handheld device, click the Add button shown in Figure 24-7. When all files have been added to the transfer list, synchronize your device by pressing the Hot Sync cradle button. Be certain your handheld is properly seated in the cradle before attempting to synchronize the unit.

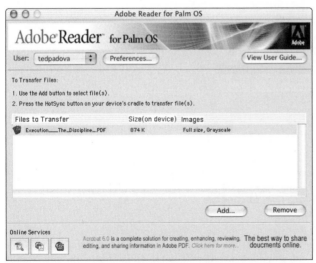

Figure 24-7: To transfer PDF files and eBooks, be certain the files to copy are listed in the Adobe Reader for Palm OS dialog box. Press the Hot Sync button on the Palm device cradle and the listed files are copied to your device.

To read eBooks on your Palm device, select the main menu and tap on the Adobe Reader icon. Adobe Reader for Palm OS loads into memory and lists the PDF documents stored on the device. Tap the book you want to read and the book opens in the Reader software. Scroll pages as you would in any document on your mobile device.

Reading eBooks

eBooks can also take advantage of the Read Out Loud command. By choosing View ➪ Read Out Loud you can listen as the book is read to you using your operating system's Text to Speech engine. For accessibility and leisure reading or group activity, Read Out Loud is a great feature in the program.

Cross-Reference   For more information on Read Out Loud options settings, see Chapter 4.

When reading eBooks or any PDF document with many pages, you may want to return to the place where you stopped reading in a previous Acrobat session. Acrobat offers you a method to return to the last viewed page via a choice in the Preferences dialog box. Select Edit ➪ Preferences (Windows) or Acrobat ➪ Preferences (Macintosh) and click on Startup in the left column. On the right side of the Preferences dialog box, open the pull-down menu for Reopen Documents to Last Viewed Page and select either the Digital Editions Only choice or the Marked Files and Digital Editions Only choice from the menu as shown in Figure 24-8. When you close an eBook and reopen it in another Acrobat session, the book opens on the last viewed page.

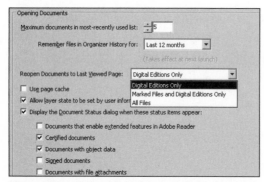

Figure 24-8: Open the Preferences dialog box and select Startup. Select either Digital Editions Only or Marked Files and Digital Editions Only to open an eBook on the last viewed page.

If you select Marked Files and Digital Editions Only from the pull-down menu in the Startup Preferences, all PDF documents you open, whether they are opened from the Digital Editions or by choosing File ➪ Open, can be returned to the last viewed page. If you select Marked Files and Digital Editions Only in the Startup Preferences, open a file and navigate pages, and then close the document, a dialog box opens as shown in Figure 24-9 where you confirm opening the document again on the last viewed page. Select Yes to open the current document on the last viewed page or select Yes to All to set the preferences to view all documents you open in Acrobat to the last viewed page. If you select Yes to All and check the box for

Do not show this message again, the defaults are set to open all PDF documents on the last viewed page without being prompted to confirm the action.

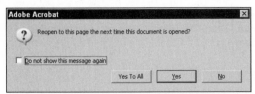

Figure 24-9: When you select Marked Files and Digital Editions Only in the Startup Preferences and close a PDF document, Acrobat prompts you to confirm opening the PDF document in another session on the last viewed page.

Commenting on eBooks

Depending on the permissions granted when an eBook was secured, you may have options for editing content and marking up a document with highlights, notes, and references you want to keep stored in the book. To see what options you have when you acquire an eBook, open the Security settings by choosing File ➪ Document Properties. Select Security in the left pane; the right side of the dialog box shows you the security settings and permissions as shown in Figure 24-10.

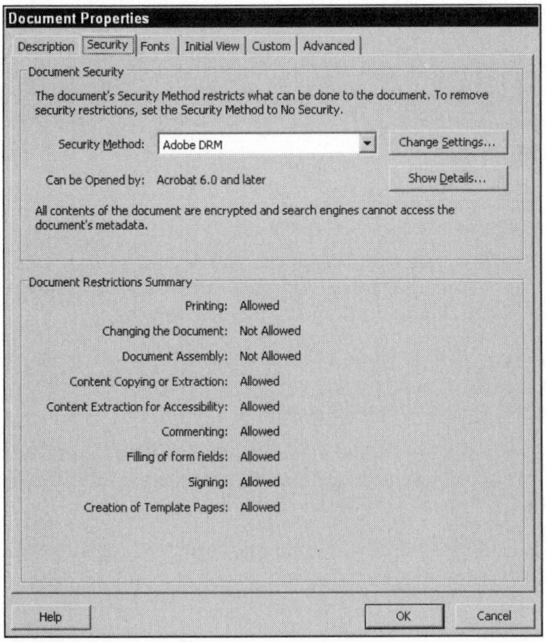

Figure 24-10: To find out what permissions are granted with an eBook you download from a Web site, open the Security Document Properties settings.

In this example, permissions for content copying and extraction, commenting, and some other permissions are allowed.

To view the book publisher's permissions, click the Show Details button in the Security preferences dialog box. The Permissions Set by the Publisher dialog box opens where additional permissions are listed. Notice in Figure 24-11 that the permissions include limited copying and a notice for when the document expires.

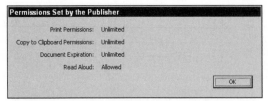

Figure 24-11: To view additional permissions, click Show Details for permissions established from the publisher for printing and the lending period.

To add comments to an eBook, use the commenting tools as you would with any Acrobat PDF file. How you use comments for eBooks is identical to how you use them in other PDF documents. You can open the Comments palette and organize comments, mark them for a status, and print the comments. You can summarize comments and export/import comments as long as the permissions grant you commenting on the document.

Cross-Reference　For information on using commenting tools, see Chapter 15

When you finish commenting, you don't need to save the file. Close the document, and the PDF is stored back on the Digital Editions. Reopening the book shows you the comments added in your previous Acrobat sessions.

Summary

✦ Before you can access eBooks online, you need to activate an account either with Adobe Systems or Microsoft.Net. You can activate your account at the time you install Acrobat or by choosing Advanced ➪ Digital Editions ➪ Activate Devices.

✦ Each computer device you use needs to have an activated account in order for you to read downloaded eBooks on that device. Again use the Digital Editions ➪ Activate Devices menu command to activate additional computers.

✦ eBooks are stored and managed in the My Digital Editions window. You access your Digital Editions through the Advanced menu in Acrobat and the Digital Editions Task Button menu in Adobe Reader (or File menu in Reader).

✦ You use tools in the My Digital Editions window to manage, read, and return books borrowed from content providers.

✦ You can organize eBooks into categories and subcategories by making menu choices from the Category1 and Category2 pull-down menus. You create custom categories with the Edit Categories command.

✦ Opening a context menu on the Digital Editions offers additional commands to manage eBooks.

✦ When you activate an account for a handheld device, eBooks can be prepared and copied to handheld devices.

✦ You view security and publisher permissions in the Document Properties Security dialog box.

✦ When the appropriate eBook permissions are granted you can copy content, add comments, and print files.

✦　　✦　　✦

Printing and Prepress

Regardless of why you create PDF files, at one time or another you'll want to print hard copy. You might be interested in printing documents to office laser printers or personal color printers, or you may be a creative professional or service center technician who wants to print to commercial printing equipment.

All Acrobat viewers including Adobe Reader offer the ability to print documents to personal desktop printers. For high-end digital prepress and commercial printing, Acrobat Professional includes all the print controls desired by the commercial printing community. Combined with features for previewing color, preflighting jobs, and printing color separations, Acrobat Professional ranks as a strong competitor against any layout or other professional applications designed to serve creative professionals. In this chapter I cover printing from Acrobat viewers, soft proofing, preflighting, and commercial printing.

Setting Up the Work Environment

You print files from Acrobat either with default tools or menu commands. In Acrobat Professional you have a toolbar used specifically for print production. Choose Tools ➪ Print Production ➪ Show Print Production Toolbar. From a context menu opened from the Toolbar Well select Advanced Editing to show the Advanced Editing toolbar. Dock the toolbars in the Toolbar Well.

For printing large documents and when soft proofing files the Loupe tool is often used. Rather than showing the Zoom toolbar, open the pull-down menu adjacent to the Zoom In tool and select Loupe.

Printing PDFs to Office Printers

You may browse information in the following sections and find that you don't need to either preflight or create PDF/X files because you're only interested in printing to office and personal printers — either laser printers or desktop color printers. If you do need to color manage files for office printers, you might want to look over the sections in this chapter related to soft proofing color and proofing separations. However, when printing to desktop laser printers or documents printed in black and white and grayscale, you don't need to be concerned about creating any special PDF-compliant file or running any preflight checks. To begin a discussion on printing, I'll start with the simple task of getting a PDF document printed to a desktop printer; later in this chapter I talk about the issues of concern for printing to commercial devices.

Print Setup

Choose File ➪ Print Setup to open the Print Setup dialog box shown in Figure 25-1. From the Name pull-down menu select a printer on your network or a local printer. Select the Orientation and Size. You can click on Properties and make additional choices specific to your printer such as manual feeds, paper trays, and so on. If you want to print the file to a specific paper size and orientation listed in the Print Setup, just click OK after checking these settings. Whenever you begin a new print job, double-checking the settings, particularly for orientation and page size, is a good idea.

Figure 25-1: Open the Print Setup dialog box and select the paper size and orientation.

Using the Print dialog box

Choose File ➪ Print or click on the Print tool in any Acrobat viewer to open the Print dialog box shown in Figure 25-2. After visiting the Print Setup dialog box and selecting the Page Orientation, you'll notice that you can select the printer in this dialog box as well as the Print Setup dialog box. If you change your mind and want to print to a different printer, make a selection from the Name pull-down menu.

Figure 25-2: Choose File ⇨ Print to open the Print dialog box.

The Print dialog box offers many controls for printing to any printer. These include

✦ **Comments and Forms:** From the pull-down menu you have choices for printing the document as you might print any document. The Document and Markups option prints the document and comments. When the item is selected, the comments on the first page, if they exist, are displayed in the Preview area. The Document and Stamps option prints just the Stamp comments and the document. The Form fields only option prints only the form fields in an Acrobat form.

✦ **Print Range:** Select All to print all pages in the document. Select Current View to print a portion of a page in a zoomed view in the Document pane. Select Current page to print the page in view in the Document pane. Select the range of pages (Pages) to print within a specified range. If Pages is selected you also have options from the Subset pull-down menu for All pages in a range, Odd pages only, or Even pages only. Select the Reversed check box to print pages in back-to-front order.

✦ **Page Handling:** Enter the number of copies you want to print. If you're printing more than one copy with more than one page per copy, select the Collate check box to collate the copies as they are printed.

✦ **Page Scaling:** Page Scaling offers options for None, Fit to Printer Margins, Reduce to Printer Margins, Tile large pages, Tile all pages, and Multiple pages per sheet. Select the option you want from the pull-down menu choices. Note that all the options listed here are available in Acrobat Professional and Acrobat Standard. Adobe Reader offers fewer options.

✦ **Auto-Rotate and Center:** When this check box is enabled, pages are auto-rotated and centered.

✦ **Preview:** A document preview shows the first page in the file (or current page) in a page preview as it prints. At the bottom of the preview image is a slider used for scaling the preview. Click and drag right and left to scale the image size up or down, respectively.

✦ **Print to file:** If you select the box, the file is printed to disk as a PostScript file when your target printer is a PostScript printer. You might use this option to send a PostScript file to a PostScript printer. As you set all the other print options in the dialog box, the PostScript file captures the print settings. This file can then be sent to a PostScript printer with a downloading utility. You might use this option for preparing multiple files to print at a later time in a batch download.

Cross-Reference For more information about creating PostScript files, see Chapter 8.

✦ **Print color as black:** Select the box to print the file with black ink only on color desktop printers.

✦ **Printing tips:** Click the button to launch your default Web browser. The target Web page is Adobe's Support Knowledgebase where you find troubleshooting information related to printing.

✦ **Advanced:** Only available in Acrobat Professional, the Advanced button opens the Advanced Print Setup dialog box.

Cross-Reference For information on using the Advanced Print Setup options, see the section "Printing PDFs for Commercial Printing" later in this chapter.

After you choose the options and click OK, the file prints to your local or network printer as defined in the Print dialog box.

Printing layers

Printing individual layers in a file is dependent on the layer state options you set in the Layers tab and the visibility of layers. As you visit the Print dialog box in all Acrobat viewers, you'll notice that there are no options for selecting layers to print. Be certain you open the Layers tab and select the layer that you want to print. If a layer state is defined for printing layers when layers are visible, you can print the selected layer by accessing the Print dialog box and printing the layer as you would any PDF document. If the layer state is set to Never Print, the layer doesn't print even though it may be visible. To enable printing for a layer that isn't printing, open the Layer Properties dialog box and change the Print layer state.

For more information on layers and layer states, see Chapter 19.

Print with Comment Summaries

When you choose File ➪ Print with Comments Summary, Acrobat Standard or Acrobat Professional performs a task similar to creating a comment summary, although a PDF file is not created. Choose File ➪ Print with Comments Summary and the Summarize Options dialog box opens as shown in Figure 25-3.

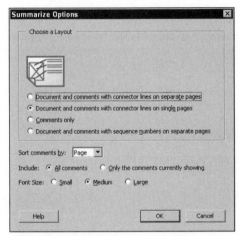

Figure 25-3: Choose File ➪ Print with Comments Summary to open the Summarize Options dialog box.

Make a selection for the type of comment summary you want to print. You have all the options for summary comments as you do when summarizing comments from menu options in the Comments pane. Click OK and the Print dialog box opens. The preview shown in the Print dialog box displays the preview of the document with the comment summary.

For information on creating comment summaries, see Chapter 15.

PrintMe Internet printing

PrintMe is a network for printing from computers, handheld devices, and fax machines to any device on the PrintMe network. You can print from within any Acrobat viewer, including Adobe Reader, to any device on the network and store files on a network-connected computer for on-demand printing. To use the service, you first need to set up an account.

Choose File ➪ PrintMe Internet Printing. Your default Web browser opens the PrintMe Web site where you find information related to the service. Follow the directions on the provider's Web pages to sign up and use the service.

Setting Up Trim and Crop Marks

 One feature you may use for both desktop printing and commercial printing is printer's marks for trim area and bleeds. For desktop printers where your printing device accommodates large page sizes, such as tabloid or color printers that print on oversized pages, you may want to create crop marks that cut off bleed areas. For commercial printing, these marks are essential when submitting film to print shops.

Cross-Reference

All the tools installed in the Print Production toolbar with the exception of the PDF Optimizer are discussed in the sections that follow. For information on using the PDF Optimizer, see Chapter 14.

To understand how page sizes are altered in Acrobat and how to include crop marks, follow these steps:

STEPS: Setting Up Printer's Marks

1. **Open the Crop Pages dialog box.** Be certain you have a file open in the Document pane. If your PDF document was created using a standard page size such as US Letter and you want to print the file with crop marks, you need to define a larger page size that's supported by your printer. To define a custom page size, click the Crop Pages tool in the Print Production toolbar. The Crop Pages dialog box shown in Figure 25-4 opens.

2. **Set the crop attributes.** From the Units pull-down menu select a unit of measure. In my example I select Inches from the pull-down menu. Click the Custom button and enter values for the width and height in the field boxes. In my example I use 9.5 x 12 (1 inch larger than the horizontal and vertical measurements). Click OK.

Note

The pull-down menu for Page Sizes lists fixed sizes according to the printer selected in the Print Setup dialog box. If you print to a fixed page size, use one of the options listed in the menu.

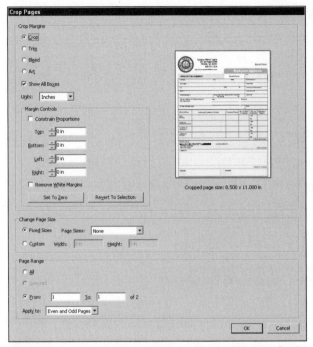

Figure 25-4: Click the Crop Pages tool in the Print Production toolbar.

3. **Add printer marks.** Click the Add Printer Marks tool in the Print Production toolbar. The Add Printer Marks dialog box shown in Figure 25-5 opens. The Style pull-down menu offers several options for printer's marks that duplicate the marks created from different design programs. Select a style from the menu options. In my example, I selected a style to match Adobe InDesign (InDesignJ2). Select the box for All Marks to show all printer's marks. Click OK to return to the Document pane.

4. **Save the file.** Choose File ➪ Save As and save a copy of the document. In Figure 25-6 you can see all printer's marks added to a PDF file.

Caution

When you create printer's marks using the Add Printer Marks tool, the marks are embedded in the PDF document. If you save the file, the marks are saved along with the document. If you print a file using the Print menu command or the Print tool and add printer's marks in the Advanced Print Setup dialog box, the printer's marks are not embedded in the PDF document. Use the Add Print Marks tool when you want to permanently apply printer's marks to a PDF document.

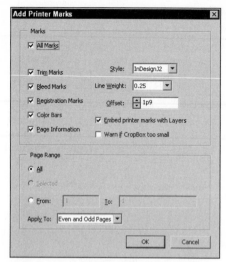

Figure 25-5: Click the Add Printer Marks tool to open the Add Printer Marks dialog box.

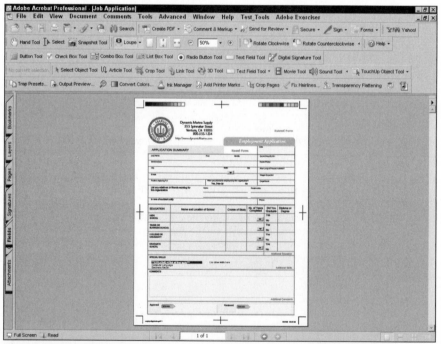

Figure 25-6: After adding printer's marks, the marks are shown on the document.

Soft Proofing Color

Soft proofing color is viewing color on your monitor with a screen preview for the way color is printed to hard copy. Rather than print a test proof and consume paper and ink, soft proofing is a digital process whereby you use your computer monitor screen to preview things such as proper color assignments, overprints, separations, transparency, and similar issues that might cause problems on printing devices.

With the exception of previewing overprints, all soft proofing options are contained only in Acrobat Professional. Most of the options you find for soft proofing apply to high-end commercial printing; however, some features can be useful when you're printing to desktop color printers.

 Note   One soft proofing option you have available in Acrobat Standard and Adobe Reader is previewing overprints.

Printing and soft proofing in Acrobat Professional is a quantum leap in Acrobat development, and the new features added in version 7 rival the best applications used today for commercial printing.

Soft proofing color is handled in the Output Preview dialog box. This dialog box does not provide you options for altering the content. It is used as a viewing tool to diagnose any potential printing problems. From a Preview menu, you select one of two categories in which to preview your document — either Color Warnings or Separations.

Color Warnings

Click on the Output Preview tool in the Print Production toolbar to open the Output Preview dialog box. From the Preview options, select Color Warnings and the Color Warnings pane opens, as shown in Figure 25-7.

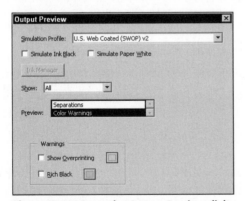

Figure 25-7: Open the Output Preview dialog box and click Color Warnings.

Simulation Profile

Simulation Profile enables you to select from a list of ICC (International Color Consortium) profiles. A number of preset profiles are available from which to choose and you can also create your own custom profiles and add them to the list. You create custom profiles with either software applications such as Adobe Gamma or hardware/software devices that are designed specifically for calibrating monitors and creating ICC profiles. As a profile is created, it is saved as a file to your hard drive.

In order for Acrobat to recognize the ICC profiles you create, you must be certain that the profiles are stored in the proper directory. By default, utilities and commercial devices used for calibrating color save profiles to a directory that makes them accessible to Acrobat. If you want to remove ICC profiles so fewer profiles show up in the Proof Colors dialog box or you have problems getting a profile to the right directory, open the folder where the profiles are stored. On Windows the path is System32\Spool\Drivers\Color. On Macintosh OS X look in Macintosh HD:Library:ColorSync:Profiles:Displays. When new profiles are added to the folder according to your operating system, you can access the profiles in Acrobat after you quit the program and relaunch it if the profile was added while Acrobat was open.

To select a profile for color proofing, open the Simulation Profile pull-down menu and choose a profile to preview. Selecting the option does not change the color in the document and you can select different profiles from the menu selections without permanently changing color in the file.

Creating Color Profiles

Covering all the aspects of creating and using color profiles is beyond the scope of this book. For a brief introduction let me say that you have two choices for creating profiles: Use a program that is shipped with an application you use for editing color images, such as the Adobe Gamma utility (Windows) or the Display Calculator Assistant (Macintosh), or purchase a calibration system. A calibration device is usually a hardware device that attaches to your computer monitor and a software program that analyzes the color from the hardware device. The result of analyzing color and making monitor hardware adjustments for correcting color is the creation of a color profile suited to an individual monitor. The systems are expensive, starting at around $3,000 U.S. Fortunately, you can calibrate monitors throughout your company with a single system.

When you use a program such as Adobe Gamma to adjust monitor brightness, the idea is to bring the monitor in sync with the printed output. You need to measure a print on the device you commonly print to against your monitor brightness and color balance. Hold a print with a wide range of color beside your monitor as you follow the steps in the calibration utility. As a general rule with quality monitors you can come close to balancing color between your screen and printed work; however, no off-the-shelf program will do the job as well as a professional calibration system.

If you use flat screen displays, adjustments with Adobe Gamma are cruder. Check your monitor's user manual for information on color calibration or look for a disk that ships with your monitor containing ICC profiles. If you don't have software support for your monitor, check your manufacturer's Web site for information or software downloads to help you calibrate your system.

From the pull-down menu you'll see a number of different profiles appear in a long list. If you have an ICC profile developed for your system as the result of calibrating your monitor, select the profile in the list. If you haven't created a profile, you can choose from one of the prein-stalled profiles. As a general rule, select a CMYK proofing profile such as U.S. Web Coated (SWOP) 2 for files you intend to print as process (CMYK) color. For Web and screen uses, select sRGB IEC61966-2.1. You can make a number of other selections, but be certain to test results of selecting one profile over another. If you select profiles such as Apple RGB or Wide Gamut RGB, you may find the color works well for your screen viewing but other Acrobat users will see much different color if they are using a different profile.

If you want to preview the PDF document as it theoretically is printed on paper, choose from either an ICC profile you created or from the preset profiles such as Euroscale, SWOP, and so on. For printing on offset press on coated stock use U.S. Web Coated (SWOP) v2. When you select one of the presets for soft proofing prints, the two check boxes for simulating ink and paper become accessible.

Tip   To ensure your color proofing uses the same profile each time you view a file onscreen, open a document in Acrobat. Select the profile you want to use as a default from the Simulation Profile pull-down menu. Quit Acrobat and re-launch the program. The last choice you made becomes the new default. You don't need to quit the program to make the profile choice a new default, but if the program crashes during a session, you lose preferences applied in that session. Quitting after making a preference choice ensures you that the preference is held in all subsequent Acrobat sessions.

Simulate Ink Black

When the Simulate Ink Black check box is enabled, the preview shows you the dynamic range of the document's profile. Dynamic range is measured in values usually between 0 and 4, although some scanner manufacturers claim dynamic ranges of 4.1, 4.2, or higher. A dynamic range of something like 3.8 yields a wide range of grays between the white point and the black point in a scanned image. If the dynamic range is high, you see details in shadows and high-lights. If the dynamic range is low, highlights can get blown out and shadows lose detail. When you enable the Simulate Ink Black check box, look for the distinct tonal differences in the preview and detail in shadows and highlights.

Simulate Paper White

If the check box for Simulate Paper White is enabled in the Output Preview dialog box, the preview shows you a particular shade of gray as simulated for the paper color by the profile you choose. You may find that the preview looks too gray or has too much black. This result may not be the profile used, but rather the brightness adjustment on your monitor. If your monitor is calibrated properly and the profile accurately displays the paper color, the pre-view should show you an accurate representation of the document as it is printed on paper.

Warnings

Two different warnings dynamically display potential printing problems. As you select a check box you can move the Output Preview aside and preview the results in the Document pane. When you select a box and preview the results, the display appears only when the Output Preview dialog box is open. Closing the dialog box returns you to the default view of the document page before you opened the Output Preview.

By default the options in the Warnings section show potential problems using default colors adjacent to the warning item. You can change the warning colors by clicking on the color swatch and selecting from a preset palette or select custom color from your operating system color palette.

Show Overprinting

Overprints are often used to *trap* colors when files are intended for printing separations. Trapping a color creates an overlap between colors so any movement of the paper when printed on a printing press prevents printing colors without gaps between the colors. In other cases, overprints may be assigned to colors in illustrations intentionally where a designer wants to eliminate potential trapping problems. For example, you might assign an overprint to text to avoid any trapping problems where black text is printed on top of a background color. In some instances, a designer might unintentionally assign an overprint to a color during the creative process. As a measure of checking overprints for those colors that you properly assign and to review a document for potential problems, you can use Acrobat's Show Overprinting preview to display on your monitor all the overprints created in a file. To view overprints in a PDF document, select the Show Overprinting check box in the Output Preview dialog box.

To understand what happens with overprints and knockouts, look at Figure 25-8. The composite image is created for printing two colors. These colors are printed on separate plates for two different inks. When the file is separated, the type is *knocked out* of the background, leaving holes in the background as in Figure 25-9. Because the two colors butt up against each other, any slight movement of the paper creates a gap between where one ink color ends and the other begins. To prevent the problem, a slight bit of overprinting is added to the type. In an exaggerated view in Figure 25-10 you can see the stroke around one of the type characters. The stroke is assigned an overprint so its color, which is the foreground color, prints on top of the background color without a knockout.

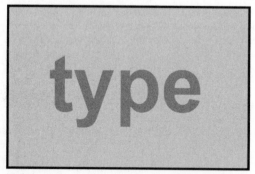

Figure 25-8: Type is set over a background. Two colors are used and the file is color separated so each color appears on a separate printing plate.

Figure 25-9: When color is separated and the background color is printed, the background appears with the type *knocked out*.

Figure 25-10: If an overprint is assigned to the type, the overprint area of the type color prints on top of the background color. If the paper moves slightly, the overprint prevents any paper color showing through gaps created by the misregistration.

Designers can apply overprints in programs like Adobe Illustrator and Adobe InDesign. If a designer inadvertently makes a mistake and selects the fill color to overprint, the color of the foreground image results in a different color created by the mix of the two colors. In Figure 25-11 a file is opened in Acrobat and viewed without an Overprint Preview. The figure shows the document as it should be printed. When you select the Show Overprinting check box, the overprints shown in Figure 25-12 appear. As you can see by comparing the figures, the overprints assigned in the file were a mistake. By using Acrobat's Show Overprinting preview command you can check for any overprint errors contained in your illustrations.

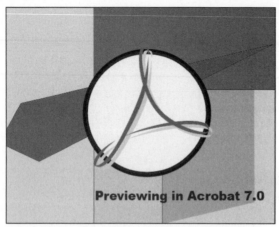

Figure 25-11: Here, a file is previewed in Acrobat without an Overprint Preview. The file appears as it is intended to be printed.

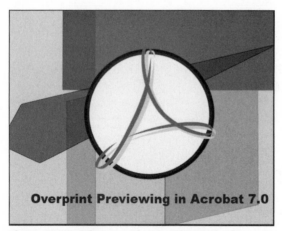

Figure 25-12: When you choose Advanced ⇨ Overprint Preview, you can preview all colors assigned an overprint on your monitor. In this example, the overprint assignments were a mistake.

Tip To carefully examine overprints assigned to type characters, select the Loupe tool in the Zoom toolbar. Move the cursor around the document to preview overprints on small type.

Rich Black

When files are printed with rich black, all the black in the document prints with more density. This is often a common setting used when printing to ink jet printers and commercial over-sized printing devices to eliminate any muddy appearance when files contain a substantial amount of black. Select the box to preview how the black will lay down on the printed output. If you see too much density in black, be certain to avoid using rich black when printing the file.

Separations

One of the great features for soft proofing color in Acrobat Professional is the ability to preview a color separation where individual colors can be viewed individually or in combinations — for example, previewing cyan and magenta instead of previewing all colors. To preview a separation, select Separations from the Preview menu in the Output Preview dialog box. The pane changes to the view shown in Figure 25-13.

Figure 25-13: Separations shows all colors contained in a file.

If you intend to print a file in four-color process, the Separation Preview dialog box helps you identify any potential problems if spot colors are contained in the file. Likewise, if a spot color job contains colors not intended to be printed, they also show up.

You can selectively view individual colors by disabling the check boxes adjacent to each color name, viewing selected colors only, and viewing spot colors converted to CMYK. When you click on the X in a check box for a spot color, the first preview is a process equivalent. Click again and the color is hidden in the document. Click a third time and the color returns as a spot color.

You evaluate color values by moving the cursor around the document with the Separation Preview dialog box open. Notice the percentage values on the far right side of Figure 25-13. These values represent the percent of ink at the cursor position.

Assessing Ink Values

As you move the cursor around a document, the values for each colorant are reported according to the profile you select in the Color Management Preferences. To open the Color Management Preferences, choose Edit ⇨ Preferences. Click on Color Management and make choices for your working spaces from the profiles you select from pull-down menus, as shown in the figure. The profiles available to you are the same as those you choose in the Output Preview dialog box discussed in the "Color Warnings" section earlier in this chapter.

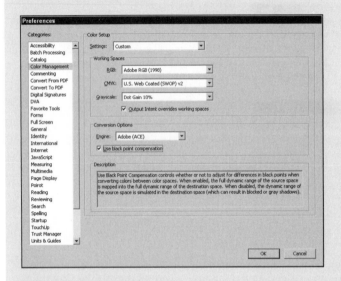

Although assessing colors in the Color Warnings pane is fine in most cases, there are situations where you might assess a color and the printed result is different from the value reported in the Output Preview dialog box. Achieving accurate proofing all depends on the proper creation of the PDF file, selecting the proper profile in the Color Management Setup preferences, and the output space that is selected when you print the file.

Tip   Color management is a complex issue and requires much research and study to fully comprehend managing color on computer systems and how color is reproduced on printing devices. To learn more about color management, click on the Search tool in the Acrobat toolbar and add *color management* as your search criteria. Click on Search PDFs on the Internet in the Search pane and the Yahoo! search engine reports all PDF documents on the Internet where the term *color management* are found. You can download many PDF documents that offer you definitions of terms and thoroughly explain color management.

Tip   For color proofing multiple files, open them in Acrobat Professional and choose Window ⇨ Tile ⇨ Vertically (or Horizontally). Open the Separations pane in the Output Preview dialog box. Move the cursor from one document to another. As the cursor enters a page in the tiled view, the separation preview displays the colors relative to the cursor position. As you move the cursor to a different document with different colors, the colors are dynamically reflected in the Separation Preview dialog box.

Ink management

The Ink Manager dialog box enables you to change ink values and convert colors. Changes you apply to the options choices aren't saved with the PDF file. If you convert spot colors to CMYK, for example, and save the document, the colors are unaffected when you reopen the file. The changes applied in the Ink Manager take effect only when you print a PDF document. To open the Ink Manager, click on the Ink Manager tool in the Print Production toolbar; the Ink Manager dialog box shown in Figure 25-14 opens.

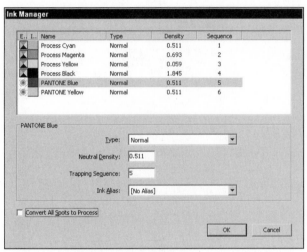

Figure 25-14: The Ink Manager enables you to change ink densities and convert color spaces.

Select from the pull-down menus options for changing type of color (Normal, Opaque, Transparent, and OpaqueIgnore). You change density values and the trapping sequence by editing the field box. To alias spot colors, select a spot color and map the color to the same angle and density as a process color.

You can also convert colors using the Convert Colors tool in the Print Production toolbar. Click the Convert Colors tool to open the Convert Colors dialog box. In this dialog box you make choices for color conversion, assign color profiles that you can choose to embed in the document, or assign profiles without embedding.

Transparency Flattener Preview

Transparency creates problems when printing to various PostScript devices. For resolving printing problems with transparency, you need to flatten the transparency, resulting in files that print successfully on almost any kind of PostScript device. When transparency is flattened in a file the vector objects are converted to raster images. Through the conversion to raster images the colors blend together to form a simulated view of transparent objects. The amount of blending transparent colors depends on the amount of transparency you apply to a file. As you move the transparency slider to the left to flatten transparency, all vector objects are rasterized. When you move the slider to the right, the transparency flattener maintains as many vector objects as needed in order to successfully print the file.

You can flatten transparency in degrees, and objects in a document are affected according to the degree of transparency flattening you apply. Determining how the other objects are affected is the purpose of the transparency flattener in Acrobat.

When you use the Transparency Flattening tool in the Print Production toolbar, the transparency changes you make to the PDF are preserved when you save the file. If you use the transparency options in the Advanced Print Setup dialog box, the settings are applied only when the file is printed and are not saved with the file. To open the Flattener Preview dialog box, click on the Transparency Flattening tool in the Print Production toolbar; the options appear as shown in Figure 25-15.

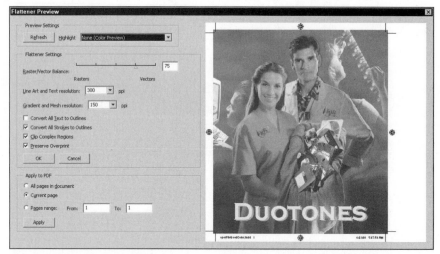

Figure 25-15: When the Flattener Preview dialog box opens, click Refresh to see a preview of the document page.

Previews are displayed only for PostScript printing devices. Be certain you have a PostScript printer selected in your Print Setup dialog box before previewing transparency. Beginning with the Highlight pull-down menu you have options for

✦ **Rasterized Complex Regions:** On the top-right side of the dialog box the slider is moved to the left to show previews with rasterization. The farther you move the slider to the left, the more rasterization you apply to objects. Click the Refresh button after moving the slider. Each adjustment requires you to click the Refresh button again to display the preview.

✦ **Transparent Objects:** All objects containing a degree of transparency, objects with blending modes, and masks with opacity are previewed. If you have overprints in the file, the overprints may also be treated as transparent objects. When you select Transparent Objects and click Refresh, all objects containing transparency are displayed with a red mask in the preview area.

✦ **All Affected Objects:** Flattening transparency affects both the transparent objects and other objects overlapping the objects assigned transparency. When type is converted to outlines and the type objects contain transparency, the entire page may be affected. When you select this option, all objects that are affected when the transparency is flattened are shown with the same red mask described in the preceding bullet.

✦ **Expanded Patterns:** If you have patterns contained in the artwork, the patterns are expanded when transparency is flattened. Gradient blends, for example, are viewed as expanded objects.

✦ **Outlined Strokes:** If type is converted to outlines, or you select the Convert All Strokes to Outlines option on the right side of the dialog box, the strokes involved with transparency are previewed.

Below the Highlight pull-down menu the remaining options include

✦ **Flattener Settings:** In addition to the slider, edit this field box to change the amount of flattening. With either adjustment, click the Refresh button to preview again with new settings.

✦ **Line Art and Text resolution:** From the pull-down menu or by editing the field box, select the resolution for rasterizing complex objects. Rasterized objects require the same considerations for output resolutions assigned to raster images.

✦ **Gradient and Mesh resolution:** Change values in the field box to edit the resolution you want to apply to gradients and gradient meshes.

✦ **Convert All Text to Outlines:** If you intend to convert text to outlines, you can see a preview for how text objects are affected in complex regions. When printing a file, you'll want to avoid globally converting text to outlines, as the files are more difficult to print.

✦ **Convert All Strokes to Outlines:** Converts all strokes to outlines.

✦ **Clip Complex Regions:** The boundaries between vector objects and raster objects change as you move the slider. Some objects remain in vector form according to the degree of rasterization you apply. This option ensures the boundaries between the vector and raster objects fall within clipping paths preventing artifacts appearing outside the path boundaries. As with any illustration artwork, the more clipping paths used in a file, the more difficult the printing.

✦ **Preserve Overprint:** Preserves all overprints assigned in the document.

✦ **Page Range:** Apply the settings to all pages or select a page range.

✦ **Apply:** After making your choices from the various options, click the Apply button. You can save the PDF document and all the transparency flattening is saved with the document. Note that saving transparency settings is a new feature in Acrobat 7.

Trapping Files

You can trap PDF files for commercial printing by applying trap presets from a selection installed as defaults or from custom trap presets you create in Acrobat.

 Before you trap a file, you may need to fix hairline rules. Click the Fix Hairlines tool in the Print Production toolbar to open the Fix Hairlines dialog box. You can adjust a rule when a hairline falls below a specified value to a new value you supply in a field box.

 Make adjustments as needed, and then click the Trap Presets tool to open the Trap Presets dialog box shown in Figure 25-16.

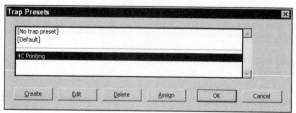

Figure 25-16: Click the Trap Presets tool to open the
Trap Presets dialog box.

The first dialog box that opens enables you to select an existing preset or create a new one. Click the Create button and the New Trap Preset dialog box opens as shown in Figure 25-17. In order to make adjustments in the dialog box you should be familiar with trapping and the acceptable amounts to apply for trap widths, miter adjustments, and attributes assigned to images and thresholds. If you know how to trap a file, you'll know what settings to apply. If you don't know anything about trapping, it's best to leave the job to your commercial printer.

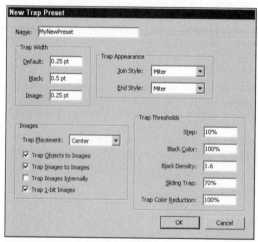

Figure 25-17: Set the attributes for the trap preset
in the New Trap Preset dialog box.

Click OK after providing a name for the new preset and making the adjustments. You are then returned to the Trap Presets dialog box where your new preset is listed in the window. Click the Assign button and the trap values are applied to the document.

Working with Job Definition Files

You use a Job Definition File (JDF) in production workflows to include information necessary for a production process and information related to the PDF creation. You assign the information in a JDF file through a collection of dialog boxes that begin with your clicking on the JDF Job Definitions tool at the far right side of the Print Production toolbar. Click the tool and the JDF Job Definitions dialog box shown in Figure 25-18 opens.

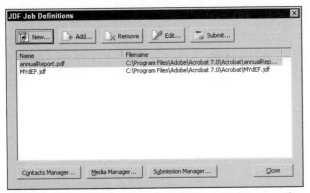

Figure 25-18: Click the JDF Job Definitions tool to open the JDF Job Definitions dialog box.

Click the New button to open the Create New Job Definition dialog box. You make choices for either creating a new definition, using the open document's structure, or applying a definition from another file saved to your hard drive. If you create a new definition, you need to supply a name in the Name field box and click OK. You return to the JDF Job Definitions dialog box. Click the Edit button and you can assign general and billing information to the file. You also specify ink values, page sizes, media descriptions, printing and scaling options. These settings are all obtained by clicking on buttons that open different dialog boxes.

The entire process for creating and using JDF files is extensive and beyond the scope of a thorough discussion in this chapter. For more information about JDF, see the Help document installed with Acrobat.

Preflighting PDF Files (Acrobat Professional Only)

Preflighting is a term used by creative professionals and service technicians to analyze a file for suitability for printing. A preflight assessment might examine a file for the proper color mode of images, whether images are compressed, whether fonts are accessible either embedded or accessible to the operating system, or any number of other conditions that might interfere with successfully printing a job.

The tools used to preflight files might be stand-alone applications or features built into programs used for printing to commercial printing equipment. Prior to Acrobat 6 you needed to preflight a file before converting to PDF with a standalone product that analyzed the original authoring application file prior to conversion to PDF or a third-party plug-in for Acrobat that performed preflighting on PDF files. Preflighting PDFs from within Acrobat was introduced in Acrobat 6 and has been polished and improved in Acrobat 7.

Preflighting a file

Acrobat requires you to have a file open in the Document pane in order to run a preflight check unless you use a batch sequence (see the "Preflighting batches of files" section later in this chapter). To preflight a document be certain a file is open and click the Preflight tool in the Print Production toolbar. The Preflight dialog box shown in Figure 25-19 opens. In the top window you see a number of preinstalled profiles listed with a description for the kind of preflighting each profile performs. Use the scroll bar on the right side of the window to display additional profiles.

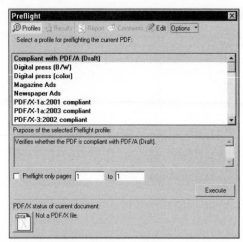

Figure 25-19: Click the Preflight tool to open the Preflight dialog box.

Note   The Options menu contains several menu commands. You can also execute a preflight by first selecting a profile in the list window and selecting Execute Preflight Profile from the Options menu.

If a profile exists containing the conditions you want to check, select a profile and click the Execute button. If the file you preflight contains errors, a report is displayed in the Preflight window after you execute the preflight. The report is listed in a hierarchy with subnotations listed under parent categories. Click the icon to the left of each category to expand the list as shown in Figure 25-20.

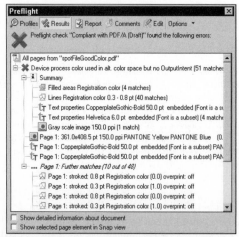

Figure 25-20: If the preflight does not match the conditions of the profile, a report lists the errors in the Preflight window.

Producing a PDF/X-compliant file

For commercial printing you'll want to create PDF/X compliant files. If a file is not converted to PDF/X during the PDF creation process you can post process the file in Acrobat to check the file for PDF/X compliance.

Cross-Reference For a detailed description of PDF/X, see Chapter 8.

To check for PDF/X compliance, first look in the lower-left corner of the Preflight dialog box. The PDF/X status of current document button displays a message reporting PDF/X compliance status. If the file is not PDF/X compliant, it is listed as such in the Preflight window, as shown in Figure 25-20. To run a check on the file, which enables you to examine the problems with the file's meeting PDF/X compliance, select one of the PDF/X profiles listed in the Preflight window and click the Execute button. Acrobat pauses momentarily as the preflight check is performed. The results of the preflight report are listed in the Preflight window. If the file does not meet compliance as shown in Figure 25-21, you can often use Acrobat to convert the document to a PDF/X-compliant file.

Figure 25-21: Click the PDF/X status of current document button to check the open document for PDF/X compliance.

Converting a document to a PDF/X-compliant file

When the Results are displayed in the Preflight window, you can return to the profile list by clicking the Profile button in the top of the Preflight window. To convert the open document to a PDF/X-compliant file, click the PDF/X status of current document button at the bottom of the Preflight dialog box. The Preflight: Convert to PDF/X dialog box opens as shown in Figure 25-22. In the dialog box you make choices for the PDF/X version, output intent, and trapping key.

Cross-Reference For information about PDF/X versions, see Chapter 8. For information about trapping see the section "Trapping files" earlier in this chapter.

Figure 25-22: Select the PDF/X file format, output intent, and trapping key and click OK to convert the open document to a PDF/X-compliant file.

Click OK in the Preflight: Convert to PDF/X dialog box and Acrobat converts the open document to a PDF/X compliant file if the file can be converted to PDF/X. In some cases files can't be converted due to problems related to the file construction. If the file cannot be converted you can examine the report and return to the original authoring program where you can fix the reported problems.

After conversion, Acrobat prompts you in a Save as PDF/X dialog box. As a default name, Acrobat adds the PDF/X version extension to the file. You can accept the new filename or change it in the File name field. By default a new filename is added to prevent you from overwriting the original file. Click Save to save the PDF/X-compliant file.

If you want to check the converted file against PDF/X compliance, return to the profile list in the Preflight window and select the PDF/X format used to convert the file. Click Execute and the Preflight window should display a message indicating no problems were found, as shown in Figure 25-23.

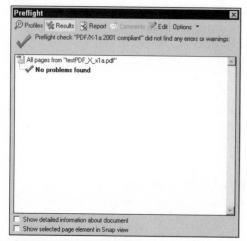

Figure 25-23: When a file meets PDF/X compliance and you run a check, the report shows no problems found.

Creating PDF/A-compliant files

PDF/A is a subset of the PDF format used for archival purposes. To make a PDF/A-compliant file you use a similar process as when creating PDF/X files. Select the Compliant with PDF/A (Draft) profile listed in the Preflight window and click the Execute button. If the file is not PDF/A-compliant, review the errors reported in the Preflight window. You need to return to the document and fix the problems in order to meet PDF/A compliance.

 Cross-Reference For more information about the PDF/A format, see Chapter 8.

Creating a new profile

If none of the preset profiles do the job of file checking for your workflow, you can create your own custom profiles. Acrobat offers you more than 400 different conditions that you can use in preflighting files. To create a new profile, click the Edit button in the Preflight dialog box; the Preflight: Edit Profile dialog box opens as shown in Figure 25-24.

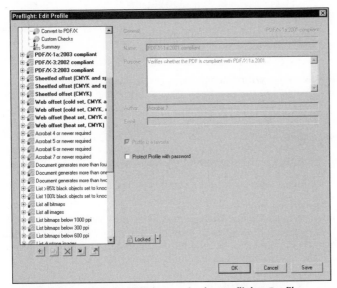

Figure 25-24: Click the Edit button in the Preflight: Profiles dialog box to open the Preflight: Edit Profiles dialog box.

At the bottom of the dialog box several tools appear for creating and managing profiles. They include

✦ **Create a new profile:** Click the icon to create a new profile. The Preflight: Edit Profile pane changes to offer options using field boxes for adding a profile name, a profile description, author name, and e-mail address. Check boxes are shown for adding a profile as a favorite, which lists the profile at the top of the Preflight window in bold type, and for password-protecting the profile. From a list of categories in the left pane shown in Figure 25-25 you select a category and specify conditions to check.

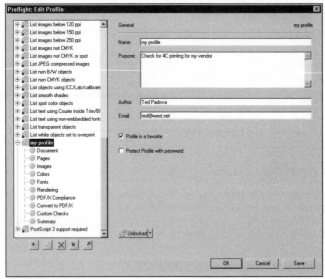

Figure 25-25: Click the Create a new profile icon to change the pane where you add conditions to a custom profile.

✦ **Duplicate the selected profile:** Click the icon to duplicate a selected profile. Once it's duplicated you can edit the profile to change conditions.

✦ **Delete the selected profile:** Select a profile and click the icon to remove the profile from the list window. You cannot delete the profile if Locked is selected in the Preflight: Edit Profile pane.

When a Profile is selected, two other buttons appear at the bottom of the column. The tools are

✦ **Import:** Click the Import tool to import a profile created by a vendor or a user in your workgroup.

✦ **Export:** If you are responsible for creating profiles at a service center or in a company where you want to implement a set of standards, click the Export button. The profile selected when you click this button is exported to a file that you can send to other users who in turn import the profile.

Adding conditions to a custom profile

After adding a name, description, author name, and e-mail address, select a category in the left pane. For each of the nine categories shown in Figure 25-26 a number of conditions appear in the right pane as you select each category. From pull-down menus you have choices to report conditions as an Error, Warning, Info, and Inactive. If you select Error, the preflight reports that condition as an error in the preflight report. Warnings also are reported as a warning in the preflight report. Info displays information if a condition is not true, and Inactive skips checking for the respective condition. In Figure 25-26 you can see a number of different conditions related to Document when it's selected in the left pane of the Preflight: Edit Profiles dialog box. The pull-down menu displays the options for one of the subcategories.

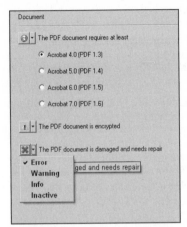

Figure 25-26: Click one of the nine categories in the left pane and make choices for the conditions to check when using the profile for a preflight.

By default, all conditions are ignored when you begin creating a new profile. Click the categories in the left pane and make choices in the right pane for the conditions you want to check. If you use the profile frequently, select the check box for Profile is a favorite.

Importing/exporting profiles

After creating a profile, you may want to send the profile to another user. Select the profile you want to export from the list of profiles in the Preflight: Edit Profile dialog box and click the Export icon. The Export Preflight profile dialog box opens. Find a location on your hard drive where you want to save the file and click the Save button. The file is saved with a default extension of .kfp.

You handle importing profiles similarly. Click the Import button and locate a file to import. Only .kfp files are listed in the Import Preflight Profile dialog box. Select the file to import and click Open. The imported profile is added to the list of profiles in the Preflight window.

Creating reports and comments

Additional tools appear in the Preflight window for creating a report and embedding comments. When you click the Report tool, a Save As dialog box opens. Provide a filename and click the Save button. The report is generated as a PDF document and opens in the Document pane. You can use the PDF file as a file attachment to send along with your job to a service center. You can save the report as PDF or XML or TXT.

If you click the Comments tool in the Preflight window, comment notes are embedded in the file, noting all the conditions met and the errors found. If you want to have comments appear in the document use the Comments tool.

Preflighting batches of files

Using the Preflight command in Acrobat Professional is handy for a single file or a few files you want to preflight or save as PDF/X-compliant. If you have many files that need to be pre-flighted, you can set up a batch sequence and preflight a folder of PDF documents.

To create a batch sequence for preflighting files, choose Advanced ⇨ Batch Processing. Click the New Sequence button in the Batch Sequence dialog box and type a name in the Name Sequence dialog box. Click OK and select Preflight in the left pane. Click the Add button to move the Preflight item to the right pane. Double-click on Preflight in the right pane to open the Preflight: Batch Sequence Setup dialog box, as shown in Figure 25-27. From the Run Preflight check using pull-down menu you can select any profile listed in the Preflight window. If checking for conditions using a custom profile, select the profile from the list. For PDF/X compliance, select one of the PDF/X-compliant file types.

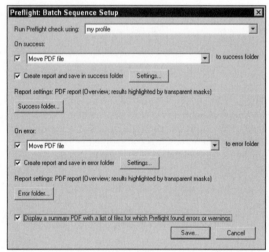

Figure 25-27: Select a profile in the Run Profile check using pull-down menu.

Cross-Reference   For a detailed description on creating and running batch sequences, see Chapter 14.

Printing PDFs for Commercial Printing

Most of the settings in the Print dialog box are the same for all Acrobat viewers, including Adobe Reader. With the exception of Print color as Black and no support for printing fields, Adobe Reader uses the same print options as Acrobat Standard and Acrobat Professional. The distinction between Acrobat Professional and the other Acrobat viewers is found in the Advanced Print Setup dialog box. Advanced print options are available in Adobe Reader and Acrobat Standard, but only a few other options for printing as image, language-level choice, and downloading Asian character sets are found in the other Acrobat viewers.

Acrobat Professional contains all the print controls you need for printing files to commercial devices. To access the options, choose File ➪ Print or click on the Print tool in the Toolbar Well. In the Print dialog box, click on the Advanced button.

Advanced print options

When you select Advanced in the Print dialog box in Acrobat Professional, the Advanced Print Setup dialog box shown in Figure 25-28 opens. There are four categories in the left pane. When you select a category, the right pane changes, just as the Preferences dialog box changes when you select a category.

Using Save as PostScript for High-End Printing

Commercial printers should note that although you can successfully print files from the Print dialog box using the Advanced print settings, there are many circumstances where saving a file to PostScript and downloading the PostScript file offers you more options and may be necessary to successfully print a job. For example, to send a PostScript file to other post-processing programs that require DCS (Desktop Color Separation)–compliant PostScript, you are required to download a PostScript file and not use the print path. In addition, PPD (PostScript Printer Description) selection is also provided in the Save As PostScript advanced settings dialog box.

Choosing File ➪ Save As ➪ PostScript (.ps) and assigning attribute choices in the Save as Settings dialog box is the path high-end commercial printers should use instead of printing files directly from the Print dialog box.

For more information on assigning attribute choices in the Save as PostScript dialog box and saving files as PostScript, see Chapter 8.

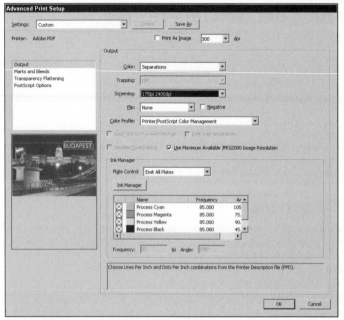

Figure 25-28: Click the Advanced button in the Print dialog box to open the Advanced Print Setup dialog box.

Output

Output options are where you set the color and frequency controls for the output. At the top of the dialog box a check box is available for printing the document as an image. For desktop printing when you have trouble printing the file, you can use the Print As Image option as a last resort. Print as Image rasterizes the PDF document and type usually looks poor on the final output. Don't enable the check box for professional printing. This option is also available in the Advanced Print options for Adobe Reader and Acrobat Standard. The remaining items are used for commercial printing and they include

✦ **Color:** Select from composite or separations. Users with PostScript 3 RIPs can choose either Separations or In-Rip Separations depending on how you set up your RIP defaults. For creative professionals printing separation proofs to desktop printers, select Separations. For composite color, select Composite from the pull-down menu. For printing RC Paper or composite images to film, select Composite Gray.

Note   If Separations is not available, you don't have a PostScript printer capable of printing separations selected for your printer. If you don't see separations active, cancel out of the dialog box and select the Adobe PDF printer in the Print dialog box; then click on Advanced to return to the Advanced Print Settings.

✦ **Trapping:** For In-RIP Separations, you can choose from Off or Adobe In-RIP. If using PostScript 3 devices supporting In-RIP trapping, you can apply the trap presets set up with the Trap Presets tool in the Print Production toolbar.

✦ **Screening:** If you're using the Adobe PDF printer as the printer driver, the screening options won't match the device where you print your job. If you're using a device printer, the screening options for the device are derived from the PPD (PostScript Printer Description). If the frequency is not available from the pull-down menu, you select custom screens and angles from the Ink Manager (discussed later in this list).

✦ **Flip:** For emulsion control, select horizontal from the Flip pull-down menu to print with emulsion down. You have options for flip vertical and flip vertical & horizontal.

Note Adobe's print controls in Acrobat Professional are *almost* perfect. However, one limitation does exist. There is no emulsion control for composite printing. Emulsion control is only available when printing separations. Therefore, service centers needing to print emulsion-down composites on LexJet, mylar, transwhite, and other substrates on large format inkjet printers need to flip files prior to PDF creation.

✦ **Color Profile:** Select from the pull-down menu items the color profile used in your workflow.

✦ **Apply Working Color Spaces:** This setting in effect applies the profile you select in the Color Management Preferences dialog box as the source space to the PDF document if the PDF is defined in Device Colors. If the PDF is calibrated, it uses the Calibrated color spaces in the PDF document as the source.

✦ **Apply Proof Settings:** This setting is available for composite printing only. If you want to apply settings made in the Proof Setup for a simulated print, enable the check box.

✦ **Simulate Overprinting:** This option, also available for composite, prints only the print results in a proof, showing the results of overprints assigned in the document. This feature emulates the overprinting previews of high-end color proofers, such as what was introduced with the Imation Rainbow printer.

✦ **Use Maximum Available JPEG2000 Image Resolution:** When the check box is enabled, the maximum usable resolution contained in JPEG2000 images is used.

✦ **Emit Trap Annotations:** Only applies to documents where trap annotations are included in the file. The trap annotations are sent to RIPs when In-Rip separations are used on PostScript 3 devices.

✦ **Ink Manager:** If spot colors or RGB colors are contained in the file, you can convert spot or RGB to CMYK color by selecting the check box. The spot color converts to CMYK color when the X in the check box turns to a fill with CMYK color. To edit the frequency and angle for each plate, double-click on a color to open the Edit Frequency and Angle dialog box. Supply the desired frequency and angle for each color by successively opening the dialog box individually for each color.

Marks and Bleeds

Select Marks and Bleeds in the left pane of the Advanced Print Setup dialog box, and the right pane changes to show options for adding printer's marks. All marks added in the Advanced Print Setup dialog box apply only to the printed file. If you want to save a file with printer's marks, use the Add Printer Marks tool in the Print Production toolbar.

Select All to show all printer's marks. If you want individual marks, deselect All Marks and select the check boxes individually below the Marks Style pull-down menu. From the pull-down menu options, you can choose Western Style or Eastern Style. Use Eastern Style for printing files in far-eastern countries.

Marks and Bleeds are also available for composite proofs as well as separations.

Transparency Flattening

Click on Transparency Flattening in the Advanced Print Setup dialog box to apply transparency flattening settings. You can determine what settings you want in the Flattener Preview dialog box and choose to not apply the settings until you want to print the document. Therefore, transparency flattening is duplicated in the Advanced Print Setup to make the choice here without having to return to the Transparency Flattener dialog box. All adjustments made in the Flattener Preview can be made in the Advanced Print Setup dialog box to be applied only when printing a file.

Cross-Reference   For information on setting the transparency flattening options, see the section "Transparency Flattener Preview" earlier in this chapter.

PostScript Options

Click on PostScript Options in the Advanced Print Setup dialog box, and the right pane changes to display options choices for PostScript attributes. The options include

✦ **Font and Resource Policy:** Three options are available from the pull-down menu. Select Send at Start to send all fonts to the printer as the print job starts. Select Send by Range to send fonts as they are encountered on the pages as new pages print; the fonts stay in memory until the job finishes printing. Select Send for Each page to conserve memory; the fonts are flushed after each page prints. The last selection takes more time to print but can overcome problems when experiencing difficulty in printing a job.

✦ **Print Method:** Choose from PostScript Level 2 or PostScript 3 depending on the level of PostScript used by the RIP.

✦ **Download Asian Fonts:** Check the box if Asian characters are in the document and not available at the RIP.

✦ **Emit TrueType Fonts as Type 2 (PS version 2015 and greater):** Converts TrueType fonts to a PostScript font equivalent.

✦ **Emit Undercolor Removal/Black Generation:** GCR/UCR removal is necessary only if the original file contained embedded settings. Deselect the box to remove any embedded settings that might have been inadvertently added and saved in Photoshop. If you want to apply any embedded settings, selecting the box to Emit the settings applies them if they were embedded in the authoring program.

✦ **Emit Halftones:** In the event that the PostScript file contained embedded halftones, you can preserve them here, and the frequency assigned in the Output options is used to print the file. Select the box to apply the frequency embedded in a file. When you want to preserve halftones is when you want an embedded halftone frequency in an image to print at a different frequency than the rest of the job.

✦ **Emit Transfer Functions:** Deselect the box to eliminate any transfer functions that might have been embedded in Photoshop images. If you know you want images to print with embedded transfer functions you may have applied according to instructions provided from a publication house, select the box to preserve the transfer functions.

✦ **Emit Flatness:** If flatness was exported from files created in Adobe Photoshop with clipping paths or a vector art image has flatness applied, the flatness values are retained in the output.

✦ **Emit PS Form Objects:** PostScript XObject stores common information in a document, such as backgrounds, headers, footers, and so on. When PostScript XObjects are used, the printing is faster, but it requires more memory. To speed up the printing, select the box to emit PostScript XObjects.

To understand more about XObjects, see Chapter 8.

✦ **Discolored background correction:** Enable this option only when printing composite proofs where backgrounds print darker or with a discolored appearance like a yellow tint.

Save As

You can capture and save the settings you select in the Advanced Print Setup dialog box as a printing profile. Click the Save As button to open the Save Print Settings dialog box. Provide a name and click OK. You select the profiles from the pull-down menu for Settings in the top-left corner of the Advanced Print Setup dialog box.

If you create a setting and want to later delete it from the Settings pull-down menu, select the setting to delete and click the Delete button.

Summary

✦ All Acrobat viewers are capable of printing composite prints to office and personal printers. Only Acrobat Professional offers high-end printing and color separations.

✦ When printing files from Acrobat viewers, first open the Print Setup dialog box to choose a printer, page size, and page orientation.

✦ You can change page sizes with the Crop Pages tool. You add trim marks with the Add Printer Marks tool in the Print Production toolbar in Acrobat Professional.

✦ Acrobat Professional provides several menu tools for soft proofing color, overprints, separation previews, and transparency flattening. Acrobat Standard and Adobe Reader offer only overprint previews.

✦ Traps are defined with the Trap Presets tool in Acrobat Professional.

✦ JDF (Job Definition Files) are defined using the JDF Job Definitions tool in Acrobat Professional.

✦ Preflighting files is a manner of checking a document for potential errors in printing. Acrobat Professional offers you an extended set of conditions to check files before sending them to prepress centers and print shops.

✦ You save PDF/X-compliant files from the Preflight dialog box. Sending PDF/X files to service centers and print shops optimizes your chances for successful output when printing to commercial printing devices.

✦ A set of preset profiles is installed with Acrobat Professional for preflighting jobs. You
  can create custom profiles by adding preset conditions in the Preflight dialog box.

✦ You can import and export profiles. You can acquire profiles from service centers and
  add them to your profile list for preflighting files.

✦ The Advanced Print Setup dialog box in Acrobat Professional offers you options for
  color separations, printer's marks, frequency control, emulsion control, and other print
  attributes associated with commercial printing.

✦   ✦   ✦

Acrobat PDF Forms

Designing PDF Forms (Windows Only)

A PDF form contains form fields that you can fill out in all Acrobat viewers. Adobe Reader cannot save form data (unless files are specially prepared by adding usage rights), but you can design forms that can submit data to URLs and e-mail addresses by all Acrobat viewers.

In earlier version of Acrobat, a form began with a PDF document created somewhere else, and you needed to create form fields manually. With the introduction of Acrobat 7 Professional on Windows you have another alternative with the Adobe LiveCycle Designer program. Note that the official name is *Adobe LiveCycle Designer*. A more common term to describe the product is Adobe Designer or simply Designer. The program is only supported on Windows, but documents created with Designer can be filled out in all Acrobat viewers on both platforms.

To create a PDF form using the tools available Acrobat Professional, look at Chapters 27 through Chapter 29. This chapter offers a brief glimpse at using Adobe Designer for the purpose of forms design.

Adobe Designer is a complex program and describing all the features in the program would require a book the size of the *Acrobat 7 PDF Bible*. Therefore, it is well beyond the scope of this chapter to cover more than a very brief introduction to the program. For more detailed information about Designer, look over the Help document you can easily access by pressing the F1 key after launching Designer.

Setting Up the Work Environment

Adobe LiveCycle Designer is a stand-alone program used to design PDF forms. When you create forms in Designer, you cannot edit the form fields in Acrobat. Therefore, the work environment in Acrobat does not require any special tools to edit forms created in Designer. To view and fill out forms in Acrobat use the default toolbar setup. Open a context menu on the Toolbar Well and select Reset Toolbars.

When working in Designer you have an elaborate set of tools and window panes. To begin your first experience in Designer, open the program and leave the tools and window panes at their default views.

Understanding the *Why* for Adobe LiveCycle Designer

When you purchase Adobe Acrobat Professional one of your first thoughts might be, "Why is Adobe providing me with a stand-alone program to design forms when I can do the job in Acrobat Professional?" This is an important question and you need to understand not only the purpose for using Designer, but also the direction Adobe is moving toward related to PDF form design and deployment.

Adobe Designer is a client-based point-and-click graphical design application that simplifies the creation of forms. It includes the ability to create the form layout as well as the form fields that your user will populate. Forms created with Adobe Designer are intended to be delivered either as PDF or HTML that support user defined data structures, like XML. In support of standards-based data formatting, like XML, Adobe is moving away from its proprietary FDF (Form Data Format) as a data exchange format and migrating to XML. With tools that help you easily design forms through drag-and-drop methods for handling images and form data fields, Adobe Designer is a tool that simplifies form designs and data exchanges.

However, the simplicity of form designs is just a small part of the power of Adobe Designer. It's data handling that takes Designer to a level well beyond the capabilities of Adobe Acrobat. Form designers using Adobe Designer can create simple data capture solutions and use the Acrobat products to consolidate data received from clients. The ability to easily transport data to and from other applications via XDP and XML format makes Designer a much less complicated and efficient solution than what you have available using Adobe Acrobat.

As of this writing, Macintosh users are at a disadvantage since Designer is only available on Windows. However, you can expect to eventually see Designer supported on both platforms as development in technology applied to Designer is likely to increase while PDF forms design support in Acrobat is likely to decrease. Considering this new direction by Adobe Systems, the more you know about Designer today, the better off you'll be when future Acrobat products are released. If you are a serious form designer, you will want to begin using Designer right away.

Creating a Form in Adobe Designer

Adobe Designer offers you several options for designing forms when you first choose a menu command to create a new form. You can create a new blank form, use one of the many supplied form templates provided to you when you install Designer, open PDF files in Designer where you add fields and buttons and you can open Microsoft Word files (even with Word form fields) in Designer where you add and or modify existing form data fields. Immediately after the program is launched, you make a decision for what kind of form design you want to use.

Launching Designer

 In Acrobat Professional on Windows, you can access Designer by selecting Create New Form from the Forms Task Button pull-down menu. Selecting the menu command leaves Acrobat open in the background and opens Adobe Designer in the foreground. You can also open Designer by selecting Edit Fillable Form from the same menu. This command is intended to be used when you have a form open in Acrobat and want to make edits to the form design. Additionally if you have a PDF document open that has no fields, you can select Make Form Fillable in Adobe Designer

Note   When you leave Acrobat and edit a form in Designer, you are prompted to save the form after making edits. After saving the form from Designer, you no longer have access to any of the editing tools in the Advanced Editing toolbar including the form tools. Any further edits to form fields and form design can only be handled in Designer.

Adobe Designer is an executable application that you can open without launching Acrobat. Open the Start menu from the Status Bar and select Programs ➪ Adobe ➪ Adobe Designer 7.0.

Using the New Form Assistant

When you open Designer, the first dialog box that appears is the Welcome Screen shown in Figure 26-1. In the Welcome Screen you have buttons for viewing a Quick Start Tutorial, Explore Sample Forms, and a What's New button that opens the Adobe LiveCycle Designer Help document. Three buttons at the bottom of the Welcome screen are commands for creating a New Form, New Form from Template, or Open a Form.

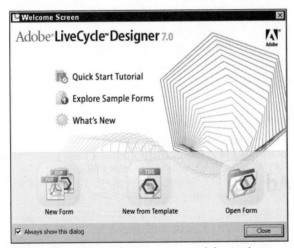

Figure 26-1: The first time you open Adobe Designer, the Welcome screen appears.

If this is your first time visiting Designer, be certain to take a look at the Quick Start Tutorial and poke around the Sample Forms and the Help document. After you start working with the program, remove the checkmark for Always show this dialog box. If you leave the checkmark on, you'll find this dialog box to be an annoyance as it always opens when you open and close documents including the Help file. You'll find yourself continually dismissing the dialog box in order to continue working.

When you click New Form in the Welcome screen or if you choose File ➪ New, the New Form Assistant opens. The first step is to select a method for creating a new form. You have choices for the method you want to use as shown in Figure 26-2.

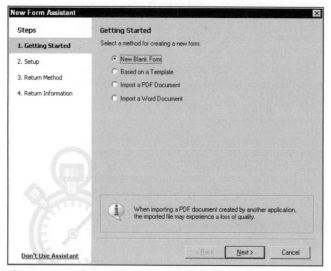

Figure 26-2: When you create a new form in Designer, you first make a choice for the method you want to use.

Creating forms based on templates

For the moment, let us skip creating a blank form and look at creating a form from a template. When you install Designer, a folder inside your Designer folder contains some pre-developed template files. Templates are saved to a .tds format. When you open a template the file opens as an *untitled* document. If you choose File ➪ Save, Designer prompts you for a file name. This method of saving new forms prevents you from overwriting the template files.

You can create custom templates complete with fields and assigned actions in Designer and save the files to your hard drive as .tds files. You can save the files to any folder, but Designer does create a folder for Custom templates for you when the program is installed. The directory path for template files and additionally the Custom folder is Acrobat 7.0/Designer 7.0/EN/Templates. Inside the Templates folder, you find a Sample folder where sample template files are saved, a Standard folder containing additional templates, and an empty folder for Custom templates.

The location of template files is not of particular importance as Designer provides you with a Template Manager that enables you to browse your hard drive to find templates saved in any folder. You can add, delete, rename, move and group templates in the Template Manager window shown in Figure 26-3. Notice the three tabs at the top of the window that correspond to the folders installed in a sub folder in your Designer folder.

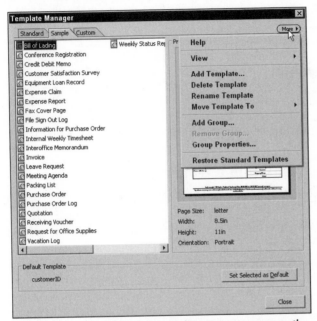

Figure 26-3: Choose Tools ⇨ Template Manager to open the Template Manager window.

When you create a new form from a template, only the Sample templates appear in a list of templates you can access from the New Form Assistant. To select a custom template or a template installed in the Standard Templates folder, click the Don't Use Assistant link at the lower-left corner of the New Form Assistant window. You are prompted in the Assistant Options dialog box to make a selection for options related to bypassing the New Form Assistant as shown in Figure 26-4.

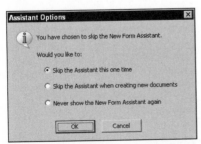

Figure 26-4: Click Don't Use Assistant and the Assistant Options dialog box opens.

If you select Skip the Assistant this one time, the next time you create a new form the New Form Assistant window opens. Selecting Skip the Assistant when creating new documents, bypasses the New Form Assistant window each time you select File ⇨ New. Selecting Never show the New Form Assistant again dismisses the dialog box and never shows it for any circumstance. If you choose to skip the New Form Assistant, the New dialog box opens. The New dialog box appears very similar to the Template Manager. However, instead of managing templates the New dialog box lets you select a template from any one of the three tabs. Therefore, you have access to your custom templates as well as the Standard templates.

It is important to understand that you need to dismiss the New Form Assistant window if you want to open a custom template and you need to open the custom template in the New dialog box. You can navigate your hard drive after selecting File ⇨ New to find a custom template, but that requires you to search through folders on your hard drive to find the template. When using the New window, you double click on any template listed in the three tabs and the file opens as a template.

To gain a better understanding for how you create a form in Designer from a preinstalled template, follow these steps:

STEPS: Creating a form from a template

1. **Open the New Form Assistant.** Launch Adobe Designer. In the Welcome Screen, click New Form. The New Form Assistant opens.

2. **Create a form based on a template.** Select the *Based on a Template* radio button. Click Next to move to the next pane.

3. **Select a template.** The Setup pane opens in the New Form Assistant. From a scrollable list, you can select a template installed in the Sample folder. Select Purchase Order in the list as shown in Figure 26-5. Click Next to move to the Return Method pane.

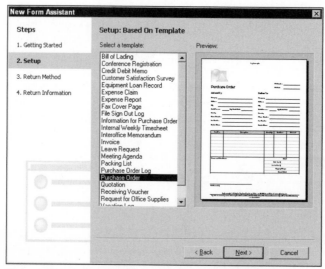

Figure 26-5: Select Purchase Order in the list of available templates and click Next to move to the next pane.

4. **Select a return method.** The Return Method pane offers options for how you want the data submitted. You can choose from options to email the form, print the form, or a combination of both email and print. Select the default option *Fill then Submit...* as shown in Figure 26-6. Click Next to open the Return Information pane.

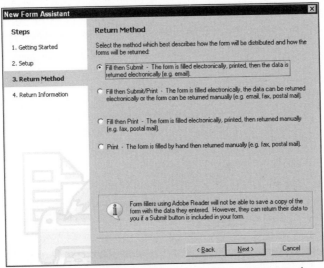

Figure 26-6: Select Fill then Submit and click next to open the Return Information pane.

5. **Add your e-mail address.** The Return Information pane contains a text box for you to type your e-mail address. Add your e-mail address in the text box shown in Figure 26-7 and click Finish. The form opens in Designer with a Submit button added to the template. When a user clicks the Submit button, the form data are sent to your e-mail address.

The form contains data fields preconfigured when the template was created. As you can see in Figure 26-8, the Submit by Email button appears at the top of the form. This data object is the only element added to the original template.

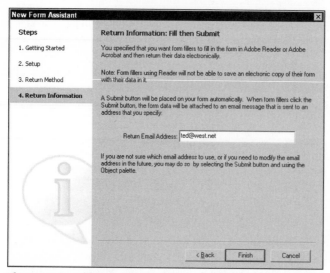

Figure 26-7: Add your e-mail address and click Finish to open the form in Designer.

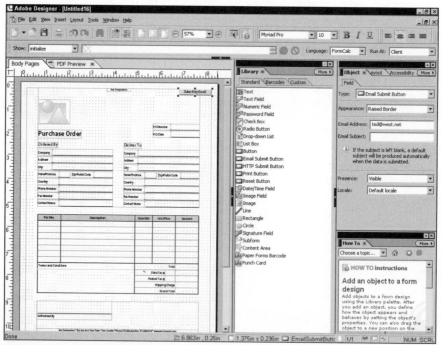

Figure 26-8: The final form contains a button to email the data to the address supplied in the Return Information pane.

Getting to Know the Designer Environment

When you first create a form in Designer or you start with a new blank page, you see your document layout and a number of palettes in the Designer workplace. Several palettes are open by default and a number of the palettes are accessible from the Window menu. Click Window to open the menu as shown in Figure 26-9 to view all the palettes and resources. Those palettes and/or resources appearing with checkmarks beside the menu names are currently visible in the Designer window.

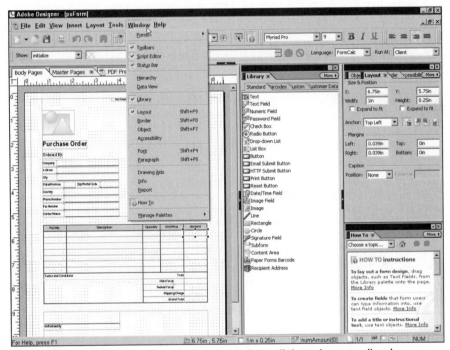

Figure 26-9: Click Window to open the menu where all the palettes are listed.

The palettes and resource items in Designer include:

✦ **Toolbars:** The tools at the top of the Designer window can be hidden if you select Toolbars and remove the checkmark. You might want to hide toolbars temporarily during a design session to provide more viewing area for your form.

✦ **Script Editor:** Drag the Separator Bar (positioned below the Show pull-down menu at the horizontal center of the Designer window as shown in Figure 26-10) down to display the Script Editor or double-click on the the separator bar to expand or contract the Script Editor window. The Script Editor is where you supply formulas for calculations. Designer supports two scripting models. FormCalc is used to supply calculation formulas for calculating field values. This language is similar to common spreadsheet calculations. JavaScript is supported in Designer and JavaScript code is added to the Script Editor window. To choose between FormCalc and JavaScript, open the Language pull-down menu appearing below the toolbars on the right side of the window and select the language option you want to use.

Tip

You can set the Script Editor default to either FormCalc or JavaScript. Select File ➪ Form Properties ➪ Defaults. From the Default Language pull-down menu, select the language you want to use. The language you choose remains as a default for all subsequent forms you create in Designer.

Figure 26-10: Drag the Separator Bar up or down to resize the Script Editor.

✦ **Status Bar:** The Status Bar appears in the same location as you find in Acrobat. Remove the checkmark in the Window menu to hide the Status Bar. Again, you might use this option to provide more viewing area for your forms.

✦ **Hierarchy:** The Hierarchy palette shown in Figure 26-11 shows you a list of all the elements on the form. Click the plus (+) symbol to expand a nested list.

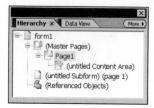

Figure 26-11: The Hierarchy palette shows you all the elements contained on a form.

✦ **Data View:** Nested in the same palette as the Hierarchy is the Data View palette. This palette is used to create, delete, and edit properties for data connections. Once a data connection is created it is listed in the palette.

✦ **Library:** The Library contains a list of objects you add to your forms by dragging from the Library to the form layout. In the Library palette, you can select an object and preview it in the palette before adding the object to your design. All field types are contained in the Library and a number of choices for bar code fields. Additionally, you can create your own objects (stored in the Custom) tab for reuse in your forms.

✦ **Layout:** The Layout palette lets you position and size fields and objects and field captions on a page. You must click an object in order to set values for positions and offsets.

✦ **Border:** The Border palette offers options for setting appearances for field borders and fills. The options available in Designer are much more than what you find available in Acrobat. Among some of the appearances you have in Designer that are not available in Acrobat are choices for different corner shapes and options for adding gradient fills.

✦ **Object:** The Object palette offers settings for assigning field types, appearances, and visibility. One feature you have available in Designer in regard to changing field types is that Designer enables you to change any field type to any other field type. In Acrobat, you have to delete the field and create a new field of a different type.

✦ **Accessibility:** The Accessibility palette offers options for adding data that can be read by screen readers. This enables you add all accessibility features at design time. Items such as Tool Tips to describe a field are found in the palette.

✦ **Font:** The Font palette provides a list in a pull-down menu of all the fonts installed in your system. You can select any installed font to use in a line of text on the form as well as assign attributes for style, face, point size, and so on.

Cross-Reference

For more information on font handling, see the sidebar "Working with Fonts in Designer" in this chapter.

✦ **Paragraph:** The paragraph palette is similar to what you might find in layout programs. Paragraph attributes for text are assigned in the paragraph palette such as indentation, hanging indents, alignment, and leading.

✦ **Drawing Aids:** The Drawing Aids palette is where you toggle rulers on and off, and set grids, guides, and object boundaries.

✦ **Info:** The Info palette displays the document metadata associated with selected objects. To view information in the Info palette select one or more objects on the page.

✦ **Report:** The Report palette provides information about a form and the form objects. You have several choices for viewing reports in the Reports palette and they include

- A list of fields with normal binding

- A list of fields that have binding by reference

- A list of fields that have global data binding

- A list of unbound data connection nodes

Note

You can bind forms in Designer to XML schemas, XML sample files, databases, and Web services. The Report palette lists data binding according to one of the options you select to view in the report.

✦ **Warnings:** The Warnings palette lists errors and messages dynamically as you work on a form. Note that the Warnings palette is not accessible from the Window menu. You access the palette by selecting Report. The Warnings palette is nested with the Report palette.

✦ **How To:** Similar to what you have in Acrobat viewers, the How To palette offers you help information. From the palette pull-down menu, you can select topical areas and click links in the text to jump to topical areas of interest.

Working with Fonts in Designer

Adobe Designer works similar to the way you might work in page layout programs. You have master pages, page size configurations, ability to import graphics and many options for setting type. Like layout programs, if you attempt to open a document when fonts contained in the document are not installed in your system, you wind up with font problems in terms of appearances and improper printing.

If you design a form using a certain font set, be certain the same font family is loaded in your system before opening the file. If you open PDF or Word documents in Designer, you need to have all the fonts contained in the file installed in your system. You may have a huge potential problem if you work with a number of legacy PDF documents that need to be redesigned in Designer. When fonts are not installed in your system and you open a PDF file in Designer, a Missing Fonts dialog box opens as shown in the following figure.

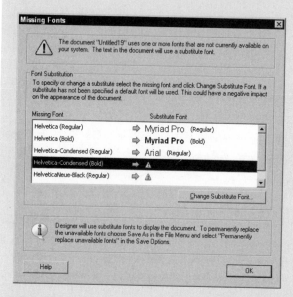

If a font is missing the font is listed with a caution symbol. To substitute the missing font with a font loaded in your system, click the Change Substitute Font button. The Specify Substitute Font dialog box opens where you select installed system fonts in a scrollable window. Select a font in the list and click OK. You need to repeat the steps for each font appearing with a caution symbol in the Missing Fonts dialog box. After identifying the font substitutions, click OK and the new substituted fonts appear in the document. When you save the file as PDF, the new fonts are embedded in the resultant PDF.

Editing a Form

Adobe Designer is just about as complex as Adobe Acrobat. As such, there is no way I can cover all the features, commands, tools, and menu options you have available in Designer. The best you can hope for in this chapter is a bit of a starting point to understand how fields are added to a form, how you assign field attributes, and how you go about creating data connections. The rest you need to explore in the Help files or search for a book dedicated exclusively to Adobe LiveCycle Designer.

Using the Library palette

The Library palette shown in Figure 26-12 contains a variety of form fields and many of these are the same as form fields you can create in Acrobat. In Designer you drag a field from the Layout palette onto the layout grid. In Acrobat you use a tool to create a form field. A feature you have available in Designer that's not available in Acrobat is the ability to group fields in a collection and add them to a personal library. When you want to use the same fields in several designs you can drag a group from your personal library to the layout grid. This group can contain validations and/or JavaScript that are preserved when you save a file.

Cross-Reference For a description of field types and attributes, see Chapter 27.

Adding fields to a form

Whether you create a form from a template or create a new blank form, you add new fields to your form by dragging and dropping the field types to your layout. Notice in Figure 26-12 I added a button to print the file by dragging from the Library to the page layout. When the grid is active, the fields snap to coordinates on the page. Additionally, all scripts assigned to the field are duplicated on the page. In this example, the Print button contains a script to open the Print dialog box when the user clicks the button.

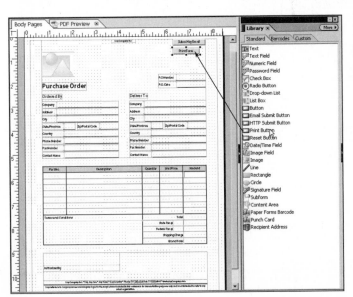

Figure 26-12: Click and drag a field from the Library palette to the layout page.

The Library palette contains three tabs. The Standard tab is shown in Figure 26-12. Here you have many standard field types similar to fields you create in Acrobat. You can modify a field for appearance properties, actions, scripts, and binding after dragging the field to the layout page. First drag a field to the layout, and then edit the field attributes while on the page. If you want to reuse the field with the same attributes click the Custom tab and drag the field from the page to the Custom panel.

Located between the Standard and Custom tabs you find the Barcodes tab. The barcode feature in Designer is one of many features that distinguish Designer from forms created in Adobe Acrobat. You have an elaborate set of different barcode samples in the barcodes tab. Barcodes created in Designer can be either static or interactive. Interactive barcodes created in Designer can automatically encode data you type in a form field.

Adding new groups to the Library

Another way to manage your custom form fields or a collection of form fields is to add new groups to the Library. Say you have a number of forms for point of sale purchases. On each form, you have fields for customers to fill out and complete when submitting orders. You typically have identifying information for client names, addresses, phone numbers and other contact information. In addition you may have a submit button for submitting data, a few different reset buttons to clear data fields, and maybe some order tables where products, quantities, unit prices, and totals are added. In addition, you may have some calculation fields for summing sub totals, adding sales tax, and adding shipping costs. All or some of these data fields might be included on several different forms you use for seasonal purchasing, general ordering, special discount programs, and so on. In Designer, you have an easy way to handle repetition when it comes to adding form fields to a new layout.

You first start by creating a new Library group. From the More pull-down menu in the Library palette select Add Group. The Add Library Group dialog box shown in Figure 26-13 opens prompting you for a Library Group name. Type a name for your new group and click OK. The new group appears as a new tab in the Library palette.

Figure 26-13: Type a name in the Add Library Group dialog box to name your new group.

Note   You can have any tab active in the Library palette when opening the More pull-down menu and selecting Add Group. Regardless of which tab is selected, the new group is created as a separate tab and docked in the Library palette.

After you create the new Library group, the tab docks in the Library palette and opens. The contents of the tab are empty. You need to add fields to the tab as you do when adding fields to the Custom tab. Yet another great feature in Designer is that you can group fields together and nest them so they appear as a single object in the Library palette. Let's say in the example for creating a group for customer information, you want to group together the name, address, city, state, and other identifying information fields. You can add these fields to the new group tab as a single object.

To group several fields as a single object and add them to a Library tab, drag a marquee on the layout page around the fields you want to group. The fields are selected when you release the mouse button. Move the cursor inside one of the selected objects and drag to the Library palette as shown in Figure 26-14.

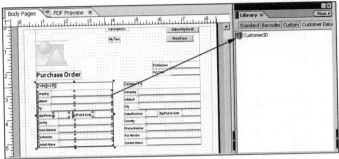

Figure 26-14: Marquee a group of fields and drag to the Library palette to create a new grouped library object.

Note   Unlike other Adobe imaging programs, Designer does not select objects when you drag through them. You need to draw a marquee completely around objects and release the mouse button to select them.

Notice in Figure 26-14 the selected objects appear on the layout page and the Library palette contains a new Library Group named *Customer ID*. When you release the mouse button the Add Library Object dialog box opens as shown in Figure 26-15. Type a Name for the new object, add a description, and select a Tab group. By default the tab group you drag to is selected in the Tag Group pull-down menu. If you want to add the grouped object to another tab group, open the pull-down menu and select the tab where you want to add the object. Click OK and the object is added to your Library tab. In Figure 26-14 you can see the CustomerID object. Note that no matter how many fields you drag together to a Library tab, only a single object is created.

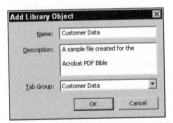

Figure 26-15: Type a name, add a description, and select a tab group to add your object to a tab group.

Editing field appearances

Another nice feature you have in Designer is the ability to change field appearances for multiple fields of different types. Additionally, you can change more appearance options and set more appearance attributes in Designer than you can in Acrobat.

To change field appearances in Designer, select one or more fields and open the Border palette. If you want to change appearances for multiple fields, open the Hierarchy palette and Click and Shift Click or Control Click. The top half of the palette handles attributes assigned to the line borders and the lower half of the palette handles fill attributes. You can change edge appearances individually or together and can select from for different border shapes. Line borders and fill styles are selected from pull-down menus and the color choices are made from color swatch palettes as shown in Figure 26-16. Click the down-pointing arrow to open a color swatch palette and click a color or select More Colors to select a custom color from your operating system color palette.

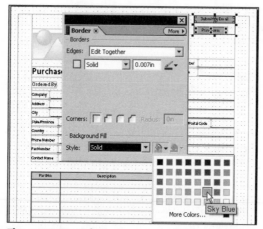

Figure 26-16: Select one or more fields and open the Border palette to change object appearances.

Adding images

Images are imported in Adobe Designer using the Object palette. You first open the Library palette and click the Standard tab. Listed in the tab are Image Field and Image. Image fields are like button faces in Acrobat. You import an image for the appearance, but the object is a data field that you can assign actions. Image is a static object that you use for a graphic as part of your form design.

Select Image from the Standard tab in the Library palette and drag to the layout page. Open the Object Palette. Type a URL to an image or click the icon adjacent to the URL field to locate a file using a dialog box. If you click the folder icon adjacent to the URL text box, the Browse for Image File dialog box opens. Navigate your hard drive and select the image you want to import. Click Open and the image imports into the image placeholder as shown in Figure 26-17.

Figure 26-17: Click the folder icon to select and open an image file.

Tip   Double-click the image placeholder to open the Browse for Image File dialog box.

Images can be imported from files saved as .bmp, .jpg, .gif, .png, and .tif. In the Object palette you can size images to the saved image size by selecting Use Image Size from the Sizing pull-down menu. Other options for sizing include Scale Image to Fit where the image is sized proportionally to the Image placeholder box or Stretch Image to Fit where the image can be sized horizontally or vertically without constraining the size to proportions.

Calculating fields

Field calculation in Designer is sophisticated and complex. You have two languages to choose from when adding calculations to fields. The FormCalc language follows similar syntax you might use with spreadsheet applications. JavaScript is a scripting language and writing JavaScript routines is similar to writing JavaScripts in Acrobat.

Learning the scripting languages requires you to review the documentation and view samples of routines developed with both languages. What's important for you as you review this chapter is not so much looking over a list of functions and routines; but rather, you need to understand where to go to start writing scripts. This feature in Designer is not entirely intuitive.

To start, you might want to create a form from a template and look over the fields. You should be able to get an idea for what fields contain calculation scripts at a quick glance. Look for total fields, sales tax fields, and summary fields at the end of columns or rows where numeric data are added. Click a field and drag the separator bar below the Show pull-down menu and above the page layout. The bar has a black bar with an up pointing arrow as shown in Figure 26-18.

Tip   To view all the scripts in a form, open the Hierarchy palette and select the root object. Select Edit ➪ Select All. Open the Script Editor window. Select Show ➪ Events with Scripts. You will now see all the scripting through the entire form.

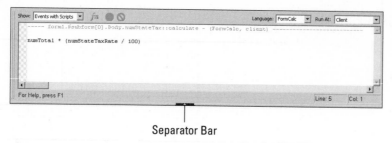

Separator Bar

Figure 26-18: Drag the separator bar down to open the scripting window.

From the Show pull-down look for events with a "*" next to the action. This event has scripting or from the Show pull-down menu select Events with Scripts to easily find all the scripts in a field. A selected field shows you a script in black text as shown in Figure 26-18 if such a script exists. You can edit the script by clicking the cursor inside the script window. If, for example, I want to change the script shown in Figure 26-18 to a fixed tax rate, I might delete the field text numStateTaxRate and replace it with a value like 8 for 8 percent.

On the right side of the scripting window, you see a pull-down menu for Language. Your options are FormCalc or JavaScript. In Figure 26-18 notice the selection is made for FormCalc.

When using either language you have a list of functions available from a menu. Select an event from the Show pull-down menu and click the *fn* button adjacent to the Show pull-down menu and a pop-up menu opens with a scrollable list of functions related to the selected language. Note that the functions change if you change languages. In Figure 26-19, you can see a partial list of the functions available for FormCalc. Scroll the list and you find math functions similar to what you find in spreadsheet programs. To add a function to a line of code, click the cursor where you want the function to appear. Click the *fn* button to open the list and scroll the list to find the function you want to use. Double click the function and the code is inserted at the cursor position.

Figure 26-19: Click on the *fn* button to open a pop-up menu where a list of functions are shown.

Calculations and scripting in Designer are extensive and a thorough description is well beyond the scope of this book. For more information on using FormCalc, open the Help menu and select Adobe Designer Help. Browse the Help document for field calculation examples.

Note   The JavaScript used in Adobe Designer is different than the JavaScript implementation used in Acrobat. For help information, be certain to visit Adobe's Web site where a reference manual will be hosted sometime after the release of Adobe Designer. As of this writing, no documentation currently exists for JavaScript used in Designer.

Previewing the form

Once you design a form complete with fields and assign field attributes, you can preview the file as it would appear in Acrobat as a PDF document. Click the PDF Preview tab in the Designer window to see a preview of how the form displays as a PDF, as shown in Figure 26-20. A preview of your form as it appears as a PDF and viewed in Acrobat viewers is shown in the Designer window. To return to layout mode click the Body Pages tab.

When you work on a document in layout mode, none of the fields are editable as a user would fill in the form. You need to view your form in PDF Preview mode in order to fill in data fields and execute scripts.

If you prepare PDFs for use by Adobe Reader users, first launch Adobe Reader. Open Adobe Designer from the Start menu or by double clicking the program icon. Since Adobe Reader is the active Acrobat viewer, all the form features used in the PDF Prerview are as an Adobe Reader user would see them.

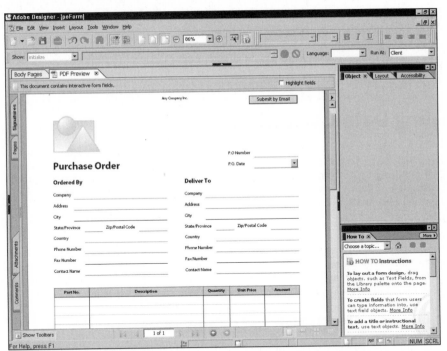

Figure 26-20: Click PDF Preview to view the form as it appears in Acrobat.

Saving the form

Choose File ⇨ Save As to save the form as a Designer template, an Adobe XML Form File, or as a PDF file. Select the desired format, and the file is saved. If you open the file in Acrobat and want to edit the form, open the Forms Task Button pull-down menu and select Edit Fillable Form. The PDF opens in Designer where you can further edit the document.

The options available for you when saving from Adobe Designer include:

✦ **Static PDF Form File:** You save the file and only static elements on your form are recognized in Acrobat. If you have dynamic elements they are unavailable when viewing in Acrobat. Static forms are just like the forms you create in Acrobat Professional. These forms are *page based* forms — that is, if you have a two page form, the form remains static as two pages.

✦ **Dynamic PDF Form File:** You save the form and all dynamic elements. Dynamic forms can grow and generate new pages. You can create elements on the forms and have the elements move down or across new pages depending on the actions you add to the form.

✦ **Acrobat 6 Compatible (Static) PDF Form File:** If you save with any of the other PDF formats, the forms can only be opened in Acrobat viewers version 7.0 and above. This option enables you to save the form that can be recognized by users of Acrobat 6 and above. (this saves as PDF 1.5)

✦ **Adobe XML Form File:** This setting saves the file as .xdp which is native to Adobe Designer. This format is recognized by Adobe LiveCycle Forms.

✦ **Adobe Designer Template:** Use this format when you want to create templates and build a form based on your custom templates.

Be aware that regardless of which PDF format you use, your form is not editable in Acrobat. You need to return to Designer to edit all form designs created with Adobe Designer.

Creating Data Connections

Binding fields in a form design to a data source is one of the true great features in Adobe Designer. If using Acrobat to bind to data sources you need to have a sophisticated level of JavaScript programming background and a lot of finesse to create the resources that successfully bind data to other sources. With Designer, the process is greatly simplified and the program does much of the mind wrenching work for you.

When binding fields on a form design to a data source, you create an association between the form and some data source that lets you capture, process, output, and print information from the data entries on a form. Designer enables you to bind data either as client-side where you might bind data locally on a hard drive to a backend database file or as server-side binding. Client-side binding enables you to make changes immediately to the data while server-side binding requires you to submit data to a server where changes are made.

Connecting to OLEDB data sources

OLE Databases (OLEDB) are sets of Component Object Model (COM) interfaces that provide applications with uniform access stored in diverse information sources. In short, these interfaces support DBMS (Database Management Systems) functionality appropriate to the data source that enables it to share data. You might have databases such as Microsoft Access files, Excel spreadsheet files or other database types that you want to share data with PDF forms. You might have a situation where you use a singe identifying field, such as an employee ID or Social Security number a user types into a form. Using this one piece of data you can connect to a database to retrieve additional information (or records) associated with this information.

To dynamically edit data in your database file, you make a connection to the database and then bind fields on the form to the corresponding columns in the database.

OLEDB is unique compared to other connection types supported by Designer as it is the only connection type that you can connect to from within Designer.

Designer supports a number of OLEDB drivers. Click the More button in the Data View palette and the New Data Connection dialog box opens. Click OLEDB Database, add a name for your connection in the Name New Connection box/field and click the Next button. The OLEDB Connection dialog box opens, Click the Build button and the Data Link Properties dialog box opens as shown in Figure 26-21. The list in the figure shows you the supported drivers.

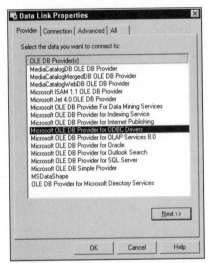

Figure 26-21: Click Build in the OLEDB Connection dialog box and the Data Link Properties dialog box opens. Select a data connection you want to make from the list of providers.

You need to name your connection and set up your database connection string. Setting up a database connection string may require you to research your database user manual. Once you've established a Connection String you are returned to the OLEDB Connection dialog box You next select from one of three options that include:

✦ **Table:** You select a table as a data source. The list is populated with a list of all the tables available within the database identified by the connection string.

✦ **Stored Procedure:** You select this option and select the record from the list. The list is populated with all of the stored procedures available from the database.

✦ **SQL Query:** Select this option and type the SQL query string.

You select one of the three options above and select next which will open the ADO Properties dialog box. Add your user name and password if required to access the DB source. Designer then validates the connection and reports that it is successful. After finishing the connection, the Data View palette lists a hierarchical tree of the data elements.

XML schema and XML data sources

You can import an XML schema definition into a form design and then bind objects in the form design to elements in the XML schema. If you have an XML file and not an XML schema you can bind objects to the XML data form. The process for binding both a schema and a file are similar. The option that differs between the two is when you select which source you want in the New Data Connection dialog box.

To create an XML schema connection, select File ⇨ New Data Connection. In the New Data Connection dialog box, select XML Schema (Sample XML Data for an XML data file). Click Next and click the Browse button adjacent to the Select XML Schema File text box. Browse your hard drive and select the XML schema file. Click Next and you need to make a selection from options in the XML Data Root Element Name menu. Select a root element that will be used to name the root subform in the form design. Additionally there are three other optional choices you can make for embedding the XML schema in the form, transforming incoming data, and transforming outgoing data. Make your selections and click Finish. When you view the Data View palette the data appears something like you might see in Figure 26-22.

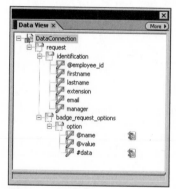

Figure 26-22: After binding to an XML schema, the data are displayed in the Data View palette.

WSDL file

Web Services are applications that run remote over the Web. For example, your form might include a field where the current mortgage rate needs to be calculated. You can connect to a Web Service that determines the daily mortgage rate based on your address. A Web Service Description Language (WSDL) is a XML document (or file) that describes the Web service and the services and operations (or methods) offered by the service. The connection supports a number of operations. The WSDL file can define for each operation an input message, an output message or both. Input messages are sent to a server. The server can then reply with an output message. Using Designer you can create and bind fields in a form design to one of many different Web services.

Aside from connecting to a WSDL via the New Data Connections wizard, you can:

✦ Bind one or more operations within one or more Web services

✦ Attach fields, subforms, and exclusion groups to the execution of a Web service operation using a button click event

✦ Execute a Web service operation from any event by way of a script

✦ Enable script access to all returned elements of a Web service regardless of whether those elements are bound to fields

✦ Use Simple Object Access Protocol (SOAP) 1.1 style communication

> **Note**
>
> SOAP is a lightweight protocol for exchange of information in a decentralized environment. SOAP is an XML based protocol that consists of three parts: an envelope that defines a framework for describing what is in a message and how to process it, a set of encoding rules for expressing instances of application-defined data types, and a convention for representing remote procedure calls and responses.

✦ Exchange data with a Web service by using doc/literal exchange format

✦ Write client-side scripts by using the Acrobat SOAP JavaScript Object which supports RPC/encoded

You create WSDL connections by selecting File ➪ New Data Connection. In the New Data Connection dialog box select WSDL File and click Next. The next pane in the New Data Connection dialog box prompts you for an HTTP address. You need assistance from your system administrator to make a file available and an address location for where the file is hosted. Click Next and select the operation you want to call. Click Finish to complete the connection.

In the Data View palette you find three objects added that include: Request, Response, and a button that makes the connection to the Web service. When you expand these objects you will see the Request fields and the Response fields similar to what is shown in Figure 26-23. Just drag and drop these fields onto your page to make the data connections.

Figure 26-23: Drag fields from the Data View palette to your form layout to make the data connections.

Tip   To see some examples of WSDL connections, visit the `http://www.xmethods.net` Web site.

If you're a form designer and not a programmer you'll need help from your system administrator using WSDL or some of the other data connections available to you with Designer. The important consideration you need to make is which data connection type works in your environment and with the users who you intend to access your forms. Choose one data connection type and solicit assistance where needed. Become familiar with the process for binding data to a given connection type and consult the user documentation supplied with your Acrobat installation.

Summary

+ You access Designer from within Acrobat or by opening the program icon.

+ Adobe Designer is a point-and-click graphical design application that simplifies creation of form templates intended to be delivered as PDF or HTML.

+ Adobe Designer represents a new direction in form design from Adobe Systems. Designer provides Windows users a more sophisticated form designer environment than adding form fields to a PDF document in Adobe Acrobat.

+ Adobe Designer supports the use of many different tools, commands and an extensive number of palettes used to create form elements and bind data to external sources.

+ You can create new form designs by starting with blank document pages or by using templates.

+ You can use preinstalled template files or create new template designs and manage your templates in the Template Manager dialog box.

+ Form elements are added to a layout from objects in the Library palette.

+ You can create custom objects and add them to custom libraries complete with scripts and attribute assignments.

+ Field calculations and actions assignments are added in a script editor window using either the FormCalc or JavaScript language.

+ Preinstalled functions are selectable from a palette and added to FormCalc formulas or JavaScripts.

+ Fields can be grouped in collections and added to custom libraries where they can be reused in subsequent forms.

+ Designer offers easy access to database connections for fields and forms.

+ You can save designer forms as templates, PDF files, and Adobe XML Form Files.

✦   ✦   ✦

Understanding the Form Tools

Certainly one of the most popular uses of the Portable Document Format has to be Acrobat PDF forms. Now with the introduction of Acrobat 7, Windows users can simplify forms design by using Adobe Designer, which makes the construction of PDF forms and data handling much easier than when working in Acrobat. However, for users in Macintosh environments and those who haven't begun to work with Adobe Designer, an abundant number of tools and commands are available that provide you the means for creating forms directly in Acrobat Professional.

Because the PDF format is so widely accepted, people often design forms documents in authoring programs, convert to PDF, and call the end result a PDF form. In a way, these documents might be termed *forms*, but to take full advantage of the power in Acrobat, you need to add live form fields and interactive elements and make your forms more dynamic with tools specifically provided for forms authoring. In this chapter you learn how to create forms with the Forms tools and how to fill in forms in Acrobat viewers.

Note   Creating, modifying, and working with form fields require the use of Acrobat Professional. Acrobat Standard does not support PDF forms creation or editing.

Setting Up the Environment

Working with PDF forms requires the use of the Forms tools. To open the Forms toolbar, choose Tools ⇨ Advanced Editing ⇨ Show Forms Toolbar. The Select Object tool in the Advanced Editing toolbar is an essential tool to use when creating and editing forms. To gain access to the tool, open the Advanced Editing toolbar from a context menu opened on the Toolbar Well. As a last item, return to the context menu on the Toolbar Well and select Properties Bar. When all toolbars are visible in the Document pane, select Dock All Toolbars from a context menu opened from the Toolbar Well.

In addition to tools, a Fields palette offers more options for editing forms. By default the Fields palette is hidden. To open the palette, choose View ⇨ Navigation Tabs ⇨ Fields. The Fields palette opens with three other palettes nested in the same window. Click on the Fields tab and drag it to the Navigation pane. Close the palette containing the other navigation tabs.

What Are Acrobat Forms?

Forms in Acrobat are PDF files with data fields that appear as placeholders for user-supplied data. In Acrobat, you can use text string fields, numeric fields, check boxes, radio buttons, date fields, calculation fields, signature fields, and a variety of custom fields created with JavaScripts. The advantage of using forms in Acrobat is that doing so enables you to maintain design integrity for the appearance of a form while providing you powerful control over data management. Rather than using a database manager, which may limit your ability to control fonts and graphics, Acrobat PDFs preserve all the design attributes of a document while behaving like a data manager.

Forms are created in Acrobat Professional or Adobe Designer. Form field data can be saved with Acrobat Standard and Professional. You can also save form data with Adobe Reader when the PDF form has been prepared with Adobe LiveCycle Reader Extensions. When opening PDFs in Adobe Reader that have not been enabled with Reader Extensions you cannot save, import, or export data. In developing PDF workflows for a company or organization, all users expected to design forms in Acrobat need to use the Acrobat Professional software. Corporations and enterprises seeking an affordable solution for extending Adobe Reader to support forms features, should look at acquiring the Adobe LifeCycle Reader Extensions Server.

The one thing to keep in mind regarding Acrobat and forms is that a form in the context of PDF is not a paper form scanned as an image and saved as PDF. Tons of these so-called forms are around offices and on the Internet. The documents originated as forms, but hopefully by the time you understand all the features available to you with Acrobat, you'll understand these scanned documents could hardly be called forms. Simply put, they're scanned images saved to PDF. The power of Acrobat gives you the tools to create *smart forms*. These forms can be dynamic, intuitive, and interactive, and save both you and the end user much time in providing and gathering information.

Understanding Form Fields

Forms contain different types of data fields that hold data, act as buttons that invoke actions, and call scripts to execute a series of actions. Form fields can assume different appearances as well as possess the capability to include graphic icons and images to represent hot links that invoke actions. Acrobat forms are more than a static data filing system—they can be as vivid and dynamic as your imagination. When designing a form in Acrobat, you are well advised to plan your work ahead of time. As you will see, with the many different choices available for field contents and appearances, creating form fields in Acrobat Professional offers an enormous number of options.

To learn how forms function in Acrobat, you need to understand how forms are developed and, ultimately, how you go about creating form fields. As Acrobat cannot be effectively used as a layout application, nor can it be used to draw rules and design elements, creation of a form begins in another application. You can use illustration or layout software for designing a form that ultimately is converted to PDF. In Acrobat, the form data fields are created with the form tools, and options are selected from the Field Properties window. Form fields can be of several different types:

✦ **Button:** A button is usually used to invoke an action or hyperlink. A button face can be text or a graphic element created in another program that you can apply as an appearance to the button. You can also use different appearance settings in the button properties for adding stroke and fill colors. Buttons are also used to import images.

✦ **Check boxes:** Check boxes typically appear in groups to offer the user a selection of choices. Yes and no items or a group of check boxes might be created for multiple-choice selections.

✦ **Combo box:** When you view an Acrobat form, you may see a down-pointing arrow similar to the arrows appearing in palette menus. Such an arrow in a PDF form indicates the presence of a combo box. When you click the arrow, a pull-down menu opens with a list of choices. Users are limited to selecting a single choice from combo boxes. Additionally, if designed as such, users can input their own choices.

✦ **List box:** A list box displays a box with scroll bars, much like windows you see in application software documents. As you scroll through a list box, you make a choice of one or more of the alternatives available by selecting items in the list.

✦ **Radio buttons:** Radio buttons perform the same function in PDF forms as radio buttons do in dialog boxes. Usually you have two or more choices for a category. Forms are usually designed so that when one radio button in a group is turned on, the other buttons in the group are turned off.

✦ **Text:** Text fields are boxes in which text is typed by the end user to fill out the form. Text fields can contain alphabetical characters, numbers, or a combination of both.

✦ **Signature fields:** Digital signatures can be applied to fields, PDF pages, and PDF documents. A digital signature can be used to lock out fields on a form.

All these form field types are available to you when you create a form in Acrobat. From the end user's point of view, one needs to examine a form and understand how to make choices for the field types in order to accurately complete a form. Fortunately, Acrobat field types relate similarly to the metaphors used by most applications designed with a graphic user interface. An example of an Acrobat form with several form field types is shown in Figure 27-1.

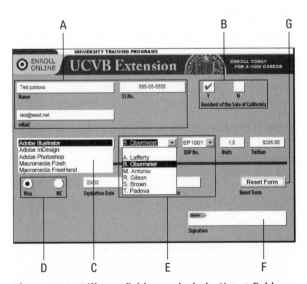

Figure 27-1: Different field types include A) text fields; B) check boxes; C) list box; D) radio buttons; E) combo boxes; F) Digital Signature field; G) button.

Filling In Forms

As you view the form shown in Figure 27-1, notice it contains several text fields, a combo box, a list box, and at least one each of the other field types. To fill out a text field, you need to select the Hand tool, place the cursor over the field, and click the mouse button. When you click, a blinking I-beam cursor appears, indicating that you can add text by typing on your keyboard.

Tip   To begin filling in a form, press the Tab key on your keyboard. When the Hand tool is selected and the cursor is not active in any field, pressing the Tab key places the cursor in the first field on the form.

To navigate to the next field for more text entry, you can make one of two choices: Click in the next field or press the Tab key on your keyboard. When you press the Tab key, the cursor jumps to the next field, according to an order you specify in Acrobat when you design the form. Be certain the Hand tool is selected and a cursor appears in a field box when you press the Tab key. If you have any other tool selected, you can tab through the fields and type data in the field boxes; however, if you click with the mouse when another tool is selected, you make edits according to the active tool.

Cross-Reference   For understanding more about tab orders, see the section "Setting field tab orders" later in this chapter.

When selecting from choices in radio button or check box fields, click in the radio button or check box. The display changes to show a small solid circle or checkmark within a box or other kind of user-defined symbol from options you select for button styles. When using a combo box, click the down-pointing arrow in the field and select from one of several pull-down menu choices.

Form field navigation keystrokes

As mentioned in the preceding section, to move to the next field, you need to either click in the field or press the Tab key. Following is a list of other keystrokes that can help you move through forms to complete them:

✦ **Shift+Tab:** Moves to the previous field.

✦ **Esc:** Ends text entry.

✦ **Return:** Ends text entry for single line entries or adds a carriage return for multi-line fields.

✦ **Double-click a word in a field:** Selects the word.

✦ **Ctrl/⌘+A:** Selects all the text in a field.

✦ **Left/right arrow keys:** Moves the cursor one character at a time left or right.

✦ **Up arrow:** Fielding combo and list boxes moves up the list.

✦ **Down arrow:** Fielding combo and list boxes moves down the list.

✦ **Up/down arrow with combo and list boxes selected:** Moves up and down the list. When the list is collapsed, pressing the down-arrow key opens the list.

✦ **Ctrl/⌘+Tab:** Accepts new entry and exits all fields. The next tab places the cursor in the first field.

Setting viewing preferences

If you design forms where fields are not distinguished from background colors by contrasting borders and/or fills, users of all Acrobat viewers can set preferences to show all fields in a highlight color. By default, the preference setting for highlights is enabled. If highlights on fields are disturbing or not necessary, you can turn the highlight off in the Preferences dialog box.

Choose Edit ➪ Preferences (Acrobat Preferences on Macintosh). Click on Forms in the left pane and the forms preference options are shown on the right side of the dialog box. Enable the check box for Show border hover color for fields in the Highlight Color section. If you want to use a color other than the default highlight color, click on the color swatch below the check box and select a color from the preset options or click on Other Color to add a custom color from the system palette. Click OK in the Preferences dialog box and the form fields appear with a highlight color as shown in Figure 27-2.

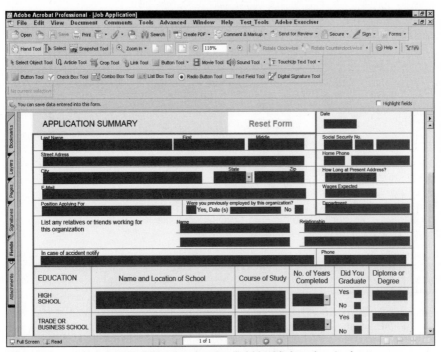

Figure 27-2: Select the check box for showing field highlight colors in the Forms preferences dialog box and all form fields appear with a highlight.

Using Auto-Complete features

While filling in a form, you can let Acrobat record common responses you supply in form fields. After recording responses, each time you return to similar fields, the fields are automatically filled in or a list is offered to you for selecting an option for auto-completing fields.

To turn the recording mechanism on, you need to address the Forms preference settings. Open the Preferences dialog box by choosing Edit ➪ Preferences (Acrobat Preferences on Macintosh) and select Forms. In the right-hand pane, open the pull-down menu under the Auto-Complete section of the Forms preferences. You can make menu choices from Off, Basic, and Advanced as shown in Figure 27-3. Selecting Off turns the Auto-Complete feature off. Selecting Basic stores information entered in fields and uses the entries to make relevant suggestions. Select Advanced from the pull-down menu to receive suggestions from the stored list as you Tab into a field. If a probability matches the list, using the Advanced option automatically fills in the field when you tab into it.

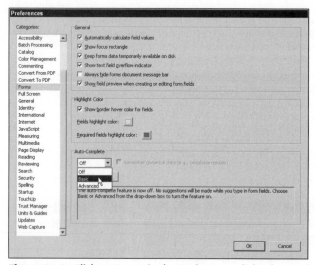

Figure 27-3: Click on Forms in the Preferences dialog box and select Basic or Advanced from the Auto-Complete pull-down menu to use the auto completion feature.

By default, numeric data are eliminated from the data stored for the suggestions. If you want to include numeric data for telephone numbers, addresses, and the like, check the Remember numerical data box.

The list grows as you complete forms when either the Basic or Advanced choice is enabled in the pull-down menu. You can examine the list of stored entries by clicking the Edit Entry List button; the Auto-Complete Entry List dialog box opens as shown in Figure 27-4. To remove an item from the list, select it and click the Remove button. To remove all entries click the Remove All button.

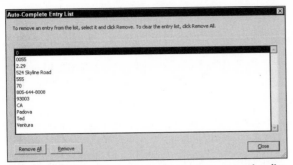

Figure 27-4: To remove entries from your suggestion list, click the Edit Entry List button in the Forms preferences. Select items in the Auto-Complete Entry List and click the Remove button.

In order to record entries, you need to first make the selection for using either the Basic or Advanced Auto-Complete feature. To have suggestions for entries submitted as you type in fields, one of the two menu options needs to be enabled. When you select Off in the pull-down menu, both recording entered data and offering suggestions is turned off. To see how the Auto-Complete operation works, follow these steps:

STEPS: Using Auto-Complete

1. **Set preferences.** Open the Preferences dialog box and click on Forms in the left pane. Open the pull-down menu under Auto-Complete and select Advanced from the menu options. Select the check box to enable adding numeric data to the field entries. Click Close to exit the Preferences dialog box.

Note If you have any data in your entry list, click on the Edit Entry List and click the Remove All button to clear the data while performing these steps.

2. **Fill in a form with your personal identifying information.** You need to create or acquire a form with fields used for name, address, phone, and so on. With the preferences set to Auto-Complete, fill in the data fields.

3. **Examine your entry list.** After filling in the data fields, open the Preferences dialog box. If you haven't changed the last preference settings, the Forms preferences should be in view. Click the Edit Entry List button and examine the entries in the list. Click Close in the Auto-Complete Entry List and click Close in the Preferences dialog box.

4. **Save the file.** To keep the entries recorded in the Entry List, choose File ➪ Save As and save the file under a new name. Close the file.

5. **Type new field entries.** To see the results of your entries and use the Auto-Complete feature, open the original file you used to record the entries. Type in each field the appropriate data and press the Tab key on your keyboard. When you tab to the next field, the list of probable responses is displayed in a menu as shown in Figure 27-5. Select the correct response for a given field from the list and tab to the next field. Continue selecting responses and tabbing until you complete the form.

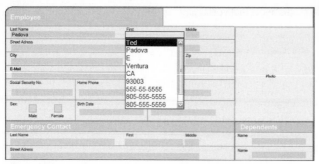

Figure 27-5: Tab to a field, and a list of probable responses is shown. Click on the correct response, and the field is populated from the selection you make in the menu.

Creating Form Fields

Now that you know something about filling out a form, it's time to learn about the attributes associated with each field type in Acrobat Professional. Creating forms in Acrobat begins with a template or PDF document and requires use of the seven Form tools. Users Acrobat 5 and earlier will notice that a single tool for creating the different fields has been replaced with separate tools to create the seven different field types.

To help with precise placement of data fields, you can use grids and guides and define attributes in the Preferences dialog box. You set major and minor gridlines in the Units preferences by choosing Edit ⇨ Preferences and selecting Units & Guides. Showing a forms grid and snapping to a grid are enabled by selecting the View menu and choosing Grid and Snap to Grid, respectively. When creating forms, showing the forms grid and using the Snap to Grid feature can be helpful. If you are not using the Grid and Snap to Grid views, you can show rulers by choosing View ⇨ Rulers and dragging guidelines from the ruler wells.

Cross-Reference

For more information on showing rulers, creating guidelines, and editing guides and grids, see Chapter 4.

All the form field types are created with the different forms tools. Select the tool of choice in the Forms toolbar and draw a rectangle. When the Snap to Forms Grid option is enabled, the rectangle snaps to the gridlines. The moment you release the mouse button after drawing a rectangle, the Field Properties window opens.

Tip

While editing a given field type, you can leave the Properties dialog box open; you don't have to close it to create more fields or edit field properties.

Field properties

The field properties vary according to the field type you create using the field tools. You change field types by creating new fields with your tool of choice. After a field has been created, you don't have an option in Acrobat 7 for changing the field type or assigning attributes that uniquely belong to a different field type. If you want to change a field type, delete the field to be changed and use the tool for the field type you want to create.

Note   A nice feature in Adobe Designer is that you can easily change field types.

When you want to edit fields, you select a specific field type with either the form tool used when creating the field or by using the Select Object tool. If you have several field types on a single page and want to modify fields, remember to use the Select Object tool to select fields where a given field's properties need to be edited. If you use the form tools, only form fields respective to the selected tool can be selected on the page. For example, when you're using the Text Field tool, only text fields can be selected. If you want to change the attributes of a button field, you need to select the Button Field tool. By using the Select Object tool, you can select all field types and make edits for the selected field properties.

Naming fields

Use the Name item in the General tab (shown in Figure 27-6) for each field type's properties to enter a name for the field. The name that appears here provides a name for the field irrespective of the field contents. By default, Acrobat adds a name for every field created on a page. The default name starts at Text1, Button1, Combo Box1, and so on for the respective field type and adds to the number following the field name as more fields are created. For example, when you create text fields, the names are created as Text1, Text2, Text3, and so on.

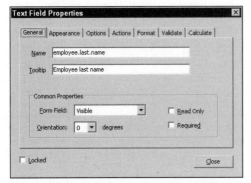

Figure 27-6: The General tab is where you add field names. By default Acrobat supplies a name in the Name field box. You can change the name at the time the field is created or later when editing field properties.

As fields are created (or after the fact), you can edit the default field name supplied by Acrobat. You can provide any name you want to use for the fields. In practice, using an identifier that closely resembles the contents of the field — something such as First or FirstName for a field where a user's first name is to be typed — is best. You could use any other identifier such as 1, F1, First Field, and so on. The name you enter is used for identifying the field when data are exported or imported, using JavaScripts, and creating calculations. If you use forms for importing data into other PDF forms, the names of fields play an important role when swapping data. It's critical that you understand the importance of field names and keep naming conventions and case sensitivity consistent among files and applications.

When naming fields, the most important thing to remember is to be consistent. Case sensitivity is important in regard to importing and exporting data. Always use the same letter case for all fields.

Using proper naming conventions will mean the difference between creating some complex forms in a short time and having them gobble up every one of your waking moments. You can choose to allow Acrobat to name fields automatically or you can name fields by editing the field names in the General tab in the Field Properties. Regardless of which method you use, you need to be aware of the advantages and disadvantages regarding field-naming conventions.

When you supply names to fields with parent/child names, you have much more opportunity to make changes to the field names when duplicating fields and when calculating fields with JavaScripts. A parent/child name contains a root name and a numeric character following the root or subroot name. Fields like total.0, total.1, total.2, or employee.name.last, employee.name.first, and employee.name.middle are examples of field names with parent/child relationships. In the first example you can create calculations on the root name of "total" and use this name in performing calculations and when writing JavaScripts. In the second example you can use the root name employee.name to globally change the name by changing just the parent name.

If you leave the default names provided by Acrobat as Text1, Text2, Text3, and so on the names do not contain parent/child relationships. Creating calculations or writing JavaScripts requires you to identify all field names in the calculation or script as opposed to using only a parent name. If you add 10, 20, or more fields that need to be calculated, the calculation or script requires more time because each field needs to be identified individually in the calculation or script.

Tooltip

The Name item in the Field Properties window identifies a particular field and plays an important part in importing and exporting form data. You must use a field name when creating fields. Tooltip, located beneath the Name field, is optional. When you add text to this field, the text you supply appears as a Tool Tip when the mouse cursor hovers over the field. The Tooltip field is helpful to users when completing forms. For example, you could name a field name.1 that you want to be the field in which users type a first name. In the Tooltip field, enter the text **First Name**. When a user moves the cursor over the field box, First Name appears as a Tool Tip. As the mouse cursor moves over fields, Tool Tips change to the short description added in the Tooltip field box.

When creating accessible forms for documents read by screen readers, be certain to provide descriptive names for Tool Tips. Screen readers read the text in the Tool Tip and can help people with vision challenges understand your forms. For more information on creating accessible documents and understanding screen readers, see Chapter 18.

Common Properties

The seven field types have the same attribute choices for Common Field Properties. Four item choices are available in the Common Properties section of the General tab of the Text Field Properties dialog box shown in Figure 27-6. The options include

✦ **Form Field:** From the pull-down menu you have choices for visibility onscreen and when printing fields. By default the choice is Visible. The Hidden menu item hides a field from view onscreen and when printing the form. Visible but Doesn't Print shows the field onscreen but the field and its contents are not printed. The last item, Hidden but printable, hides the field onscreen but the field and its contents are printed.

✦ **Orientation:** A field and a field's contents can be rotated in 90-degree rotations. By default fields are at a 0 (zero)-degree rotation. Select from 90, 180, and 270 to rotate fields in fixed rotations.

✦ **Read Only:** When a field is marked as Read Only, the field is not editable. The user is locked out of the field. A Read Only field might be something you use to show fixed price costs where you don't want users changing a fixed purchase price on an order form. Another example is a value that is pre-populated from a database.

✦ **Required:** If a field needs to be filled in before the data is submitted, select the Required box.

In the General tab of the properties dialog box for each field type are two additional items. The check box for Locked appears on all tabs for all field types. Select this box to lock a field position on a page. When a field is locked, the field sizing, movement, and attributes cannot be changed. Disable the Locked check box to edit, move, or resize a field.

The Close button in all field properties dialog boxes closes the dialog box. Notice that the button is not an OK button. Clicking the Close button simply eliminates the dialog box from view. Clicking on Close is not required to change values for any field properties. The changes are dynamic and are made as you work through the options among the various tabs.

Appearance

The Appearance tab relates to form field appearances. The rectangle links you draw can be assigned border colors and content fills. The text added to a field box or default text you use for a field can be assigned different fonts, font sizes, and font colors. These options exist in the Appearance properties for all field types. Figure 27-7 shows the Appearance properties for a selected text field.

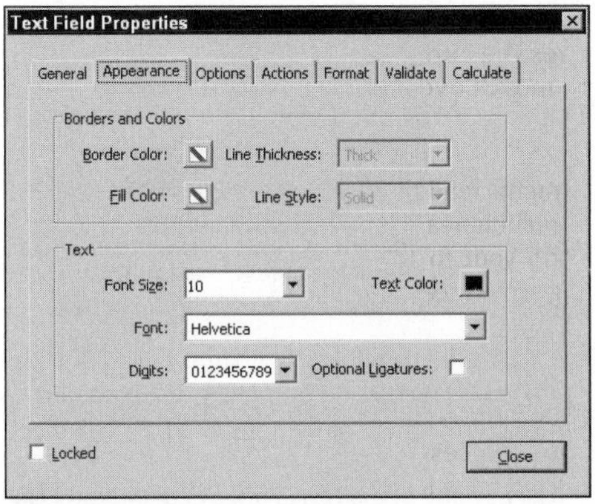

Figure 27-7: Click the Appearance tab for any field properties and make choices for the appearance of fields and text.

The Appearance options include the following:

✦ **Border Color:** The keyline created for a field is made visible with a rectangular border assigned by clicking the Border Color swatch and choosing a color.

✦ **Background Color:** The field box can be assigned a background color. If you want the field box displayed in a color, enable this option, click the color swatch next to it, and choose a color the same way you do for the borders. When the check box is disabled, the background appears transparent.

✦ **Line Thickness:** Options are the same as those available for link rectangles. Select the pull-down menu and choose from Thin, Medium, or Thick. The pull-down menu is grayed out unless you first select a Border Color.

✦ **Line Style:** You can choose from five style types from the pull-down menu. The Solid option shows the border as a keyline at the width specified in the Width setting. Dashed shows a dashed line; Beveled appears as a box with a beveled edge; Inset makes the field look recessed; and Underline eliminates the keyline and shows an underline for the text across the width of the field box. See Figure 27-8 for an example of these style types.

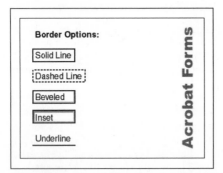

Figure 27-8: Five choices for a border style are available in the Appearance tab when selecting from the Line Style pull-down menu.

✦ **Font Size:** Depending on the size of the form fields you create, you may have a need to choose a different point size for the text. The default is Auto, which automatically adjusts point sizes according to the height of the field box. Choices are available for manually setting the point size for text ranges between 2 and 300 points.

✦ **Text Color:** If you identify a color for text by selecting the swatch adjacent to Text Color, the field contents supplied by the end user change to the selected color.

✦ **Font:** From the pull-down menu, select a font for the field data. All the fonts installed in your system are accessible from the pull-down menu. When designing forms for screen displays, try to use sans serif fonts for better screen views.

Note   When designing forms for cross-platform use, use one of the Base Fonts. Custom fonts loaded in your system may not be available to other users. Base Fonts appear at the top of the font list and are separated from the fonts installed on your system with a space between the Base Fonts and your system fonts. For more information about Base Fonts, see Chapter 7.

The Appearance settings are identical for all field types except Digital Signature fields, Radio Button fields, and Check Box fields. The latter two field types use fixed fonts for displaying characters in the field box. You choose what characters to use in the Options tab. When creating Radio Button and Check Box fields you don't have a choice for Font in the Appearance properties. By default, the Adobe Pi font is used.

Options

The Options tab provides selections for specific attributes respective to the type of fields you add to a page. Options are available for all fields except the Digital Signatures field. Options tab attributes for the other six field types include options for text, radio buttons, combo and list boxes, and buttons.

Text options

When you use the Text Field tool to create a field and you click on the Options tab, the Properties window appears as shown in Figure 27-9.

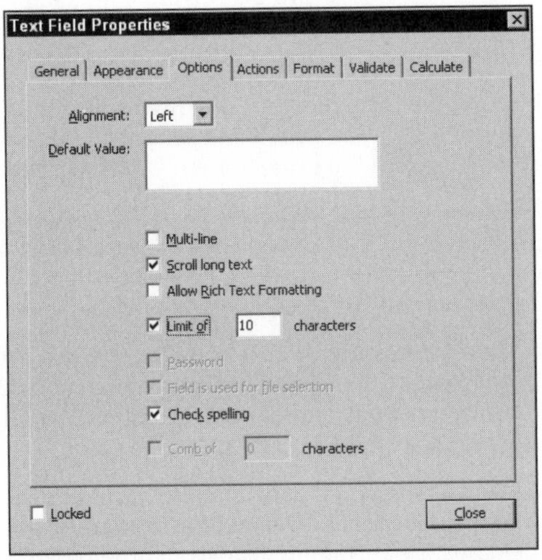

Figure 27-9: The Options settings for Text field properties

Each of the following attribute settings is optional when creating text fields:

✦ **Alignment:** The Alignment pull-down menu has two functions. First, any text entered in the Default field is aligned according to the option you specify from the pull-down menu choices. Alignment choices include Left, Center, and Right. Second, regardless of whether text is used in the Default field, when the end user fills out the form the cursor is positioned at the alignment selected from the pull-down menu choices. Therefore, if you select Center from the Alignment options, the text entered when filling out the form is centered within the field box.

✦ **Default Value:** The Default Value field can be left blank or you can enter text that appears in the field when viewing the form. The Default item has nothing to do with the name of the field. This option is used to provide helpful information when the user fills out the form data. If no text is entered in the Default field, when you return to the form, the field appears empty. If you enter text in the Default field, the text you enter appears inside the field box and can be deleted, edited, or replaced.

✦ **Multi-line:** If your text field contains more than one line of text, select the Multi-line option. When you press the Return key after entering a line of text, the cursor jumps to the second line where additional text is added to the same field. Multi-line text fields might be used, for example, as an address field to accommodate a second address line.

✦ **Scrolling long text:** If Multi-line is selected and text entries exceed the height of the field, you may want to add scroll bars to the field. Enable the check box to permit users to scroll lines of text. If the check box is disabled, users won't be able to scroll, but as text is added, automatic scrolling accommodates the amount of text typed in the field.

✦ **Allow Rich Text Formatting:** When you check this box, users can style text with bold, italic, and bold italic font styles. You may want to enable the check box if you want users to emphasize a field's contents.

✦ **Limit of [ ] characters:** The box for this option provides for user character limits for a given field. If you want the user to add a state value of two characters, for example, check the box and type 2 in the field box. If the user attempts to go beyond the limit, a system warning beep alerts the user that no more text can be added to the field.

✦ **Password:** When this option is enabled, all the text entered in the field appears as a series of asterisks when the user fills in the form. The field is not secure in the sense that you must have a given password to complete the form; it merely protects the data entry from being seen by an onlooker.

✦ **Field is used for file selection:** This option permits you to specify a file path as part of the field's value. The file is submitted along with the form data. Be certain to enable the Scrolling long text option described earlier in this list to enable this option.

✦ **Check spelling:** Spell checking is available for comments and form fields. When the check box is enabled, the field is included in a spell check. This can be helpful so the spell checker doesn't get caught up with stopping at proper names, unique identifiers, and abbreviations that may be included in those fields.

✦ **Comb of [ ] characters:** When you create a text field box and enable this check box, Acrobat automatically creates a text field box with subdivision lines according to the value you supply in the Characters field box. Be certain to disable all other check boxes. You can set the alignment of the characters by making a choice from the alignment pull-down menu, but all other check boxes need to be disabled to access the Comb of check box.

Note Comb fields are limited to single characters. If you need to create comb fields where two characters are contained in each subdivision, you need to create separate field boxes for each pair of characters.

Check box and radio button options

Check boxes and radio buttons have similar Options attribute choices. When you select either field and click on the Options tab, the settings common to both field types include

✦ **Button/Check Box Style:** If a radio button is selected, the title is Button Style. If the field is a check box, the title is listed as Check Box Style as shown in Figure 27-10. From the pull-down menu, you select the style you want to use for the check mark inside the radio button or check box field.

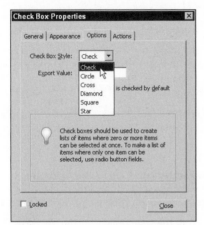

Figure 27-10: You can choose various options for radio buttons and check boxes, including those for the style of the checkmarks or radio buttons.

✦ **Export Value:** When creating either a check box or radio button, use the same field name for all fields in a common group where you want one check box enabled while all the other check boxes or radio buttons are disabled. To distinguish the fields from each other, add an export value that differs in each field box. You can use export values such as Yes and No or other text, or number values such as 1, 2, 3, 4, and so on.

The creation of radio buttons and check boxes on Acrobat forms has been confusing to many users and users often inappropriately create workarounds for check boxes and radio buttons to toggle them on and off. To help eliminate confusion, notice the Options properties in Figure 27-10 includes a help message informing you to name fields the same name but use different export values.

✦ **Button/Check box is checked by default:** If you want a default value to be applied for either field type, like Yes, for example, enter the export value and select the box to make the value the default.

In the Options tab for the check boxes or radio buttons, use the Check box/Button is checked by default item to place a mark in all data fields by default. When the user fills out a form, she or he needs to click a check box or radio button field to toggle the checkmark on and off. Among the different marks applied to the field boxes are six different characters shown in Figure 27-11.

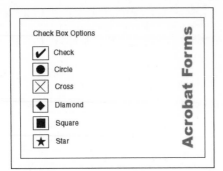

Figure 27-11: Six icon options are available for check boxes and radio buttons.

Combo box and list box options

Combo boxes enable you to create form fields with a list of selections appearing in a pull-down window. The user completing a form makes a selection from the menu items. If all items are not visible, the menu contains scroll bars made visible after selecting the down-pointing arrow to open the menu. A list box is designed as a scrollable window with an elevator bar and arrows like you see in authoring application documents as shown in Figure 27-12.

The two field types differ in several ways. First, combo boxes require less space for the form field. The combo box menu drops down from a narrow field height where the menu options are shown. List boxes require more height to make them functional to the point where at least two or three options are in view before the user attempts to scroll the window. Second, you can select only one menu option from a combo box. List boxes enable users to select multiple items. Finally, combo boxes can be designed for users to add text for a custom choice by editing any of the menu items. List boxes provide no option for users to type text in the field box and the menu items are not editable.

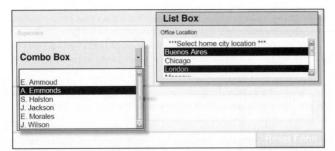

Figure 27-12: View the combo box items by clicking the down arrow. After you open the menu the scroll bars become visible. List boxes enable users to select multiple items in the scrollable window.

The data exported with the file include the selected item from the combo boxes and all selected items for list boxes. The item choices and menu designs for the field types are created in the Options tab for the respective field type. Attributes for list boxes, shown in Figure 27-13, are also available for combo boxes. The options include

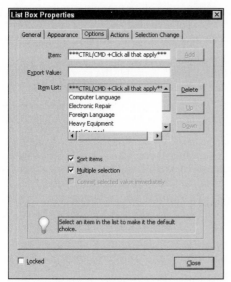

Figure 27-13: The Options settings for list boxes have common properties also found in combo boxes.

✦ **Item:** You enter the name of an entry you want to appear in the scrollable list in this field.

✦ **Export Value:** When the data are exported, the name you enter in this field box is the exported value. If the field is left blank, the exported value is the name used in the item description typed in the Item field. If you want different export values than the name descriptions, type a value in this field box. As an example, suppose you created a consumer satisfaction survey form. In that form, the user can choose from list items such as Very Satisfied, Satisfied, and Unsatisfied, and you've specified the export values for these items to be 1, 2, and 3, respectively. When the data are analyzed, the frequency of the three items would be tabulated and defined in a legend as 1=Very Satisfied, 2=Satisfied, and 3=Unsatisfied.

✦ **Add:** After you enter the Item and Export Values, click the Add button to place the item in the Item List. After adding an item, you can return to the Item field and type a new item in the field box and, in turn, a new export value.

✦ **Delete:** If an item has been added to the list and you want to delete it, first select the item in the list. Click the Delete button to remove it from the list.

✦ **Up/Down:** Items are placed in the list according to the order in which they are entered. The order displayed in the list is shown in the combo box or list box when you return to the document page. If you want to reorganize items, select the item in the list and click the Up or Down button to move one level up or down, respectively. To enable the Up and Down buttons, the Sort Items option must be disabled.

✦ **Sort items:** When checked, the list is alphabetically sorted in ascending order. As new items are added to the list, the new fields are dynamically sorted while the option is enabled.

✦ **Multiple selection (List box only):** Any number of options can be selected by using modifier keys and clicking on the list items. Use Shift+click for contiguous selections and Ctrl/⌘+click for non-contiguous selections. This option applies only to list boxes.

✦ **Commit selected value immediately:** The choice made in the field box is saved immediately. If the check box is disabled, the choice is saved after the user exits the field by tabbing out or clicking the mouse cursor on another field or outside the field.

With the exception of the multiple selection item, the preceding options are also available for combo boxes. In addition to these options, combo boxes offer two more items that include

✦ **Allow user to enter custom text:** The items listed in the Options tab are fixed in the combo box on the Acrobat form by default. If this check box is enabled, the user can create a custom value. Acrobat makes no provision for some items to be edited, and others are locked out from editing.

✦ **Check spelling:** Spell checking is performed when a user types in a custom value. As text is typed the spelling is checked.

Button options

Buttons differ from all other fields when it comes to appearance. You can create and use custom icons for button displays from PDF documents or file types compatible with Convert to PDF from File. Rather than entering data or toggling a data field, buttons typically execute an action. You might use a button to clear a form, export data, import data from a data file, or use buttons as navigation links. When you add a button to a page, the Options tab attributes change to those shown in Figure 27-14.

Figure 27-14: The Options tab for the Button field properties includes options for button face displays and several different mouse behaviors.

When you create a button, you make choices from the Options tab for the highlight view of the button, the behavior of the mouse cursor, and the text and icon views. The Options attributes for buttons are as follows:

✦ **Layout:** Several views are available for displaying a button with or without a label, which you add in the Label field described later in this list. The choices from the pull-down menu for Layout offer options for displaying a button icon with text appearing at the top, bottom, left, or right side of the icon, or over the icon. Figure 27-15 shows the different Layout options.

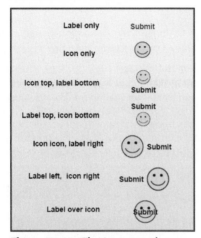

Figure 27-15: The Layout options include Label only; Icon only; Icon top, label bottom; Label top, icon bottom; Icon left, label right; Label left, icon right; and Label over icon.

✦ **Behavior:** The Behavior options affect the appearance of the button when the button is clicked. The None option specifies no highlight when the button is clicked. Invert momentarily inverts the colors of the button when clicked. Outline displays a keyline border around the button, and Push makes the button appear to move in on Mouse Down and out on Mouse Up.

✦ **Icon and Label State:** Three choices are available in the list when you select Push in the Behavior pull-down menu. Up displays the highlight action when the mouse button is released. Down displays the highlight action when the mouse button is pressed. Rollover changes the icon when a second icon has been added to the rollover option. When the user moves the mouse cursor over the button without clicking, the image changes to the second icon you choose—much like a rollover effect you see on Web pages.

✦ **Label:** If you've selected a layout type that includes a label, type text in the field box for the label you want to use. Labels are shown when one of the options for the layout includes a label view with or without the icon.

✦ **Choose Icon:** When you use an icon for a button display, click Choose Icon to open the Select Icon dialog box. In the Select Icon dialog box, use a Browse button to open a navigation dialog box where you locate a file to select for the button face. The file can be a PDF document or a file compatible with converting to PDF from within Acrobat. The size of the file can be as small as the actual icon size or a letter-size page or larger. Acrobat automatically scales the image to fit within the form field rectangle drawn with the Button tool. When you select an icon, it is displayed as a thumbnail in the Select Icon dialog box.

Tip   An icon library can be easily created from drawings using a font such as Zapf Dingbats or Wingdings or patterns and drawings from an illustration program. Create or place images on several pages in a layout application. Distill the file to save out as a multiple-page PDF document. When you select an icon to use for a button face, the Select Icon dialog box enables you to scroll pages in the document. You view each icon in the Sample window as a thumbnail of the currently selected page. When the desired icon is in view, click OK. The respective page is used as the icon.

✦ **Clear:** You can eliminate a selected icon by clicking the Clear button. Clear eliminates the icon without affecting any text you added in the Layout field box.

✦ **Advanced:** Notice the Advanced button at the top of the Options tab. Clicking the Advanced button opens the Icon Placement dialog box where you select attributes related to scaling an icon. You can choose from icon scaling for Always, Never, When the icon is too big to fit in the form field, or When the icon is too small to fit in the form field. The Scale option offers choices between Proportional and Non-proportional scaling. Click Fit to bounds to ensure the icon placement fits to the bounds of the field rectangle. Sliders provide a visual scaling reference for positioning the icon within a field rectangle.

Actions

The Actions tab enables you to set an action for any one of the seven field types; the attribute choices are identical for all fields. The same action items available for links, Bookmarks, and page actions are also available to form fields.

Cross-Reference   For more information on selecting action types, see Chapter 17.

From the Select Trigger pull-down menu, you make choices for different mouse behaviors that are assigned to invoke the action. From the menu options you have choices for

✦ **Mouse Up:** When the user releases the mouse button, the action is invoked.

✦ **Mouse Down:** When the user presses the mouse button, the action is invoked.

✦ **Mouse Enter:** When the user moves the mouse cursor over the field, the action is invoked.

✦ **Mouse Exit:** When the user moves the mouse cursor away from the field, the action is invoked.

✦ **On Focus:** Specifies moving into the field boundaries through mouse movement or by tabbing to the field. As the cursor enters the field, the action is invoked.

✦ **On Blur:** Specifies moving away from the field boundaries through mouse movement or by tabbing to the field. As the cursor exits the field, the action is invoked.

Actions assigned to the cursor movements are similar to those in the context of creating links. You first select the trigger, and then select an action type from the Select Action pull-down menu. Click the Add button to add the action to the Actions list.

The action is assigned to the mouse cursor option when you click Add. The default is Mouse Up. When Mouse Up is selected, the action is invoked when the mouse button is released.

Caution Trigger choices other than Mouse Up may sometimes complicate filling in form fields for end users. Just about any program dealing with link buttons has adopted the Mouse Up response to invoke an action. Many users often click down, think about what they are doing, and then move the mouse away without releasing the button. This behavior enables the user to change his/her mind at the last minute. Deviating from the adopted standard might be annoying for a user.

When you click the Add button, a dialog box specific to the action type you are adding opens. The actions listed in this dialog box are the same as those in the Link Properties dialog box discussed in Chapter 17. Turn back to Chapter 17 for examples of how the following action types work. A few of the more important action types used with form fields include importing form data, resetting a form, submitting a form, and showing and hiding a field.

Importing form data

You can export the raw data from a PDF file as a Form Data File (FDF) that can later be imported into other PDF forms. To import data, you use a menu command or a JavaScript, or use the Execute Menu Item action and select the Import Data to Form command. Rather than retyping the data in each form, you can import the same field data into new forms where the field names match exactly. Therefore, if a form contains field names such as First, Last, Address, City, State, and so on, all common field names from the exported data can be imported into the current form. Those field names without exact matches are ignored by Acrobat.

 The Import Data to Form command enables you to develop forms for an office environment or Web server where the same data can easily be included in several documents. When designing forms, using the same field names for all common data is essential. If you import data and some fields remain blank, recheck your field names. You can edit any part of a form design or action to correct errors.

Acrobat's Data Search

When a data file is identified for an import action, Acrobat looks to the location you specified when creating the action. Acrobat also searches other directories for the data. On the Macintosh, Acrobat looks to the Reader and Acrobat User Data directories for the data file. On Windows, Acrobat looks to the Acrobat directory, Reader directory, current directory, Windows directory, and Application Data directory. If Acrobat cannot find the data file, a dialog box opens containing a Browse button to prompt the user to locate the data file.

Resetting a form

This action is handy for forms that need to be cleared of data and resubmitted. When the Reset a form action is invoked, data fields specified for clearing data when the field was added are cleared. When you select Reset a form and click the Add button, the Reset a Form dialog box opens. You make choices in this dialog box for what fields you want to clear. Click the Select All button and all data fields are cleared when a user clicks on the button you assign with a Reset a form action. When you use this action, associating it with Mouse Up to prevent accidental cursor movements that might clear the data and require the user to begin over again is best. Reset a form can also be used with a Page Action command. If you want a form to be reset every time the file is opened, the latter may be a better choice than creating a button.

Cross-Reference   For more information on using page actions, see Chapter 17.

Submitting a form

Form data can be e-mailed or submitted to Web servers. You can design forms so users of the Adobe Reader software can submit data via e-mail or to Web servers when the PDF is viewed as an inline view in a Web browser. When using the Submit a form action, you have access to options for the type of data format you want to submit.

Cross-Reference   For more information on submitting form data, see Chapter 28. For more information on viewing PDFs as inline views in Web browsers, see Chapter 22.

Showing/hiding a field

You'll find many uses for the Show/hide a field action type. You may want to set up conditional responses in which a user answers a question, and based on the answer, another field is made visible. Or you may want to add some help information where a user can click on a button to show a field containing a description to help the user complete the form. These actions occur with showing fields that are hidden when you select Hidden in the field General tab and create a button to show the hidden field(s). From a dialog box, you select what fields are to be made visible.

Format

The General, Appearance, and Actions tabs are available for all field types. Option attributes are available for all field types except digital signatures. The options vary significantly depending on which field type is used. For a quick glance at the tab differences according to field type, take a look at Table 27-1.

Table 27-1: Tab Options for Field Types in the Field Properties Window

Field Type	Appearance	Options	Actions	Format	Validate	Calculate	Selection Change	Signed
Button	X	X	X					
Check Box	X	X	X					
Combo Box	X	X	X	X	X	X		
List Box	X	X	X				X	
Radio Button	X	X	X					
Text	X	X	X	X	X	X		
Signature	X		X					X

As shown in Table 27-1, the Format, Validate, and Calculate tab options are only available for Combo Box and Text field types. To access the Format tab, select either of these field types. The Format options are the same for both field types.

When you click the Format tab, you'll find a pull-down menu for selecting a format category. To define a format, open the Select format category and choose from the menu choices the format you want to assign to the Text or Combo Box field. As each item is selected, various options pertaining to the selected category appear directly below the pull-down menu. When you select Number from the menu choices, the Number Options appear as shown in Figure 27-16.

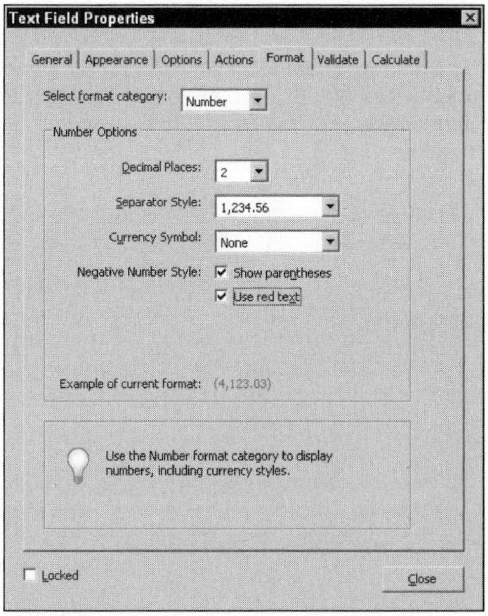

Figure 27-16: When you choose either Combo Box or Text as the field type, you can select data format options from the Format tab.

The Select format category menu options include

✦ **None:** No options are available when None is selected. Select this item if no formatting is needed for the field. An example of where None applies would be a text field where you want text data such as name, address, and so on.

✦ **Number:** When you select Number, the Number Options choices appear below the Select format category pull-down menu. The options for displaying numeric fields include defining the number of decimal places, indicating how the digits are separated (for example, by commas or by decimal points), and specifying any currency symbols. The Negative Number Style check boxes enable you to display negative numbers with parentheses and/or red text.

✦ **Percentage:** The number of decimal places you want to display for percentages is available when you select Percentage from the pull-down menu. The options are listed for number of decimal places and the separator style.

✦ **Date:** The date choices offer different selections for month, day, year, and time formats.

✦ **Time:** If you want to eliminate the date and identify only time, the Time category enables you to do so, offering choices to express time in standard and 24-hour units and a custom setting where custom formats are user-prescribed in a field box.

✦ **Special:** The Special category offers formatting selections for Social Security number, Zip code, extended Zip codes, phone numbers, and an arbitrary mask. When you select Arbitrary Mask, a field box is added where you define the mask. The acceptable values for setting up an arbitrary mask include

  • **A:** Add *A* to the arbitrary mask field box, and only the alphabetical characters A–Z and a–z are acceptable for user input.

  • **X:** When you add *X* to the arbitrary mask field box, most printable characters from an alphanumeric character set are acceptable. ANSI values between 32–166 and 128–255 are permitted. (To learn more about what ANSI character values 32–166 and 128–255 are translated to, search the Internet for ANSI character tables. You can capture Web pages and use the tables as reference guides.)

  • **O:** The letter *O* accepts all alphanumeric characters (A–Z, a–z, and 0–9).

  • **9:** If you want the user to be limited to filling in numbers only, enter *9* in the Arbitrary Mask field box.

✦ **Custom:** Custom formatting is available by using a JavaScript. To edit the JavaScript code, click the Edit button and create a custom format script. The JavaScript Editor dialog box opens where you type the code. As an example of using a custom JavaScript, assume that you want to add leading zeros to field numbers. You might create a JavaScript with the following code:

```
event.value = "000" + event.value;
```

The preceding code adds three leading zeros to all values supplied by the end user who completes the form field. If you want to add different characters as a suffix or prefix, enter the values you want within the quotation marks. To add a suffix, use

```
event.value = event.value + "000";
```

Validate

Validate helps ensure proper information is added on the form. If a value must be within a certain minimum and maximum range, select the radio button for validating the data within the accepted values (see Figure 27-17). The field boxes are used to enter the minimum and maximum values. If the user attempts to enter a value outside the specified range, a warning dialog box opens, informing the user that the values entered on the form are unacceptable.

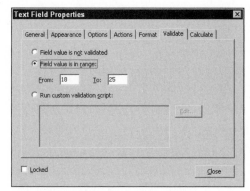

Figure 27-17: Validate is used with Combo Box and Text field types to ensure acceptable responses from user-supplied values.

Selecting the Run custom validation script radio button and clicking the Edit button enables you to add a JavaScript. Scripts that you may want to include in this window would be those for validating comparative data fields. A password, for example, may need to be validated. If the response does not meet the condition, the user is denied access to supplying information in the field.

Calculate

The Calculate tab in the Field Properties window enables you to calculate two or more data fields. You can choose from preset calculation formulas or add a custom JavaScript for calculating fields as shown in Figure 27-18.

The preset calculation formulas are limited to addition, multiplication, averaging, assessing the minimum in a range of fields, and assessing the maximum in a range of fields. For all other calculations you need to select the Custom calculation script radio button and click the Edit button. In the JavaScript Editor you write JavaScripts to perform other calculations not available from the preset formulas.

Cross-Reference   For more information on calculating data, see Chapter 29.

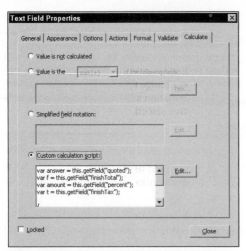

Figure 27-18: The Calculate tab offers options for calculating fields for summing data, multiplying data, and finding the average, minimum, and maximum values for selected fields. In addition, you can add custom calculations by writing JavaScripts.

Selection Change

The Selection Change tab shown in Figure 27-19 is available for List Box fields only. If a list box item is selected, and then a new item from the list is selected, JavaScript code can be programmed to execute an action when the change is made. Like the other dialog boxes, clicking the Edit button opens the JavaScript Editor dialog box where you create the JavaScript code.

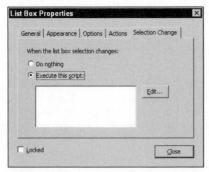

Figure 27-19: The Selection Change tab is available only for List Box fields. When using a Selection Change option, you'll need to program JavaScript code to reflect the action when a change in selection occurs.

A variety of uses exist for the Selection Change option. You might want to create a form for consumer responses for a given product — something such as an automobile. Depending on information preceding the list box selection, some options may not be available. For example, a user specifies "four-door automobile" as one of the form choices, and then from a list, that user selects "convertible." If the manufacturer does not offer a convertible for four-door automobiles, then through use of a JavaScript in the Selection Change tab, the user is informed that this selection cannot be made based on previous information supplied in the form. The displayed warning could include information on alternative selections that the user could make.

Digital Signature fields

The Digital Signature Field tool enables you to create a field used for electronically signing a document with a digital signature. The Signed tab offers options for behavior with digital signatures as follows:

✦ **Nothing happens when signed:** As the item description suggests, the field is signed but no action will take place upon signing.

✦ **Mark as read-only:** When signed, the selected fields are changed to read-only fields, locking them against further edits. You can mark all fields by selecting the radio button and choosing All fields from the pull-down menu. Choose All fields except these to isolate a few fields not marked for read-only, or select Just these fields to mark a few fields for read-only.

✦ **This script executes when field is signed:** Select the radio button and click the Edit button to open the JavaScript Editor. Write a script in the JavaScript Editor that executes when the field is signed.

Digital signatures can be used to lock data fields. You can also use them to indicate approval from users or PDF authors, or you may want to display a message after a user signs a form. In Figure 27-20, a JavaScript was added to the Digital Signature Signed Properties.

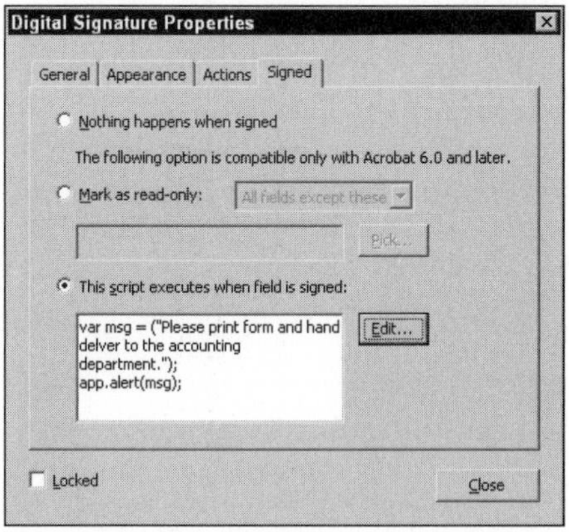

Figure 27-20: For custom actions when a user signs a form, use a JavaScript.

The script in this example instructs a user to print the form and hand-deliver it to the accounting department. A dialog box opens after the user signs the form.

Cross-Reference   For setting up digital signatures and finding out more information related to signing documents, see Chapter 21.

Using the Properties bar

Many of the appearance attributes you apply in the Field Properties Appearance settings you can also apply with the Properties bar. The Properties bar can be used if the Field Properties window is either opened or closed. As a matter of standard practice, you'll often use the Properties bar while the Field Properties window is closed. Notwithstanding the options excluded for font selection with check boxes and radio buttons, the options in the Properties bar are identical for all form tools.

The options available to you include changing field appearances and text. You can make selections for field fills and strokes, line widths, font selection, and font point sizes. To make an appearance change on a field, select the field with the Select Object tool. Make appearance and font changes by clicking buttons in the Properties bar or making selections from pull-down menus.

Editing fields

For purposes of explanation, I'll use the term *editing fields* to mean dealing with field duplication, deleting fields, and modifying field attributes. After you create a field on a PDF page, you may want to alter its size, position, or attributes. Editing form fields in Acrobat Professional is made possible by using one of several menu commands or returning to the respective Field Properties window.

To edit a form field's properties, use the Select Object tool or the form tool for the respective field type and double-click the field rectangle. The Properties window opens after you double-click with either tool. You can also use a context-sensitive menu opened from using either tool and clicking on the form field to be edited. At the bottom of the context-sensitive menu, select the Properties command as shown in Figure 27-21.

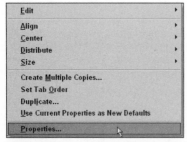

Figure 27-21: Double-click on a field with either the Select Object tool or the tool used to create the field, or open a context menu from the selected field with either tool and choose Properties from the menu options to open the Field Properties.

To select multiple fields you must use the Select Object tool if you want to select fields of different types. If you want to select the same field types, you can use the tool that was used to originally create the fields. Ctrl/Shift+click each field to be selected. You can drag through fields to select them, but you can do so only with the Select Object tool.

When you select multiple fields and choose Properties from the context-sensitive menu, options in the General tab, the Appearance tab, and the Actions tab are available for editing. Specific options for each different field type require that you select only common field types. For example, you can edit the appearance settings for a group of fields where the field types are different. However, to edit something like radio button field options for checkmark style, you need to select only radio button fields in order to gain access to the Options tab.

Tip   If the fields you want to select are located next to each other or you want to select many fields, use the Ctrl key (Windows) or ⌘ key (Macintosh) and drag with the Select Object tool to place a marquee through the fields to be selected. When you release the mouse button, the fields inside the marquee and any fields intersected by the marquee are selected. The marquee does not need to completely surround fields for selection — just include a part of the field box within the marquee.

Duplicating fields

You can duplicate a field by selecting it and holding down the Ctrl/Option key while clicking and dragging the field box. Fields can also be copied and pasted on a PDF page, between PDF pages, and between PDF documents. Select a field or multiple fields, and then choose Edit ⇨ Copy. Move to another page or open another PDF document and choose Edit ⇨ Paste. The field names and attributes are pasted together on à new page.

Tip   To ensure exact field names match between forms, create one form with all the fields used on other forms. Copy the fields from the original form and paste the fields in other forms requiring the same fields. By pasting the fields, you ensure all field names are identical between forms and can easily swap data between them.

Moving fields

You can relocate fields on the PDF page by selecting the Select Object tool in the Advanced Editing toolbar, and then clicking and dragging the field to a new location. To constrain the angle of movement, select a field with the Select Object tool, press the Shift key, and drag the field to a new location. For precise movement, use the arrow keys to move a field box left, right, up, or down. When using the arrow keys to move a field, be certain to not use the Shift key while pressing the arrow keys because doing so resizes field boxes as opposed to moving them.

Deleting fields

You delete fields from PDF documents in three ways. Select the field and press the Backspace key (Windows) or Delete key (Macintosh). You can also select the field and then choose Edit ⇨ Delete, or open a context menu and choose Edit ⇨ Delete. In all cases, Acrobat removes the field without warning. If you inadvertently delete a field, you can Undo the operation by choosing Edit ⇨ Undo.

Aligning fields

Even when you view the grids on the PDF page, aligning fields can sometimes be challenging. Acrobat simplifies field alignment by offering menu commands for aligning the field rectangles at the left, right, top, and bottom sides as well as for specifying horizontal and vertical alignment on the PDF page. To align fields, select two or more fields and then open a context menu and select Align. The alignment options for Left, Right, Top, Bottom, Horizontally, and Vertically appear in a submenu. Acrobat aligns fields according to the first field selected (the anchor field appearing with a red highlight). In other words, the first field's vertical position is used to align all subsequently selected fields to the same vertical position. The same holds true for left, right, and top alignment positions. When you use the horizontal and vertical alignments, the first field selected determines the center alignment position for all subsequently selected fields. All fields are center aligned either vertically or horizontally to the anchor field.

Tip
Fields are aligned to an anchor field when multiple fields are selected and you use the align, center, distribute, and size commands. The anchor field appears with a red border whereas the remaining selected field highlights are blue. If you want to change the anchor (the field to be used for alignment, sizing, and so on), click on any other field in the selected group. Unlike other multiple object selections, you don't need to use the Shift key when selecting different fields from among a group of selected fields. All fields remain selected until you click outside the field boundaries of any selected field.

You can distribute fields on a PDF page by selecting multiple fields and choosing Distribute from a context-sensitive menu. Select either Horizontally or Vertically for the distribution type. The first and last fields in the group determine the beginning and ending of the field distribution. All fields within the two extremes are distributed equidistant between the first and last fields.

Cross-
Reference
For an example of how to use the Distribute command, see "Creating multiple copies of fields" later in this chapter.

Center alignment is another menu command available from a context menu. When you choose Center ⇨ Vertically or Horizontally from a context menu, the selected field aligns to the horizontal or vertical center of the page. Choose Center ⇨ Both to align a field to the center of a page. If multiple fields are selected, the alignment options take into account the relative positions of the field boxes and center the selected fields as a group while preserving their relative positions.

Sizing fields

Field rectangles can be sized to a common physical size. Once again, the anchor field determines the size attributes for the remaining fields selected. To size fields, select multiple field boxes, and then open a context menu and choose Size ⇨ Height, Width, or Both. Size changes are made horizontally, vertically, or both horizontally and vertically, depending on which menu option you choose. To size field boxes individually in small increments, hold down the Shift key and move the arrow keys. The left and right arrow keys size field boxes horizontally, whereas the up and down arrow keys size field boxes vertically.

Creating multiple copies of fields

To create a table array, select fields either in a single row or single column and open a context menu. From the menu options select Create Multiple Copies. The Create Multiple Copies of Fields dialog box opens as shown in Figure 27-22.

Note   You can also create a table array by first creating a single field and selecting options for both Copy Selected Fields down and Copy Selected Fields across.

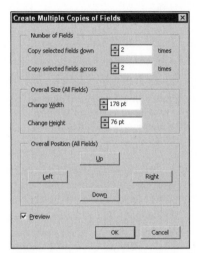

Figure 27-22: To create a table array, select a row or column of fields and open a context menu. Select Create Multiple Copies and make selections in the Create Multiple Copies of Fields dialog box for the number of rows or columns to be duplicated.

In the Create Multiple Copies of Fields dialog box, enter a value in the field box for Copy selected fields down (for creating rows of fields) or Copy selected fields across (to create columns of fields). If you want to add both rows and columns, you can supply values in both field boxes for the desired number of columns and rows. The Change Width and Change Height field boxes enable you to adjust the field distance respective to each other — editing the values does not change the physical sizes of the fields. Click the Up/Down buttons for moving all fields vertically or the Left/Right buttons to move fields horizontally. When the preview box is enabled, you'll see a preview of the duplicated rows and columns before you accept the attribute choices by clicking OK.

If, after you click OK, you need to polish the position of the new fields, you can move the top and bottom fields (for aligning single columns), then open a context menu and choose Distribute ➪ Vertically or Horizontally — depending on whether you're adjusting a row or column. In Figure 27-23 you can see the Vertical adjustment of the second column being applied.

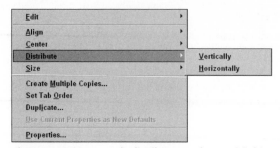

Figure 27-23: To evenly distribute a column of fields, select the fields in a given column and open a context menu. Choose Distribute ⇨ Vertically to position the fields equidistant between the first and last fields.

When using the Distribute command, you can only distribute single rows or columns. If you attempt to select all fields in a table and distribute several rows or columns at once, the results render an offset distribution that most likely creates an unusable alignment.

Duplicating fields

Using the Create Multiple Copies menu command from a context menu enables you to create table arrays or individual columns or rows only on a single page. If you want to duplicate fields either on a page or through a number of pages, another menu command exists for field duplication.

After creating a field, open a context menu and select Duplicate. The Duplicate Field dialog box opens as shown in Figure 27-24. Most often you'll use the Duplicate command when duplicating copies of fields throughout all pages or selected pages in a document.

Figure 27-24: To duplicate fields across a range of pages, select From and enter the page numbers where you want to duplicate the fields.

Duplicating fields is particularly helpful when you create navigation buttons and want to duplicate buttons for navigating to the next and previous pages. By combining button faces and rollover effects, you can add some creative button designs for users to easily navigate pages.

Cross-Reference   For information on creating navigation buttons and duplicating buttons in a PDF document, see Chapter 17.

Setting attribute defaults

If you spend time formatting attributes for field appearances, options, and actions, you may want to assign a default attribute set for all subsequent fields created with the same form tool. After creating a field with the attributes you want, open a context menu and select Use Current Properties as New Defaults. The properties options used for the field selected when you choose the menu command becomes a new default for that field type. As you change form tools and create different fields, you can assign different defaults to different field types.

Setting field tab orders

To set tab order, open the Pages palette and open a context menu on the page where you want to set tab order. Select Properties from the menu options and the page Properties dialog box opens, as shown in Figure 27-25. Click the Tab Order tab and the options for setting tab order appear as radio button selections.

Figure 27-25: To set tab order, open the Pages palette and open a context menu on the page where you want to edit the tab order. Select Properties from the menu choices and click on Tab Order in the Pages Properties dialog box.

The options for setting tab order include

✦ **Use Row Order:** Tabs through rows from left to right. If you want to change the direction for tabbing through fields, choose File ➪ Document Properties. Click on Advanced in the left pane and select Right Edge from the Binding pull-down menu. When you select Use Row Order and the document binding is set to Right Edge, the tab order moves from right to left.

✦ **Use Column Order:** Tabs through columns from left to right, or right to left if you change the binding as described in the preceding bullet.

✦ **Use Document Structure:** When selecting this option, you first need to use a PDF document with structure and tags. The tab order is determined by the structure tree created by the original authoring application when the file was exported to PDF.

✦ **Unspecified:** The default for all documents you created in earlier versions of Acrobat that you open in Acrobat 6 or 7 have the Unspecified option selected. Unless you physically change the tab order to one of the preceding options, the tab order remains true to the order set in Acrobat 5 or earlier.

The order in which you create fields and add them to a page is recorded. If you happen to create a row of fields, and then change your mind and want to add a new field in the middle of the row, Acrobat tabs to the last field in the row from the last field created. Changing the tab orders in the Page Properties won't help you fix the problem when the fields need to be reordered.

Fortunately, you do have an option to manually set tab order on forms. First, click the Select tool. With the Select tool active, select Advanced ⇨ Forms ⇨ Fields ⇨ Set Tab Order. You can also open a context menu and select Set Tab Order when opening a context menu with the Select tool on any field. If you have the Hand tool selected, the Set Tab Order menu command is grayed out.

After selecting Set Tab Order, the fields on the page appear with a number in the top left corner of each field, The number indicates the tab order. If you click on a field, that field becomes the first filed in the tab order. Clicking subsequent fields numbers the fields in ascending order.

If you want to start in the middle of a group of fields press Ctrl/⌘+click on the field preceding the filed you want to reorder. For example if you want to change a field order from any number to number 6, Ctrl/⌘+click field number five. Move the cursor where you want number 6 to follow. When finished ordering the fields, press the Esc key.

Using the Fields Palette

To access the Fields palette, choose View ⇨ Navigation Tabs ⇨ Fields. The Fields palette contains a list of all fields in a PDF document. The fields are listed in alphabetical order much like Bookmarks are. For fields where parent/child names are used, you can expand or collapse the list of child names by clicking the icon adjacent to the parent name. In Figure 27-26 the Fields palette is opened with a list of field names and expanded views.

Figure 27-26: The Fields palette shows all fields in the document. You can expand child names by clicking the plus (+) symbol (Windows) or the right-pointing arrow (Macintosh).

If no fields are contained in a document, the palette appears empty. As you add new fields, each field is dynamically listed in the palette. From the Options menu you have choices for importing and exporting form data, creating multiple copies of fields or duplicating them, creating page templates, and setting the calculation order of fields.

If you open a context menu on a field name in the palette you have more menu options for navigating to a selected field, renaming a field, deleting fields, or opening the field's properties. When renaming a field, you can choose to rename a parent name, which renames all child names in the field group. For example, if you have field names like total.1, total.2, and total.3, you can rename the fields to subtotal.1, subtotal.2, subtotal.3, and so on by simply selecting the parent name *total* and renaming it to *subtotal*. All child names are renamed according to the new name you modified for the parent name.

Summary

✦ Acrobat forms are not scanned documents converted to PDF. They are dynamic and can include interactive elements, data fields, buttons, and JavaScripts.

✦ Automatic form fill-in is enabled in the Preferences dialog box. Form fields can be displayed on PDF pages with a highlight color to help identify field locations.

✦ Data fields are created from many different field types including text, buttons, combo boxes, list boxes, signatures, check boxes, and radio buttons.

✦ You set all data field attributes in the Field Properties window. Properties can be described for fields by selecting the tabs labeled Appearance, Options, Actions, Calculations, or other tabs associated with specific field types.

✦ You can edit fields with a context-sensitive menu. Acrobat has several editing commands used for aligning fields, distributing fields, and centering fields on a PDF page.

✦ Field duplication is handled in a context menu. You can duplicate fields on a page to create tables with the Create Multiple Copies command, or duplicate fields across multiple pages with the Duplicate command.

✦ The Forms palette dynamically lists all fields created in a PDF file. The palette menus and options can be of much assistance in editing field names and locating fields.

✦ Field names need to be unique for each field you add to a form. By using root names and extensions, you can reduce the amount of time needed for designing forms and creating calculations.

✦　　✦　　✦

Working with Form Data

After you get a handle on creating form fields as covered in
Chapter 27, you'll want to know some things about managing
data to help economize your efforts when working with forms and
performing routine calculations on data fields. When forms are completed, you have the option of printing a form or sending the data off
to a host that processes the field data. In this chapter I cover data
management from calculating field data to importing, exporting, and
submitting data.

As is the case with most of the content in Chapter 27, this chapter is
also targeted at users who aren't using Adobe Designer. Most of what
is covered in this chapter can be handled by Designer. However, if
you're a Macintosh user or you want to do some editing in Acrobat
Professional, what follows is strictly related to working with data and
form fields in Acrobat.

For Windows users, the best opportunity you have when working
with form data is to create your form designs in Adobe Designer.
Designer provides you with XDP, XML, and TXT as export data format
options and XDP, XM, TXT, and XFD as import format options. With
Acrobat form data imports and exports you get only FDF, XFDF, and a
version of XML much different than what is provided with Designer. If
you're a serious PDF form designer, Adobe Designer is your best solution for forms creation and handling data.

Setting Up the Environment

As described in the previous chapter, creating form fields requires
use of the Forms tools. The same toolbars used in Chapter 27 are
used to handle form field editing and field creation. For setting up the
Toolbar Well, refer to Chapter 27.

In addition to using form fields, having access to menu commands
helps you manage data while working with forms. Nothing specific
needs to be opened for menu access. As you move through this chapter, I'll cover the various menu options used for data management.

Calculating Field Data

More often than not, you'll want to create forms that use some kind of calculation for data fields. Calculations might be used for summing data, calculating averages, adding complex formulas, assessing field responses, or many other conditions where results need to be placed in separate fields.

Acrobat offers you a few limited built-in functions for performing math operations. When your needs extend beyond these simple functions, you need to write JavaScripts. Some math operations, as simple as subtracting data or producing a dividend, require use of a JavaScript.

Even though I address JavaScript in detail in the next chapter, you need to begin learning about JavaScript as it pertains to calculating data. Therefore, I'll start this chapter with some details on using the built-in functions for calculations in Acrobat and move on, later in this section, to cover some JavaScript basics.

Formatting for calculations

Math operations can be performed on data fields without any formatting applied to either the fields to be calculated or the result field. Although doing so is not required, as a matter of practice applying formats to all fields where calculations are made and to those fields participating in the calculation result is a good idea. As you create a PDF form, you may need to use a particular format that eventually is required either in the formula or for the text appearance in the result field. Rather than going back to the fields and changing the format, you'll save time by supplying proper formats as you create fields.

When creating text fields, open the Format tab in the Text Field Properties window and select the format you want for the field. If Number is the desired format, select Number from the pull-down menu and make choices for the number of decimal places, the display for negative numbers if it applies, and the use of a currency symbol if it applies.

Cross-Reference   For more information on using the Text Field tool, see Chapter 27.

When you set the attributes for one field, select the field with the Text Field tool or the Select Object tool and open a context menu. Select Use Current Properties as New Defaults. As you create additional fields, the new defaults are applied to all subsequent text fields. If you create a field that needs a different format, you can change the format for the new field without affecting the defaults.

Using the preset calculation formulas

Preset math calculations include sum, product, average, minimum, and maximum. After formatting fields, select the field where you want the result to appear and click the Calculate tab in the Text Field Properties dialog box as shown in Figure 28-1. For adding a column or row of data, select the *Value is the* radio button. The default is sum (+). Click the down-pointing arrow to open the pull-down menu to make formula choices from the list of other preset formulas.

Note   Be certain numeric data are formatted using number format options in the Format tab of the Text Field Properties dialog box when creating form fields.

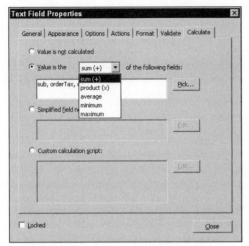

Figure 28-1: To add a preset calculation to a field, click the Calculate tab in the Text Field Properties dialog box. Select the calculation formula from the pull-down menu next to the Value is the radio button.

For summing data, leave the default as it appears and click the Pick button. The Field Selection dialog box opens as shown in Figure 28-2. You can see the fields added to your form and grouped together. To sum a group of fields, select the check box to the left side of each field you want to add to the formula.

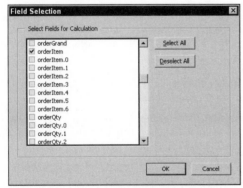

Figure 28-2: Identify the fields used for the calculation in the Field Selection dialog box by selecting the check box for each field name.

Click OK to leave the Field Selection dialog box and return to the Calculate properties. Click Close, and the calculation is ready. In this example the sum of the data for the selected fields updates as the user enters data in the fields assigned to the calculation.

For performing other preset calculations, you follow the same steps. Select the formula you want to use from the pull-down menu options and select the check boxes for all fields you want to add to the calculation.

Note When using the Average formula, Acrobat averages all fields regardless of whether the fields used in the formula contain data. If you have three fields, but only two have values—for example 3 and 3—Acrobat returns a result of 2 ((3+3+0) ÷ 3=2). The preset formula doesn't take into consideration whether or not a field has data in it. To perform an average calculation where you want to average only fields containing a response, you need to write a JavaScript.

Summing data on parent names

If you've read Chapter 27 you may remember that I mentioned advantages when using parent/child names for form fields. As you can see in Figure 28-2, all the fields in your form are listed in the Field Selection dialog box. If you want to sum data in large tables, clicking on all the boxes in the Field Selection dialog box to select fields for columns or rows in a table can take some time. However, when you use parent/child names, the task is much easier.

Assume you have fields with names like total.1, total.2, total.3, and so on. You want to calculate the sum of all the fields with the parent name *total*. In a subTotal field, open the Field Selection and check the field where you see the parent name. Notice in Figure 28-2 the parent name orderItem is checked and fields below the parent name are the parent/child named fields orderItem.0, orderItem.1, orderItem.2, and so on.

Imagine a table that contains 25 rows of data with a total field at the bottom of each column; it has 10 columns across the page. By using the parent name in the formula, you can easily create total fields at the bottom of the page by duplicating fields and editing the parent names in the Calculate properties.

Using hidden fields

Complex formulas can be written in the JavaScript Editor. However, if you aren't up to speed in JavaScript programming or you want to simplify the code you write, you may want to break down a series of calculations and place results in separate fields. For example, suppose you want to calculate the result of A – B * C. If you don't know the code to create the calculation to first subtract two values and multiply the result times another value, you can use separate fields to hold results. In this example you need a field to hold the result of A – B. In another calculation you take the result field containing A – B and multiply it by C.

On the PDF form, the result of A – B is not needed for user input—it's simply a container to use as part of the larger formula. To help avoid confusion, you can hide the field. When data are contained in hidden fields, the data can still be used for calculations.

To create such a field, add a text field anywhere on a page and add the calculation in the Calculate properties. In the General properties, select Hidden from the Form Field pull-down menu. If you need to edit a hidden field, you can do so with either the Text Field tool or the Select Object tool.

When using hidden fields, you can create calculations and access the fields in the Field Selection dialog box or use parent names in the Calculate properties as described in the preceding section.

Using Simplified field notation

In addition to letting you perform simple calculations and write JavaScripts, the Calculate pane also offers you an option for using Simplified field notation. When you select the radio button for Simplified field notation and click Edit, the JavaScript Editor dialog box opens. In the dialog box you don't write JavaScript code. The code added for this calculation type is based on principles used with spreadsheet formulas.

Simplified field notation can be used in lieu of writing JavaScripts for many different math operations. As an example, suppose you want to calculate a sales tax for a subtotal field. To calculate an 8 percent sales tax with a JavaScript you would open the JavaScript Editor and type the following code:

```
1. var f = this.getField("subtotal");
2. event.value = Math.round(f.value * 8) / 100;
```

As an alternative to using JavaScript, select the Simplified field notation radio button and click the Edit button. In the JavaScript Editor you type the following code to produce the same sales tax calculation:

```
1. subTotal * .08
```

Notice in the JavaScript code you need to identify each field used in a calculation and assign a variable to the field name. Line 1 of the preceding JavaScript code assigns the variable f to the field `subtotal`. Notice that in the Simplified field notation the field name does not get assigned to a variable. You simply use all field names as they appear on the form and introduce them in your formulas.

Using JavaScripts

You need to write JavaScripts for all calculations that cannot be made with either the preset formulas or the Simplified field notation method. If you are a novice, you'll find writing simple JavaScripts to be a relatively easy task if you understand a few basic concepts in regard to performing simple calculations:

✦ **Variables:** Variables consist of using characters (alphabetical and numeric) to identify a field, a result, or other variable used in the formula. You can use something as simple as a character name or a long descriptive name. Variables might be `f`, `amt`, `item0grandTotal`, `Price Amount`, and so on.

✦ **Identifying fields:** You need to tell Acrobat in the JavaScript code that you want to assign a variable name to a field that exists on your form. The syntax for assigning a field to a variable name might look like

```
var f = this.getField("item");
```

In the preceding code the field name appears in quote marks and the quote marks are contained within parentheses. The variable `f` is assigned to the field name `item` on `this` (the current open) document.

✦ **Algebraic formulas:** After identifying the variables, you use standard algebraic notation. Therefore, to divide one value by another (something not available to you with the preset formulas), you might enter the code shown in Figure 28-3 in the JavaScript Editor as

```
1. var f = this.getField("amount");
2. var g = this.getField("itemNumber");
3. event.value = f.value / g.value;
```

Figure 28-3: Select Custom calculation script in the Calculation properties and enter the code to perform the calculation in the JavaScript Editor.

The first line assigns the variable f to the field amount. The second line of code assigns the variable g to the field itemNumber. The third line of code is the formula where f is divided by g. The result is placed in the field where you add this script in the JavaScript Editor. The trigger to put the result in the field where the calculation is coded is the event.value item.

Without going into loops and more complex formulas, the beginning Acrobat forms designer can do quite a bit by just following the preceding simple example. The code is all case sensitive and your field names need to be identical to the name of the field on the form as you code in the JavaScript Editor.

Managing Form Data

The field boxes in an Acrobat form are placeholders for data. After data are added to a form, they can be exported. When the data are exported from Acrobat, they are written to a new file as a Form Data File (FDF), XFDF, or XML. These files can be imported in a PDF document or managed in an application that can recognize the data formats. When you submit data to a Web server, the server must have a Common Gateway Interface (CGI) application that can collect and route the data to a database. Using form data on the Web requires advanced programming skills. You can acquire more information about handling data on Web servers on Adobe's Web site. Because Adobe is revising many aspects for handling data in PDF forms and because there are constant changes in supported data formats, I can't yet direct you to a specific URL. If you want to view new information on Adobe's Web site, search the site for the specific areas of interest you want to explore.

Importing and exporting data

One of the great benefits of importing and exporting data is the ability to eliminate redundancy in recreating common data used in different forms. Among the most common redundant data entries is your personal identifying information. Adding your name, address, phone number, and so on to forms is often a common practice. In an environment where you need to supply your personal identity information, you could keep an FDF file on your hard drive and load it into different PDF forms, thereby eliminating the need to re-key the data.

In order to swap data between forms, you need to observe one precaution. All data fields used to import FDF data must have identically matched names to the fields from which the data were exported, including case sensitivity. Therefore, the data from a field called *Name* in a PDF that exports to FDF cannot be introduced in a PDF with a field called *name*. Setting up the fields is your first task, and then you can move on to data exports and imports. To clarify this concept further, I first show you how to design forms with common fields, and then export and import data.

Creating common fields

To be certain your field names match exactly between two forms, the easiest and most efficient way to duplicate the fields is to copy fields from one form and paste them into another form. In Figure 28-4, I have a form used for customer identity. In Figure 28-5, I have a form that uses the same data for customer identity. As yet, the fields on this form have not been created. The customer identity form has all the identifying information, but nothing specific for placing an order. This form is designed to be the source for a customer's individual identity. From this form, I want to take the data and place it on order forms when the customer places an order. To do so requires all forms to have the exact same field names for the identity information.

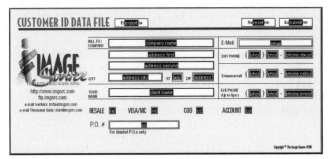

Figure 28-4: The customerID.pdf file contains all the fields used for a customer's identity. Field names on the form you're importing need to match field names on the form where the data were exported.

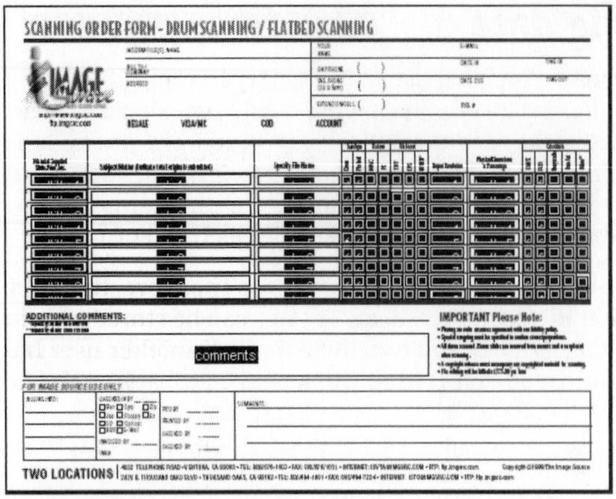

Figure 28-5: The order form uses the same identifying information as the customerID.pdf file. As yet, the form contains no fields for customer identity.

To ensure the field names have an exact match in other files, copy and paste the fields from the original document to the secondary documents. Open the document where the fields are to be pasted and keep it in the background. On the form containing the fields, select the Select Object tool and marquee the fields to be copied. After you select the fields, open a context menu and choose Edit ➪ Copy from the menu choices or choose Edit ➪ Copy from the main menu.

Tip   If you need to copy all fields on the form, select the Select Object tool and press Ctrl+A (Windows) or ⌘+A (Macintosh) to select all fields. Press Ctrl+C (Windows) or ⌘+C (Macintosh) to copy all the selected fields to the Clipboard.

Choose Window ➪ *filename* where *filename* is the name of the file where the fields are to be pasted. When the destination PDF appears in the Document pane, choose Edit ➪ Paste. If the fields are not pasted to exact position, you need to move the fields to the proper location on the form. Click and drag the group into position or nudge the fields with the arrow keys on your keyboard. Be certain to keep the fields selected if they overlap existing fields on the page.

Exporting FDF data

After the forms have been created with matching fields, complete a form and fill in all the data fields. If you have some fields on one form that have been excluded on a second form, Acrobat ignores any field data where it can't find a matching field name. Therefore, you need not worry about having the same number of fields on both documents.

Exporting data from a PDF file is handled with a menu command. If you want to export the data from a form choose Advanced ➪ Forms ➪ Export Data from Form. A dialog box opens where you name the file and designate a destination for the FDF data. If you want a user to export data from a button action, create a Button field on the form. Click the Actions tab and select Execute a menu item from the Select Action pull-down menu. In the Menu Item Selection dialog box (Windows) or the top-level menu bar (Macintosh), choose Advanced ➪ Forms ➪ Export Data from Form.

Cross-Reference   For more information on using the Execute Menu Item action, see Chapter 17.

Click OK to return to the Button Properties. When you click the button or select the menu command, the Export Form Data As dialog box opens. By default the name of your PDF file and an .fdf extension are supplied in the File name field box. This name is used as the FDF filename. If you want to change the name, edit text in the File name field, but be certain to leave an .fdf extension after the filename. Click Save and the file is saved as a Forms Data Format file.

The file you save as FDF contains only the data from the form fields. Therefore, the file size is considerably smaller than the PDF that produced the data. The file can be stored on a local disk, network server, or sent as an e-mail attachment to another user. If another user has a PDF with the same field names, the data can be imported with either Acrobat Standard or Acrobat Professional.

Importing FDF data

As with form data exports, importing FDF data in PDF forms is handled with menu commands. Choose Advanced ➪ Forms ➪ Import Data to Form or create a button like the export button mentioned in the preceding section. In either case the Select File Containing Form Data dialog box opens where you can navigate your hard drive and find the FDF file to import.

To create a button, follow the same steps used for exporting form data (see the preceding section). In the Menu Item Selection dialog box (Windows) or the top-level menu bar (Macintosh) choose Advanced ➪ Forms ➪ Import Data to Form.

Click OK and click Close in the Field Properties dialog box to complete creating a Button field. When you click the button the Select File Containing Form Data dialog box opens. The default file type from the Files of type pull-down menu is Acrobat FDF Files (*.fdf). When the dialog box opens, only files saved as FDF appear in the window list.

Select the FDF file to be imported and click the Select button in the dialog box. When you import data from common field names the fields are populated for all matching fields. Acrobat ignores all data where no matching fields are found.

Importing text data

The discussion thus far has been limited to FDF data in Acrobat forms. In addition to using FDF data, you have other options available with different data types. You may receive data files created in database managers or spreadsheets that you want to use in your Acrobat forms. As long as the data exports are properly formatted with text-delimited fields, you can import data saved as text from spreadsheet and database programs.

To understand how Acrobat supports text data, follow these steps:

STEPS: Importing text data

1. **Create a database.** You can use any program capable of exporting data as a text file. In this example, I use Microsoft Excel to create a data file with three records and a row for field names. For the first row in a spreadsheet application, add the exact same names as the field names used in the Acrobat form. All subsequent records (rows) contain the data like the example shown in Figure 28-6.

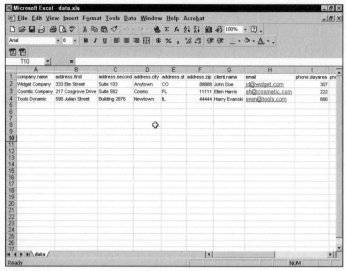

Figure 28-6: A data file is created in Microsoft Excel with three data records. Each row is a separate record and the cells across each row horizontally represent the field data for the respective record. Row one contains the field names that match the PDF form.

2. **Add export values for radio buttons and check boxes.** For fields such as check boxes, the data used to denote a checked box is equal to the export value associated with the field in Acrobat. If you use export values like Yes and No, add Yes or No in a data field for the data imported in Check Box fields.

3. **Save the spreadsheet.** Save as text only from your database manager. In this example I chose File ➪ Save As and selected Text (tab delimited)(*.txt) in the Microsoft Excel Save As dialog box.

4. **Open the PDF document.** Quit your database manager and open the form to import the data in Adobe Acrobat.

5. **Open the text file.** Choose Advanced ➪ Forms ➪ Import Data to Form. The Select File Containing Form Data dialog box opens. From the Objects of type pull-down menu, select Text Files (*txt). Find the file exported from the database manager and select it. Click the Select button to open the file.

Note   Each time you use the Advanced ➪ Forms ➪ Import Data to Form menu command, Acrobat defaults to the *.fdf Files of type, expecting you to select an FDF file. Be certain to select Text Files (*.txt) from the Files of type pull-down menu when importing text data. You need to manually access the pull-down menu choice each time you want to import data other than FDF.

6. **Import the data.** The Import Data From Delimited Text File dialog box opens. In the dialog box you see the names of the fields appearing at the top of the dialog box. Below the title fields are the records in the database. Only one record can be imported in the form. Therefore, you need to tell Acrobat which record you want to import. Click anywhere in a record row to select the desired record as shown in Figure 28-7. In this example, the first record data is selected for import. Click OK and the data are imported in the form for all matching field names.

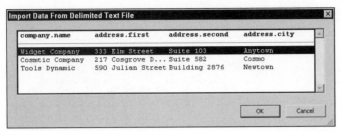

Figure 28-7: Select a record to import by clicking anywhere in the record row you want to import.

Creating spreadsheets from form data

If you aren't an Adobe Designer user and you need to convert rows and columns of data from PDF forms to spreadsheets, you can use a workaround to get what you see on a PDF page to a spreadsheet program. If a PDF form is populated with data and you export the data as an FDF file, a spreadsheet program won't import the data without a lot of formatting problems. Essentially, there's just not an easy way to use data exports from Acrobat to create a file suitable for spreadsheet use through exporting form data. You do have an alternative by using another tool to export text, but the data needs to be on the page and not contained within form fields. Therefore the method for getting data to a spreadsheet requires you to first eliminate the form fields while retaining the data and then export the data as text. To understand how this method can help you, follow these steps:

STEPS: Creating a spreadsheet from form data

1. **Open a PDF form in Acrobat.** Use a PDF form containing rows and columns of data that you want to open in a spreadsheet application.

2. **Convert the file to PostScript.** The form fields cannot be selected with any text tools in Acrobat. You need to eliminate the form fields and retain the data as text on the page. The only way to do this is to save the PDF as PostScript and distill the file in Acrobat Distiller. To save the file as PostScript, select File ➪ Save As and select PostScript (*.ps) from the Save as Type (Windows) or Format (Macintosh) pull-down menu. Save the file to a target folder you can easily find on your hard drive.

Tip

If eliminating form fields while retaining the data is a frequent function you perform routinely, you can acquire third-party plug-ins to do the job. Look at ARTS PDF Stamper. You can find information about ARTS PDF Stamper and other third party solutions on the Planet PDF Store Web site as www.planetpdf.com/browse_software.

3. **Distill the PostScript.** Select Advanced ➪ Acrobat Distiller in Acrobat. Use the Standard settings and open the PostScript file in Distiller. The file is converted to a PDF. All the form fields are removed from the file and the data are retained as text on the page.

Cross-Reference

For more information on using Acrobat Distiller, see Chapter 8.

4. **Open the PDF in Acrobat.** Click the Open tool and open the PDF file you converted in Distiller.

5. **Select the text.** Click the Select tool and drag through the text appearing in columns and rows to select it as shown in Figure 28-8.

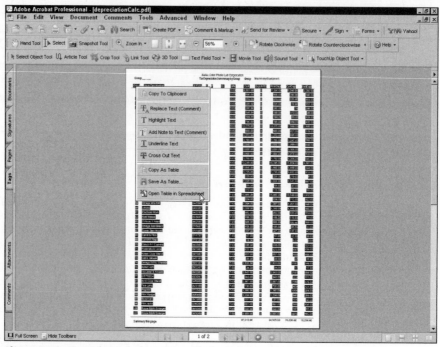

Figure 28-8: Drag through the table with the Select tool.

6. **Open the text in a spreadsheet.** Move the cursor to the beginning of the selected text. Pause a moment and you see a text icon. Place the cursor over the icon and a popup menu opens. From the menu selections, click Open Table in Spreadsheet.

7. **Edit the data in your spreadsheet.** After selecting Open Table in Spreadsheet, the data are copied to a new document window in your spreadsheet application. If using Microsoft Excel, Excel opens and you see the data placed in columns and rows as shown in Figure 28-9.

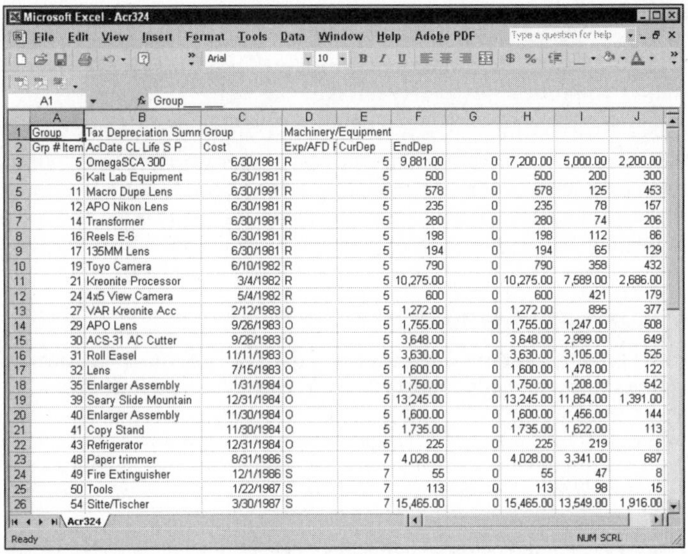

Figure 28-9: The data opens in a new document in Microsoft Excel.

Microsoft Excel - Acr324

	A	B	C	D	E	F	G	H	I	J
1	Group	Tax Depreciation Summ Group		Machinery/Equipment						
2	Grp # Item	AcDate CL Life S P	Cost	Exp/AFD F	CurDep	EndDep				
3	5	OmegaSCA 300	6/30/1981 R		5	9,881.00	0	7,200.00	5,000.00	2,200.00
4	6	Kalt Lab Equipment	6/30/1981 R		5	500	0	500	200	300
5	11	Macro Dupe Lens	6/30/1991 R		5	578	0	578	125	453
6	12	APO Nikon Lens	6/30/1981 R		5	235	0	235	78	157
7	14	Transformer	6/30/1981 R		5	280	0	280	74	206
8	16	Reels E-6	6/30/1981 R		5	198	0	198	112	86
9	17	135MM Lens	6/30/1981 R		5	194	0	194	65	129
10	19	Toyo Camera	6/10/1982 R		5	790	0	790	358	432
11	21	Kreonite Processor	3/4/1982 R		5	10,275.00	0	10,275.00	7,589.00	2,686.00
12	24	4x5 View Camera	5/4/1982 R		5	600	0	600	421	179
13	27	VAR Kreonite Acc	2/12/1983 O		5	1,272.00	0	1,272.00	895	377
14	29	APO Lens	9/26/1983 O		5	1,755.00	0	1,755.00	1,247.00	508
15	30	ACS-31 AC Cutter	9/26/1983 O		5	3,648.00	0	3,648.00	2,999.00	649
16	31	Roll Easel	11/11/1983 O		5	3,630.00	0	3,630.00	3,105.00	525
17	32	Lens	7/15/1983 O		5	1,600.00	0	1,600.00	1,478.00	122
18	35	Enlarger Assembly	1/31/1984 O		5	1,750.00	0	1,750.00	1,208.00	542
19	39	Seary Slide Mountain	12/31/1984 O		5	13,245.00	0	13,245.00	11,854.00	1,391.00
20	40	Enlarger Assembly	11/30/1984 O		5	1,600.00	0	1,600.00	1,456.00	144
21	41	Copy Stand	11/30/1984 O		5	1,735.00	0	1,735.00	1,622.00	113
22	43	Refrigerator	12/31/1984 O		5	225	0	225	219	6
23	48	Paper trimmer	8/31/1986 S		7	4,028.00	0	4,028.00	3,341.00	687
24	49	Fire Extinguisher	12/1/1986 S		7	55	0	55	47	8
25	50	Tools	1/22/1987 S		7	113	0	113	98	15
26	54	Sitte/Tischer	3/30/1987 S		7	15,465.00	0	15,465.00	13,549.00	1,916.00

Creating and Using Submission Buttons

All the previous discussions for importing and exporting data work well on local hard drives and network servers. When you use the Internet for data transfers and extend data submission to users of the Adobe Reader software, then you need to use other measures. Users of any Acrobat viewer can submit Adobe form data. This feature offers you a powerful tool for collecting data from anyone. Because the Adobe Reader is a free download from Adobe Systems, you can be assured all potential customers can place orders for your products or any employee can remotely complete any form you create and submit the data to you.

The primary concept to understand with regard to submitting data to Web servers is that after the data leave Acrobat, Acrobat is no longer in control of the data. Whatever programming you add to a PDF file, remember that after Acrobat executes its action to send the data to a destination, some other form of programming is needed to collect the data and route it to the proper location. If you find errors in submitting PDFs or FDF data on servers and the data disappear, you most likely have a problem in the programming outside of Acrobat. Look to your system administrator or individual responsible for server-side programming to help you with a solution.

Submitting data to URLs

Data from a PDF form can be sent to a Web server in several different formats and with different attributes. You can also use either an Acrobat built-in action type or a JavaScript action. The submission of data, regardless of the format exported, is a relatively simple process. Things get more complex with scripting actions; however, the real complexity is involved at the server end. In terms of a simple explanation—you need a script at the server to know what to do with your data. For the server-side issues, you can find a wealth of information on the Web related to CGIs (Common Gateway Interface) and scripting languages such as Perl, which is one of the most popular scripting languages for writing CGI scripts. Start your browsing by logging on to `www.perl.com` and downloading the free Perl software for your platform. Next, log on to `www.planetpdf.com` and search for Perl on the Web site. You can find examples of how to process PDF data and use Perl scripts for collecting PDF data. If Planet PDF doesn't answer your questions, start searching the Web for PDF and Perl or PDF and CGIs. Many sites offer sample code and documentation to help you get started.

If you are a forms designer and not a programmer, you'll be best served by passing on the preceding information to your system administrator. The task at hand is not to be concerned with what happens at the server end, but how to get the data from the PDF file on your computer to the server. In this regard, the next section discusses using a Submit Form action and some JavaScript actions.

Using the Submit a form action type

The Submit a form action type is created from a choice in the Select Action pull-down menu for all interactive functions that support adding actions. You can create a Button field or a link, use a page action, or use a document action to invoke the Submit a form action. Most often you'll want to use a Button field so the user knows when the data are submitted to the server. Submit buttons work equally from all Acrobat viewers and you can submit any of the data types from the free Adobe Reader software.

Note Adobe Reader prior to version 6 required you to submit data from within a Web browser. In Acrobat 6 and greater, you can create submit buttons that enable users of Adobe Reader 6 and above to submit data without using a Web browser.

Cross-Reference For more information on inline views in Web browsers, see Chapter 22.

To create a submit button on a PDF form, start with creating a Button field and select the Actions tab. Select Submit a form from the Select Action pull-down menu and click the Add button. The Submit Form Selections dialog box opens as shown in Figure 28-10.

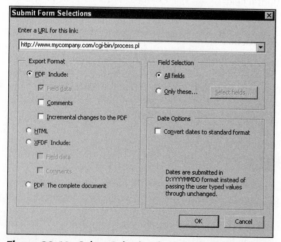

Figure 28-10: Select Submit a form in the Select Action pull-down menu and click the Add button. The Submit Form Selections dialog box opens, offering you many different options for the type of data to be submitted.

At the top of the dialog box, enter the URL where the data are to be sent. Include the script name for the script that post-processes the form data. Under the Export Format section on the left side of the dialog box you have four data type options from which to choose.

The four data options are

✦ **FDF Include:** The FDF data are sent to the server. The three options below the FDF Include item offer you choices for sending the Field data; Comments, which includes any comments created on a form; and Incremental changes to the PDF, which should be used when digital signatures have been used to save updates. Any one or all of the selections can be made for this data type.

✦ **HTML:** The data are sent in HTML format. Much as you might create a form on a Web page using HTML and JavaScript, the HTML option processes the same data type.

✦ **XFDF Include:** The data are sent in XML format. Two options are available for sending the Field data or the Comments data or both. You cannot submit digital signatures via XFDF.

✦ **PDF The complete document:** This option enables you to submit the PDF populated with the field data. This option is useful for Digital Signature workflows or for archiving the complete document.

On the right side of the dialog box are options for including all or selected field data in your submission. If there are fields to be eliminated, select the Only these button and then click the Select fields button. The Field Selection dialog box opens where you select which fields to use for the data export. Dates are converted from the format specified on the form to standard date formats when the Date Options check box is enabled.

When the user clicks the button, the form data from the choices you made in the dialog box are sent to the specified URL. Keep in mind that if you do not have the necessary server-side programming, nothing happens to the data and it won't be found on your server. You need intervention from the host to collect and route the data.

Tip   If you have a form containing button fields and you want to export the buttons as well as the text field data, select the Only these radio button in the Submit Form Selections dialog box. The Field Selection dialog box opens after you click the Select Fields button. In the Field Selection dialog box, select the check boxes for all fields you want to submit.

E-mailing forms

For a simple exchange of data between you and a limited number of users you might want to have data submitted via e-mail attachments. Any user of the Adobe Reader software as well as other users can e-mail forms to you by adding a simple statement in the Enter a URL for this link field box in the Submit Forms Selections dialog box. Rather than send the form to a Web address, change the line of code in the field box to

```
mailto:you@company.com
```

Enter your own e-mail address after the `mailto:` item in the preceding line of code and the PDF form is e-mailed to you. Users of the Adobe Reader software viewing your PDF document either in or outside a browser window can e-mail the form data back to you by clicking the Submit button you added to the form with one of the statements in the preceding section.

Users of Acrobat Standard or Acrobat Professional can export data and attach the FDF data file as an e-mail attachment. When sending the data file instead of the PDF document, you'll see much smaller file sizes for the FDF files. If form file sizes are large, using the FDF data speeds up transmissions for both the end user and you. After you receive an FDF data file, choose Advanced ➪ Forms ➪ Import Data to Form to populate a form with the data submitted as an e-mail attachment.

Summary

✦ Acrobat offers a few preset calculation formulas used for calculating data. For more sophisticated calculations, you need to use JavaScripts.

✦ When using parent/child names you can easily sum data by adding a parent name in the Calculate properties and selecting the sum (+) menu command.

✦ Form data can be exported from populated PDF forms to an FDF file. The data can be introduced into any form having matching field names as from where the data were exported.

✦ To ensure creating fields with exact names between different forms, copy fields from one document and paste the fields in all other documents.

✦ Button fields can be created to submit form data from any Acrobat viewer. After the data leaves an Acrobat PDF file a server-side application needs to collect and route the data.

✦ Data can be exported from a PDF document directly to a spreadsheet program.

✦ By adding a simple line of code in the Submit Forms Selections dialog box, users of the Adobe Reader software can e-mail PDF form data when viewing the forms in a Web browser.

✦   ✦   ✦

Understanding JavaScript

With JavaScript you can create dynamic documents for not only forms, but also many other uses such as adding interactivity to files, and viewing options, animation, and similar features not available with Acrobat tools. JavaScript helps you add flare and pizzazz to your PDF files. In Acrobat Standard, you can edit JavaScripts create JavaScripts using Bookmarks, links, and page actions. However, to get the full range of editing JavaScripts and applying JavaScripts to form fields, you need to use Acrobat Professional.

This chapter offers you a brief introduction to using JavaScript by example. The contents of this chapter are intended only to provide the novice some examples that can be easily duplicated without much description for understanding coding syntax and programming methods. For more sophisticated uses and some sound reasoning for coding forms, look at the Acrobat JavaScript Scripting Reference and the Acrobat JavaScript Scripting Guide. Both documents are available from Adobe Systems by logging on to `http://partners.adobe.com/public/developer/pdf/topic_js.html`

Setting Up the Environment

As described in Chapter 27, creating form fields requires use of the Forms tools. You also use the same toolbars used in Chapter 27 to handle form fields where you add JavaScripts. For setting up the Toolbar Well, refer to Chapter 27.

In addition to using form fields, you'll use several menu commands related to writing JavaScripts. As you move through this chapter, the menu options related to accessing and writing JavaScripts are covered.

JavaScripts can be written using an internal editor in Acrobat or an external editor such as WordPad on Windows or TextEdit on the Macintosh. If you write a lot of JavaScript code, open the Preferences dialog box by pressing Ctrl/⌘+K. Click JavaScript in the left pane and check the radio button for *Use external JavaScript editor* at the bottom of the right pane. Click the Browse button and locate the editor you want to use.

Getting Started with Acrobat JavaScript

Before I begin to explain some coding, let me start by making a few suggestions to the novice user who may find the programming aspects of Acrobat confusing and beyond your reach. For those who haven't coded a single line, you can easily search and find samples of code used in Acrobat forms that you can copy and paste into your designs. Search the Internet and find PDF forms that are not secure, which enables you to examine the code. If, for example, you need a calculation for sales tax, search for one of the many examples of forms where a sales tax calculation is coded in a form field. You can copy and paste fields into your designs and often only need to change a variable name to make it work. Poke around and experiment, and you'll find some worthwhile routines in existing PDF forms.

Tip

Create a blank page in a program and convert it to PDF. To create a blank new page, press Ctrl/⌘+J to open the JavaScript Debugger and type the following code:

```
app.newDoc();
```

Press the Num Pad Enter key (or Control+Enter if you are on a laptop) on your keyboard with the cursor at the beginning or end of the line of code and a new page is created in the Document pane. On the PDF blank page you can paste JavaScript form fields and add comments as to what the JavaScripts do. A collection of common scripts will make your task easier when it comes time to code a new form. Open the file and search through the comments to find the routine you want for a given task. Copy the form field, complete with the JavaScript, and paste it into your new form design. Test it out and make changes that might be needed to get the routines to work in your form.

Finding JavaScripts

As you peruse documents searching for JavaScripts either to paste into your own designs or to learn more about using JavaScript in Acrobat, you need to know where scripts are contained. You might copy and paste a script and find that the script doesn't execute properly. One reason is that the script relies on a function contained in another area in the document. Therefore, to gain a complete understanding of how a form works, you need to examine all the potential containers for scripts. As a matter of practice, you'll want to examine several areas in a form where JavaScripts are found.

Tip

If you want a quick glance at JavaScripts contained in a document, select Advanced ➪ JavaScript ➪ Edit All JavaScripts. The JavaScript Editor opens and displays all JavaScripts in the document in a scrollable window.

Examining field scripts

The most frequent use of JavaScript in Acrobat forms is when scripts are written for field actions. To examine JavaScripts associated with fields, select the Select Object tool and open the Field Properties. Depending on the field type, there may be several places where a script can be located. The first logical place to look is the Actions tab. Actions can contain JavaScripts for all field types. Click the Actions tab to see what actions are assigned to the field as shown in Figure 29-1.

Button Properties
General
Appearance
Options
Actions
Add an Action
Select Trigger:
Mouse Up
Select Action:
Run a JavaScript
Add...
Actions
Mouse Up
Run a JavaScript
Up
Down
Edit
Delete
Locked
Close

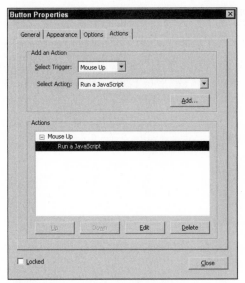

Figure 29-1: Click the Actions tab to see whether a JavaScript action has been added to the field.

If you see JavaScript assigned to a mouse behavior, click on Run a JavaScript in the Actions list and click the Edit button. Acrobat opens the JavaScript Editor and displays the code written for the script as shown in Figure 29-2. The code in the JavaScript Editor can be copied from one field and pasted into the editor when you assign a script to another field. In addition, the field can be copied and pasted into another form. When you paste fields with JavaScript in them, the code is preserved in the pasted field.

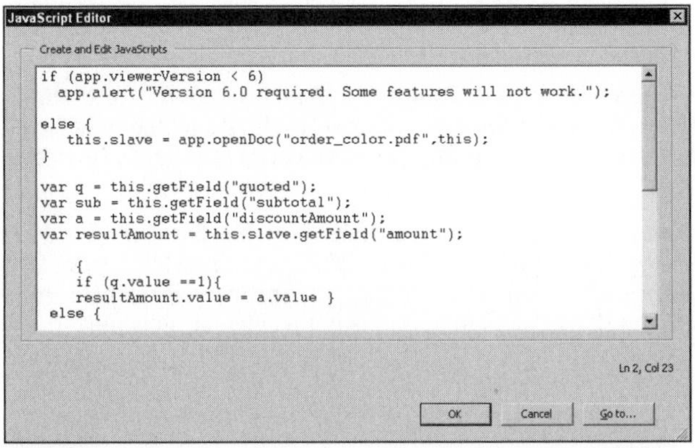

JavaScript Editor
Create and Edit JavaScripts
if (app.viewerVersion < 6)
app.alert("Version 6.0 required. Some features will not work.");
else {
this.slave = app.openDoc("order_color.pdf",this);
}
var q = this.getField("quoted");
var sub = this.getField("subtotal");
var a = this.getField("discountAmount");
var resultAmount = this.slave.getField("amount");
{
if (q.value ==1){
resultAmount.value = a.value }
else {
Ln 2, Col 23
OK
Cancel
Go to...

Figure 29-2: Select JavaScript in the Actions tab and click the Edit button. The JavaScript Editor dialog box opens, displaying the code.

With Text and Combo Box fields you can find JavaScripts in the Actions properties as well as the Format, Validate, and Calculate properties. If you are examining a form to understand how the field actions are executed, be certain to select each of these tabs to see whether any custom formatting or validation is used. Click the Format tab and look for Custom selected in the Select format category pull-down menu, as shown in Figure 29-3. If a JavaScript appears in either the Custom Format Script window or the Custom Keystroke Script window, click the Edit button adjacent to where the script is written. The JavaScript Editor opens where you can edit the script or copy the text.

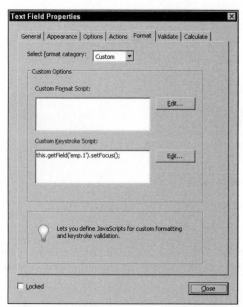

Figure 29-3: Select the Format tab and click Edit to see a script appear in the dialog box.

The Validate properties offer the same options. Follow the same procedures for finding JavaScripts as described earlier in this section by clicking the Validate tab and clicking Edit where you see a JavaScript in the Run custom validation script window to open the JavaScript Editor dialog box.

Field calculations are often handled in the Calculate properties. When JavaScript produces data calculations, be certain to examine the Calculate properties as shown in Figure 29-4. However, not all field calculations are assigned to the Calculate properties, so be certain to check the Actions properties as well as Calculate in the event a calculation is performed on an action.

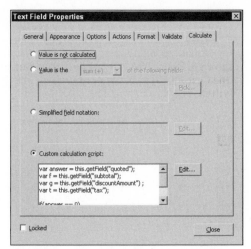

Figure 29-4: Click Calculate to see whether a custom calculation script has been added to the field. If a script appears in the dialog box, click Edit to open the JavaScript Editor dialog box.

List Boxes offer different properties. If a List Box is used, click the Selection Change tab. A JavaScript can execute when a selection in the List Box changes. If a script appears in the dialog box, click the Edit button to open the JavaScript Edit dialog box.

Digital signatures can also be assigned custom JavaScripts. Click the Signed tab for a Digital Signature field and examine the dialog box for a custom script.

Buttons, Radio Buttons, and Check Boxes can only have JavaScripts added to the Actions properties. When opening these field types, click the Actions tab described earlier.

Bookmarks and links

Both Bookmarks and links use the same action types as form fields. You might use a Bookmark for navigating documents rather than creating form field buttons or links on every page to open and close files. When the Bookmarks tab is open, users can click on a Bookmark to open secondary files or perform other actions such as spawning pages.

To check for JavaScripts contained in Bookmark actions, open the Bookmark Properties dialog box and click the Actions tab. JavaScripts are listed the same as when examining actions for form fields (described in the preceding section). Likewise, when you open Link Properties you can check to see whether a JavaScript has been added as a Link action.

Examining document-level JavaScripts

You may copy a field and paste it into another document and find an error reported when executing the JavaScript action. Notwithstanding variable names that are explained later, you can experience problems like this because the routine in the JavaScript might be calling a JavaScript function or global action that was contained in the original document as a document-level JavaScript. Among your tasks in dissecting a form should be an examination of any document-level JavaScripts. To find document-level JavaScript functions contained in a form, choose Advanced ➪ JavaScript ➪ Document JavaScripts. The JavaScript Functions dialog box opens as shown in Figure 29-5.

Figure 29-5: Open JavaScript functions by choosing Advanced ⇨ JavaScript ⇨ Document JavaScripts.

In the JavaScript Functions dialog box, search for any names in the box below the Script Name box. All document-level functions are listed in this dialog box. To examine a script, select the script name and click the Edit button. The JavaScript Editor window opens where you can examine the script.

Writing functions and accessing them in JavaScript code written for field actions is much more complex. If you are new to JavaScript you may want to start with simple scripts in form fields until you learn more about how JavaScript is coded and implemented in Acrobat. As you learn more you can develop more sophisticated routines that include functions.

Examining page actions

Page actions execute when a user opens or closes a PDF page. You can assign any action type available from the Select Action types for field actions, including Run a JavaScript. When examining forms, open the Page Properties dialog box by opening a context menu in the Pages tab and selecting Properties. Click on Actions when the Page Properties dialog box opens. If a JavaScript or any other page action is assigned to either the Page Open or the Page Close action, the action types are listed in the Actions window. Notice in Figure 29-6 that both a Page Open and Page Close action appear in the Actions window showing Run a JavaScript for both Page Actions.

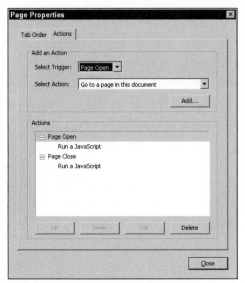

Figure 29-6: When you open the Page Properties dialog box and click the Actions tab, both Page Open and Page Close actions are shown in the Actions window.

Like the other dialog boxes described earlier in this chapter, click on Run a JavaScript and click the Edit button. The JavaScript Editor window opens where you can view, edit, and/or copy the JavaScript.

Examining document actions

Document actions execute JavaScripts for any one of five different Acrobat functions. On a document close, during a save, after a save, during a print, or after a print a JavaScript action can be executed. To view any document actions assigned to the PDF document, choose Advanced ➪ JavaScript ➪ Set Document Actions.

Cross-Reference

For information on creating JavaScripts on Document Actions, see the section later in this chapter "Using Document Actions."

The Document Actions dialog box opens. If a JavaScript is assigned to a document action an icon appears adjacent to the action type. You can view a script in the dialog box as shown in Figure 29-7 or you can open the JavaScript Editor window by selecting the action name and clicking Edit.

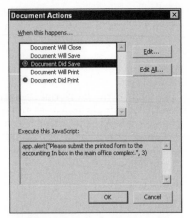

Figure 29-7: Any document actions assigned to the PDF are displayed with a green circle adjacent to an action type in the Document Actions dialog box.

Searching for page templates

Although not a JavaScript action, page templates can be called upon by JavaScript routines or additional fields can be created from template pages. Because templates can be hidden, the only way to examine JavaScripts on template pages is to first display a hidden template. As a matter of routine, you should search for page templates when examining forms.

To display a hidden template, choose Advanced ➪ Forms ➪ Page Templates. The Page Templates dialog box opens. If a Page Template is used in the PDF file a template name appears in a list box in the Page Templates dialog box. If the Page Template is hidden the square adjacent to the template name appears empty. To show the template page, click on the icon adjacent to the template name. The icon changes to an eye icon inside the square as shown in Figure 29-8.

Figure 29-8: Clicking on the icon to the left of a template name for hidden templates makes the template visible in the PDF.

The template likely appears at the end of the document. After you make a template visible, click the GoTo button to navigate to that page. If form fields or links are on the page, you can open them and examine them for JavaScripts.

Using the JavaScript Debugger

All of the aforementioned JavaScript locations can also be found in the JavaScript Debugger. The JavaScript Debugger dialog box enables you to examine JavaScripts from a list in the Scripts window shown in Figure 29-9. Select an item in the list and click the arrows to open scripts nested in a hierarchical order. When you select the script, the code is shown in the View window.

Figure 29-9: Choose Advanced ⇨ JavaScript ⇨ Debugger to open the JavaScript Debugger, or press Ctrl/⌘+J.

At the top of the hierarchy in the Scripts window, you'll see all the scripts associated with different actions. Click the right-pointing arrow to expand a listed item. You can expand individual items until you arrive at the action. Select the action, and the code for the item is listed in the lower View window when you select either Script or Script and Console from the pull-down menu options.

The JavaScript Debugger also helps you debug scripts you write. You can set break points that halt routines to help narrow down bugs in your code. To set a break point, click on the left side of each line of code where you want a break to occur. A red circle appears after you set a break point. Notice in Figure 29-9 that a break point was set at the second line of code for the discountAmount field selected in the Scripts window.

Using the JavaScript Console

The JavaScript Console is a part of the same dialog box where you find the JavaScript Debugger. In the console window you can type a line of code to test it for errors or you can copy code from a field and paste it into the console window. To execute a segment in a routine, select the segment to be tested and press the Num Pad Enter key (or press Control+Enter).

You can also execute a statement by placing the cursor at the beginning of the line to be executed. Press the Enter key on the Num Pad and the routine runs.

Be certain to check the Preferences dialog box when using the JavaScript Debugger and Console. Open the Preferences dialog box and click on JavaScript in the left pane. On the right side of the dialog box are options for enabling the Debugger and the Console. Be certain these items are enabled before you begin editing scripts.

Creating Viewer Options Warning Alerts

There are some circumstances where it will be helpful for users to know the limitations of completing your forms before they attempt filling in data fields. If users open your forms in Adobe Reader, they cannot save the data after filling in the form. In other cases, some scripts you add to a form cannot be performed in Adobe Reader. Some examples of such scripts might be adding a Comment note from a button action or spawning a page from a template. These actions require Acrobat. In other cases, new features in Acrobat 7 make some actions unusable for users with viewers earlier than Acrobat 7. Therefore, you may want to assess the viewer type and viewer version when a user opens your forms. If a version or viewer type cannot be used with the form you created, you can alert the user immediately when the file opens.

Tip

Although some features such as viewing page templates or creating fields are not available in Acrobat Standard, you can often execute JavaScripts in Acrobat Standard that produce actions not available through menu commands. For example, you cannot add templates or write JavaScript code to spawn pages from templates using Acrobat Standard. However, you can write a script for a button to spawn a page from a template in Acrobat Professional. An Acrobat Standard user can open the file, click the button, and a page is spawned via the button action. Before you create viewer version alerts, you need to run all your scripts in Acrobat Standard to determine what scripts cannot be executed in Acrobat Standard. Use viewer version alerts for Acrobat Standard users only when scripts don't execute properly. You can also find a key in the JavaScript Reference Guide that describes which objects and methods work in Acrobat Standard.

Creating viewer type alerts

A viewer type is the Acrobat viewer used to view the PDF form. Adobe Reader, Acrobat Standard, and Acrobat Professional are the viewer types that are used in filling out PDF forms. If you have forms submitted via an Internet connection, any viewer type is capable of submitting data if you have the proper server-side programming and create a button to submit the data to a URL.

Cross-Reference

For more information on submitting data, look over Chapter 28.

In a local environment where PDF forms may be completed on local hard drives or network servers, users of the Adobe Reader software may not be aware that they cannot save the form data after completion. If a user realizes this only after filling in a long form, users are likely to become annoyed and frustrated. To help the user out, follow these steps to create an alert dialog box informing a user that the current viewer type has limitations:

STEPS: Adding viewer type alerts

1. **Open the Page Properties dialog box.** Open a PDF and navigate to the default page view when the file opens. Open the Pages tab and from a context menu opened on the first page, select Properties. The warning message you create appears immediately after a user opens the PDF form. To ensure the message is displayed upon opening the file, be certain to navigate to the first page and open the context menu. Unless the default has been overridden in the Initial View Options dialog box, the opening page is always the first page in the PDF file.

2. **Add a page action.** Click the Actions tab. Select Page Open from the Select Trigger pull-down menu and select Run a JavaScript from the Select Action pull-down menu. Click the Add button to open the JavaScript Editor.

3. **Add a JavaScript.** Enter the following code in the JavaScript Editor dialog box:

```
1. //is Reader (as opposed to Acrobat)
2. if (typeof(app.viewerType)!="undefined")
3.  if(app.viewerType == "Reader")
4.  {
5.    var msg = "To save form data you need to purchase Adobe Acrobat
Standard or Adobe Acrobat Professional. This form can be completed
and printed from Reader; however to save the data, you need one of
the viewers noted above.";
6.    app.alert(msg);
7.  }
```

Note The preceding line numbers are for clarification only. The line numbers are not included in the code you write in the JavaScript Editor.

This routine begins with a comment denoted by // where a programmer's comment is added to the script. In line 2, the if statement assesses the viewer. If the viewer type in line 3 is equal (==) to Adobe Reader ("Reader"), then an alert dialog box opens — line 6: app.alert(msg). The variable msg is defined in the line 5 var msg statement. Therefore, the variable msg value appears when the alert dialog box opens. If the viewer type is not Reader, the warning dialog box does not open.

4. **Save the file.** Select File ➪ Save or File ➪ Save As and save the file.

5. **Open the file in Adobe Reader.** Click OK in the JavaScript Editor dialog box and click Close in the Page Properties dialog box. Save the file and close it. Open the file in Adobe Reader and you see an alert dialog box open when the file is launched, as shown in Figure 29-10.

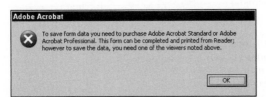

Figure 29-10: When the PDF is opened in Acrobat Reader, the alert dialog box displays the message created in the JavaScript routine.

Creating viewer version alerts

You may create JavaScripts to perform actions that are not available in earlier versions of Acrobat. The newer Acrobat 7.0 implementation of JavaScript adds more statements and reserved words than earlier versions. If it is essential for a user to complete your form in Acrobat 7, you can add a page action and inform the user in an alert dialog box that Acrobat 7 is needed to complete the form. Follow these steps to assess the viewer version:

STEPS: Create a viewer version alert

1. **Create a age action.** Create a page action following the steps listed earlier for opening the Page Properties dialog box. Select Run a JavaScript from the Select Action pull-down menu and click the Edit button.

2. **Add a JavaScript.** Type the following code in the JavaScript Editor:

```
1. if (typeof(app.viewerVersion)!="undefined")
2.  if(app.viewerVersion < 7.0)
3.  {
4.  var msg = "Not all features in this document work in Acrobat
viewers lower than version 7.0. Upgrade to Adobe Acrobat Standard 7.0
or Adobe Acrobat Professional 7.0 before proceeding.";
5.  app.alert(msg);
```

   In line 1, `app.viewerType` is used instead of the viewer version noted in the earlier example. This routine assesses the current Acrobat viewer version and displays the message in line 4 if the viewer version is less than Acrobat 7.0.

JavaScript Calculations

Going back to the form created in the previous chapter where I discussed calculating sales tax with a Simplified Field Notation, assume you want to create a sum of a total column and add sales tax with a JavaScript. For the sales tax, you need to first create the sum of values in a column or row. If you aren't up to speed in writing complex formulas, you can create a temporary field for summing the data and use the temporary field data to compute the sales tax. The field can be placed anywhere on the form and be hidden from the user.

To create a temporary field, drag open a field with the Text Field tool; the Text Field Properties dialog box opens. I'll call this field `subtotal`. Click the Calculate tab and either use the Select Field dialog box to select fields for summing a group of fields, or type the parent name in the field box as described in Chapter 26. To hide the field, select the General tab and choose Hidden from the Form Field pull-down menu at the bottom of the dialog box.

The field name is `subtotal` and the field is now hidden. I'll use this field data to calculate my sales tax. For the sales tax field, I'll create a new form field and name it `tax`. In the Calculate dialog box I enter the following code:

```
1. var f=this.getField("subtotal");
2. event.value=Math.round(f.value*7.25)/100
```

The variable name f gets the contents of the `subtotal` field. The second line of code performs the calculation for variable f to compute sales tax for a tax rate of 7.25 percent. If you want to duplicate the code for one of your forms, change the tax rate accordingly.

Calculating dates

You can add a date to a form with a simple JavaScript. To add a date to a form, create a text field. Set the attributes for the text appearance and font in the Appearance tab and click the Calculate tab. Add a JavaScript action and enter the following code:

```
1. event.value = util.printd ("mm/dd/yy", new Date());
```

In the preceding example the date is reported in the format 07/31/03. You can change date formats by editing the text within quotes. For example, change the text to read "mmm dd, yyyy", and the date is reported in the format Jul 04, 2003.

Using loops

For summing columns of data you can use the sum + preset formulas where you need results at the end of a column or row. However, at times, summing column or row data with a JavaScript is necessary. You might have a need to multiply an item by a quantity for a subtotal, and then add all the subtotals together to create a grand total. For summing data in columns, you need to create a loop that loops through all the fields used in the calculation.

For a simple loop to calculate a row of data, use the following example:

```
1. var amount = "price";
2. var sum = 0;
3. for (var i=0; i < 12; i++)
4. {
5.   var total = amount + "." + i;
6.   sum += this.getField(total).value;
7. }
8. event.value = sum;
```

Line 1 assigns the variable amount to a parent name price. The fields in a column are named price.1, price.2, price.3, and so on. Line 2 assigns the variable sum to zero. Line 3 begins the loop and the loop continues through 12 iterations (< 12). Line 5 inside the loop assigns variable total to price.1—the first pass through the loop. Line 6 takes the variable sum and collects the value of total with each pass through the loop. Line 8 places the total value sum in the field where the script is written.

Note   The above script works when you have 12 fields. If using fewer or more than 12 fields, change line 3 to the number of fields in a column or row you want to loop through.

Assume you want to calculate a grand total and place the result in the grand total field. A loop like the following example is used to take the product of each row and calculate the sum of the products:

```
1. var quantity = "qty";
2. var amount = "unit";
3. var sum = 0;
4. for (var i=0; i < 12; i++)
5. {
6.   var total = quantity + "." + i;
7.   var unit = amount + "." + i;
8.   sum += this.getField(total).value * this.getField(unit).value;
9. }
10. event.value = sum;
```

In the preceding code, I added a second variable `item` and used it along with the `amount` variable from the earlier example. The `sum` variable takes the product of `item` and `amount` with each pass through the loop and sums the values until the loop halts.

Using Document Actions

Document actions are actions from JavaScript routines that are implemented when a file is printed, saved, or closed. Rather than using a button to execute an action, Acrobat executes the action during one of five conditions. A document action is executed when a file is closed, when a file is saved, after a file is saved, when a file is printed, and after a file is printed. There are many uses for executing actions on one of the document action items. You might want to delete unused fields on a form, delete all page templates, or perhaps offer a message to the user after a form has been saved or printed. In environments where Adobe Reader is used, users can't delete fields or page templates, but alert dialog boxes can be displayed from Reader on all the document action types.

As an example, suppose forms need to be routed in printed form. You can provide instructions on what to do with the form after it finishes printing. You may have Adobe Reader users who cannot save data. For the Adobe Reader users it is necessary to circulate printed documents. In this case, you can set up a document action after a file has finished printing. You are assured the user sees the message because the form needs to be printed as the last step in completing the form.

Follow these steps for creating an alert dialog box with a message to instruct a user what to do with a form after it has printed:

STEPS: Create a document action showing an alert dialog box

1. **Open the Document Actions dialog box.** Open a PDF file by choosing Advanced ⇨ JavaScript ⇨ Set Document Actions. The Document Actions dialog box opens.

2. **Select the Document Did Print action type.** Select one of the five items in the list box for the type of action to be used. In this example, I'll use Document Did Print as the action type.

3. **Open the JavaScript Editor.** Click Edit in the Document Actions dialog box. The JavaScript Editor dialog box opens.

4. **Code the script.** Enter the following code:

   ```
   app.alert("Please submit the printed form to the accounting In box in
   the main office complex.",1)
   ```

5. **Exit the JavaScript Editor.** Click OK in the JavaScript Editor.

Note   The Document Actions dialog box displays an icon adjacent to the action type and the code appears in the window below Execute this JavaScript. If you later want to delete the script, click the Edit button and highlight the text in the JavaScript Editor. Press Delete (Backspace) on the keyboard to eliminate the text.

6. **Print the form.** Print the document to your desktop printer. After the PDF finishes printing, the dialog box opens.

Working with Page Templates

One very useful tool available to you with page templates and JavaScript is the ability to create new pages from a template page. You can make templates either visible or hidden in your forms. You create new pages from template pages by spawning a page from a template. The spawned pages are duplicates of the template pages, but any fields on spawned pages are created with new field names if desired. The scripts and actions for fields added to template pages are duplicated when you spawn pages from templates. The only changes that occur are field names, so each field in your new document contains unique field names if desired.

Page templates can be spawned to create new pages or you can also use page templates to overly data on existing pages. For example, adding a watermark, graphic, text, and so on like you might add with headers and footers can be overlaid on pages using page templates.

Creating a page template

To create a page template, open a PDF form in which you want to convert one of the pages to a template. You may have a form to which you want to add pages for users to make comments. As more comments are needed, the user can create new pages by spawning new pages from the template page. In the following example, I have a form where one page on the form is a page designed for comments. In Figure 29-11 I designed an employee application form. At the bottom of the section for education history is a button used to create a new page if the applicant needs to add comments.

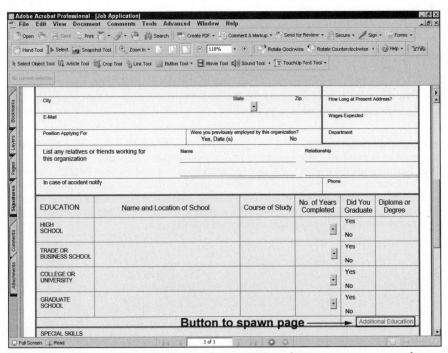

Figure 29-11: The employee application form contains a button to spawn a page from a template for adding additional comments related to education history.

Figure 29-12 shows a page used to amplify comments regarding educational background. The page is optional and all potential candidates won't need to fill out this page. To eliminate the page from view, you can create a page template and then hide the template. When a user needs to fill in the template page, the button action creates a new page from the template.

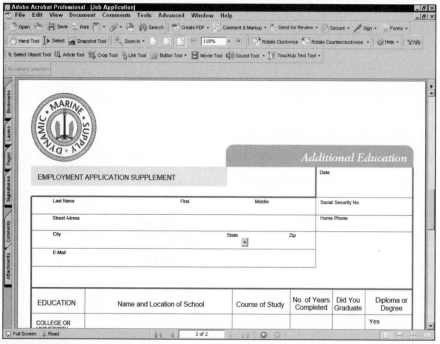

Figure 29-12: You can hide a page in the document that is not necessary for all users to fill in. To hide the page, create a page template.

To create a template, be certain to navigate to the page in the document that needs to be converted to a template. Choose Advanced ⇨ Forms ⇨ Page Templates. In the Page Templates dialog box, provide a name in the Name field and click the Add button. To hide the template, click the icon adjacent to the template name in the list window. By default templates added to the list window appear with an eye icon (Windows and Macintosh). Click the eye icon and the icon disappears as shown in Figure 29-13. The page template is hidden in the PDF document, and you can see the page disappear when you click the icon.

Figure 29-13: Hide page templates by clicking the icon adjacent to the template name in the list window.

Spawning a page from a template

To create new pages from your template, create a button on the page from which you want the user to spawn a new page. Either a link button or form field can be used. In the link or button properties dialog box select Run a JavaScript as the action type.

The following code is used to spawn a page from a template.

```
1. var a = this.getTemplate("additionalEducation");
2. a.spawn ({
3.    nPage:this.numPages,
4.    bRename:true,
5.    bOverlay:false
6. })
```

The template name is additionalEducation as defined in the first line of code. In the second line of code the instruction a.spawn spawns a page from a template. Lines 3 to 5 set the attributes for the spawned page. In line 3 the spawned page is placed after the last page in the template. You can change the value this.numPages to a page number and place the spawned page anywhere in the file. In line 5 any fields contained on the template page are renamed on the spawned page to provide unique field names. If the line is changed to bRename:false, all fields are duplicated with duplicate field names. In line 5 the code instructs Acrobat to create a new page in the document. If you change the code to bOverlay:true, the spawned page is superimposed over the last page in the file.

Lines 3 through 5 in the preceding script are default values. If you write the script as follows, Acrobat assumes using the defaults without specific notation for the attributes:

```
1. var a = this.getTemplate("additionalEducation");
2. a.spawn();
```

This two-line script works fine in Acrobat 6 and 7; however. there are problems executing the script properly in earlier versions of Acrobat. Be certain to use the script with six lines of code and specify all attributes of the spawned page and you can be certain the script works in all versions of Acrobat.

You can also use an action type to instruct Acrobat to go to the newly created page. By default, spawned pages are created at the end of the PDF document. When pages are spawned, the page containing the button used to spawn a new page remains in view. To help a user navigate to the new spawned page, you can add another line of code to go to the new page. Add the following script after the last line of code used to spawn a page:

```
this.pageNum = this.numPages-1;
```

This line assesses the number of pages in the document, subtracts one from the number and opens the last page. JavaScript is zero based; therefore, the –1 item subtracts one from the total number of pages. In JavaScript terms, page 1 is page 0.

Tip   If you have a document with many pages and need to spawn pages periodically as the user browses the document, use a Bookmark instead of adding buttons on all the pages. A single Bookmark takes up much less memory than button fields added to every page.

Creating Pop-up Menus

Application pop-up menus can be useful for nesting action items so you can save some space on a form. You might want to have a contents page where a user navigates via menu commands to many different files stored on a CD-ROM or network server. Rather than listing all files on a page or in Bookmarks you can categorize groups and nest them in submenus for a more economical use of space.

As an example, suppose you want to create links to other PDF documents. You have a small page and don't have enough room to display all the titles of the documents you want the user to access. By creating an application pop-up menu like the one shown in Figure 29-14, you can create categories, subcategories, and links to destinations that assist users in opening files in a relatively small section on a contents page.

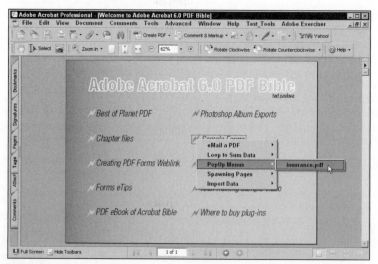

Figure 29-14: By adding application pop-up menus, you can create lists of destination documents in categorical groups.

When you select the menu option the file associated with the link opens in the Document pane. In Figure 29-15, a document is opened after selecting a submenu item from a popup menu.

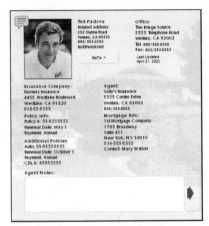

Figure 29-15: After selecting the submenu item in the popup menu the file link opens in the Document pane.

Writing document-level JavaScripts

If you use JavaScript to open and close files, all destination files need to have a document-level JavaScript to make the open actions workable. In each file being addressed with a JavaScript, to open the file you need to add one line of code at the document level.

For each file you want to open from a pop-up menu, open each target document and choose Advanced ➪ JavaScript ➪ Document JavaScripts. In the JavaScript Functions dialog box type a name for the script in the field box at the top of the dialog box. Click the Add button to open the JavaScript Editor. Delete all the default text in the JavaScript Editor and type the following code:

```
this.disclosed = true;
```

Click OK in the JavaScript Editor to return to the JavaScript Functions dialog box. Click Close and save the file. Repeat the steps for all files you want to open with a JavaScript.

If you don't add the aforementioned code to the document level, the files won't open with a JavaScript. Be certain to verify that all documents contain this one line of code at the document level.

Creating a pop-up menu

After coding functions in the destination documents, create a button field on a form used as a contents page and add the following JavaScript:

```
1. var c = app.popUpMenu
2. (["Category 1", "1a.pdf", "1b.pdf"],
3.  ["Category 2", "2a.pdf", "2b.pdf"],
4.  ["Category 3", "3a.pdf", "3b.pdf"],);
5. this.slave = app.openDoc(c, this);
```

The first line of code assigns the variable c to the `app.popUpMenu` method. In lines 2 to 4 are three categories. The category name is the first item in quote marks on each line. Following the category names are the filenames that open when the menu item is selected. Line 5 instructs Acrobat to open the selected file.

To create your own pop-up menus, change the category names to menu titles you want to use. Following each category, type the name of the respective document to open. Be certain to begin line 2 with an open parenthesis (and use a closed parenthesis) after the last line of code used to identify the category and filenames (line 4). Each line of code where the categories and filenames appear is contained within brackets.

The code used above works in Acrobat 7 as well as earlier viewers. Updates to the JavaScript implementation in Adobe Acrobat support more refinement for coding application popup menus. These newer code listings can be found in the Acrobat JavaScripting Reference Manual for version 7 of Acrobat. An example of a script using an application popup menu that opens your default Web browser and takes you to Adobe's Web site where Web pages open for Acrobat and Adobe Reader is coded as follows:

```
var aParams = [
{cName: "Adobe Web Page", cReturn: "www.adobe.com"},
{cName: "-"},
{cName: "The Adobe Acrobat family",
cReturn: "http://www.adobe.com/products/acrobat/main.html"},
{cName: "Adobe Reader",
cReturn: "http://www.adobe.com/products/acrobat/readstep2.html"}
];
// apply the function app.popUpMenuEx to the app object, with an array
// of parameters aParams
var cChoice = app.popUpMenuEx.apply( app, aParams );
```

There's much more to creating application popup menus and many changes to app.openDoc in version 7 of Acrobat. Be certain to review the Acrobat JavaScripting Reference Manual for code samples using these and other routines you want to implement in Acrobat.

Submitting E-mail Attachments

You may have a need to ask a user to fill out a form and return the populated form to you or another user. A user could fill out a form and attach it to an e-mail message like any other file. However, by using a little JavaScript you can help the user out by creating a button that automatically launches the default e-mail application and attaches the data to a message window when the user clicks on a button field. Depending on your need you can choose to send the complete PDF file or an FDF file. In order for a user to see the FDF data the PDF form is needed at the recipient end so the data can be imported. Conditions vary, so becoming familiar with both methods is a good idea.

The Submit a form action type enables you to submit documents and e-mail files. However, by using JavaScript you can also include as part of your script other items such as code that assesses fields for completion, response dialog boxes, and conditional statements.

Cross-Reference

The foregoing examples illustrate how to create e-mail attachments with JavaScripts for users of either the Acrobat Standard or Acrobat Professional product. To learn how to create submit buttons for Adobe Reader users, see Chapter 26.

Attaching PDF forms to e-mails

At the user end, the user can select the Email tool in Acrobat or choose File ➪ Email; the current active PDF document is attached to an empty e-mail message ready for the user to type the message and send the e-mail. You can achieve the same effect by creating a button field and a JavaScript action on your form. By using a JavaScript you can check the form for empty fields before the button action is invoked. When you add a button, a user unfamiliar with the Acrobat tools or menu commands can easily send an e-mail attachment by clicking the button you create on the form.

In this example I'll use a routine for assessing the viewer type and show you how to write a conditional statement. If the viewer type is not Adobe Reader, the routine executes a statement to attach a PDF document to an e-mail attachment.

```
1. if (typeof(app.viewerType)!="undefined")
2. if(app.viewerType == "Reader")
3. {
4.  var msg = "You must use Acrobat Standard or Acrobat Professional to
send the application back to us. To find out more information on
purchasing Adobe Acrobat Standard or Acrobat Professional visit:
http:www.adobe.com.";
5.  app.alert(msg);
 }
6. else
7.  {
8. this.mailDoc ({
bUI: true,
9.  cTo: "management@company.com",
10.  cCc:"supervisor@company.com",
11.  bCc:"ceo@company.com",
12.  cSubject: "Employment Application Form"});

13.  }
```

In the preceding routine, I start by examining the viewer version. If the user attempts to e-mail the file from Adobe Reader, an application alert dialog box opens, informing the user that Acrobat is needed to submit the form. The user is instructed as to where to acquire Acrobat Standard and Acrobat Professional to submit the form properly.

If the user's viewer is either Acrobat Standard or Acrobat Professional, the statement after else (line 7) executes. this.mailDoc instructs Acrobat to attach the active PDF document to an e-mail message. The three items in quotes begin with the recipient, the cc recipient, and the bcc recipient, respectively. The last item in quotes is the subject title for the e-mail message. If you want to eliminate a cc and a blind cc, the code in lines 10 and 11 would read as

```
8. this.mailDoc ({
    bUI: true,
9.  cTo: "management@company.com",
10:  cCc: "",
11:  bCc: "",
12. cSubject: "Employment Application Form"});
```

If you want to add multiple recipients, cc, or bcc recipients, just add a comma after the name of the recipient within the quotation marks for the respective recipients.

When the user clicks the button, the e-mail application launches with the active PDF file attached and the specified recipients placed in their respective locations, as shown in Figure 29-16.

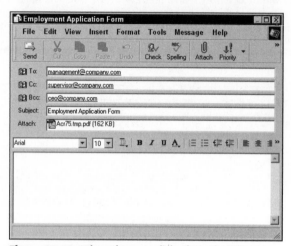

Figure 29-16: When the user clicks the submit button, the default e-mail application is launched, the PDF file is attached, the recipients are designated, and the subject line is filled in.

Attaching FDF data to e-mails

In the example in the preceding section an e-mail attachment was used to submit an employee application form to several users. The entire PDF file was distributed to various parties. As a practical measure, submitting the entire form makes sense because some parties may not have the original PDF at hand. In other cases you may not need the original PDF document. For example, the employee application form is routed to the human resources department that screens all applications. The HR department certainly has the original PDF file and therefore only needs the data from the form that they import into an empty employment application form. In this regard, the company personnel need only receive the FDF data. Sending the data requires much less storage space and the file transfer is much faster, especially if the form is complex and contains many pages.

To send the data instead of the PDF file, you need to make one slight change in the JavaScript. Using the previous example, change the code in line 8 to

```
8. this.mailForm( {
     bUI: true,
9.  cTo: "management@comany.com",
10.  cCc: "",
11.  bCc: "",
12. cSubject: "Employment Application Form"});
```

Suppose a user completes a form on a home computer or on the road on a laptop computer. Assume for a moment that the user has a different e-mail address for office and home or on the road. If you want to offer an option to enable the user to e-mail a copy of the FDF data to a second e-mail address, you might want to ask for the address in a dialog box. The response from the dialog box can be placed in the cc line of the e-mail message. This way you can use a generic form suited for all users.

To send FDF data with a cc to an address specified from an application response dialog box, use a script as follows:

```
1. var cResponse = app.response({
2. cQuestion: "To copy yourself, enter your email address. Click cancel
to send data without sending a copy to yourself",
3. cTitle: "emailAddress", }); // title of the dialog box
4. {
5.  if ( cResponse == null)
6.   this.mailForm(true, "finance@company.com", "", "", "Purchase
Order");
7. else
8.   this.mailForm(true, "finance@company.com", cResponse, "", "Purchase
Order");
9. }
```

> **Note**
>
> The code in lines 6 and 7 are a simplified method for adding the To, cc, bcc, and Subject to the e-mail message. The results are the same as when using the code samples noted previously for sending a form or form data.

The beginning of the routine asks the question, "Do you want to copy yourself?" If not, the user clicks the Cancel button in the response dialog box and the data are sent to the recipient (finance@company.com). If yes, the user types an address in a dialog box and clicks OK; the data from the response dialog box are posted in the cc line of the e-mail message.

Clicking OK opens the dialog box shown in Figure 29-17.

Figure 29-17: The e-mail address to send a copy of the FDF data to is supplied in a response dialog box.

After the user adds an e-mail address and clicks OK, the e-mail message window appears with the FDF data attached, and the cc line includes the address from the response dialog box.

Summary

✦ One method for learning JavaScript is to examine forms with scripts. You can copy JavaScripts in the JavaScript Editor dialog box or copy form fields and links.

✦ JavaScripts are found in several places in PDF documents including fields, links, Bookmarks, page actions, document-level scripts, and document actions.

✦ The JavaScript Debugger lists all JavaScripts in a document. When you're learning how a form executes JavaScripts, examining all potential areas where scripts are written is a good idea.

✦ Viewer types and viewer version alerts are used to inform users whether their Acrobat viewer is the correct version and type to complete a form.

✦ Sums of data in rows and columns are calculated with JavaScripts using loops to gather data through each pass in a loop.

✦ Document actions are used to execute a JavaScript when a file opens, closes, or prints.

✦ Pages can be spawned in a document to create new pages from a template page. When pages are spawned, all fields, links, and JavaScripts on the new spawned pages are duplicated from the template page with new field names.

✦ Pop-up menus can save some space on a form where lists in nested menus are scripted to open documents.

✦ Using JavaScripts to e-mail PDFs and data offers you more flexibility than using the Submit a form action type. With JavaScript you can open response dialog boxes, add conditional statements, and check a form for any blank fields.

✦   ✦   ✦

Index

Symbols and Numerics

A

Continued

Continued

Continued

Continued

Continued

Continued

Continued

Continued

Continued